LEAVING CERTIFICATE GEOGR
HIGHER AND ORDINARY LEVELS

EARTH

MICHAEL ORGAN

PUBLISHED BY:

Educate.ie

Walsh Educational Books Ltd

Castleisland, Co. Kerry, Ireland

www.educate.ie

EDITOR:

Ciara McNee

DESIGN:

Kieran O'Donoghue

COVER DESIGN:

Kieran O'Donoghue

LAYOUT:

Design Image

PRINTED AND BOUND BY:

Walsh Colour Print, Castleisland,

Co. Kerry, Ireland

ISBN: 978-1-910468-73-9

ACKNOWLEDGEMENTS

I would like to thank the following people for helping me throughout the writing of this book. To my partner Ciara, for being a source of unconditional love, support and happiness. To Pat for his comic relief in stressful times. To Barry for his help, advice and insights. To my colleagues and staff of Scoil Pól, Kilfinane for making my job a constant source of happiness. To my family for their love and support, and finally the team at Educate.ie for their guidance, care and sheer hard work

PHOTOGRAPHS AND ILLUSTRATIONS:

For permission to reproduce photographs, the author and publisher acknowledge the following copyright holders:

© **Alamy:** 28T, 30T, 35, 37C, 39, 48C, 49CL, 49CR, 51C, 53, 66, 71, 74, 97B, 110, 111T, 130T, 130C, 132C, 133, 144, 156B, 164, 168, 184, 185, 186, 188BR, 193T, 204, 206, 207, 212, 216T, 222, 223T, 223B, 228T, 235, 286L, 286R, 289, 304CL, 304B, 333, 334, 338, 355, 364, 369T, 369B, 373T, 377, 381B, 383C, 383B, 384T, 384C, 390T, 390C, 398T, 404T, 412C, 423, 426B, 429, 455, 456C, 456B, 459, 460, 462R, 475T, 479C, 481, 482, 489B, 492C, 493T, 494, 498, 501T, 503C, 503B, 510C, 516, 526, 528, 532T, 544T, 562, 567, 570, 572C, 573T, 574, 575, 578T, 580 • © **Barrow Coakley Photography:** 285CR, 285BL, 287, 290, 294, 295, 296, 297, 298, 299, 280 • © **Bigstock.com:** 3, 34, 129, 134T, 143, 151T, 151C, 182, 183, 208, 209, 215T, 215B, 232T, 234 • **Courtesy of Canterbury Of New Zealand, Photograph Perry Ogden:** 501B • © **Getty Images:** 48B, 54, 193C, 245, 344, 398C, 486BL, 486BR, 510T, 540B, 543, 577 • © **Google Earth:** 305T (A–D), 305C (A–E), 306T (A–D), 306C (A–D), 306B (A–D), 363, 381T, 382 • © **The Irish Times:** 409 • **Courtesy of the Islamic Cultural Centre of Ireland, Clonskeagh:** 346BL • © **iStockphoto.com:** 113T, 153, 156T, 167C, 167B, 255, 399, 405, 407T, 447C, 477, 521, 540C, 541, 544B, 557T, 558, 559B, 563, 568, 579 • **NASA:** 188BL, 301, 302TL, 302TR, 302BL, 302BR, 303T, 303CL, 303CR, 304TL, 321BL, 322TL • **Courtesy of the National Library of Ireland:** 190B • © **Ordnance Survey of Ireland:** 150, 177, 194, 195, 216B, 237, 240CL, 240T, 257T, 257CR, 259, 261C, 261B, 263L, 264, 265, 267, 268, 270, 272, 274, 276, 278, 281 • **Courtesy of Pfizer Ireland:** 404B • © **Richard Jolley/cartoonstock.com:** 371T • © **Shutterstock.com:** 26, 36, 41, 42T, 42B, 43, 49B, 51T, 55, 65, 86, 87T, 90, 91, 93, 96B, 97T, 104, 106, 108, 109, 111B, 113B, 114, 135, 141, 146T, 146B, 147, 148, 159C, 161T, 165, 174, 180, 192C, 192B, 200, 202R, 210, 215C, 217C (1–4), 226, , 227T, 227C, 236, 240T (A–D), 240CR, 256, 285CL, 332T, 332C, 242, 346CL, 361, 362, 368, 370, 376, 377, 394, 396, 397, 402, 406, 407B, 412BR, 424, 426C, 434B, 435T, 439T, 439C, 439B, 447B, 457, 461, 468, 470, 471, 473TL, 473TC, 473TR, 473B, 474C, 474B, 475C, 478, 479T, 486T, 487T, 487C, 487B, 489T, 490, 492T, 493B, 504, 507, 508, 520, 532B, 550, 554, 557B, 559T, 560, 571CR, 571BC, 571BR, 572T, 573C • **Wikicommons:** 9, 11T, 11B, 12C, 37B, 46, 47T, 47C, 47B, 96C, 132T, 134C, 134B, 145, 160, 162T, 201, 217, 232B, 233, 304TR, 304CR, 343, 353, 434C, 506

Ordnance Survey Ireland Permit No. 9061
© Ordnance Survey Ireland/Government of Ireland

Contents

REGIONAL GEOGRAPHY — CORE 3

GEOECOLOGY (HIGHER LEVEL ONLY) — OPTION 7

Preface

Earth is an up-to-date and comprehensive package for Higher and Ordinary Level Geography students. The *Earth* package includes a textbook, elective books, a Teacher's Resource Book, posters and digital resources.

The textbook covers the three core units of the course:

- Patterns and Processes in the Physical Environment
- Geographical Skills
- Regional Geography

The most popular option (Geoecology) is also covered for Higher Level students.

Key Features of the Earth textbook:

- Content is developed in line with the requirements of the marking scheme.

- The text is written with both Higher and Ordinary Level students in mind.

- Fully developed, Significant Relevant Points (SRPs) give students exactly what they need to know. Text in bold clearly shows the information required to gain marks for SRPs. This allows for independent learning and study.

- Each topic begins with **Key Words** and **Learning Outcomes** to inform the student and to facilitate teacher planning.

- The **Geo Dictionary** feature provides a focus on literacy throughout and gives simple definitions of key terms and new words. The **Geo Numeracy** feature gives information on how to carry out important calculations.

- **Active learning** questions and tasks are included throughout each chapter to engage students. The questions range from comprehension questions to more detailed ones involving class discussion.

- Relevant, accurate diagrams are carefully drawn in a style that is easy for students to reproduce. Up-to-date maps, photographs, satellite images and statistical data further aid learning.

- **FACT** boxes provide additional information to enhance student interest and promote further independent research.

- **Why** textboxes explain difficult concepts.

- There is a strong study and exam focus:

  - The **Educate Yourself** feature highlights key points in each topic. These promote focused and logical ordering of information and enable the student to write informative answers that are topic specific.

  - End-of-chapter Higher and Ordinary Level past-exam questions give students an insight into the wording of exam questions and test their knowledge.

  - End-of-chapter Exam Focus model answers show clear links to the marking scheme.

  - End-of-chapter Topic Maps aid understanding and revision.

I hope you enjoy your journey through this wonderful subject and that this book becomes the perfect companion.

Michael Organ

CORE UNIT 1

Patterns and Processes in the Physical Environment

CHAPTER 1

Plate Tectonics

In this chapter, you will be introduced to some of the most important features of our planet. You will learn about the unique, layered structure of the Earth and about one of the most important theories – the theory of plate tectonics. Everything you learn in this chapter provides the basis for Chapters 2–6 in this book. A good understanding of this chapter will be of great benefit as you progress through the rest of the physical section.

KEY WORDS

- Inner core
- Outer core
- Mantle
- Asthenosphere
- Lithosphere
- Continental crust
- Oceanic crust
- Molten

- Plates
- Convection currents
- Continental drift
- Continental fit
- Matching fossils
- Glacial deposits
- Matching mountain ranges
- Mid-ocean ridges

- Seafloor spreading
- Magma
- Lava
- Basalt
- Ocean sediments
- Subduction

LEARNING OUTCOMES

What you MUST know

- Each layer of the Earth and their functions
- The difference between continental and oceanic crusts
- The major crustal plates of the Earth and how they form boundaries
- The difference between magma and lava
- How convection currents move plates
- The theory of continental drift and its proofs
- The theory of seafloor spreading and its proofs
- The formation of mid-ocean ridges

What you SHOULD know

- A number of minor plates, such as the Cocos Plate
- Slab pull

What is USEFUL to know

- Who discovered the theories of contintental drift and seafloor spreading

Introduction

The Earth formed roughly 4.6 billion years ago. Early Earth was a much different place to the planet we live on today. Meteorite collisions caused the Earth to become very hot, reaching surface temperatures of up to 2000 °C (the melting point of iron). At this stage, much of the Earth was **molten,** with oceans of **magma** at the surface. Gradually, the Earth began to cool down. Heavier materials such as nickel and iron sank to the centre to form the core of the planet. Lighter materials stayed near the surface, forming the mantle and crust. It is this **core, mantle** and **crust** structure that makes up the Earth today.

GEO DICTIONARY

Molten: liquid

Magma: liquid rock that is underneath the crust

Earth's Structure

The Earth is made up of the following:

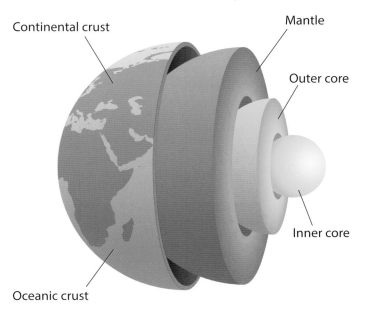

Continental crust

Mantle

Outer core

Inner core

Oceanic crust

⊙ **Fig. 1.1** The layers of the Earth: each layer has an effect on the geography of the surface.

FACT

The Earth's inner core accounts for just 1 per cent of the planet's mass, yet it is roughly the same size as the moon.

The outer core is approximately the same size as the planet Mars.

1.1 The Core

The core is the most centre point of the Earth. The core is made up of dense, heavy metals which sank to the centre as the Earth began to cool. The core is divided into two parts:

- The inner core
- The outer core

The Inner Core

The Earth's inner core is a solid sphere made of the metals **nickel and iron.** Despite being the hottest layer of the Earth at **6000 °C** (slightly hotter than the temperature of the surface of the sun), it is **solid due to intense pressure.** The inner core **transfers this heat to the upper layers.** This transfer of heat is a vital process in making life possible on Earth.

Pressure increases the melting point of metal. While iron normally melts at 1538 °C, the Earth's inner core remains solid at 6000 °C because of intense pressure.

The Outer Core

The outer core is a **2000 km thick** layer also made of **nickel and iron.** The outer core is not under as much pressure as the inner core. This, along with **intense heat,** causes the outer core to be **fully molten.**

The outer core spins around the **static** inner core, causing the metals to become charged (much like a turbine used to generate electricity). This movement **generates the Earth's magnetic field** which protects us from the sun's harmful radiation.

GEO DICTIONARY

Static: not moving or changing

Note!
Identifying or labelling the different layers of the Earth is a frequently asked question in the Leaving Certificate exam.

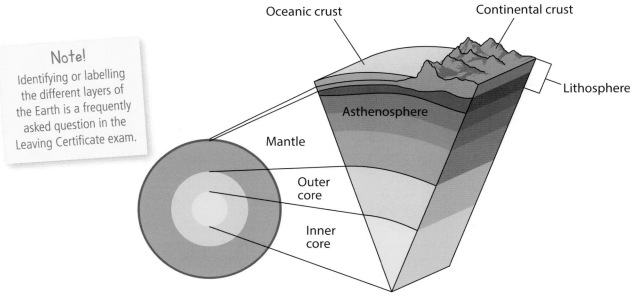

Oceanic crust

Continental crust

Lithosphere

Asthenosphere

Mantle

Outer core

Inner core

🔺 **Fig. 1.2** A closer look at the Earth's layers

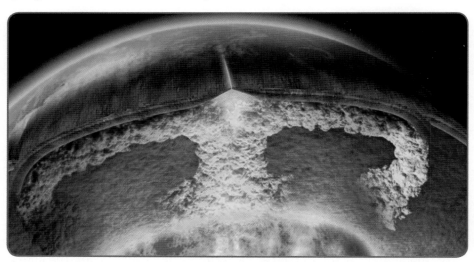

🔺 **Fig. 1.3** Huge convection currents rise from the lower mantle towards the crust. As the semi-molten magma moves laterally (sideways) underneath the lithosphere, friction causes the plates to move.

1.2 The Mantle

The mantle is the largest layer in the Earth, making up **75 per cent of its volume.** The mantle is made up of layers of rock which are **molten close to the core,** as it is so hot. Closer to the crust, the rock is **semi-molten** or solid as it is cooler. The **mantle** can be **divided into three layers:** the **lower mantle, asthenosphere** and **lithosphere.**

GEO DICTIONARY

Semi-molten: when magma begins to cool, it becomes thick and pasty

The Lower Mantle

The **lower part of the mantle is its hottest part.** It is made up **entirely** of **molten** magma due to this intense heat. As the magma becomes hot, it **rises upwards towards the crust.** As the magma rises, it **begins to cool** again before **sinking to the lower mantle** again. This is a very important process known as **convection currents.** We will look at this more closely in Section 1.4 on the **theory** of plate tectonics.

The Asthenosphere

The asthenosphere is the name given to the **semi-molten part of the mantle.** It consists of a **thin layer** of semi-molten rock roughly **100–200 km below** the Earth's surface. The semi-molten rock **acts like a lubricant** and allows the lithosphere to slide on top of it.

The Lithosphere

The lithosphere is the term given to the **upper mantle and crust combined.** It is between **50 and 100 km thick,** with the crust making up only a small percentage on top. It is **solid and rigid** but also quite **brittle.** It sits on the semi-molten asthenosphere which **allows it to slide.** The boundary where the upper mantle meets the crust is called the **Moho.** The lithosphere is **cracked in many places,** forming segments **called plates.**

The crust can be divided into the **continental crust** (land) and **oceanic crust** (oceans and seas).

1.3 The Crust

The crust is the **outermost layer of the Earth** and makes up the top part of the lithosphere. It is made of solid rock.

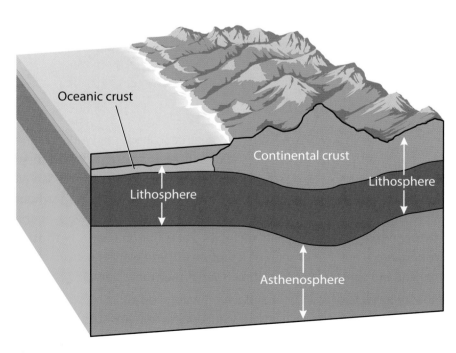

🔼 **Fig. 1.4** The continental crust is thicker and lighter than the oceanic crust.

 **GEO DICTIONARY**

Convection currents: when air or liquid is heated, it becomes buoyant, causing it to rise. When it is cooled, it becomes less buoyant and sinks

Moho: the boundary between the crust and the solid upper mantle (collectively known as the lithosphere)

Theory: A proposed idea or group of ideas to help explain events. A theory is widely held to be true but has not been proven

ACTIVE LEARNING

1. Describe the following:
   (a) The inner core
   (b) The outer core
   (c) The lower mantle
   (d) The asthenosphere
2. Go to the following website:
   scienceline.ucsb.edu
   Explore the geography section where scientists and geographers answer commonly asked questions.

The Continental Crust

The continental crust is, on average, **45 km thick.** In places, it can be as **thin as 30 km** where **continents are pulling apart** and as **thick as 70 km** underneath **mountain ranges.** The rocks which form the **continental crust are light,** e.g. **granite.** Rocks such as granite are rich in the minerals **silica and aluminium** – known collectively as **sial.**

Note!

Continental crust = sial

The Oceanic Crust

The oceanic crust is **much thinner** than the continental crust. It is **8 km thick on average,** but is as thin as 3 km in parts. The rocks which form oceanic crust are **heavy,** e.g. **basalt.** This means that the oceanic crust is **heavier than the continental crust,** even though it is thinner. Rocks such as basalt are rich in the **minerals silica and magnesium** – known collectively as **sima.**

Note!

Oceanic crust = sima

ACTIVE LEARNING

Describe the differences between continental crust and oceanic crust.

GEO DICTIONARY

Motion: movement of any kind

Natural disaster: a major event caused by nature such as an earthquake that has negative effects on life on the Earth

EDUCATE YOURSELF

Earth's Structure		
Core	Inner core: nickel and iron, solid, hottest layer, 6000 °C, transfers heat to upper layers	
	Outer core: iron, molten, spins around inner core, generates magnetic field	
Mantle	Lower mantle: molten magma, convection currents begin here	
	Asthenosphere: semi-molten rock, 100–200 km below surface, lithosphere slides on top of it	
	Lithosphere: solid upper mantle and crust, slides on asthenosphere, 50–100 km thick, broken sections called plates	
Crust	Continental crust: average thickness 45 km; light, granite, sial	
	Oceanic crust: average thickness 8 km; heavy, basalt, sima	

1.4 Plate Tectonics

Over the last century, we have learned a great deal about the workings of our planet. This short period of time has led to a greater understanding of the world we live in. Like most major discoveries, this greater understanding began with a simple observation. Over a number of decades that followed, large amounts of information and other ideas were gathered and made into a working theory: the theory of plate tectonics. Plate tectonics states that the Earth's **lithosphere is broken** into a number of slabs called **plates.** These plates float on top of the mantle and are constantly **in motion** – even if they move very slowly.

The theory helps to explain how and where natural disasters such as earthquakes occur. It also explains how and where features such as volcanoes and fold mountains occur. To do well in the Leaving Certificate geography exam, it is vital that you understand plates and plate boundaries.

ACTIVE LEARNING

Look at a map of the world before you begin studying plate tectonics:

1. Do you notice anything about the shapes of all the continents?

2. If the continents were pieces of a (very old) jigsaw, what pieces could you join together easily?

3. Go to **bbc.co.uk/science** and search for 'Pangaea' to watch a video about continental drift.

Plates

There are **seven major plates** and several smaller ones. As these plates move, they collide with, separate from, or slide past each other along their **boundaries.** It is along these plate boundaries that nearly all **earthquakes, fold mountains and volcanoes occur.** Plate tectonics explains **how** and **why** this movement occurs.

As these plates move, they interact with each other, greatly shaping our planet.

Theories

The theory of plate tectonics was formed as a result of evidence from several earlier theories:

- The theory of continental drift – Alfred Wegner (1912)
- The theory of convection currents – Arthur Holmes (1928)
- The theory of mid-ocean ridges – Maurice 'Doc' Ewing (1947)
- The theory of seafloor spreading – Harry Hess (1962)

These theories served as building blocks of information. They combined to make up the theory of plate tectonics.

FACT

The Earth's plates move at roughly 1 cm per year (roughly the same speed as human fingernails grow!). However some plates move faster at up to 4 cm per year.

Note!

Familiarise yourself with a map of the world. Make sure you can identify the following:

- All continents
- All major oceans
- Iceland

In Chapter 2, we will look at plate boundaries and how they interact with each other in more detail.

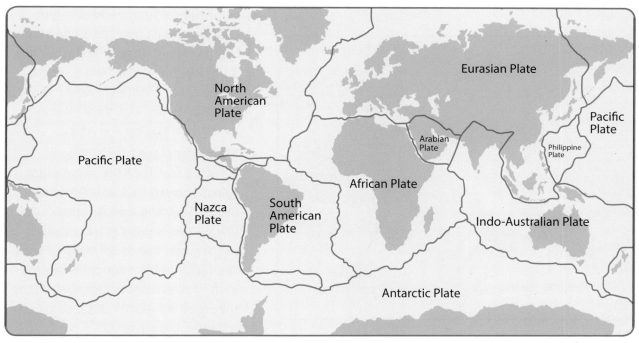

⊙ **Fig. 1.5** The Earth's crust is broken into sections called plates.

Continental Drift

Alfred Wegner was a German **meteorologist.** He developed the theory of continental drift, which states that the world's continents are constantly moving. This theory provided the foundations of what was eventually to become the theory of plate tectonics.

GEO DICTIONARY

Meteorologist: a scientist who studies atmospheric conditions and weather patterns

▶ **Fig. 1.6** Alfred Wegner

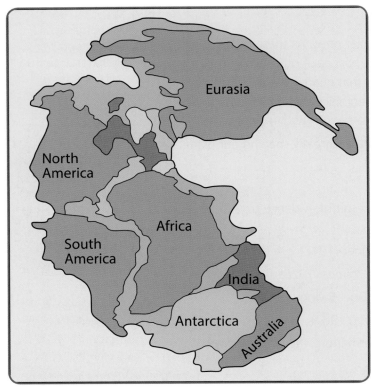

Fig. 1.7 Pangaea

Continental drift began as a simple observation. Wegner noted that the east coast of South America and the west coast of Africa fit together almost perfectly. From this observation, Wegner proposed that **all landmasses were** originally **joined together** in one super continent he called **Pangaea** (Greek for 'all land'). He suggested that this supercontinent **began to break apart** roughly **200 million years ago.** Wegner suggested that Pangaea first broke into two smaller supercontinents he named **Gondwanaland** and **Laurasia,** before **eventually forming the continents and oceans we see today.** Wegner collected large amounts of data to help prove his theory, dividing it into five main proofs.

Proof of Continental Drift

- **Continental fit:** If we look at the continents on a map, their **coastlines** look as though they **fit together like a jigsaw.** These matching coastlines suggest that continents were previously joined together, e.g. the Americas joined with Europe and Africa.

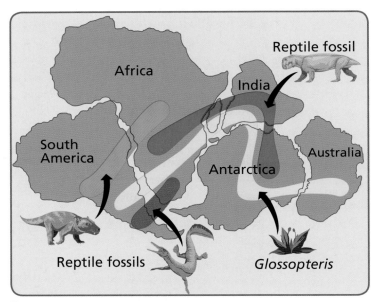

Fig. 1.8 Matching fossils of plants and animals

- **Matching plant fossils:** Wegner collected **fossils of the same plant (*glossopteris*) in South America, India, Australia and Antarctica.** Usually plants grow in specific parts of the world due to differing climates. The fact that the same plant grew in each of these continents showed that they must have been closer or joined together in the past.

- **Matching animal fossils:** Wegner also collected **fossils of the same reptile in both South America and Africa.** At the time, it was suggested that land bridges connected the continents, allowing animals to spread throughout the world. However, Wegner suggested that animals could not have travelled those distances.

- **Matching rock folds:** Identical **fold mountains** are found on the **east coast of the USA and the western and northern coasts of Europe,** e.g. Ireland, Scotland and Scandinavia.

- **Glacial deposits:** Evidence of **materials left behind from glaciers** is found in several continents, such as Africa, which are largely far too warm to have these ice flows.

GEO DICTIONARY

Glossopteris: a type of fern that is now extinct

Glaciers: huge sheets of ice that covered large parts of the Earth during ice ages

---

Despite having a lot of evidence, Wegner's theory was not accepted by his fellow geographers. The main reason for this was his **failure to explain how such huge slabs of rock could move.** It was not until Arthur Holmes presented the idea of **convection currents** that Wegner's idea began to be taken seriously.

Convection Currents

In 1928, Arthur Holmes discovered a way in which plates could move. He suggested that **magma deep in the mantle** was **heated by the Earth's core.** As magma becomes hotter, it rises towards the crust in the same way that boiling water rises when it boils. As the magma reaches the **upper mantle,** it cools and becomes semi-molten. The cooling magma moves **laterally,** before sinking downwards again. As the **semi-molten rock moves sideways,** it rubs off the Earth's lithosphere causing friction. This **friction causes the plates** to **pull apart, collide** or **slide** past each other at their boundaries.

⬆ **Fig. 1.9** Arthur Holmes

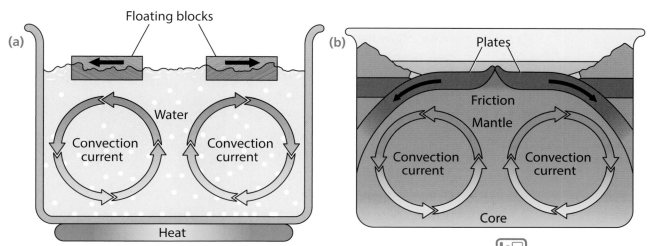

⬆ **Fig. 1.10** (a) Convection currents can be seen in a pot of boiling water. As the water is heated closest to the stove at the bottom of the pot, it rises towards the top of the pot where some of its heat escapes as steam. Once the steam escapes, the water sinks down to the bottom again and the process is repeated. If you place two pieces of wood into the water, they will move away from each other. This is caused by friction between the wood and the water. (b) The same process is occurring in the Earth's mantle on an enormous scale. Friction between cooling magma and the Earth's lithosphere causes entire continents to move.

Mid-Ocean Ridges

In 1947, Maurice Ewing discovered a **chain of underwater volcanoes** and mountains along the middle of the Atlantic Ocean. This chain became known as the **Mid-Atlantic Ridge.** Ewing also discovered that the **ocean floor was made of basalt and was much thinner** than usual **close to the ridge.** This suggested that **plates were pulling apart at this point.** Many other mid-ocean ridges have since been discovered.

⬆ **Fig. 1.11** Maurice Ewing

ACTIVE LEARNING

1. Explain how convection currents cause plate movement with reference to Fig. 1.10.

2. Place the palm of your hand flat on your desk and press down hard. Try to slide your hand backwards and forwards along the desk. What happens? What causes this to happen?

3. Press your hands tightly together and rub them rapidly. What happens? Why?

CORE 1 CHAPTER 1

ACTIVE **LEARNING**

1. Explain the theory of continental drift and describe three pieces of evidence to support it.

2. Why was the theory of continental drift not accepted at first?

3. Explain how convection currents help to prove that continental drift is occurring.

4. Using Fig. 1.13, name the two plates pulling apart to form the Mid-Atlantic Ridge.

GEO **DICTIONARY**

Lava: the name given to magma when it reaches the Earth's surface

Seafloor Spreading

In 1962, Harry Hess, a naval officer, added to the discoveries made by Ewing. Hess discovered that **mid-ocean ridges were points where new seafloor was made.** As convection currents cause plates to pull apart from each other, **magma pushes upwards** between them. When it reaches the ocean floor, the **lava cools rapidly to form basalt rock.** This basalt rock forms new seafloor.

⬆ **Fig. 1.12** Harry Hess

As **new seafloor is created,** the **older floor is pushed further away from the ridge,** making the ocean wider. For example, the **North American Plate** and **Eurasian Plate** began to move apart **60 million years ago,** opening up the Atlantic Ocean.

Proof of Seafloor Spreading

* **Age of seafloor:** Rock samples taken from the floor of the Atlantic Ocean show that **the ocean floor gets progressively older further from the ridge.** Ocean floor beside the **Mid-Atlantic Ridge is 10 million years old,** while ocean floor near the **North American and Eurasian continents is over 180 million years old.**

* **Ocean sediments:** In the same way as house furniture gets covered in dust, ocean floors are gradually covered in sediment over time. **Ocean floor further away from mid-ocean ridges has much thicker sediment** than floor close to it. This shows ocean floor further away from mid-ocean ridges is older.

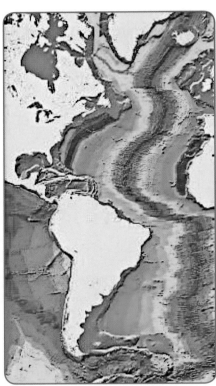
⬆ **Fig. 1.13** The youngest seafloor is found along mid-ocean ridges.

➤ **Fig. 1.14** Ocean sediments gather like dust on the wreck of the *Titanic*.

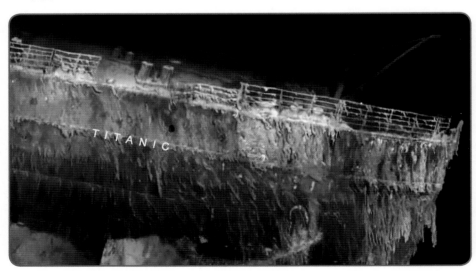

1.5 Subduction

Having learned about the theory of plate tectonics, you now know that the **Earth's plates are constantly in motion** due to convection currents. You also know that, **where plates pull apart, new seafloor is created** along mid-ocean ridges. **Mid-ocean ridges are underwater volcanoes** which form as lava reaches the surface through the gap between the **separating plates.** Separating plate boundaries can be called any of the following:

- Separating boundaries
- Divergent boundaries
- Constructive boundaries

If new ocean floor is constantly being made, does that mean the Earth is getting bigger?

After the discovery of seafloor spreading, scientists puzzled over this question. The answer is no. As **new ocean floor is created at mid-ocean ridges, the older ocean floor is destroyed close to the continents** where plates collide with each other. **Colliding plates** can be called any of the following:

- Colliding boundaries
- Convergent boundaries
- Destructive boundaries

As you already know, **oceanic crust is heavier than continental crust.** Therefore, when an **oceanic plate collides with a continental plate**, the **oceanic plate's heavier weight means it sinks back down into the mantle.** Here, it is **melted back into magma** by the extreme heat (*see* Fig. 1.15). When **two oceanic plates collide**, the **heavier plate sinks** underneath the lighter one. This process is called **subduction.** This means that the Earth is constantly **recycling its lithosphere.** We will look at subduction and other processes along plate boundaries in more detail in Chapter 2.

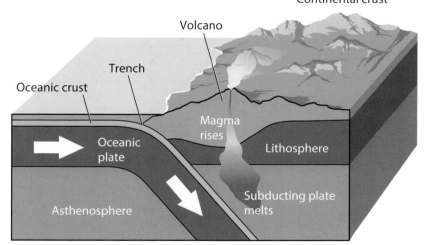

Fig. 1.15 Subduction zone

When the oceanic plate first sinks into the mantle, it is **much heavier than the surrounding magma.** As it is **surrounded by liquid**, it begins to **sink further downwards** before melting, **dragging more of the plate with it.** This process is known as **slab pull.** This dragging down of plates helps to explain why some plates move faster than others.

ACTIVE **LEARNING**

Explain why the process of subduction (melting plates) is not causing the Earth to get smaller.

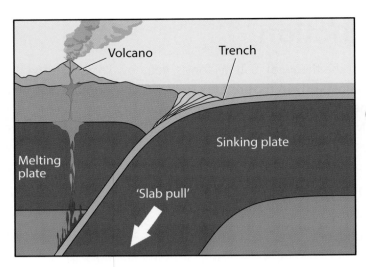

 Fig. 1.16 Slab pull drags the plate down into the mantle.

EDUCATE YOURSELF

Theory of Plate Tectonics	
Continental drift	Pangaea, Gondwanaland, Laurasia, continental fit (jigsaw), matching plants and animal fossils, matching fold mountain ranges
Convection currents	Magma heated in lower mantle, rises towards lithosphere, cools and becomes semi-molten, moves sideways and sinks, sideways movement causes friction, friction moves plates
Mid-ocean ridges	Chain of underwater volcanoes, plates separating, ocean floor thinner here
Seafloor spreading	New seafloor made at mid-ocean ridges, older seafloor pushed towards continents, oceans getting bigger, age of seafloor and ocean sediments proof of theory
Subduction and slab pull	Heavy oceanic plate collides with light oceanic plate, oceanic plate sinks into mantle and melts, before the plate melts it sinks into mantle, drags the rest of the plate with it

EXAM QUESTIONS

ORDINARY LEVEL

SHORT QUESTIONS

1. Examine the diagram and match each letter in the diagram with one of the descriptions:

Outer core	
Mantle/convection currents	
Inner core	
Mid-ocean ridge	
Ocean trench	

5 x 2m

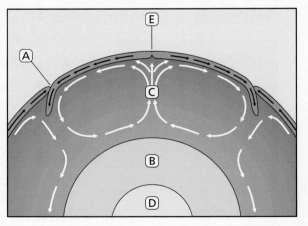

2010 Q1 8M

14   EARTH

ORDINARY LEVEL

2. (i) Match each of the letters A, B and C on the map with the correct tectonic plate in the table.

Tectonic plate	Letter
African	
North American	
Pacific	

(ii) Name the two plates that are colliding together.

(iii) Name the plate on which Ireland lies.

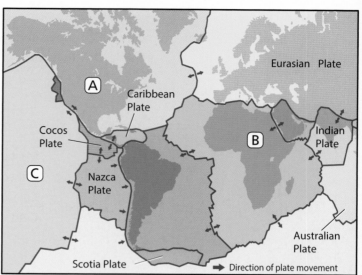

2014 Q6 8M

(i) 3 x 2m	
(ii) 2m	
(iii) 2m	

LONG QUESTIONS

1. Examine the diagram and answer the following questions:

(i) Describe briefly how the currents at A move.

(ii) Name the landform at B which is found on the seafloor of the Atlantic Ocean.

(iii) Are the plates colliding or separating at C?

(iv) Explain briefly the process of subduction.

(v) Briefly describe the difference between lava and magma.

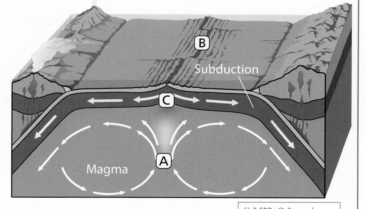

2013 Q1A 30M

(i) 2 SRPs @ 3m each
(ii) 6m
(iii) 6m
(iv) 2 SRPs @ 3m each
(v) 2 SRPs @ 3m each

2. Match each of the following names with the correct letter from the diagram:

- Crust
- Outer core
- Mantle
- Inner core

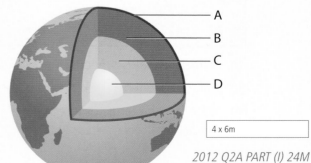

4 x 6m

2012 Q2A PART (I) 24M

SHORT QUESTIONS

1. Examine the diagram below which shows the structure of the Earth.
Match each of the letters A to D with its correct name in the table.

Structure of the Earth

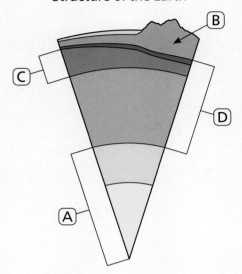

Name	Letter
Mantle	
Asthenosphere	
Core	
Crust	

4 x 2m

2011 Q8 8M

2. Examine the map and answer the following questions.

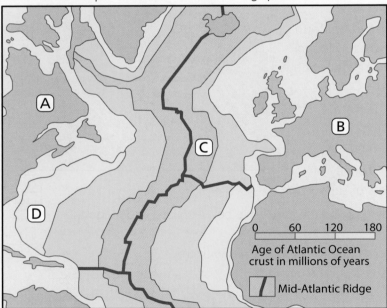

Age of Atlantic Ocean crust in millions of years

Mid-Atlantic Ridge

(i) Name the plates A and B.

(ii) Name the igneous rock most commonly found at C.

(iii) State the age range of the ocean crust at C and the age range of the ocean crust at D.

(i) 2 x 1m

(ii) 2m

(iii) 2 x 1m

2013 Q1 PARTS I–III 6M

LONG QUESTIONS

1. Examine the map showing major crustal plates of the Earth and answer the following questions:

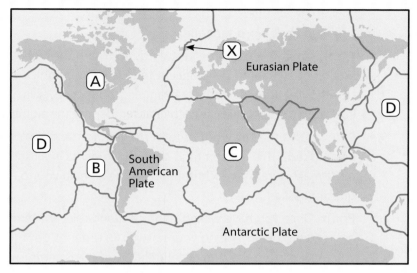

(i) Name the plates A, B, C and D.

(ii) Name the plate boundary at X.

(i) 4 x 4m
(ii) 4m

2011 Q2A 20M

2. Examine the diagram showing the internal structure of the Earth and answer the following questions:

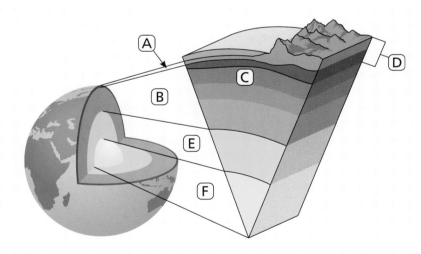

(i) Name each of the layers of the Earth A, B, C, D, E and F.

(ii) Describe briefly the main difference between the composition of layer C and layer D.

(iii) Explain briefly why plates move.

(i) 6 x 2m
(ii) 2 SRPs @ 2m each
(iii) 2 SRPs @ 2meach

2014 Q2A 20M

What Is an SRP?

SRP stands for **S**ignificant **R**elevant **P**oint. It is the method used to correct the Leaving Certificate geography exam. While the thought of sitting the exam can be stressful, acquiring good exam habits now will make the journey much easier. So what does the term mean and how difficult is it to write in an SRP format?

Let's look at each word separately:

- **Significant:** These are the key words you learn throughout each section of a chapter. A significant term is a geographical term, fact or statistic you have learned, for example, subduction, lava, volcano. The Educate Yourself tables in each chapter identify the significant terms.

- **Relevant:** Is the key word or term relevant to the question you have been asked? This is a common issue for students in all subjects. You must make sure that each term you pick will help you to answer the question asked.

- **Point:** Once you have picked significant and relevant terms, you are ready to begin writing your answer. In order to get full marks, you must explain the significant, relevant pieces of information in a sentence that shows the examiner that you fully understand what they mean and in a way that fully answers the question.

Each SRP you write is worth 2 marks at Higher Level and 3 marks at Ordinary Level. The marks for each SRP are shown in the sample answer below. SRPs are also awarded for named examples, labelled diagrams and so on.

Plate tectonics is a very important part of the physical geography section. It often appears in exam questions, alongside related topics such as:

- Volcanoes
- Earthquakes
- Fold mountains

> It is important that you can link plate tectonics to these topics.

The theory of plate tectonics has appeared as a 30-mark question on the Ordinary Level paper but not yet on the Higher Level paper. But it is only a matter of time! It is vital that you understand, and are able to describe the theory under the main headings. In order to practise this, we will answer a possible exam question.

SAMPLE **QUESTION**

Explain the theory of plate tectonics and describe the evidence used to prove it.

> This is a straightforward question that asks you to explain a theory in a logical manner. In order to answer this question, you must understand the theory fully.

Marking Scheme
Definition 1 SRP @ 2m
General discussion 14 SRPs @ 2m each
Allow 1 SRP for (optional) diagram

The following table includes all of the key terms and elements needed to fully answer this question.

Convection currents	Continental drift	Seafloor spreading
Moves plates	Pangaea	New seafloor
Magma heated and rises	Gondwanaland	Mid-ocean ridges
Cools	Laurasia	Widening of oceans
Semi-molten	Continental fit	Ocean sediments
Moves sideways/sinks	Matching fossils	
Friction	Matching fold mountains	

SAMPLE ANSWER

The theory of plate tectonics states that the Earth is divided up into seven major plates that float on the mantle [2m]. The theory explains how and why these plates interact with each other to cause earthquakes, volcanoes and other natural events [2m].

Convection Currents

Convection currents are the process that causes tectonic plates to move through the constant heating and cooling of magma in the mantle [2m]. Molten magma deep in the mantle is heated by the core, causing it to rise towards the lithosphere [2m]. As it rises it cools, becoming semi-molten [2m]. The semi-molten magma moves laterally along the Earth's lithosphere before sinking down towards the core. Friction between the semi-molten magma and the plates cause them to collide, separate or slide past each other [2m].

Continental Drift

Continental drift proposes that all of the Earth's continents and landmasses were joined together as one giant continent called Pangaea [2m]. Convection currents caused Pangaea to break apart roughly 200 million years ago [2m]. Pangaea broke into two large continents called Gondwanaland and Laurasia, before forming the continents we have today [2m]. There are three proofs of this theory: continental fit, matching fossils and sediments, and matching folding patterns [2m].

Continental fit suggests that the coastal edges of continents fit together like a jigsaw, e.g. the west coast of Africa and the east coast of South America [2m]. Wegner noticed similarities between plant and animal fossils on either side of the Atlantic, in places

A **definition** of the theory is given before examples and description.

The description is organised, starting with the basic theory of how plates move, before moving to the separate theories and proofs that led to the theory of plate tectonics.

Many students fail to link plate tectonics to the activities that occur along plate boundaries. If you understand the causes and proofs of this theory, it will make the next four chapters much easier to understand.

As always, ask yourself whether you have answered the question asked!

that now have very different climates. This suggested that the continents must have been joined together at some point, e.g. South America and Antarctica [2m]. Fold mountains found in northern Europe (Scandinavia) match fold mountains found in eastern US, suggesting that both ranges were created at the same time, on the same plate boundary [2m].

Seafloor Spreading

A chain of underwater volcanoes, known as the Mid-Atlantic Ridge, was discovered on the floor of the Atlantic [2m]. It was suggested that new seafloor was being formed at this point. Lava cooled on the bottom of the ocean as plates separate from each other, causing magma to rise up to fill the cracks in the crust [2m]. Through this process, oceans are widened, as older rock moves away from the ridge and is replaced by younger rock. Ocean sediments are the main proof for seafloor spreading [2m]. The depth of sediment resting on the ocean floor allows scientists to tell which ocean floor is oldest: the thicker the sediment, the older the ocean floor [2m].

Note!

Many of the sample answers will include more SRPs than are needed to answer the question. If you write extra relevant SRPs in the exam, you will be awarded on your best ones.

Logical order of theories and proofs showing a clear understanding and knowledge of topic

Marks Awarded
Definition of plate tectonics 1 SRP @ 2m
Best 14 SRPs @ 2m each
Total 30/30

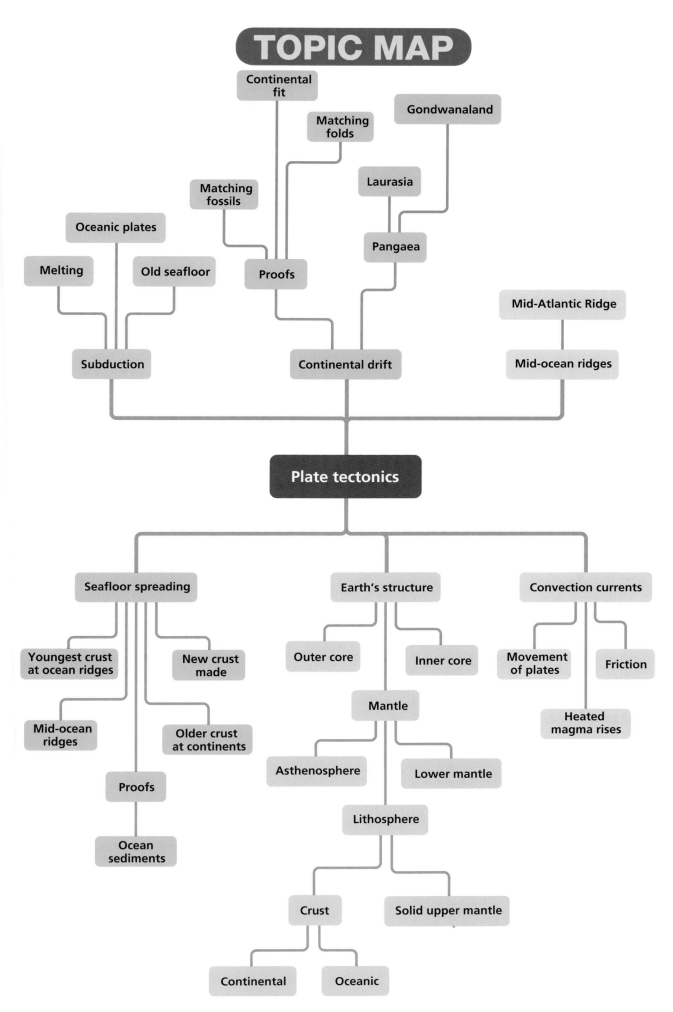

TOPIC MAP

Continental fit

Matching folds

Gondwanaland

Matching fossils

Laurasia

Oceanic plates

Melting

Old seafloor

Proofs

Pangaea

Mid-Atlantic Ridge

Subduction

Continental drift

Mid-ocean ridges

Plate tectonics

Seafloor spreading

Earth's structure

Convection currents

Youngest crust at ocean ridges

New crust made

Outer core

Inner core

Movement of plates

Friction

Mid-ocean ridges

Older crust at continents

Mantle

Heated magma rises

Proofs

Asthenosphere

Lower mantle

Ocean sediments

Lithosphere

Crust

Solid upper mantle

Continental

Oceanic

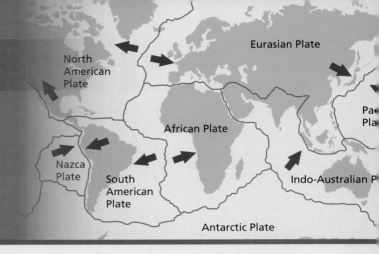

CHAPTER 2

Plate Boundaries

In Chapter 1, you learned about one of the most important theories discovered about the workings of our planet. Key points of the theory of plate tectonics are that:

- The Earth's crust is divided into sections called plates.
- These plates are moved by convection currents.

In this chapter, we will look at the effects of this plate movement on the surface of the planet. We will look specifically at the effects of plates colliding, separating and sliding past each other. This chapter is important as it links directly to the next three chapters of the book. Therefore, a good understanding of this will make progress in the next chapters much easier.

KEY WORDS

- Convection currents
- Convergent/destructive/colliding plate boundaries
- Divergent/constructive/separating boundaries
- Transform/passive/neutral plate boundaries
- Continental-continental
- Continental-oceanic
- Oceanic-oceanic
- Earthquakes
- Fold mountains
- Subduction
- Ocean trenches
- Mid-ocean ridges
- Rifting
- Volcanoes
- San Andreas Fault
- Mid-Atlantic Ridge

LEARNING OUTCOMES

What you **MUST** know
- The three types of plate boundary
- How each of the three plate boundaries is formed
- The three types of convergent/destructive plate boundary
- Examples of each type of plate boundary between major plates
- The processes and landforms that occur at each type of plate boundary

- Global examples of landforms at plate boundaries
- Formation of the Andes Mountains
- Ireland's tectonic journey

What you **SHOULD** know
- Additional examples of boundaries between plates

What is **USEFUL** to know
- Iceland CASE STUDY

Introduction

As you now know, the Earth's **plates are constantly in motion** due to the effects of **convection currents** and slab pull. This motion leads to plates separating, colliding and sliding past each other. This movement leads to the crust at the edges of the plates being changed or destroyed or, in some cases, new crust being created.

There are three types of plate boundary.

- When two or more **plates separate** from each other, it creates a **divergent plate boundary.** Divergent boundaries are also called constructive or separating boundaries as **new crust is created** between them.

- When two or more **plates collide** into each other, it creates a **convergent plate** boundary. Convergent boundaries are also called destructive or colliding boundaries as crust is destroyed.

- Some plates neither collide nor separate. Instead, they **slide past each other,** creating a **passive plate** boundary. These are also called transform or neutral boundaries. Crust is neither created nor destroyed at these boundaries.

2.1 Divergent Boundaries

Convection currents rise towards the crust and move away from each other. As they move away from each other, the friction from the currents pulls the plates apart. This is the process that forms divergent plate boundaries.

The boundary between the **Eurasian and North American Plates** is an example of a major divergent boundary. This has formed as convection currents move the plates away from each other

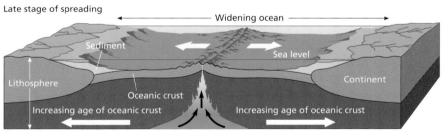

Fig. 2.1 Divergent boundaries lead to rifting and seafloor spreading.

at a rate of **2.5 cm per year.** As plates separate, **magma rises from the mantle** to fill the gap left between them. This leads to the formation of **ocean ridges** and **volcanoes** along the plate boundary. Over millions of years, **parts of the ocean ridges rise above sea level.** When this happens **volcanic islands form,** creating new land. **Iceland** is an example of a newly formed volcanic island. It forms part of the **Mid-Atlantic Ridge.**

Divergent boundaries occur underneath oceanic crust and continental crust, leading to different formations:

- Separating continental plates lead to the formation of rift valleys.

- Separating oceanic crust leads to seafloor spreading and the formation of mid-ocean ridges.

Rift Valleys

Rift valleys are formed when continental plates are pulled apart by convection currents. The convection currents begin to **stretch land** within a continent. As an area of crust is stretched, it becomes **thinner** than the surrounding crust. This creates a **valley**. Eventually the **crust tears apart**, creating a new divergent plate boundary. Currently, **East Africa is rifting apart** from the rest of the African continent. The Red Sea has formed as a result of water from the Indian Ocean rushing in to fill the north part of the rift valley.

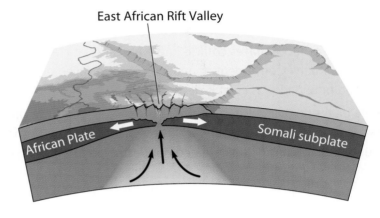

🔺 **Fig. 2.2** East African Rift Valley

Seafloor Spreading

As you learned in Chapter 1, seafloor spreading occurs when separating oceanic plates allow magma to rise through the gap before cooling to form new oceanic crust. As new seafloor is created, oceans are widened. The Atlantic began to open up roughly **130 million years ago** and continues to grow wider today. Mid-ocean ridges are **chains of underwater volcanoes** that form along the gap between the separating plates. They are created over millions of years as **layers of hardened lava form layers of basalt rock,** which build up to form volcanic mountains. The Mid-Atlantic Ridge marks the **line of divergence** along the Atlantic Ocean. Over time, certain mountains build up to break the surface of the ocean. When this occurs, they form volcanic islands such as Iceland.

Note!
Revise Chapter 1 for more detail on seafloor spreading.

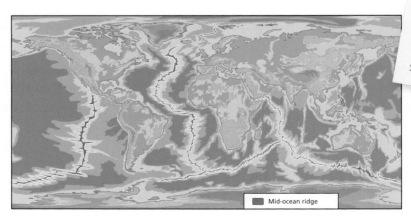

Mid-ocean ridge

🔺 **Fig. 2.3** The red lines show the mid-ocean ridges of the world's oceans. The light blue areas bordering the continents are continental shelves (the edges of continents that have been submerged by the ocean).

Case Study: Iceland

Iceland is a volcanic island that sits on the Mid-Atlantic Ridge. It is one of the youngest pieces of land on Earth, having formed between 16 and 18 million years ago.

The land formed after a series of volcanic eruptions caused the ridge to rise above sea level. Half of Iceland lies on the Eurasian Plate, while the other half lies on the North American Plate. As the plates separate, Iceland is split apart, allowing magma to rise upwards. The magma erupts onto the surface to form volcanoes along the country's surface. Lava from these volcanoes cools on the surface to form new basalt rock, causing the island to grow in size.

As a result, Iceland is **one of the most volcanically active** places in the world. There are over **130 active volcanoes** dotted along the island, with most concentrated along the line of divergence between the two plates. On average, an Icelandic volcano erupts every 5 to 10 years.

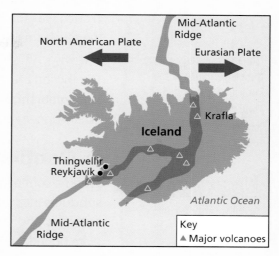

🔺 **Fig. 2.4** Iceland lies on the divergent plate boundary between the North American and Eurasian Plates, making it volcanically active.

2.2 Convergent Boundaries

Convergent plate boundaries are formed where convection currents cause two or more plates to **collide with one another.** For example, a convergent plate boundary exists between the **Eurasian Plate and the Pacific Plate.** Convergent boundaries are often called **destructive boundaries.** There are three types of convergent plate boundary.

- Oceanic-oceanic
- Continental-oceanic
- Continental-continental

The type of boundary depends on the type of plates that collide.

> **Note!**
> Subduction and uplifting are the key processes active along convergent plate boundaries.

1. Oceanic-Oceanic

When two oceanic plates collide, the **heavier plate subducts** underneath the lighter plate. The subducting plate **sinks into the mantle and melts** at a depth of roughly 100 km. Magma from the melting plate **rises upwards through the overlying plate.**

Eventually, the magma **reaches the surface, forming volcanoes.** As material from the volcanoes build up, **volcanic arc islands are formed,** e.g. the Mariana Islands in the Pacific Ocean.

> 📱 **ACTIVE LEARNING**
> Research the following:
> 1. The 2004 Indonesian tsunami
> 2. The 2011 Japanese tsunami
> If possible, present your findings to your class.

Oceanic-oceanic convergence

◀ **Fig. 2.5** Oceanic-oceanic boundary

CORE 1 CHAPTER 2

The point where one plate sinks underneath another (the zone of subduction) leads to the formation of a **deep ocean trench.** For example, the **Marianas Trench** was formed from the subduction of the Pacific Plate underneath the much smaller Philippine Plate. Reaching a depth of over 11 000 m, the Marianas Trench is the deepest part of ocean floor in the world.

The friction caused between a subducting and an overlying plate leads to **strong earthquakes occurring along the boundary.** When an earthquake occurs under water, it **can trigger a tsunami.**

2. Continental-Oceanic

When a continental and an oceanic plate collide, the **heavier oceanic plate subducts** into the mantle. As with oceanic-oceanic convergences, **ocean trenches and strong earthquakes** are created along a continental-oceanic plate boundary. Volcanic arcs are also formed along the continental plate as **magma** from the subducting plate is **forced upwards.** Eventually, the magma forces its way through the continental plate to form **volcanic mountains.** This occurs where the Pacific Plate subducts underneath the Eurasian Plate. The magma from the melting Pacific Plate rises through the Eurasian Plate to form volcanic mountains. Over time, layers of lava from the volcanoes build up to break the surface of the ocean. This has led to the formation of the **Japanese archipelago islands.**

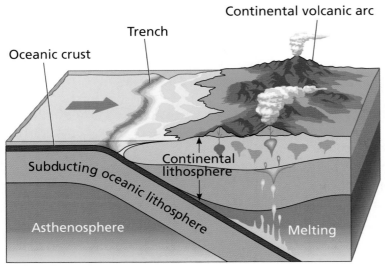

Fig. 2.6 Continental-oceanic boundary

Fold mountains are also formed along the **edges of the non-subducting (continental) plate.** A large amount of friction is caused between the subducting oceanic plate and overlying continental plate. As the oceanic plate subducts, sudden movement releases pressure that **triggers powerful earthquakes.** This pressure also causes **layers of rock** at the edge of the continental plate to **buckle upwards,** forming tall mountain ranges. This is currently happening on the west coast of South America, where the **Nazca Plate is subducting underneath the South American Plate.** This has led to the formation of the Andes Mountains.

Fig. 2.7 The Andes Mountains have formed as a result of the Nazca Plate subducting beneath the South American Plate.

3. Continental-Continental

When two continental plates collide, **neither plate is subducted.** This is because continental plates are **too light to be forced downwards.** Instead, the movement is **mainly upwards.** This process is called uplift.

As the plates collide, a huge amount of pressure is caused, which **forces layers of rock to buckle.** As the layers of rock buckle, they fold upwards to create fold mountains. Currently, the **Indo-Australian Plate is colliding with the Eurasian Plate.** This has led to the formation of the **Himalaya Mountains,** which are the tallest mountains in the world. The highest peak is Mount Everest, which is **8848 m above sea level.** As the plates continue to collide, the mountains are slowly getting taller each year.

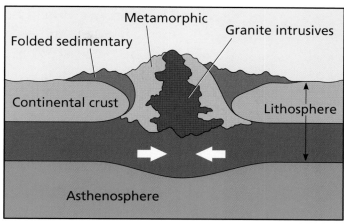

Fig. 2.8 Continental-continental boundary causing the crust to uplift

Earthquakes are common along continental-continental plate boundaries as friction between the plates causes the crust to vibrate. On 25 April 2015, such an earthquake occurred in Nepal killing more than 9000 people.

2.3 Passive Boundaries

Passive plate boundaries are created where **plates slide past each other.** The best-known passive boundary in the world exists between the **North American and Pacific Plates.**

Both the North American and Pacific Plates are moving in a north-westerly direction, but at different speeds. The Pacific Plate is moving at roughly **7 cm per year.** The **North American Plate** is moving at roughly **2 cm per year.** This movement is not smooth, as the edges of the plates generate huge amounts of friction as they move beside each other. This **friction causes the plates to become stuck,** or to lock together.

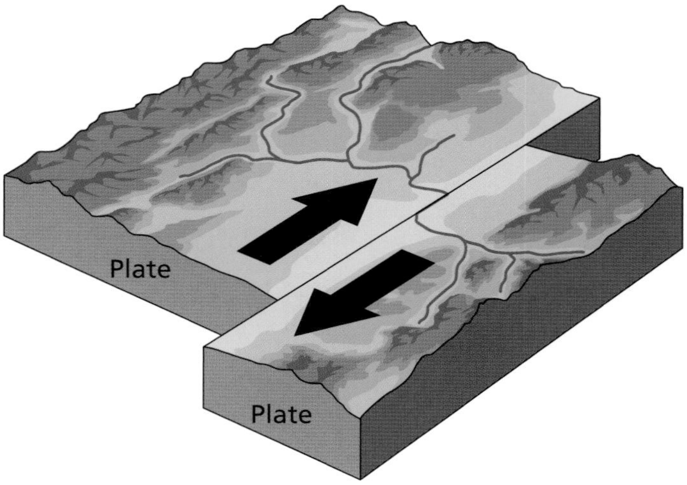

Pressure builds over time as the faster-moving Pacific Plate tries to jolt free from the slower-moving North American Plate. This pressure builds until **one plate slips** or **jolts free.** The sudden movement of the plate triggers **powerful earthquakes.** Generally, the longer the plates are locked together, the more powerful the earthquake will be when they finally slip. The movement of the plates has created a **large crack in the crust** that is over 1300 km long. This is known as the **San Andreas Fault.** The fault formed when **layers of rock were torn apart by the plates.** Most of the earthquakes caused by the passive boundary occur along this fault.

Plates move laterally

Fig. 2.9 Passive boundaries occur where plates slide past each other.

Fig. 2.10 The San Andreas Fault is one of the most earthquake-prone areas in the world. The picture shows the damage caused to the Earth's crust as the Pacific and North American Plates slide past each other.

2.4 Plate Boundaries and Ireland

Although Ireland lies over 1500 km away from its nearest plate boundary, plate movement has played a major role in shaping its landscape. While volcanic eruptions, fold mountain building and violent earthquakes no longer occur here, the landscape of Ireland provides visual evidence that Ireland was once a very tectonically active country. In this section we will look at:

- Ireland's tectonic journey across the globe
- Ireland's tectonic history and rock formations

Ireland's Tectonic Journey

Ireland's journey began in two very different locations. Roughly 850 million years ago, north-west Ireland and Scotland were part of the North American Plate, which lay close to the equator. South-east Ireland lay 25° south of the equator, just below the Tropic of Capricorn.

GEO DICTIONARY

Tropic of Capricorn: a circle of latitude about 23.5° south of the equator. It is the most southerly point where the sun can be directly overhead

(a)   **The seam across Ireland**

Northern half (Laurentia)

Southern half (Avalonia)

Point where Ireland joined together

(b)

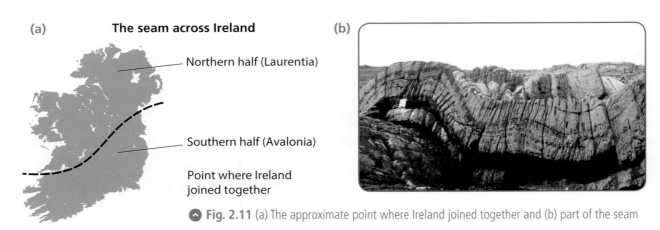

Fig. 2.11 (a) The approximate point where Ireland joined together and (b) part of the seam

Roughly **400 million years ago,** the ocean between the two sections had **closed due to subduction.** The two sections **collided and welded together** under intense pressure. The collision led to **intense folding,** which created the **Caledonian mountains.** The mountains created ran in a **north-west to south-east direction.** Magma rose up underneath the arched folds, creating the **Leinster Batholith.** Layers of sedimentary rock covering the magma were **metamorphosed** due to the intense heat. These metamorphic rocks created **resistant caps** on the peaks on many of the Caledonian mountains, e.g. the **Sugarloaf Mountain** in Co. Wicklow.

By **380 million years ago**, Ireland lay **15–30° south of the equator** and had a desert climate. At this time, the newly formed **Caledonian mountains** to the north and east were **above sea level**, while the **south and south-west** of Ireland were **covered by a shallow sea**. Sediments which were broken down by **weathering and erosion** were **washed into the shallow sea** by flash floods. Over time, the bottom layers of these sediments were crushed and compacted, before **lithifying to form sandstone**. Due to the high iron content, the sandstone formed had a dark red colour, leading to its common name of **Old Red Sandstone**.

Some **320 million years ago**, global **sea levels rose** significantly, **submerging all of Ireland except** for its highest mountain **peaks**. The **warm tropical sea** was a perfect breeding ground for fish. As fish died, their **fossils built up in layers**, before compressing and **lithifying to form limestone**.

Roughly **250 million years ago**, the **African and Eurasian Plates collided**, which **folded the southern half of the country**. As the folding occurred, **land was uplifted above sea level**, creating the **Munster Ridge Valley**. The collision lead to all the landmasses **joining together** as one supercontinent called **Pangaea**. This folding orogeny also **uplifted the area of the Burren** above sea level. At this time, the **underlying limestone was covered** by thick layers of mudstone.

With the **break-up of Pangaea 200 million years ago**, Ireland began to drift **northwards**. Marine sediments continued to be deposited along the ocean floors surrounding Ireland. Over time, these sediments **partly decomposed** to form **natural gas and oil**.

Approximately **65 million years ago**, the **North American Plate began to separate from the Eurasian Plate**. This separation led to the **formation of the Atlantic Ocean**. As the two landmasses split apart, **intense volcanic activity** began along the newly formed **divergent boundary**. Evidence of this is seen along the **Antrim-Derry Plateau**, where layers of basic lava spilled along the landscape to form basalt, e.g. the **Giant's Causeway** in Co. Antrim.

Volcanic activity ceased in Ireland approximately **15 million years ago**. Despite this, Ireland's **landscape is still changing** due to the processes of **denudation** (weathering and erosion).

Ireland is still on the move, travelling **northwards at 5 cm per year**. This might not seem very fast, but it means Ireland moves some **10 km northwards every 1 million years**. You must remember the timescale involved in tectonic history when considering this movement.

ACTIVE LEARNING

1. Name and give an example of the three different types of convergent boundary.
2. Explain the causes and effects of an oceanic-continental plate boundary.
3. Explain both ways in which fold mountains can occur as a result of convergent plates.
4. Explain how volcanoes can form along convergent boundaries.
5. Research 'The Big One', which is a large earthquake expected to occur along the San Andreas Fault. If possible, present your findings to your class.

GEO DICTIONARY

Flash flood: a sudden and destructive flood caused by very heavy rainfall over a very short space of time

Lithify: when sediments are compacted together to form solid rock

Orogeny: a period of time in which fold mountains are created

Batholith: a large area of igneous rock that forms when magma cools inside Earth's crust

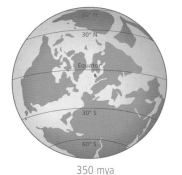

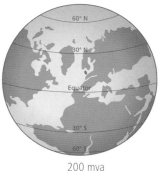

| 850 mya | 350 mya | 200 mya | present day |

Fig. 2.12 Ireland's tectonic journey

2.5 Continental Drift and Ireland

⌃ **Fig. 2.13** Inishtrahull Island off the coast of Malin Head

In Section 2.4, we examined Ireland's continual journey across the globe. The small rocky island of Inishtrahull which lies just 10 km off the coast of Malin Head in Donegal, offers further proof of the effects of continental drift. The island is composed of rock that is over 1.7 billion years old, making it the oldest part of Ireland. Geologists puzzled over the origins of the island as its rock structures are unlike any other rock type found in Ireland. Due to the age of the island, the rocks have been heavily folded and altered by denudation, causing their minerals to separate and form multicoloured layers of gneiss.

⌃ **Fig. 2.14** Multicoloured gneiss rock

Twenty years ago, it was discovered that the island is not part of Ireland at all. Instead the island is a piece of Greenland that broke off as the North American Plate separated from the Eurasian Plate 60 million years ago. As the plates rifted apart, the rock separated from Greenland due to convection currents and positioned itself off the coast of Donegal.

EDUCATE YOURSELF

Plate Boundaries	
Process of movement	Convection currents
Divergent boundaries	E.g. North American and Eurasian Plates, plates separate, land rifts apart, e.g. East African Rift Valley, magma rises to fill gap, cools and forms new seafloor, seafloor spreading, volcanoes form, mid-ocean ridges form along boundary, e.g. Mid-Atlantic Ridge, new land is created, e.g. Iceland
Convergent boundaries	Plates collide, three types of boundary
	Oceanic-oceanic: heavier plate subducts, subducting plate melts, magma from melting plate rises, forms volcanoes on overlying plate, arc islands develop, friction between plates cause earthquakes
	Continental-oceanic: e.g. Pacific and Eurasian Plates, oceanic plate subducts, subducting plate melts, magma from melting plate rises, forms volcanoes on overlying plate, arc islands develop, e.g. Japanese archipelago, friction causes earthquakes
	Continental-continental: e.g. Indo-Australian and Eurasian Plates, neither plate subducts, movement is upwards, layers of rock buckle, fold mountains form, e.g. Himalayas, earthquakes occur
Passive boundaries	E.g. North American and Pacific Plates, plates slide past each other, land neither created nor destroyed, friction causes plates to lock, pressure builds, plate slips suddenly, sudden movement causes earthquake, San Andreas Fault, layers of rock torn apart

ACTIVE **LEARNING**

Visit **www.geolsoc.org. uk** and search for 'plate tectonics' and 'San Andreas Fault' to read interesting articles on these topics.

EXAM QUESTIONS

ORDINARY LEVEL

LONG QUESTIONS

1. Describe and explain what happens at plate boundaries.

   | 10 SRPs @ 3m each |

   2011 Q3C 30M

2. Examine the map and answer the following questions.

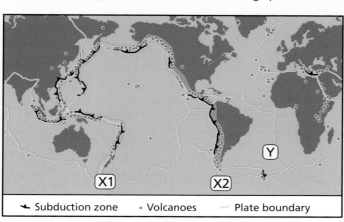

Subduction zone   • Volcanoes   — Plate boundary

   (i) What is the name given to the region from X1, along the shaded line to X2?

   (ii) Name the ridge running north from Y.

   (iii) Name any two volcanoes.

   (iv) Name any two crustal plates.

   (v) Explain briefly what is meant by subduction.

   | (i) + (ii) 4m each |
   | (iii) + (iv) 2 x 4m |
   | (v) 2 x 3m |

   2011 Q2A 30M

3. Study the diagrams and answer the following questions:

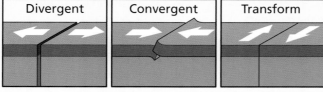

Divergent   Convergent   Transform

   (i) Match each of the descriptions below with the correct plate boundary above:

   • Plates pushing together

   • Plates sliding past each other

   | (i) 3 x 5m |
   | (ii)–(iv) 5m each |

   • Plates pulling apart

   (ii) At which of the above plate boundaries is the mid-ocean ridge?

   (iii) At which of the above plate boundaries would you find fold mountains?

   (iv) Name an example of fold mountains.

   2010 Q1A 30M

HIGHER LEVEL

LONG QUESTIONS

1. Describe and explain destructive plate boundaries.

15 SRPs @ 2m each

2014 Q3B 30M

2. Explain, with reference to examples you have studied, how plate tectonics help us to understand the forces at work along crustal plate boundaries.

Name two forces 2 x 2m
Name examples of different boundaries 2 x 2m
Discussion 11 SRPs @ 2m each

2009 Q1B 30M

3. 'Plate boundaries are zones where crust is both created and destroyed.' Examine the statement with reference to examples you have studied.

Example of each boundary 2 x 2m
Discussion of creation/destruction (2 headings) 7(6) SRPs and 6(7) SRPs @ 2m each

2007 Q1B 30M

Plate boundaries is a vital section of physical geography as it explains the activity of the Earth's crust. It also accounts for the distribution of geographical phenomena such as earthquakes, volcanoes and fold mountains across the globe. It is important to keep in mind that this chapter has introduced you to many of the topics you will study over the next three chapters. Therefore, it is important that you fully understand the processes occurring along each boundary type.

Questions on plate boundaries typically ask you to explain the effects of boundaries or the processes occurring along them. We will look at a question from the 2009 Higher Level Paper.

HIGHER LEVEL

EXAM QUESTION

Explain, with reference to examples that you have studied, how plate tectonics help us to understand the forces at work along plate boundaries.

Marking Scheme
2 forces @ 2m each
2 examples of boundaries @ 2m each
General discussion 11 SRPs @ 2m each

2009 Q1B 30M

First, let's examine the wording of the question.

Note that examples and forces are in plural, meaning you are being asked for more than one of each. Therefore, you can assume that marks are awarded for two examples and two forces. If each example/force is awarded 2m, then 8m are awarded for them in total.

The remaining 22m means you are required to write 11 SRPs.

As you can see, studying the wording of a question carefully gives you a good idea of the marking scheme.

SAMPLE ANSWER

The main forces occurring along plate boundaries are collision and separation [2m + 2m]. The Earth's crust is split into several sections called plates, which float on the mantle [2m]. These plates are moved by convection currents which rise from the lower mantle towards to crust. When the currents move laterally beneath the crust, they generate friction which moves the plates – towards or away from each other [2m].

Force 1: Collision

Where plates collide is referred to as convergent or destructive plate boundaries as land is destroyed [2m]. There are three different types of convergent plate boundary: oceanic-oceanic, continental-continental and oceanic-continental boundaries [2m]. An example of an oceanic-oceanic convergence is the collision of the Pacific and Philippine Plates [2m]. When oceanic plates collide, the heavy plate sinks into the mantle and melts. This process is known as subduction [2m]. As the plate melts, magma rises through cracks in the overlying plate to form volcanoes [2m]. As layers from volcanic materials build up, they reach the surface of the ocean and form chains of arc islands above the subduction zone, e.g. the Mariana Islands [2m]. An example of continental-continental convergence is the collision of the Indo-Australian and Eurasian Plates [2m]. As continental plates are lighter than oceanic plates, the main movement is upwards. This process is known as uplifting [2m]. The collision of the Indo-Australian and Eurasian Plates has caused the plates to fold upwards to form the Himalaya Mountains, with Mount Everest being its tallest peak at 8848 m [2m]. Earthquakes are common along continental-continental plate boundaries as friction and pressure cause sudden movement of plates, e.g. the Nepal earthquake in April 2015 [2m].

An example of oceanic-continental convergence is the collision of the Pacific and Eurasian Plates [2m]. The oceanic plate subducts beneath the continental plate before melting [2m]. The magma from the subducting plate rises through the overlying continental plate to form arc islands along the subduction zone, e.g. the Japanese archipelago [2m]. Tsunamis can be triggered by earthquakes which occur along these boundaries, e.g. the Japanese earthquake and tsunami of 2011 [2m].

Note!

More detail than necessary is given in this answer to show you a number of additional SRPs and how to write them. Remember the technique used in Chapter 1 where you chose your headings and organised your key words before writing.
It will help you to structure your answers before you begin writing.

Force 2: Separation

Where plates separate is referred to as divergent or constructive plate boundaries as new crust is created [2m]. Divergent boundaries can form along oceanic plates, creating mid-ocean ridges and causing seafloor spreading [2m]. An example of this plate boundary is between the North American and Eurasian Plates, which are separating at a rate of 2 cm per year [2m]. As the plates separate, magma rises through the gaps in the crust before cooling to form new basalt rock on the ocean floor [2m]. This rock creates new oceanic crust and gradually widens the Atlantic Ocean. This is called seafloor spreading [2m]. Along the boundary, a chain of underwater volcanoes form the Mid-Atlantic Ridge, which reaches the surface in places, e.g. Iceland [2m]. Iceland formed as layers of newly formed rock piled up before eventually reaching the ocean's surface to form the island [2m].

Convection currents can also slowly rift continents apart as friction causes the crust to stretch before eventually tearing apart to form a new divergent boundary [2m]. As the crust is stretched, it becomes thinner forming a rift valley, e.g. the East African Rift Valley [2m].

Marking Scheme
Forces identified 2 x 2m
Examples given 2 x 2m
Best 11 SRPs @ 2m each
Total 30/30m

TOPIC MAP

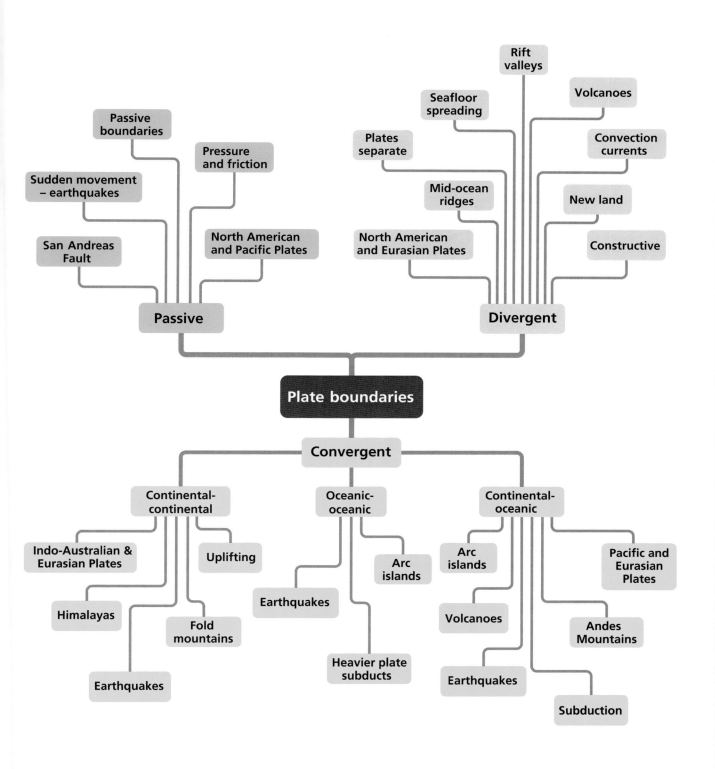

CHAPTER 3

Volcanoes

In Chapter 2, you learned how the theory of plate tectonics causes a variety of natural phenomena at plate boundaries. In this chapter, you will look at one of these phenomena – volcanoes. Volcanoes are openings or vents in the Earth's lithosphere. They allow magma from the mantle to reach the surface.

KEY WORDS

- Active
- Dormant
- Extinct
- Acidic lava
- Basic lava
- Pyroclast
- Tephra
- Lahar

- Convergent boundary
- Divergent boundary
- Hotspot
- Mid-Atlantic Ridge
- Subduction
- Antrim-Derry Plateau
- Leinster Batholith
- Intrusive

- Extrusive
- Seismometers
- Volcanic tourism
- Geothermal energy
- Nevada del Ruiz
- Mount Pinatubo

LEARNING OUTCOMES

What you must know
- The three locations where volcanoes occur
- The differences between active, dormant and extinct volcanoes
- The two types of lava emitted from a volcano
- The different parts of a volcano
- How batholiths and lava plateaux are formed
- How volcanoes are measured and predicted
- Two positive and two negative effects of volcanoes

What you should know
- All materials emitted from a volcano
- Mount Pinatubo CASE STUDY
- Geothermal energy CASE STUDY 📁
- Nevada del Ruiz CASE STUDY 📁

What is useful to know
- The different volcanic cone structures

TOPIC MAP

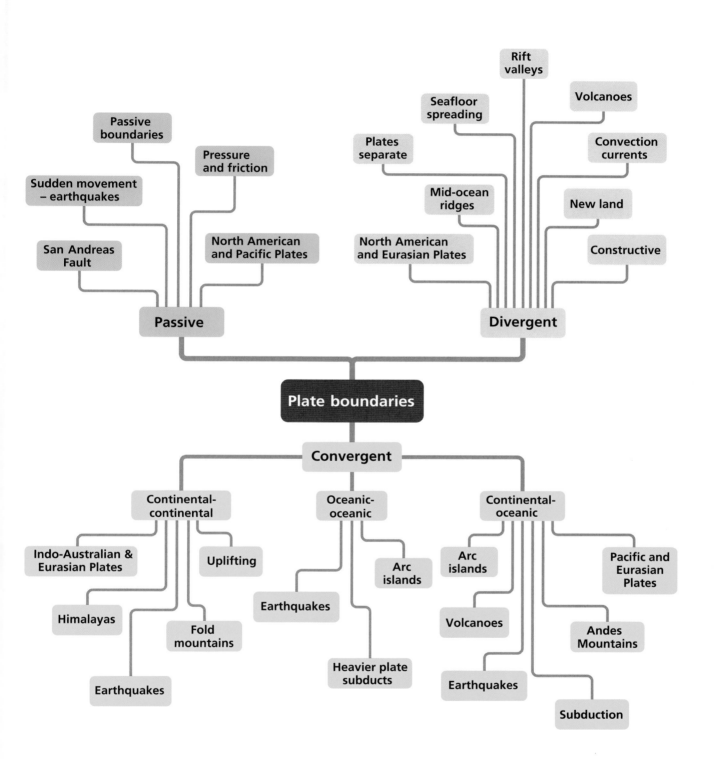

In Chapter 2, you learned how the theory of plate tectonics causes a variety of natural phenomena at plate boundaries. In this chapter, you will look at one of these phenomena – volcanoes. Volcanoes are openings or vents in the Earth's lithosphere. They allow magma from the mantle to reach the surface.

KEY WORDS

- Active
- Dormant
- Extinct
- Acidic lava
- Basic lava
- Pyroclast
- Tephra
- Lahar

- Convergent boundary
- Divergent boundary
- Hotspot
- Mid-Atlantic Ridge
- Subduction
- Antrim-Derry Plateau
- Leinster Batholith
- Intrusive

- Extrusive
- Seismometers
- Volcanic tourism
- Geothermal energy
- Nevada del Ruiz
- Mount Pinatubo

LEARNING OUTCOMES

What you must know
- The three locations where volcanoes occur
- The differences between active, dormant and extinct volcanoes
- The two types of lava emitted from a volcano
- The different parts of a volcano
- How batholiths and lava plateaux are formed
- How volcanoes are measured and predicted
- Two positive and two negative effects of volcanoes

What you should know
- All materials emitted from a volcano
- Mount Pinatubo CASE STUDY
- Geothermal energy CASE STUDY
- Nevada del Ruiz CASE STUDY

What is useful to know
- The different volcanic cone structures

Introduction

Volcanoes occur when **molten magma reaches the Earth's surface** due to **vents or fissures** in the crust. As convection currents force the magma into these fissures, gas bubbles force it towards the surface. When pressure from the **rising gas and magma** becomes too high, lava is released onto the surface. This is called a volcanic eruption. It is estimated that between 30 and 60 volcanoes erupt each year. Across the globe, there are more than 10 000 volcanoes that are capable of erupting some time in the future.

GEO DICTIONARY

Fissure: a narrow crack in the Earth's crust

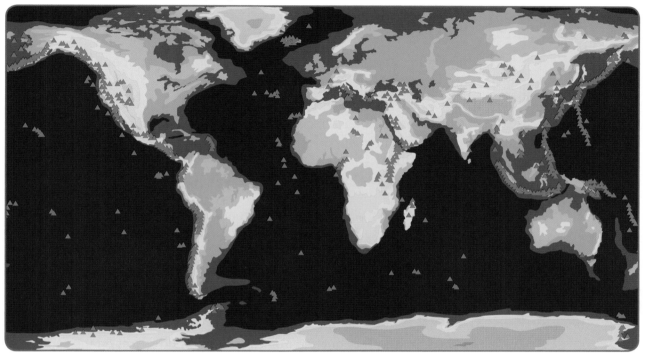

🔼 **Fig. 3.1** The global distribution of active volcanoes

3.1 Categories of Volcanoes

The following diagram shows the different parts of a volcano.

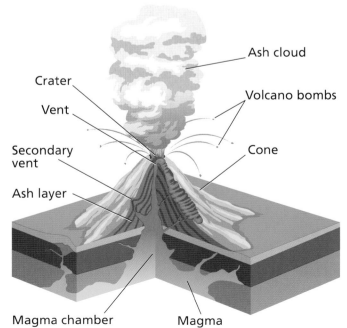

Volcanoes are divided into one of **three general categories** based on their level of activity:

- Active
- Dormant
- Extinct

🔼 **Fig. 3.3** Slemish in Co. Antrim is an extinct volcano.

◀ **Fig. 3.2** The parts of a volcano

Crater
Vent
Secondary vent
Ash layer
Ash cloud
Volcano bombs
Cone
Magma chamber
Magma

Active

There is no universal definition for an active volcano. A volcano is generally said to be active if it has **erupted recently,** is **erupting** or is **likely to erupt** again in the near future. Mount Vesuvius in Italy is an active volcano.

Dormant

A **dormant** volcano has **not erupted in recent history,** but is **likely to erupt again in the future.** For example, the volcano in Yellowstone National Park is estimated to erupt once every 700 000 years.

Extinct

An **extinct** volcano is one which has not erupted in recorded history and is **not expected to erupt again** in the future.

For example, **Slemish in Co. Antrim** is the site of an extinct volcano. It was active at one point. Eruptions ceased roughly 15 million years ago as Ireland moved away from its position on a plate boundary.

3.2 Volcanic Emissions

Five general substances are emitted from volcanic eruptions:

- Lava
- Pyroclast/Pyroclastic flow
- Gases
- Tephra
- Water vapour

Fig. 3.4 An ash cloud rises from a volcano

Lava

Lava is **molten rock** emitted from **volcanoes and fissures** on the Earth's crust. Volcanoes produce two types of lava.

- **Acidic lava:** This type of lava is emitted from volcanoes at **destructive plate boundaries** where subduction occurs. Acidic lava is **rich in silica,** giving it a **high viscosity** (meaning it is thick and pasty). Due to its thick, sticky texture, **gases are unable to escape,** causing pressure to build in the magma chamber. Eventually the pressure becomes too great and an eruption occurs. Acidic lava is emitted from the volcano at temperatures of roughly **800 °C.** Due to its **viscous texture,** it **moves slowly, cooling and solidifying** quickly to form steep-sided volcanoes such as **Mount Pinatubo** in the Philippines or Mount St Helens in the US.

- **Basic lava:** This type of lava is emitted from volcanoes at **constructive plate boundaries** and at hotspots. Basic lava contains much **less silica** than acidic lava, which makes it **runny**. Due to its liquid texture, **gases escape easily,** meaning that violent eruptions do not occur. Instead, lava flows from the vent at temperatures of roughly **1200 °C,** travelling **long distances before cooling.** As it travels a long distance before cooling, basic lava forms gently sloping volcanoes such as **Mauna Loa in Hawaii.**

Note!

It is important to know the difference between acidic and basic lava as it appears regularly in questions.

Pyroclast/Pyroclastic Flow

Pyroclast, or pyroclastic flow, is emitted from volcanoes at **destructive plate boundaries**. It is often referred to as volcanic bombs. It consists of **rock fragments, lava** and **ash** that are emitted from a volcano during

 GEO **DICTIONARY**

CE: means Common Era and is the same as AD, but non-religious

an eruption. Pyroclastic flows occur when clouds of scorching ash and rock **flow down the slopes of the volcano,** destroying everything in their path. Pyroclastic flows reach **temperatures of between 200 and 700 °C** and reach speeds of up to **600 km/h.** The most famous pyroclastic flow occurred in **79 CE** when the town of **Pompeii** was destroyed after the eruption of **Mount Vesuvius.**

🔺 **Fig. 3.5** Pyroclastic flow

Once a pyroclastic flow has stopped, there is still danger of destruction from lahars. **Lahars** are **mudflows** made up **of volcanic material.** Lahars form when **rainfall mixes with rock and ash** deposited from the pyroclastic flow. Lahars can also generate directly from an eruption when **volcanic ash mixes with snow or ice** on the slopes, or with rainfall, before flowing down the valley. You will learn more about lahars later in this chapter in the case study on **Nevada Del Ruiz** in Colombia.

🔺 **Fig. 3.6** A lahar engulfs Nevada Del Ruiz in Colombia

Tephra

Tephra is the **collective name** given to **ash, dust** and **pumice**. Ash is formed during **explosive eruptions** as **rock is pulverised** inside the vent. This ash and dust are emitted from the volcano and **rise high into the atmosphere,** disrupting air travel. **Pumice** is created when **lava mixes with air,** causing it to fill with air bubbles.

Gases

Dangerous gases such as **carbon dioxide, chlorine** and **sulphur dioxide** are released during volcanic eruptions. These gases can suffocate people and animals. This occurred in **Lake Nyos** in Cameroon in **1986**. Carbon dioxide from the crater's lake leaked into the atmosphere, **killing over 1700 people** and 3500 livestock.

Water Vapour

Volcanoes along **subduction zones** often emit large amounts of water vapour during an eruption. This water is **sea water carried into the mantle** by the **subducting plate**. This water vapour **rises into the atmosphere** during an eruption, before cooling and condensing rapidly. This rapid cooling leads to **torrential rainfall** which can cause devastating **lahars**.

 EDUCATE YOURSELF

Volcanic emissions		
Lava	Acidic lava: destructive plate boundaries, subduction zones, high silica content, high viscosity, build-up of gases/pressure, violent eruption, 800 °C, steep-sided volcanoes, e.g. Mount St Helens	
	Basic lava: constructive plate boundaries, hotspots, low silica content, low viscosity (fluid), gases escape easily, lava flows, 1200 °C, gently sloping volcanoes, e.g. Mauna Loa	
Pyroclast	Destructive plate boundaries, rock fragments, lava, ash, moves downslope at up to 600 km/h, 200–700 °C, e.g. Pompei 79 CE, Mount Vesuvius	
	Lahars, volcanic material mixes with rainfall/snow, e.g. Nevada Del Ruiz, block rivers/lakes, annual lahars, e.g. Mount Pinatubo	
Tephra	Mixture of ash, dust and pumice, violent eruptions, rises high into atmosphere	
Gases	Carbon dioxide, sulphur dioxide, chlorine, e.g. Lake Nyos 1986	
Water vapour	Subduction zones, sea water evaporated, vapour rises into atmosphere, condenses, torrential rainfall, can cause lahars	

3.3 Volcanic Distribution

Volcanoes are not distributed randomly across the globe. They are usually clustered together in **lines along plate boundaries.** Only a few volcanoes occur away from plate boundaries in areas known as **hotspots.** Most of the world's volcanoes are found along the edges of the Pacific Plate, which forms an almost circular ring of volcanoes. This ring is known as the Pacific Ring of Fire.

Volcanoes at Constructive/Divergent Boundaries

Volcanoes occur at constructive/ divergent boundaries as **plates pull apart** from each other. As they separate, **fissures form** in the Earth's crust. Pressure from **convection currents** and **gases** in the mantle **force the magma upwards** through these fissures. Eventually, this magma **forces its way on to the surface** in an eruption.

As the plates are separating, the fissures in the crust allow much of the volcanic **gases to escape.** This means that the eruptions are **not very volatile**, releasing **basic lava** onto the surface. Most constructive boundaries occur in the middle of oceans at **mid-ocean ridges** (seafloor spreading), so eruptions are underwater.

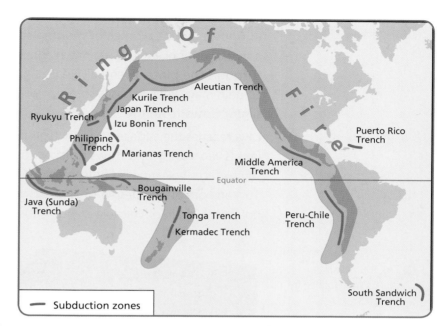

Fig. 3.7 The Pacific Ring of Fire

The lava **cools quickly** in large blobs known as 'pillow' lava before hardening to form **basalt** rock. Over time, these volcanic deposits **build up** to break the surface of the ocean and form new land. Iceland, which lies on the **Mid-Atlantic Ridge**, was formed from the build-up of basalt rock. Generally, volcanoes at constructive boundaries have **small cones** composed of volcanic debris. As basic **lava is runny**, it **travels long distances**, producing an almost flat lava field.

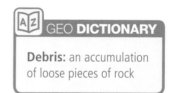

GEO **DICTIONARY**

Debris: an accumulation of loose pieces of rock

Volcanoes at Convergent/ Destructive Boundaries

Volcanoes occur at **convergent/destructive plate boundaries** as two plates collide with each other, causing **subduction.** As the **heavier oceanic plate subducts into the mantle**, it begins to melt. This **forces magma upwards** towards the lighter **overlying plate.** The magma begins to melt its way upwards through the crust to **form a magma chamber.**

The magma has a **high silica content.** This makes it **thick and pasty,** which means that volatile **gases cannot escape.** As a result, **pressure begins to build** in the magma chamber until it becomes too great, leading to a **violent eruption.** Volcanoes at convergent boundaries are **steep-sided** and **composed of alternating layers** of volcanic debris (tephra) and lava. They are known as composite or stratovolcanoes, e.g. **Mount St Helens.**

Fig. 3.8 An explosive eruption

Volcanoes at Hotspots

Unlike other volcanoes, volcanoes at hotspots **form away from plate boundaries** on both **continental and oceanic plates**. Hotspots occur due to **unusually hot plumes of magma** rising through the mantle beneath a thin layer of oceanic plate. The magma is so hot that it begins to **melt through the plate,** eventually reaching the surface. The magma does not contain many volatile gases so **eruptions are not violent**. Instead, the lava simply **flows from the vent.**

Lava reaches the surface at a very high temperature **(1200 °C)**. The basic lava is very **runny** and **flows quickly** away from the vent before cooling on the surface. Volcanoes at hotspots are very **gently sloping** (between 2 and 10°) and are often referred to as shield volcanoes. As a plate moves over a hotspot, a chain of volcanic islands is formed, e.g. Hawaii.

◉ **Fig. 3.9** Hawaiian Islands were formed by hotspots

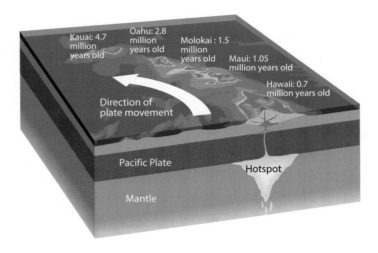

Kauai: 4.7 million years old

Oahu: 2.8 million years old

Molokai : 1.5 million years old

Maui: 1.05 million years old

Hawaii: 0.7 million years old

Direction of plate movement

Pacific Plate

Hotspot

Mantle

ACTIVE LEARNING

Using Fig. 3.10, explain the different ways in which volcanoes can form.

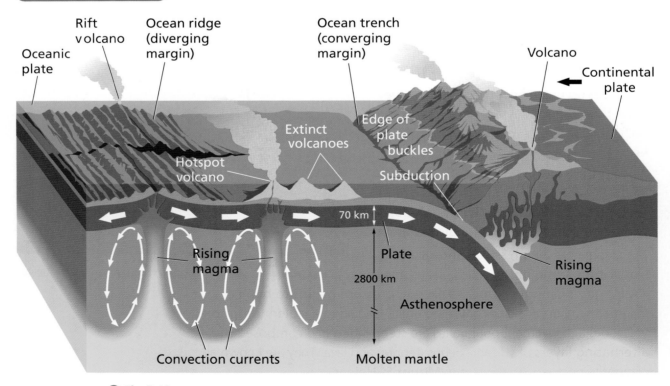

Rift volcano

Ocean ridge (diverging margin)

Ocean trench (converging margin)

Volcano

Oceanic plate

Continental plate

Extinct volcanoes

Edge of plate buckles

Hotspot volcano

Subduction

70 km

Rising magma

Plate

2800 km

Rising magma

Convection currents

Asthenosphere

Molten mantle

◉ Fig. 3.10

Distribution of Volcanoes	
Constructive/divergent boundaries	Plates separate, magma rises through fissures/cracks, gases escape, basic lava, cools on the surface, forms basalt, mid-ocean ridges, e.g. Mid-Atlantic Ridge
Convergent/destructive boundaries	Plates collide, oceanic plate subducts, plate melts, magma rises, forms magma chamber, high silica content, gas builds, violent eruption, steep sided, composite/strata, e.g. Mount St Helens
Hotspots	Away from plate boundaries, continental and oceanic crust, hot plumes of magma, gases escape, non-violent eruptions, basic lava flows, 1200 °C, gently sloping cones

3.4 Volcanic Landforms

Volcanic activity creates a variety of different landforms, both on the Earth's surface and inside the Earth's crust. Landforms created **on the surface** are called **extrusive** or **volcanic** features, while landforms created **within the crust** are called **intrusive** or **plutonic** features.

Extrusive/Volcanic Landforms

Cones

Volcanic cones are the **most common feature** associated with volcanic activity. Volcanic cones can form in many ways and vary in structure and composition.

- **Composite cones:** Composite volcanoes are also called **stratovolcanoes.** Composite cones form at both **constructive and destructive** boundaries from explosive eruptions and from gentle eruptions, leading to a build-up of **alternating layers of pyroclastic material** and **lava.** Composite cones have a **broad base and steep sides,** which get steeper towards the summit. **Mount Fuji** in Japan is an example of a composite volcano.

GEO DICTIONARY

Extrusive: volcanic materials that have cooled and solidified on the Earth's surface

Plutonic: volcanic materials that have cooled and solidified within the Earth's crust

(a)

(b)

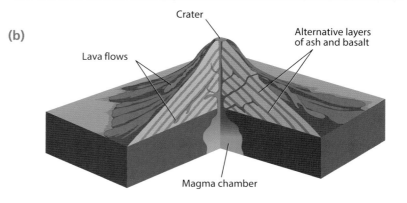

Crater
Alternative layers of ash and basalt
Lava flows
Magma chamber

▲ **Fig. 3.11** (a) Mount Fuji in Japan, a composite volcano, and (b) a cross-section of a composite cone

CORE 1 **CHAPTER 3**

ACTIVE **LEARNING**
Go to the following website
and click on Volcano photos to
observe the various volcanic
shapes and parts:
www.volcanodiscovery.com

- **Cinder cone:** Cinder cones are the **smallest type of volcano,** rarely reaching heights of more than **300 m.** They are the **most common type of volcano** found on Earth. Cinder cones consist of **pyroclastic material** formed from relatively **explosive eruptions.** Cinder cones have very **steep sides** with a **wide crater** at the summit. While many volcanic cones erupt many times, cinder cones **usually erupt only once** in their lifetime as the eruption destroys their structure. They are usually found **surrounding shield volcanoes** and **composite cones.** For example, there are more than 100 cinder cones surrounding Mauna Loa in Hawaii.

(a)

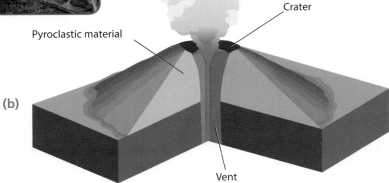

Pyroclastic material

Crater

(b)

Vent

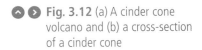
Fig. 3.12 (a) A cinder cone volcano and (b) a cross-section of a cinder cone

(a)

Shield Volcano

Shield volcanoes usually form at **hotspots,** and occasionally at **constructive plate boundaries.** Shield volcanoes form from **gentle eruptions** where **basic lava** reaches the surface and **spreads** out over a **large area. Layers of lava** build up very slowly to form a volcanic mountain with **gently sloping sides.** The base of the volcano can be more than 100 km in diameter. An example is **Mauna Kea** in Hawaii.

Summit caldera

Central vent

Gently sloping sides

Lava flow

(b)

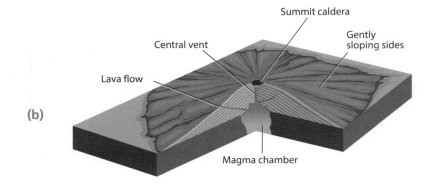

Magma chamber

Fig. 3.13 (a) Mauna Kea in Hawaii and (b) a cross-section of a shield volcano

Lava Plateau

Lava plateaux are formed when large **floods of basic lava** are released from a crack or **fissure** in the ground, before flowing over a large area and solidifying. The fissures allow **gases to escape,** meaning that **eruptions are not violent.** Multiple eruptions cause the plateau to build up **layer by layer.** The **Antrim-Derry Plateau** was created in this way approximately **60 million years ago,** when the **Eurasian Plate** and **North American Plate** began to separate. As the crust tore apart, large fissures formed, causing huge lava flows to cover the surrounding area.

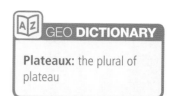

GEO DICTIONARY

Plateaux: the plural of plateau

These flows continued for over **2 million years,** forming a plateau up to **1800 m thick.** As the lava cooled and contracted, it formed **hexagonal columns of basalt.** These are best seen in part of the Antrim-Derry Plateau known as the **Giant's Causeway.** The Causeway has become a popular tourist attraction.

Evidence of these ancient fissures can still be seen surrounding the plateau. Lava hardened in the vents creating what is known as a **volcanic plug.** Slemish in Co. Antrim is an example of a volcanic plug.

🔼 **Fig. 3.14** The Giant's Causeway, Co. Antrim

Intrusive/Plutonic Landforms

Intrusive landforms are created when **volcanic material cools and solidifies within the Earth's crust.** Over time, the material covering these landforms is removed by **weathering and erosion** to leave them exposed on the surface.

Batholith

A batholith is a large area of **igneous rock** that forms when magma cools inside the Earth's crust. As magma rises into the crust, it melts surrounding layers of rock. Over millions of years, this magma cools to form **granite** rock. Batholiths **vary in shape and size,** but are usually larger than 100 km². Most batholiths form **underneath mountain folds** and are **capped by a layer of metamorphic rock.**

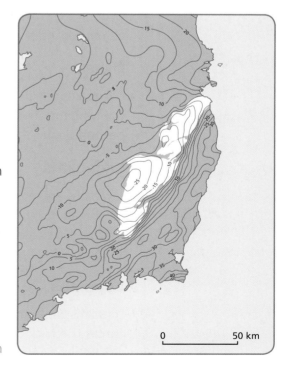

🔵 **Fig. 3.15** The location of the Leinster Batholith

CORE 1 **CHAPTER 3**

PATTERNS AND PROCESSES IN THE PHYSICAL ENVIRONMENT **45**

Fig. 3.16 Exposed granite in the Wicklow Mountains

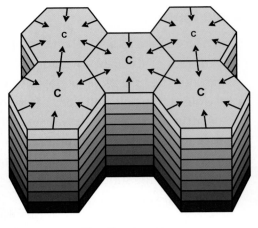

C = Contraction

Fig. 3.17 Contracting basalt

The **Leinster Batholith** is an Irish example of such a formation. It was **formed over 400 million years** when the **North American Plate collided with the Eurasian Plate.** When the plates collided, **layers of sedimentary rock** were **pushed upwards, forming fold mountains.** Magma rose upwards underneath the fold, before cooling slowly over millions years. A layer of **sedimentary rock** above the magma was **subjected to heat and pressure,** forming a layer of **metamorphic rock** above the batholith. Over time, the **overlying mountains** were **weathered and eroded** away to expose the underlying batholith. This metamorphic rock acts like a shield that protects the underlying granite from erosion. An example of this is the peak of the **Sugarloaf** in the Wicklow Mountains, which is protected by the metamorphic rock quartzite. The Leinster Batholith occupies over 1500 km² encompassing the Dublin, Wicklow and Blackstairs Mountains.

Sills

Sills are **horizontal layers of granite rock** that form when magma moves through the crust and forces its way **between layers of sedimentary rock** before cooling slowly. Slieve Gullion in Co. Armagh is an example.

Dykes

Dykes are formed when magma forces its way **upwards** through layers of overlying rock before cooling. Once cooled, a **layer of granite** is formed **perpendicular** to the layers of rock.

Laccoliths

Laccoliths are formed when magma forces its way through layers of rock. As more magma intrudes (forces its way) between the layers, the pressure of the magma forces the rock to **push upwards.** It cools slowly to form a **dome-shaped** layer of **granite** rock, e.g. Pine Valley Laccolith, Utah in the US.

Lopoliths

Lopoliths are formed in a similar way to laccoliths. As magma intrudes, its weight **forces the rock downwards** to form a **bowl-shaped** layer of granite, e.g. Great Dyke, Zimbabwe.

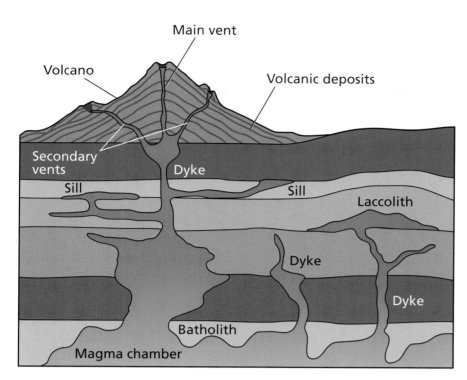

ACTIVE **LEARNING**

1. Describe how volcanic activity has affected the landscape of Ireland.
2. Using Fig. 3.18, describe how intrusive/plutonic landforms form.

◀ **Fig. 3.18** Plutonic features

 EDUCATE YOURSELF

Volcanic Landforms	
Extrusive/volcanic: Volcanic cones	Composite/stratovolcanoes: constructive and destructive boundaries, gentle and violent eruptions, alternating layers, pyroclastic material and lava, broad base, steep sides, e.g. Mount Fuji
	Cinder cone: small, most common, explosive, steep sides, wide crater, usually erupt once, e.g. volcanoes surrounding Mauna Loa, Hawaii
	Shield volcano: hotspots, gentle eruptions, basic lava, gently sloping sides, wide base, e.g. Mauna Kea
Extrusive/volcanic: Lava plateau	Divergent boundaries, basic lava, builds in layers, Antrim-Derry Plateau, 60 million years ago (mya), divergence of North American and Eurasian Plates, lava flows for 2 million years, 1800 m thick, cooled and contracted, hexagonal columns, e.g. Giant's Causeway
Intrusive/plutonic	Batholith: granite, underneath folds, Leinster Batholith, 400 mya, North American and Eurasian Plates collided, sedimentary layers buckled, cooled slowly, capped by metamorphic rock, quartzite, e.g. Sugarloaf, 1500 km², Wicklow, Dublin and Blackstairs Mountains
	Sills: horizontal layers of granite, between layers of sedimentary rock, e.g. Slieve Gullion, Co. Armagh
	Dykes: magma forced upwards, perpendicular layers of granite
	Laccoliths: magma intrudes between rock, pushes rock upwards, cools slowly, dome-shaped granite
	Lopoliths: magma intrudes between rock, pushes rock downwards, bowl-shaped granite

3.5 Measurement and Prediction of Volcanoes

It is **extremely difficult** to predict volcanic eruptions as each has **different patterns** and shows **different signs** before erupting. Accurate prediction requires volcanologists to carefully **monitor a volcano's vital signs**. Despite these difficulties, volcanic prediction has developed greatly over the past number of decades. The eruptions of **Mount St Helens in 1980, Mount Pinatubo in 1992** and Mount Merapi in 2010 were all successfully predicted. These predictions helped to save the lives of tens of thousands of people living close to the volcanoes.

Fig. 3.19 A volcanologist at work on a lava flow

Instruments Used and Eruption Indicators

Volcanologists use a variety of instruments and tools to detect and record volcanic activity.

Seismic Activity

Earthquake activity always increases beneath a volcano prior to an eruption. Seismometers and seismographs are used to measure movements in the Earth's crust, detecting and recording earthquakes. Seismometers are placed within a 20 km radius of a volcano's vent. It is vitally important that seismometers are placed in the correct locations as many **earthquakes that occur prior to eruption** are very small and difficult to detect. If seismometers are placed too far away, these small earthquakes could go undetected.

The earthquakes occur as **magma and volcanic gas force their way upwards through cracks and vents in the crust.** As the magma rises upwards, it **causes rock to vibrate,** triggering earthquakes. These earthquakes serve as **warning signs** that an eruption is going to occur. This is how the eruption of **Mount Pinatubo** was predicted.

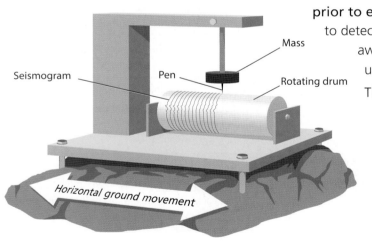

Horizontal seismograph

Mass

Seismogram

Pen

Rotating drum

Horizontal ground movement

Fig. 3.20 A seismograph

Ground Deformation

Electronic distance measurement **(EDM)** devices, **tiltmeters, GPS** and **satellite radar** are used to check for any **ground deformation**. Ground deformation is one of the most **obvious signs** that a volcano is close to erupting. As pressure from rising magma and gases increases, **volcanic mountain peaks swell shortly before eruption.**

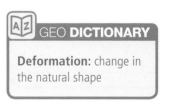

GEO DICTIONARY

Deformation: change in the natural shape

- EDMs measure any **horizontal movement** of a volcano. The device sends a **laser signal** to a reflector which then returns it. If the **volcano grows or shrinks**, the signal will take a **longer or a shorter time to return**.

- A **tiltmeter** operates much like a carpenter's spirit level. A **small bubble in water** is used to detect any **change in slope level**. Even a slight change in the slope angle on a volcanic mountain indicates a **build-up of pressure** inside the volcano. Tiltmeters were **used to monitor Mount St Helens** prior to its eruption in 1980.

- **GPS satellites** are used to monitor the Earth's surface, recording any changes in volcanic shape.

- Satellite radar (Interferometric Synthetic Aperture Radar – InSAR) records images of volcanoes. This allows volcanologists to **accurately record changes of deformation** in the volcanic mountain.

⬆ **Fig. 3.21** A tiltmeter

Gas Emissions

Carbon dioxide (CO_2) **sensors** are used to measure the **release of CO_2** from volcanoes. Gas releases from volcanoes **can lead to a large loss of life,** such as the disaster which occurred at Lake Nyos, **Cameroon in 1986. Lake Nyos** is a water-filled crater that formed as the result of a volcanic eruption over 500 years ago.

On 21 August, 1986, large deposits of **carbon dioxide seeped from the lake, killing over 1700 people** and **3500 livestock.** As a result of the disaster, **CO_2 monitors** were **placed in the lake** and it was discovered that there were still large deposits of CO_2 deep in the crater. In 2001, scientists decided to **degas the lake** using an electric pump that would mimic the effects of an eruption. Vertical pipes connect the bottom of the lake to the surface. Water near the bottom of the lake is saturated in CO_2. This water is continually pumped to the surface, releasing the CO_2 into the atmosphere in small amounts. Since the disaster, **monitoring gas emissions** has become a **regular part** of volcanic prediction.

⬆ **Fig. 3.22** Lake Nyos in Cameroon

◀ **Fig. 3.23** Pipes were used to release CO_2 from Lake Nyos

ACTIVE LEARNING

1. For more information on the Lake Nyos disaster, watch the BBC Documentary *Killer Lakes* which is available on YouTube.

2. For information on a similar disaster, research Lake Monoun. If possible, present your findings to your class.

3. Describe the ways in which volcanic eruptions can be predicted.

Historical Records

Historical records are used to help **predict when an eruption may occur again.** If volcanologists know the history of the volcano's eruptions, they can **combine** this knowledge **with the information found using modern instruments** to provide a fairly accurate prediction of the next eruption.

EDUCATE YOURSELF

Measurement and Prediction of Volcanoes	
Seismic activity	Seismometers/seismographs, 20 km radius, earthquakes prior to eruption, movement of magma, vibration of rock, e.g. Mount Pinatubo
Ground deformation	Electronic Distance Meters (EDMs), laser signals, horizontal movement, tiltmeters, spirit level, changes in slope indicate pressure levels, satellite and GPS, deformation changes, mountain swelling e.g. Mount St Helens 1980
Gas emissions	CO_2 – carbon dioxide, Lake Nyos 1986
Historic records	Historic eruptions, combined with information from modern instruments

3.6 Positive Effects of Volcanoes

Fig. 3.24 Tourists getting close to an eruption

Volcanic activity has many positive effects for the regions in which they occur. Human's ability to take advantage of volcanic activity dates as far back as the Roman Empire, nearly 2000 years ago. Advantages of volcanic activity include:

* Creation of new land
* Creation of fertile soils
* Tourism
* Geothermal energy

Creation of New Land

Volcanic activity can create new land, most recently seen off the coast of Japan. As **lava is emitted** from the volcano, it **cools rapidly forming basalt** rock. Over time, these layers of basalt build up and break the surface of the ocean, forming a volcanic island.

Fig. 3.25 A new Japanese island forming

Japan itself was created from volcanic activity resulting from the **subduction** of the **Pacific Plate underneath the Eurasian Plate.** Magma rising from the melting plate created the **Japanese archipelago 60 million years ago.** In November 2013, a volcanic eruption led to the creation of a new island in the Pacific Ocean. The island is located 1000 km south of Tokyo and is just 200 m in diameter. Although it may be eroded away by the sea, there is a possibility that the island will grow from further eruptions and become a permanent island in Japanese territory.

Iceland was created **16–18 million years ago** by a **build-up of basalt** rock formed from cooling lava on the **Mid-Atlantic Ridge**. Iceland is **still getting bigger** as the **North American Plate and Eurasian Plate continue to separate** from each other, and also due to the creation of a **hotspot** from a fissure on the south-east of the island. Lava escapes on to the surface of the island before cooling rapidly.

In **1963**, volcanologists' attention was drawn away from the island to a section of the Atlantic Ocean 32 km off the southern coast of Iceland. A **series of volcanic eruptions** caused the surface of the water to start bubbling. Between 1963 and 1967, continuous eruptions led to the creation of a **new island,** now named **Surtsey.** The island is a **protected heritage site** and does not have any human settlement. The island has enabled scientist to monitor how plants, bacteria and birds colonise new land over time.

Fig. 3.26 Plants colonising Surtsey

Fig. 3.27 Surtsey Island in 2014

Creation of Fertile Land

Volcanic soils are among the most fertile in the world as a result of the **weathering of volcanic materials** such as ash and lava. This weathering **provides nutrients and minerals** to the soil, making it extremely **fertile for agriculture.** The Bay of Naples in southern Italy has **benefited greatly from** volcanic deposits from Mount Vesuvius. Eruptions from Mount Vesuvius blanketed the area with thick **deposits of tephra**, which has since been broken down into fertile soil. As a result, the regions surrounding the mountain are **farmed intensively,** with vines, vegetables, fruits and flowers being grown throughout the year. In areas away from Mount Vesuvius, the land is too barren to grow crops successfully.

Fig. 3.28 A pineapple plantation in Hawaii

ACTIVE LEARNING

1. For more information on volcanic tourism, visit the following website:
www.volcano-tourism.net

2. Research the following volcanic areas for information on the positive effects of volcanoes:
   - Iceland
   - Yellowstone
   - Mount Fuji

If possible, present your findings to your class.

Mount Merapi in Java, Indonesia is **densely populated.** Over 1 million people live within 30 km of the slope. The volcanic soils surrounding the mountain allow for the **intensive growing of rice.** Hawaii's pineapple and sugar plantations are also located on volcanic soils.

Tourism

Tourism in volcanic landscapes has **grown in popularity** over the past two decades. This is especially the case since a number of eruptions were widely reported in the media because of the disruption they caused, such as Eyjafjallajökull in 2010. There are a number of volcanic regions which are visited by large numbers of tourists.

Iceland

Iceland is one of the **most volcanically active regions in the world** as a result of its position on the Mid-Atlantic Ridge. There are over **130 active volcanoes** scattered across the island. Despite this, Iceland has seen a large increase in tourism partly due to the **media interest** caused by the eruption of Eyjafjallajökull in 2010. Iceland has a population of just under 330 000. Roughly **600 000 tourists** visit Iceland each year, most of whom are attracted by its unspoilt volcanic landscape. In 2012, Iceland earned **€700 million** from tourism.

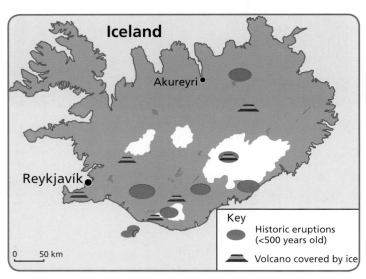

Fig. 3.29 Volcanic activity in Iceland

In what is referred to as 'volcanic tourism', tourist companies and airlines offer trips to Iceland, where tourists can go **hiking** around volcanic mountains, take **sightseeing** flights over volcanic craters and cycle through volcanic landscape.

Iceland also attracts tourists who want to **bathe** in volcanically heated waters. The water reaches average temperatures of 37–39 °C. The **Blue Lagoon Spa** company is one of the most popular tourist attractions in Iceland. Their volcanically heated waters are **rich in minerals** such as silica and sulphur, which many believe are good for the skin.

Yellowstone National Park, US

Yellowstone National Park in the US is located on both a **hotspot** and the **San Andreas Fault.** Underneath the park is the magma chamber of a 'super volcano', which is constantly monitored as it is capable of devastating eruptions.

Despite this threat, Yellowstone has become a popular destination for tourists due to its **geysers and hot springs.** Old Faithful is the most famous geyser in Yellowstone. It is visited by over **3.6 million tourists** each year. Old Faithful erupts **every 45–110 minutes,** with its water and steam reaching a height of between 35 and 55 m. On average, eruptions last for four minutes and are regarded as a must-see attraction.

GEO DICTIONARY

Geyser: a vent in the Earth's surface which periodically ejects a column of volcanically heated water and steam

 Fig. 3.30 Old Faithful erupting in Yellowstone National Park

Note!

The Geothermal Energy case study ties in with Human Interaction with the Rock Cycle in Chapter 6.

CASE STUDY 📁

Geothermal Energy

In areas with active volcanoes, geothermal energy can be exploited to our advantage. Intense **heat from volcanic activity is capable of boiling ground water** that is close to the surface. This creates underground **reservoirs of superheated water** or steam. Geothermal energy is mainly used to **generate electricity** but can also be used to **heat homes** and **grow crops** out of season.

 Fig. 3.31 Harmless steam emitted from a power station

Iceland is one country which has been able to fully exploit geothermal energy. As magma rises up through fissures, it generates high temperatures at relatively shallow depths. This causes the surrounding **igneous rock** to absorb the heat, which in turn **heats the groundwater.**

Despite Iceland's high level of volcanic activity, over 10 per cent of its landmass is covered in glaciers. **Meltwater from these glaciers provides an almost constant supply of groundwater** which can be heated by volcanic activity. In total, 30 high-temperature spots have been identified, where water temperatures of over **200 °C** are reached at a depth of **1000 m**. Wells are drilled into the igneous rock and the hot water is pumped out of the ground. As the water reaches the surface, it **decompresses and turns into steam.** This steam is **funnelled through turbines,** causing them to turn and **generate electricity.** On rare occasions, when there is a shortage of groundwater, water is pumped into the ground to be heated. The water comes into contact with hot rock before returning to the surface as steam.

A/Z GEO **DICTIONARY**

Geothermal energy: a renewable energy source, in which water in the ground flows across rocks that have been heated by volcanic activity. This heat turns the water to steam. The steam is then piped to the surface to turn turbines and generate electricity

Decompresses: expands

CORE 1 CHAPTER 3

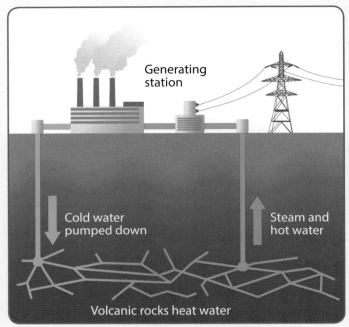

Fig. 3.32 Workings of a geothermal power plant

After flowing through the turbines, the steam is piped to another plant, where it is used to heat water from another lake. Once the water has been **heated to 80 °C**, it is **piped to homes and businesses** to be used in **central heating**. Some **90 per cent of Iceland's homes and businesses** are heated in this way. Currently, **25 per cent of Iceland's electricity is generated through geothermal energy** sources. By 2030, the Iceland Deep Drilling Project (IDDP) aim to have increased this figure to 50 per cent. They plan to do this by drilling deeper into the rock to reach water heated to temperatures of 450 °C.

Once the water has been used for central heating in homes and businesses, it is **pumped to greenhouses,** allowing vegetables, fruits and flowers to be grown throughout the year. Some **50 per cent** of the water is used for **growing vegetables and fruits, 26 per cent** for **potted plants** and **24 per cent** for **nurseries** and forest plants.

Geothermal energy could be part of the solution to our overreliance on fossil fuels, which contributes to global warming. Many Icelandic companies sell their technology to other countries which have volcanic activity.

Note!

The benefits of volcanoes, distribution of volcanoes and measurement and prediction of volcanoes have all appeared as exam questions. So, it is important that you understand these topics and are able to answer questions on them.

ACTIVE LEARNING

Discuss the positive effect of volcanoes using two of the following headings:

1. Geothermal energy
2. Tourism
3. Fertile land
4. New land

 EDUCATE YOURSELF

Benefits of volcanoes	
Creation of new land	Lava flows, cools rapidly, basalt, Japanese archipelago 60 mya, Iceland 20 mya, Mid-Atlantic Ridge, Surtsey, repeated eruptions, heritage site
Fertile soils	Weathering, nutrients/minerals, fertile agricultural land, Mount Vesuvius, tephra, intensively farmed, Mount Merapi, rice, Hawaii, pineapple plantations
Tourism	Iceland, hiking, sightseeing, Blue Lagoon Spa, 600 000 visitors, €700 million; Yellowstone, Old Faithful geyser, 3.6 million tourists
Geothermal energy	Boiling groundwater, superheated reservoirs, igneous rock heats water, 200 °C, steam turns turbines, generates electricity, central heating, 90% homes and businesses, growing crops out of season, nurseries

3.7 Negative Effects of Volcanoes

While volcanic activity provides many advantages, volcanoes remain a dangerous force of nature. Two disadvantages of volcanic activity are:

- Loss of life
- Disruption to air travel

Loss of Life

Loss of life can be caused either directly or indirectly by volcanic activity. On **1 February 2014, Mount Sinabung** in Indonesia erupted suddenly, **killing 15** people who were within a 3 km radius of its crater. The eruption occurred after a **build-up of gas pressure,** sending pyroclastic material over 1.5 km into the sky, before falling back down on the surrounding area. The 15 people who died were **killed by ash and lava** as it travelled down the volcano's slopes. Loss of life can also occur from **gas leaking from a volcano's crater,** as occurred in Lake Nyos, Cameroon in 1986.

> **FACT**
> Despite what you might think, lava is the least likely volcanic emission to kill you in a volcanic eruption. Pyroclast, rocks, gases and ash are far more dangerous.

 **Fig. 3.33** Pyroclast from Mount Sinabung on 1 February 2014, which claimed the lives of 15 people

CASE STUDY 📁

Nevada del Ruiz

One of the most devastating losses of life from volcanic activity occurred in the Colombian town of Armero in 1985. Armero is just over 100 km from the Nevada del Ruiz volcano. In 1985, three-quarters of the town's 28 700 inhabitants were killed by a devastating lahar which swept down the slopes of the volcano.

Nevado del Ruiz is part of a chain of volcanic mountains that stretches along the Andes Mountain Range. Standing at 5389 m, it is the highest volcano in Colombia. Due to its height, its peak is covered in snow and ice which increases the chance of generating lahars.

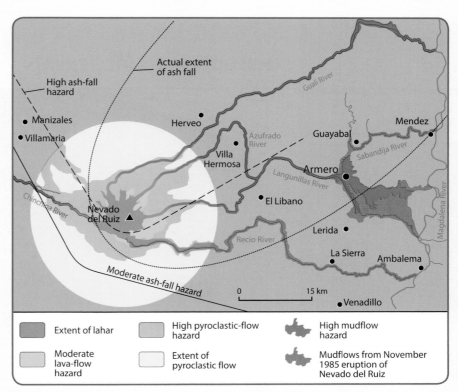

Fig. 3.34 The area affected by the lahar

On 13 November 1985, Nevada del Ruiz erupted violently, sending huge volumes of ash and pumice into the air. This ash and pumice began to rain down on the town of Armero almost immediately. However, this did not cause any alarm for the town's residents. Both the town mayor and the local priest announced over loud speakers that there was no need to evacuate the town and that the residents were in no danger. Despite this, the Red Cross ordered an evacuation shortly after the eruption, which was called off once the ash stopped falling.

The heat from pyroclast and lava ejected during the eruption began to melt the 25 km^2 of snow and ice that lay on the peak of the volcano. Bad weather meant that the town's residents were unable to see the mountain clearly.

As the pyroclast mixed with the water from the melted snow, it formed a river of boiling mud (lahar). Travelling at over 50 km/h, the lahar burst through an upstream dam and submerged Armero in over 2 m of mud. Just two hours after the eruption began, over 23 000 people were killed and another 4500 were seriously injured. As well as the loss of life, the damage caused by the lahar was estimated to be US$1 billion.

Fig. 3.35 A young girl being pulled from the rubble

Could it have been avoided?

A number of failures lead to the devastating loss of life in Armero. For nearly a year prior to the eruption, Nevado del Ruiz had experienced several earthquakes and minor eruptions. Despite the townspeople being nervous of the volcano, they were not fully convinced that it was an immediate danger to their lives.

Colombia had neither the technology nor the skilled geologists to properly monitor the volcano. As a result, they depended on experts from other countries to study the volcano. A report carried out by a number of scientists concluded that even a relatively small eruption would produce 'a 100 per cent chance of mudflows'. Only ten copies of the report were made and it was widely dismissed as being too cautionary.

Disruption to Air Travel

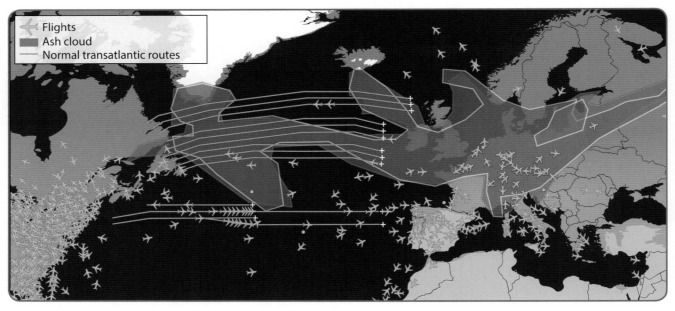

Fig. 3.36 Flight disruption from the ash cloud from the Eyjafjallajökull eruption in 2010

During an eruption, ash, dust and other materials emitted from volcanoes can reach **heights of several kilometres** into the atmosphere. This material puts aircraft overhead in danger as the planes' engines can become clogged, causing them to stall. As a result, airline companies cancel flights whose paths put them near potential ash clouds. In 2010, the eruption of Eyjafjallajökull led to the **cancellation of flights for over 8 million passengers** as huge ash clouds affected the airspace of 20 countries. The ash cloud reached an extraordinary **height of 9 km,** with flight disruption lasting from 14 to 20 April.

EDUCATE YOURSELF

Negative effects of volcanoes	
Loss of life	1 Feb 2014, Mount Sinabung, Lake Nyos, gas emitted; Nevado del Ruiz, lahar
Disruption to air travel	Ash cloud, Eyjafjallajökull 2010, flights cancelled, over 8 million passengers affected

CASE STUDY

Mount Pinatubo

On 15 June 1991, Mount Pinatubo began what was the second largest volcanic eruption in the twentieth century. Mount Pinatubo is one of a chain of composite volcanoes on the Philippine arc island of Luzon. The chain of volcanoes formed due to the subduction of the eastern edge of the Eurasian Plate underneath the Philippine Mobile Belt. This formed the Manila Trench.

Warning Signs

The first warning sign arrived in the form of an **intense earthquake** that occurred **100 km north-east of the volcano.** This was said to have been **triggered by movement of magma** building up in the volcano's chamber. **On 2 April, a small explosion** occurred in vents on Pinatubo which **dusted local villages** in ash. As earthquakes and explosions continued, a **Level 3 warning was issued** which led to the **evacuation of 5000** villagers due to the possibility of a major eruption.

On **9 June**, the appearance of a lava dome led to the government issuing a **Level 5 warning** (the highest warning level), indicating an **eruption in progress.** An evacuation area of 30 km was declared on 12 June, leading to 58 000 people having to leave their homes.

Eruption

On 15 June, a full eruption of Mount Pinatubo began, lasting for **nine hours.** Large quantities of **ash, dust and sulphur** were released **34 km into the atmosphere,** covering an area **400 km wide.** The eruption caused **numerous earthquakes** and the collapse of the summit of Mount Pinatubo. The collapse of the summit led to the creation of a **large caldera.** Unfortunately, the eruption **coincided** with the **passing of tropical storm** Yunya whose 190 km/h winds blew ash over a large distance, while **torrential rain** caused falling ash to turn to mud.

 **Fig. 3.37** The lake-filled caldera of Mount Pinatubo

GEO DICTIONARY

Lava dome: a mound of viscous lava that appears as a volcano erupts

Caldera: a large cauldron-shaped volcanic crater that forms after a volcanic eruption. In the years after the eruption, it fills with water, forming a caldera lake

CORE 1   CHAPTER 3

Effects of the Eruption

 Fig. 3.38 A wall of pyroclast descends from Mount Pinatubo.

Note!

Go to **www.livescience.com** and search for the 'the 12 largest eruptions' to find an interesting article on volcanoes.

The Mount Pinatubo eruption killed 847 people, with a further 100 000 left homeless. Most of the fatalities occurred due to roofs of houses collapsing under the weight of ash deposited by the volcano. Healthcare facilities on the island were damaged while disease spread rapidly in temporary shelters for the homeless. This led to rising death tolls in the month following the eruption.

As well as widespread destruction from ash deposits, **some 20 million tonnes of sulphur dioxide** were released into the atmosphere which mixed with water and oxygen, making sulphuric acid. Sulphuric acid depletes ozone. During 1992 and 1993, the hole in the ozone layer over Antarctica increased dramatically. Dust and gases released into the atmosphere formed a dust cloud that spread across the entire globe. This cloud over the Earth led to a **reduction in global temperatures of 0.5 °C** on average.

The eruption of Mount Pinatubo has also been linked to other natural disasters across the globe. The eruption is believed to have influenced the 1993 floods along the Mississippi River and the drought in the Sahel region of Africa.

Agriculture in the area was also greatly affected by the eruption as many afforestation projects, rice plantations and livestock herds were destroyed. Education for thousands of children was disrupted as schools were destroyed. Each year, heavy rainfall mixed with sediment deposited from the eruption has produced lahars which flow from the mountain and major rivers. These lahars have caused extensive damage to housing in the area.

The evacuation of the areas surrounding Mount Pinatubo saved the lives of tens of thousands of people and was regarded as a major success for volcanologists and volcanic prediction.

 ACTIVE **LEARNING**

For information on well-known volcanic eruptions (besides the examples given in this chapter) research the following:

1. Mount St Helens
2. Krakatoa
3. Tambora
4. Mauna Loa
5. Eyjafjallajökull
6. Mount Pelée
7. Thera

If possible, present your findings to your class.

ACTIVE **LEARNING**

1. You have been commissioned to carry out a hazard report on the current danger to towns surrounding Nevado del Ruiz. Using your knowledge of measurement and prediction of volcanic eruptions, explain what equipment you would use to assess the likelihood of an eruption

   You may also find historical reports of previous eruptions useful.

2. As well as the 1985 eruption, the Nevado del Ruiz volcano has a history of eruptions and mudflows. Research the mountain to learn more about these events. If possible, present your findings to your class.

ORDINARY LEVEL

SHORT QUESTIONS

5 x 2m

1. Match each of the letters A, B, C, D and E in the diagram with the correct volcanic feature in the table below.

2012 Q4 10M

Volcanic feature	Letter
Magma chamber	
Vent	
Lava	
Ash cloud	
Crater	

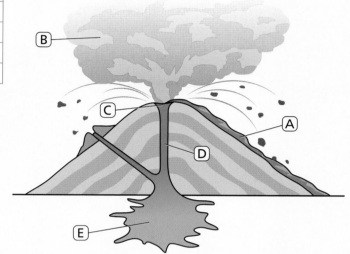

LONG QUESTIONS

1. (i) Define and name an example of each of the volcano types listed below:
- Active volcano
- Extinct volcano
- Dormant volcano

(iii) Explain in detail how volcanoes occur.

(i) 3 definitions @ 3m each
3 examples @ 3m/2m/2m

(ii) 8 SRPs @ 3m each

2015 Q3B 40M

2. (i) Name two examples of volcanoes.

(ii) Describe the negative effects of volcanoes.

(iii) Describe the positive effects of volcanoes.

(i) 2 x name @ 2m each

(ii) 6 SRPs @ 3m each

(iii) 6 SRPs @ 3m each

2014 Q1B 40 M

3. (i) Name one tectonic plate on the Earth's crust.

(ii) What is the name given to the area of earthquakes and volcanoes that stretches around the Pacific Ocean?

(iii) Describe in detail how volcanoes occur.

(i) Named @ 3m

(ii) Named @ 3m

(iii) 8 SRPs @ 3m each

2012 Q1C 30M

4. Explain, with the aid of a diagram(s), how volcanic eruptions occur.

Diagram 3 labels @ 2m each

Explanation@ 8 SRPs@ 3m each

2011 Q1C 30M

HIGHER LEVEL

SHORT QUESTIONS

1. Examine the diagram and answer each of the following questions.

   (i) Match each of the letters A, B, C and D with the feature that best matches it in the table below.

   (ii) Indicate whether plutonic processes or volcanic processes are most associated with each of the features, by ticking the correct box in the table below.

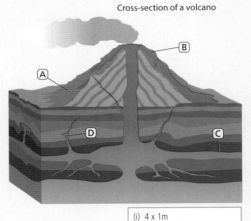

Cross-section of a volcano

Feature	(i) Letter	(ii) Plutonic	(iii) Volcanic
Sill			
Pyroclastic sediment			
Dyke			
Lava flow			

(i) 4 x 1m

(ii) 4 x 1m

2015 Q1 8M

LONG QUESTIONS

1. Discuss the positive impacts of volcanic activity.

Positive Impacts 2 x 2m

Discussion 13 SRPs @ 2m each

2011 Q1B 30M

2. Using an example you have studied, describe the causes and effects of a volcanic eruption.

Named example 1 x 2m

Discussion of causes 7 x 2m

Discussion of effects 7 x 2m

SAMPLE QUESTION 30M

3. Describe the effects of volcanic activity on the Irish landscape.

Effects identified 2 x 2m

Effect 1 discussed 7/6 x 2m

Effect 2 discussed 6/7 x 2m

SAMPLE QUESTION 30M

In the previous two chapters, you have learned about the movement of plates and the activities that occur along different plate boundaries. Volcanoes are the first of these activities that you have now studied in detail. Volcanoes have appeared in some section on every exam paper since 2006 at both Higher and Ordinary Levels so it is a vital topic to know well.

In this section, we will examine both a Higher level and an Ordinary Level question. In the previous two chapters, you learned two different techniques of preparing your answer: first by picking your 'significant' terms and writing them under your headings in a logical order and, second, by analysing the wording of the question. These techniques will be repeated in later chapters so you can become more familiar with them.

In this chapter, you will learn how to write an answer in bullet point form. When the new geography syllabus was introduced in 2006, students' answers were marked on 'overall coherence' as well as on the content. In other words, your answer had to be written in paragraph form and be well structured. Today, only the Higher Level Option Essay is marked for overall coherence, which allows us to use bullet points to answer 30m questions. In my teaching experience, some students find they can better organise their answers if they use bullet points. So let's try it here:

ORDINARY LEVEL

EXAM QUESTION

(i) Name two examples of volcanoes.

(ii) Describe the negative effects of volcanoes.

(iii) Describe the positive effects of volcanoes.

Marking Scheme
2 x name @ 2m each
6 SRPs @ 3m each
6 SRPs @ 3m each

2014 Q1B 40M

SAMPLE ANSWER

(i) Two examples of volcanoes are Mount Pinatubo in the Philippines and Mount St Helens in the US. [2m + 2m]

(ii) The negative effects of volcanoes are loss of life and disruption to air travel. [3m + 3m]

Loss of life

- Loss of life can occur directly from the eruption of a volcano such as in Mount Sinabung in Indonesia or indirectly such as Nevado del Ruiz in Colombia. [3m]

- When a volcano erupts, it emits pyroclast, ash, lava, gases and water vapour. Anyone who is close to the volcano when it erupts is in danger of being smothered or crushed by falling debris and pyroclast, e.g. Mount Vesuvius. [3m]

- In 1985, the town of Almero was hit by a mudflow after the snow covering the peak of Nevado del Ruiz melted during an eruption. The melted snow mixed with pyroclast to make a boiling mudflow (lahar). [3m]

- The lahar covered the town in boiling mud and killed over 28 000 people. [3m]

Disruption to air travel

- During a volcanic eruption, ash, dust and other materials are blown several kilometres into the atmosphere, putting aircraft flying overhead in danger. [3m]

- The biggest danger is that engines become clogged with material and stall. As a result, airline companies cancel any flights that would come near ash clouds. [3m]

- In 2010, the Icelandic volcano Eyjafjallajökull erupted, sending ash and other materials over 9 km into the atmosphere. As a result, flights across Northern Europe were cancelled. In total 8 million passengers had their flights cancelled. [3m]

(iii) Two positive effects of volcanic activity are the creation of new land and tourism. [3m + 3m]

New land

- When a volcano erupts, it emits lava onto the surface. This lava cools rapidly to form basalt rock. [3m]

- Over time these layers of basalt build up and reach the surface of the ocean to form new islands. [3m]

- Iceland was created 20 million years ago from a build-up of basalt rock. This basalt formed from cooling lava on the Mid-Atlantic Ridge. [3m]

- Just south of Iceland, the island of Surtsey formed after a series of volcanic eruptions in 1963. This new island helped scientists to understand how plants and animals colonise new land. [3m]

Tourism

- Volcanic tourism has become increasingly popular over the past two decades, especially in Iceland, which has over 130 active volcanoes. [3m]

- Tourist companies offer trips to Iceland where tourists can hike along volcanic mountains, or bathe in the Blue Lagoon, which is an outdoor spa with volcanically heated water. [3m]

- Roughly 600 000 tourists visit Iceland each year, generating over €700 million in revenue [3m]

- Yellowstone National Park in the US attracts over 3.6 million tourists per year, many of whom go to witness the volcanic geyser Old Faithful. [3m]

Bullet points make it much easier to keep track of your points and how many SRPs you have written.

In this answer, you can clearly see that each section is answered fully.

It also gives answers a structure as the points are written in stages similar to a scientific experiment report.

All parts are answered fully and accurately. Answers are focused on answering the question asked.

Marks Awarded
Volcanoes named 2 x 2m
Negative impacts described 6 @ 3m each
Positive impacts described 6 @ 3m each
Total 40/40m

HIGHER LEVEL

For this section I will answer a question that requires knowledge of all three chapters studied so far.

EXAM QUESTION

Examine how plate tectonics help us to understand the global distribution of volcanoes.

2008 Q2B 30M

SAMPLE ANSWER

- The theory of plate tectonics states that the Earth's lithosphere is broken up into seven major plates that float on the Earth's mantle. [2m]

- These plates are moved by the process of convection currents. [2m]

Marking Scheme
2 locations of volcanoes 2 x 2m
Discussion 13 SRPs @ 2m each

So, what is this question asking us? We can look at the three components of this question:

- Plate tectonics: the movement of plates by convection currents is the process that makes volcanoes possible.

- The plates collide and separate at their boundaries which causes subduction and seafloor spreading.

- Describe the types of volcanoes that are created at each boundary, i.e. explosive/non-explosive.

- Convection currents occur as magma is heated by the Earth's core, becomes buoyant and rises towards the lithosphere, before cooling and sinking again in a circular motion. [2m]
- These cooling currents create friction with the plates, causing them to collide (convergent), separate (divergent) or slide past (passive) each other. [2m]
- Volcanoes occur in three locations: at convergent and divergent plate boundaries and at hotspots. [2m]

Convergent boundaries [2m]

- As plates converge, the heavier oceanic plate subducts into the mantle and melts. [2m]
- The molten magma from the melting plate rises parallel to the plate boundary, forcing its way through the crust of the lighter plate before erupting on the surface. [2m]
- Volcanoes at subduction zones are volatile due to the high silica content, which allows the pressure from gases to build before erupting explosively. [2m]
- Repeated volcanic eruptions can eventually lead to the creation of a volcanic or island arc such as the Japanese archipelago. [2m]
- Examples of volcanoes at subduction zones can be seen around the Pacific Ring of Fire, where the Pacific Plate converges with the Eurasian, North American and Indo-Australian Plates. [2m]

Divergent boundaries [2m]

- Volcanoes occur where plates separate from one another and magma is forced through the fissures/cracks before reaching the surface. [2m]
- Volcanoes at divergent plate boundaries are less volatile as they have a low silica content, meaning that gas does not build up. [2m]
- Divergent boundaries are now known as the point where seafloor is renewed, as lava hardens to form new basalt rock, which gets older as you move towards the continents. [2m]
- Mid-ocean ridges are formed at the point of divergence, leading to the formation of a chain of underwater volcanoes, e.g. the Mid-Atlantic Ridge. [2m]
- Over time, lava from these eruptions builds up to form volcanic islands, e.g. Iceland. [2m]
- At 20 million years old, Iceland is the youngest country in the world. It formed from the separation of the Eurasian and North American Plates. [2m]

Marks Awarded	
Locations of volcanoes 2 x 2m	
Discussion best 13 SRPs @ 2m each	
Total 30/30m	

Volcanic distribution clearly links to plate tectonics. Named examples are also provided.

CORE 1

CHAPTER 3

TOPIC MAP

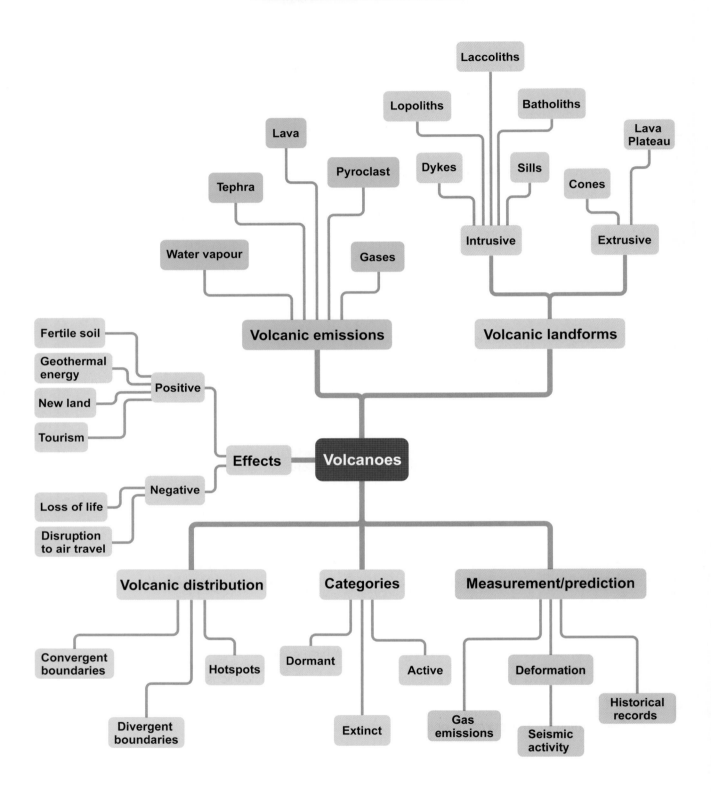

Laccoliths

Lopoliths

Batholiths

Lava

Lava Plateau

Tephra

Pyroclast

Dykes

Sills

Cones

Water vapour

Gases

Intrusive

Extrusive

Volcanic emissions

Volcanic landforms

Fertile soil

Geothermal energy

New land

Tourism

Positive

Effects

Volcanoes

Loss of life

Disruption to air travel

Negative

Volcanic distribution

Categories

Measurement/prediction

Convergent boundaries

Hotspots

Dormant

Active

Deformation

Divergent boundaries

Extinct

Gas emissions

Seismic activity

Historical records

CHAPTER 4

Earthquakes

In Chapter 3, you learned how plate tectonics can cause volcanoes to form. In this chapter, you will learn another effect of plate movement – earthquakes. Earthquakes are violent vibrations in the Earth's crust caused by the sudden movement of tectonic plates. The strength of the earthquake depends on the type of fault, the depth at which the earthquake occurs and the level of plate movement.

KEY WORDS

- Seismic waves
- Seismograph
- Richter scale
- Modified Mercalli scale
- Fault line
- Focus
- Epicentre

- Tremors
- Aftershock
- Convergent boundaries
- Divergent boundaries
- Passive boundaries
- Rift valleys
- San Andreas Fault

- Historic records
- Animal behaviour
- Tsunami
- Earthquake-proof buildings

LEARNING OUTCOMES

What you MUST know
- The locations of earthquakes
- How earthquakes are measured and predicted
- Named examples of earthquakes
- The different parts of an earthquake
- The effects of earthquakes

What you SHOULD know
- Japanese earthquake CASE STUDY 📁
- How to prevent earthquake damage

What is USEFUL to know
- Named examples of plate boundaries where earthquakes occur
- The different types of seismic waves

CORE 1 CHAPTER 4

Introduction

Every day, there are several hundred earthquakes across the globe. Most of these are minor and cause little or no damage. All of the Earth's **major earthquake zones are found in the faults at plate boundaries.** The Indonesian earthquake of 2004 and the Japanese earthquake of 2011 were huge earthquakes and caused destructive waves known as tsunamis. Luckily, these are very rare. In total since 1950, there have been **11 earthquakes with a magnitude higher than 8.6** on the Richter scale. However, when large earthquakes do occur, the effects are devastating.

Fig. 4.1 Devastation after the Indonesian earthquake in 2004

4.1 Seismic Waves

Seismic waves, also known as shockwaves, are the **vibrations of energy** created from the **plate movement** that causes an earthquake. There are several types of seismic waves generated by an earthquake. Each type of seismic wave travels at a different speed to the others, meaning that they arrive at different times. These **different waves can be seen in the readings from seismographs,** which are instruments used to record any movements in the Earth's crust.

- The first waves to arrive are known as **primary waves,** or P-waves, and can travel through liquids, solids and gases. Despite being the fastest-travelling wave, they **do not have much energy** and do not cause any damage. Primary waves **push and pull** at rock as they move through the crust, much like sound waves move through the air. For example, if you were to slam the door of a room, the windows in the room might rattle. This is because the P-waves generated push and pull at the window in the same way waves push and pull at rock in the crust during an earthquake.

Types of seismic waves produced by an earthquake

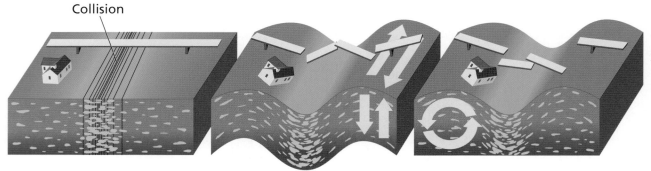

Primary waves arrive first, pushing and pulling at the crust.

Secondary waves move the crust up and down, causing more noticeable crustal movement.

Surface waves travel in a circular motion, causing buildings and bridges to collapse.

Fig. 4.2 (*From left to right*) Primary waves, secondary waves and surface waves

- **Secondary waves** arrive after P-waves and have much **more energy.** Secondary waves **cause the crust to move up and down,** making the ground shake more noticeably than the P-waves do.

- **Surface waves** arrive after secondary waves and are **responsible for almost all damage caused during an earthquake.** The waves move slowly along the surface, moving it **up and down as well as from side to side.** This movement causes buildings, roads and other infrastructure to sway violently and often collapse.

EDUCATE YOURSELF

Seismic Waves
Energy from earthquake, caused by plate movement, recorded by seismograph; primary waves, travel fast, low energy, no damage, push and pull rock; secondary waves, move crust up and down; surface waves, cause damage, roads and buildings collapse, move crust up and down and from side to side

4.2 Parts of an Earthquake

Seismologists are scientists who study earthquakes. They divide earthquakes into the following four parts in order to describe them:

- The **fault line** refers to the gap between two **tectonic plates,** or fractures in rock caused by plate movement. Nearly all **earthquakes originate along a fault line** due to the build-up of huge pressures between plates. As plates attempt to move, against or past each other, **friction is caused between layers of rock.** This causes the plates to become stuck. **Pressure builds up over many years,** before a layer of rock breaks, allowing the plates to jolt free, causing an earthquake.

- The **focus is the point where the earthquake begins.** The focus can be deep in the fault line or at a shallow depth. The focus marks the point where pressure is released, allowing the plates to move. Seismic waves are created from the sudden movement, travelling from the focus to the surface.

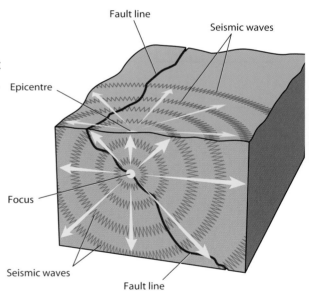

● Fig. 4.3 Parts of an earthquake

- The **epicentre** is the point on the surface, directly above the focus. The epicentre is the shortest distance from the focus for shockwaves to travel before reaching the surface.

- **Seismic waves,** also known as tremors or shockwaves, are the vibrations caused by the earthquake. These are strongest at the epicentre. The further from the epicentre that seismic waves travel, the less energy they will have. If the epicentre of an earthquake is in, or close to, an urban area, then it can lead to widespread damage and loss of life. Such an event happened in Haiti in 2010 when an earthquake struck close to the capital city of Port-au-Prince.

Parts of an Earthquake	
Fault	Gap between tectonic plates, earthquakes originate along fault, friction, build-up of pressure
Focus	Point of pressure release, where earthquake begins, seismic waves created and travel from here
Epicentre	Directly above focus, shortest distance to surface, seismic waves strongest here, most damage occurs
Seismic waves	Vibrations from focus, cause damage in urban areas, e.g. Haiti 2010

4.3 Measuring Earthquakes

Seismologists use an instrument called a seismograph or seismometer to record the waves of energy released by an earthquake. The data collected is then expressed on three different scales.

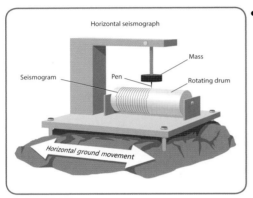

⊙ **Fig. 4.4** A seismograph is used to measure earthquakes.

- **Seismograph/seismometer:** This instrument **records movements in the crust,** which is also used to detect earthquakes near active volcanoes. Seismographs are **placed along fault lines,** which allows seismologists to **record and locate earthquake activity.** When an earthquake occurs, seismographs record **vertical and horizontal movement,** allowing it to be charted on a graph.
The **focus and epicentre of an earthquake can be located** along a fault line by determining which seismograph recorded the strongest tremors and which seismograph began recording first.

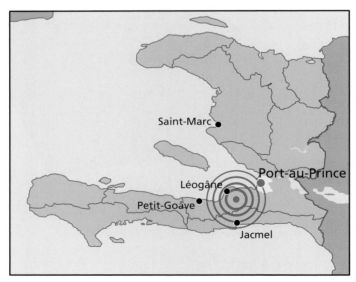

⊙ **Fig. 4.5** The epicentre of the 2010 Haitian earthquake

- **Richter scale: Readings from a seismograph** can be recorded on a Richter scale, which was named after its inventor, Charles Richter. The Richter scale **measures the magnitude** (size) of earthquakes. The scale begins at 0 and has no upper limit, although the highest magnitude ever recorded on the scale was 9.5, from the Chilean earthquake of 1960. Each step on the Richter scale represents a **tenfold increase** in the energy of an earthquake. For example, a 2.0 on the Richter scale is ten times stronger than a 1.0 recording. A magnitude **7.0 is a million times stronger than a 1.0** (10^6).

- **Moment magnitude scale:** Most seismologists now use the moment magnitude scale (MMS), which **combines seismograph readings with the amount of rock movement** at a fault. MMS readings are considered to be **more accurate** than the Richter scale for earthquakes above 7.0 and usually record a higher reading. Like the steps on the Richter scale, each step represents a tenfold increase in the energy released. **Media reports use the MMS** to report the magnitude of earthquakes.

Note!
These scales are regularly asked in the exam. It is important that you understand what each one does.

- **Modified Mercalli scale:** The Modified Mercalli scale is an older form of assessing the power of an earthquake. The scale does not use any mathematical formula for measurement, instead relying on the **visual damage caused as an indication of strength.** There are 12 grades on the Mercalli scale, with each higher number indicating a greater amount of damage. The scale uses roman numerals (I–XII), with I representing little or no damage and XII representing the total destruction of an area hit by an earthquake. The reading on the Mercalli scale is not connected to readings on the Richter or moment magnitude scales. For example, **a weak reading on the MMS or Richter scale does not mean a low rating on the Mercalli scale,** as a weak, shallow earthquake close to the surface can cause a great deal of damage at its epicentre.

ACTIVE LEARNING

1. Go to the Pacific Disaster Website to find information on the latest earthquakes across the globe:

   www.pdc.org

   If possible, present your findings to your class.

2. How would a seismograph reading help emergency services to send aid to the areas most affected by an earthquake?

EDUCATE YOURSELF

Measuring Earthquakes	
Seismograph	Records movements/waves, placed along fault lines, records and locates earthquake activity, vertical and horizontal activity, locates focus and epicentre
Richter scale	Readings from seismograph, measures magnitude (strength), each step equals a tenfold increase, e.g. 7.0 is ten times stronger than a 6.0
Moment magnitude scale	More accurate than Richter scale, combines seismograph readings and rock movement, each step equals a tenfold increase
Modified Mercalli scale	Not mathematical, records visual damage, low rating on Richter/moment scales does not mean low damage rating

4.4 Locations of Earthquakes

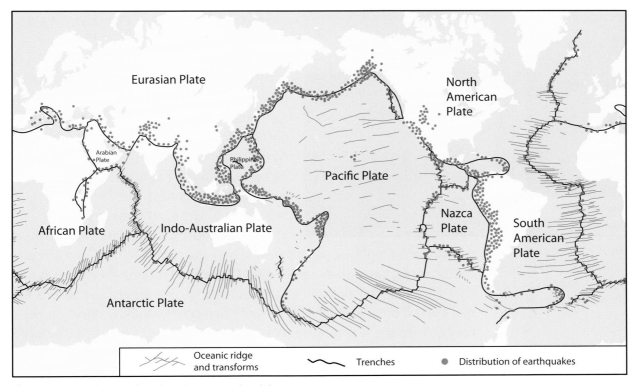

Fig. 4.6 Distribution of earthquakes across the globe

GEO DICTIONARY

Elastic rebound: when huge force pulls at rock, it stretches until it suddenly breaks. Like when you stretch and break an elastic band: it does not stay in the same position. Instead it snaps backwards quickly, releasing huge amounts of pressure as it does so. These sudden movements trigger earthquakes

ACTIVE LEARNING

1. Why does Ireland not experience strong earthquakes?

2. What is the most common cause of earthquakes?

3. Using Fig. 4.6, name the plates causing earthquakes along the western coast of the US and along the west coast of South America.

Nearly all earthquakes across the globe **occur at plate boundaries,** with 80 per cent of all seismic activity occurring along the Pacific Ocean's subduction zones. Earthquakes mainly occur along **destructive and passive** plate boundaries, but can also occur at constructive boundaries where the crust is being torn apart by convection currents. **Elastic rebound** is the most common cause of earthquakes, as layers of rock are exposed to pressure from opposite sides. This causes them to be **stretched and bent.** Eventually, the layers of rock are unable to bend any more and snap, releasing pressure suddenly. This sudden release of pressure results in an earthquake.

Destructive Boundaries

The most common and intense earthquakes **occur along subduction zones** at oceanic-oceanic or oceanic-continental plate boundaries. This can clearly be seen through examining the distribution of earthquake activity across the world (*see* Fig. 4.6). When plates converge, **the heavier oceanic plate is forced downwards** into the mantle. As the plate slides underneath the overlying plate, a great deal of **friction is created** between layers of rock. This friction causes the subducting plate to become stuck, allowing pressure between the two plates to build over several years. Eventually, the **rock breaks,** allowing the subducting plate to sink further into the mantle before becoming stuck once again. This process means that the **movement of the plate is not smooth.** Sudden movements occur after a long build-up of pressure. This **sudden movement triggers strong earthquakes,** capable of causing widespread damage.

Earthquakes at subduction zones can be at **deep, intermediate or shallow** depths as the focus can be located at any point along the sinking plate. The deepest earthquakes occur at depths of greater than **650 km below the surface.** Japan experiences earthquakes as a result of the Pacific Plate subducting underneath the Eurasian Plate. In 2011, an intense earthquake occurred due to movement from the Pacific Plate. As the plate subducted, it pushed the Eurasian Plate upwards, creating a tsunami (tidal wave). Earthquakes also occur along the **boundaries between destructive continental plates.** As the plates collide, the pressure generated causes layers of rock to buckle upwards, forming fold mountains. The force of this movement causes **earthquakes to occur at shallow depths.** Earthquakes formed in this way occur regularly along the plate boundary between India and China. This occurs as the **Indo-Australian and Eurasian Plates** collide, forming the Himalaya mountains. Although these earthquakes are not as powerful as those which occur at subduction zones, the relatively **shallow depth of the focus** means the seismic waves have a short distance to travel to the surface. This means that the seismic waves do not lose energy before they reach the surface and can cause a lot of damage.

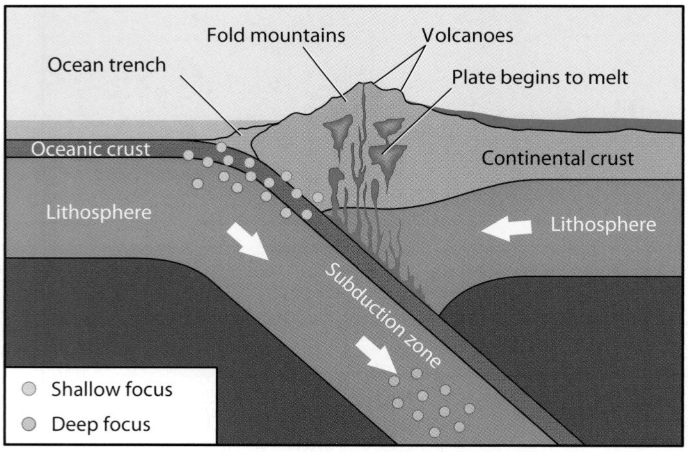

Labels: Fold mountains, Volcanoes, Ocean trench, Plate begins to melt, Oceanic crust, Continental crust, Lithosphere, Lithosphere, Subduction zone, Shallow focus, Deep focus

Fig. 4.7 The depth of earthquakes can determine how destructive they are on the surface.

Passive Boundaries

Earthquakes also occur at passive plate boundaries where plates slide past each other. The **San Andreas Fault** is the world's best-known passive boundary. The San Andreas Fault formed between the **Pacific and North American Plates.** Over the past century, movement of the Pacific Plate has increased from an **average of 1 cm per year to 5 cm per year.**

The Pacific Plate and North American Plate are moving in a **north-westerly direction.** As the plates slide past each other, friction is caused between them. This friction leads to the plates locking together for many years, causing pressure to build up. Eventually, this **pressure is released,** causing a violent earthquake. These earthquakes can occur anywhere along the 800 km boundary.

In 1906, movement in the northern section of the San Andreas Fault caused an earthquake measuring 8.3 on the Richter scale. A similarly strong earthquake occurred again in 1989 near San Francisco. Seismologists have noticed pressure levels building rapidly in the southern section. When this pressure is released, it will cause a large earthquake, already referred to as **'The Big One'.** Although they are unsure of when this earthquake will occur, seismologists predict it will have happened by 2032. In April 2014, a number of earthquakes, measuring over 7.5 on the MMS were recorded, leading seismologists to believe they are entering a phase of increased seismic activity along the fault.

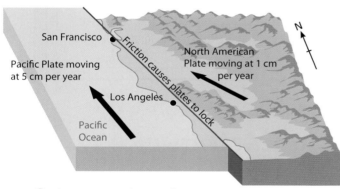

◔ **Fig. 4.8** San Andreas Fault pressure zones

ACTIVE LEARNING

The 2015 Nepal earthquake killed more than 9000 people. There are fears that there are going to be even more powerful earthquakes hitting the area in the near future. Find out the following:

1. What two plates collided to cause the earthquake?
2. How powerful was the earthquake?
3. Was the focus of the earthquake shallow, intermediate or deep?
4. How many homes/ buildings were destroyed?
5. Is Nepal a developed or a developing country?
6. What caused the most fatalities?
7. Where was the epicentre located?
8. Was aid able to access the area rapidly?

ACTIVE LEARNING

1. Visit the San Andreas Fault website to discover more information about 'The Big One': **www.sanandreasfault.org**

   If possible, present your findings to your class.
2. Explain how plate tectonics influence the distribution of earthquakes across the globe.
3. What precautions do you think could be taken by the major cities on the west coast of the US to reduce the damage caused by a large earthquake?

◔ **Fig. 4.9** An aerial view of the San Andreas Fault

Divergent Boundaries

Although much less frequent, earthquakes occur at divergent boundaries. These earthquakes occur at **shallow depths along mid-ocean ridges** and along points where the crust is rifting apart. Earthquakes occur along the **Mid-Atlantic Ridge** as **plumes of magma are forced through gaps** in the crust. The movement of magma can trigger low-magnitude earthquakes, much **like those which occur prior to a volcanic eruption.**

Earthquakes also occur along rift valleys, such as the East African Rift Valley, as **convection currents split the continent apart.** As the crust rifts apart, layers of **rock are bent and broken,** leading to strong earthquakes as a result of elastic rebound. In 2006, an earthquake in Mozambique measuring 7.0 on the MMS occurred along the southern section of the rift.

EDUCATE YOURSELF

Location of Earthquakes	
Convergent	Subduction zones, oceanic plate subducts, plates lock, pressure builds, sudden movement, shallow/intermediate earthquakes, continental-continental boundaries, buckling rock, shallow earthquakes, e.g. Indo-Australian and Eurasian Plates
Passive	San Andreas Fault, Pacific and North American Plates, 1 cm to 5 cm per year, Pacific and North American Plates north-westerly direction, plates stick, pressure builds, release triggers earthquake
Divergent	Shallow depths, mid-ocean ridges, e.g. Mid-Atlantic Ridge, plumes of magma rise, movement of magma triggers earthquakes, rift valleys, continent splits apart, rock bent and broken, strong earthquakes, e.g. East African Rift Valley

4.5 Predicting Earthquakes

Despite large amounts of time and money being spent on the prediction of earthquakes, it remains an **almost impossible task.** The difficulties are due to the **large number of variables** involved in earthquake prediction. Even if possible indicators are found in one area, no two fault lines are the same, making those indicators unreliable elsewhere. Generally, there are three methods of earthquake prediction, none of which is universally accepted as being accurate.

GEO DICTIONARY

Variables: differences or changes

Behaviour of animals

Although there is **no scientific evidence,** some people believe that monitoring animal behaviour can be used to help predict earthquakes. **China** is one such country which uses this method of prediction. Behaviours such as **rats fleeing towns, animals coming out of hibernation early and cattle and sheep refusing to enter their shelters** have been noted as indicators of earthquake activity.

Scientific **evidence suggests that animals are unable to foretell seismic activity.** Animals who behave strangely in the moments before an earthquake strikes are believed to be **responding to primary waves** (P-waves), which **go largely undetected by humans.** In 2011, the National Zoo in Virginia, US, reported that its animals predicted the earthquake that occurred there. Despite the media interest it caused, reliable reports suggest that the strange **behaviour occurred during the earthquake** rather than before it. Despite its unreliability as a predictor of earthquake activity, animals' ability to sense P-waves can provide **valuable seconds' warning** to occupants of buildings, allowing them to get to a safer part of the room, turn off electrical appliances, drop kitchen utensils and so on.

Historical Records

Historical records can be used to generate a **general prediction** of when the next earthquake is due to strike in an area. Seismologists using historical records attempt to provide a long-term forecast for future seismic activity. Studying historical records of an area can allow seismologists to identify a pattern or frequency of earthquake activity. For example, if a major earthquake occurs along a particular fault once every 100 years, there is a **10 per cent chance of it occurring in any given decade,** if the earthquake activity is randomly spaced. However, historical records are also unreliable as each plate movement changes the characteristics of the fault line, meaning that previous timelines become irrelevant.

Measuring Rock Stress

Monitoring stress levels in rock along fault lines is seen as the **most reliable form** of earthquake prediction. Seismologists use a variety of instruments to help them to monitor the build-up of stress at earthquake zones. As **pressure builds** along a fault line, the **likelihood of a strong earthquake increases.**
For example, monitoring of the San Andreas Fault has led seismologists to predict that the next major earthquake will have occurred by 2032.

⊙ **Fig. 4.10** A strainmeter measures the strain on rock either side of a fault line.

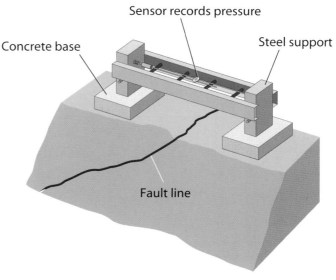

Sensor records pressure

Concrete base

Steel support

Fault line

- **Strainmeters** are used to monitor the build-up of stress at fault lines. As rocks can only withstand certain pressures before breaking, strainmeters provide information that will help to predict when they will reach breaking point.

- **Tiltmeters** (also used in volcano eruption prediction) detect any changes in the slope level of land. Any bulging on the surface can indicate increased pressure on the rock underneath.

- **Satellite/GPS** is also used to monitor any ground deformation taking place.

- **Seismographs** can be used to detect any minor movements or vibrations in the Earth's crust. These vibrations, known as **foreshocks,** often occur prior to an earthquake.

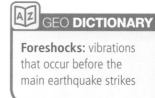

A|Z GEO **DICTIONARY**

Foreshocks: vibrations that occur before the main earthquake strikes

Although these methods work towards earthquake prediction, they mainly provide a location of where the earthquake will occur rather than a prediction of when it will occur.

EDUCATE YOURSELF

Predicting Earthquakes	
Behaviour of animals	No scientific evidence, monitor strange activities, responding to P-waves, undetected by humans, behaviour occurs during earthquake
Historical records	General prediction, once every 100 years = 10% chance per decade, unreliable
Measuring rock stress	Most reliable technique, monitor pressure, strainmeters, tiltmeters, satellite/GPS, foreshocks

4.6 Effects of an Earthquake

● **Fig. 4.11** Railway tracks damaged after the Christchurch earthquake in 2010

Damage to Infrastructure

Earthquakes can cause **damage to buildings** and other infrastructure. The vibrations in the crust cause buildings and bridges to sway and crumble. This falling debris is very dangerous and **causes many deaths.** In the aftermath of an earthquake, rescue workers must **search through the rubble** and debris in search of survivors trapped underneath.

The **Haitian earthquake** of 2010 caused widespread damage to infrastructure in the capital Port-au-Prince. The buildings in Port-au-Prince were poorly built, meaning that the 7.0 magnitude earthquake caused them to collapse. The only airport in the country was unusable after the earthquake as the control tower was badly damaged. In total, **160 000 people died,** with a further **300 000 people estimated to have been injured** – mostly from falling debris. In total, some **19 million cubic tonnes of rubble** had to be removed from Port-au-Prince.

The 2010 earthquake in **Christchurch, New Zealand** caused extensive damage to the city centre. For example, it toppled two of the bell towers on the Christchurch Catholic Cathedral.

◄ **Fig. 4.12** Widespread destruction of Haiti in 2010

Tsunami

When earthquakes occur beneath the sea, they can produce **huge waves** known as tsunamis. As one plate subducts, the **overlying plate** can be **forced upwards** in a sudden movement. The uplifting of the plate causes an **excess hump of water** on the surface of the ocean. If, for example, the plate is **uplifted by 4 m,** a 4 m hump of water is created on the ocean's surface. This excess water radiates (spreads) outwards in all directions, travelling across oceans at **speeds of up to 800 km/h.**

Most tsunamis are created by uplifts of less than 1 m. However, more powerful earthquakes, such as those that occurred in **Indonesia in 2004 or in Japan in 2011,** create much larger waves.

For boats out in the open sea, a tsunami is barely noticeable. However, as the waves approach the coastline, the **bottom of the wave comes into contact with the shore,** slowing it down. This causes the rest of the wave to stand upwards, often **quadrupling in size** before hitting the coastline at speed.

On 26 December, 2004, the devastating Indonesian tsunami was triggered by a **9.0 magnitude** earthquake on the MMS scale underneath the **Indian Ocean.** A large amount of water was displaced due to the uplifting of the Burma Plate. This wave travelled across the Indian Ocean, before hitting the coastlines of 14 different countries at heights of **between 24 and 30 m.** An estimated **220 000 people were killed,** most of whom were drowned. Since the devastating tsunami, an advanced tsunami warning system has been set up in the Indian Ocean.

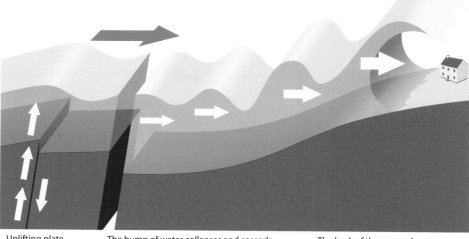

Uplifting plate displaces water causing an excess hump on surface

The hump of water collapses and spreads out causing a series of waves that travel across the open ocean – as the waves reach land, the front of the waves comes into contact with land causing it to slow down

The back of the waves does not slow down, causing them to rise upwards, quadrupling in size

⊙ **Fig. 4.13** How a tsunami forms

Liquefaction

During an earthquake, the **intense shaking of the crust** can cause soil to become **saturated with groundwater.** When this occurs, soil takes on the **properties of a liquid** (like quicksand). This process referred to as liquefaction. Due to the liquefaction, the soil is **unable to support buildings** on top of it, causing them to collapse. Liquefaction caused widespread damage in **Christchurch in New Zealand** during an earthquake in 2010. Liquefaction occurred after the 1995 earthquake in Kobe, Japan which caused entire apartment blocks to collapse as their **foundations sank. Gas and sewage pipes** also sank into the ground causing them to bend and break. This led to the outbreak of fires across the city and played a large part in the **5000 deaths** that occurred.

⊙ **Fig. 4.14** Liquefaction caused a car to sink into the ground in Christchurch, New Zealand in 2010.

4.7 Factors Affecting Damage

Earthquakes have many negative effects. However, the extent of the damage they cause depends on a number of factors.

Economic Development

Nearly 2 million people have been killed by earthquakes in the past 100 years. Most of these deaths have occurred in **developing or underdeveloped** countries. This is because buildings and other infrastructure are not built to the same quality as in developed countries. As a result, even minor earthquakes can cause a lot of damage, destroying buildings, roads and bridges. This leads to a large loss of life.

Population Density

Urban areas have much higher populations than rural areas. Earthquakes with epicentres close to urban areas usually result in a larger loss of life.

Time of Day

The **time of day that an earthquake strikes** is directly linked to the number of deaths that occur. An earthquake that strikes during the day will have a higher casualty rate than an earthquake of similar magnitude at night. By night, roadways and bridges are largely free of traffic, while streets are unpopulated. This means there are far fewer deaths as a result of bridges collapsing or falling debris crushing pedestrians.

Magnitude/Aftershocks

The **higher the magnitude** of an earthquake, the more likely it is to cause damage. A shallow earthquake (close to the surface) is likely to cause more damage than a deep earthquake.

4.8 Reducing the Effects of an Earthquake

Although earthquakes are nearly impossible to predict, the damage caused can be greatly reduced through the **correct planning of cities** and efficient emergency response plans.

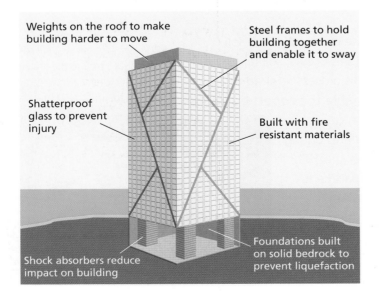

Weights on the roof to make building harder to move

Steel frames to hold building together and enable it to sway

Shatterproof glass to prevent injury

Built with fire resistant materials

Shock absorbers reduce impact on building

Foundations built on solid bedrock to prevent liquefaction

◀ **Fig. 4.15** Earthquake-proof building technology can reduce the damage caused by earthquakes.

Earthquake-proof Infrastructure

In earthquake zones such as California and Japan, strict building regulations have reduced the damage caused to infrastructure, saving countless lives. High-rise buildings are designed to be **slightly elastic rather than rigid,** allowing the building to move from **side to side** during an earthquake. This means that the energy from seismic waves does not harm the building. The **foundations of the buildings are built on stone rather than on soil** to avoid damage caused by liquefaction. Buildings are also fitted with **mechanical dampers** which act as shock absorbers that reduce the energy of the vibrations. The frames of the buildings are reinforced with steel, which join together to allow the building to move as a single unit. This prevents buildings from splitting apart during an earthquake. Bridges are built to similar specifications, allowing them to **sway gently without breaking.**

Efficient Urban Planning

In these areas, buildings are also spaced apart to prevent them from collapsing on others. This prevents a **'domino effect'** from occurring, when one building collapses and causes other buildings to also collapse. Also, in cities prone to earthquake activity, it is important that services such as hospitals, schools and fire stations are built in areas least likely to be affected by the tremors. This ensures that **children are safer** and that vital **emergency services are not disrupted.**

Early Warning Systems

Early warning systems for earthquakes and tsunamis **alert people to seismic activity** before it arrives. Early warning systems work by receiving messages from a network of seismographs that detect primary waves. The length of time between the alarm warning and the arrival of the destructive secondary and surface waves depends on the distance of the epicentre from the area. Sometimes the alarms sound only seconds before the earthquake begins, while other times they can provide up to a minute's warning. Nevertheless, even a slight advanced warning can allow **people to brace themselves, trains to slow down, factory assembly lines to stop** and so on.

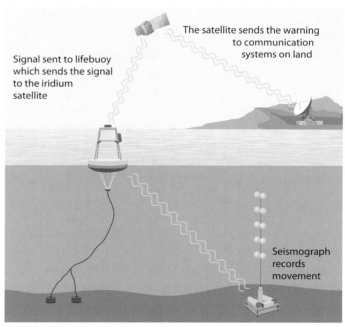

Signal sent to lifebuoy which sends the signal to the iridium satellite

The satellite sends the warning to communication systems on land

Seismograph records movement

🔺 **Fig. 4.16** Early warning system used in Japan

Japan has the most advanced warning system in the world, currently detecting **85 per cent of all earthquakes** in the area. Since the earthquake and tsunami of 2011, the system has been updated and improved. If the warning of a strong tremor or tsunami is detected, a message is immediately sent to all televisions, radios and mobile phones followed by **two chimes of an alarm.** This system is continually improving. For example, people can now download an early warning app to their smartphones and tablets.

Effects of an earthquake	Damage to infrastructure, vibrations cause buildings to collapse, high casualties, Christchurch 2010, Haitian 2010 160 000 deaths, 300 000 injuries, 19 million tonnes of rubble
	Tsunami, huge wave, uplifting of plate, excess hump of water, quadruples in size, Indonesia 2004, 220 000 killed
	Liquefaction, intense shaking, groundwater mixes with mud, mud turns to liquid, foundations collapse, Kobe, Japan, 5000 deaths
Factors affecting damage	Developing or underdeveloped, higher deaths than developed, building standards
	Population density urban population higher than rural, more deaths
	Time of day, more people outside by day, larger chance of injury, night-time means fewer casualties, magnitude, stronger earthquakes means more damage
Reducing effects	Earthquake-proof buildings, elastic rather than rigid, move side to side, foundations are solid, mechanical dampers, sway without breaking
	Efficient urban planning, avoids domino effect, schools/hospitals away from earthquake zones
	Early warning systems, forewarning, machinery and trains shut down, Japan detects 85% of its earthquakes

CASE STUDY

Japan 2011

On **11 March 2011**, an earthquake measuring **9.0 on the Richter scale** struck off the coast of Japan. The earthquake occurred on a **subduction zone** along the **Eurasian Plate and Pacific Plate** boundary.

As the Pacific Plate subducts beneath the Eurasian Plate, it causes **huge amounts of friction** and pressure. The pressure had been building up over centuries before the Pacific Plate finally jolted free. This sudden movement caused a strong earthquake **70 kilometres off the coast** of Japan, at a depth of 32 kilometres beneath the crust.

Early Warning

Japan has the most advanced **earthquake/tsunami warning** system in the world. The system delivered warning to the Japanese a **full minute before the tremors reached land**. This allowed **high-speed trains** to stop safely, **production lines to stop** and dangerous machinery to be deactivated before the shaking began. All residents also received a **text message to their phones** warning them of the earthquake.

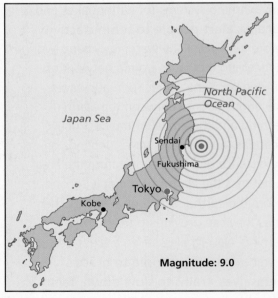

Fig. 4.17 Location of epicentre of the Japanese earthquake

A tsunami warning was sent soon after the earthquake, telling civilians to go to higher ground for protection. However, the height of the **tsunami was hugely underestimated,** causing a large percentage of those who received the warning to ignore safety precautions. It was predicted that a 20 m wave would hit and it was assumed that the tsunami walls would be easily able to withstand it.

Effects

As the Pacific Plate subducted, it caused the Eurasian Plate to uplift suddenly, creating an **excess hump of water** on the surface of the Pacific Ocean. The earthquake triggered a **39 m high tsunami** that devastated the eastern coast of Japan.

Less than an hour after the earthquake had struck, the first of many tsunami waves hit Japan's coastline. The waves were so high that they **breached Japan's tsunami defense system**. The waves rushed as far as **10 km inland,** destroying buildings and other infrastructure. Many buildings that were destroyed contained people who had fled to the higher floors for safety.

The waves also destroyed the cooling system for the **Fukushima Daiichi Nuclear Power Plant,** causing a catastrophic meltdown. **Radioactive waste** still leaks from the power plant into the Pacific Ocean every day. This has **destroyed marine habitats** and made the surrounding area uninhabitable. In total, over **18 000 people were killed**, most of whom were drowned by the tsunami. Some **130 000 buildings** were completely **destroyed,** while a further **1 million buildings** were **damaged.**

Fig. 4.18 The tsunami breaching highway barriers

FACT

The convergence of the two plates that caused the earthquake was so powerful that it shortened the length of a day on Earth by a microsecond.

Fig. 4.19 Radioactive smoke rising from the Fukushima Plant

Aftermath

After its failure to accurately predict the size of the wave, Japan upgraded its tsunami warning system. The disaster cost the Japanese economy over **€200 billion** as the expensive clean-up operation continues. Radiation from the Fukushima Plant continues to leak despite the best efforts of experts and volunteers. Over **1000 aftershocks** have hit Japan since the earthquake, with **magnitudes of up to 7.9.**

EDUCATE YOURSELF

Case Study: Japan

11 March 2011, 9.0, subduction zone, Eurasian and Pacific boundary, friction, 70 km offshore, 32 km deep; earthquake/tsunami warning, one minute warning, text messages, tsunami underestimated; 39 m high wave, excess hump of water, breached defensive system, reached 10 km inland, meltdown of Fukushima Power Plant, 300 tonnes radioactive waste per year, destroyed marine habitats, 18 000 people killed, 130 000 buildings destroyed, 1 million buildings damaged; cost €200 billion, 1000 aftershocks, strongest 7.9 magnitude

CORE 1   CHAPTER 4

ORDINARY LEVEL

SHORT QUESTIONS

1. (i) Match each of the letters A, B and C in the diagram with the correct feature in the table.

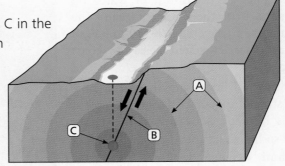

Feature	Letter
Focus	
Shock waves	
Fault line	

(ii) Name a scale used to measure earthquakes.

(iii) What is the name given to a large wave caused by an earthquake under the water in the ocean?

2014 Q5 10M

(i) 3 x name @ 2m each

(ii) Name 2m

(iii) Name 2m

2. Study the table and answer the following questions:

Number of Earthquakes Worldwide 2006 to 2010					
Magnitude	2006	2007	2008	2009	2010
8.0 to 9.0	2	4	0	1	1
7.0 to 7.9	9	14	12	16	21
6.0 to 6.9	142	178	168	144	151
Estimated deaths resulting from earthquakes	6605	712	88 011	1790	226 896+

(i) In what year was the largest number of earthquakes of magnitude between 8.0 and 9.0?

(ii) In what year did the greatest estimated number of deaths occur?

(iii) How many earthquakes of the strongest magnitude occurred over the period shown?

(iv) What is the name of the scale used for measuring the strength of an earthquake?

(v) Read the statement below and place and X in the correct box.

'Earthquakes occur where plates collide.'

True	
False	

5 x 2m

2011 Q4 10M

LONG QUESTIONS

1. (i) Name one location where an earthquake has occurred.

(ii) Name a scale used to measure the force of an earthquake.

(iii) Describe how earthquakes occur and describe their main effects.

(i) 2m

(ii) 2m

(iii) 12 SRPs @ 3m each

2013 Q1B 40M

2. Read the newspaper article and answer each of the following questions.

Earthquake in the Irish Sea

A 3.8 magnitude earthquake struck this morning. The epicentre was located approximately 2 km off the coast of the Lleyn Peninsula in Wales and was 97 km southeast of Dublin. The quake was followed four minutes later by a smaller 1.7 magnitude tremor.

Moderate shaking was felt in Carlow, Kildare, Wicklow, Wexford and Dublin. Earthquake stations as far away as Valentia, Donegal and Galway also recorded the earthquake.

Adapted from the *Irish Independent*, 28 June, 2013

(i) What direction from Dublin was the epicentre of the earthquake and how far, in kilometres, was the epicentre from Dublin?

(ii) Name two locations in Ireland where the earthquake was felt.

(iii) What is the term given to the smaller tremors which follow the main earthquake?

(iv) State two effects of earthquakes.

(v) Explain briefly why Ireland has not experienced major earthquakes.

(i) 2 x 3m	
(ii) 2 x 3m	
(iii) 6m	
(iv) 2 x 3m	
(v) 2 x 3m	

2014 Q1A 30M

3. Study the map of an earthquake in Italy and answer the following questions:

(i) What was the magnitude (strength) of the earthquake at the epicentre?

(ii) At what time did the earthquake take place?

(iii) How many towns reported deaths as a result of the earthquake?

(iv) Explain in detail how earthquakes occur.

2010 Q2B 40M

(i) 2m	
(ii) 2m	
(iii) 3m	
(iv) 11 SRPs @ 3m each	

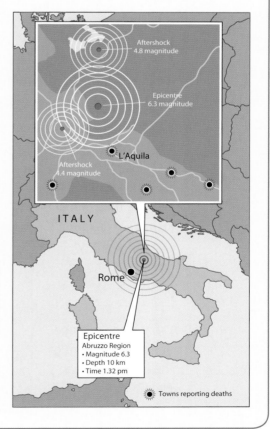

ITALY

Aftershock 4.8 magnitude

Epicentre 6.3 magnitude

L'Aquila

Aftershock 4.4 magnitude

Rome

Epicentre
Abruzzo Region
• Magnitude 6.3
• Depth 10 km
• Time 1.32 pm

● Towns reporting deaths

SHORT QUESTIONS

1. (i) Match each of the letters A, B, C and D on the diagram with the correct feature on the table.

Feature	Letter
Focus	
Epicentre	
Seismic waves	
Fault line	

(ii) Explain briefly each of the following terms:

Seismologist

Seismometer

2013 Q2 8M

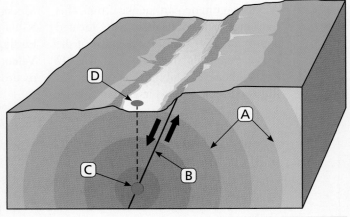

(i) 4 x 1m
(ii) 2 x 2m

LONG QUESTIONS

1. Examine the map relating to the earthquake in Haiti in January 2010 and answer the following questions:

(i) Activity along which two plates resulted in the earthquake in Haiti?

(ii) What type of fault caused the earthquake?

(iii) Describe the fault responsible for the earthquake.

(iv) What tectonic activity along the subduction zone created the island arc on the map?

(i) 3m + 3m
(ii) 5m
(iii) 2 x 2m
(iv) 5m

2010 Q3A 20M

2. Examine the map and answer the following questions.

(i) Name the plates marked X and Y.

X	
Y	

(ii) What is the average annual movement of the Indo-Australian Plate?

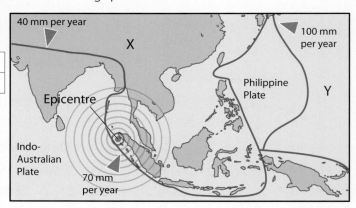

HIGHER LEVEL

(iii) Explain what is meant by the term 'epicentre'.

(iv) Given that the epicentre of the earthquake shown is offshore, name and briefly explain the main effect of this earthquake on the sea.

(v) Name the two scales that measure the magnitude/intensity of an earthquake.

2012 Q2A 20M

(i) 2 x 2m
(ii) 2m
(iii) 2m + 2m
(iv) 4m + 2m
(v) 2m + 2m

3. Explain how the occurrence of earthquakes and volcanic eruptions can be monitored and predicted.

2013 Q3C 30M

15 SRPs @ 2m each

4. Explain, with reference to examples that you have studied, how the theory of plate tectonics helps to explain the distribution of earthquakes around the world.

2012 Q1C 30M

Global examples/locations 2 x 2m
Discussion 13 SRPs @ 2m each

Earthquakes are a topic that regularly appear on exam papers at both Higher and Ordinary Levels. Familiarise yourself with a case study as most questions will ask you for a named example. Added to this, all case studies give details of the magnitude of the earthquake and the effects it had on the region it struck. In this section, we will look at Q3C from the 2008 Higher Level exam paper.

HIGHER LEVEL

EXAM **QUESTION**

Examine, with reference to actual examples, the measurements and effects of earthquakes. *2008 Q3C 30M*

Marking Sheme
Measurement identified 2m
Effects identified 2m + 2m
Named examples 2m + 2m
Discussion 10 SRPs (5 SRPs per aspect)

For this answer, I have used a second case study: the Haitian earthquake of 2010. The first half of the answer describes the measurement of the earthquake, and the second half deals with the effects of the earthquake on Haiti and also the effects of the Japanese earthquake of 2011.

SAMPLE **ANSWER**

• An earthquake struck Haiti on 12 January 2010 with devastating effects. [2m] Haiti is situated to the north of the Caribbean Plate, on a passive plate boundary with the North American Plate. [2m] It is on a boundary with the North American Plate which is moving west.

Measurement

- This movement is not smooth, and a great deal of friction occurs between the plates. [2m] Pressure built up between the two plates, eventually ending in a powerful earthquake measuring 7.0 on the Richter scale. [2m] Despite the tremors only lasting for one minute, the focus of the earthquake was relatively shallow, at 13 km below the surface of the Earth. [2m] The epicentre of the earthquake was 16 km south-west of Port-au-Prince due to the slipping of a plate along a nearby fault. [2m] As the earthquake was shallow, the seismic waves had to travel a very small distance through the Earth's crust to reach the surface. This means that the earthquake kept most of its energy. [2m]

Effects

- The earthquake struck in the most densely populated area of the country. Port-au-Prince has a population of 3 million, with the majority living in slum conditions. [2m] The buildings in Port-au-Prince and other areas of Haiti were in very poor condition in general, and were not designed to be earthquake resistant. This meant that many buildings collapsed easily. [2m]

- Haiti is considered to be the poorest country in the entire Western Hemisphere, and was not able to deal with the destruction the earthquake caused. [2m] Haiti has only one airport with a single runway. The control tower was badly damaged in the earthquake, as was the port, making them both unusable. [2m] As a result, rescue teams from around the world took up to 48 hours to arrive in Haiti. During this time, local volunteers used their bare hands to dig through the rubble in search of survivors. [2m] The country has a very limited number of doctors, meaning that a large percentage of injured civilians did not receive the treatment they needed. Many people died due to common injuries such as broken limbs. [2m]

- When aid did arrive, it piled up at the airport due to a lack of trucks and people to distribute it. Water and food took many days to arrive at its destinations, with not enough to go around. [2m] After the earthquake, there were 19 million cubic metres of rubble and debris in Port-au-Prince. In total 160 000 people are estimated to have died, with a further 300 000 injured and 1 million left homeless. [2m]

- In 2011, an earthquake measuring 9.0 on the Richter scale struck off the coast of Japan, generating a large tsunami which hit the island three hours later. [2m] The tsunami killed 18 000 people and caused a nuclear power plant to go into meltdown. [2m]

This answer draws on a correct number of examples and the effects they had on the regions they occurred in.

Marks Awarded
Named examples 2 x 2m
Effects 2 x 2m
Discusion best 11 SRPs @ 2m each

TOPIC MAP

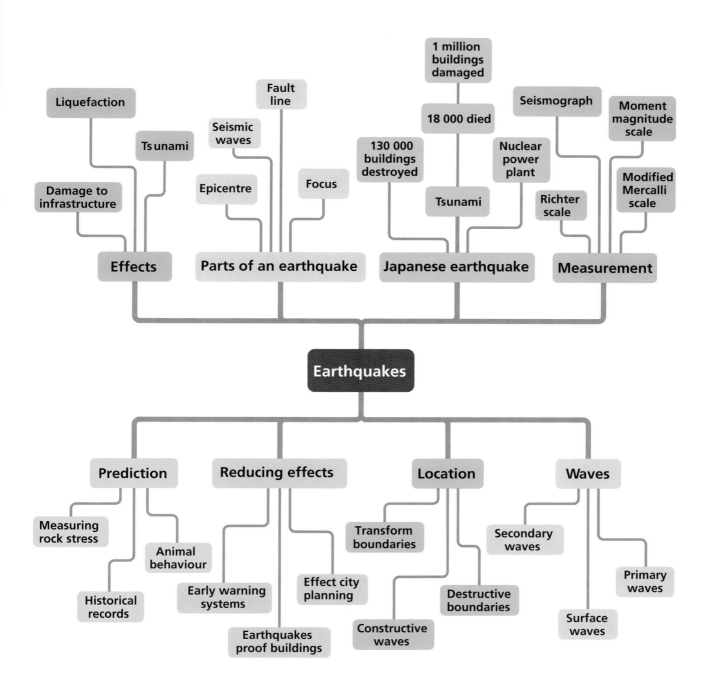

- **Effects**
  - Liquefaction
  - Tsunami
  - Damage to infrastructure
- **Parts of an earthquake**
  - Fault line
  - Seismic waves
  - Epicentre
  - Focus
- **Japanese earthquake**
  - 1 million buildings damaged
  - 18 000 died
  - 130 000 buildings destroyed
  - Tsunami
  - Nuclear power plant
- **Measurement**
  - Seismograph
  - Moment magnitude scale
  - Modified Mercalli scale
  - Richter scale

Earthquakes

- **Prediction**
  - Measuring rock stress
  - Animal behaviour
  - Historical records
- **Reducing effects**
  - Early warning systems
  - Earthquakes proof buildings
  - Effect city planning
- **Location**
  - Transform boundaries
  - Constructive waves
  - Destructive boundaries
- **Waves**
  - Secondary waves
  - Surface waves
  - Primary waves

CHAPTER 5

Folding and Faulting

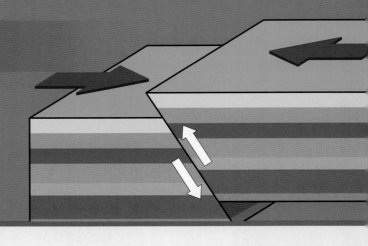

So far, you have learned how the Earth's crust is divided into several sections of rock which float on molten magma. Moved by convection currents, the plates collide, separate and slide past each other. In Chapters 3 and 4, you learned about two effects of this movement: volcanoes and earthquakes. In this chapter, we will look at the creation of fold mountains and rock faults, which is the third effect of moving tectonic plates.

KEY WORDS

- Ductile
- Anticline
- Syncline
- Limb
- Symmetrical
- Asymmetrical
- Overturned

- Caledonian
- Armorican
- Alpine
- Compression
- Tension
- Shearing
- Normal fault

- Reverse fault
- Transform fault
- Escarpment
- Heave
- Throw

LEARNING OUTCOMES

What you **MUST** know
- The types of plate boundaries where folding occurs
- The three main periods of folding
- How folding has shaped the Irish landscape
- The three main types of faulting
- The three processes of faulting
- Irish examples of folds and faults
- Anticlines and synclines
- How fold mountains form
- How to identify the parts of a fault

What you **SHOULD** know
- How domes and monoclines form

What is **USEFUL** to know
- Additional global examples of faults

5.1 Folding

Fold mountains are areas of rock that have been **pushed high above the surrounding landscape.** This is due to the **influence of plate tectonics,** as **convection currents** push plates together causing the rock to uplift. The rock is then shaped through weathering and erosion. The shaping of folds forms peaks, valleys and other features. Rocks that are **close to the Earth's surface are hard and brittle,** meaning that they break easily when subjected to pressure. However, **rocks that are buried deeper** in the Earth's crust are **heated and compressed,** causing them to become **ductile.** This allows the rock to be **folded and deformed without breaking.** Layers of ductile **sedimentary rock can buckle** and bend into a variety of curved shapes. This ability to buckle and bend, combined with pressure from plate movement, leads to the formation of fold mountains.

Fig. 5.1 Ductile rock bends without breaking.

Parts of a Fold Mountain

There are three parts of a fold mountain: the **anticline, syncline** and **limb.**

- The **anticline** is the **rock which has been folded upwards.**
- The rock in between the anticlines, which has been **folded downwards, is known as a syncline.**
- The slopes that separate the anticlines and synclines are known as **limbs.**

Note!
To remember which is which: for anticline, think of an anthill (rises up) and for syncline think of sink (goes down).

(a)

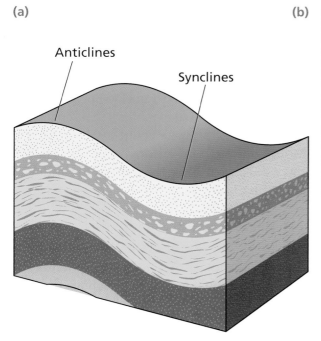

Anticlines

Synclines

(b)

Fig. 5.2 (a) Anticlines and synclines are the most predominant feature of folding. (b) A series of anticlines and synclines run across Munster, creating what is known as the Munster Ridge Valley.

5.2 Types of Folds

There are three main types of folds: **symmetrical**, **asymmetrical** and **overturned**. The type depends on the amount of pressure exerted from each of the plates that are colliding.

- When **even pressure** is exerted from each of the convergent plates, a **symmetrical**, or even, fold is created. This means that both plates **folded evenly**.

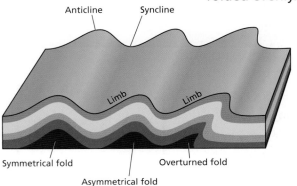

Anticline   Syncline

Limb   Limb

Symmetrical fold   Overturned fold

Asymmetrical fold

Fig. 5.3 The type of fold formed depends on the pressure from each of the convergent tectonic plates.

- When the **pressure from one plate is slightly greater** than from the other plate, an **asymmetrical** fold is formed. When this occurs, one limb is steeper than the other.

- An **overturned** fold is created when **one plate exerts much more pressure** than the other, causing it to fold over on itself.

GEO DICTIONARY

Symmetrical: evenly shaped (i.e. both sides match)

Asymmetrical: lopsided (i.e. one side has pushed over more than the other)

Overturned: one plate has folded over on itself

5.3 Location of Fold Mountains

Fold mountains are evidence that plate tectonics are or were active in that region at some point in the past. Folding occurs at two different types of convergent plate boundaries: continental-oceanic and continental-continental.

The convergence of **continental-oceanic** plates creates fold mountains **along the coastlines of the continental plate.** When a continental plate and an oceanic plate collide, the **heavier oceanic plate subducts** into the mantle before melting. As the oceanic plate subducts underneath the continental plate, pressure causes the **edges of the continental plate to buckle** upwards. This creates a series of fold mountains that run along the full edge of the plate boundary. The **Andes Mountains** in South America have been created in this way as the oceanic **Nazca Plate is subducting underneath the South American Plate.** Many of the peaks in the Andes are volcanically active as magma from the subducting Nazca Plate rises through the overlying South American Plate.

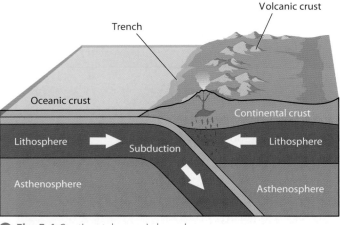

Volcanic crust

Trench

Oceanic crust

Continental crust

Lithosphere   Subduction   Lithosphere

Asthenosphere   Asthenosphere

Fig. 5.4 Continental-oceanic boundary

Mountain range

Continental crust

Lithosphere   Lithosphere

Asthenosphere

Fig. 5.5 Continental-continental boundary

The convergence of **continental-continental** plates also create series of fold mountain ranges. When two continental plates collide, **neither plate subducts** as they are much lighter than oceanic plates. As convection currents push the plates together, the increased pressure eventually causes **layers of sedimentary rock to buckle upwards,** creating anticlines and synclines.

It is through this process that most of Ireland's mountain ranges have been created. For example, the **Macgillycuddy's Reeks** in Co. Kerry were formed by the **collision of the African and Eurasian Plates.**

Note!

The Himalaya Mountains are a global example of continental-continental convergence.

EDUCATE YOURSELF

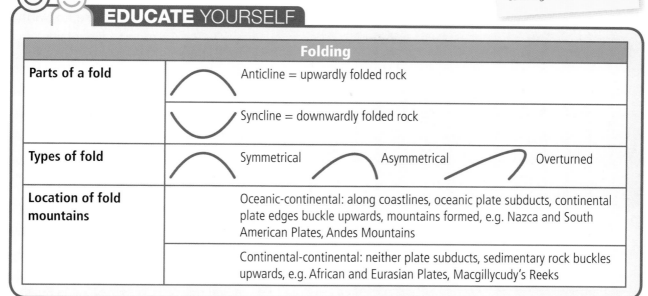

Folding			
Parts of a fold	Anticline = upwardly folded rock		
	Syncline = downwardly folded rock		
Types of fold	Symmetrical	Asymmetrical	Overturned
Location of fold mountains	Oceanic-continental: along coastlines, oceanic plate subducts, continental plate edges buckle upwards, mountains formed, e.g. Nazca and South American Plates, Andes Mountains		
	Continental-continental: neither plate subducts, sedimentary rock buckles upwards, e.g. African and Eurasian Plates, Macgillycudy's Reeks		

5.4 Periods of Folding

There have been many periods of fold mountain building across the globe. These periods of mountain building are known as **orogenies** and occur due to plate tectonics. We can tell how, why, where and when folding occurred in the past and is still occurring today There have been three main orogenies in recent geological history. These are:

- The **Caledonian folding** period (450–400 million years ago)
- The **Armorican folding** period (270–250 million years ago)
- The **Alpine folding** period (60 million years ago to present)

ACTIVE LEARNING

1. Name and describe the three main types of fold.

2. Describe how fold mountains are formed at two different types of convergent boundaries.

Note!

The Caledonian and Armorican orogenies had a huge impact on the Irish landscape.

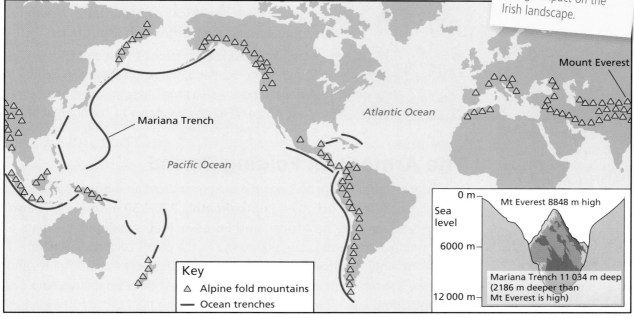

Fig. 5.6 The location of the world's Alpine fold mountains. The presence of an ocean trench shows that an oceanic plate is subducting at this point. All other folds are continental-continental convergences.

The Caledonian Folding Period

Fig. 5.7 The quartzite peak of Mount Errigal in the Derryveagh Mountains, Co. Donegal

The Caledonian folding period occurred approximately **450–400 million years ago,** creating mountains that extend from Scotland, through Ireland, to North America. The Caledonian mountains are the **oldest mountains in Ireland,** running in a north-east to south-west direction. The Caledonian orogeny began when the **North American and Eurasian Plates collided,** creating a **continental-continental plate boundary.** When the plates collided 450 million years ago, there followed 50 million years of folding. The pressure from the colliding plates caused **layers of shale, mudstone and sandstone to buckle** upwards.

As the folds arched upwards, magma rose beneath them and cooled, forming **igneous rock beneath the anticlines.** The heat from the rising magma caused some of the overlying sedimentary rock to cook, turning it into metamorphic rock. For example, layers of **sandstone metamorphosed into quartzite,** which forms a **cap along the peak of Croagh Patrick** in Co. Mayo (we will examine this in Chapter 6). As the Caledonians are the oldest mountains in Ireland, they are also the smallest as **weathering and erosion have worn them down** over time. Most Caledonian peaks in Ireland are **between 600 and 700 m in height.** Examples in Ireland include the **Wicklow Mountains,** Maumturk Mountains and the **Derryveagh Mountains.**

Matching folds can be traced to Greenland, Scandinavia, Scotland, the Appalachians in North America and the Avalonian Mountains of North West Africa (proving the theory of continental drift).

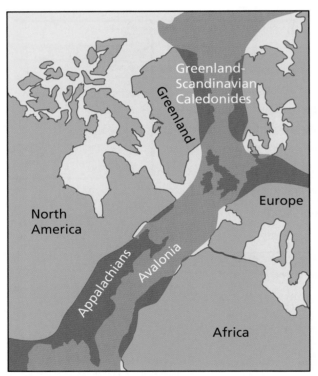

Fig. 5.8 Caledonian mountains stretch from Scotland, through Ireland, to Africa and North America.

The Armorican Folding Period

The Armorican folding period was the next major folding orogeny to affect the Irish landscape. It **occurred approximately 270–250 million years ago.** The folds occurred as the **African and Eurasian Plates collided,** creating a continental-continental plate boundary. As the plates collided, layers of **sandstone and limestone were buckled,** creating a series of anticlines and synclines. The folded mountains have an **east-west direction,** stretching from the Comeragh Mountains in Co. Waterford to the Macgillycuddy's Reeks in Co. Kerry.

This folding created the **Munster Ridge Valley,** which shapes the landscape of Munster today. The ridges of Munster are the **anticlines of sandstone** folded during this time. The sandstone ridges were covered by layers of limestone. As limestone is a much softer rock than sandstone, it was worn away by weathering and erosion at a much faster rate. The faster weathering of limestone **created deep valleys** between the anticlines of sandstone. The rivers Lee, Bandon and Blackwater flow through the valleys of Munster, which aided in the wearing down of limestone synclines. The tallest mountain peak in Ireland is **Carrantouhill (1037 m),** which is part of the Macgillycuddy's Reeks.

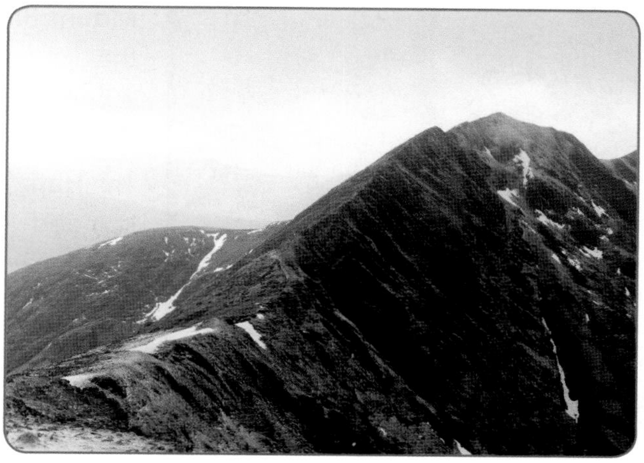

Fig. 5.9 Carrantouhill is Ireland's highest peak.

The Armorican orogeny also led to the **uplifting of the karst region of the Burren** above sea level. The Burren's limestone formed under the sea 100 million years **before the orogeny began.**

GEO DICTIONARY

Karst: an area of limestone that has been exposed to the surface

The Alpine Folding Period

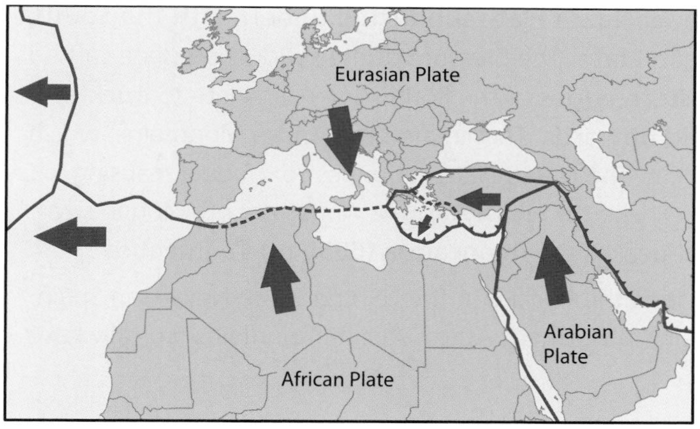

Fig. 5.10 Convergent boundary between the African and Eurasian Plates

Unlike the Caledonian and Armorican folding period, the Alpine orogeny **has not affected the Irish landscape.** The Alpine folding period, which **began 40–60 million years ago,** is still taking place. It refers to any mountain range created during this time. The Alps, Himalayas and Andes Mountains have been formed during this time.

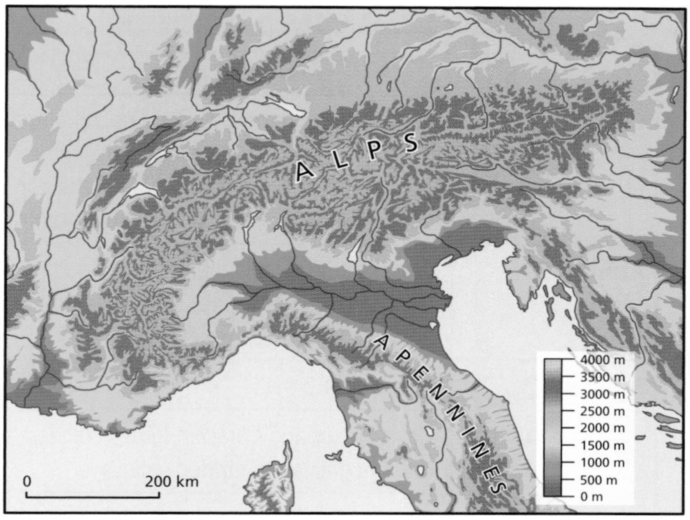

Fig. 5.11 The extent of the Alps

The **Alps were created due to the collision of the Eurasian and African Plates**. As the plates collided, sediment from the surface was uplifted, **forming weak mudstone folds.** The mountains grew rapidly as **sandstone was buckled and folded into anticlines** of more than **4000 m in height.** The synclines in between the peaks have been **worn down due to glaciation** over the past 2 million years, creating steep Alpine valleys.

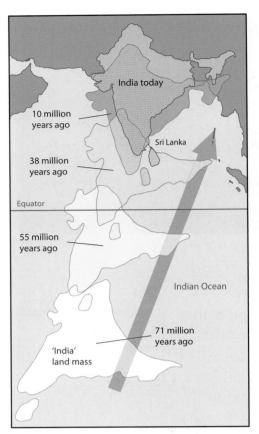

Fig. 5.12 Movement of the Indian subcontinent

ACTIVE **LEARNING**

1. Explain how folding has impacted on the landscape of Ireland.

2. Describe the effects of the Alpine folding period on the global landscape.

Mount Blanc in France, which reaches a height of **4807 m,** is the highest peak in the Alps. The Alps stretch for over 1050 km in an arc along southern Europe in a west-to-east direction, from southern France to Austria.

The **Himalayas** occurred when the **Indo-Australian Plate collided with the Eurasian Plate 50 million years ago.** The Himalayas stretch over 2400 km across Pakistan, India, Nepal and Bhutan. The **Indian subcontinent** began moving northwards **70 million years ago** at a speed of **15 cm per year.** As the Indian subcontinent moved closer to the Eurasian Plate, it closed the ancient Tethys Sea. Approximately 50 million years ago, the Indian subcontinent **collided with the Eurasian Plate,** causing layers of sedimentary rock to **buckle and form steep anticlines.** The force of the collision has shortened the length of the Indian subcontinent by over 2000 km and created the tallest mountains in the world. The highest peak is **Mount Everest at 8848 m** above sea level. Mount Everest continues to rise slowly each year as the plates continue to push together.

The **Andes Mountains were formed 50 million years ago** as the **Nazca Plate collided with the South American Plate.** The heavier **Nazca Plate subducted underneath the South American Plate.** The pressure of the subducting plate caused the **western edges** of the South American Plate to **buckle and fold upwards.** This created the Andes Mountains, which stretch for over 7200 km. The Nazca Plate continues to subduct, causing further folding to occur. Like the Himalayas, the Andes are growing in size each year. The highest peak is the **Aconcagua (6959 m)** in Argentina.

Other Alpine folds include the Rockies in the US, the Sierra Nevada in Spain and the Atlas Mountains in Northern Africa. Alpine mountains typically have peaks of over 6000 m.

EDUCATE YOURSELF

Periods of Folding	
Caledonian	450–400 mya, oldest mountains in Ireland, North American and Eurasian Plates collided, shale and sandstone folded, magma rose underneath folds, cooled to form igneous rock, sedimentary rock turned to metamorphic, quartzite cap on Croagh Patrick, worn down by weathering and erosion, 600–700 m, e.g. Wicklow Mountains
Armorican	270–250 mya, African and Eurasian Plates collided, sandstone and limestone buckled, folded into sandstone anticlines and limestone synclines, Munster Ridge Valley, limestone weathered away, making steep valleys
Alpine	Began 40–60 mya
	Alps: African and Eurasian Plates collided, mudstone and sandstone folded, anticlines over 4000 m, glaciation eroded valleys
	Himalayas: Indo-Australian and Eurasian Plates collided, Indian subcontinent moved northwards, 15 cm per year, buckled and formed steep anticlines, peaks over 8000 m
	Andes: 50 mya, Nazca and South American Plates collided, Nazca subducting, western edge of South American Plate buckling, peaks above 6000 m

5.5 Monoclines and Doming Structures

Monoclines

As you have learned, folding occurs due to intense pressure from colliding plates. Monoclines are mountains and other upland structures **formed from smaller earth movements.** They form when **sedimentary rock is uplifted slightly and faulted** due to compression. Generally, the rocks uplifted in this way **tilt slightly in one direction.** This uplifting of land can lead to the formation of **plateaus** such as Ben Bulben in Co. Sligo, which has a flat, or 'tabletop' appearance. Over time, these structures are **broken down by weathering,** erosion and mass movement. As some rocks are more resistant to weathering and erosion than others, a stepped landscape can develop.

Fig. 5.13 A side view of Ben Bulben shows layers of rock tilted in one direction. This is known as a monocline.

Doming

A dome refers to a **round, or an oval, anticline** structure similar in shape to that of an upturned bowl. It has a **high peak in the centre and slopes down to its base.** The most common cause of doming is **pressure from rising magma** underneath the crust. As the magma rises upwards, pressure causes the **overlying sedimentary rock to bulge** upwards. Doming can also occur due to **ground deformation as rocks are compressed** from several directions. **Weathering and erosion break down the overlying material,** exposing older rock layers in the centre of the dome. **Slieve Bloom** in Co. Laois/Co. Offaly is an example of a dome. It formed during the formation of the Leinster Batholith, **400 million years ago** due to pressure from rising magma.

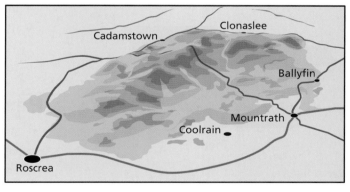

Fig. 5.14 The Slieve Bloom dome in Laois/Offaly formed from pressure due to rising magma.

ACTIVE LEARNING

Explain the following processes:
1. Monoclines
2. Doming

EDUCATE YOURSELF

Monoclines and Doming	
Monocline	Formed from small earth movements, sedimentary rock uplifted, rock tilted to one side, plateaus formed, e.g. Ben Bulben, broken down by weathering
Doming	Round/oval anticline, high peak in centre, slopes to its base, formed from pressure of rising magma or ground deformation from compression, broken down by weathering and erosion, e.g. Slieve Bloom, formed 400 mya

5.6 Faulting

As we have seen from fold mountain formation, rocks are capable of withstanding huge amounts of pressure without breaking. However, when **rocks are put under too much strain,** they **fracture and break, forming faults.** In Chapter 4, we learned that faults are **where earthquake activity occurs.** When the rock finally breaks, the sudden release of pressure causes it to move rapidly in a **vertical** (upwards or downwards) or **lateral** (sideways) direction. We refer to this movement as **rock 'displacement'.** This rock displacement has a major impact in shaping landscape.

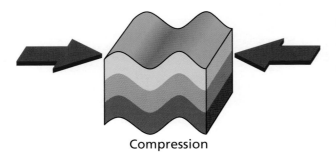

Compression

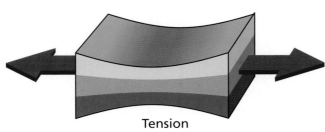

Tension

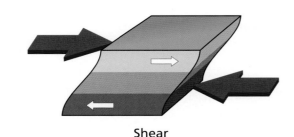

Shear

Fig. 5.15 The processes of faulting

Processes of Faulting

Faulting is caused by **compression, tension** or **shearing** of rock:

- **Compression** occurs when rock is **pushed together** as **pressure is exerted from both sides.** When this occurs, the main **movement of the crust is upwards.** Compression is the key process involved in the formation of a **reverse fault.**

- **Tension** occurs when **rocks are pulled apart** as they are **strained from both sides.** Generally, this causes the **crust to sink downwards.** Tension is the key process involved in the formation of a **normal fault.**

- **Shearing** occurs when sections of **rock are moved laterally in opposite directions.** This causes the **crust to tear apart.** Shearing is the process associated with the formation of a **transform fault.**

Parts of a Fault

- A **scarp,** or **escarpment,** is the **cliff formed** by the **vertical displacement of rock.** When part of the crust slips downwards, the rest of the crust remains elevated above it. The **face of this elevated rock** is called the scarp.

- The **throw** is the amount of **vertical displacement of the rock.** It is the distance the crust has moved upwards or downwards.

- The **heave** is the **horizontal displacement of the rock.** As the crust is pushed upwards or sinks downwards, it also moves horizontally.

- The section of **crust above the fault** is called the **hanging wall** and the section of **rock that is under the fault** is the **footwall.** The hanging wall slides along the footwall.

Processes of faulting	
Compression	Rock is pushed together, movement of crust is upwards, forms a reverse fault → ←
Tension	Rock is pulled apart, movement of crust is downwards, forms a normal fault ← →
Shearing	Rock is moved laterally in opposite directions, crust is torn apart, forms a transform fault ↗ ↙
Parts of a fault	Scarp: the cliff formed
	Throw: vertical displacement
	Heave: horizontal displacement
	Hanging wall: section of rock above fault
	Footwall: section of rock underneath fault

Types of Fault

Generally, there are three types of fault that occur, each formed by a different type of movement:

- Normal fault
- Reverse fault
- Transform fault

These faults are created through compression (being pushed together), extension (being pulled apart) or shearing (being torn apart).

Note!
Each type of fault is classified by the direction of movement that forms it.

Normal Faults

Normal faults are created by the **stretching of crust**. The tension caused by this stretching is so strong that it **causes rock to pull apart.** As the crust pulls apart, tension **causes the crust to get thinner** (much like when you stretch a rubber band). Eventually, the stress **causes the rock to fracture** and pull apart. When the rocks fracture, **one side of the fault sinks downwards** under the influence of gravity, leaving the **other section above.** Normal faulting eventually leads to the **formation of a constructive boundary** between two plates.

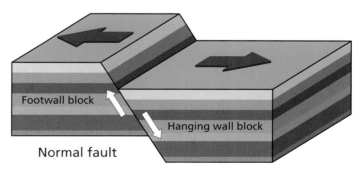

Footwall block

Hanging wall block

Normal fault

🔺 **Fig. 5.16** A normal fault formed by tension

The **East African Rift Valley** is an example of this. Currently, in East Africa, a series of normal faults has developed due to the stretching of crust by convection currents underneath the continent. The crust between these fault lines is between **40 and 60 km wide.** The crust has sunk downwards, creating a rift valley.

The **Red Sea has formed** in the valley of the **northern section** of the rift, as the crust has dropped below sea level. Once, the land was below sea level, water from the Indian Ocean flowed in and submerged it. It is estimated that in the next 10 million years, the east section of Africa will completely separate from the rest of the continent. This will lead to the **formation of a divergent boundary between the African Plate and the newly formed plate.** As they continue to separate, a new ocean will develop between the two plates.

Killary Harbour in Co. Mayo is an Irish example of a rift valley which is part of the larger Scottish Rift Valley that formed over 400 million years ago. A rift valley is also known as a graben.

⌃ **Fig. 5.18** The Rift Valley is dotted with volcanoes.

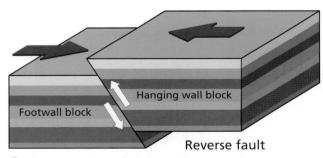

⌃ **Fig. 5.17** A map of the East African Rift Valley

Reverse Faults

A reverse fault, also known as a thrust fault, occurs when the **crust is compressed together.** The pressure from the compression **causes the crust to buckle upwards,** forming an anticline. As the pressure continues, the rock is put under increased pressure, **eventually causing it to fracture along its anticline.** When this occurs, one section of rock slips upwards on top of the other. This leads to the **formation of an escarpment.**

The **Killarney–Mallow** thrust fault was created in this way **250 million years ago,** during the Armorican folding period. As the African Plate collided with the Eurasian Plate, sandstone was buckled upwards. Continued pressure eventually **caused the Old Red Sandstone to fracture,** creating a thrust fault. As a result, the sandstone was pushed upwards onto the limestone which lay north of it.

⌃ **Fig. 5.19** A reverse fault formed by compression

⌃ **Fig. 5.20** Evidence of a reverse fault in rock

Block mountains can also form as a result of parallel reverse faults. They are formed when the **crust at either side of the faults converges, pushing the section in the middle upwards** above the surrounding land. The **Ox Mountains in Co. Sligo** are examples of block mountains. The Ox Mountains are a result of block of granite that has been left elevated above the down-faulted limestone rock to the north and south of it. A block mountain is also known as a horst.

Transform Faults

Transform faults, also known as tear faults or strike-slip faults, occur when **two sections of crust move in opposite directions or in the same direction at different speeds.** This eventually leads to the **formation of a passive plate boundary.** The **San Andreas Fault** is the largest transform fault on Earth. It lies between the North American and Pacific Plates. The movement of the crust in opposite directions puts pressure on layers of rock within the crust. Eventually, the pressure becomes too great and the **rock fractures, causing the crust to tear apart.**

Imagine you are tearing a sheet of paper: one hand moves towards your chest, while the other moves away. This is the same horizontal motion that causes transform faults to form. As the **movement is horizontal** rather than vertical, no escarpment is formed.

The movement of these faults is not constant, as the opposing sections of rock can become stuck, allowing pressure to build. When movement does occur, it is very sudden, **leading to violent earthquakes.**

Right lateral strike-slip fault

⊙ **Fig. 5.21** A transform fault, or strike-slip fault, formed by shearing

⊙ **Fig. 5.22** The San Andreas Fault line

ACTIVE LEARNING

Describe how one of the following influences the development of landscape:

1. Folding
2. Faulting

Types of Fault	
Normal fault	Stretching of crust, tension, pulls rock apart, crust gets thinner, movement is downwards, forms a constructive boundary, two parallel faults leads to a rift valley, e.g. East African Rift Valley, 40–60 km wide, Red Sea in northern part, Irish example is Killary Harbour
Reverse fault	Crust is compressed, buckles, eventually fractures, movement is upwards, forms escarpment, Mallow–Killarney fault, 250 mya, Old Red Sandstone faulted, 400 mya, block mountains when crust either side converge
Transform fault	Crust moves laterally in opposite directions, forms passive boundary, e.g. San Andreas Fault, crust tears apart, crust moves horizontally, earthquakes occur here

Folding and Faulting in Ireland

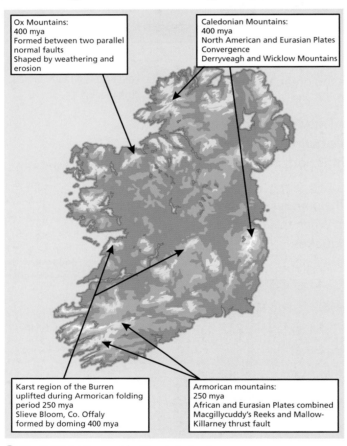

Ox Mountains:
400 mya
Formed between two parallel normal faults
Shaped by weathering and erosion

Caledonian Mountains:
400 mya
North American and Eurasian Plates Convergence
Derryveagh and Wicklow Mountains

Karst region of the Burren uplifted during Armorican folding period 250 mya
Slieve Bloom, Co. Offaly formed by doming 400 mya

Armorican mountains:
250 mya
African and Eurasian Plates combined
Macgillycuddy's Reeks and Mallow-Killarney thrust fault

Fig 5.23 Folding and faulting in Ireland

ACTIVE LEARNING

1. Explain what is meant by the term 'ductile'.

2. Draw a labelled diagram of an anticline and a syncline.

3. Name the three types of folds and explain how each is formed.

4. With reference to Fig. 5.24, explain how fold mountains are formed at continental-continental boundaries.

Fig. 5.24

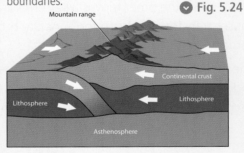

5. With the aid of a labelled diagram, explain how fold mountains are formed at subduction zones.

6. What is meant by the term 'orogeny'?

7. Name three major folding periods and give examples of the plate boundaries involved for each.

8. Examine how the Caledonian folding period affected the Irish landscape.

9. Name the folding period that led to the formation of each peak and explain why they differ in height.

    Croagh Patrick   739 m

    Carrantouhill   1037 m

    Mount Everest   8848 m

HIGHER LEVEL

LONG QUESTIONS

1. Examine the diagram and answer the following questions.

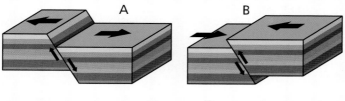

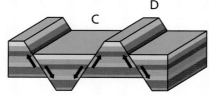

   (i)   Name the type of fault at A and the type of fault at B.

   (ii) Explain briefly what causes the type of faulting at A or at B.

   (iii) Name the landform at C and the landform at D that result from faulting.

(i) 2 x 4m
(ii) 2 x SRP @ 2m each
(iii) 2 x 4m

2013 Q2A 20M

2. Explain, with reference to examples you have studied, how folding impacts on landscape development.

2010 Q3C 30M

Named examples 2 x 2m
Discussion 13 x SRPs
1 SRP awarded for diagram

3. Examine the impact of folding and faulting on the landscape. In your answer, refer to one landform in each case.

2007 Q3B 30M

Folding	Named landform 2m
	Discussion 7/6 SRPs @ 2m each
Faulting	Named landform 2m
	Discussion 6/7 SRPs @ 2m each

4. Describe, with the aid of a labelled diagram, the processes involved in the formation of fold mountains which you have studied.

SEC SAMPLE PAPER 2 Q2B

Named example 2m
Discussion 14 SRPs @ 2m each

EXAM FOCUS

The topic of folding and faulting does not appear as a long question on Higher Level or Ordinary Level papers as frequently as the other plate boundary activities of earthquakes and volcanoes. At Ordinary Level, the topic of folding and faulting has appeared as a long question in 2009 and 2012, while at Higher Level it has been asked in 2007, 2012 and 2015. In order to prepare yourself to answer short questions and Part A questions, you must learn what each fold and fault type looks like and the processes involved, something which you will automatically do while preparing longer questions.

ORDINARY LEVEL

The following question appeared on the 2012 Ordinary Level paper as Q2C. It is worth 30 marks and requires you to provide a named example, diagram and explanation of how folding occurs.

ORDINARY LEVEL

EXAM **QUESTION**

(i) Name one fold mountain that you have studied.

(ii) With the aid of a diagram(s), explain how fold mountains are formed.

2012 Q2C 30M

Marking Scheme	
Named example 1 x 3m	
Diagram 3 x 2m	
Explanation 7 SRPs @ 3m each	

This marking scheme is useful for those of you who find it difficult to organise answers. We are given three tasks to complete: name, draw, explain.

Now, we can use the question to organise our answer.

Folding	Armorican folding period
Macgillycuddy's Reeks/Carrantouhill	African/Eurasian Plates
Destructive boundaries	Anticlines/synclines
Continental/continental boundary	Old Red Sandstone/limestone
Oceanic/continental boundary	Munster Ridge Valley
Buckle	South-west of Ireland

While you are free to discuss any aspect of fold mountain building, I linked my example to my explanation. Note that the question did not ask for an Irish example or a global example, so we are free to choose any we wish.

Perhaps you could practise using the Caledonian or Alpine folding periods as your named example and explanation.

Can you explain the terms on the left? If so, then you are ready to answer!

SAMPLE **ANSWER**

(i) A fold mountain that I have studied is Carrantouhill, which is the highest peak of the Macgillycuddy's Reeks. [3m]

(ii) Fold mountains are formed at destructive plate boundaries as plates collide. [3m] They occur at two types of destructive boundary: continental-continental and at oceanic-continental boundaries. [3m] As continental plates are light, when they collide, both plates buckle upwards, forming a series of anticlines and synclines. [3m] When an oceanic plate collides with a continental plate, the heavier oceanic plate sinks into the mantle and melts, while the edges of the continental plate are buckled upwards. [3m]

Continental-continental folding

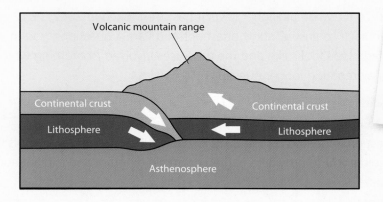

> **Note!**
> Your diagram does not need to have the range of colour shown here. Once you have clearly drawn and labelled the diagram, you will be awarded the marks.

The Macgillycuddy's Reeks were formed during the Armorican folding period, 250 million years ago [3m]. This happened when the African and Eurasian Plate collided, which folded layers of Old Red Sandstone and limestone [3m]. This led to the formation of the Munster Ridge Valley that shaped the south-west of Ireland [3m].

The three aspects of the question are all dealt with in a clear and logical manner. This shows a clear understanding of both the task given and the topic being examined.

Note that the answer in Part (i) is written as a full sentence rather than as a single word answer.

Part (ii) is divided into two parts: general explanation and explanation linked to an example. For the general explanation, the focus is on what happens when the different types of plate collide. The linked-to example shows that you are able to link the process of folding to an example of the action.

The answer is written is a logical order and each sentence contains a 'building block' for the explanation, meaning that each sentence leads clearly to the next.

Diagram: The diagram shows two plates colliding (be sure to insert arrows) as well as rock being buckled. Be sure to clearly label the type of boundary you have drawn and the type of crust.

Marks Awarded
(i) mountain identified 3m
(ii) diagram given and labelled 3 x 2m
Best 7 SRPs @ 3m each
Total 30/30

HIGHER LEVEL

The following question is a sample question based on the impact of folding on the Irish landscape. It is worth 30 marks and requires you to explain the processes of folding while linking it specifically to how folding has shaped the Irish landscape.

When we read the question carefully, it is possible to work out the marking scheme before we begin.

Being asked to name more than one example allows you to divide the question into two sections:

example 1 + SRPs of explanation and example 2 + SRPs of explanation.

A general introduction on the process of folding should also be given at the beginning of the answer.

SAMPLE QUESTION

Using examples that you have studied, describe how the process of folding has impacted on the Irish landscape.

Marking Scheme
Named examples 2 x 2m = 4m
Discussion 13 SRPs @ 2m each
A labelled diagram 1 SRP
Additional Information on labelled diagram = up to 2 SRPs

Example 1: Derryveagh Mountains	Example 2: Munster Ridge Valley
Caledonian orogeny	Armorican orogeny
North American + Eurasian Plates	African + Eurasian Plates
450–400 mya	270–250 mya
Shale/mudstone/sandstone folded	Old Red Sandstone/limestone
Magma/metamorphose	Anticlines/synclines
Caps on mountains peaks	Weathering and erosion
Weathering and erosion	Uplifted Burren region

SAMPLE ANSWER

Folding occurs when layers of sedimentary rock are buckled upwards at convergent plate boundaries due to the influence of convection currents [2m]. In this answer, I will discuss two major folding orogenies that have had a major impact on the Irish landscape.

One impact of folding on the Irish landscape has been the formation of the Derryveagh Mountains in Co. Donegal [2m]. This is just one example of the mountain ranges formed in Ireland during the Caledonian orogeny, which began 450 million years ago [2m]. The orogeny took place due to the collision of the North American and Eurasian Plates, creating a continental-continental destructive boundary [2m]. As the plates collided, layers of sedimentary rock, such as shale, sandstone and mudstone were uplifted and folded, creating anticlines and synclines [2m]. As the rock folded, magma rose up underneath the anticlines, before cooling slowly to form igneous rock underneath the mountains [2m]. Heat from the rising magma caused the overlying layers of sedimentary rock to cook and metamorphose [2m]. The formation of metamorphic rock created a resistant peak on the tops of mountains such as Mount Errigal, which is capped by quartzite. [2m] The peaks of the Derryveagh Mountains are between 600 and 750 m, as weathering and erosion has greatly reduced their height over millions of years [2m].

Another major impact on the Irish landscape by folding was the creation of the Munster Ridge Valley in Munster [2m]. The Munster Ridge Valley was created during the Armorican orogeny, which began 270 million years ago [2m]. The orogeny took place due to the collision of the African and Eurasian Plates, creating a continental-continental destructive boundary [2m]. As the plates collided, layers of Old Red Sandstone and limestone were buckled and uplifted [2m]. The layers of sandstone were folded upwards into anticlines, while the layers of limestone were folded downwards into synclines [2m]. As limestone is a much softer rock than sandstone, it was broken down by weathering and erosion at a much faster rate, creating deep valleys in between the anticlines [2m]. As the folding of the Munster region occurred, the karst region of the Burren was also uplifted above sea level [2m]. As the Armorican orogeny was more recent than the Caledonian orogeny, it has higher peaks, such as the Macgillycuddy's Reeks, which have peaks of over 1000 m [2m].

A definition of folding is given before the examples and description.

The description is well organised, starting with the oldest folding orogeny in Ireland and describing its effects, before moving to a more modern orogeny and then describing how it has also affected the landscape.

A common mistake students make is failing to link explanations to the examples given. If you fail to link your answer, you are not displaying a clear understanding of the topic.

Irish examples given are linked to description showing a clear understanding and knowledge of topic.

Marks Awarded
Irish examples given 2 x 2m
Best 13 SRPs@ 2m each
Total 30/30

Note!
Visit the following website and search for 'folding and faulting' to see a series of animations on these processes.
www.physicalgeography.net

TOPIC MAP

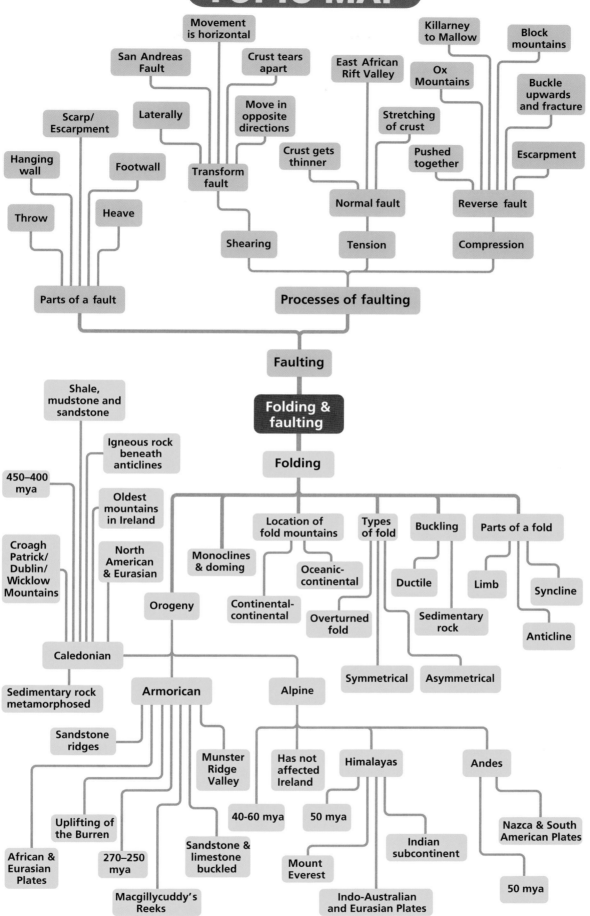

CHAPTER 6

The Rock Cycle

In this chapter, we will look at the formation, change and destruction of rocks in and on the Earth's crust. Much of the information you have learned in the previous five chapters is also relevant for this chapter. For example, you will be revisiting basalt and granite rock, plutonic and volcanic landforms, the Munster Ridge Valley and the Burren. You will also revisit plate boundaries, where rocks are changed due to extreme heat and pressure. The case study of geothermal energy from Chapter 3 can also be used instead of Irish gas exploration in this chapter. Therefore, you will be building on the knowledge and understanding you have gained so far in your geographical studies.

KEY WORDS

- Igneous
- Metamorphic
- Sedimentary
- Basalt
- Granite
- Marble
- Quartzite
- Limestone
- Sandstone
- Batholith

- Antrim-Derry Plateau
- Munster Ridge Valley
- Karst
- Cooling
- Solidifying
- Mica
- Quartz
- Lithification
- Bedding plane
- Strata

- Organic rock
- Inorganic rock
- Compaction
- Compression
- Regional metamorphism
- Contact metamorphism
- Foliated
- Non-foliated

LEARNING OUTCOMES

What you MUST know
- The formation of two igneous rocks
- The formation of two sedimentary rocks
- The formation of two metamorphic rocks
- Landscapes associated with igneous rocks
- Landscapes associated with sedimentary rocks
- Human interaction with the rock cycle: oil and gas

What you SHOULD know
- How to identify each rock by appearance

What is USEFUL to know
- Additional rocks in each of the three categories
- Uses of each rock

Introduction

The Earth's crust is made up of solid materials known as rocks. Most of these rocks are **naturally occurring combinations of minerals** that have become cemented together. Rocks formed from these combinations of minerals are referred to as **aggregates.** Over millions of years, large numbers of different rock types have formed in the crust. These rocks can be grouped into **categories according to how they were formed.** There are three main groups in which we can place rocks: **igneous, sedimentary and metamorphic.** These rock types are formed, changed and destroyed in a continuous linked cycle – referred to as the **rock cycle.**

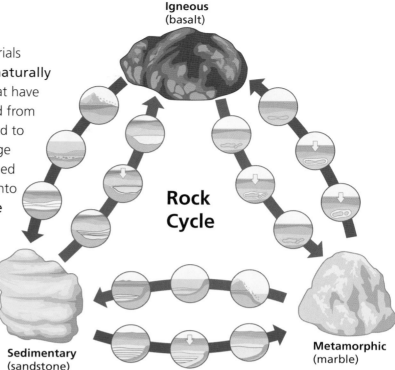

Rock Cycle

Igneous (basalt)

Sedimentary (sandstone)

Metamorphic (marble)

Fig. 6.1 The rock cycle shows the continuous formation and deformation of rocks on the Earth's crust.

The Rock Cycle

- **Igneous rock** is created through **volcanic activity** on, or within, the crust.

- The rock is then broken down into sediments by **weathering and erosion,** before being washed into lakes and seas.

- These sediments are buried in the beds of lakes and seas, slowly **cementing together** to form **sedimentary rock.**

- Both igneous and sedimentary rocks are exposed to **heat and pressure** at plate boundaries, or from rising magma, which changes them into **metamorphic rocks.**

- Metamorphic rock is then either broken down by **weathering and erosion** forming sediments, or **subducted** into the mantle and recycled.

In this chapter, we will examine the formation of the following categories and examples:

Rock Type	Examples
Igneous	Basalt, granite
Sedimentary	Limestone, sandstone
Metamorphic	Marble, quartzite

6.1 Igneous Rock

Igneous rocks are created by **volcanic activity,** when molten rock **cools and solidifies** in, or on, the Earth's crust. **Basalt** and **granite** are two common igneous rocks. Igneous rocks are divided into **intrusive and extrusive** rocks, also known as **plutonic** and **volcanic.** Intrusive/plutonic rocks form when magma cools **beneath the surface,** while extrusive/volcanic rocks form when lava cools **on the surface.**

GEO DICTIONARY

Aggregates: rocks that are made from a number of different minerals

Igneous: rocks that are made from cooled volcanic material. They can occur on the surface or in the crust

Sedimentary: rocks made from the compacted sediments of other rocks or fossils

Metamorphic: sedimentary or igneous rocks that have been changed by heat and/or pressure

Granite

Granite is a **coarse-grained, multicoloured** rock that forms mainly at **convergent boundaries**. Granite is an **intrusive rock,** forming from magma cooling slowly inside the crust over millions of years. It is made up of **silica-rich** minerals such as **quartz, feldspar** and **mica,** which give it a **multicoloured appearance.**

Granite forms in two ways:

- through **folding** at convergent boundaries
- through **subduction** at convergent boundaries

Note!

Questions on the formation of igneous, sedimentary or metamorphic rocks or a question on landscapes associated with a rock type have appeared every year on the exam papers.

Fig. 6.2 Granite rock

Folding

When two continental plates collide, layers of sedimentary rock are **pushed upwards,** forming fold mountains. As this occurs, **magma rises** upwards, **underneath** the arched folds. This magma cools slowly over millions of years, as the surrounding **layers of sedimentary rock trap heat.** Due to this slow cooling process, **large crystals develop** as different minerals cool at different temperatures. The folded sedimentary rock is sometimes 'cooked' by the heat from the magma, changing it to metamorphic rock. This acts as a **'cap' of resistant rock** which protects the underlying granite from weathering and erosion. An Irish example of granite formed in this way is the **Leinster Batholith,** which encompasses the Wicklow, Dublin and Blackstairs Mountains.

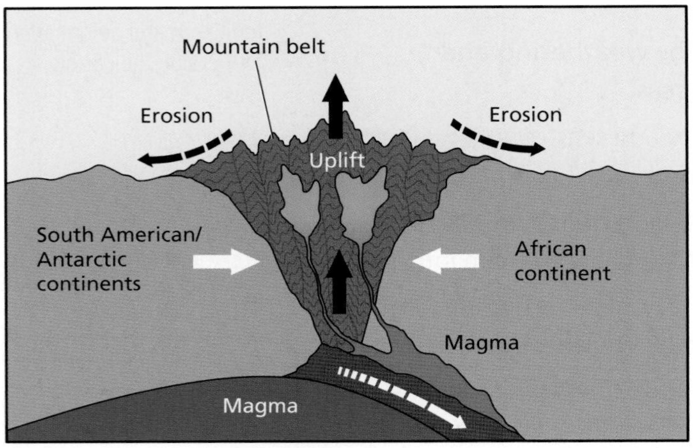

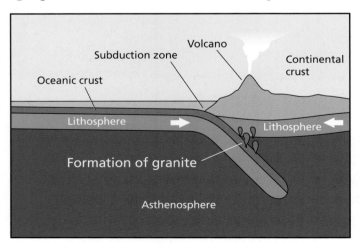

Fig. 6.3 Granite/batholith formation due to folding

Fig. 6.4(a) Granite/ batholith formation at subduction zones

Subduction

Granite is also formed at **subduction zones,** as an oceanic plate sinks underneath a continental or another oceanic plate. As the plate subducts it melts, allowing magma to rise upwards **underneath the overlying plate.** This magma seeps into the overlying plate, forcing its way through layers of sedimentary rock, before **cooling slowly** to form granite.

The areas of cooled magma that form granite are referred to as **batholiths.** These cover large areas, often thousands of kilometres in size. However, they also form on a smaller scale as small amounts of magma is forced between layers of sedimentary rock to form sills, lopoliths and laccoliths. As granite forms deep in the Earth's crust, it is **exposed to the surface** only after long periods of **weathering and erosion** or tectonic **uplifting** (folding, etc.).

When granite is **metamorphosed**, it is turned into **gneiss** (pronounced 'nice').

Landscape Associated with Granite

- The **Leinster Batholith** is an example of a landscape associated with granite.

- It is the largest area of granite rock in Ireland, covering **1500 km²**, encompassing the Dublin, Wicklow and Blackstairs Mountains.

- The Leinster Batholith formed approximately **400 million years ago** when the **North American and Eurasian Plates** collided.

- As the layers of **sedimentary rock buckled,** magma rose underneath the arched folds before cooling slowly.

- The **intense heat** from the **magma,** combined with the heat caused by the **friction** of the colliding plates, **metamorphosed** much of the sedimentary rock.

- Sandstone was turned into **quartzite,** while shale was turned into **schist.**

- These layers of metamorphic rock **'capped' many of the taller mountain peaks,** which protected the underlying granite from erosion.

- An example of this is the peak of the **Sugarloaf Mountain,** which is protected by a cap of **quartzite.**

- Over millions of years, much of the soil covering the batholith has been removed by weathering and erosion, exposing granite to the surface.

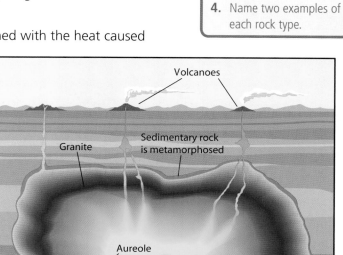

 **Fig. 6.4(b)** The formation of a batholith

Basalt

Basalt is a **fine-grained, dull-coloured** rock which forms mainly at **divergent plate boundaries.** It can also form anywhere **volcanic activity** occurs. Basalt is an **extrusive rock,** forming when lava **cools rapidly** on the Earth's surface. Basalt is made up of the minerals **magnesium** and **iron,** which often give it a rusty colour. Basalt forms when two plates separate, creating gaps in the Earth's crust, allowing magma to rise to the surface. Once on the surface, the lava cools rapidly as it is exposed to **surface temperatures** and **ocean water.**

ACTIVE LEARNING

Using the information about the Leinster Batholith below as evidence, explain how plate tectonics have impacted the Irish landscape.

ACTIVE LEARNING

1. What is an aggregate?
2. Name the three main categories of rock.
3. What is meant by the term 'rock cycle'?
4. Name two examples of each rock type.

ACTIVE LEARNING

1. Explain how folding led to the formation of granite.
2. Explain the term 'subduction'.
3. Explain fully how granite is formed at subduction zones.
4. Explain the following terms:
   - Intrusive/plutonic
   - Extrusive/volcanic

● Fig. 6.5 Basalt rock

Basalt is the world's most **common rock,** making up the **floors of the oceans.** Currently, new basalt rock is being created at the **Mid-Atlantic Ridge** as seafloor spreading occurs. As the North American and Eurasian Plates continue to separate, lava escapes through the gaps before cooling and solidifying. As basalt forms rapidly, large **crystals do not develop** like they do in granite. Instead crystals are **small and not visible** to the naked eye.

Landscape Associated with Basalt

The **Antrim-Derry Plateau** is an example of a landscape associated with basalt. It formed **65 million years ago** when the **North American and Eurasian Plates** began to separate. This marked the opening of the **Atlantic Ocean.** As the plates separated, lava flowed from the newly formed **constructive boundary.** As the lava had a **low viscosity,** it spread out across a large area, before cooling rapidly. Gradually, these layers of basalt built up to form a mixed, **flat-topped basalt plateau.**

● Fig. 6.6 Basalt columns at the Giant's Causeway

The plateau is estimated to once have been 1800 m thick, but has since been worn down by weathering and erosion. As the basalt cooled and contracted, it began to split apart into a series of **hexagonal columns.** These columns can be seen at the **Giant's Causeway** in Co. Antrim.

FACT

The Giant's Causeway gets its name from an old Irish story in which the giant Fionn MacCumhaill built the causeway to get to Scotland to battle another giant called Benandonner.

ACTIVE LEARNING

1. Describe the appearance of basalt.
2. Explain fully how basalt is formed.
3. Explain how basalt can produce a distinctive landscape using an example that you have studied.
4. Explain, using examples, how volcanism has led to the formation of two distinctive rock landscapes in Ireland.

EDUCATE YOURSELF

	Igneous Rock
Granite	Coarse, multicoloured, convergent boundaries, intrusive, cool slowly, quartz, mica, feldspar, folding, subduction, magma rises under folds, heat trapped by sedimentary rock, crystals develop, cap of resistant rock, Leinster Batholith, exposed by weathering and erosion
	Landscape: Leinster Batholith, 1500 km², 400 mya, North American and Eurasian Plates, sedimentary rock buckled, metamorphosed into quartzite, quartzite forms protective cap, e.g. Lugnaquilla
Basalt	Fine grained, dull coloured, divergent boundaries, extrusive rock, magnesium, iron, cooled on surface, ocean water, e.g. Mid-Atlantic Ridge, small crystals
	Landscape: Antrim-Derry Plateau, 65 mya, North American and Eurasian Plates, opened Atlantic Ocean, constructive boundary, low viscosity, flat-topped plateau, hexagonal columns, Giant's Causeway

6.2 Sedimentary Rock

Sedimentary rocks are defined according to the **parent material** they formed from.

- Sedimentary rocks formed from the **fragments of other rocks** are called **inorganic**, e.g. **sandstone**.
- Sedimentary rocks which are formed from the **fossils of plants or animals** are called **organic** rocks, e.g. **limestone**.

Regardless of the parent material, sedimentary rocks are formed through a similar process. Sediments are deposited in thick **layers called strata,** which are **crushed** and **compacted** by their own weight or the weight of water above them. Eventually, these compacted layers are **cemented together** by minerals such as silica or iron, creating solid rock. This process is known as **lithification**. Often, the different strata of rock are separated by a **thin layer of mud** called **bedding planes**. Bedding planes can be easily identified as they **differ in colour and texture** from the rest of the rock strata. As sedimentary rocks are layered, they are referred to as foliated rocks.

Chemical sedimentary rocks are formed from the compacting of tiny sea creatures on the sea bed (forming oil) or the compaction of sea salt (forming gypsum).

Sandstone

Sandstone is an example of a **coarse-grained, inorganic rock,** which forms when **grains of quartz** (sand particles) were deposited in layers on land or on the bed of a **shallow sea**. The deposits of quartz accumulate in two different ways: from **flood deposits** or from **wind deposits**.

Sandstone was created in Ireland roughly **350 million years ago** as a result of **flash-flooding.** Heavy rainfall eroded the newly formed **Caledonian Mountains,** washing the eroded sediments into the bed of a shallow sea bed, which now makes up much of the Munster landscape. Gradually, these layers were **compacted by their own weight** and the weight of the water above them. **Lithification** occurred as iron and silica cemented these sediments together, forming **strata** of sandstone. The sandstone created during this time has **high levels of iron oxide,** which gives it a reddish appearance. It is commonly called **'Old Red Sandstone'** as a result.

⌃ **Fig. 6.7** Sandstone rock

 **ACTIVE LEARNING**

Explain the following terms:

1. Convergent boundaries
2. Mid-Atlantic Ridge
3. Caledonian orogeny

 FACT

At one point, the Caledonian mountains of Ireland were over 4000 m high, but have been worn down by weathering and erosion.

CORE 1

CHAPTER 6

Landscape Associated with Sandstone

Fig. 6.8 Ridges of sandstone rise above the flat limestone floor of the Munster Ridge Valley

- The **Old Red Sandstone** of Munster remained submerged in a shallow sea until approximately **250 million years ago.** As the **African and Eurasian Plates** collided, layers of sandstone and overlying limestone were buckled and uplifted during the formation of the Armorican mountains.

- This process of folding created **parallel ridges of sandstone and valleys of limestone.** The limestone overlying the sandstone ridges was easily weathered and eroded, exposing it to the surface.

- These sandstone ridges rise above the surrounding landscape, creating ridge mountains such as the Macgillycuddy's Reeks. The limestone valleys were weathered and eroded downwards creating flat, fertile land between the ridge mountains.

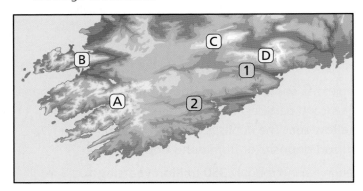

Fig. 6.9 The Munster Ridge Valley

- The ridge mountains run in a west-to-east direction with rivers flowing along the valley floors in between. This landscape is referred to as the **Munster Ridge Valley.**

Limestone

Limestone is an example of an **organic rock** formed from the **compressed** remains of sea creatures. Limestone is composed of the mineral calcium carbonate ($CaCO_3$), from the bones of the marine fossils. Limestone formed in Ireland roughly **320 million years ago,** just after the formation of **Old Red Sandstone.** At this time, Ireland was close to the equator and mostly submerged in a **shallow tropical sea.** Over millions of years, the fossils of small tropical fish built up in layers, forming coral reefs similar to the Great Barrier Reef in Australia. Gradually, the weight of the fossils began to crush its bottom layers, **removing seawater** and **air from the pores** of the bones. Once the water and air had been removed, **lithification** occurred as **calcium carbonate cemented the fossils** together, forming limestone. Similar to sandstone, limestone is made up of strata which are separated by **bedding planes.** As limestone is a **brittle** rock, movements within the crust cause **vertical cracks,** making it **permeable.**

Limestone is typically a **fine-grained** rock and slightly greyish in colour. While **pure calcium carbonate is white,** limestone gets its **grey colour from impurities.** It is the most common rock in Ireland and can be found in the karst region of the **Burren in Co. Clare.**

Landscape Associated with Limestone

- **Karst** is an example of a landscape associated with limestone. Karst is the name given to areas of exposed limestone that have similar characteristics to the Karst region of Slovenia, along the coast of the Adriatic Sea.

△ **Fig. 6.10** Limestone rock

- The **Burren in Co. Clare** is an Irish example of a karst region. The Burren covers an area of **250 km²,** which slopes gently into the Atlantic Ocean. The area of the Burren was submerged in a shallow tropical sea until 250 million years ago, when the folding of the **Armorican Mountains** in Munster raised it above sea level.

- The limestone remained protected by a layer of soil until the last ice age. During this time, large **glaciers scraped it away,** exposing the limestone to the surface. The limestone, then exposed to the Earth's environment, was **shaped by the chemical weathering** process of carbonation.

- **Carbonation** occurs as limestone is dissolved by **acidic rain.** This process led to the development of limestone pavement on the surface of the landscape.

- **Limestone pavement** is formed as carbonation widens and deepens the **vertical cracks** in the rock, leaving isolated sections of rock in between. These sections of rock are called **clints,** while the widened cracks separating them are called **grikes.**

△ **Fig. 6.11** The landscape of the Burren

CORE 1 CHAPTER 6

Sedimentary Rocks	
Sandstone	Coarse grained, inorganic, quartz, strata, shallow sea, flood deposits, wind deposits, 350 mya, flash flooding, Caledonian mountains, compaction, lithification, iron oxide, Old Red Sandstone
	Landscape: Old Red Sandstone, 250 mya, African and Eurasian Plates, folding, ridges of sandstone exposed, overlying limestone, limestone weathered, Munster Ridge Valley
Limestone	Organic rock, compressed fossils, 320 mya, shallow tropical sea, removing seawater and air, lithification, calcium carbonate, bedding planes, brittle, vertical cracks, permeable, fine grained, white if pure, normally greyish, Burren, Co. Clare
	Landscape: Karst, Burren, Co. Clare, 250 km², Armorican folding period, glaciers scraped away surface, chemical weathering, carbonation, acidic rain, limestone pavement, vertical cracks – grikes, clints

GEO **DICTIONARY**

Metamorphism: the physical and chemical changing of rock through heat and/or pressure

6.3 Metamorphic Rock

Metamorphic rocks are formed when existing sedimentary or igneous rocks are exposed to **intense heat and pressure**. This heat and pressure cause the rock to change both in its **physical appearance** and **chemical composition**. Metamorphism can occur in two different ways:

- Contact metamorphism
- Regional metamorphism

Types of Metamorphism	
Contact Metamorphism	**Regional Metamorphism**
Contact metamorphism occurs when **magma intrudes** on the Earth's crust, causing the surrounding layers of sedimentary rock to cook.	**Regional metamorphism** occurs at **plate boundaries** as heat and pressure occur over a **wide area**.
This heat alters the physical and chemical properties of the rock, creating an **aureole** (or zone) of metamorphic rock in the crust.	This normally occurs during a period of **folding or at subduction zones** as two plates collide.
Magma reaches temperatures of between **700 °C and 1200 °C,** with the surrounding rock trapping the heat.	Friction between the colliding plates generates a large amount of heat, which adds to the heat from the rising magma underneath the plates.
Contact metamorphism tends to be **localised** and does not affect a wide area.	The intensity of this **heat cooks the surrounding rock in the Earth's crust,** changing its physical and chemical properties.

GEO **DICTIONARY**

Mudstone: a dark sedimentary rock formed from the lithification of compacted layers of mud

There are several examples of metamorphic rock:

- **Granite becomes gneiss.**
- Basalt becomes amphibolite.
- Shale becomes slate.
- Mudstone becomes schist.
- **Sandstone becomes quartzite.**
- **Limestone becomes marble.**

In this section, we will focus on the metamorphism of limestone into marble and sandstone into quartzite.

Marble

- **Marble** is formed from the **regional metamorphism** of its parent rock of **limestone** or chalk. The intense heat created at the **convergent boundaries** causes minerals in the limestone to melt.

- As it melts both its layered structure and the remains of marine fossils are destroyed. As a result of this process, marble is a **non-foliated rock** (meaning it does not have any layers).

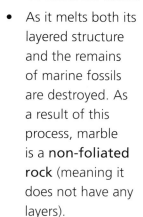

Fig. 6.12 Marble rock

- As the limestone rock is cooked by the heat, minerals in the rock expand, which causes **large crystals develop.** The outer layer of these crystals melt slightly, causing them to become stuck together once it cools.

- The colour of the rock depends on the purity of the limestone it formed from. **Pure marble,** like that found in Rathlin Island, is **white.**

Fig. 6.13 Connemara marble is an attractive green colour.

- There are many varieties of limestone found across Ireland. For example, **green marble** is found in **Connemara, Co. Galway** due to the presence of serpentine (copper ore), while the presence of **carbon** has led to the formation of **black marble** in **Co. Kilkenny.**

Fig. 6.14 Quartzite rock

ACTIVE LEARNING

Explain the differences between contact and regional metamorphism.

GEO DICTIONARY

Chalk: a soft limestone formed from the fossils of sea creatures

FACT

Connemara marble was formed over 600 mya. A 2000-year-old spearhead carved from the marble was excavated in Suffolk, England.

CORE 1

CHAPTER 6

ACTIVE **LEARNING**

1. Describe the process of regional metamorphism.

2. Explain how limestone is metamorphosed into marble.

3. Explain why the colour of marble differs in different locations across Ireland.

4. Using your knowledge of plate tectonics in Ireland and regional metamorphism, can you figure out what other landforms were created at the same time as Kilkenny marble? (Hint: Kilkenny marble formed approximately 400 mya.)

ACTIVE **LEARNING**

1. Describe the process of contact metamorphism.

2. Explain how sandstone is metamorphosed into quartzite.

3. Name two locations where quartzite is found in Ireland.

4. Describe the differences between organic and inorganic sedimentary rock.

5. Explain the following terms:
   (a) Lithification
   (b) Compaction
   (c) Karst
   (d) Calcium carbonate
   (e) Permeable

GEO DICTIONARY

Recrystallise: when melted minerals cool and become solid once again

Quartzite

- **Quartzite** is formed from **regional or contact** metamorphism of its **parent rock, sandstone.**

- Quartzite is formed mainly from quartz that has been **recrystallised** from intense heat and pressure. It was formed in Ireland when magma intruded on the Earth's crust, causing **deeply buried layers of sandstone** to cook.

- During this process, quartz and silica minerals melted as the intense heat caused the silica to fuse together. As the minerals melt, the layers of strata are destroyed, meaning quartzite is a **non-foliated rock.**

- The silica fuses together as it cools, creating larger grains than those in sandstone.

- The **absence of pores** and strata means that quartzite is a **much harder rock** than sandstone, making it much more **resistant to weathering** and erosion.

Landforms Associated with Metamorphic Rock

- As metamorphic rock is resistant to weathering and erosion, it often leads to the formation of **sharp mountain peaks.**

- This can be seen on the peak of the **Great Sugarloaf in Co. Wicklow,** which is covered by schist. **Mount Errigal in Co. Donegal** and Croagh Patrick in Co. Mayo are also protected from erosion by a cap of quartzite on their peaks.

◀ **Fig. 6.15** The Great Sugarloaf Mountain

 EDUCATE YOURSELF

Metamorphic Rocks	
Processes	Heat and pressure, contact metamorphism, regional metamorphism
Marble	Regional metamorphism, parent rock limestone, convergent boundaries, non-foliated, large crystals, pure white in colour, green in Connemara, black marble in Co. Kilkenny
Quartzite	Regional/contact, parent rock is sandstone, recrystallised, buried sandstone, non-foliated, absence of pores, resistant to weathering Landforms: sharp mountain peaks, Sugarloaf Co. Wicklow, Mount Errigal Co. Donegal

Uses of Rock
Due to its durability, basalt is used for road chipping. It is not suitable for decoration due to its dull rusty colour.
Granite is used for worktops in kitchens as it does not scratch easily.
Limestone is used to make cement and concrete blocks. It is also ground up and used for agriculture.
Sandstone is used to make red bricks for housing.
Marble can be used for making tiles and fireplaces. It is also used to make headstones as it is not weathered easily.
Quartzite is a durable rock which is sometimes used for wall decoration. It has also become popular for kitchen worktops due to its durability.

6.4 Active and Trailing Plate Margins of North America

To help you to understand this section, let's recap on what you already know:

- The Earth is divided up into sections called plates which float on the mantle.

- These plates collide and separate, leading to activity such as volcanoes, earthquakes, folding and faulting.

- Volcanic activity leads to the formation of igneous rocks (granite and basalt) while folding and subduction lead to metamorphism of existing rock.

If you are familiar with these three points, then you are already on your way to understanding plate margins.

Active Plate Margins

An **active plate margin** occurs where an **oceanic plate is subducting** underneath a continental plate. The **Pacific Plate is subducting underneath the eastern section** of the **North American Plate**. As a result, a number of **geographical activities occur here**, such as folding, faulting, volcanoes and earthquakes. This means it is an active margin.

- As the margin is active, the continent's **newest igneous metamorphic rock** is **formed** here.

- Due to **denudation** (weathering and erosion), **overlying sedimentary rock has been removed** to reveal underlying igneous and metamorphic rock.

- The metamorphic process has formed **valuable minerals** such as diamonds, iron ore and copper.

GEO **DICTIONARY**

Active plate margin: the leading edge of an continental plate which crashes into an oceanic plate. It is tectonically active (volcanoes, earthquakes, folding, etc.)

Trailing plate margin: the trailing edge of the continent that is not tectonically active. Here weathering and erosion are the main processes that shape the landscape

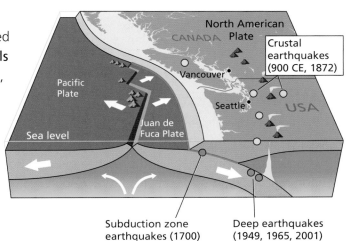

Fig. 6.16 Earthquake zones along an active plate margin

Trailing Plate Margins

A **trailing plate margin** occurs where there is **an absence of seismic, volcanic or folding activity**. As the plate margin is **not active,** the main processes occurring are **erosion and deposition**. The processes of erosion and deposition form sediments which are compacted to form **sedimentary roc**k such as **limestone and sandstone**. In North America, the trailing plate margin can be divided into two main areas:

1. The Canadian Shield
2. Coastal plains

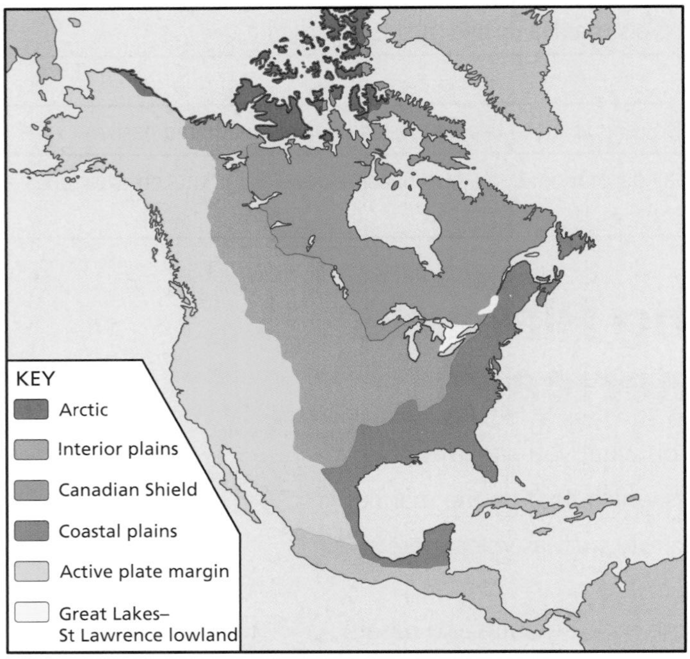

1. The Canadian Shield

The Canadian Shield is a large area of low-lying crystalline rock covering over **8 million km²**. The shield, originally formed from igneous rock, **was metamorphosed by folding and faulting** nearly **4 billion years ago.** Thin layers of sedimentary rock were eroded away during the last ice age, exposing metamorphic rock to the surface. Due to intense metamorphism, **valuable minerals** such as copper, gold and iron ore have formed.

2. Coastal Plains

Sediments eroded from mountain ranges along the interior continent were **deposited into shallow seas** on the eastern coast. Over time, these sediments compressed and **lithified to form sandstone**. The sandstone was **uplifted** above sea level, while limestone formed in warmer seas further offshore. **Oil and gas deposits formed** in the region as **organic sediments** partially decayed in shallow seas.

6.5 Human Interaction with the Rock Cycle

The exploitation of oil and gas is an example of human interaction with the rock cycle.

Natural Gas Exploration in Ireland

- Natural gas is mainly made up of **methane gas**. It is an odourless, colourless fossil fuel that forms when plants, animals or other gasses are exposed to **intense heat and pressure over millions of years.** As gas is non-renewable, it is a valuable natural resource.

- Natural gas is found deep underneath layers of rock in **large reservoirs**. Before it can be used as a fuel, it must be processed to **remove impurities** such as water.

Fig. 6.17 Active and inactive margins in North America

GEO DICTIONARY

Canadian Shield: an 8 million km² area of low-lying crystallised rock along the north-east American continent

Coastal plains: a low-lying area along the south-eastern coast of North America made up of sandstone

Note!

The geothermal energy case study in Chapter 3 Volcanoes can also be used to answer questions on human interaction with the rock cycle.

GEO DICTIONARY

Non-renewable: a resource that, once used, cannot be used again

Formation

- Natural gas formed when **decomposed plant and animal fossils** were buried under layers of sand or mud. This typically occurred under **shallows seas.**

- Over millions of years, **intense heat and pressure** caused the decomposed remains to change both **physically and chemically** to form droplets of natural gas. As further layers of sedimentary rock formed, it forced the gas upwards through the crust. The gas moved upwards until it reached a layer of **overlying impermeable rock** such as shale or mudstone.

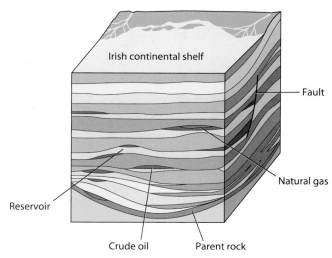

Fig. 6.18 Gas and oil form under layers of ocean sediments.

Ireland

- Oil and gas exploration off Irish shores began in the early 1970s. Marathon Oil, operating as **Marathon Petroleum Ireland Ltd,** bought the rights to explore for oil off the southern coast of Ireland.

- Since then, a number of large **gas deposits** have been found, while a number of potential oil fields have also been discovered.

- To date, only gas fields have been exploited. The **Kinsale Gas Field** and the **Corrib Gas Field** are in production.

- Although there are no oil fields in production in Irish waters, the **Ballyroe Oil Field** is estimated to have 1.6 billion barrels of oil. There is also estimated to be 2.3 billion barrels underneath the main Kinsale Field.

Kinsale Gas Field

- Marathon Petroleum Ireland Ltd found gas off the Old Head of Kinsale after **drill samples** were taken by the ship *Glomar North Sea*. The field was located **50 km off the coast,** 915 m beneath the ocean floor.

- The gas reservoirs are trapped in thin layers of **porous sandstone** rock. The sandstone rock formed approximately **100 million years ago** and was covered by layers of shale and chalk. As shale and chalk are **impermeable to gas,** it could not escape.

- Although the **reservoirs are shallow,** at less than **120 m deep,** the gas field covers an area of over **100 km².** Also, the gas found at Kinsale is **high in purity,** consisting mainly of **methane.**

- Two steel platforms named Alpha and Bravo were built to allow the gas to be brought to the surface. In 1978, production began by supplying gas to the **Aghada Power Station** in Co. Cork before eventually supplying the whole country.

- Since production began, a number of gas fields surrounding the Old Head of Kinsale have been found.

  - Ballycotton Gas Field in 1991

  - South-west Kinsale Gas Field in 1999

  - Seven Heads Gas Field in 2003

> **FACT**
>
> Marathon's gas storage facility in Kinsale can keep up to 2 billion cubic metres of gas and can deliver up to 9 million cubic metres per day. Nine million cubic metres is approximately 5 per cent of Ireland's annual demand.

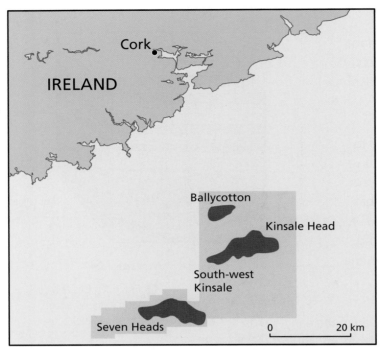

Fig. 6.19 The Kinsale Gas Field

- Gas is **pumped distances of over 35 km** from these fields to the main Alpha and Bravo platforms. At these platforms, all gas is **combined and compressed** before being piped to Inch Terminal, near Midleton, Co. Cork. From here the gas is transferred to **Bord Gáis Energy,** which then distributes it nationwide.

- Production reached its **peak in 1995** and has been declining since.

Currently **only 3 per cent of the gas reserve** at Kinsale remains. As the reserves of natural gas have nearly been exploited, some of the empty reservoirs have been developed as **offshore gas storage** facilities, e.g. the South-west Kinsale Gas Field. This has the potential to reduce Ireland's gas emissions into the atmosphere by 6 per cent annually.

Oil Underneath Kinsale?

- Sample drillings have found evidence to suggest that over **2.3 billion barrels of oil** could exist beneath the Kinsale Gas Fields.

- Due to the importance of the Kinsale Gas Fields, drilling beneath them for oil was seen as too much of a risk as it would disrupt gas supply. Due to global collapse in oil prices, many companies who were licensed to drill for oil off the coast of Ireland have not done so. An example of this is Fastnet Oil (now Fastnet Equity) which had planned to start drilling for oil in 2015.

Corrib Gas Field

- The Corrib Field was discovered in 1996 by Enterprise Oil (now Shell), **83 km off the coast** of Erris Head in Co. Mayo.

- The gas was found in layers of sandstone created **250 million years ago.** Overlying layers of **shale and mudstone** have **prevented the gas from escaping.**

- Much like the gas at Kinsale, the gas at Corrib is very pure, consisting mainly of **methane and ethane gas.**

- The Corrib Field is roughly **70 per cent the size of the Kinsale gas field** and is expected to supply **60 per cent of Ireland's gas needs** when operating at its peak.

- It has started production and has a production life of between **15 and 20 years.**

- A pipeline over 80 km long has been built. This will bring the gas ashore, before being piped to a processing plant at **Bellanaboy.** From here, processed gas will be piped to the Bord Gáis Energy grid.

GEO **DICTIONARY**

Ethane: a mixture of methane and petroleum

FACT

Shell to Sea was an organisation set up to protest Shell's plan to refine gas inland rather than offshore. Unrefined gas is extremely unstable, which caused fear among the residents of Belmullet and Rossport in Co. Mayo, towns near Bellanaboy. Protests continued throughout the building process and continue today. For more information, visit **www.shelltosea.com**.

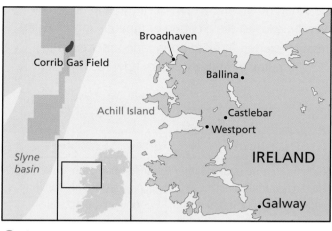

Fig. 6.20 Corrib Gas Field

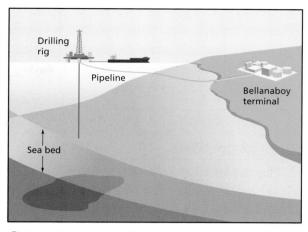

Fig. 6.21 How gas will be pumped ashore at Corrib

- Production has been delayed by **conflict** between Shell and locals, who object to the building of a gas pipeline through their village.

(a)

(b)

Fig. 6.22 (a) and (b) Protests against the site of the gas refinery

 EDUCATE YOURSELF

Oil and Gas Exploration in Ireland	
Gas	Odourless, colourless, fossil fuel, non-renewable, large reservoirs, decomposed plants and animals, heat and pressure, physical and chemical change, overlying impermeable rock
Kinsale	50 km off coast, porous sandstone, 100 mya, overlying shale, impermeable, 100 km², reservoir, high purity, Marathon Petroleum Ltd, Aghada Power Station, combined and compressed, Bord Gáis, peak 1995, 3 per cent remains, offshore storage, oil deposits, 2.3 billion barrels underneath
Corrib	83 km off coast, 250 mya, overlying shale/mudstone, 70 per cent size of Kinsale, 60 per cent of gas needs, Shell, 15–20 year life, Bellanaboy, conflict

In the six chapters you have studied so far, you have learned how plate tectonics create and alter rock structures on our landscape. For example, volcanic activity leads to the creation of igneous rock; folding and faulting reshapes sedimentary rock; heat and pressure exerted at plate boundaries alter existing igneous and sedimentary rock into metamorphic rock. The following table outlines how tectonic activity has altered the rocks of Ireland:

Ireland's Tectonic Landscape			
Landscape Type	Force at Work	How?	Example
1. Plutonic landscape	Collision of North American and Eurasian Plates 400 mya (convergent boundary)	Magma rose up underneath the arched folds of sedimentary rock before cooling slowly to form a large area of granite rock.	Leinster Batholith: 1500 km² encompassing the Dublin, Wicklow and Blackstairs Mountains, exposed to the surface denudation
2. Volcanic landscape	Separation of the North American and Eurasian Plates 60 mya (divergent boundary)	As the plates separated, lava poured out of the fissures and onto the surface, before cooling quickly to form thick plateaux of basalt rock.	Antrim-Derry Plateau: 1800 m in depth, characterised by the Giant's Causeway, an area of hexagonal basalt columns formed by the rapid cooling of lava
3. Fold mountains	Buckling and uplifting due to pressure from colliding plates. Two orogenies: the Caledonian orogeny 400 mya caused by the collision of the North American and Eurasian Plates; the Armorican orogeny 250 mya caused by the collision of the African and Eurasian Plate boundary (both continental-continental convergent boundaries)	Caledonian: As the North American and Eurasian Plates collided, layers of mudstone and shale were buckled upwards to form a range of mountains running from the north-west to south-east of the country. Armorican: As the African and Eurasian Plates collided, layers of sandstone and overlying limestone were uplifted to form the Munster Ridge Valley.	Wicklow Mountains: Largest upland region of Ireland. Its highest peak is Lugnaquilla at 925 m. Most of the Caledonian mountain ranges are approximately 600 m as they have been broken down by weathering and erosion. Lugnaquilla is protected by a layer of metamorphic rock (schist). McGillycuddy's Reeks in Co. Kerry is the highest mountain range in Ireland, averaging 1000 m in height. The Armorican mountains of Munster are higher than the Caledonian mountains as they are newer and therefore have not been weathered or eroded as much.

SHORT QUESTIONS

1. **A.** Match the name of the rock with the location most associated with it, by writing the correct letter in each case, in the table.

Rock Type	Rock Type
A	Limestone
B	Marble
C	Basalt

Location	Letter
The Giant's Causeway	
The Burren	
Connemara	

B. State whether each of the following rocks is an igneous or a sedimentary or a metamorphic rock.

- Marble

- Basalt

2013 Q2 10M

A 3 x 2m
B 2 x 2m

2. Examine the photograph of a basalt area in Ireland and answer the following questions:

A. Is basalt an igneous or a sedimentary or a metamorphic rock?

B. Read the statement and place an X in the correct box. 'Basalt is formed by the cooling of lava on the Earth's surface.'

True	
False	

C. Was this photograph taken in the Burren, Co. Clare or in the Giant's Causeway, Co. Antrim?

D. Read the statement and place an X in the correct box. 'Basalt consists of mainly large crystals.'

True	
False	

E. Name one use of rocks.

2012 Q2 10M

5 x 2m

LONG QUESTIONS

1. (i) Name one igneous rock, and name one metamorphic rock.

(ii) Name one sedimentary rock, and name one Irish location where this rock is found.

(iii) Describe how sedimentary rocks are formed.

2015 Q2B 40M

(i) Each named @ 3m each
(ii) Named and located 3m and 4m
(iii) Explanation 9 SRPs @ 3m each

EXAM QUESTIONS

2. Examine the diagram of the rock cycle and answer each of the following questions.

   (i) Name the category of rock at X and name one rock in this category.

   (ii) Name the category of rock at Y and name one rock in this category.

   (iii) Name any two ways rocks are used.

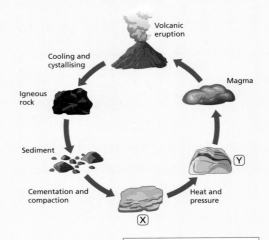

(i) Category 6m Named example 6m
(ii) Category 6m Named example 6m
(iii) Any two uses @ 3m each

2015 Q3A 30M

3. (i) Name one type of igneous rock.

   (ii) Name one Irish location for this type of rock.

   (iii) Explain in detail how this rock was formed.

(i) Named 3m
(ii) Location 3m
(iii) Explanation 8 SRPs @ 3m each

2007 Q2B 30M

4. With reference to the boxes labelled A, B and C on the diagram of the rock cycle, state which letter represents each of the following:

   • Sedimentary rock

   • Metamorphic rock

   • Igneous rock

   This type of rock is formed when sediments sink to the floor of seas and oceans.

   The Rock Cycle

   B

   A — This type of rock is formed when rocks themselves are changed by heat or pressure.

   C — This type of rock is formed when magma cools on or below the Earth's surface.

   2008 Q3A 30M

Each correctly labelled @ 10m each

HIGHER LEVEL

SHORT QUESTIONS

1. The table contains information on rocks regarding their name, category, location in Ireland and the name of the metamorphic rock they can become following metamorphosis.

Name of Rock	Category of Rock	Location in Ireland	Metamorphic Rock
Limestone	Sedimentary	Central Plain of Ireland	Marble

~~Sedimentary~~   ~~Central Plain of Ireland~~   Sandstone   Gneiss

Igneous   ~~Marble~~   Wicklow Mountains   Granite

Mountains of Munster   Quartzite   ~~Limestone~~   Sedimentary

Complete the table by inserting the correct term from the list in its correct position in the table.

2013 Q12 8M

8 @ 1m each

2. Examine the geological map of Ireland. Match each of the letters A to D with its correct rock type in the table below.

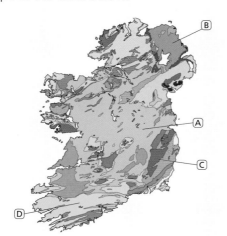

Rock Type	Letter
Basalt	
Limestone	
Sandstone	
Granite	

2011 Q9 8M

4 @ 2m each

LONG QUESTIONS

1. Explain the formation of sedimentary rocks, with reference to Irish examples.

2015 Q2B 30M

Irish examples of sedimentary rock 2 + 2m

Explanation 13 SRPs @ 2m each

EXAM FOCUS

2. Examine how humans interact with the rock cycle, with reference to one of the following:

- Mining
- Extraction of building materials
- Oil/gas exploration
- Geothermal energy production

2015 Q3C 30M

Examination of any one 15 SRPs @ 2m each

3. Explain the formation of igneous rocks with reference to Irish examples.

2014 Q1B 30M

2 Irish igneous rocks named 2 + 2m
Examination 13 SRPs @ 2m each

4. Examine how different rock types produce distinctive landscapes, with reference to examples you have studied.

2014 Q2C 30M

Rock 1 + associated landscape 2 + 2m
Rock 2 + associated landscape 2 + 2m
Examination 11 SRPs @ 2m each

5. Explain the formation of metamorphic rocks, with reference to example(s) that you have studied.

2013 Q1B 30M

2 metamorphic rocks named 2 + 2m
Explanation 13 SRPs @ 2m each

6. Examine the diagram of the rock cycle and answer the following questions.

(i) Name the category of rock formed at A and name one example of this category of rock.

(ii) Name the category of rock formed at B and name one example of this category of rock.

(iii) Name one example of an igneous rock formed at C.

(iv) Name one example of igneous rock which is formed at D.

(v) Briefly explain the difference between the process of weathering and the process of erosion.

2012 Q3 A 20M

(i) Named category + example 2 + 2m
(ii) Named category + example 2 + 2m
(iii) Example 4m
(iv) Example 4m
(v) Any valid explanation 2 + 2m

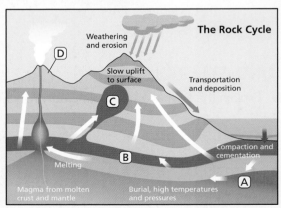

The Rock Cycle

Weathering and erosion

Slow uplift to surface

Transportation and deposition

Compaction and cementation

Melting

Burial, high temperatures and pressures

Magma from molten crust and mantle

The rock cycle is an extremely important topic, so it is vital that you completely understand it. So far, a question relating to the rock cycle or distinctive rock landscapes has appeared on the exam paper every year since 2006. Questions are generally one of three types:

- How a category of rock is formed and where examples can be found in Ireland
- How an example of a rock type is formed and the distinctive landscape it forms
- How humans interact with the rock cycle

Another question that can be asked is how one sedimentary rock is formed and how it is metamorphosed, e.g. how limestone is formed and how it is metamorphosed into marble.

In this section, we will look at one Ordinary Level and one Higher Level question. For this topic, there is very little difference between the type of question asked between Higher and Ordinary Levels. However, the level of detail required differs greatly.

ORDINARY LEVEL

The following question is a regular one at both levels. A surprisingly common mistake made by students is to answer the question using more than one example of interaction. It is vital that you use only one and know it in sufficient detail to answer a full question on it.

EXAM QUESTION

Describe any one of the following examples of human interaction with the rock cycle:

- Quarrying
- Mining
- Oil/gas exploration
- Geothermal energy

Marking Scheme
10 SRPs @ 3m each

2014 Q1C 30M

SAMPLE ANSWER

An example of human interaction with the rock cycle that I have studied is Ireland's gas exploration. Natural gas forms from intense heat and pressure, which caused physical and chemical change of partially decomposed particles [3m]. As gas forms, it rises upwards before coming trapped under impermeable layers of rock such as shale or chalk [3m].

In the 1970s, Marathon Petroleum Ltd bought rights to explore for offshore oil and gas deposits, which resulted in gas finds off the shore of Kinsale and in the Corrib Basin [3m]. Drill samples from the *Glomar North Sea* 50 km off the shore of Kinsale found gas deposits in the pores of sandstone, beneath an impermeable layer of shale and chalk [3m]. The Kinsale Gas Field is located 915 m beneath the ocean floor, is 120 m deep and covers an area of 100 km^2 [3m]. Two steel platforms, Alpha and Bravo, were built to bring gas to the surface where it is combined and compressed before being pumped over 35 km to Inch Terminal near Midleton, Co. Cork [3m]. Once refined, this gas is transferred to Bord Gáis Energy where it is then piped to homes and businesses [3m]. Production of gas at Kinsale peaked in 1995 and now only 3% of the original gas deposits remain [3m]. Empty reservoirs are now being used to store gas, which has the potential to reduce Ireland's atmospheric gas emissions by 6% annually [3m].

In 1996, Shell discovered gas 83 km off the coast of Mayo. The gas was trapped under shale and mudstone that formed 250 mya [3m]. The deposit at the Corrib Gas Field is just under 70% of the original Kinsale find and is capable of supplying 60% of Ireland's gas needs over the next 15–20 years [3m]. An 80 km pipeline has been built to bring the gas ashore to Bellanaboy, where it will be processed and piped to the Bord Gáis grid [3m]. Conflict has arisen between locals of Belmullet and Rossport and Shell due to the pipeline running through their village [3m].

Marks Awarded
Best 10 SRPs @ 3m each
Total 30/30

The first two sentences name the human interaction you have studied and how the gas is formed.

The main body of the answer provides detail of the two main gas finds in Ireland:

- Marathon Petroleum Ltd found the Kinsale Gas Field.
- Shell found the Corrib Gas Field.

Specific statistics are provided regarding the size of each find, the years they were found and their current status.

An explanation of how the gas is extracted and piped ashore for consumer use is also provided.

EXAM QUESTION

Examine, with reference to an example you have studied, the formation of one rock type and how it produces a distinctive landscape.

2008 Q3B 30M

Marking Scheme
Rock formation: Identification 2m
Named example 2m
Examination 5/6 SRPs @ 2m each
Distinctive landscape: Identification 2m
Named example 2m
Examination 5/6 SRPs @ 2m each

SAMPLE ANSWER

1. Intrusive (plutonic rock) is formed when molten magma intrudes into the crust of the Earth, cooling and hardening very slowly beneath the surface, e.g. granite [2m].

2. Granite is formed when a subducting oceanic plate melts, turning to magma [2m].

3. The magma forces its way upward before cooling slowly, deep in the Earth's crust [2m].

This answer is written as a numbered list. This method can be useful if you find it difficult to keep track of your SRPs, and it also helps you to avoid repetition. It is a particularly useful for practising writing answers as part of your exam preparation.

4. Over millions of years the magma cools, as the surrounding layers of rock trap the heat allowing crystals to develop [2m].

5. Granite is made up of three minerals called mica, feldspar and quartz, giving the rock a multicoloured appearance, varying from grey to pink [2m].

6. Granite was formed in Ireland 400 mya during a period of volcanic activity that coincided with a period of folding (Caledonian) [2m].

7. The overlying rock that covered the granite has been removed by weathering and erosion over time to leave it exposed, e.g. Wicklow and Dublin Mountains [2m].

8. The largest area of granite rock in Ireland is the Leinster Batholith that stretches from Dublin to Kilkenny, covering an area of 1500 km² [2m].

The Leinster Batholith [2m] (formed by granite)

1. The Leinster Batholith was created during the Caledonian folding period over 400 mya [2m].

2. It occupies over 1500 km² of the Irish landscape, encompassing the Dublin, Wicklow and Blackstairs Mountains [2m].

3. The Leinster Batholith is a plutonic feature formed as convection currents caused the tectonic plates to collide, buckling the surrounding sedimentary rock, allowing magma to rise underneath the arched folds [2m].

4. This magma cooled over millions of years to form the granite batholith [2m].

5. A combination of the intense heat and pressure cause by the folding plates and rising magma, metamorphosed much of the sedimentary folds into quartzite and schist [2m].

6. Batholiths are usually surrounded by a zone or aureole of metamorphic rocks that were formed in this way [2m].

7. These metamorphic rocks often make a 'cap' on mountain peaks, which protect the underlying granite from weathering and erosion, e.g. the peak of Lugnaquilla in the Wicklow Mountains is protected by schist [2m].

Marks Awarded
Rock formation named 2m
Example named 2m
Examination of formation best 6 SRPs @ 2m each
Associated landscape identified 2m
Named example 2m
Examination best 5 SRPs @ 2m each
Total 30/30

TOPIC MAP

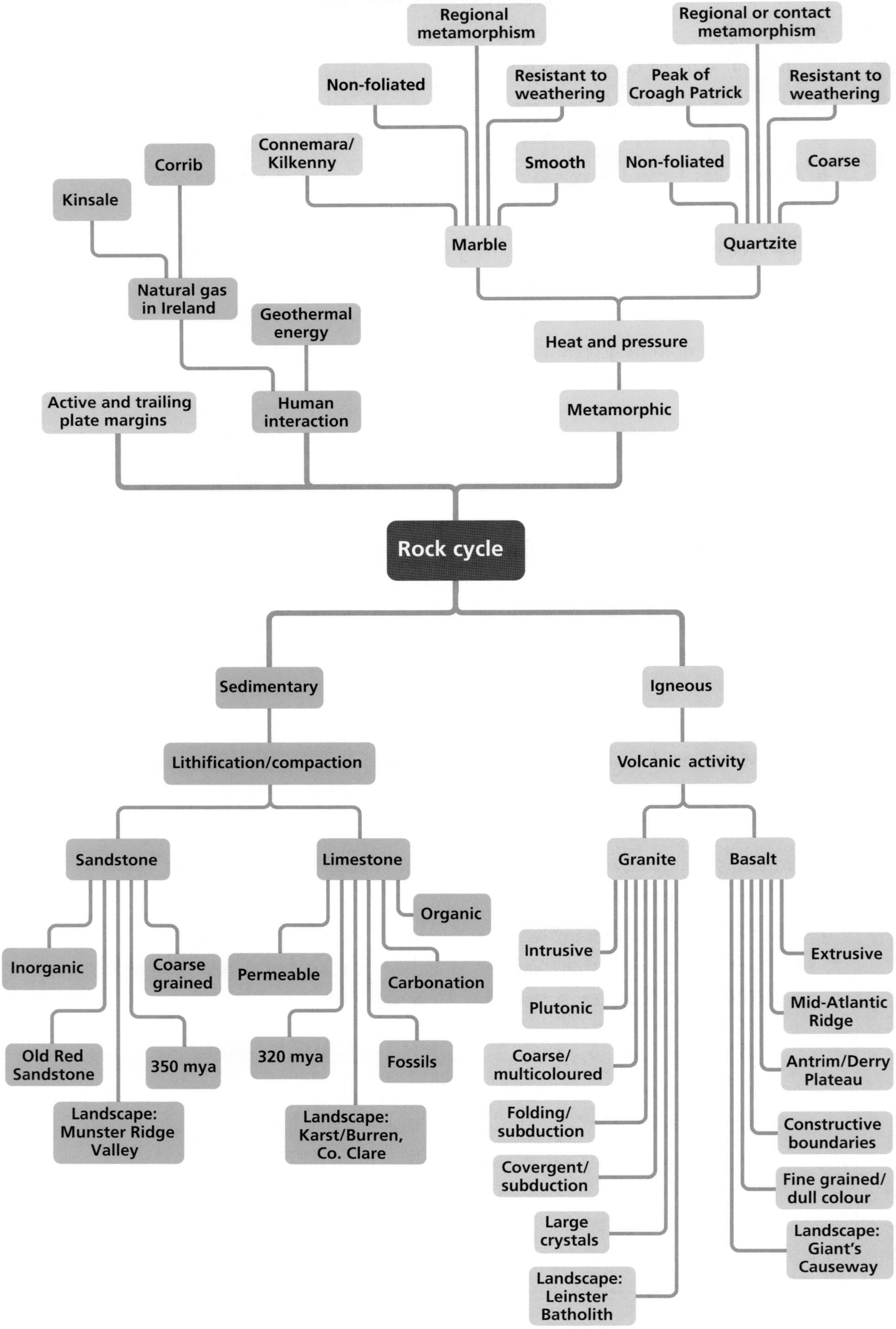

Regional metamorphism

Regional or contact metamorphism

Non-foliated

Resistant to weathering

Peak of Croagh Patrick

Resistant to weathering

Connemara/Kilkenny

Smooth

Non-foliated

Coarse

Corrib

Kinsale

Marble

Quartzite

Natural gas in Ireland

Geothermal energy

Heat and pressure

Active and trailing plate margins

Human interaction

Metamorphic

Rock cycle

Sedimentary

Igneous

Lithification/compaction

Volcanic activity

Sandstone

Limestone

Granite

Basalt

Organic

Inorganic

Coarse grained

Permeable

Carbonation

Intrusive

Extrusive

Plutonic

Mid-Atlantic Ridge

Old Red Sandstone

350 mya

320 mya

Fossils

Coarse/multicoloured

Antrim/Derry Plateau

Folding/subduction

Constructive boundaries

Landscape: Munster Ridge Valley

Landscape: Karst/Burren, Co. Clare

Covergent/subduction

Fine grained/dull colour

Large crystals

Landscape: Giant's Causeway

Landscape: Leinster Batholith

CHAPTER 7

Weathering

Up until this point, you have been studying how forces from within the Earth (endogenic forces) have altered the Earth's surface through creating tectonic landscapes. In this chapter, you will begin studying how forces on the surface – namely weathering and erosion – gradually break down these landscapes. These are known as exogenetic forces. Although we think of rocks as permanent features, they are gradually changed and destroyed by the Earth's environment over a long time. This wearing down of rocks by the Earth's environment is called weathering.

KEY WORDS

- Weathering
- Erosion
- Physical
- Chemical
- Disintegration
- Decomposition
- Freeze-thaw action

- Exfoliation
- Carbonation
- Hydrolysis
- Hydration
- Oxidation
- Expansion
- Contraction

- Diurnal range
- Carbonic acid
- Calcium carbonate
- Calcium bicarbonate
- Karst
- Kaolin
- Feldspar

LEARNING OUTCOMES

What you MUST know
- The difference between weathering and erosion
- Two processes of physical weathering
- Two processes of chemical weathering

What you SHOULD know
- Examples of where each process occurs
- The difference between disintegration and decomposition

What is USEFUL to know
- How to identify the type of weathering from a photograph

Introduction

In this chapter, we will look at the various processes that weather rock. The processes are slow. Rocks are gradually broken down by the Earth's environment through the processes of **weathering** and **erosion**.

Weathering is the **breaking up and decay** of rocks on the Earth's surface through natural **mechanical and chemical** processes.

 GEO **DICTIONARY**

Erosion: the breaking down and transportation of rock by water, wind and ice

Fig. 7.1 Weathered rock is visible in the foreground of the photograph.

Erosion is the **breaking down and transportation** of rock by **water, wind and ice.** In this way, erosion removes the debris broken down by weathering, exposing fresh rock. Weathering produces **regolith,** which is made up of **small rock particles** and **mineral fragments.** When regolith mixes with organic matter, it produces soil.

There are two types of weathering:

- Physical/mechanical weathering
- Chemical weathering

When rock is broken down by **physical weathering,** it is known as **disintegration.**

When rock is broken down and **altered** by **chemical weathering,** it is known as **decomposition.**

7.1 Physical Weathering

Physical weathering, also known as mechanical weathering, is **the breaking down of rocks into smaller pieces** by stress acting on them. These pieces of rock range in size from large boulders to small grains. Two **main forms** of physical weathering are **freeze-thaw action** and **exfoliation.** Neither forms a new substance or changes the physical appearance of rocks.

1. Freeze-Thaw Action

Freeze-thaw action is the **most common form of mechanical weathering.** It occurs in **cold climates** or in **upland areas** where **temperatures regularly rise and fall above and below freezing point.** Freeze-thaw action occurs regularly in Arctic and Alpine environments which have numerous freezing and thawing cycles throughout the year. **Upland areas** in the **West of Ireland** are also affected by freeze-thaw action.

Fig. 7.2 Sandstone split apart by physical weathering

Three conditions are necessary for freeze-thaw action to occur:

1. There is an adequate **supply of water.**
2. **The rock has pre-existing fractures and joints where water can enter,** e.g. sedimentary rock.
3. **Temperatures** regularly rise and fall **above and below freezing point.**

Freeze-thaw action occurs when **rainwater seeps into fractures and joints** in beds of rock by day. By night, **temperatures drop below 0 °C** (freezing point), turning the water into ice. When water freezes, it **expands by 9 per cent.** The expanding ice **causes stress** on the joints and fractures in the rock, **prising them apart like a wedge.** This is known as wedging. The force produced by the expanding ice is very strong: it applies **110 kg/cm²** of pressure on the rock. When the temperature rises above 0 °C again, the ice turns back into water, and **flows deeper into the joints** of the rock. Repeated freeze-thaw cycles **enlarge the cracks and joints** of the rock further until the rock eventually breaks apart.

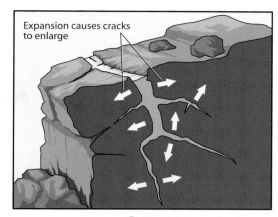

Expansion causes cracks to enlarge

🔼 **Fig. 7.3** Expanding ice forces joints of rock apart.

- Freeze-thaw action is much **more effective** in areas where **freezing and thawing occur many times a year,** rather than in areas where water is permanently frozen.

- The result of freeze-thaw action can clearly be seen in the mountains around Ireland, as the **pieces of broken rock** accumulate at the **bottom of slopes.** These broken, angular pieces of rock are called **scree.** Croagh Patrick in Co. Mayo and Carrantouhill in Co. Kerry are examples of mountains in Ireland with large accumulations of scree.

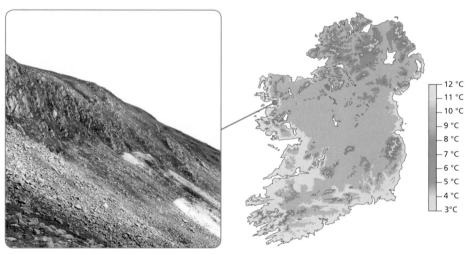

12 °C
11 °C
10 °C
9 °C
8 °C
7 °C
6 °C
5 °C
4 °C
3 °C

🔼 **Fig. 7.4** *(left)* Scree accumulation on the slopes of Glendalough, Co. Wicklow
Fig. 7.5 *(right)* A temperature map showing the colder upland areas of Ireland where freeze-thaw action is likely to occur

2. Exfoliation

Exfoliation is the process by which **layers of rock are peeled away** as a result of repeated **expansion and contraction cycles.** Exfoliation is commonly known as 'onion weathering' as the layers peel off. Like, freeze-thaw action, it **relies on temperature change.** However, unlike freeze-thaw action, it does not rely on a water supply. Exfoliation occurs in regions with a **large temperature range,** such as a hot desert region. **Diurnal range** is the difference between the **highest and lowest temperature** each day. Exfoliation is most effective in rock that has **strata or joints,** as it makes it easier for the outer layers to peel off.

CORE 1 CHAPTER 7

By day, temperatures in the desert exceed **40 °C**. This causes the outer layers of rock to become much hotter than the inner layers. This **uneven heating** by the sunlight causes the **outer layers to expand.** By night, **temperatures fall** close to freezing point, causing the outer **layers** to **contract** again. Repeated expansion and contraction mean the outer **layers loosen and crack,** before peeling away layer by layer. The gradual removal of these layers causes the rock to become rounded.

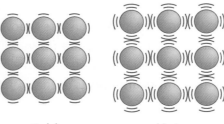

Cold   Hot

◀ **Fig. 7.7** Objects expand when heated.

◀ **Fig. 7.6** The effects of exfoliation are seen in this photograph. The rock has been 'rounded' and a thin layer has broken off due to repeated expansion and contraction.

Some minerals in rock heat faster than others, which can cause increased stress on the rock. For example, **quartz expands three times as much as feldspar** when it is heated. As the quartz expands, it causes the layers in the rock to separate from each other.

Sometimes, **dew falls in deserts** at night and **freezes,** resulting in **freeze-thaw action,** as well as contraction. A **combination** of exfoliation and freeze-thaw action **weakens the rock** more rapidly, causing them to break into large rectangular blocks. This is referred to as **block disintegration.** This can be seen in **Monument Valley** in the **Arizona Desert.** Block disintegration most likely occurs if the rock is jointed and layered.

Exfoliation also occurs when underlying layers of rock are exposed to the Earth's surface. As **overlying materials are removed,** there is **less pressure on the underlying layers of rock,** causing them to expand. As the underlying layers expand, the rigid top layers of rock fracture into **pieces of scree.** These expanding layers can lead to the formation of a dome mountain.

▲ **Fig. 7.8** Doming occurs when underlying rock is exposed.

Often, rock surrounding the dome is **more resistant to weathering,** forming blocks of rock around the mountain. These blocks are known as **tors. Three Rock Mountain in Co. Dublin** is an example.

▲ **Fig. 7.9** Three Rock Mountain in Co. Dublin is an example of a tor.

Physical Weathering (Rock Disintegration)	
Freeze-thaw action	Stress, upland areas, fluctuating temperatures, freezing point (0 °C), expansion, joints/fractures, 110 kg/cm², West of Ireland, scree, Croagh Patrick
Exfoliation	Peeling, onion weathering, expansion, contraction, diurnal temperature range, strata, joints, 0–40 °C, desert climate, quartz, feldspar, scree, block disintegration, doming, Arizona Desert

 ACTIVE **LEARNING**

1. Explain the difference between exfoliation and freeze-thaw action.
2. Where is exfoliation most likely to occur?
3. Why is exfoliation referred to as 'onion weathering'?
4. What is block disintegration? Give an example of where it occurs.
5. What are tors and how do they form?

7.2 Chemical Weathering

Chemical weathering refers to the **breaking down of rock through chemical reactions between minerals in rock and the Earth's environment.** Unlike physical weathering, chemical weathering causes both the **physical appearance** and the **chemical composition** of rock to change. During chemical weathering, rocks are decomposed as the mineral structure in the rock is changed. Most rocks are **aggregates,** meaning that they are made of two or more minerals **cemented together through bonding agents.** Over time, exposure to the Earth's surface weakens the bonding of these minerals, causing the rock to decompose. **Water is the essential substance** needed for chemical weathering to occur.

There are three types of chemical weathering:

1. Carbonation
2. Hydration and hydrolysis
3. Oxidation

● **Fig. 7.10** Evidence of chemical weathering

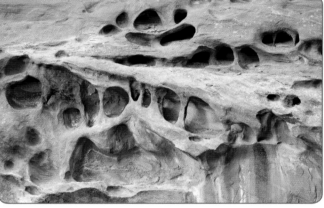

1. Carbonation

Carbonation is a very common form of chemical weathering. As **rainwater falls through the atmosphere, it mixes with carbon dioxide (CO_2)** forming a **weak carbonic acid.**

As the rainwater hits the ground, it **reacts with rocks made from calcium carbonate,** e.g. **limestone** and chalk. When the carbonic acid reacts with limestone, it causes the **calcium carbonate** to **change into calcium bicarbonate,** which is a **soluble mineral.**

This mineral is removed by water in solution. Limestone is particularly prone to chemical weathering through carbonation as it has **lines of weakness** in its **bedding planes and joints.** As acid runs along these joints and cracks, it causes them to widen, forming **limestone pavement.** Carbonation **produces a very distinct landscape known as karst,** which can be seen in the **Burren in Co. Clare,** or in the Marble Arch Caves in Co. Fermanagh.

[A-Z] GEO **DICTIONARY**

Aggregate: rocks that are made from two or more minerals cemented together through bonding agents

Carbonic acid: an acid formed from the mixing of carbon dioxide and water

Calcium carbonate: naturally occurring solid, forming limestone, chalk, etc.

Calcium bicarbonate: solution composed of calcium, carbon dioxide and bicarbonate

Soluble: a mineral that can be dissolved in water

CORE 1 CHAPTER 7

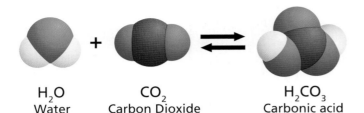

H_2O
Water

$+$

CO_2
Carbon Dioxide

$\rightleftharpoons$

H_2CO_3
Carbonic acid

Equation

$$H_2O + CO_2 = H_2CO_3$$

Water + Carbon dioxide = Carbonic acid

ACTIVE LEARNING

1. Explain the difference between physical weathering and chemical weathering.

2. What is the essential agent for chemical weathering?

3. Explain how carbonic acid is formed.

4. Name two rocks affected by carbonation.

5. What happens when limestone reacts with carbonic acid?

6. Why is limestone so prone to carbonation?

7. Name a distinctive landscape produced by carbonation.

GEO DICTIONARY

Hydration: the absorption of water by rock minerals, which causes them to expand and break apart. Hydration means 'to split using water'

Hydrolysis: the turning of feldspar into kaolin (clay) through a chemical reaction between feldspar and carbonic acid

2. Hydration and Hydrolysis

Hydration refers to the **absorption of water** by **rock minerals**. Soil-forming minerals in rock do not contain any water. As they are **exposed to humid conditions** on the Earth's surface they are hydrated by absorbing water. When these minerals absorb water, they expand. As these minerals expand, they **cause stress** to develop **within the rock. Increased stress causes the rocks to fracture** and eventually shatter. Once hydration causes fractures in the rock, mechanical weathering processes further the disintegration. **Some minerals also become soft** when hydrated causing the rock to fall apart.

Hydrolysis is the most **common form of chemical weathering** and leads to the **formation of clay.** It occurs when **water reacts with minerals in rock.** Acidic water (carbonic acid) causes rock-forming minerals such as **feldspar to turn into a softer, weaker mineral called kaolin** (china clay).

Kaolin **does not bond well** and breaks down easily, weakening the rock's structure. Gradually, the rock breaks down and decomposes causing more resistant rock minerals, such as **mica and quartz,** to **move down slope** due to gravity.

Hydrolysis occurs at a much **faster** rate than **in regions with a wetter and warmer climate.** For every **10 °C increase in** temperature, the rate of **hydrolysis doubles.** Hydrolysis is an **important** factor in the **formation of soils** containing clay minerals. It was an important process in shaping the granite of the Leinster Batholith when Ireland had a much warmer climate and the process was much more effective.

Fig. 7.11 Limestone pavement

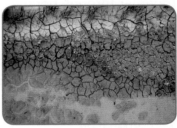

Fig. 7.12 Evidence of hydration in the rock's centre, where chemical reactions has led to a softening of materials

Fig. 7.13 The outer layers of the rock show evidence of hydrolysis as clay is forming.

3. Oxidation

Oxidation takes place when **oxygen reacts with minerals in rock.** Oxygen dissolved in **water reacts with metal in rocks,** usually iron. This process produces **oxides of iron** and causes the **rusting of rock particles.** This chemical reaction gives rocks and soil a **reddish brown** appearance. Clay formed through the process of hydrolysis, turns red when it is exposed to oxygen.

Fig. 7.14 Evidence of oxidation

 ACTIVE **LEARNING**

1. Explain the factors which control the type and speed of weathering.
2. Explain how carbonic acid forms in the atmosphere.
3. Explain the process of hydrolysis.
4. Where in Ireland is freeze-thaw action most likely to occur?
5. Why is exfoliation of rock unlikely to occur in Ireland?
6. Explain the effects of carbonation on limestone.
7. Copy the Venn diagram below. Write in the numbers of the terms to show the similarities and differences between freeze-thaw action and exfoliation.
8. What evidence of oxidation can you see in Fig. 7.14?

 GEO **DICTIONARY**

Feldspar: the glue that holds mica and quartz together in granite rock

Kaolin: commonly known as 'china clay'. It forms when feldspar reacts with carbonic acid

Oxidation: oxygen in water causes metal, especially iron, in rocks to rust

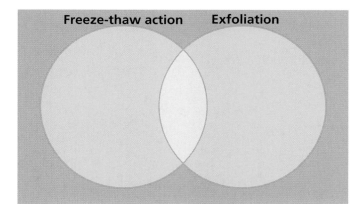

Freeze-thaw action   Exfoliation

1. Expansion
2. Contraction
3. Water
4. Temperature change
5. Joints/cracks
6. Upland
7. Desert
8. Wedging
9. Scree
10. Doming
11. Feldspar

Note!
Go to the following websites for more resources on weathering:

- **www.youtube.com** and search for 'freeze-thaw action' and 'carbonation' for a selection of videos and experiments on these processes

- **www.geolsoc.org. uk** and search for 'rock cycle' for basic definitions, explanations and images showing evidence of the various weathering processes

 EDUCATE YOURSELF

Chemical Weathering (Rock Decomposition)	
Carbonation	Chemical weathering, aggregates, carbon dioxide, carbonic acid, calcium carbonate, limestone, calcium bicarbonate, solution, decomposition, joints/bedding planes, karst, Burren, Co. Clare
Hydration	Humid, absorption, expand, stress
Hydrolysis	Formation of clay, carbonic acid, feldspar, kaolin, mica, quartz, warm and wet climate, 10 °C increase = hydrolysis doubling, formation of soils
Oxidation	Oxygen, rock minerals, iron oxides, rusting, reddish soil

ORDINARY LEVEL

SHORT QUESTIONS

1. Examine the diagram of a karst landscape and answer each of the following questions.

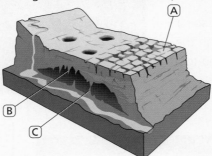

(i) 3 @ 2m each	
(ii) 2 @ 2m each	

(i) Match each of the letters A, B and C in the diagram with the landform that best matches it, in the table.

Landform	Letter
Pillar/column	
Clint	
Stalactite	

(ii) Indicate whether each of the statements is true or false, by ticking the correct box.

(a) The Giant's Causeway is an example of a karst landscape.

True	
False	

(b) Permeable rock allows water to pass through it easily.

True	
False	

2015 Q3 10M

LONG QUESTIONS

1. Study the diagram of the karst landscape and answer the following questions:

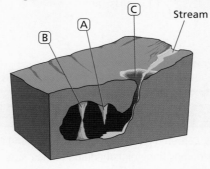

(i) Three named @ 3m each
(ii) Feature named 2m
(iii) Naming 2m
Diagram with 3 labels @ 2m each
Explanation 7 SRPs @ 3m each

2012 Q3C 40M

(i) Name the features marked A, B and C.

(ii) Name one other feature found in karst landscapes.

(iii) Explain, with the aid of a diagram, how any one feature in a karst region is formed.

ORDINARY LEVEL

Weathering has appeared on both the Higher Level and Ordinary Level exam papers. Usually, short questions are combinations of weathering and karst landscapes, which we will look at in Chapter 8. Weathering appears frequently as a 30-mark question on the Ordinary Level Paper, while it has appeared only once as a 30-mark question on the Higher Level Paper.

The following question appeared on the 2013 Ordinary Level paper. It is worth 30 marks and requires you to know the process of freeze-thaw action **or** carbonation.

EXAM QUESTION

Describe and explain any one of the following weathering processes that you have studied:

- Freeze-thaw action

- Carbonation

Marking Scheme
Explanation of one of the weathering processes 10 SRPs @ 3m each

2013 Q2C 30M

The following table includes all of the key terms and elements needed to fully answer this question.

Freeze-thaw action		Carbonation	
Physical weathering	Stress	Chemical weathering	Joints/bedding planes
West of Ireland	Joints/fractures	Carbonic acid	Karst landscape
Temperature change	Enlarged	Calcium carbonate	Burren, Co. Clare
Upland areas	Scree	Limestone	Limestone pavement
Freezing point	Croagh Patrick	Calcium bicarbonate	
Expansion	Solution	Solution	

Can you explain each of these terms? If so, you can answer this question.

SAMPLE ANSWER

Freeze-thaw action

Freeze-thaw action is a process of physical/mechanical weathering that I have studied [3m]. Physical weathering occurs in upland regions, such as the mountainous regions in the West of Ireland [3m]. It occurs in areas such as this as the temperature regularly rises and falls above and below freezing point [3m].

There are three factors needed for freeze-thaw action to occur:

- There is a plentiful supply of water.

- The rock has cracks/joints where the water can enter.

- Temperatures regularly rise and fall above and below freezing point. [3m]

Freeze-thaw action occurs when water seeps into the cracks and joints of rock during the day. [3m] At night, when temperatures drop below freezing point, the water freezes and turns to ice. [3m] When water freezes, it expands by 9%, causing pressure on the

The introduction clearly states the process of weathering, and gives a general location of where it occurs. A clear knowledge of the factors which cause this process is shown. The explanation is broken into two distinct stages: what happens by day and what happens by night. A clear description of the effects of freeze-thaw action on the rock is given. A specific Irish example of where this process occurs is given.

CORE 1 CHAPTER 7

ORDINARY LEVEL

joints. [3m] The expanding ice acts like a wedge and causes the cracks and joints of the rock to enlarge. [3m]

Over time, repeated freeze-thaw cycles cause the rock to break apart into pieces of angular rock called 'scree' [3m]. This is referred to as rock disintegration [3m]. Scree rolls down the slopes of mountains under the influence of gravity, accumulating in piles at the bottom [3m]. Examples of scree accumulations can be seen in mountains along the West coast of Ireland, such as Croagh Patrick in Co. Mayo and the peak of Carrantouhill in Co. Kerry [3m].

Answer is well structured and is written in a logical sequence (i.e. from the beginning of the process to the end). Sentences have clear SRPs, with each key term developed to show understanding.

Now, try to answer the above question, by explaining the process of carbonation.

Marks Awarded
Best 10 SRPs @ 3m each
Total 30/30

HIGHER LEVEL

The following question appeared on the 2013 Higher Level paper. It is worth 30 marks and requires you to know at least one process of physical weathering **or** one process of chemical weathering.

Marking Scheme
Name and discuss one/two processes of physical or chemical weathering: 2m each
Explanation 14 SRPs @ 2m each
Labelled diagram 1 SRP @ 2m

EXAM QUESTION

Explain the process(es) of physical weathering **or** the process(es) of chemical weathering.

2013 Q3C 30M

The following table includes all of the key terms and elements needed to fully answer this question. You may answer on physical or chemical weathering.

You have the options of including a diagram or dividing your answer into two headings (i.e. discussing two processes of chemical/physical weathering).

Physical Weathering		Chemical Weathering	
Freeze-thaw Action	**Exfoliation**	**Carbonation**	**Hydrolysis**
Disintegration	Peeling	Carbonic acid	Helps form clay
Stress	Expansion	Calcium carbonate	Carbonic acid
Upland areas	Contraction	Limestone/chalk	Feldspar
Fluctuating temperature	Diurnal range	Calcium bicarbonate	Kaolin
Freezing point (0 °C)	Desert climate	Solution	Quartz/mica
Expansion	Strata/joints	Joints/bedding planes	Decomposition
Joints/fractures	Quartz/feldspar	Karst landscape	Warm/wet climate
Wedging	Scree	Limestone pavement	10 °C increase
Scree	Block disintegration	Burren, Co. Clare	Soil formation
Croagh Patrick	Doming	Marble Arch caves	Leinster Batholith
	Arizona Desert		

SAMPLE ANSWER

Chemical weathering refers to the breaking down of rock through chemical reactions between rock minerals and water [2m].

Chemical reactions change the physical appearance and chemical composition of the rock [2m]. Most rocks are aggregates, meaning they are made up of more than one mineral [2m].

When rocks are exposed to the Earth's environment, the bonds between minerals weaken, causing them to decompose [2m].

Water is necessary for chemical weathering to occur, while temperature greatly affects the rate at which it occurs [2m].

Carbonation

Carbonation is a common form of chemical weathering [2m].

Carbonation occurs when acidic water reacts with rocks made from calcium carbonate [2m]. Limestone is an example of a rock made from calcium carbonate [2m]. As water falls through the atmosphere, it mixes with carbon dioxide, forming a weak carbonic acid: $H_2O + CO_2 = H_2CO_3$ [2m].

When the rain hits the ground, it causes the calcium carbonate in rock such as limestone to turn into calcium bicarbonate [2m]. Calcium bicarbonate is a soluble mineral which is then washed away by water in solution [2m]. The bedding planes and cracks in limestone mean that carbonation is very effective, enlarging the joints and cracks [2m]. This process leads to the formation of a unique limestone landscape known as karst [2m]. An example of a karst landscape is the Burren in Co. Clare [2m].

Hydrolysis

Hydrolysis is the most common form of chemical weathering [2m].

It occurs when carbonic acid softens rock minerals such as feldspar [2m]. When this occurs, feldspar turns into a softer, weaker mineral called kaolin [2m]. Kaolin does not bond well with other minerals, and this weakens the structure of the rock [2m]. As a result, the rock decomposes, leaving behind more resistant minerals such as mica and feldspar [2m].

Hydrolysis is most effective in regions that have a warm and wet climate [2m]. For every 10 °C increase in temperature, the rate of hydrolysis doubles [2m]. Hydrolysis is a very important process in the formation of clay soils [2m]. When Ireland was close to the equator, hydrolysis helped to shape the granite of the Leinster Batholith [2m].

A clear definition is given at the beginning of the answer. The explanation of chemical weathering shows a clear understanding of the topic. Two processes of chemical weathering are clearly identified, while each of their effects is clearly described. An Irish example of where both processes occur or have occurred is given.

Answer is well structured and is written in an examiner-friendly fashion, with each sentence containing a key word and clear explanation to show understanding.

Marks Awarded	
Process named 2m	
Additional process 2m	
Best 13 SRPs @ 2m each	
Total	30/30

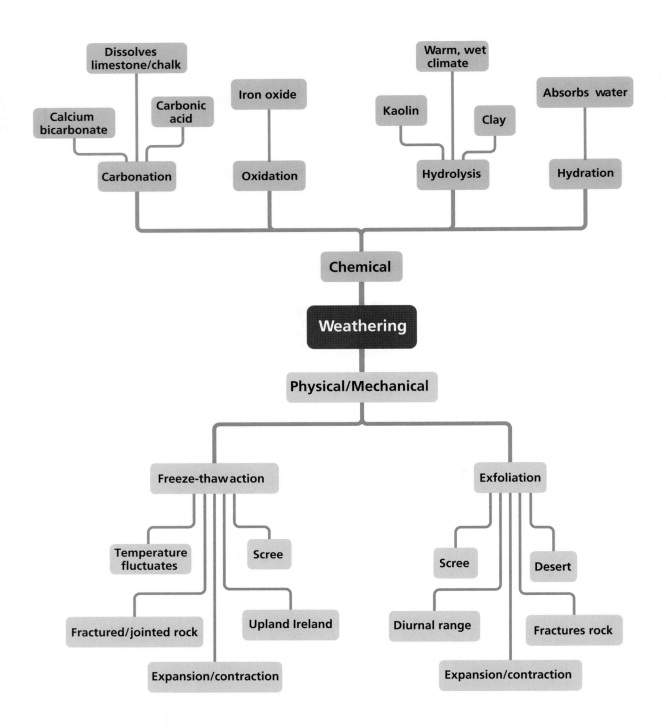

TOPIC MAP

CHAPTER 8
Karst Landscapes

In Chapters 6 and 7, you learned how limestone rock is created, before being gradually worn down by chemical weathering. In this chapter, we will examine how carbonation of limestone creates a distinct landscape known as karst. Your knowledge of limestone formation and carbonation will make this chapter much easier to understand. The chapter is divided into two sections: the creation of surface karst features and the creation of underground karst features.

KEY WORDS

- Karst
- Carbonation
- Porous
- Pervious
- Dissolve
- H_2CO_3 (carbonic acid)
- $CaCO_3$ (limestone)
- Burren
- Marble Arch

- Surface features
- Underground features
- Limestone pavement
- Clints
- Grikes
- Swallow holes
- Dry valleys
- Caves/caverns
- Dripstone features

- Evaporate
- Calcite
- Stalactites
- Stalagmites
- Youthful
- Mature
- Old

LEARNING OUTCOMES

What you MUST know
- How limestone is weathered
- Two surface features in detail
- Two underground features in detail
- How to correctly draw and label a diagram of surface and underground features

What you SHOULD know
- The three stages of karst landscapes
- How to identify karst features on an OS map

What is USEFUL to know
- Additional surface and underground features

Note!

Questions on karst landscapes regularly appear in the short questions and physical section at both Higher and Ordinary Levels.

Introduction

Karst landscape refers to an area of **exposed limestone** that has been shaped by the chemical weathering process of carbonation. The term 'karst' comes from the name of a limestone region of Slovenia along the eastern coast of the Adriatic Sea. As you have already learned in Chapter 6 The Rock Cycle and Chapter 7 Weathering, limestone is a permeable rock, meaning that water can drain through it. It is permeable due to the following three reasons:

Fig. 8.1 The features of a karst landscape

- It is **porous:** limestone contains small holes that can hold water.
- It is **pervious:** it has joints that allow water to pass through it.
- It is **dissolved** by **carbonic acid,** causing it to be weathered.

In Chapter 7, you learned exactly how limestone is weathered. Water in the atmosphere mixes with carbon dioxide, forming a **weak carbonic acid.** When this carbonic acid falls on the limestone, it **reacts with the calcium carbonate,** causing it to turn into **calcium bicarbonate.** Calcium bicarbonate is soluble (dissolves in water) and is **washed away in solution.**

Equation

Formation of carbonic acid: $H_2O + CO_2 = H_2CO_3$

Weathering of limestone: $CaCO_3 + H_2CO_3 = Ca(H_2CO_3)_2$

Calcium bicarbonate: $Ca(H_2CO_3)_2$

This process causes large sections of limestone to dissolve. This enlarges joints on the surface, carving out an underground drainage system. This underground drainage allows more water to pass through the limestone and leads to the creation of unique underground karst features. Global examples of karst landscapes are Karst in Slovenia and Guilin in China.

 GEO **DICTIONARY**

Porous: full of small holes that hold water

Pervious: something that can be entered, is permeable

ACTIVE **LEARNING**

1. Where does the name karst come from?
2. Explain three reasons why water can flow through limestone.
3. How does carbonic acid form?
4. What happens when carbonic acid reacts with limestone?

GEO **DICTIONARY**

Glacio-karst: limestone landscape that has been affected by glaciation

8.1 Irish Karst

Limestone is the **most common rock** in Ireland. This has led to karst landscapes forming in the **Burren, Co. Clare** and the **Marble Arch in Co. Fermanagh.** During the last ice age, large glaciers moved across the Burren, **eroding away the topsoil** and exposing the limestone rock that lay underneath. The Burren is referred to as **'glacio-karst',** meaning that it has been affected by glaciation. As karst is weathered away, several unique features or landforms are created which we will divide into two categories:

- Surface features
- Underground features

Surface Features

In this section, we will examine the formation of unique features on the surface of karst landscape: **limestone pavement, swallow holes** and **dry valleys**.

Limestone Pavement

Limestone pavement is an area of **flat, exposed blocks** of limestone, which are separated by **deep, intersecting joints.**

Fig. 8.2 Limestone pavement in the Burren, Co. Clare

Limestone pavement can be seen throughout the **Burren in Co. Clare.**

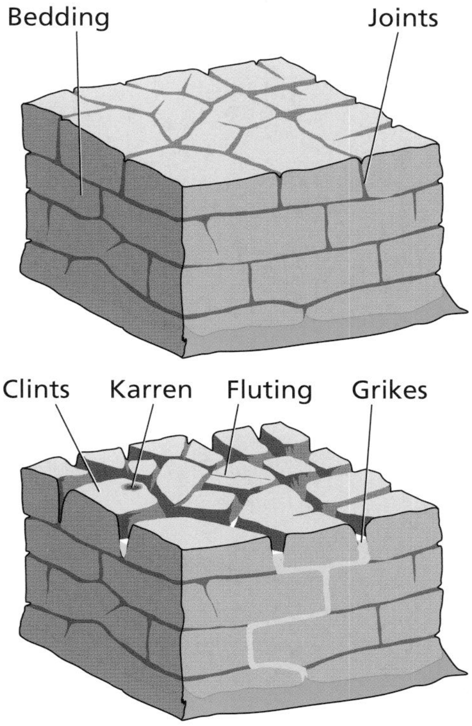

- **Carbonation** is the most important process in the formation and shaping of limestone pavement.

- Once **glaciers** had **stripped away the overlying soil** and rock, the underlying limestone was exposed to the environment. As limestone is **naturally jointed and cracked,** carbonation from rainwater is very effective at dissolving it.

- Carbonic acid falls on the limestone, before flowing through its cracks and joints. This is known as **percolation.** As the water percolates through the limestone, it dissolves the rock, **widening the gaps** between the cracks and joints.

- The widening and deepening of the joints form a series of **intersecting lines** known as **grikes.** Once a grike develops, more acidic water drains into the crack, causing it to deepen. As the grikes deepen, the remaining limestone is divided into sections called **clints.**

- Sometimes water lodges on the top of clints, dissolving a small hollow through carbonation. These hollows are known as **karrens.**

- As these small hollows overflow, the water runs across the clint before flowing into the grike. Over time, the water cuts a channel into the clint, connecting the karren to the grike. This carving of a channel is known as **fluting.**

Fig. 8.3 Surface features of limestone pavement

Note!
The best way to answer questions on this topic is to use DEED:
Definition, Example, Explanation, Diagram.

Swallow Holes and Dry Valleys

A swallow hole is a **narrow, funnel-shaped hole** into which a river flows and disappears. Swallow holes and dry valleys are common features formed in all karst regions.

Many examples of swallow holes, such as **Poll na gColm,** can be found in the Burren region.

- Also known as **sluggas,** swallow holes normally form from the top down due to a **combination of erosion, carbonation** and **solution.**

GEO DICTIONARY

Percolation: the movement of water through pores/holes in the rock

Grikes: intersecting lines formed in limestone which has been exposed to the surface through carbonation

- A swallow hole marks the point where a **river disappears underground** in a limestone region.

- Once the river flows into the swallow hole, it **dissolves a channel** underneath the surface. As you have seen in the formation of limestone pavement, when water lands on the surface of a karst region, it quickly disappears underground **through grikes.**

- As grikes are widened and deepened by the process of carbonation, they begin to join with other grikes, creating a large **vertical passage.**

- The river flows into this passage and disappears underground. The erosive power of the moving water from the river **(hydraulic action) widens** the swallow hole.

- A common point of formation is where limestone borders with an **impermeable rock such as shale.** The water flows across the **impermeable rock** before seeping through the limestone and disappearing.

- This water dissolves the limestone underneath the surface, carving out an underground passage. Eventually, after carbonation has dissolved more limestone, the **roof of the passage is weakened and collapses.** This opens up a swallow hole.

- Swallow holes can also appear along river valleys causing the river to disappear underground before **reappearing further down the valley.** This occurs when a thin layer of impermeable rock lies over the underlying limestone.

- As the river erodes vertically downwards, it removes the impermeable rock and flows over the limestone, before disappearing.

- As part of the river valley is left without water, it is called a **dry valley.** The point where the river reappears on the surface is known as the **point of resurgence.** Over time, new swallow holes may form further up the river valley, which lengthens the dry valley.

⬆ **Fig. 8.4** A dry valley

- During winter in Ireland, many **dry valleys are temporarily filled** with water once again as the water table rises above the height of the swallow hole.

- The water usually disappears once again during the summer as it is **drained away by the underground passage.**

EDUCATE YOURSELF

Surface Features	
Karst	Exposed limestone, porous, pervious, dissolved, carbonic acid, $H_2O + CO_2 = H_2CO_3$, $CaCO_3 + H_2CO_3 = Ca(H_2CO_3)_2$, surface and underground features
Limestone pavement	Flat exposed blocks, intersecting joints, Burren, Co. Clare, carbonation, soil removed by glaciers, naturally faulted and cracked, percolation, dissolves, grikes, clints, karrens, fluting
Swallow holes and dry valleys	Narrow, funnel-shaped, Poll na gColm, erosion, carbonation, solution, river disappears underground, dissolves a channel, hydraulic action, impermeable rock, roof collapses, point of resurgence, dry valleys, temporarily filled

⬆ **Fig. 8.5** Pollaphuca in the Burren, Co. Clare is an example of a swallow hole.

 ACTIVE **LEARNING**

1. Define the following features:
   (a) Limestone pavement
   (b) Swallow hole and dry valley
2. Give an example of where limestone pavement can be found.
3. Explain how carbonation of limestone occurs.
4. Explain how limestone pavement forms as a result of carbonation.

5. Draw a labelled diagram of limestone pavement, showing the following:
   - Clints
   - Grikes
   - Karrens
   - Fluting
6. Name an example of a swallow hole in Ireland.
7. Explain how dry valleys form.

8.2 Underground Features

In this section, we will examine how a cave is formed underneath the limestone surface and how dripstone features are formed inside the cave.

Caves/Caverns

As you have already learned, when a river disappears down through a swallow hole, it carves out large passages. These passages are known as **caverns.**

Examples include the Aillwee Cave in the Burren or the Crag Cave in Castleisland, Co. Kerry.

- Caves in limestone areas are formed at, or below, the **zone of saturation.** The zone of saturation is the term given to rock and soil that is below the **water table.**

- Any limestone rock in this zone can be **weathered by carbonation** as the acidic water causes it to **dissolve.** As rainwater seeps down through the soil and rock close to the surface, it **absorbs more CO_2** and forms an even stronger **carbonic acid.**

- Just as it does on the surface, the carbonic acid dissolves the limestone along its cracks and joints (lines of weakness). Over time, large areas of underground limestone are dissolved, forming an underground cave, e.g. Aillwee Cave.

Note!
Visit the following website to explore the landscape, wildlife and history of the Burren National Park:
www.burrennationalpark.ie

Fig. 8.6 A limestone cave

- Caverns are formed from running water (rivers) carving a passage through the limestone. **Hydraulic action** (the erosive power of moving water) breaks the limestone rock, carving a long underground passage.

- **Abrasion** widens the passage as broken pieces of limestone hit off the sides of the passage. When the water table falls, caverns form at a lower level. This can lead to a series of caverns at different levels if the water table continues to fall.

- The caverns above the water table, such as at Aillwee Cave, are left dry and can be viewed by the public.

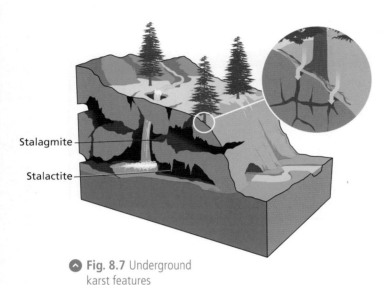

Stalagmite

Stalactite

Fig. 8.7 Underground karst features

Dripstone Formations

- As you have already learned, when a weak carbonic acid reacts with limestone, the rock is changed into **calcium bicarbonate.** The calcium bicarbonate is dissolved by the rainwater and removed in **solution**.

- Within limestone caves and caverns, a variety of features are formed by **dissolution**. Dissolution is the **reversal of carbonation**. Dissolution occurs when the **water evaporates,** allowing the **carbon dioxide** in the solution to escape.

- Once the water has evaporated, a speck of **calcite** (hardened calcium bicarbonate) is left behind. As calcite builds up over time, it creates a variety of features known as **dripstone features.**

Stalactites

- Stalactites form on the roofs of caves and caverns, **hanging downwards** towards the floor.

- They form as water containing **dissolved limestone** seeps down through the limestone and into the roof of the cave or cavern.

- The drops of **water hang** on the roof of the cave, before **losing their carbon dioxide** and **evaporating.**

- Once the water has evaporated, it leaves behind a small speck of calcite. This process is repeated over thousands of years, causing calcite to build up.

- Gradually, an **icicle-shaped** feature made of calcite is formed. This is known as a stalactite.

Fig. 8.8 Stalactites hanging from a cave roof

> **Note!**
> Dissolution is the process by which dripstone features form.

Stalagmites

- Stalagmites form on the floors of caves and caverns and **grow upwards.**

- Stalagmites form when water on the roof of the cave drops onto the floor before evaporating. As the **water evaporates,** the CO_2 in the solution also escapes, leaving behind a speck of **calcite.**

- Over thousands of years, this **calcite builds upwards** to form stalagmites. Stalagmites are much more **shapeless** than stalactites, as the water splashes when it hits the floor.

- When the **water splashes,** the calcite is spread out over a wider area meaning that the bases of stalagmites are thicker. They usually form directly below a stalactite.

Pillars

- Pillars form when stalactites and stalagmites **grow towards each other** and eventually **join together.** Pillars are sometimes referred to as **columns.**

Curtains

- Curtains form when water containing dissolved limestone runs along a **crack in the roof** of a cave.

- As the water moves along the crack, it deposits tiny amounts of calcite, which then hardens. Gradually, a **thin layer of calcite** builds up to form a sheet of calcite. More rarely, this can also occur on the floors and walls of caves, creating **sheets of calcite.** When this occurs they are referred to as **flowstones.**

Fig. 8.9 Pillars form when stalactites and stalagmites join together.

 GEO **DICTIONARY**

Pillars: form when a stalactite and a stalagmite join together

Curtains: a ridge of dripstone that forms along the roof of a cave

Flowstones: sheets of dripstone that form on the walls and floors of caves

GEO **DICTIONARY**

Dissolution: the opposite of solution. Calcium carbonate is washed away in solution by acidic water. When the water evaporates, only calcium carbonate remains, which then hardens into calcite

Calcite: a hard mineral made of calcium carbonate

Dripstone: rock features made from calcium carbonate which formed from dripping water

Stalactites: icicle-shaped dripstone features which hang downwards from the roof of a cave

Stalagmites: shapeless mounds of dripstone that form from water dripping from stalactites onto the floor below

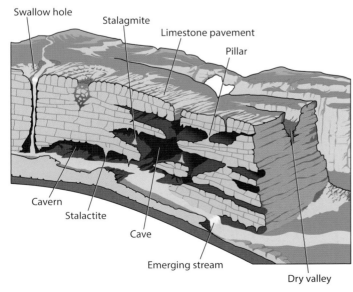

Swallow hole
Stalagmite
Limestone pavement
Pillar
Cavern
Stalactite
Cave
Emerging stream
Dry valley

 Fig. 8.10 Surface and underground features of a karst landscape

ACTIVE **LEARNING**

1. Name two underground features that form in karst landscapes.
2. Name five dripstone features.
3. Why are stalagmites less regularly shaped than stalactites?
4. Explain how stalactites form.
5. Explain how stalagmites form.
6. Explain how pillars form.
7. What are flowstones?

Note!

Students often mix up stalagmites and stalactites, so here are ways to remember which is which:

- Stala**c**tites: C for **C**eiling
- Stala**g**mites: G for **G**round
- Stalac**tites**: hold on tight to the ceiling
- Stalag**mites**: burrow into the ground

Underground Features	
Caves/caverns	Aillwee Cave, Crag Cave, zone of saturation, water table, carbonation, absorbs CO_2, carbonic acid, hydraulic action, abrasion, enlarging joints
Dripstone features	Dissolution, calcium bicarbonate, solution, water evaporates, carbon dioxide, calcite, dripstone features; stalactites, hanging downwards, dissolved limestone, icicle shaped; stalagmite, grow upwards, shapeless, water splashes; pillars, stalactites and stalagmites join together; curtains, crack in roof, thin layer of calcite, sheets of calcite, flowstones, naturally white, impurities

FACT

Calcite is naturally white, but varies in colour from green to red due to impurities. If you look at the heating element in your kettle at home, you may see hardened calcite stuck to it. When you boil your kettle, some of the water is evaporated, leaving behind specks of calcite. As a result, this calcite builds up on the heating element. If you have calcite in your kettle, it is evidence that the water supplied to your home flows across a limestone area.

8.3 Stages of Karst

The weathering and erosion of karst landscapes goes through three stages:

Youthful karst   Mature karst

Old karst   Hums/tower karst

● **Fig. 8.11** Stages of karst development

● **Fig. 8.12** Hums or tower karst are blocks of limestone rock that remain in the old stage of karst development.

1. **Youthful:** At this stage, the limestone rock is **protected by layers of soil** and/or impermeable rock. **Rivers and glaciers** gradually **erode away** the soil and rock, creating river valleys and exposing the limestone to the surface. Carbonation and erosion from the rivers shape the landscape, creating **limestone pavements** and **swallow holes.**

2. **Mature:** At this stage, **rivers disappear** underground, creating **caves** and **caverns. Dripstone features** and **dry valleys** are also formed at this stage. The **Burren** is an example of a mature karst landscape.

3. **Old:** At this stage, the roofs of **caves** and **caverns collapse** as the remaining limestone is completely weathered away. Once the limestone has been weathered away, the more resistant rock is left behind. Only **blocks of limestone** rock, known as **hums** or **tower karst,** remain. Rivers once again flow along the surface of the landscape over impermeable rock.

FACT

The most famous tower karst landscape in the world can be found in Guilin, in south-west China. Search for 'Guilin China' or 'Karst China' on the following websites to explore its landscape:
www.geotimes.org
www.guilinchina.net

Stages of Karst	
Youthful	Protected by soil/rock, rivers/glaciers erode surface, limestone pavements, swallow holes
Mature	Rivers disappear, caves/caverns, dripstone features, dry valleys, Burren
Old	Roofs collapse, limestone weathered away, hums/tower karst, Guilin China

The Burren

The Burren is a 250 km² area of karst landscape located in the north-west of Co. Clare.

Carbonation shaped the surface of the Burren, creating limestone pavement (clints and grikes). A number of small streams which flow from Slieve Elva disappear into swallow holes after flowing through shale and onto the limestone rock. Many swallow holes can be identified on Ordnance Survey maps of the region, as their names start with 'Poll' or 'Poul' (from the Irish for 'hole'). These streams carved out caves and caverns under the surface, e.g. the Aillwee Cave. A number of dripstone features form in these caves, such as stalagmites, stalactites, pillars and curtains. During winter, a number of dry valleys fill with water before disappearing again during the drier summer months.

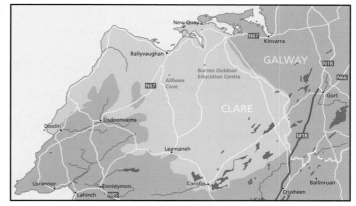
▲ **Fig. 8.13** The Burren

There is evidence of a number of karst landscape features on the OS map of the Burren shown (Fig. 8.14 on page 150).

1. **Turlough:** This is a seasonal lake that typically occupies lowland areas. Turloughs appear when the water table rises above the surface during times of flood. Usually they appear during the wetter winter months and disappear again during the summer. Examples of turloughs can be seen on the map at M 282 046, with the name also giving you an indication. Other turloughs can be seen on the map at R 288 992 and R 264 963.

2. **Caves:** These are found throughout the Burren, with the best-known example being Aillwee Cave, located at M 23 04. As the parking sign beside the Aillwee Cave suggests, it has become a popular tourist attraction. This contrasts with the limestone cave found at R 291 977,W which is not accessible by road.

3. **Swallow hole:** Castletown River disappears underground at R 288 990, suggesting an unnamed swallow hole is located here. Other swallow holes can be found in areas with the prefixes 'Poll' or 'Poul', e.g. Pollaphuca (M 26 02) or Poulbaun (M 25 02). The point where Castletown River appears before disappearing underground again is referred to as the 'point of resurgence' (R 284 980).

4. **Dry valley:** This is a valley carved out by a river which then disappeared underground leaving the valley dry. A steep dry valley can be seen at M 295 021 or at R 30 96.

Note!

The limestone of the Burren formed roughly 350 million years ago, when much of Ireland was submerged in a shallow tropical sea. The area of the Burren was raised above sea level during the Armorican orogeny which occurred 250 million years ago. Layers of soil and overlying rock were scraped away during the last ice age, exposing the limestone to the surface.

CORE 1 CHAPTER 8

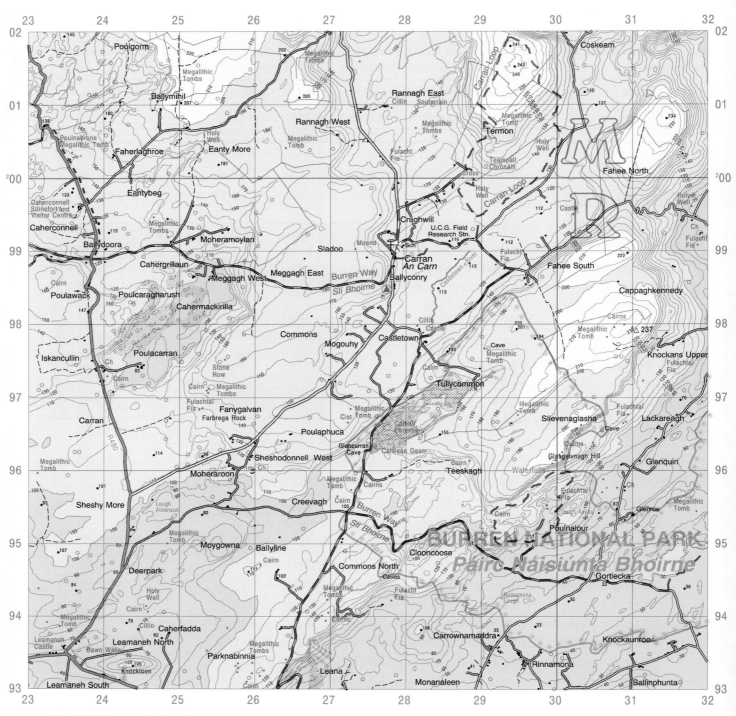

Fig. 8.14 OS map showing the Burren

ORDINARY LEVEL

SHORT QUESTIONS

1. (i) Name the limestone features A and B.

(ii) Name one location in Ireland where features like this are formed.

(iii) Name two underground features which can be found in karst regions.

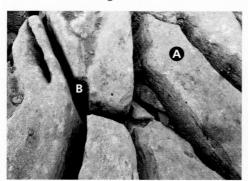

(i)	Features named 2m each
(ii)	Any valid location 2m
(iii)	Two named features @ 2m each

2014 Q4 10M

2. Select the correct words from the table to complete the paragraph below.

Clints
Pavement
Limestone
Grikes
Carbonation

The sedimentary rock in the photograph is called

_____. It is weathered by the process

of _____. This dissolves calcium

carbonate in the rock to form deep grooves

called _____. These grooves are

separated from each other by upright blocks called

_____. This forms a landscape which is known as limestone

_____.

Five words inserted in the correct location @ 2m each

2010 Q6 10M

LONG QUESTIONS

1. (i) Name one example of a karst landscape that you have studied.

(ii) Explain, with the aid of a diagram, how one surface feature in a karst landscape is formed.

(iii) Explain, with the aid of a diagram, how one underground feature in a karst landscape is formed.

(i)	Landscape named 2m
(ii)	Surface feature named 1m Diagram 3m Explanation 5 SRPs @ 3m each
(iii)	Underground feature named 1m Diagram 3m Explanation 5 SRPs @ 3m each

2014 Q2B 40M

2. Examine the diagram of a karst landscape and answer the following questions:

   (i) Name the three features marked A, B and C.

   (ii) Name one other feature found in karst landscapes.

   (iii) Explain, with the aid of a diagram, how any one feature in a karst region is formed.

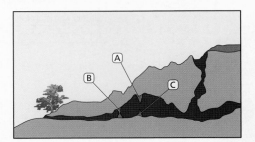

(i)	Three features named 3m each
(ii)	Feature named 2m
(iii)	Naming 2m Diagram 3 labels @ 2m each Explanation 7 SRPs @ 3m each

2012 Q3C 40M

3. (i) Name an example of a karst region in Ireland.

   (ii) Explain, with the aid of a diagram(s), how one surface feature in a karst region is formed.

   (iii) Explain with the aid of a diagram(s), how one underground feature in a karst region is formed.

(i)	Named Irish example 1m
(ii)	Landform named 1m Diagram 2 labels @ 1m each Explanation 6 SRPs @ 3m each
(iii)	Landform named 1m Diagram 2 labels @ 1m each Explanation 5 SRPs @ 3m each

2011 Q3B 40M

LONG QUESTIONS

1. Examine the diagram and answer each of the following questions:

   (i) Name each of the landforms A, B, C, D, E and F.

   (ii) Name any two processes of chemical weathering.

   (iii) State what is meant by the term 'permeable rock' and name an example of a permeable rock.

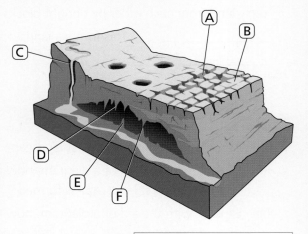

(i)	Six landforms named @ 2m each
(ii)	Two processes named @ 2m each
(iii)	Term and example @ 2m each

2015 Q1A 20M

2. Examine the photograph and answer the following questions:

(i) What is the name of the feature marked A?

(ii) What is the name of the feature marked B?

(iii) What is the name of the overall feature in the photograph?

(iv) Name one process which helped to form the features.

(v) Name the type of rock most associated with these features.

(i)	Feature named 4m
(ii)	Feature named 4m
(iii)	Feature named 4m
(iv)	Any valid process 4m
(v)	Rock named 4m

2010 Q2A 20M

3. With reference to an Irish landscape, examine the processes which have influenced the development of any one underground landform in a karst region.

Named process 2m
Underground landform identified 2m
Irish example 2m
Discussion 12 SRPs @ 2m each

2010 Q3C 30M

In this section we will look at a question from the 2006 Higher Level paper.

EXAM QUESTION

With reference to any one rock type, explain how it was formed and how it can produce a distinctive landscape.

2006 Q1B 30M

This question asks you to combine information from Chapter 6 The Rock Cycle and Chapter 8 Karst Landscapes. This means you must plan your SRPs and order them before you begin to avoid repetition. While the answer is related to limestone and karst landscape, this question can be related to other rock types and related landscape.

Try answering the above question by using one of the following combinations:

- Sandstone and the Munster Ridge Valley

- Granite and the Leinster Batholith

- Basalt and the Antrim-Derry Plateau

Marking Scheme	
Rock type identified 2m	
Formation 7 SRPs @ 2m each	
Distinctive landscape identified 2m	
Formation 6 SRPs @ 2m each	

SAMPLE ANSWER

Rock Formation

Limestone is an example of a sedimentary rock that produces a distinctive landscape [2m]. Limestone was formed in Ireland roughly 350 mya when Ireland was close to the equator [2m]. Over millions of years, the fossils of tropical fish and other marine animals sank to the sea floor and built up in layers (much like to coral reefs of Australia) [2m]. Over time, the weight of fossils began to crush the bottom layers, removing water from the pores, allowing the calcium carbonate to cement the grains together – a process called lithification [2m].

Limestone, like sandstone, contains strata (layers) that are separated by bedding planes with vertical cracks (joints) also present [2m]. Vertical cracks formed in the rock during folding or other Earth movements, making limestone a permeable rock (meaning that water can pass through it) as it trickles through these gaps [2m]. Limestone is made up of a chemical compound called calcium carbonate [$CaCO_3$], which was received from minerals in the bones of the coral [2m]. Pure calcium carbonate is white in colour, but impurities give most limestone a greyish colour. Limestone is Ireland's most common rock, and can be found in areas such as the Burren in Co. Clare [2m].

> Rock type is identified and is linked to the landscape named.
>
> Formation of rock type is sufficiently explained.

Karst Landscape

Karst landscape is the term given to areas that display a similar pattern of denudation as the Karst region of Slovenia along the eastern coast of the Adriatic Sea [2m]. The Burren in Co. Clare is Ireland's best example of such a landscape and was formed by a combination of glacial erosion and carbonation [2m].

These landscapes are best developed in moist, temperate regions that are underlain with thick and widespread soluble rocks, e.g. when Ireland was close to the equator 350 mya [2m]. During the Armorican folding period 250 mya, the area of the Burren was lifted above sea level by folding [2m]. Large glaciers eroded much of the overlying impermeable rock, leaving the underlying limestone exposed to the surface [2m]. Karst regions are formed by carbonation, a chemical reaction that occurs when limestone reacts with carbonic acid [2m].

> Landscape is identified and is linked to the rock type.
>
> Irish example is named and a clear explanation of how the landscape was formed is provided in sufficient detail.

Equation

$$H_2O + CO_2 = H_2CO_3 \text{ (carbonic acid)} + CaCO_3 \text{ (limestone)}$$
$$= Ca(HCO_3)_2 \text{ (calcium bicarbonate) [2m]}$$

This chemical weathering process leads to the cracks of the limestone being widened and deepened, leading to the formation of clints and grikes, creating limestone pavement [2m].

Marks Awarded
Rock type identified 2m
Formation of rock type 7 SRPs @ 2m each
Distinctive landscape identified 2m
Formation of landscape 6 SRPs @ 2m each
Total 30/30

TOPIC MAP

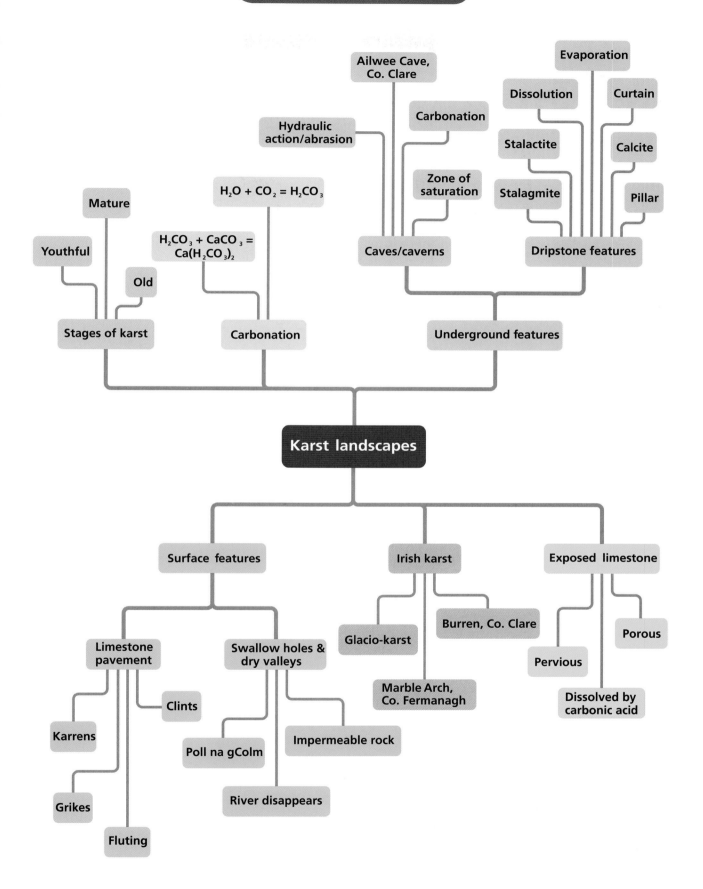

Ailwee Cave, Co. Clare

Hydraulic action/abrasion

Carbonation

Evaporation

Dissolution

Curtain

Stalactite

Calcite

Mature

$H_2O + CO_2 = H_2CO_3$

Zone of saturation

Stalagmite

Pillar

Youthful

$H_2CO_3 + CaCO_3 = Ca(H_2CO_3)_2$

Old

Caves/caverns

Dripstone features

Stages of karst

Carbonation

Underground features

Karst landscapes

Surface features

Irish karst

Exposed limestone

Glacio-karst

Burren, Co. Clare

Porous

Limestone pavement

Swallow holes & dry valleys

Clints

Pervious

Marble Arch, Co. Fermanagh

Dissolved by carbonic acid

Karrens

Poll na gColm

Impermeable rock

Grikes

River disappears

Fluting

CHAPTER 9
Mass Movement

In Chapters 7 and 8, you learned how rock is gradually broken down through weathering. In this chapter, we will examine how these pieces of broken and weathered rock are moved down slopes by gravity. These movements can be slow or fast depending on a number of factors. The movement of these masses of soil and rock is known as mass movement or mass wasting. Mass movement can occur due to natural or human processes.

KEY WORDS

- Regolith
- Slope
- Water content
- Slope material
- Vegetation
- Human activity

- Tectonic activity
- Soil creep
- Earthflow
- Slumping
- Rockfall
- Landslide

- Mudflow
- Lahar
- Avalanche
- Terracettes
- Overcropping
- Overgrazing

LEARNING OUTCOMES

What you MUST know
- A slow process of mass movement in detail
- A fast process of mass movement in detail
- The factors affecting mass movement
- How human processes affect mass movement

What you SHOULD know
- How to draw diagrams of processes of mass movement
- Examples of disasters caused by mass movement

What is USEFUL to know
- Additional processes of mass movement

▲ **Fig. 9.1** Regolith is loosely bound together.

Introduction

Mass movement is the process by which **loose, weathered material** such as rock, soil and mud is moved downslope under the **influence of gravity**. The loose material is collectively known as **regolith**. Regolith is held together poorly, making it easy to move.

Mass movement occurs on nearly all slopes, in small or large movements. This movement can be fast or slow depending on a number of factors. Generally, these movements can occur due to **natural weathering** processes, natural disasters or **human interference.**

9.1 Factors Affecting Surface Processes of Mass Movement

There are a number of factors that affect both the type and speed of mass movement:

Fig. 9.2 Human activity can trigger mass movement.

- **Slope:** The slope, or **gradient,** of the landscape is a major factor in **determining the speed of mass movement.** If the **slope is steep,** then the movement will be **rapid,** while a **gentle slope** causes **slow** movement.

- **Water content:** Water content also **controls the speed of mass movement.** When a small amount of water soaks through the soil, it acts as a **binding agent,** slowing the rate of mass movement. However, when **heavy rainfall** occurs, water **saturates the soil** and **acts as a lubricant.** Therefore, the more water in a soil, the more likely mass movement is to occur. Mass **movement in saturated soils is rapid** and can cause large-scale destruction.

- **Slope material:** The **composition of slopes** will determine the likelihood and speed of mass movement. Slopes made of **consolidated or compacted** materials, e.g. solid rock, are **less likely to move.** However, if the slope is made of loose or **unconsolidated material,** movement is more **likely to occur.**

- **Vegetation:** The **roots** of trees and other vegetation help to **bind soils together,** making mass movement less likely to occur. The **removal of vegetation** through human activity or weathering can **make the slope unstable,** leading to mass movement.

- **Human activity:** Human activity is often the cause of the most destructive forms of mass movement. The **construction of roads,** especially through mountains and hilly landscapes, often causes **disturbed materials to move.** The **digging of road foundations** can leave slopes unsupported, causing them to collapse. The soil removed is often piled on either side of the road to make high embankments. If the embankments are not compacted properly, they can become saturated and collapse. Cutting down forested or wooded areas can also lead to mass movement as there are no longer roots to anchor the soil.

- **Natural disasters/tectonic activity:** **Volcanic activity** often results in **lahars and mudflows.** Lahars are boiling mudflows caused by **volcanic eruptions on snowy slopes.** Earthquakes can also trigger mass movement, as **sudden vibrations** or changes on the surface can **cause the ground to become unstable.**

 GEO **DICTIONARY**

Composition: what something is made of

Consolidated: made firm, strengthened, brought together in a single whole

Unconsolidated: the opposite of consolidated, loosened, not strengthened

Lubricant: a substance which lessens friction

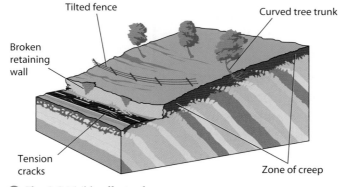

1. What is meant by the term 'regolith'?

2. Why is mass movement more likely to occur on unconsolidated material?

3. List six factors that influence mass movement.

4. Explain how water content and slope influence mass movement.

5. How can human activity trigger mass movement?

6. How does vegetation help prevent mass movement?

9.2 Types of Mass Movement

Processes of Mass Movement		
Type of Movement	Speed of Occurrence	Causes
Soil creep	Slow	Naturally occurring
Earthflow	Moderate	Naturally occurring
Slumping	Moderate	Naturally occurring/human interference
Rockfall	Fast	Naturally occurring/human interference
Landslide	Fast	Naturally occurring/human interference
Mudflow/lahar	Fast	Naturally occurring/human interference
Bogflow/bog burst	Fast	Naturally occurring/human interference
Avalanche	Fast	Naturally occurring/human interference

The speed at which mass movement occurs is **dependent on a combination** of the **factors already mentioned**. In general, mass movement can be divided into four general categories:

- Creeps: soil creep
- Slides: rockslides, slumping
- Flows: mudflows, lahars, bogflows, earthflows
- Falls: rock falls, avalanches, landslides

Soil Creep

Soil creep is the **slowest** form of **mass movement**, occurring on **gentle slopes** of greater than 5°. Typically, soil creep occurs when there is a slope between **10° and 15°**. The two most important processes in causing soil creep are freeze-thaw action and **wetting and drying cycles**. These processes help to **loosen the regolith** on the slope, allowing it to move.

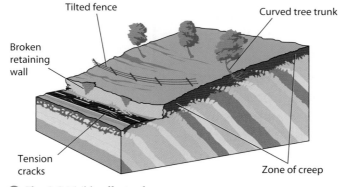

Fig. 9.3 Visible effects of soil creep

Tilted fence

Curved tree trunk

Broken retaining wall

Tension cracks

Zone of creep

Soil creep occurs very slowly, with the fastest movements occurring in regions, such as the **West of Ireland,** that experience **frequent cycles of freeze-thaw action** throughout the year. In regions such as these, soil creep occurs at a maximum of **0.5 cm per year.** Due to the slow rate of movement, it takes many years for the effects of soil creep to become visible.

When **water** becomes **frozen** between particles of rock and soil in the ground, it **expands by 9 per cent, forcing the material upwards.** When the **ice melts,** the particles **sink downwards** again. However, due to the presence of the slope, the particles also move **forwards due to gravity.** This means that the particles come to rest further down the slope than their previous position.

Wetting and Drying

During periods of rainfall, **soil absorbs water,** causing it to **expand.** As the soil expands, pressure causes soil particles to **rise upwards.** Once the soil **dries** again, the **particles shrink** back to their original size and **sink downwards.** As there is now **space between the particles,** they are able to **move down the slope** under the influence of gravity.

Both of these processes are **common in Ireland.** This is due to our **cool temperate oceanic climate** (*see* Chapter 20), which brings **frequent rainfall,** and our **upland relief,** which allows for freeze-thaw cycles throughout the year. The greatest rate of movement **occurs on the surface** where there is **less weight** and **compaction.** Deeper in the soil, **less movement occurs** due to a **higher level of compaction and binding of regolith.** The rate of soil creep **slows to nothing close to the bedrock** as it is composed mainly of **solid rock.**

Vegetation cover is an important factor in determining the speed at which mass movement occurs. Generally, if a landscape is **covered in vegetation,** the rate of soil **creep is very slow** as the roots of the plants and trees bind the regolith together.

Although it is not possible to observe soil creep as it takes place, we can see the **impact it has on the landscape.**

- **Terracettes** are ridges that form on slopes due to the forward movement of soil. These ridges run **parallel across the slope,** giving it a **stepped appearance.**

- Other evidence of soil creep comes from **vertical objects** embedded in the soil, such as **trees and telephone poles.** As a result of soil creep, they **tilt downslope,** while some trees have **bent or curved trunks** as they continue to grow after being tilted.

- At the base of the slope, stone and other regolith can build up behind stone walls, causing them to **bulge or collapse.**

Rockslide

Rockslides occur when **large sections of rock fracture.** Fractures that cause such rockslides often occur along the **bedding planes of sedimentary rock.** When the fractures occur, the **rock dips downwards,** causing the **loose regolith** on top of the bedrock to **slide off** it. For example, if you tilt your table, the items on top of it will slide off.

1. What is meant by the term 'freeze-thaw action'? Explain how it occurs.

2. Draw a diagram showing the visual effects of soil creep.

3. What conditions are needed for soil creep to occur?

Fig. 9.4 Soil creep causes trees to bend.

Fig. 9.5 Terracettes form across a slope.

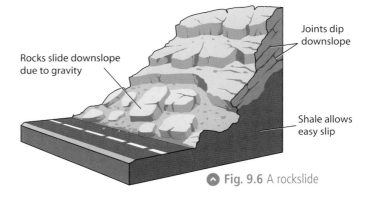

Rocks slide downslope due to gravity

Joints dip downslope

Shale allows easy slip

Fig. 9.6 A rockslide

CORE 1 CHAPTER 9

PATTERNS AND PROCESSES IN THE PHYSICAL ENVIRONMENT **159**

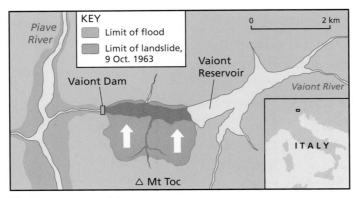

Fig. 9.7 Extent of the disaster in Vaoint, Italy, 1963

Heavy rainfall increases the speed of a rockslide as it acts like a **lubricant**. As this means there is **less friction** between the bedrock and overlying regolith, the rockslide moves at a faster speed. Rockslides can lead to **high numbers of fatalities** if they occur **close to towns and villages.**

One of the most infamous rockslides occurred in **Vaiont, Italy in 1963.** The rockslide was directly associated with **human interference.** Although the rockslide did not directly cause any fatalities, it triggered a tsunami that led to the **deaths of over 2600 people.**

A **dam** was constructed along the narrow Vaiont Valley in order to generate **hydroelectric power** (HEP). As the valley was narrow, the **dam was 260 m high** to allow for an adequate supply of water to build up. The valley was made of **layers of sedimentary rock** that **sloped** gently downwards **towards the reservoir.** As the dam caused the level of the lake to rise, rain that fell on the slopes of the valley was unable to drain away as it had when the river was free-flowing. The **clay soil overlying the shale became saturated** as it absorbed large amounts of water. The water acted as a lubricant, allowing the materials on the slope to **slide into the water,** triggering a 'mega-tsunami'. Waves **250 m high** flowed down the valley, destroying

Fig. 9.8 Rescue work in the aftermath of the rockslide

towns and village below and drowning their inhabitants. It is regarded as a major **engineering catastrophe.** No preventative action was taken, despite evidence that a major landslide was likely to occur.

Slumping

Slumping is mostly associated with **steep slopes.** Slumping occurs when a large **block of regolith breaks free from a slope** and moves downwards under the influence of **gravity.** Slumping is usually caused when the **base of the slope is removed** by weathering or human activity, leaving the **upper part of the slope unsupported.** Due to the force of gravity, the upper section of the slope slides downwards. Typically, the mass of regolith moves along an **inward-curving surface,** causing it to slide **downwards and outwards** (much like the scoop shape of a spoon). As a result of this movement, it is referred to as 'slump rotational slide'. Often, a steep cliff, or **scarp,** is formed on the **upper point of the slope** and the mass of regolith slumps downwards.

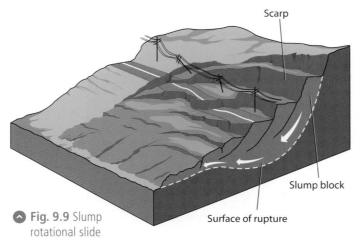

Fig. 9.9 Slump rotational slide

Slumping occurs on slopes made of **unconsolidated material** such as **sand and gravel** and on **cliffs made of boulder clay** (mixture of rocks and clay). Slumping typically leads to **movement over a short distance** and can occur in isolation or in a number of places.

Slumping is commonly caused by **human activity**, such as **road construction**, which can involve digging into the base of the slopes. When the slope is undercut too much, it is unable to support its own weight and moves. Naturally occurring slumping is common along **coastlines and river banks**, as the moving water causes **undercutting**. Slumping is particularly evident along boulder-clay cliffs such as **Cregg Beach** in Lahinch, Co. Clare.

⊙ **Fig. 9.10** Evidence of slumping

Flows

Earthflow

Earthflows are usually localised events that occur on individual hills and valleys after heavy rainfall. Earthflows occur on slopes made of disintegrating rock and loose soil, which cover a layer of impermeable rock such as shale. When heavy rainfall occurs, the water is unable to pass through the rock, causing the soil to become saturated. The high water content acts as a lubricant, allowing the soil to move downslope.

Earthflows can also occur where forestry cover is removed from a hillside. As trees are removed, so too are the roots that bind the soil together. Cutting down of forestry removes shelter from rain and other weathering agents, allowing the soil to become saturated before moving downslope. Earthflows can be fast or slow depending on the water content and vegetation above them. Normally, they are slow moving and not a threat to human life. However, they can cause roadblocks, extensive damage to property and other damage to infrastructure. Visible signs of earthflows are **small bulges** or **torn vegetation** on the landscape.

⊙ **Fig. 9.11** Vegetation tearing and bulging

Mudflow/Lahar

Mudflows occur as a result of **severe saturation of regolith** by heavy **rainfall**, or from **snow melts**. Heavy rainfall or snowfall **soak into the soil**, causing it to become saturated. Once the regolith becomes over **30 per cent water**, it takes on **fluid-like properties** (i.e. the ability to flow), allowing it to move downslope. The high water content **acts as a lubricant**, removing any friction between the **bedrock and overlying regolith**. This allows the mud to move down slopes and valleys at speeds of up to **80 km/h**.

Fig. 9.12 The destruction of Armero

Mudflows usually occur on **steep slopes with little vegetation** cover as the soil is loosely bound. As the mud flows down the slope, it **accelerates due to its own weight** and the additional weight of water. Therefore, the higher the water content, the faster the rate of movement. If the water content is **far above 30 per cent,** the mud has a **low viscosity,** meaning it **travels faster and over longer distances.** A **lower water content** means the mud has a **higher viscosity,** travelling at a **slower pace** over a much **shorter distance.**

More debris is added as the mud flows down the valley as **trees and rocks are swept away** by the mud. When the mud reaches **flat,** open land, it **spreads out and slows down.**

The most deadly form of mudflow is a **lahar,** which occurs as a **result of volcanic activity.** Typically, lahars occur when **ash and lava are emitted from a volcanic eruption,** causing snow on the **slopes of the mountain to melt.** As the lava mixes with water from the melting snow, it turns into boiling mud. The boiling mud **travels rapidly** down the mountain slope, destroying everything in its path, such as trees and houses.

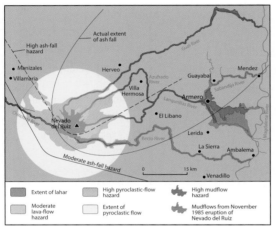

Fig. 9.13 Extent of the lahar from Nevado del Ruiz

Both mudflows and lahars can lead to a **high loss of life** if they occur near towns and villages. The most destructive lahar in history killed over **21 000 people** and destroyed more than **5000 homes** in the town of Armero, Colombia in 1985. The lahar occurred after the **eruption of the Nevado del Ruiz** volcano, which emitted large quantities of lava and ash. The heat from the eruption **melted the snow** on the mountain peak, saturating the volcanic materials. As a result, a river of boiling mud flowed down the valley, destroying the town below.

Bogflow

Bogflows, also known as bog bursts, occur when **peat becomes saturated** after heavy rainfall. Bogflows occur on **blanket bogs** in the mountainous regions of the **West of Ireland.** During summer months, the upper layer of **peat dries,** causing the sparse vegetation on top to wither. In late autumn and winter, **heavy rainfall saturates the peat,** causing it to flow down the slope. Human activity can also lead to bogflows.

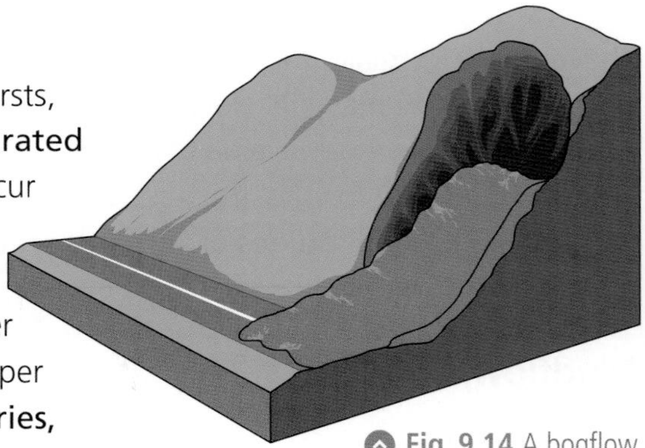

Fig. 9.15 The 2013 bogflow in Derrybrien

Fig. 9.14 A bogflow

Excavation work was being carried out in preparation for the construction of a wind farm in **Derrybrien,** Co. Galway. Large quantities of peat were **excavated from the blanket bogs** of the Slieve Aughty Mountains and left in piles beside the excavation site.

Over the summer, the **piles of peat dried and contracted.** As the peat contracted, **cracks opened** up, making the peat less stable and more susceptible to saturation. During a spell of heavy rain in November 2013, a large bogflow occurred as saturated peat from the excavated piles flowed downslope. The peat became so **saturated** that it flowed for **3.4 km** down through a river valley. Although there were **no fatalities,** water sources were contaminated, which **killed large quantities of fish.** Several acres of forestry were also destroyed, and many **roads were blocked.**

Falls

Rockfall

A rockfall is one of the **fastest forms of mass movement,** occurring on very **steep or vertical slopes.** Rockfalls occur when a **rock, or several rocks, break free from a slope.** When they break free, they roll or fall down the slope at very high speeds. Large rocks can reach speeds of **up to 300 km/h** on vertical slopes. Rockfalls normally occur as a result of **physical weathering** – in particular freeze-thaw

▲ **Fig. 9.16** A rockfall that has reached a roadway

action. As weathering **enlarges cracks and joints,** a piece of rock eventually breaks free and falls down the slope. Over time, rocks accumulate at the base of slopes in **piles called scree.** Generally the largest pieces of scree are farthest from the slope as **larger rocks travel a greater distance.**

Avalanche

Avalanches **are one of the fastest** and most deadly forms of mass movement. They can be divided into two categories:

- Rock avalanches
- Snow avalanches

Rock avalanches occur on **steep slopes** when **scree begins to move** downslope. As it does, it bounces off **other rock** and scree, **dislodging** them also. As the rocks move down the valley, their **speed increases** as more debris is dislodged. Usually, avalanches occur on slopes of between **25° and 60°.** Slopes of **less than 25°** are generally **too gentle** to produce an avalanche, while slopes of **greater than 60°** are **too steep** to allow a build-up of scree.

▲ **Fig. 9.17** Large boulders dislodging more scree

Rock avalanches are extremely dangerous if they occur on slopes **close to roads or housing** as they can crush people and cars and damage buildings. On steep slopes close to roadways, **mesh and fencing** are used as protection.

GEO DICTIONARY

Liquefied: when a substance becomes so saturated with water that it can flow, i.e. it becomes liquid

ACTIVE LEARNING

1. Explain the term 'earthflow'.
2. How can human activity trigger earthflows?
3. What is a mudflow?
4. Explain how mudflows occur.
5. What is a lahar?
6. Give an example of a mudflow or lahar which led to a large loss of life.
7. Nevado del Ruiz is in the Andes Mountains. What plates are colliding to form these mountains?
8. How do volcanoes form at this plate boundary?
9. How do bogflows occur?
10. Name an example of a bogflow.

CORE 1 CHAPTER 9

Fig. 9.18 A snow avalanche in the Swiss Alps

Snow avalanches are probably the best known type of mass movement. Like rock avalanches, snow avalanches occur on slopes of **between 25° and 60°**. They are caused by a **layer of weak or poorly compacted snow** underlying a layer of fresh snowfall (much like loose regolith on top of bedrock). The weight of the fresh snow eventually causes the **poorly compacted layer to break free** and to slide down the mountain slope. Despite what many people think, avalanches are not caused by people making loud noises. Instead, they are caused by either **natural triggers such as a change in the weather or a falling tree,** or by **human activities such as winter sports.**

As the snow flows down the mountain, more loose snow is picked up and carried along, allowing the avalanche to **increase in speed**. Avalanches consisting of '**dry snow**' can travel at speeds of **300–500 km/h,** while heavier '**wet-snow**' travels at a much slower speed of **40 km/h**. Avalanches can occur at any time of the year and can lead to a **high number of fatalities**. On 10 December 2011, an avalanche at the **Titlis ski resort** in Switzerland **killed 11 people**. The avalanche reached speeds of over 480 km/h and travelled nearly 1 km down the slope.

 ACTIVE LEARNING

1. What process commonly triggers rockfalls?
2. How do rock avalanches occur?
3. How can human activity trigger avalanches?
4. Search for 'the most deadly avalanches in history' on **www.independent.co.uk**

 **GEO DICTIONARY**

Dry snow: freshly fallen powdered snow, which is loose and not compacted

Note!
Landslides do not need to be studied in detail.

EDUCATE YOURSELF

Types of Mass Movement	
Soil creep	Slowest type of movement, gentle slopes 10°–15°, e.g. West of Ireland: upland relief, 0.5 cm per year
	Processes of movement: freeze-thaw action, rain freezes and expands by 9%, forces soil upwards, thaws and sinks downwards, moves forward due to gravity; wet/dry cycles: absorption of rainwater, expansion, regolith forces upwards, dries and shrinks, space created allows forward movement, common in Ireland, cool temperate oceanic climate; most movement at surface, less compaction and weight; less movement at depth, more compaction and weight; no movement at bedrock, solid, vegetation cover slows creep, roots bind soil, terracettes, tilted poles, bent tree trunks, bulging walls
Slides	Slumping: steep slopes, regolith breaks free from slope, gravity, base of slope removed, upper slope unsupported, inward-curving surface, movement is downward and outward, slump-rotational slide, scarp formed on upper slope; unconsolidated material, sand, gravel, boulder clay; human activity, road construction; naturally occurring, coasts and rivers, undercutting
	Rock slides: sections of rock fracture, along bedding planes of sedimentary rock, dip downwards, loose regolith slides, rainfall increases speed, can cause fatalities close to settlement, Vaiont 1963, human interference, 2600 dead, 260 m HEP dam, sloping sedimentary rock, clay overlying shale, absorption and saturation, slid into reservoir, 250 m tsunami, engineering catastrophe

EDUCATE YOURSELF

Flows	Mudflow/Lahar: severe saturation, heavy rainfall and snow melts, absorbed by soil, over 30% water content, fluid-like properties, 80 km/h, occurs on slopes with little vegetation, accelerates, speed according to viscosity; volcanic activity: lahar, eruption melts snow, mixes with ash/lava, boiling mud, travels rapidly, Nevado del Ruiz 1985, 21 000 people killed
	Bogflow: peat becomes saturated, blanket bogs, West of Ireland, peat dries, vegetation withers; during winter: rain saturates peat, Derrybrien 2003, excavation work, piles of peat dried, rainfall liquefied peat, flowed down mountain, killed fish, destroyed forestry, blocked roads
	Earthflow: localised, hills and valleys, heavy rainfall, loose regolith, impermeable bedrock, saturation, lubricant, removal of forestry, roots bind soil, exposed to weathering agents, speed varies according to water content, usually slow moving, damage to infrastructure, small bulges, torn vegetation
Falls	Rockfalls: very fast, vertical or steep slopes, rock(s) break free, 300 km/h, usually caused by weathering, enlarges cracks and joints, scree, larger rocks travel further
	Rock avalanche: steep slopes, 25°–60°, scree moves, dislodges more scree, speed increases, protective fencing at base of slope
	Snow avalanche: 25°–60°, weakly compacted layer, loose snow on top, triggered by natural activity or human activity, cause fatalities, e.g. Titlis December 2011, 11 killed

9.3 Human Interference and Mass Movement

As you already know from studying mass movement processes, **human activity is closely linked to most types of movement.** Human activity often alters the balance of conditions on slopes through excavation work, deforestation, extracting minerals and agricultural practices.

Excavation work

Excavation work is one of the most **common causes** of mass movement, as it often leads to the removal of slope bases, causing the upper slope to become unstable. This frequently occurs during the **construction of roads** in mountainous regions where workers use blast explosives to break through bedrock as they **cut into the mountain.** Although engineers are used to assess the safety of such construction projects, the slope's stability can change greatly as a result of interference. A perfect example of this is the Derrybrien bogflow.

⬆ **Fig. 9.19** The road through Fagaras Mountains in Romania involved huge excavation work.

Deforestation

Deforestation is also a common cause of mass movement. Trees **act as anchors** for soil as their roots help to **bind the soil** and other regolith together. The cutting down of trees removes this anchor and causes it to become much more unstable. Added to this, the **trees act as a canopy** (umbrella) which **shelters the soil from wind and rain.** With the trees removed, more rain falls on the soil, allowing it to become more saturated. The more saturated a soil is, the more likely it is to move.

Mining and quarrying

Mining and quarrying can trigger **landslides and rockslides** as explosives are used to break through overlying rock. Also, roads are constructed to the sites to allow for transportation to and from the site. In order to construct the roads, deep excavation work is necessary, which can cause **slopes to lose their stability.** Now unstable, heavy rainfall or **vibrations from work and vehicles** can cause the slopes to collapse.

Agriculture

Agriculture can also lead to mass movement. In the **West of Ireland,** poor farming practices have led to mass movement with the **soil in upland areas becoming thinner** as a result. Agriculture in the West of Ireland is largely subsistent. Many farms are **overstocked** in order to generate as much income as possible. Previously, EU grants and subsidies for sheep farmers further encouraged farmers to overstock, which in turn led to **overgrazing** occurring in mountainous areas. The Irish Government added to the problem as they recommended a stocking rate that was five times greater than that recommended for similar land in Great Britain. Overgrazing led to **less vegetation cover** to bind soil together. Gradually, the peat and gley soil cover in these mountains was eroded away, exposing more bare rock. Two of the areas most affected were **Nephin Beg Mountains** in Co. Mayo and large parts of the **Connemara uplands**.

Changes to the EU Common Agricultural Policy has meant the problem of overstocking has been greatly reduced. This has allowed some of the damage to be reversed naturally. However, **17 per cent of farms in the West are still overstocked,** meaning that these areas will continue to be affected by mass movement and soil erosion.

Fig. 9.20 Exposed bedrock in the Nephin Beg Mountains

CASE STUDY

Note!
This case study links to the Electives of Geoecology and Global Interdependence.

The Sahel Region

The **Sahel region** is an area of **2.6 million km² of arid and semi-arid land.** It stretches along the southern edge of the Sahara Desert, from the Atlantic Ocean to the Red Sea. In 1950, the region was home to 31 million people, while today it is **home to over 100 million people.** This rapid population growth (expected to have tripled by 2050) has had a major impact on the resources available in the region. This **overuse of resources and deforestation,** combined with climate change, has led to soil erosion and desertification occurring in the Sahel. **Desertification is the spread of desert** over arid and semi-arid regions. Currently, the **Sahara Desert is advancing into the Sahel** at a rate of between 5 km and 10 km per year.

Intensive Farm Practices

Soil erosion and desertification in the Sahel are largely caused by human activities such as intensive farming (**overgrazing, overcropping** and **deforestation**), which is triggered by population growth. As these activities are carried out, soil becomes weathered as it is **exposed to extreme sunshine and wind.**

Overgrazing

Until the second half of the twentieth century, overgrazing was not as large a problem in the Sahel. Nomadic farmers moved their animals to areas where there had been rainfall. This prevented certain areas from being overused. However, a 20-year period between 1950 and 1970 saw increased rainfall, leading to **greater amounts of vegetation for cattle** to graze on. **Herd sizes increased** and food supply became more stable as a result. **Nomadic farmers began to settle** in one location, fencing their cattle in and allowing **cattle to graze the same area** of land for a prolonged time. This, combined with **increased drought** since the 1970s, led to the soil structure being damaged, and much soil being blown away.

⌃ **Fig. 9.21** The Sahara Desert is spreading south into the Sahel Region.

Due to rapid population growth and a rise in the number of farmers, the **number of goats and sheep grazing** has also increased. This has led to **widespread overgrazing** in the Sahel region. The animals' **hooves have compacted the soil,** further destroying its structure. Young trees and shrubs are also destroyed by grazing. This reduced the amount of soil humus and **removed the roots necessary to bind the soil together.** The increasingly sparse cover of grasses increased the level of erosion and allowed desertification to occur.

Overcropping

Overcropping occurs when land is **continuously farmed,** which **drains the nutrients from the soil,** making it less fertile. The soil becomes dry, dusty and is **easily removed by wind erosion** and rain. Like overgrazing, overcropping has been caused by the **rapid population growth** in the Sahel region, which has increased the demand for food from the already weakened soil. Despite improvements in farming methods, many areas of the Sahel are being continuously **overcropped and not properly fertilised.**

⌃ **Fig. 9.22** A cattle herd in need of water

Farmers in many countries in the Sahel have been forced into overcropping. Many of the Sahel countries took advantage of cheap loans being offered by developed countries in the 1960s, but are now struggling to repay them. They have had to increase the amount of **cash crops produced from the**

◁ **Fig. 9.23** A cash crop plantation in the Sahel

GEO DICTIONARY

Nomadic: people who travel from place to place to find new pasture for their herd

ACTIVE LEARNING

1. List and explain three ways that human activity can impact on the surface processes of mass movement.

2. Explain how poor farming practices has caused mass movement in the West of Ireland.

3. Where is the Sahel Region?

4. What is meant by the term 'desertification'?

FACT

In the Sahel Region, the number of cattle you own is a measure of how wealthy you are.

GEO DICTIONARY

Cash crops: crops grown to sell on the international market – often to pay off debts

land to sell on the international market to pay off these national debts. The land used for these plantations is intensively cultivated as a **monoculture** (meaning that the same crop is grown there each year). As a result, each year the same particular **nutrients are taken** from the soil. As the land is not properly fertilised, the nutrients are not replaced, and the **land becomes sterile and useless.**

The plantation workers live and use the land on the **edges of the plantations to grow their own food** crops. This leads to overcropping and overgrazing in these areas. As the workers need this land for their food, it is never left fallow. Once the nutrients have been depleted, the soils become dry and dusty, causing the soil to blow away.

Deforestation

Deforestation occurs where **large areas of forest are cut down,** leaving the landscape bare. As well as binding the soil together, **trees provide natural protection** from the intense sunshine and wind. Once the trees have been removed, the **soil is weakened and dried,** allowing mass movement to occur. When rain falls in the region, it tends to be in short, heavy bursts which can wash away the weakened soil in **flash floods and landslides.** As the population rises, more and more trees are cut down to make way for agricultural land and also for firewood (as many people cannot afford any other fuel). Generally, the **trees that are cut down are not replaced.** Once the trees have been cleared, cattle dung, which was once used for fertilising the land, is now dried and used as a fuel for cooking. Without fertiliser, the carrying capacity of the area is further reduced.

The combination of overgrazing, overcropping and deforestation has led to much of the soil in the Sahel becoming useless for future farming. **Land is abandoned,** causing the desert to spread over these vacant farmlands. The land is also becoming drier due to the increasing demand for water (human and animal consumption), and for irrigation. More wells are sunk, and this, along with climate change, is **causing the water level to drop.** Due to this, the Sahel region is now **classified as being overpopulated.** Currently, between **12 and 18 million people are starving** in the region. This figure is increasing significantly each year as droughts are increasing in both frequency and intensity.

Better farming techniques are being introduced slowly but the situation is still getting worse.

Fig. 9.24 Clearing of forestry in the Sahel Region

ACTIVE LEARNING

Draw a topic map of the Sahel Region case study using overgrazing, overcropping and deforestation as your three headings. You can use the topic map at end of this chapter as a guide.

Human interference	Excavation, road construction, deforestation, removes soil anchor, removes canopy, mining and quarrying, rockslides, agriculture, West of Ireland, soils get thinner, overstocking, overgrazing, Nephin Beg, Connemara uplands, 17% still overstocked
Sahel Region	2.6 million km², population 100 million, overuse of resources
	Overgrazing: drains nutrients, increased herd size, increased drought, less vegetation cover, remove soil anchor
	Overcropping: nutrient-deprived soil, not fertilised; rapid population growth, demand for food, high debts, cash crops, monoculture, land becomes sterile, workers' food grown on edges, soil removed by wind
	Deforestation: large areas of forestry cut down, soil protection removed, soil weakened and dried, removed by floods and landslides, land is abandoned, classified as overpopulated, 1–18 million people starving

EXAM QUESTIONS

ORDINARY LEVEL

LONG QUESTIONS

1. Describe and explain any two processes of mass movement.

Two processes @ 20m each
Process stated @ 2m each
Explanation of each process 6 SRPs @ 3m each

2013 Q3C 40M

2. Describe and explain how humans attempt to control the following surface process:
   • Mass movement

Control named 3m
Explanation 9 SRPs @ 3m each

2012 Q3B 30M

HIGHER LEVEL

SHORT QUESTIONS

1. (i) Match each of the letters A, B, C and D with the process that best matches it in the table.

Process	Letter
Rotational slump	
Soil creep	
Landslide	
Mudflow	

(ii) Name any two factors that influence the operation of mass movement processes.

(iii) Name one example of a very rapid mass movement process and name one example of a very slow mass movement process.

A   B   C   D

All answers 1m each

2015 Q6 8M

LONG QUESTIONS

1. Describe and explain two processes of mass movement that you have studied.

Two processes named 2 x 2m
Examination of each process 6/7 SRPs @ 2m each

2014 Q2C 30M

2. Human activity impacts on surface processes. Examine this statement with reference to how human activity impacts mass movement.

Impact on process identified 2m
Examination of impact on process 14 SRPs @ 2m each

2014 Q1C 30M

ORDINARY LEVEL

Mass movement has appeared as a long question on every exam paper since 2006 at both Higher Level and Ordinary Level. So it is very important that you become familiar with all aspects of this chapter. Initially it was not a popular question for students to answer in the exam, but it has become increasingly popular over the past number of years. In this section, we will look at both a Higher Level and an Ordinary Level question.

ORDINARY LEVEL

EXAM QUESTION

(i) Match each of the following examples of mass movement with the letter that best matches it from the images:

A    B    C    D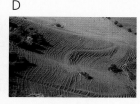

- Soil creep
- Landslide
- Rockfall
- Slumping

(ii) Explain briefly what is meant by mass movement.

Marking Scheme
Each feature correctly matched to images 6m each
2 SRPs @ 3m each

2013 Q2A 30M

SAMPLE ANSWER

Marks Awarded
Processes correctly matched with images 4 x 6m
Two SRPs explaining mass movement @ 2m each
Total 30/30

(i) Soil creep is shown in picture D.
The landslide is shown in picture A.
A rockfall is shown in picture B.
Slumping is shown in picture C.

(ii) Mass movement is the process by which loose, weathered material such as rock, soil, mud and other loose material (known as regolith), moves downslope under the influence of gravity [3m]. Mass movement occurs on nearly all slopes and can be fast or slow depending on a number of factors such as natural weathering, natural disasters and human interference [3m].

The explanation of mass movement is clear and precise, without falling into the trap of discussing individual processes such as soil creep.

HIGHER LEVEL

EXAM QUESTION

Describe and explain any two processes of mass movement.

Marking Scheme
Two processes named 2 x 2m
Examination of each process 6/7 SRPs @ 2m each

2014 Q2B 30M

SAMPLE ANSWER

Two processes of mass movement that I have studied are soil creep and mudflows [2m + 2m].

Soil creep is the slowest form of mass movement, occurring on slopes of between 5° and 15° [2m]. Soil creep occurs at a maximum speed of 0.5 cm per year [2m]. It occurs in areas which experience frequent freeze-thaw action and wet-dry cycles, e.g. the West of Ireland [2m]. Freeze-thaw action loosens regolith through expansion and contraction. When water in the ground freezes it expands by 9°, pushing the soil upwards [2m]. When it thaws again, the soil shrinks back down. However, due to the slope, soil also moves slightly downslope due to gravity [2m]. Wet-dry cycles also loosen regolith, allowing it to move downslope. When soil absorbs water it expands, before shrinking once again when the weather is dry [2m]. Most movement caused by soil creep occurs close to the surface, with very little movement occurring deeper due to more compaction [2m]. Eventually, terracettes form ridges of soil on the slope giving it a stepped appearance [2m].

It is important that you choose two processes that you know enough about to write the number of SRPs required. For this answer, we will look at soil creep and mudflows. The processes explained here are very different, meaning you are far less likely to get information mixed up.

Two processes are clearly identified.

- Each process is explained in a logical manner. Focus is on the process, which is what was asked, rather than the effects.

- Each process is described in a separate paragraph which makes it clear and precise.

Mudflows occur due to severe saturation of regolith on a slope, usually after heavy rainfall [2m]. Once soil has become more than 30% water, it takes on fluid-like qualities meaning it can flow [2m]. The water acts as a lubricant, which removes friction between the bedrock and the regolith, making it easier to move [2m]. Mudflows usually occur on slopes with little or no vegetation as the soil is loosely bound together [2m]. Mudflows move at up to 80 km/h, with a higher water content meaning a faster speed [2m]. When the mud reaches flat, open land it spreads out and loses speed [2m]. Lahars are a deadly form of mass movement caused when volcanic material melts and mixes with snow, leading to a boiling mudflow, e.g. Nevado del Ruiz [2m].

Marking Awarded
Processes identified 2 x 2m
Process 1 explained best 7 SRPs @ 2m each
Process 2 explained best 6 SRPs @ 2m each
Total 30/30

TOPIC MAP

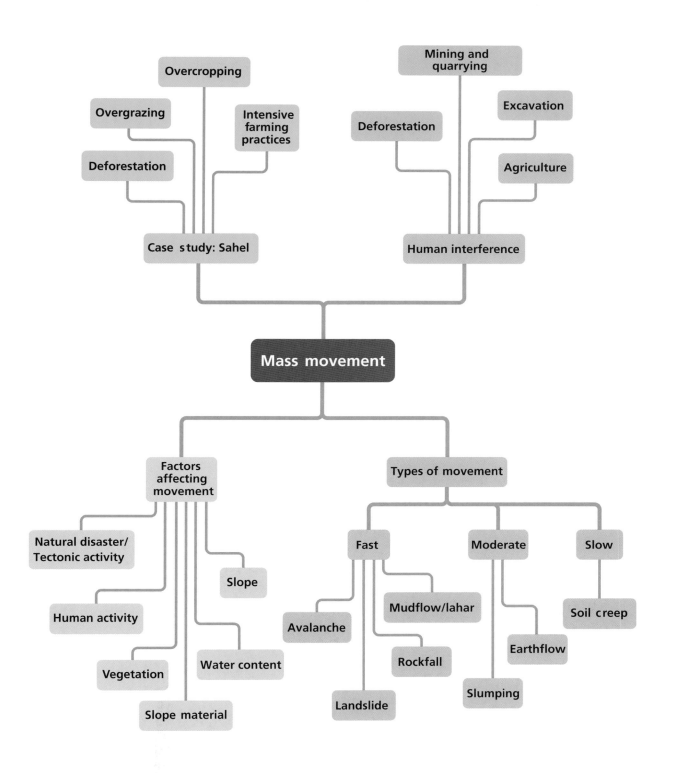

Overcropping

Overgrazing

Intensive farming practices

Deforestation

Case study: Sahel

Mining and quarrying

Excavation

Deforestation

Agriculture

Human interference

Mass movement

Factors affecting movement

Natural disaster/ Tectonic activity

Human activity

Vegetation

Slope material

Slope

Water content

Types of movement

Fast

Avalanche

Mudflow/lahar

Rockfall

Landslide

Moderate

Earthflow

Slumping

Slow

Soil creep

CHAPTER 10

Rivers

In the previous chapters, you learned how rock is gradually broken down through weathering. You also learned the difference between weathering and erosion. In this chapter, you will learn how rivers erode and deposit materials as they flow towards the sea. As rivers erode and deposit along the landscape, they create unique landforms. These landforms are not permanent and disappear over time. River processes are also referred to as fluvial processes.

KEY WORDS

- Erosion
- Transportation
- Deposition
- Discharge
- Velocity
- Gradient
- Turbulent flow
- River basin
- Tributaries

- Watershed
- Drainage patterns
- Dendritic
- Trellised
- Radial
- Deranged
- Upper course/youthful stage
- Middle course/mature stage
- Lower course/old age

- Hydraulic action
- Abrasion
- Attrition
- Solution
- Waterfall
- V-shaped valley
- Meander
- Oxbow lake
- Delta

LEARNING OUTCOMES

What you MUST know
- The processes of erosion
- The river profile
- The processes of transportation
- A landform of erosion
- A landform of deposition
- Human interaction with rivers
- River rejuvenation
- How to identify the main features of erosion and deposition on OS maps, aerial photographs and diagrams

What you SHOULD know
- About a river's energy
- A second process of erosion
- A second process of deposition

What is USEFUL to know
- Additional named Irish examples of studied features

Introduction

Rivers are the most powerful erosive force on Earth, capable of wearing down entire mountains and shaping landscapes over millions of years. The main functions of a river are **drainage, erosion, transportation** and **deposition.** Over 20 billion tonnes of eroded land are deposited by rivers each year. The effects of a river on its surrounding landscape depend largely on its discharge, velocity and flow.

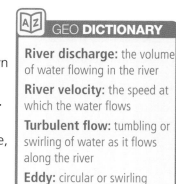

AZ GEO **DICTIONARY**

River discharge: the volume of water flowing in the river

River velocity: the speed at which the water flows

Turbulent flow: tumbling or swirling of water as it flows along the river

Eddy: circular or swirling movement of water

River's Energy	
Discharge	The discharge of a river refers to the volume, or amount, of water it carries. The greater the discharge, the more effective a river will be at eroding and transporting material. Discharges are highest in Irish rivers during the winter months as high levels of rainfall increase the volume.
Velocity	The velocity of a river refers to the speed with which its water flows.
	Gradient: The **steeper** a river's course is, the **faster it will flow**, giving it more energy.
	Discharge: The more water a river contains, the faster it will flow. Irish rivers flow **faster during the winter months** when their volume is greater than in the summer months.
	Shape of the river channel: The shape of the river's channel (also known as its 'wetted parameter') refers to its width and depth. As water comes into contact with the river's bed and bank, it causes **friction which reduces velocity.** If a river has a **wide, flat channel,** then more of its water will come into contact with the river bed, causing it to **slow** down. If a river has a **deep, narrow channel,** less of its water will come into contact with the river bed, allowing it to flow **faster.**
	Roughness of the river channel: If a river channel is uneven, it will cause the river to **slow down** due to increased friction. **A smooth river channel** will allow the river to flow at a **faster rate.**
Flow	Water in rivers flows in a confused or 'chaotic' manner creating what is known as **turbulent flow.** Turbulence, which is caused by the unevenness of the river's banks, causes the water to **tumble or swirl** as it flows. This swirling/tumbling motion is necessary for the erosion and transportation of rock and soil. The greater the velocity of a river, the greater the turbulent flow will be. Young rivers experience turbulence due to obstructions like big boulders in the path of the stream causing it to eddy and scour the river bed (vertical erosion).

10.1 River Basin

A river basin refers to the **entire area drained by a river** and **its tributaries.** It is also referred to as a drainage basin. Each river basin is **separated** from the next by **areas of high ground** known as a **watershed.** The point where the tributaries join the river is known as the **confluence** of a river.

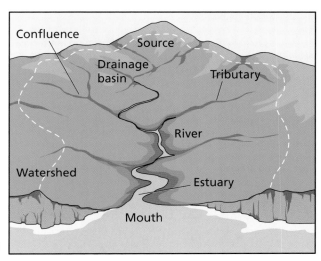

⊙ **Fig. 10.1** A river valley

Differential erosion: erosion that occurs at different speeds due to the difference in the resistance of rocks

Parts of a River	
Source	The beginning or start of a river
Course	The path the river flows along to the sea
Confluence	The point where two or more rivers join together
Tributary	A smaller river that flows into a bigger river
Mouth	The point where the river enters the sea
Drainage basin	Area of land drained by the river
Watershed	A highland area that marks the boundary of the drainage basin
Estuary	Part of a river mouth that is tidal, e.g. the Shannon Estuary

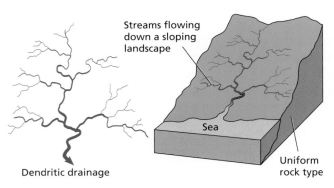

Streams flowing down a sloping landscape

Sea

Dendritic drainage

Uniform rock type

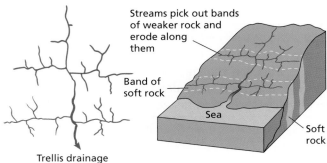

Streams pick out bands of weaker rock and erode along them

Band of soft rock

Sea

Trellis drainage

Soft rock

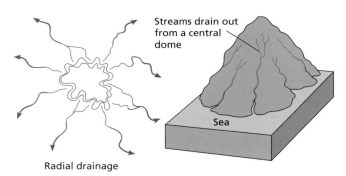

Streams drain out from a central dome

Sea

Radial drainage

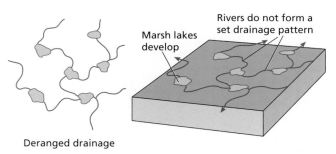

Rivers do not form a set drainage pattern

Marsh lakes develop

Deranged drainage

🔺 **Fig. 10.2** Drainage patterns

10.2 Drainage Patterns

Drainage patterns refer to the shapes a **network of rivers** create over an area. The drainage patterns of a river basin are affected by the landscape and rock types over which the river flows. Generally, there are four different types of drainage pattern:

- Dendritic
- Radial
- Trellised
- Deranged

Dendritic

The dendritic drainage pattern is the **most common type** found in river basins. The name 'dendritic' comes from the Greek word for **'tree'**, which is used because the drainage pattern **resembles** a tree trunk and its branches. **Tributaries (branches)** meet the **main river (trunk)** at acute angles (less than 90°). Dendritic drainage normally occurs on **gently sloping land** with a similar rock type where **differential erosion does not occur.** The tributaries flow **from narrow valleys** into the main river, which occupies the largest valley in the area.

Trellised

Trellised drainage occurs where **tributaries meet** the main river at a **right angle.** Trellised drainage normally occurs where the **larger river has eroded the softer rock** in a valley, leaving the landscape of **harder rock elevated above it.** Tributaries from these ridges of harder rock then flow downwards, meeting the river at right angles.

Radial

Radial drainage forms when tributaries **flow outwards** in **all directions** from a single upland area (like the spokes of a bicycle wheel). This pattern is most commonly seen on a **circular or oval-shaped mountain** peak. As the rivers flow outwards from the mountain peak, they may form other patterns before joining a main river.

Deranged

Deranged drainage occurs where tributaries flow in a **chaotic or disorganised** manner. This typically occurs in **swamp or marshlands** where the river has a **low velocity.** Often the rivers appear to double back and intersect each other. Areas that experience heavy glacial erosion (e.g. drumlin belts) may experience deranged drainage, e.g. Co. Cavan, Co. Mayo.

ACTIVE LEARNING

1. What are the four main functions of a river?
2. Name three factors that determine a river's energy.
3. Explain four factors which influence the velocity of a river.
4. Name and explain four types of drainage pattern.
5. Using an OS map extract of Kenmare (Fig. 14.20 on page 270). Identify and give a four-figure grid reference for:
   (a) Dendritic drainage
   (b) Radial drainage
   (c) Trellised drainage
   (d) Deranged drainage

Fig. 10.3(a) Dendritic drainage on an OS map

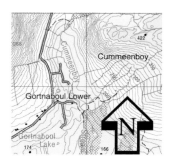

Fig. 10.3(b) Trellised drainage on an OS map

Fig. 10.3(c) Radial drainage on an OS map

Fig. 10.3(d) Deranged drainage on an OS map

EDUCATE YOURSELF

Drainage Patterns	
Dendritic	Most common type, 'tree trunk and branches', gently sloping land, equal erosion, tributaries have narrow valleys
Trellised	Tributaries join at right angles, main river, rapid vertical erosion, tributaries elevated above, flow down to river
Radial	Tributaries flow from single point, oval shaped mountain, 'spokes of a wheel'
Deranged	Chaotic/disorganised, swamp/marshland, low-velocity rivers

10.3 River Processes

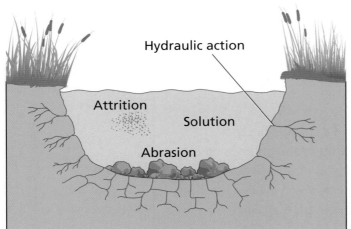

Rivers have three main surface processes: erosion, transportation and deposition. **Erosion** mainly takes place in the **upper course of a river** as water flows fastest here. Erosion also takes place in the middle course. From here, eroded material, referred to as its load, is transported downstream. At the **old age stage,** the river slows down and is unable to carry its load. The material is **deposited** along the bed and banks of the river.

◀ **Fig. 10.4** Processes of erosion

GEO DICTIONARY

Hydraulic action: the force of moving water

Cavitation: shockwaves caused by air bubbles bursting, which loosen pieces of mud and stone

Abrasion: the river using its load to erode

Attrition: when the river's load swirls, causing stones to hit off each other and wears them down

Alluvium: sorted material made of sand, silt and clay which is deposited in sorted layers

Solution: rocks such as limestone or chalk are dissolved in acidic water

Erosion

Large, fast-flowing rivers use their energy to erode the surface of the land. **Vertical erosion** deepens the river bed, while **lateral erosion** widens the banks of the river. There are four main processes of erosion: hydraulic action, abrasion, attrition and solution.

Hydraulic Action

Hydraulic action refers to the **sheer force of turbulent water.** As water flows rapidly downstream, it hits off the beds and banks of the rivers, **dislodging and breaking** fragments of rock as it does so. The greater the velocity of the water, the greater the erosive power a river will have. Hydraulic action can **undercut river banks,** causing them to collapse into the river. This is known as bank caving. A form of hydraulic action known as **cavitation** also erodes the banks of rivers. This occurs when millions of **air bubbles burst,** causing tiny **shockwaves** to loosen fragments of clay and sand.

Abrasion

Abrasion occurs when the river **uses its load to erode the river bed and banks.** Hydraulic action breaks pieces of rock and clay (its load) which are then **transported downstream.** As the river transports its load, it hits off the river bed and banks, loosening other fragments of rock as it does so. Abrasion is the most effective form of fluvial erosion, particularly in **times of flood** when the river is capable of carrying a larger load.

Attrition

Attrition refers to the wearing down of the river's load by a **sandpapering effect.** As a river transports its load, particles of **rock and soil hit off each other.** As they collide, they are worn down, becoming rounder and smaller. Eventually, they are reduced to **fine particles** called **alluvium.**

Solution

Solution refers to the breaking down of rock through **chemical reaction.** Rocks such as limestone and chalk are **dissolved by weak acid** in the river water before being carried away in solution.

Transportation

A river transports its load downstream through **solution, suspension, saltation** and **traction.**

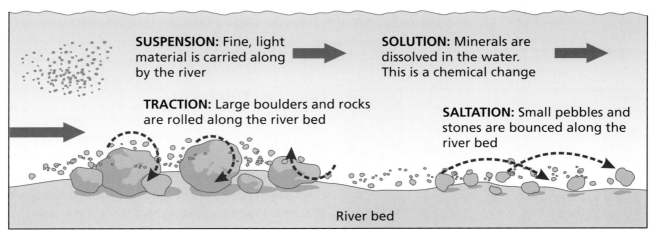

SUSPENSION: Fine, light material is carried along by the river

SOLUTION: Minerals are dissolved in the water. This is a chemical change

TRACTION: Large boulders and rocks are rolled along the river bed

SALTATION: Small pebbles and stones are bounced along the river bed

River bed

 **Fig. 10.5** The processes of river transportation

Solution

Solution occurs when soluble rocks such as limestone and chalk are **dissolved and carried away** in solution. Solution accounts for only a **small percentage** of the river's load transported downstream. Transport by solution needs very **little energy,** unlike the other processes of transportation.

Suspension

Clay and silt particles are **lifted off the river bed** by hydraulic action and **carried in suspension.** A large percentage of the river's load is carried in suspension which gives rivers a **brown or muddy appearance,** especially in times of flood.

Saltation

Saltation occurs when small pebbles that are too heavy to be carried in suspension for a long time are **bounced along the bed** of the river. Hydraulic action lifts the pebbles off the river bed and the turbulent water **carries them a short distance** before dropping them again.

Traction

Traction occurs when large stones that are too heavy to be transported by suspension or saltation are **dragged along the river bed.** This process of transportation requires large amounts of energy and only occurs **during times of flood** or at certain times of year. Most traction occurs during **winter** as the volume and velocity of rivers are greater.

GEO DICTIONARY

Suspension: eroded particles are carried by the river

Saltation: heavier pebbles are bounced along the river bed

Traction: larger rocks are dragged along the river bed during times of flood

Deposition

Deposition occurs when a river **loses its energy,** or is unable to carry all of its load. Sediment deposited by a river is **usually stratified** (layered) as **heavier materials are deposited first.** Finer silt and clay are carried further downstream. Deposition takes place due to three main reasons: **reduced velocity, reduced discharge** or an **increased load.**

Reduced Velocity

As a river slows down, it **loses its energy.** This normally occurs at the **mature and old age** stages of rivers as the **slope of the landscape is reduced.** Human interference can also reduce the speed of a river, especially through **dam construction.** When dams block a river's course, sedimentation occurs.

Reduced Discharge

If a river loses some of its **volume,** its **energy is reduced.** This can occur at **distributaries,** where streams separate from the main river, during hot weather or when a river flows through a hot region. Evaporation occurs in hot regions or during hot spells of summer months, leading to a reduction in river discharge. Again, human interference can cause a **reduction in discharge.** Irrigation schemes use huge quantities of water to grow crops during times of drought. As water is taken from the river, there is a reduction in the river's volume.

 Fig. 10.6 During the summer, reduced discharge leads to sediment being deposited in the river channel.

Increased Load

An increase in the amount of sediment can occur during times of heavy rainfall or when a tributary carrying a lot of sediment joins the main river. During spells of heavy rainfall, more soil erosion occurs in the upland parts of the river valley. This soil is washed into the river, **increasing its load.** When this occurs, the river is **unable to transport all of its load,** leading to the river channel becoming clogged with sediment.

EDUCATE YOURSELF

River Processes	
Erosion	Lateral erosion, vertical erosion; processes: hydraulic action, abrasion, attrition, solution, cavitation
Transportation	Solution, suspension, saltation, traction
Deposition	Reduced velocity, reduced discharge, increased load

10.4 Stages of a River

Most rivers have three distinct stages: the upper or youthful course, the middle or mature course and the lower or old age course. Each stage has its own characteristics and unique landforms. These three stages combined make the river's profile.

- **Upper course:** The upper course of a river is characterised by **steep slopes,** causing the river to move at a **high velocity.** As the water moves quickly, it erodes downwards into the bed of the river (vertical erosion) creating a valley with **steep sides** and a **narrow floor** (a V-shaped valley). **Erosion** at the youthful stage leads to the formation of **V-shaped valleys, potholes, interlocking spurs, waterfalls** and **gorges.** The youthful stage of a river can be identified on an Ordnance Survey map as **contour lines will be close together,** indicating a steep slope.

- **Middle course:** The mature stage of a river has more **gentle slopes** than the youthful stage, meaning that the river's **velocity is reduced.** Both **erosion and deposition** take place here. Erosion widens the valley (**lateral erosion**) as meanders sweep across the valley floor. **Meanders** (*see* page 184) are the most common landforms in this stage, with **braids and alluvial fans** also forming. The mature stage of a river can be identified on an Ordnance Survey map as **contour lines are widely spaced,** indicating a gentle slope.

- **Lower course:** The old age stage of a river is **almost flat,** meaning the **river flows very slowly** towards its entry point to the sea. As the river flows slowly, it is unable to carry the sediment eroded upstream and deposits it. The old age stage is characterised by **wide sweeping meanders** and other **features of deposition** such as **floodplains, levees, oxbow lakes** and **deltas** (*see* pages 185–88). The old age stage can be identified on Ordnance Survey maps as there are **few or no contour lines** present. Also, a map will normally show the river's point of entry to the sea.

 GEO **DICTIONARY**

Contour lines: lines on a map which connect areas of equal height

Braids: where deposited material causes the river to split into several small channels before joining together again further downstream

Alluvial fan: a fan-shaped or cone-shaped deposit of sediment that forms when a river's velocity is reduced

 ACTIVE **LEARNING**

1. What features would you expect to find in the upper stage of a river?
2. Are these features formed as a result of erosion or deposition?
3. What features would you expect to find in the middle course of a river?
4. Why does erosion typically not take place in the lower course of a river?
5. What features would you expect to find in the lower course?

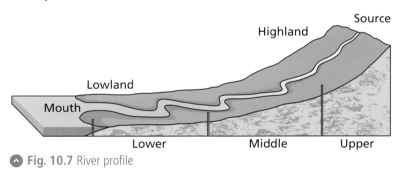

⬆ **Fig. 10.7** River profile

 EDUCATE YOURSELF

Stages of a River	
Upper	Youthful, high velocity, steep sides, narrow floor, V-shaped valleys, potholes, interlocking spurs, waterfalls, gorges, contour lines close together
Middle	Gentle slopes, velocity reduced, erosion and deposition, lateral erosion, meanders, braids, alluvial fans, contour lines are spaced
Lower	Flat, low velocity, wide sweeping meanders, features of deposition, floodplains, deltas, levees, oxbow lakes, deltas, few or no contour lines

10.5 River Landforms

Upper Course/Youthful Stage

Landforms created in the **upper course** of a river are formed by the processes of **erosion**.

V-Shaped Valley

V-shaped valleys are **deep, steep-sided valleys** carved out by rivers. The **river fills the base** of the valley.

Examples of V-shaped valleys are found in the **upper stages** of nearly all rivers in Ireland, including the **Shannon, Blackwater** and **Moy**.

V-shaped valleys are formed in the **youthful stage** of a river as a result of vertical erosion. At the youthful stage, a river has **more energy** than is needed to carry its load. As a result, it **erodes downwards** into the river bed, a process known as **downcutting**. As the water moves down the valley, **hydraulic action dislodges stones and sediment**. These stones hit off the river beds and banks, eroding them further through **abrasion**. The uneven river bed causes the water to swirl, carving out hollows, called **potholes**. Over time, these potholes are **enlarged by abrasion** and eventually **join together**. When the potholes join together, the **river bed is deepened** further.

> **Fig. 10.8** A V-shaped valley has steep sides and a narrow floor.

As the river flows down the youthful stage, it forms a winding course. This occurs as the river **erodes** the **less-resistant rock** in the valley and **flows around** the **more-resistant rock**. The course of the river takes on a **zigzag pattern** as it continues to **vertically erode** the river channel. As vertical erosion continues, the **more-resistant rock is left elevated above** the river channel. The river flows in between these areas of high ground that appear to 'lock' into each other. These areas are referred to as **interlocking spurs**.

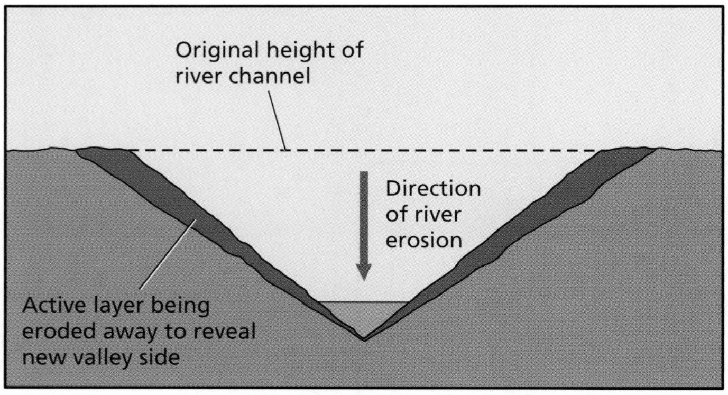

> **Note!**
>
> A question on the formation of landscapes as a result of erosion or deposition has been asked in the exam every year since 2006.
>
> The best way to answer questions on formation of landscapes is to use DEEPD:
>
> Definition, Example, Explanation, Processes, Diagram.
>
> I recommend describing how the processes form the feature as part of the explanation rather than keeping them separate as it helps to explain the formation process in a logical manner.

Waterfall

Waterfalls are **vertical interruptions** in the river's profile that occur due to **vertical erosion** in the **youthful stage** of a river.

There are several examples of waterfalls in Ireland with notable examples being:

- **Torc Waterfall** in Killarney, Co. Kerry
- **Aasleigh Falls,** Co. Mayo
- **Powerscourt Falls,** Co. Wicklow

Original height of river channel

Direction of river erosion

Active layer being eroded away to reveal new valley side

> **Fig. 10.9** Diagram of a V-shaped valley

- Waterfalls can occur due to **faulting,** when a section of **rock is uplifted** above the rest, causing the river to **flow over the edge.** However, most waterfalls occur where a band of **hard rock lies upstream of soft rocks** such as **limestone** or chalk.

- At the youthful stage, the river has a **high velocity** and therefore **large erosive power** which **vertically erodes** the river bed. The soft rock is eroded at a much faster rate than the hard rock, a process called differential erosion. The swirling water **carves out hollows** across the river bed through the process of **hydraulic action** (which is the force of moving water).

- The process of **abrasion increases the rate of erosion** as broken rocks become trapped in these hollows causing them to deepen and widen. Eventually, the hollows spread across the river channel to form a **vertical drop** in the river bed, which the river now plunges over.

Fig. 10.10 Torc Waterfall in Killarney, Co. Kerry

- As the water now **freely flows** over this drop, the rate of **hydraulic action** is increased. Its impact **shatters the rock at the base** of the fall. This constant impact of water at the base of the fall carves out a deep hole known as a **plunge pool.**

- The combined processes of hydraulic action and abrasion **widen the plunge pool,** causing it to **erode into the back wall** of the waterfall. This is known an undercutting. As undercutting continues, the layer of hard rock is left elevated above the plunge pool, creating an **overhang.**

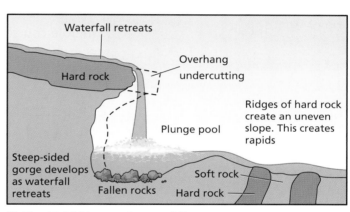

Fig. 10.11 Diagram of a waterfall

- Eventually, the overhang becomes **unstable and collapses** into the plunge pool. This increases the rate of abrasion as **pieces of hard rock collide** with the bed and bank of the river. As these pieces swirl in the water, they collide with each other and are gradually **worn away by attrition.**

- **Solution** also aids the **undercutting** process as water sprays back on the wall of the waterfall, causing it to dissolve. Evidence of solution can be seen by the presence of a **cave** behind the falling water.

- As **undercutting and collapsing** are repeated, the waterfall gradually **retreats upstream,** which is known as **headward erosion.** As the waterfall retreats upstream, a **steep-sided valley** referred to as a **gorge** is created downstream. As the **headward erosion** continues, the length of the gorge is increased.

- Over time, physical weathering **reduces the height** of the gorge as rock is broken down into scree and transported away by the river. When vertical erosion is much more rapid than the rate of weathering occurring in the V-shaped valley, huge gorges such as the **Grand Canyon** in Arizona, USA are formed.

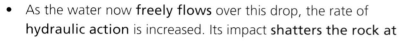

ACTIVE LEARNING

1. Name two features of erosion found in the upper course of a river.
2. Name two Irish rivers where a V-shaped valley is found.
3. Explain how the processes of hydraulic action and abrasion help to form a V-shaped valley.
4. Define a waterfall.
5. Name two examples of waterfalls found on Irish rivers.
6. Explain how a waterfall is formed.

Upper Course: Landforms of Erosion	
Processes	Hydraulic action, abrasion, attrition, solution
V-shaped valley	Steep-sided valley, river fills base, upper stages, River Shannon, River Moy, youthful stage, more energy, erodes downwards/downcutting, hydraulic action, abrasion, potholes join, river bed deepened, erodes less-resistant rock, flows around resistant rock, zigzag pattern, vertically erode, resistant rock elevated, interlocking spurs
Waterfall	Vertical interruptions, vertical erosion, youthful stage, torc waterfall, faulting, rock uplifted, hard rock/soft rock, limestone, high velocity, large erosive power, vertical erosion, potholes, hydraulic action, abrasion, potholes join, vertical drop, plunge pool, solution, back wall eroded, overhang, unstable and collapses, pieces of rock collide, attrition, undercutting, retreats upstream, headward erosion, steep sided valley, gorge, Grand Canyon

Fig. 10.12 Well-developed meanders along the middle course of a river

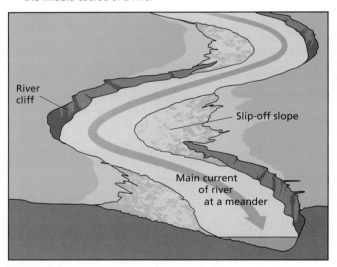

Fig. 10.13 Diagram of a meander

Middle Course/Mature Stage

Landforms created in the middle course of a river are formed by both **erosion and deposition.**

Meanders

Meanders are a series of **S-shaped loops** that develop along the **middle course** of a river. Meanders can be found in all rivers across Ireland, such as the **Rivers Shannon,** Liffey and Moy.

- Meanders are formed as a result of **erosion and deposition** in a series of stages. Almost all river beds are uneven, with some areas of **shallow water (riffles)** and others of **deep water (pools).**

- These differences in depth affect the current of the river, causing the water to **flow from side to side.** The water moves towards the outer bank before hitting off it and turning towards the inner bank again in a snaking motion.

- This movement creates a **small bend** in the river and is the first stage in the development of a meander.

- Water flows faster on the **outer bend** of a river, which causes **lateral erosion** to occur. **Hydraulic action** occurs as the water crashes on the outer bank of a river, dislodging rocks and clay, gradually **undercutting** the bank.

- **Abrasion** increases the rate of **undercutting** as the river's load hits off the outer bank of the meander. **Cavitation** also aids in the erosion as **shockwaves** from bursting air bubbles dislodge more material. Eventually, the bank becomes unstable and collapses into the river, forming a **river cliff.**

- Water flows slowly on the **inner bank** of the meander as it is slowed by friction between itself and the river bank. This causes it to have **less energy** to carry its load. As a result, the **river deposits** some of its load on the inner bank of the meander.

- As deposition on the inner bank continues, sand and gravel build up to form a slip-off slope or **point bar.** Erosion of the outer bank continues, as does deposition on the inner bank, leading to the meander moving from side to side **across the valley** floor.

- Meanders also **migrate slightly downstream,** cutting into interlocking spurs and **widening the valley** floor as they do so. As most of the **interlocking spurs are removed,** their remnants form a slope which marks the widest point to which meanders migrate. This slope is referred to as the **bluff line.**

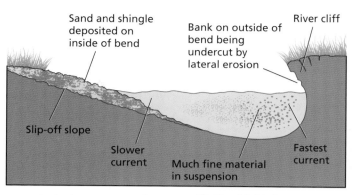

Fig. 10.14 Cross-section of a meander

Floodplains

A floodplain is a **wide, flat floor** of a river valley that floods during times of **heavy rainfall.** Bluff lines mark the farthest border that the water reaches during flood. Floodplains are located in the **mature and old age stage** of most rivers, such as the **Shannon,** Liffey and Lee.

- As meanders migrate downstream, they **erode interlocking spurs.** This widens the river valley. Sediment eroded from the outer bend is **deposited on the inner bend** allowing **point bars** to develop. Over time, this process creates a **flat landscape** either side of the river, known as an **erosional floodplain.**

- During times of heavy rainfall, the **river bursts it banks** causing water to flow over the valley floor. A flood may occupy the entire valley floor, from bluff lines on one side to the other.

- As the water flows along the floodplain, it **loses its energy** and **deposits its load** in thin layers. The material deposited is called **alluvium** and mainly consists of sand and silt. Each time a river floods, an additional layer of alluvium is added to the floodplain. This is referred to as a **depositional floodplain.** These floodplains are extremely **fertile for agricultural** production.

Fig. 10.15 A depositional floodplain

ACTIVE **LEARNING**

1. Name two features of erosion found in the middle course of a river.
2. Name two Irish rivers that have floodplains.
3. Explain how the processes of erosion and deposition help form a meander.
4. What is the difference between an erosional and a depositional floodplain?
5. How are floodplains of benefit to humans?

 EDUCATE YOURSELF

Middle Course: Landforms of Erosion and Deposition	
Processes	Hydraulic action, abrasion, cavitation, deposition
Meander	S-shaped loops, middle course, River Shannon, erosion and deposition, shallow water (riffles), deep water (pools), water flows side to side (outer to inner bank), small bend, outer bend – lateral erosion, hydraulic action, undercutting, abrasion, cavitation, shockwaves, river cliff, inner bank – less energy, river deposits, moves across valley floor, migrates downstream, widening valley, interlocking spurs removed, bluff line
Floodplain	Wide and flat floor, bluff lines, mature and old age stage, River Shannon, erode interlocking spurs, deposition inner bend, point bars, flat landscape, erosional floodplains, river bursts banks, loses its energy, deposits its load, depositional floodplain, fertile for agriculture

Lower Course/Old Age Stage

By the old age stage, a river has stopped eroding as it has lost most of its energy. **Deposition** is the **main process** that occurs as the **slow-moving river** is no longer able to carry its load. At this stage, both the **river and its valley have been widened.**

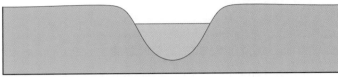

A. Normal river volume

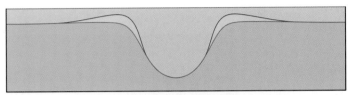

B. Heavy rain leads to flooding – water flows along the floodplain, as it does so, it loses its energy and deposits the heavier and more coarse material close to the river bank. The lighter sediments are spread out along the floodplain

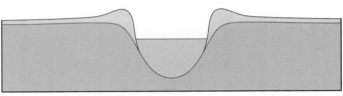

C. The coarse material builds up over time to form a natural flood barrier – these are levees

⌃ **Fig. 10.16(a)** How levees form

⌃ **Fig. 10.16(b)** Developed levees

Levees

A levee is a natural ridge of material deposited along the banks of a river in its old age stage. Natural levees can be found along the old age stage of the **River Moy.**

- Levees are built up over many years after **repeated flooding.** When a river bursts its banks, the water flows over its floodplain, **depositing alluvium** as it does so.

- This occurs as the **water loses its velocity** and ability to carry its load. The larger, **heavier sediments** are deposited **closest to the river bank,** causing a **ridge** to form over time. These ridges build up, eventually forming a **natural flood barrier.**

- During summer months or prolonged dry spells, deposition occurs only on the bed of the river channel. This raises the height of the river, which then overflows during times of flood.

- With floods, the height of the river and levees increase until they are raised above the height of the floodplain. This is known as a **raised river channel.**

- When the river overflows again, the floodplain is unable to drain back through the **alluvium levee.** As a result, marshland known as a **back swamp develops** on the floodplain.

Oxbow Lakes

An oxbow lake is a **horseshoe-shaped lake** that has been cut off from a river. Examples of oxbow lakes can be found on the old age stage of most Irish rivers, including the **Shannon,** the Nore and the **Moy.**

- Oxbow lakes are a **continuation of meander formation.** Although oxbow lakes are a feature of **deposition,** the processes of erosion play a part in their formation.

- **Lateral erosion** continues in the old age stage of a river as the meander continues to **migrate downstream.** At this stage, the meanders have become more twisted and have **pronounced bends.**

- As the meanders bends become more pronounced, only a **narrow neck of land** separates the two outer meander banks. During times of flood, the **discharge and velocity** of the river are increased, as is its erosive power.

- The fast-flowing water is unable to flow around the meander, so it **cuts through the narrow strip** of land between the outer bends of the meander, straightening the river's course.

- Once the flood has subsided, deposition occurs once again. Deposition **seals off the ends** of the meander, completely cutting it off from the main river. This is called an oxbow lake.

- As the oxbow lake is **deprived of water** from the river, it slowly dries up as its **water is evaporated**. Once the lake has dried up, it is referred to as a meander **scar or mort lake**.

- Repeated floods from the river fill the mort lake with **alluvium**, eventually causing it to disappear completely.

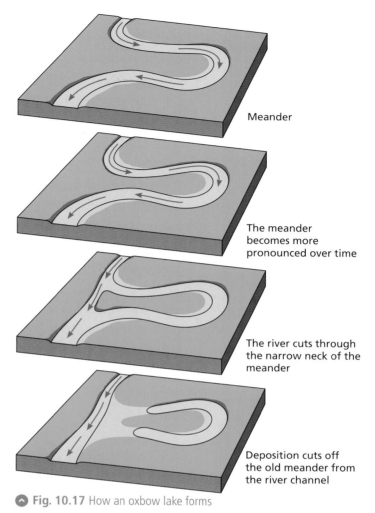

Meander

The meander becomes more pronounced over time

The river cuts through the narrow neck of the meander

Deposition cuts off the old meander from the river channel

▲ **Fig. 10.17** How an oxbow lake forms

Deltas

A delta is a **flat area of alluvium** deposited at the **mouth of a river** as it enters a lake or the sea. Examples of deltas can be seen in the **old age stage** of many rivers throughout Ireland such as **Lough Tay** in Co. Wicklow and the **Shannon Delta** in Co. Limerick.

- Deltas form when a river **loses its velocity** as it enters a sea or lake. When a delta enters the sea, it is called a **marine delta**. A delta that enters a lake is called a **lacustrine delta**.

- Deltas are formed by a combination of **erosional and depositional** processes. When a river flows through its old stage, its **water loses its velocity** and its ability to transport its load. As the river flows into a sea or lake, it slows and begins to **deposit its load** along its mouth.

- In order for a delta to form, a river must have **large amounts of sediment** and a **rate of deposition that is greater than the rate of erosion**.

- Marine deltas normally only form along **calm seas** such as the Mediterranean Sea as it does not wash away the sediments deposited.

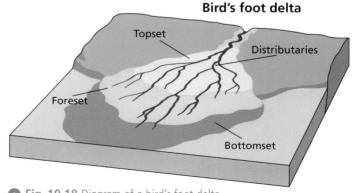

Bird's foot delta

Topset

Distributaries

Foreset

Bottomset

▲ **Fig. 10.18** Diagram of a bird's foot delta

- Due to deposition at the delta, the mouth of the river becomes clogged with sediment, forcing the river to break into several channels caused **distributaries.**

- The deposited material is sorted and deposited into three distinct beds called **bottomset, foreset** and **topset.** Eventually, the sediment breaks the surface of the water.

- Bottomset beds are made up of **horizontal layers** of fine sediment that are carried **furthest into the sea or lake** ahead of the main delta.

- Foreset beds are deposited **closer to the mouth** of the river and are made up of **thick layers of coarse material.**

- As the material is heavier, the river does not have the energy to carry it further into the river or lake. Instead, the **foreset bed lies on top of the bottomset** bed and slopes gently towards the sea.

- As more material is deposited, the delta advances further outwards from the mouth of the river. The topset beds are made of the material deposited closest to the mouth of the river and cause the mouth to become **clogged with sediment.**

There are three types of marine delta:

1. Arcuate
2. Bird's foot
3. Estuarine

- **Arcuate deltas** are the **most common** form of **marine delta.** They are composed mostly of **coarse alluvium.** They extend outwards in a **bow-like shape** and are characterised by **several distributaries** that flow into the sea. The best-known arcuate delta is formed at the mouth of the **River Nile.**

- **Bird's foot deltas** form when deposition occurs along the banks of the distributaries. When this occurs, **small levees** are formed which grow outwards into the sea. As they do, they take on the appearance of a **bird's foot.** A well-known example is the delta that has formed at the mouth of the **Mississippi River.**

- **Estuarine deltas** form when sediment builds up around the banks of river estuaries. The **Shannon Delta** is an example of estuarine delta.

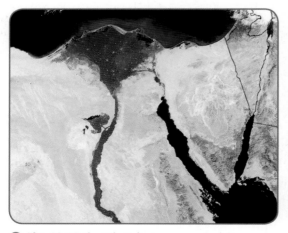

⬆ **Fig. 10.19** The Nile Delta is an arcuate delta.

⬆ **Fig. 10.20** The Mississippi Delta is a bird's foot delta.

Lower Course: Landforms of Deposition	
Processes	Deposition
Levee	Natural ridge, deposition along banks, old age stage, River Moy, repeated flooding, alluvium deposits, sediments are sorted, natural flood barrier, raised river channel, swamp develops
Oxbow lake	Horseshoe-shaped lake, River Shannon, continued meander formation, deposition, lateral erosion, meander migration downstream, pronounced bends, narrow neck of land, flood, meander cut off, deposition, deprived of water, water evaporates, scar/mort lake
Delta	Flat area alluvium, mouth of river, old age stage, Lough Tay, Shannon Delta, low velocity; sea: marine delta; lake: lacustrine delta; estuary: estuarine delta; erosional and depositional processes, river deposits at mouth, large amounts of sediment, greater deposition than erosion, calm seas, bottomset, foreset, topset, arcuate delta, triangular, River Nile Delta, bird's foot delta, Mississippi Delta

10.6 Human Interaction with Rivers

Rivers are an important resource for humans. This can be seen by the **distributions of populations** along rivers throughout the world. As well as providing a source of **fresh water,** rivers are also used in a variety of different ways. Although human interference with river processes can provide many advantages, it can also have negative effects. Some of the main uses of rivers are:

- Hydroelectric power (HEP)
- Transportation
- Flood control
- Irrigation
- Urban water supply
- Recreational use

In Ireland, the River Shannon has been interfered with greatly by humans, as has the River Liffey. Internationally, the Sacramento River in California and the River Rhine in Germany have been changed by human interaction.

1 The River Shannon

The Shannon is Ireland's longest river, flowing over **360 km through 11 different counties.** It divides the West of Ireland from the rest of the country with very few bridging points to allow for crossing. Human interference with the Shannon began nearly **300 years ago,** with the focus originally being on the issues of **drainage and transportation.**

Drainage and Transport

Despite the length of the River Shannon, its **course is very flat,** falling only **76 m from its source** to its mouth. Due to its **flat profile,** the river has a **low velocity** for most of its course, meaning it provides **poor drainage** for the surrounding agricultural land. The issue of drainage is worsened by the natural relief (lay of the land) of Ireland, which has **high mountainous coastlines** with a **flat central plain.**

> **Note!**
>
> A question on human interference with rivers has appeared as a long question at both Higher Level and Ordinary Level approximately every second year since 2006.

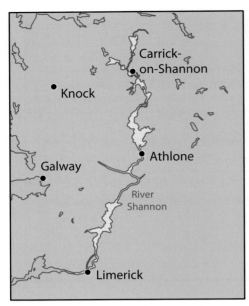

Fig. 10.21 The course of the River Shannon

From 1755 until 1920, the issue of drainage and transport navigation was the focus of human interference on the River Shannon. During British rule, it was seen as vital to improve the drainage for the large expanses of **peat and boulder clay soils** along the Central Plain of Ireland. These soils are **impermeable,** meaning that they flood easily as the water cannot drain away. A number of schemes were undertaken to improve drainage in the Shannon Basin by **widening the channels** of tributaries flowing into the river. Despite sizeable investment and drainage schemes being carried out, the issue has not greatly improved, with **annual floods** still occurring along the river's course.

A number of **canals** were built during this time to allow for the navigation of both **passengers and freight** along the river. Several canals, such as the **Jamestown Canal** and the **Royal Canal,** connected the Shannon to Dublin, making it a **valuable economic asset.** The opening of a railway line from Limerick to Dublin in the 1850s saw a sharp decrease in the number passengers using the river for transport, causing many of the canals' infrastructure to **deteriorate** over the next number of decades. It was not until the construction of the **Ardnacrusha Hydroelectric Power** plant in the 1920s that navigation on the river improved once again. **Artificial flooding** of loughs along the course of the Shannon **raised water levels** for transport. From the 1950s onwards, **tourism and recreational activities** (such as boating and angling) have developed greatly on the river as a result of canalisation, making it a valuable asset to the Irish economy.

Fig. 10.22 Recreational boating is popular on the Shannon.

Fig. 10.23 At the time of its completion, Ardnacrusha was the largest HEP station in the world.

Hydroelectric Power

In the early 1920s, the newly formed **Irish Free State** looked to the Shannon as a potential source of hydroelectric power (HEP). A 1922 report by the German engineering company Siemens suggested building a HEP plant, which was accepted by the Irish Government. The Shannon Scheme **began in 1925** and took four years to complete. At its time of completion in 1929, it was the largest HEP station in the world.

Ardnacrusha in the lower course of the Shannon in Co. Clare was chosen as the site for the power station. HEP plants are normally constructed in the upper or middle courses of rivers to make use of **higher water velocity to turn turbines.** However, the Shannon's flat profile meant that the upper and middle courses were not suitable. The upper course of the river is relatively flat, falling only 18 m in the first 224 km. However, in the lower course of the Shannon, the river falls by **30 m in just 20 km.**

A **weir and canal** were built in the nearby village of Parteen. The weir directed two-thirds of the water from the Shannon to the **Headrace Canal.** The weir also allowed the water in three major loughs to rise: **Lough Derg, Lough Allen** and **Lough Ree.** As the water levels rose, the loughs **flooded bordering farmland.** The farmers affected were paid compensation. These loughs are kept at artificially high levels to ensure enough water remains available to the Ardnacrusha station.

From the weir, the water flows for 12.8 km along the canal to the turbines at Ardnacrusha. The canal was constructed by building **embankments** of up to **18 m in height** to stop the surrounding land from flooding. As the path of the canal cut through several roads, three large bridges had to be built across it.

⬆ **Fig. 10.24** Ardnacrusha Dam

Positive Impacts of Interference

The building of several canals has made the Shannon more accessible for **tourism and recreation.** Lough Derg has become a popular tourist attraction for **watersports, fishing** and **scenic tours.**

At the time of its completion, Ardnacrusha was capable of producing enough **electricity to power the whole of Ireland** and was hailed around the world as a **major engineering accomplishment.** Although it is no longer able to meet the energy demands for Ireland, it is still an important producer of electricity for the country.

⬆ **Fig. 10.25** Flooding along the River Shannon

Negative Impacts of Interference

As much of the Shannon's volume is now diverted to the HEP station, the amount of **water flowing downstream** is greatly **reduced.** As the demand for electricity increased across the country, more water was diverted to the canal. The ESB are in charge of the water flow and are required to allow a certain volume of water to flow down the natural river channel. However, due to the high demand for electricity only the minimum discharge allowed flows down the natural channel. This has led to **river losing its energy** and caused large amounts of **sediment to be deposited** in the river channel. In some areas, parts of the **river bed** have **dried up** completely, which has destroyed much of the **aquatic life** in this section of the river.

Fish stocks such as the salmon and eel have been **depleted** on the lower course of the Shannon. As the level of water flowing down the natural channel has been reduced, salmon migrating downstream are choosing the Headrace Canal instead of the traditional course.

Winter floods on the Shannon have become much **more severe** due to the **artificially high levels** of its loughs. During the wettest months of the year, the water levels rise, causing the **river to burst its banks.** The floods of **December 2015 and January 2016** saw the Shannon burst its banks in several locations, causing damage to several towns built on its banks, such as Carrick-on-Shannon.

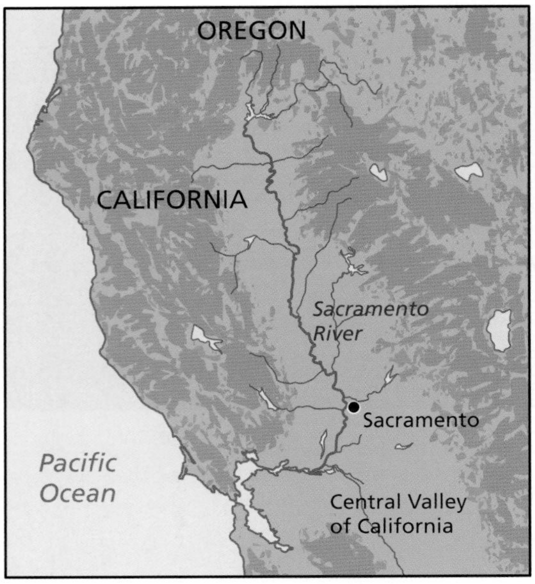

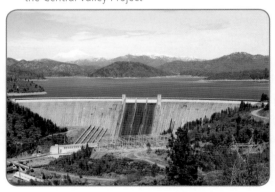

Fig. 10.26 Central Valley California

2 Central Valley Project

The Central Valley Project began in the late **1937** as an attempt to **irrigate agricultural land** in the drought-stricken **San Joaquin Valley** in California. The project also aimed to provide a **water supply** to nearby urban cities such as San Francisco.

The Central Valley is occupied by two rivers: the **Sacramento River,** which **drains the northern section** of the valley, and the **San Joaquin River,** which **drains the southern section** of the valley. Rain falls **unevenly** in the valley, with **75 per cent of precipitation** occurring in the **northern half** of the valley and just **25 per cent in the south.** Rainfall does not occur throughout the year, with most precipitation occurring **during a five-month spell** from December to April. During the wet season, the land surrounding the Sacramento River was **flooded by intense rainfall.** During the dry summer months, **drought occurred,** especially in the **southern half** of the valley.

GEO **DICTIONARY**

Aqueduct: a bridge carrying a waterway over a valley or other gap

This left a **shortage of water** during the **summer months** when crops were growing. Initially, farmers began irrigating their crops by **pumping water from local wells.** However, as the amount of groundwater being used for irrigation during this time was far greater than the amount being replenished by winter rains, the **wells began to dry up.** This caused two major problems for the population of Central Valley.

- First, by using groundwater during dry season, less water was returning to the rivers, **lowering their discharge.** The low water discharge allowed salt water from the **San Francisco Bay** to flow further inland to areas where crops were grown. This damaged the crops and farmland further.
- Second, **soil erosion** began to occur due to a lack of water in the soil. As the soil dried, it turned to dust before being **blown away by winds.**

Fig. 10.27 One of the dams constructed as part of the Central Valley Project

Starting in 1937, dams were built to store water that falls during the rainy months for use during the summer. In total, **22 reservoirs were built** on the Sacramento and San Joaquin Rivers. These store over **13.5 billion cubic metres** of water. A series of **canals and aqueducts** were built to transport water to the southern part of the valley to be used for the irrigation of agricultural land.

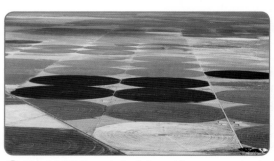

Fig. 10.28 Crop circles irrigated from water piped from the Sacramento River

Positive Impacts of Interference

The project **transformed agriculture** in the region, making it one of the most **intensive food-producing regions** in the world. More than **230 crops are now grown in the region,** accounting for **8 per cent of the United States' food output.** It produces a total of 50 per cent of the fruit and vegetables grown in the United States. It is now known as the **'breadbasket of America'.**

More of the water is used to provide a **safe water supply to urban areas** such as San Francisco. In total, the Central Valley provides water to more than **2 million people.**

Negative Impacts of Interference

Although agriculture improved, there have been a number of **negative effects** caused by human interference with the Central Valley. The construction of reservoirs caused sections of the river to rise to **unnatural heights,** which **flooded land** nearby. In doing so, historical Native American lands were submerged and the remaining tribe members forced to leave.

Intense heat during the summer months **evaporates millions of litres** of water from the reservoirs. This causes the **salt content** of the water to increase. This high salt content can **burn the crops** it is used to irrigate and gradually **turn the soil toxic.**

A **severe drought** began in December 2013 and is still ongoing. The drought has threatened to **destroy the livelihoods of farmers** throughout the valley. The normally reliable **rains** that fall for five months of the year have **failed to arrive,** causing many of the reservoirs to completely dry up. If this drought continues, agriculture in the region will become unviable.

▲ **Fig. 10.29** The Central Valley Project allows for intense cultivation of land.

▲ **Fig. 10.30** The ongoing Californian drought has seen many of the reservoirs dry up and irrigation schemes fail.

FACT

As part of the New Deal, an economic plan for recovery during the Great Depression of the 1930s, the US government invested in the building of several HEP plants along the western coast of the country.

 EDUCATE YOURSELF

	Human Interaction
River Shannon	Drainage, transportation, hydroelectric power
	Drainage and transport: flat course, low velocity, poor drainage, high mountainous coastline, flat central plain, peat and boulder clay, impermeable, widened channel, annual floods, canals for transport, passengers and freight, Jamestown Canal, Royal Canal, valuable economic asset, infrastructure deteriorated, artificial flooding, tourism and recreation
	HEP: 1925, Ardnacrusha, high velocity, 30 m drop in 20 km, Headrace Canal, Lough Derg, Lough Allen, Lough Ree, flooded bordering farmland, 18 m embankments
	Impacts: tourism and recreation, water sports, fishing, scenic tourism, electricity for Ireland, reduced discharge, loses energy, sediment deposited, river bed dries up, depleted fish stocks, severe winter floods, December 2015 and January 2016
Central Valley Project	1937, irrigate agricultural land, San Joaquin Valley, Sacramento Valley, uneven precipitation, floods in winter, drought in summer, shortage of water, wells reduced groundwater, soil erosion, dams built, 22 reservoirs, 13.5 billion m³ of water, canals, aqueducts, water to 2 million people
	Impacts: transformed agriculture, intense food production, 230 crops, 8% of US food output, safe water supply, flooding of land, water evaporates, high salt content, poisons land, burns crop, severe drought December 2013, ongoing, crops destroyed

10.7 Identifying Fluvial Landforms on an OS Map

Upper Course

Fig. 10.31(a) Waterfall

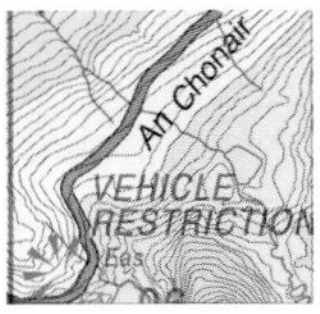

Fig. 10.31(b) V-shaped valley

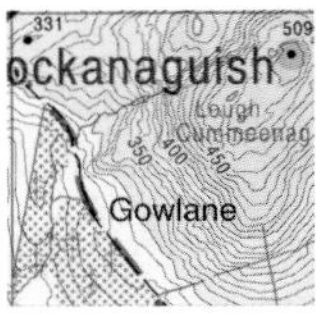

Fig. 10.31(c) Interlocking spurs

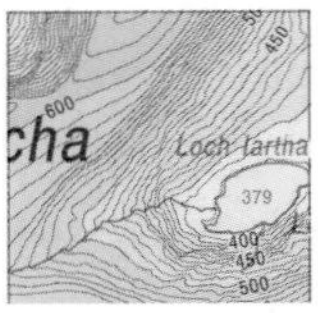

As you have already learned, upper course landforms are created as result of erosion. The three most common upper course landforms identifiable on an OS map are:

- Waterfalls, which occur where there is a sudden change in the river's profile, causing a vertical drop. It is often marked on an OS map with a blue label saying 'Waterfall' but can also be identified where closely packed contour lines cross a river.

- V-shaped valleys, which are narrow, steep-sided valleys with contour lines normally joining at close to right angles.

- Interlocking spurs, which occur as the river winds its way around obstacles such as resistant rock. On an OS map, interlocking spurs look similar to meanders, but they occur in upland areas (youthful stage). You can identify interlocking spurs on an OS map by bends in a river surrounded by upland areas, which have steep contour lines.

Middle Course

Landforms on the middle course of a river occur due to a combination of erosion and deposition:

- Meanders are naturally occurring bends that are formed in a river by erosion on the outer bend and deposition on the inner bend. You can identify meanders on the map as the river will wind and will be surrounded by flat land with few or no contour lines.

- Floodplains are level areas of land at either side of the river. During times of heavy rain, the river floods over this area covering it in alluvium. It is noticeable on an OS map by an absence of contour lines close to a river's banks.

- Braiding typically occurs along the middle course of rivers with a large load. You can identify braiding on the map, as the river splits into several small channels of water running through deposited sediment.

Fig. 10.32(a) Meander

Fig. 10.32(b) Floodplain

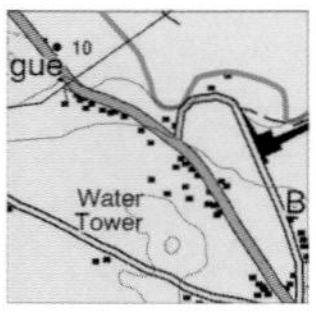

Fig. 10.32(c) Braiding

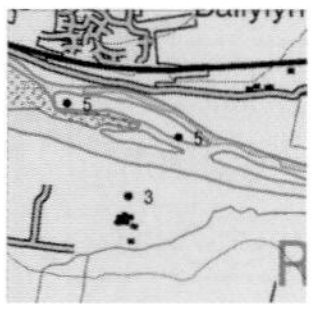

Lower Course

Landforms on the lower course of a river occur due to deposition. The most common features are:

- Oxbow lakes, which form when a river cuts through a meander to take a more direct path. In Fig. 10.33(a), deposition has not yet cut the old meander away from the main river channel.

- Levees, which form when ridges of material build up along the banks of a river. Irish rivers do not have many well-developed natural levees, with only small ones evident along the River Moy.

⌃ **Fig. 10.33(a)** Oxbow lake

⌃ **Fig. 10.33(b)** Levees

EXAM QUESTIONS

ORDINARY LEVEL

SHORT QUESTIONS

2015 Q2 10M

1. Examine the diagram showing river landforms and answer each of the following questions.

   (i) Match each of the letters A, B, C and D with the landform that best matches it.

Landform	Letter
Levee	
Floodplain	
Meander	
Oxbow lake	

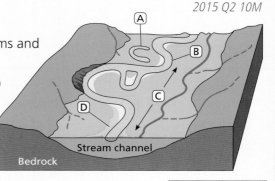

(i) 4 letters @ 2m each
(ii) Correct box 2m

   (ii) Indicate whether the landforms named above are most associated with the youthful stage of a river or the old age stage of a river, by ticking the correct box.

   ☐ Youthful Stage
   ☐ Old Age Stage

LONG QUESTIONS

1. Explain, with the aid of diagrams, the formation of any two landforms.
   2015 Q1 B 40M

Each landform @ 20m each
Landform named 1m
Diagram(s) 2 aspects @ 2m each
Formation explained 5 SRPs @ 3m each

2. Examine how humans interact with river processes.
   2015 Q3 C 30M

Interaction named 3m
Examination 9 SRPs @ 3m each

3. Describe and explain how humans attempt to control river processes.
   2014 Q2 C 30M

Control identified 3m
Description and explanation 9 SRPs @ 3m each

4. Explain, with the aid of a diagram, how any one Irish landform is formed from river action.
   2010 Q1 B 30M

Landform named 2m
Diagram 2 aspects @ 2m each
Formation explained 8 SRPs @ 3m each

LONG QUESTIONS

1. Explain the formation of one landform of erosion and one landform of deposition that you have studied.

| Landform of erosion named 2m |
| Landform of deposition named 2m |
| Landform of erosion explained 6/7 SRPs @ 2m each |
| Landform of deposition explained 6/7 SRPs @ 2m each |

2014 Q2B 30M

2. Explain, with the aid of a labelled diagram, the formation of one landform of deposition that you have studied.

| Named landform 2m |
| Labelled diagram 4m |
| Explanation 12 SRPs @ 2m each |

2012 Q2B 30M

3. Examine, with reference to examples you have studied, how human activities have impacted on river processes.

| Human activity identified 2m |
| Impact identified 2m |
| Named example 2m |
| Examination 12 SRPs @ 2m each |

2012 Q1C 30M

Questions on landscape development and surface processes have appeared every year since 2006 at both Higher Level and Ordinary Level. So it is an important section to be prepared. A question on human interaction appears regularly on papers at both levels. In this section, we will look at a question on each of these topics. The answers will both be answered to a Higher Level standard as the information required at both levels is almost identical.

Marking Scheme	
Impact on process identified 2m	
Examination 14 SRPs @ 2m each	

EXAM QUESTION

'Human activity impacts on surface processes.'
Examine this statement with reference to the impact of dams on rivers.

2014 Q1C 30M

SAMPLE ANSWER

The River Shannon in Ireland and the Sacramento River in Central Valley, California are two examples of rivers whose natural processes have been altered as a result of damming [2m]. A hydroelectric power station was built along the lower course of the River Shannon at Ardnacrusha in Co. Clare [2m]. Normally dams are constructed along the upper and middle courses of rivers, however the Shannon's flat profile limited the options to Ardnacrusha. The Shannon's profile drops 30 m over 20 km in the lower course, increasing the velocity

This question is more specific than those asked in many other years. Information can refer only to the impact of dams on river processes.

of the river [2m]. A weir was built across the river to allow water levels to rise in three major loughs: Lough Derg, Lough Allen and Lough Ree [2m]. As the water levels rose to an artificially high level, farmland bordering the river was flooded and farmers were paid compensation for their loss of land [2m]. 18 m high embankments were built along the banks of a newly constructed canal, which brought water to the power station, in order to stop the surrounding land from flooding [2m].

As much of the water from the river is diverted away from its natural course towards the station, the volume of water flowing downstream is greatly reduced, causing it to lose energy [2m]. With less energy, the river is no longer able to transport much of its load, leading to large amounts of sediment being deposited in the river channel downstream [2m]. In some areas, the water has dried up completely and destroyed much of the river's aquatic life. Winter flooding has become much more severe due to the artificially high water levels of its loughs [2m]. In December 2015, the Shannon burst its banks in several locations after heavy rainfall, causing damage to many towns [2m]. Deposition has also impacted on flooding as alluvium dropped on the river bed raises the water levels leading to increased flooding [2m].

The Sacramento River was dammed in order to provide a water supply to the drought-stricken San Joaquin Valley. Reservoirs were built across the river to allow water levels to rise to unnatural heights [2m]. The damming of the river has trapped billions of litres of water behind the dam, which reduced the river's volume [2m]. However, due to the intense heat of the summer months, millions of litres of water evaporate, which increases the salts levels [2m]. This salt content poisons farmland. The loss of the water through evaporation of the river, combined with drought, has seen the Sacramento River's volume drop more each year [2m]. An ongoing drought which began in 2013 has led to many reservoirs drying up completely, leaving only dry river channels [2m].

Named examples are given which provide a focus for the answer.

Damming has been linked to increased river flooding, reduced river energy, reduced volume and increased deposition.

Marks Awarded
Impact on process identified 2m
Examination best 14 SRPs @ 2m each
Total 30/30

EXAM **QUESTION**

Examine the impact of the processes of erosion on the formation of one fluvial landform that you have studied.

Marking Scheme
Processes of erosion 2 + 2m
Landform named 2m
Examination 12 SRPs @ 2m each

2015 Q1B 30M

SAMPLE **ANSWER**

D A waterfall is a vertical interruption on a river's profile, found in the youthful stage of a river. It is formed as a result of erosional processes [2m].

E.g. An example of a waterfall is Torc in Killarney, Co. Kerry [2m].

E/P Most waterfalls occur where a band of hard rock lies upstream of soft rock such as limestone or chalk [2m]. The main processes involved in the formation of a landform are hydraulic action – the force of moving water – and abrasion – the river using its load to erode [2m]. A river leading to a waterfall has a steep gradient which means the water has a high velocity, giving it more erosive power. This allows it to erode vertically and deepen the river channel [2m]. As the water crashes off the river bed, hydraulic action wears away the soft rock at a much faster rate than the hard rock. This is known as differential erosion [2m]. The process of abrasion increases the rate of vertical erosion as the rock broken off by hydraulic action becomes trapped in hollows, deepening and widening them further [2m]. Eventually, these processes form a drop in the river channel, causing the water to flow from the resistant hard rock and plunge onto the softer rock below [2m]. Hydraulic action increases as the water flows freely over the edge and shatters the rock below, carving

A clear definition is given.

A correct example of the feature is named.

The explanation uses the processes of hydraulic action and abrasion clearly in terms of their role in creating the landform.

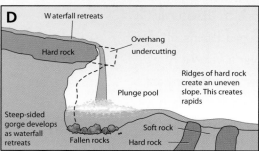

out a deep hole called a plunge pool [2m]. Both processes widen and deepen the plunge pool. They erode backwards into the wall of the waterfall, underneath the layer of hard rock. This is known as undercutting [2m].

As undercutting continues, the layer of hard rock is left sticking out above the plunge pool, creating an overhang [2m]. Eventually, the overhang becomes unstable and collapses into the plunge pool below, increasing the rate of abrasion as the pieces of hard rock collide with the bed and bank of the river [2m]. Solution also aids undercutting as slightly acidic water sprays against the wall of the waterfall, causing it to dissolve [2m]. Evidence of this process can be seen by the presence of a cave behind the falling water [2m]. As the undercutting and collapsing are repeated, the waterfall gradually retreats upstream. This referred to as headward erosion [2m].

Answer is clear and well structured with the DEEPD method of answering.

Marks Awarded
Processes of erosion 2m + 2m
Landform named 2m
Explanation 12 SRPs @ 24m
Total 30/30

TOPIC MAP

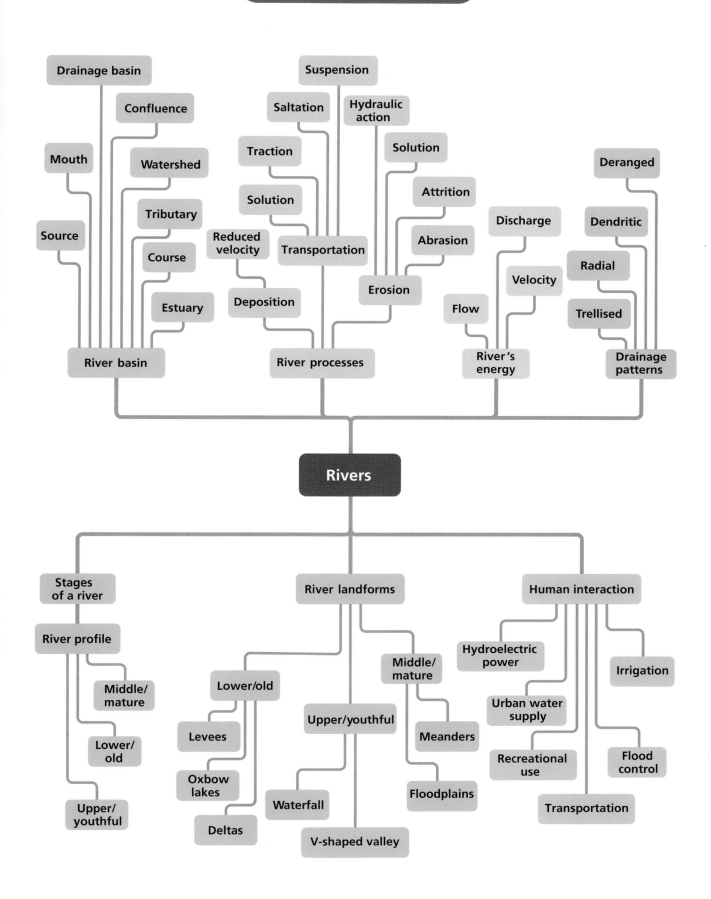

CHAPTER 11

Coasts

In this chapter, you will learn about how the movement of the Earth's oceans can alter the coasts of continents and countries.

Note!
You must study either Chapter 11 or Chapter 12 in detail, but make sure to familiarise yourself with the appearance of the landforms in both chapters.

KEY WORDS

- Waves
- Fetch
- Crest
- Swash
- Backwash
- Destructive waves
- Constructive waves
- Wave refraction
- Hard/soft coasts
- Hydraulic action
- Abrasion
- Attrition

- Compression
- Solution
- Cliff
- Wave-cut platform
- Undercutting
- Coastal retreat
- Bays and headlands
- Sea stump
- Blowhole
- Geo
- Longshore drift
- Beach

- Youghal
- Shingle
- Backshore
- Foreshore
- Storm beach
- Marram grass
- Dunes
- Sandspit
- Tombolo
- Lagoon
- Coastal protection

LEARNING OUTCOMES

What you MUST know

- The processes of erosion, transportation and deposition
- A landform of erosion
- A landform of deposition
- Human interaction with coasts
- Coastal protection methods
- How to recognise coastal landforms on diagrams, photographs and OS maps

What you SHOULD know

- A second process of erosion
- A second process of deposition
- Destructive/constructive waves
- How wind drives waves

What is USEFUL to know

- The parts of a wave

Introduction

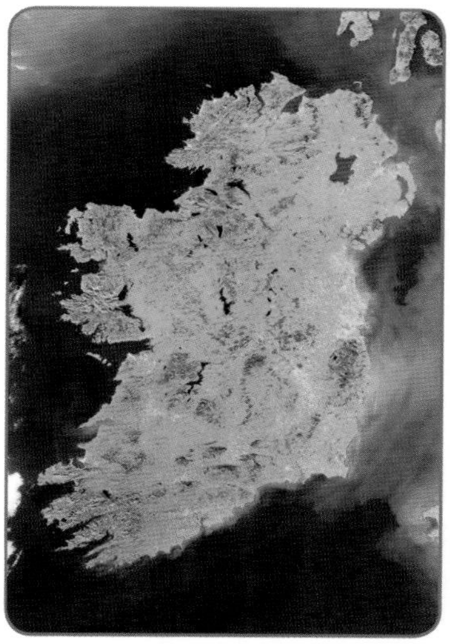

The Earth's oceans are constantly in motion. They are moved by the **wind,** which **creates waves,** and by tides. As it moves, the ocean has the power to change the shape of the coastlines of the world's continents through constant erosion and deposition.

The **coastline** refers to the point where the **ocean meets land.** The Irish coastline is attacked by the Atlantic Ocean on the west and by the Irish Sea on the east. The Atlantic has much more erosive power, as its open waters are driven by the strong south-westerly winds. These winds have greatly changed the shape of Ireland's western coastline. The Irish Sea is much more sheltered and does not have the power to change the eastern coast to the same degree. As you can see from the satellite image in Fig. 11.1, the western coast of Ireland is indented and greatly altered by wave activity, while the east coast remains relatively smooth and unchanged.

Fig. 11.1 A satellite image showing Ireland's indented western coastline

11.1 Waves

- Waves are produced by the **friction** caused between **moving air (wind)** and the **water** at the surface of the sea. The energy of the moving wind is transferred to the water by this friction and pressure, causing waves.

- **Light winds** will produce **slight ripples** on the surface of the ocean. **Faster winds** cause more turbulence on the surface, making the water 'choppy', before eventually developing into **bigger waves.**

- The size of the waves generated depends on the **wind speed, wind duration** and **fetch.** The fetch refers to the **distance of open sea** that the **wave travels** before reaching the shore. The **shore** is the area of beach exposed between **high tide** and **low tide.** The **largest waves** are produced by a combination of a **long fetch** and **strong winds.**

- The Atlantic Ocean regularly produces large waves as it provides a long fetch, combined with strong south-westerly winds. The Irish Sea has a much shorter fetch and is much more sheltered than the Atlantic, meaning it produces smaller waves.

GEO **DICTIONARY**

Fetch: distance of open sea the wave travels over

Shore: the area of beach exposed between high tide and low tide

Crest: the top of a wave

Trough: the bottom of a wave

Parts of a Wave

- The **top of a wave** is called its **crest** and the **bottom of a wave** is called its **trough.** The wavelength is calculated by measuring the distance **between the crests** of two waves.

- As waves approach the shore, friction causes the troughs of the waves to slow down. The faster-moving crest begins to catch up to the trough, making the wave steeper. Shortly after this, the **crest collapses over the trough.**

- This is known as a **breaking wave.** When the wave breaks it rushes up the shore, carrying beach material with it. This is known as the **swash.** When the swash has no more energy, it flows back down the shore to the sea, dragging lighter beach material with it. This is called the **backwash.**

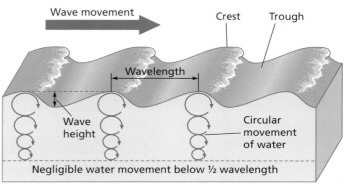

Fig. 11.2 Parts of a wave

Types of Waves

There are two types of waves: constructive and destructive.

Constructive Waves

Constructive waves are small, **low-energy** waves that break onto the shore of beaches.

As constructive waves break, the swash pushes sand and other material up along the beach. The swash quickly loses energy, causing some of the water to soak into the sand. This reduces the size of the backwash.

As the backwash is weaker than the swash, the waves **add more material** to the shore than they take away. As they are building up the material on the shore, these waves are said to be **constructive**.

Destructive Waves

Destructive waves are large, powerful waves that are generated during high winds or storms.

(a)

(b)

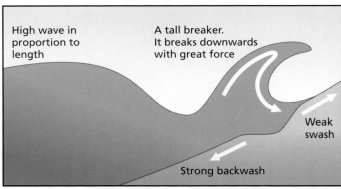

Fig. 11.3 (a) and (b) Constructive waves

They have a **high wave frequency** with more than **10 per minute** breaking on the shore. They break rapidly and plunge almost vertically onto the shore. As the wave does not lose much energy when it breaks, it crashes against the coastline, removing **weakened rock.** The backwash is much stronger than the swash, meaning that **material is removed** from the shore and brought out to sea. As these waves erode and break rock on the coastline, they are said to be **destructive**.

(a)

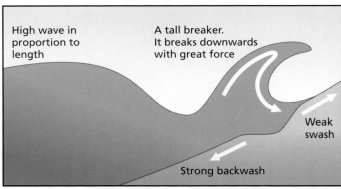

(b)

Fig. 11.4 (a) and (b) Destructive waves

ACTIVE LEARNING

1. Why is Ireland's western coastline more indented than its eastern coastline?
2. How are waves produced?
3. Why are waves on the Atlantic Ocean larger than waves on the Irish Sea?
4. Visit *The Irish Times* website to find the high and low tides for areas nearest to you:
   www.irishtimes.com/weather/tides

Wave Refraction

- As waves approach the shore, friction with the seabed causes them to **bend** and **change direction**. This is known as **wave refraction**.

- Sections of waves in **shallow water** begin to drag against the ocean floor, causing the waves to **slow down**. Sections of the same waves in **deeper water** move on at the **normal speed**. This causes the waves to **bend inward** towards the shallow water.

- The most shallow water tends to be close to **headlands**, meaning that the waves' energy is concentrated towards them. This means that the **bays** located between headlands are **not affected** by strong waves, allowing deposition to occur.

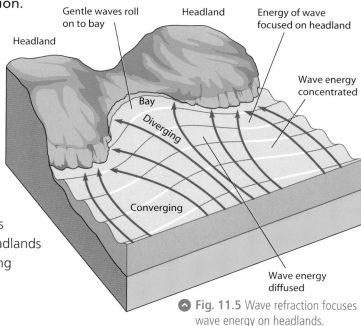

Gentle waves roll on to bay

Headland

Headland

Energy of wave focused on headland

Wave energy concentrated

Bay

Diverging

Converging

Wave energy diffused

Fig. 11.5 Wave refraction focuses wave energy on headlands.

EDUCATE YOURSELF

Waves	
Breaking waves	Crest, trough, wavelength, break, swash, backwash
Constructive waves	Low energy, strong swash, weak backwash, material added
Destructive waves	High winds, storms, high wave frequency, plunge vertically, remove rock, strong backwash, weaker swash
Wave refraction	Friction with seabed, bend/change direction, slows in shallow water, normal speed in deep water, headlands eroded, bays not affected

11.2 Coastal Erosion

Coastal erosion is caused by **destructive waves hitting off the coastline**. The rate of erosion depends on the **type of coastline** being eroded and the **strength of the waves** attacking them. Seven main factors influence erosion:

1. **Make up of coasts:** Hard coasts are made of **resistant rock structures** such as sandstone cliffs, or human-made objects such as sea walls or piers. These structures are eroded very slowly by waves. **Soft coasts** are made up of **weak rock, boulder clay, sand** or **shingle**, etc. They are **eroded very quickly** by destructive waves.

2. **Wave strength:** Destructive waves cause erosion. Waves are at their **strongest during storms**, especially when **high winds coincide with high tides**, e.g. the storms along the West of Ireland in December 2013.

GEO DICTIONARY

Hard coasts: resistant rock structures which can be natural or human-made

Soft coasts: weak or unconsolidated material such as boulder clay, sand or shingle

Boulder clay: clay soil mixed with pebbles and stones

Shingle: rounded pebbles

Fig. 11.6 Storm waves

3. The **shape of coast determines the amount of wave refraction** that occurs. **Coastlines that jut out** towards the sea are **more prone to erosion** than sheltered coasts such as bays.

4. **Slope of shore:** Steeply sloping shores are **more likely to generate destructive waves** than gently sloping ones. Waves break closer to the coastline where there are steep shores, meaning that they do not lose as much energy. Instead they crash against the coastline, causing erosion.

5. **Human activity:** Humans have the power to increase or decrease the rate of erosion on coastlines. The **removal of beach material** makes coasts **more susceptible to erosion.** The building of sea walls, rock armour and other protective structures can reduce the rate of erosion.

6. **Rising sea levels:** Rising sea levels are inevitable as a result of **melting ice caps and glaciers.** It is predicted that waters around Ireland will rise by as much as **30 cm in the next 20 years.** This will result in **more flooding and increased erosion** along our coasts.

7. **Increased storm frequency:** Climate change has resulted in an **increase in storm frequency** and strength across Ireland. Stronger storms are capable of destroying coastal protection efforts and **increasing the rate of erosion in unprotected areas.**

Processes of Erosion

The processes of coastal erosion are similar to those in the upper course of a river. However, coastal retreat, also known as **headward erosion, is dominant at coastlines rather than vertical erosion.**

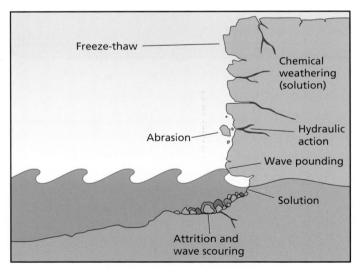

Fig. 11.7 Processes of erosion

Hydraulic Action

Hydraulic action refers to the **erosive power of the waves crashing against the coastline.** Hydraulic action is most effective during storms, exerting pressure of up to **25 tonnes per square metre** on the coastline. As the waves hit off the coast, **hydraulic action fractures rock, enlarges joints and washes away loose pieces of debris.** It is particularly effective on weaker sections of coastline, such as boulder clay cliffs.

Abrasion

Abrasion refers to the **sea using its load to erode the coastline.** It is the most effective process of erosion, especially during storms. **Rocks, pebbles and other materials are carried by waves and thrown against the coastline.** The impact of these materials **weakens and fractures rock and clay,** making hydraulic action more effective. Driving or walking along coast roads during storms can be dangerous as this debris is often hurled onto roads.

Attrition

As rocks are **hurled against each other and against the coastline,** they are **worn down by friction.** As this occurs the pebbles become **rounder, smaller and easier** to transport by waves and tides. As a result, attrition is also referred to as the sandpapering effect.

Compression

As waves hit off the coastline, **air is compressed between the cracks** and **joints of rock.** When the **waves retreat,** the compressed **air expands rapidly** as it escapes. This rapid expansion creates an **explosive effect** that **weakens and shatters rock.**

Solution

Solution refers to the **dissolving of rock by salts in the sea water.** This is common along **limestone or chalk** coastlines. Once the rock is dissolved, it is **removed in solution.**

Landforms of Coastal Erosion

Eroded coastlines provide some spectacular features such as cliffs, bays, headlands and sea arches. Each of these landforms is created by a combination of erosional processes.

Cliffs and Wave-Cut Platforms

Cliffs are **vertical or steep slopes** on the coastline that are formed as a result of coastal erosion and sometimes mechanical weathering. Examples of cliffs are the **Cliffs of Moher** in Co. Clare or Slieve League in Co Donegal.

- Cliffs are mainly formed due to coastal erosion, but boulder clay cliffs can also form due to mechanical weathering and slumping. Weathering is particularly effective on **boulder clay** cliffs as coastal material is **unconsolidated** (loose).

- However, most cliffs are formed by **destructive waves** hitting off the coast. A combination of the erosional processes of **hydraulic action, abrasion, attrition** and **compression** breaks down rock on the coastline to form a steep or vertical slope.

- Hydraulic action weakens rock as destructive waves crash against the coastline. The power of the moving water enlarges and **weakens the rock,** as well as removing loose materials. As the waves hit the coastline, the pressure caused forces the water through cracks and joints in the rock compressing the air in between.

- When the waves retreat, the **air decompresses and escapes** with an explosive effect. This weakens and shatters the rock, making it easier to erode.

- Abrasion occurs as pebbles and rocks are picked up by the waves and thrown against the coastline. This is particularly effective during **storms,** when there is more eroded material in the water.

ACTIVE LEARNING

1. Research why ice caps are melting and how this will cause sea levels to rise. If possible, present your findings to your class.

2. Research how climate change increases storm frequency. If possible, present your findings to your class.

3. Explain the following terms:
   (a) Hydraulic action
   (b) Abrasion
   (c) Attrition
   (d) Compression
   (e) Solution

Note!

The best way to answer questions on landforms created from erosion and deposition is to use DEEPD:

Definition, Example, Explanation, Processes, Diagram.

It is a good idea to describe how the processes form the feature as part of the explanation rather than keeping them separate as it helps to explain the formation process in a logical manner.

CORE 1 CHAPTER 11

● **Fig. 11.8** Headward erosion of a coastal cliff

🔤 GEO **DICTIONARY**

Undercutting: when the base of the coast is eroded away, leaving the upper part unsupported

Wave-cut platform: the base of an eroded cliff which acts as a break for incoming waves

● **Fig. 11.9** The formation of a sea cliff

- Attrition occurs as the **pebbles hit off each other** in the waves, causing a sandpapering effect as the rocks wear away.

- A cliff is formed in stages and is caused by **undercutting** of the coastline. As the waves attack the coast, they erode a **wave-cut notch** at the base of the coastline. Notches are located just above the high tide mark and are the first stage in cliff development.

- Hydraulic action and compression enlarge the notch further, leaving the upper part of the **slope unsupported.** Eventually the **overhanging rock** is unable to support its own weight and **collapses.** As a result, a steep cliff face is formed.

- This cycle of undercutting continues as the **cliff face retreats** inland. This repeated cycle of undercutting and collapse is called **coastal retreat.** Each time a cliff is undercut and collapses, a higher cliff is formed.

- As the cliff retreats, the base of the eroded coastline forms a **flat surface** in front of the cliff. This platform is visible at low tide and is known as a **wave-cut platform.** As the platform widens, it acts as a brake for incoming waves, causing them to slow down and lose their energy.

- The fallen debris from the collapsed overhang collects at the base of the cliff. This rock is **gradually worn down by attrition** and carried away by currents. This debris collects at the edge of the wave-cut platform, forming a ridge called a **wave-built terrace.**

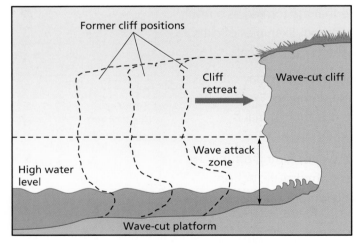

- Eventually the wave-cut platform becomes large enough to stop destructive waves from eroding the cliff. At this stage the cliff is said to be **inactive.**

- Signs that a cliff is inactive include **vegetation growth on the face of the cliff** or piles of material at its base.

- Cliffs on the west coast of Ireland that **face south-west** are more open to erosion by waves from the Atlantic. This is because Ireland's **prevailing winds blow from the south-west.** Cliffs that face in this direction are hit head on by waves.

Cliffs that **face in a different direction are more sheltered** from erosion. The direction a cliff faces is **known as its aspect.**

Bays and Headlands

Bays are **curved indents** on the coastline formed by destructive waves. A headland is a section of land that **protrudes** further into the sea than its surrounding coastline. Normally, a bay is formed in between two headlands. Examples of bays include Liscannor Bay in Co. Clare, **Galway Bay** and **Dublin Bay.** Examples of headlands include Mizen Head in Co. Cork, Slea Head in Co. Kerry and Wicklow Head.

💬 ACTIVE **LEARNING**

1. Why are south-westerly facing slopes more prone to erosion in Ireland?

2. Name one example of a cliff in Ireland.

3. What is a wave-cut platform?

4. How does a wave-cut platform reduce erosion of a cliff?

- Bays and headlands typically form where **bands of hard rock** and **bands of soft rock** are beside one another on a coastline, for example, where a band of basalt is beside a band of shale.

- As destructive waves attack the coastline, the less-resistant rock is eroded much faster than the more-resistant rock, which is an example of **differential erosion.**

- As the **less-resistant rock** is broken down, the coastline **retreats** inland to form a **bay.** **Headlands** are composed of **more-resistant rock,** meaning they are eroded at a much slower rate. The resistant rock sticks out as a result, forming a headland.

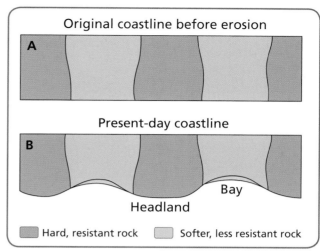

Original coastline before erosion

A

Present-day coastline

B

Bay

Headland

☐ Hard, resistant rock   ☐ Softer, less resistant rock

⊙ **Fig. 11.10** The formation of a bay and headland

- **Hydraulic action** and **compression** are the two most effective processes of erosion in the formation of bays and headlands. During stormy weather, **destructive waves** crash against the coast causing the rock to weaken. It is particularly effective on rock with bedding planes and joints such as limestone and sandstone.

- As the incoming waves hit off the coastline, air is trapped and compressed in between joints and cracks in the rock. As the waves retreat, the air escapes rapidly with an explosive effect. This **weakens the rock** and widens cracks and joints, making hydraulic action more effective.

- The materials broken off the coast are worn down further by **attrition** before they are carried away by currents. As the headland becomes more pronounced, due to the retreat of the weaker rock around it, **wave refraction** increases.

⊙ **Fig. 11.11** A bay and headland

- The shallow waters around the headland create friction, slowing down the section of wave flowing towards it. The section of wave in deeper waters continues on at its normal speed. This causes the waves to bend towards the headland, concentrating their energy on the protruding rock.

- **Weaker waves** flow onto the shore of the bay, **depositing** material along the shore. Often, bays are **occupied by beaches** as a result.

Beach deposits

Headland

Sea Stumps

A sea stump is a small, **flat plateau** of rock that is **cut off** from the coastline. It is the final landform produced in the erosion of a headland, before it too is destroyed by waves. It is created in stages: a **wave-cut notch is created first, then a sea cave, a sea arch, a sea stack** and, finally, a sea stump. Examples of these landforms can be seen off the **Head of Kinsale** in Co. Cork or off the coast of Kilkee in Co. Clare.

⊙ **Fig. 11.12** Wave refraction focuses wave energy towards the headland while deposition occurs along the bay.

 Fig. 11.13 Sea stumps

- **Wave refraction** focuses wave energy on headlands, causing erosion. The **destructive waves** attack **lines of weakness** in the rock, opening up cracks and joints.

- **Hydraulic action** enlarges the lines of weakness in the rock as the waves crash off the headland. **Undercutting** occurs in areas of weakness as the waves attack the base of the headland.

- Gradually, a wave-cut **notch develops** along the base of the headland. The rock at the back of the wave-cut notch is cracked and jointed, allowing hydraulic action and compression to erode it further.

- As the waves hit the back of the notch, air is compressed in the cracks and joints. As the waves retreat, the air escapes with an explosive effect, shattering and weakening the rock. These processes **widen and deepen** the notch, forming a **sea cave**.

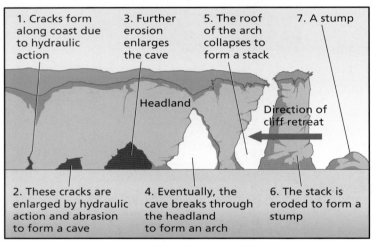 **Fig. 11.14** The formation of a sea stump

1. Cracks form along coast due to hydraulic action
2. These cracks are enlarged by hydraulic action and abrasion to form a cave
3. Further erosion enlarges the cave
4. Eventually, the cave breaks through the headland to form an arch
5. The roof of the arch collapses to form a stack
6. The stack is eroded to form a stump
7. A stump

Headland

Direction of cliff retreat

- During storms, rocks and pebbles are hurled against the walls of the cave, deepening it further by **abrasion**. In narrow headlands, the cave is **eroded through** to the other side, creating a **sea arch**.

- Sea arches can also form when caves at opposite sides of the headland join together. As erosion continues, the **arch becomes wider**. As this happens, the roof of the arch is also eroded, making it **thinner and weaker**.

- Eventually the **roof** of the arch **collapses** into the sea and is carried away by currents. The seaward section of the coastline is cut off from the coastline forming a **sea stack**.

- Waves erode the sea stack, **undercutting** its base and making it unstable. Eventually the **stack collapses** into the sea.

- All that remains is the base of the stack. This is called a **sea stump**. Eventually, the stump is worn away by waves completing the **coastal retreat**.

ACTIVE **LEARNING**

1. Give an example of a bay and headland in Ireland.
2. Explain how a bay and headland are formed.
3. Draw a diagram of a bay and headland.
4. Name the four features that are formed before eventually creating a stump.
5. Draw a diagram showing how a sea stump is formed.

Blowholes and Geos

Sometimes, the roof of a cave is eroded to form a **tunnel** to the land above. This occurs as **compression** shatters the rock between the **cave roof** and the top of the cliff. This feature is called a blowhole. It gets its name as a result of sea spray blown up through it during stormy weather. The 'Two Pistols' in Co. Donegal are examples of blowholes.

⌄ **Fig. 11.15** A blowhole

A **geo** is a small, **narrow coastal inlet.** Geos form as a result of a line of weakness along a cliff or from the collapse of a sea cave.

EDUCATE YOURSELF

Coastal Erosion	
Process of coastal erosion	Hydraulic action: erosive power of waves, fractures rock, enlarges joints, washes away debris, weaker coastlines and boulder clay cliffs
	Abrasion: load hits off coastline, weakens and fractures rock
	Attrition: rocks collide, worn down, pebbles become rounder
	Compression: waves compress air in cracks/joints, waves retreat, air expands, explosive effect
	Solution: dissolved by salt, limestone, chalk
Landforms of coastal erosion	Cliff and wave-cut platform: vertical/steep slopes, Cliffs of Moher, boulder clay, unconsolidated, destructive waves, hydraulic action, abrasion, attrition, compression, weakens rock, air decompresses and escapes, rock shattered, effective in storms, undercutting, wave-cut notch, slope unsupported, overhanging rock collapses, cliff retreats, coastal retreat, flat surface, wave-cut platform, wave-built terrace, inactive
	Headland: protrudes, Dublin Bay, Mizen Head, hard/soft rock, differential erosion, less-resistant rock
	Bay: curved indent, more resistant rock, headland, hydraulic action, compression, destructive waves, weakens rock, attrition, wave refraction, weaker waves deposit on bay, bays occupied by beaches
	Sea stack: flat plateau, notch, cave, arch, stack, Head of Kinsale, wave refraction, destructive waves, lines of weakness, hydraulic action, undercutting, notch develops, compression enlarges notch, cave formed, abrasion, eroded through, sea arch, arch widens, roof collapses, sea stack, undercutting, stack collapses, stump formed, stump eroded, coastal retreat
	Blowholes and geos: tunnel, compression, cave of roof shattered, Two Pistols, geo, narrow coastal inlet

11.3 Transportation

Materials eroded by waves are broken down further by the process of attrition before being transported away by waves and currents. This material is referred to as the **sea's load.** Most of the sea's load comes from sediment deposited by rivers, while some of it comes from sediment eroded by waves.

Processes of Transportation

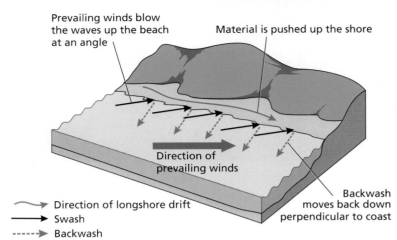

Prevailing winds blow the waves up the beach at an angle

Material is pushed up the shore

Direction of prevailing winds

Backwash moves back down perpendicular to coast

→ Direction of longshore drift
→ Swash
-----▸ Backwash

Fig. 11.16 Processes of transportation

Longshore Drift

When waves approach the shore, friction causes them to slow down and **break onto the shore.** As they break onto the shore, the **swash carries pebbles** and other material **up along** the beach. The water then flows back down the shore to the sea, **dragging some of the material** with it.

The direction that waves hit the coast at is determined by the direction of the wind. Sometimes the direction of the wind causes the waves to flow onto the beach at a **sharp angle.** This means the swash from the breaking waves pushes the sediment up along the beach at an angle. The backwash flows back to sea at a 90° angle. As it does, it drags some of the material down along the shore once again. This process is repeated, causing deposited sediment to be moved along the shoreline. This process is called **longshore drift.**

11.4 Landforms of Deposition

Beaches

A beach is a build-up of **loose material,** deposited by **constructive waves,** between the **low and high tide mark.** Examples of beaches in Ireland are Kilkee Beach, Co. Clare, **Youghal,** Co. Cork and Ballybunion, Co. Kerry.

- Beach material is typically made up of **loose material** such as boulders, pebbles, sand, mud and **shingle.** Most beaches are formed on **gently sloping shores.**

Fig. 11.17 A beach is a landform of deposition.

- **Constructive waves** deposit the beach sediments on the shore, allowing the beach to form. The **powerful swash** of constructive waves pushes material up the shore. As it loses energy, the swash slows down and spreads out over the shore.

- Some of the water **soaks into the sand,** causing materials to be deposited on the shore. The powerful swash is capable of **pushing large materials,** such as pebbles, to the upper part of the beach. The weaker backwash does not have the energy to drag the material back to the sea. Instead, the larger materials are deposited on the upper beach, while **smaller sand** and mud is **dragged down to the foreshore.**

- This processes sorts the beach material, with larger materials located at the backshore and finer materials located on the foreshore.

- **Longshore drift** also contributes to beach formation. When the waves break at an angle to the beach, longshore drift occurs. Sediments are dragged along the coastline in a **zigzag motion** before being deposited.

- Beaches range in size from long straight beaches that stretch along coastlines, to small curved beaches that form in sheltered bays. These smaller beaches are sometimes called 'pocket beaches'.

- A typical beach is made up of two distinct parts: the **backshore** and the **foreshore.** The backshore is the upper part of the beach. It is the **steepest part** of the beach and is made up of **coarse material** such as shingle. Waves only reach this part of the beach during storms and high tides when the sea has increased energy.

- The foreshore is the lower part of the beach. The foreshore has a **gentle slope** and is made of fine sand and mud.

- **Storm beaches** develop at the very back of a beach. They are made of ridges of large stones and gravel that are hurled onto the shore by destructive storm waves. Storm beaches lie beyond the reach of normal waves breaking on the shore.

Beach Features

Several features are formed on beaches.

- **Berms:** Berms are small ridges of slightly **coarse gravel** that are deposited **parallel to the shore.** They mark the highest point reached by the swash during each high tide. They are destroyed and rebuilt by the next higher tide.

- **Runnels:** Gently sloping ridges of sand develop on the **seaward edge of the foreshore.** They run parallel to the coastline as a result of constructive waves. They form near the point where the waves break. If a series of ridges develop, they are separated by **depressions called runnels.**

- **Sand dunes:** Sand dunes are small **hills of sand** that develop inland, behind beaches. They are beyond the reach of the sea. In order for dunes to develop, there must be a plentiful supply of fine beach sand and the prevailing wind must come in from the sea. During low tide, the sand dries and is blown inland by the wind. The sand is **deposited by the wind** when it comes into contact with obstacles such as fences or vegetation. Gradually, sand builds up to form hills of sand called dunes. These dunes are unstable as the sand is not compacted.

- **Marram,** is a coarse, strong grass that grows in sand. Marram colonises the dunes and binds the sand together with its long roots, which **act as an anchor.** Marram grass allows the dune to grow larger as it traps more sand.

GEO **DICTIONARY**

Berms: ridges of coarse gravel deposited parallel to the shore

Runnels: depressions that separate berms

Sand dune: hills of sand that form at the back of a beach

ACTIVE **LEARNING**

1. Explain fully the difference between constructive and destructive waves.
2. Describe the backshore and foreshore of a beach.
3. Name two Irish examples of beaches.
4. What are berms and runnels?
5. What are sand dunes and how do they form?
6. How does Marram grass help dunes to grow larger?

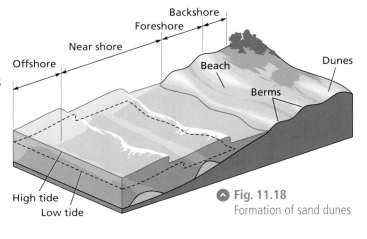

▲ Fig. 11.18
Formation of sand dunes

Sandspits, Tombolos, Baymouth Bars and Lagoons

A **sandspit** is a long, **narrow ridge of sand** that extends from the coastline out to sea. An example of a sandpit can be seen in **Inch Beach** in Co. Kerry.

Fig. 11.19 A tombolo

ACTIVE LEARNING

1. Name three features of deposition found along a coastline.

2. What is a tombolo?

3. Give an example of a sandspit which can be found along the Irish coastline.

4. What is a lagoon?

5. State whether constructive or destructive waves are in operation in the formation of:
   (a) Cliffs
   (b) Beaches
   (c) Arches
   (d) Wave-cut platforms
   (e) Lagoons
   (f) Geos
   (g) Headlands
   (h) Berms

6. Draw a labelled diagram to show the following:
   (a) Cliff
   (b) Beach
   (c) Lagoon, tombolo and sandspit

7. Explain four factors which influence the rate of erosion occurring along a coastline.

- Spits form in areas where there is a **sudden change** in the **shape of the coastline**. This change in shape can be as a result of a **sheltered bay** or inlet.

- The change of shape **disrupts** the process of **longshore drift,** causing the **sediment** to be **deposited** in a single area rather than spread along the coastline. Sediment is deposited on the seabed of **shallow waters** and is gradually **built up to sea level.**

- Continued deposition causes the spit to grow **across the bay** or inlet. The spit will continue to grow outwards until it reaches an area where tides and currents remove more sediment than longshore drift deposits.

- The sandpit is **stabilised by Marram grass** as its roots bind the sediment together. Constructive waves deposit **sand on the seaward side** of the spit to form a narrow beach. Some of this sand is blown onto the top of the spit by the wind to form **sand dunes.**

- As the spit gets bigger, wave refraction or a change in wind direction causes its tip to **bend inwards** towards the land. A **tombolo** is formed when a **sand spit joins an offshore island,** connecting it to the mainland. An example of a tombolo can be seen in **Howth,** Co. Dublin.

- A baymouth bar forms when a spit extends **across the mouth of a bay.** They typically form on **gently sloping** shores. The waves break far from the shore and the powerful swash pushes sediment ahead of it to form a bar.

- **Constructive waves** add sediment, increasing its height while **longshore drift** increases its length. The former bay is now blocked off from the sea and becomes a lake. This lake is called a **lagoon.**

- If a river does not flow into the lagoon it may eventually dry up to become a salt marsh. An example of a baymouth bar can be seen at **Our Lady's Island,** Co. Wexford.

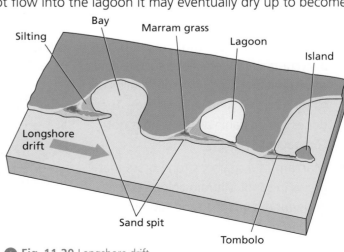

Fig. 11.20 Longshore drift

Landforms of Deposition	
Beach	Loose materials (shingle), constructive waves, low/high-tide mark, Youghal, gently sloping shore, swash deposits material, backshore, foreshore, powerful swash, large materials pushed up beach, finer sand dragged to foreshore, longshore drift, zigzag motion, storm beaches, berms, ridges, runnels, sand dunes, Marram grass
Sandspit	Long ridge of sand, Inch Beach, change in coastal shape, sheltered bay, disrupts longshore drift, sediment deposited in shallow water, builds to sea level, grows across bay, Marram grass, beach on seaward side, sand dunes develop, tip bends inwards
Tombolo	Sandspit joins island, Howth
Baymouth bar	Across mouth of bay, gently sloping, constructive waves, longshore drift, lagoon, Our Lady's Island

11.5 Human Interference with Coasts

An example of the positive and negative effects of human interference with marine processes can be seen in **Dublin Bay.**

Dublin Bay

- In the past, deposition of sand and silt blocked the mouth of **the Liffey channel,** causing ships to run aground as they entered Dublin Harbour. This was a major issue as it hindered the importing and exporting of goods.

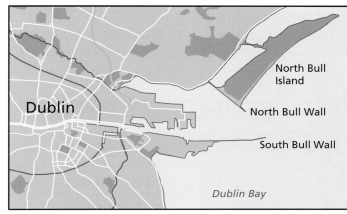

▲ Fig. 11.21
A map of Dublin Bay

- Authorities attempted to prevent the build-up of silt by **dredging** the mouth of the Liffey, but this did not solve the issue. To prevent **longshore drift** from depositing sand and silt, two walls were built to the **north and south** of the Liffey channel.

- The North Bull Wall and the South Bull Wall were constructed between 1818 and 1825 and had an **immediate positive effect for ships** entering and exiting the harbour.

- The depth of the harbour increased by 3 m in 50 years as tides and currents **washed away the silt that had accumulated at the mouth of the harbour.**

- As the sand and silt was blocked from entering the harbour, it began to accumulate on the north side of the North Bull Wall. Sediment **accumulated rapidly** leading to the formation of an island.

- This island, which has now grown to a size of **5 km long and 700 m wide,** is called **Bull Island.** It continues to grow in size as more sand is trapped.

- The island is described as a 'gift from the sea', and is an example of an **unexpected consequence of human interaction** with coastal processes.

GEO DICTIONARY

Dredging: scooping mud and sediment from the bottom of something

CORE 1 CHAPTER 11

Fig. 11.22 Bull Island

Advantages

- The island has become a **valuable amenity** for the people of Dublin. Two of Dublin's best known golf courses: Royal Dublin and St Anne's, have been built there as the high dunes make it an ideal location for links courses.

- Bull Island is home to a wide range of flora and fauna. The island became a **bird sanctuary** in 1930 and an official wildlife sanctuary in 1986. A visitor centre provides information about the wildlife of the island.

Disadvantages

- Some human activity has had negative effects on the physical structure of the island. People driving and parking their cars on the beach have led to the **compaction of sand.** This means that less sand is blown inwards by the wind, considerably slowing the growth of sand dunes.

- People walking and playing on sand dunes have damaged the dunes' structure as they trample on the Marram grass that anchors them. As the **dunes become unstable,** they are more likely to be eroded by the wind.

GEO **DICTIONARY**

Amenity: a service that is of benefit to the locality

EDUCATE YOURSELF

Human Interference

Liffey channel, dredging, longshore drift, North and South Walls, sediment accumulated, Bull Island, 5 km long, 700 m wide, valuable amenity, bird and wildlife sanctuary, compaction of sand, dunes becoming unstable

Coastal Management

Ireland has approximately 3171 km of coastline, roughly **half of which is in danger due to flooding and erosion**. Human interference with coastal processes can have positive or negative effects on coastal processes. Even slight interference can lead to increased erosion or deposition in an area. In order to protect coastlines, two types of structures are used:

1. Hard structures
2. Soft structures

Hard Structures

Hard structures are used to **prevent erosion**. They are usually large structures made from **resistant rock or reinforced concrete**. Once constructed, these structures are considered to be permanent features as they are rarely removed. Hard structures are particularly popular along coastal towns as they protect buildings and streets from erosion. Examples of hard structures include sea walls, gabions, groynes and rock armour.

Sea Walls

Sea walls are used to **protect coastlines from destructive waves.** They are made from concrete reinforced with steel. Their walls are **curved** in order to deflect the breaking wave back onto the next incoming wave. This reduces the energy of the incoming wave and makes it less likely to breach the top of the protective wall. Sea walls are used in the coastal town of **Lahinch in Co. Clare** to protect businesses built along the coast.

▲ **Fig. 11.23** A sea wall

Gabions

Gabions are **steel mesh cages** that are filled with stones. They are used to **reduce the energy of incoming waves.** When a wave hits a line of gabions, it is broken up as the wave filters through the stones in the mesh. As the wave's energy is spread out, its **erosive power is reduced.** Although gabions are effective, they are not long-lasting as the mesh wire can break during storms and the stones can be washed away. Sea walls are seen as a better choice as they require less maintenance.

▲ **Fig. 11.24** Gabions

Groynes

Groynes are low walls made of **cement or wood** that are built at **right angles to the shore.** They are used to **trap sediment** being moved along the coast by longshore drift. This allows material to accumulate and prevents the erosion of beaches. Several groynes have been built along **Youghal Beach in Co. Cork.** A negative effect of groyne construction is that this deprives nearby coastal areas of natural deposition. This can lead to increased erosion in those areas.

▲ **Fig. 11.25** Groynes

Rock Armour

Rock armour is a basic but effective form of coastal protection. **Large boulders** are placed along a coastline to reduce sea erosion. When waves crash off these boulders, their energy is reduced, preventing erosion from occurring. Although they are effective, rock armour is not a popular choice of coastal defence as it is bulky and takes up too much space on the beach.

▲ **Fig. 11.26** Rock armour

Fig. 11.27 Beach nourishment

Soft Structures

Soft structures are considered to be a more **environmentally friendly** method of coastal protection. They are not permanent structures and are used to **repair damage** caused by destructive waves. The most common forms of soft coastal protection are beach nourishment and sand dune repair.

Beach Nourishment

Beach nourishment involves adding new sand to beaches, increasing their thickness and width. This is done by dredging sand from offshore and transporting it to the beach. This helps to prevent erosion and increases the recreational value of the beach. This was carried out in Rosslare, Co. Wexford in the 1960s. Although effective, beach nourishment is a very **expensive and labour-intensive** method of coastal protection.

Sand Dune Repair

Sand dunes are protected from erosion by **planting Marram grass.** The roots of the Marram bind the sand together and make it more resistant to wind erosion. It is the most **environmentally friendly** form of coastal protection as it does not affect other coastal areas.

EDUCATE YOURSELF

Coastal Management	
Hard structures	Sea walls, gabions, groynes, rock armour
Soft structures	Beach nourishment, sand dune repair

11.6 Identifying Coastal Features on OS Maps

As part of the exam, students are often asked to identify coastal features of erosion and deposition on an OS map.

A = Cliff:	packed contour lines at the coastline indicate a steep fall
B = Headland:	a piece of land jutting out into the sea next to a bay/beach
C = Sea stack:	a speck of land separated from the coastline
D = Geo:	a narrow inlet indicating a line of weakness
E = Beach:	the most obvious feature of deposition as it is marked in yellow on a map
F = Bay:	a curved inlet surrounded by headlands, usually occupied by a beach

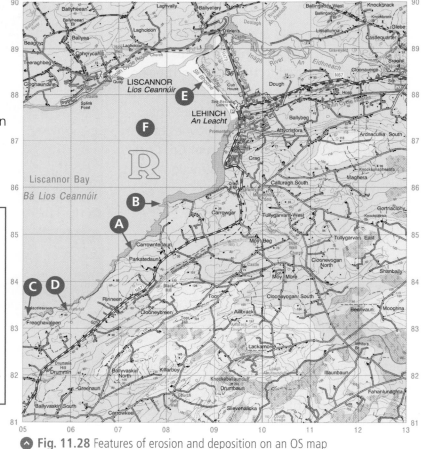

Fig. 11.28 Features of erosion and deposition on an OS map

ORDINARY LEVEL

SHORT QUESTIONS

1. (i) Examine the photograph showing coastal landforms and match each of the letters A, B, C and D with the landform that best matches it, in the table.

Landform	Letter
Sea stack	
Sea arch	
Sea cave	
Sea cliff	

(ii) Indicate whether the statement below is true or false, by ticking the correct box.
'All of the landforms named above are formed by coastal deposition.'

True	
False	

(i) Each letter correctly inserted 4 @ 2m each
True/false correctly answered 2m

2009 Q1 10M

2. (i) Examine the photographs of coastal landforms and correctly match each of the letters on the photographs with one of the named landforms in the box.

Landform	Letter
Sea arch	
Blowhole	
Cliff	
Beach	

(ii) Which of the landforms named above was formed by the process of deposition?

Each letter correctly inserted 4 @ 2m each
Landform correctly named 2m

2015 Q1 10M

LONG QUESTIONS

1. Explain, with the aid of diagrams, the formation of any two landforms.

Each landform @ 20m each
Landform named 1m
Diagram(s) two aspects @ 2m each
Formation explained 5 SRPs @ 3m each

2015 Q1B 40M

2. Examine how humans interact with coastal processes.

Interaction named 3m
Examination 9 SRPs @ 3m each

2015 Q3C 30M

3. Describe and explain how humans attempt to control coastal processes.

| Control identified 3m |
| Description and explanation 9 SRPs @ 3m each |

2014 Q2C 30M

4. Explain, with the aid of a diagram, how any one Irish landform is formed from coastal action.

| Landform named 2m |
| Diagram 2 aspects @ 2m each |
| Formation explained 8 SRPs @ 3m each |

2010 Q1B 30M

SHORT QUESTIONS

1. Examine the aerial photograph and answer each of the following questions.

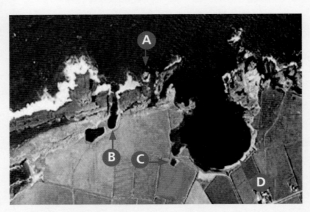

(i) Match each of the letters A, B, C and D with the landform that best matches it in the table.

(ii) Indicate whether processes of coastal erosion or coastal deposition are most associated with the formation of each of the landforms, by ticking the correct box in the table.

Landform	Letter	Processes of Coastal Erosion	Processes of Coastal Deposition
Blowhole			
Sea stack			
Bayhead beach			
Geo			

| Landform correctly labelled with letter 4 @ 1m each |
| Correct processes identified 4 @ 1m each |

2015 Q2 8M

LONG QUESTIONS

1. Examine the impact of the processes of erosion on the formation of one coastal landform that you have studied.

| Processes of erosion 2m + 2m |
| Landform named 2m |
| Examination 12 SRPs @ 2m each |

2015 Q1B 30M

HIGHER LEVEL

2. Explain the formation of one landform of erosion and one landform of deposition that you have studied.

| Landform of erosion named 2m |
| Landform of deposition named 2m |
| Landform of erosion explained 6/7 SRPs @ 2m each |
| Landform of deposition explained 6/7 SRPs @ 2m each |

2014 Q2B 30M

3. Explain, with the aid of a labelled diagram, the formation of one landform of deposition that you have studied.

| Named landform 2m |
| Labelled diagram 4m |
| Explanation 12 SRPs @ 2m each |

2012 Q2B 30M

4. Examine, with reference to examples you have studied, how human activities have impacted on coastal processes.

| Human activity identified 2m |
| Impact identified 2m |
| Named example 2m |
| Examination 12 SRPs @ 2m each |

2012 Q1C 30M

HIGHER LEVEL

Questions on landscape development and surface processes have appeared every year since 2006 at both Higher Level and Ordinary Level. So it is important that you prepare for this section. Similarly, a question on human interaction often appears on papers at both levels. In this section, we will look at human interaction question from a Higher Level paper.

EXAM QUESTION

'Human activity impacts on surface processes.'

Examine this statement with reference to the impact of coastal defence work on coastal processes

Marking Scheme	
Impact on process identified 2m	
Examination 14 SRPs @ 2m each	

2014 Q1C 30M

SAMPLE ANSWER

Roughly half of Ireland's 3171 km of coastline is in danger due to flooding and coastal erosion [2m]. In order to prevent the loss of endangered coastlines, a number of coastal protections in the form of hard and soft structures have been built [2m]. Human interaction through coastal protection can have both positive and negative results, as it will usually increase or decrease changes to coastal erosion or deposition processes [2m].

Hard Structures

Hard structures are made from resistant rock or reinforced concrete and are used to prevent erosion from occurring along a coastline [2m]. Examples of hard coastal protection structures are sea walls, gabions, groynes and rock armour [2m]. Sea walls are curved and reduce the erosional power of plunging waves by deflecting the breaking wave back on the next incoming wave [2m]. This reduces the incoming waves' energy, making them less likely to remove coastal materials. This greatly reduces erosion in the area [2m]. Examples of sea walls in use can be seen in Lahinch, Co. Clare [2m]. While sea walls are seen as a cheap and effective way of stopping erosion, they disrupt the natural processes of the region. This can lead to increased erosion in other areas, or the prevention of the natural movement of sand along the coast [2m]. In some cases, entire coastal habitats are destroyed.

Gabions are steel mesh cages that are filled with tightly packs stones which cause waves to spread out as they hit the coast. This reduces the wave's energy and erosional power [2m]. Sea walls are seen as a better option than gabions, as the mesh that keeps the stones together often breaks and is expensive to replace. Groynes are low walls made from wood or cement that are designed to interrupt the process of longshore drift [2m]. They are built at right angles to the shore and allow material to accumulate and prevent the erosion of beaches. While they are effective, they deprive nearby coastal areas of natural deposition which can lead to increased erosion of these areas [2m].

Soft Structures

Soft structures are a more environmentally friendly method of coastal protection as they are used to repair damage caused by destructive waves [2m]. The most common forms of soft coastal protection are beach nourishment and sand dune repair [2m]. Beach nourishment involves adding new sand to beaches by dredging sand from offshore, which increases their thickness and width [2m]. This helps to prevent erosion of beaches and adds to their value as recreational areas [2m]. The planting of Marram grass is seen as the most environmentally friendly method of coastal protection as it does not affect other coastal areas [2m]. Planting Marram grass on sand dunes roots binds the sand together and makes it more resistant to wind erosion [2m].

Impact on process identified (reduced erosion).

Hard and soft structures purposes and impacts clearly discussed.

Marks Awarded
Impact on process identified 2m
Examination of impact best 14 SRPs @ 2m each
Total 30/30

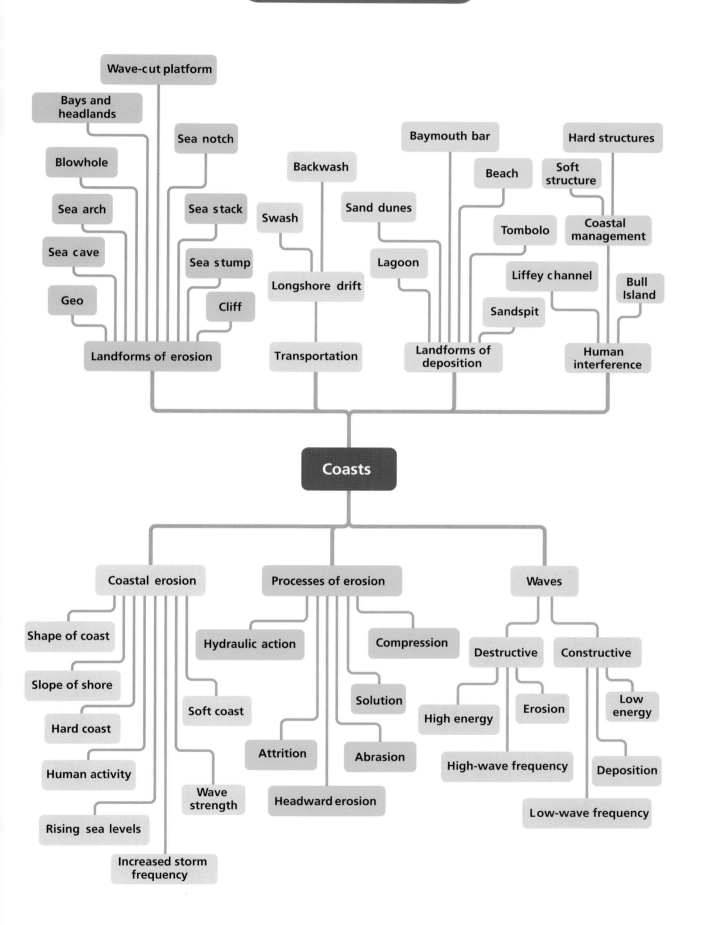

TOPIC MAP

Wave-cut platform

Bays and headlands

Sea notch

Blowhole

Sea arch

Sea stack

Sea cave

Sea stump

Geo

Cliff

Landforms of erosion

Backwash

Swash

Sand dunes

Longshore drift

Lagoon

Transportation

Baymouth bar

Beach

Tombolo

Sandspit

Landforms of deposition

Hard structures

Soft structure

Coastal management

Liffey channel

Bull Island

Human interference

Coasts

Coastal erosion

Processes of erosion

Waves

Shape of coast

Slope of shore

Hard coast

Human activity

Rising sea levels

Increased storm frequency

Hydraulic action

Soft coast

Attrition

Wave strength

Headward erosion

Compression

Solution

Abrasion

Destructive

Constructive

High energy

Erosion

Low energy

High-wave frequency

Deposition

Low-wave frequency

CHAPTER 12
Glacial Landscapes

In this chapter, you will learn about the different features of erosion and deposition that occur as a result of glaciation. You will also learn about the effect of the last ice age on the Irish landscape.

> **Note!**
> You must study either Chapter 12 or Chapter 11 in detail, but make sure to familiarise yourself with the appearance of the landforms in both chapters.

KEY WORDS

- Pleistocene
- Firn
- Zone of accumulation
- Interglacial period
- Compaction
- Basal slide
- Plastic flow
- Plucking
- Abrasion
- Striations
- Cirques
- Glaciated valleys
- Glacial spillways
- Tarn
- Freeze-thaw action
- Crevasses
- Bergschrund
- Rotational slide
- Arête
- Pyramidal peak
- Vertical/lateral erosion
- Ribbon lakes
- Paternoster lake
- Truncated spurs
- Hanging valleys
- Fiords
- Fluvioglacial landforms
- Rock flour
- Drumlins
- Eskers
- Outwash plain
- Erratics

LEARNING OUTCOMES

What you MUST know
- How glaciers move
- The processes of erosion
- A landform of erosion
- A landform of deposition
- How to recognise features from diagrams, photographs and OS maps

What you SHOULD know
- Fluvioglacial landforms
- A second feature of erosion
- A second feature of deposition
- How materials are transported

What is USEFUL to know
- Effects of glaciation on the Irish landscape

Introduction

Today, **10 per cent of the Earth's landscape is covered in glaciers** that are mainly concentrated in the North and South Poles. However, throughout the Earth's history there have been **several periods** when glaciers covered entire continents. These periods are known as ice ages.

As glaciers move across a landscape, they alter its shape and characteristics through erosion and deposition.

12.1 The Last Ice Age

The last ice age **began roughly 2.6 million years ago** and **ended 10 000 years ago.** This period of time is referred to as the **Pleistocene.** During this era, large ice sheets covered Greenland, Antarctica, Northern Europe and North America. This period was characterised by huge temperature fluctuations (rises and falls). Scientists believe that there were at least **five periods of glacial advance,** with warmer, **interglacial periods** in between.

Glaciers form during glacial periods, which are long periods of very cold temperatures. As temperatures are low, snowfalls do not melt, causing the snow to build up and be compacted into glaciers. As these glaciers moved across the landscape, they **joined together to form vast ice sheets.**

Fig. 12.1 Louis Agassiz developed glacial theory.

The ice sheets shaped the landscape over which they travelled through both erosional and depositional processes. Several examples of glacial landscape can be seen throughout Ireland, where glaciers that were over **1 km thick moved** across the country.

Eventually, temperatures rose once again, causing snow and ice to melt. This is called an interglacial period. Currently, we are in an interglacial period. Ice sheets from the last ice age remain in Greenland, Antarctica and mountainous regions such as the Alps.

Effects of Ice Ages

As well as creating **features of erosion and deposition,** an ice age leads to:

- Large-scale isostatic movement (*see* Chapter 13)
- The interruption of river processes
- Interrupted wind and ocean currents as warm currents no longer travels as far from the equator

How Glaciers Form

A glacier is a build-up of many layers of ice and snow over hundreds and thousands of years. In order for glaciers to develop, snow must accumulate faster than it melts. Where this occurs is called a **zone of accumulation.** Zones of accumulation are usually located **along mountain ranges,** where **temperatures are lower.**

FACT

The idea of the Earth experiencing an ice age was first proposed by Louis Agassiz, a Swiss-born biologist.

GEO DICTIONARY

Pleistocene: the name given to the era between 1.6 million years and 10 000 years ago

Compact: to join or pack closely together

Isostatic movement: the rising and sinking of the Earth's crust due to removal/addition of weight

Accumulate: build/pile up

Zone of accumulation: the area where snow and ice builds up

ACTIVE LEARNING

There are many interesting theories and facts about the cause of ice ages. Research some of the following and, if possible, present your findings to your class:

- Milankovitch theory
- Ice age and ocean currents
- The 100 000-year problem
- Snowball Earth

Fig. 12.2 Snowball Earth

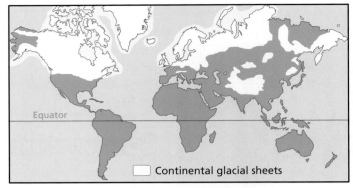

Fig. 12.3 The extent of continental ice sheets

These glaciers grow to occupy entire valleys, before **moving downslope due to gravity.** As they move downslope, the glaciers join together to form ice sheets. These sheets can cover entire continents, and are also called **continental glaciers.**

Glacial ice is formed in three stages, which can occur quickly or slowly depending on the rate of accumulation.

1. Fresh snow falls and accumulates on the ground. Newly fallen snow is soft and easy to **compact** as it is **90 per cent air.**

2. As more snow falls, the layers beneath it are compacted. Due to the pressure, the snow melts slightly before refreezing again. This changes the snow into rounder, **small grains of ice called firn.**

3. As more snow falls, the grains of ice are compacted further into a solid block of dense glacial ice. Glacial ice is also referred to as **'blue ice'**. It is blue as compaction has removed all oxygen from it.

Fig. 12.4 The formation of glacial ice

EDUCATE YOURSELF

The Last Ice Age
Snow – compaction – firn – compaction – blue ice

12.2 Glacial Movement

As glaciers build up, they are pushed downslope by gravity and their own weight. This movement occurs in two ways:

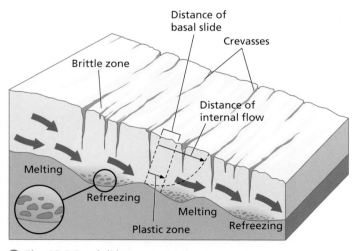

Fig. 12.5 Basal slide

1. **Basal slide** (also called basal slip) occurs in the same way as an ice sheet forms. Pressure from the weight of the ice melts a **thin layer of water** at the base of the glacier. This layer of water acts as a **lubricant** and allows the glacier to **slide downslope.** The gradient of the slope the glacier lies on **reduces friction** between ice and rock and affects the amount of movement that takes place. Most basal sliding takes place on **steep slopes** with a **smooth profile.** Basal sliding is most active during the summer months as higher temperatures allow more ice to melt.

2. **Plastic flow** is a slightly more difficult concept to understand than basal sliding. Plastic flow occurs in **extremely cold climates** such as those found in Greenland and Antarctica. In these regions, the bottom layers of glaciers are too cold to melt ice, so basal sliding cannot occur.

Instead, the weight of the overlying ice pushes down on the ice crystals, creating horizontal layers (much like the way sedimentary rock is organised into layers). This allows the layers to creep past each other. The upper and middle layers of the glacier move faster than the layers near the bottom, which is slowed down by friction between the ice and valley. In this way, plastic flow is able bend and flow over uneven rock surfaces. Plastic flow **does not occur in glaciers that are less than 50 m thick** as there is not enough pressure.

• If you have ever gone ice-skating, you technically have created basal slide. The pressure of your ice skates melts a film of ice which allows you to slide around.

• To see how plastic flow operates, place your hand on top of a deck of cards. Push your hand forward and you will notice that only the top layers move significantly, while the middle layers move slightly. The bottom layers will not move at all.

EDUCATE YOURSELF

Basal slide	Thin layer of water, lubricant, reduces friction, steep slopes, smooth profile
Plastic flow	Cold climates, glacier >50 m, horizontal layers, slide or flow past

ACTIVE LEARNING

1. When did the last ice age occur?
2. How do glaciers form?
3. Explain the terms 'plastic flow' and 'basal slide'.

12.3 Glacial Erosion

As glaciers move, they erode rock and other materials at their base and sides. The two main processes of glacial erosion are **plucking** and **abrasion**.

Plucking

Plucking (also called quarrying) occurs when pressure melts water at the base and sides of a glacier.

As this happens, melt water from the glacier seeps into the **cracks and joints** of the rock. When the water **refreezes** it expands by 9 per cent, weakening and loosening the rock. As the glacier is now frozen around the weakened rock, it **plucks the rock** away as it moves downslope.

This process is most effective in rock with well-developed joints, such as sedimentary rocks. The pieces of rock carried away by the glacier are referred to as its **load.**

GEO DICTIONARY

Plucking: when water in a glacier melts and then refreezes around rock, and then lifts and transports pieces of rock as the glacier moves

Abrasion: jagged pieces of rock stuck onto the slide of the glacier cut and scrape the sides and floor of the valley

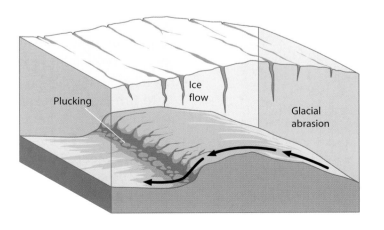

Plucking

Ice flow

Glacial abrasion

▶ **Fig. 12.6** Processes of glacial erosion

CORE 1 CHAPTER 12

Abrasion

Due to plucking and freeze-thaw action, large pieces of **jagged rock** are frozen onto the **base and sides** of a glacier. As the glacier moves downslope, these fragments of rock **smooth and polish** the rock over which they move. Larger fragments of rock can cause **deep scratches** in the bedrock called **straie** or **striations**. These deep scratches further aid the process of plucking.

Rate of Erosion

The rate at which erosion occurs is dependent on the following factors:

- **Glacial thickness:** The thickness of a glacier impacts the rate of erosion. The **greater the depth** of the ice, the **greater the rate of erosion.**
- **Gradient:** Glaciers move **faster on steep slopes.** Just like rivers, faster-moving glaciers have more erosive power.
- **Resistance of rock:** Softer rock is **eroded more quickly** than harder rock.

Landforms of Erosion

Cirques and glaciated valleys are the most common landforms that occur as a result of glacial erosion.

Fig. 12.7 A cirque

Cirques

Cirques are also known as **corries or cooms.** Cirques are **basin-shaped hollows** that are formed on the **side of a mountain.** They mark a **zone of accumulation,** where a glacier originally formed. Cirques have **three steep sides** and one gently sloping side. The **gently sloping side** is the point where the glacier exited the mountain and moved into the valley below. The remaining three sides consist of a **back wall** and **two side walls** which form cliffs. Some cirques are filled with water, forming a small, round lake called a **tarn,** also known as a **corrie lake.**

Irish examples of cirques are the **Devil's Punchbowl** in Mangerton Mountain, Co. Kerry and Lough Nahanagan, Wicklow Gap, Co. Wicklow.

- Many cirques in Ireland have formed on the **north or north-east of mountains** as they receive the least amount of sunshine, allowing snow to accumulate.
- As snow falls, it gathers in a pre-existing hollow on the mountainside. The **expansion of ice** through **freeze-thaw action** shatters and breaks the bedrock causing the hollow to enlarge.
- As further snow falls on the hollow, the bottom layers are **compressed into firn** before eventually forming glacial ice. As the glacier grows, its weight causes it to move downslope. Pressure on the base and sides of the glacier cause a layer of ice to melt as it moves.
- The **water seeps into the cracks and joints** in the rock before refreezing again. The frozen water expands, further weakening the rock. **Plucking** of the back wall creates a **deep crevasse** in the glacier called a **bergschrund.**

- Freeze-thaw action along the mountain causes scree to fall into the bergschrund. Fresh snow gathers in the bergschrund from a combination of precipitation and avalanches from the mountain above it. This snow is compressed into glacial ice and picks up the weathered scree as it moves downslope.

- The pieces of **scree** stick out from the glacier, causing abrasion as it moves down the mountain. As the glacier moves, it does so in a semicircular motion known as **rotational slide** (*see* Chapter 9). This rotational movement further **deepens the cirque** through plucking and abrasion.

- When two cirques **form at either side** of the same mountain, an **arête** is formed. An arête is a **narrow ridge of steep-sided rock**.

- When three or more cirques form along the sides of the same mountain, they form a steep **pyramidal peak.** Several arêtes join to the central peak, marking the back walls of each cirque. **Carrantouhill,** which is the highest mountain in Ireland, is an example of a pyramidal peak.

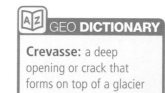
GEO **DICTIONARY**

Crevasse: a deep opening or crack that forms on top of a glacier

⬆ **Fig. 12.8** An arête

Glaciated Valley

Glaciated valleys are also known as **U-shaped valleys** or **glacial troughs.** Glacial valleys are characterised by their steep sides and a flat, wide valley floor, which gives them their U shape. Irish examples include **Glendalough,** Co. Wicklow, the Horse's Glen in Mangerton, Co. Kerry and Glenveagh, Co. Donegal.

- Almost all U-shaped valleys were **originally V-shaped river valleys** as they provided the easiest route downslope. Glaciers occupy most of the valley and greatly **change its shape.** The large glaciers **widen and deepen the valley** through **vertical** and **lateral erosion.**

- Pressure caused by the weight of the ice caused a layer of ice at the base of the glacier to melt. The melt water seeps into the cracks and joints of the bedrock, before freezing again. As the water freezes, it expands, **shattering and loosening the rock.**

- As the glacier moves downslope, it **plucks** the loose rock from the valley floor, **deepening** it further. The pieces of rock plucked from the valley stick out from the glacier, causing **abrasion** to occur as it moves downslope. Abrasion has a sandpaper effect on the bedrock creating a flat, **smooth valley** floor.

⬆ **Fig. 12.9** A pyramidal peak

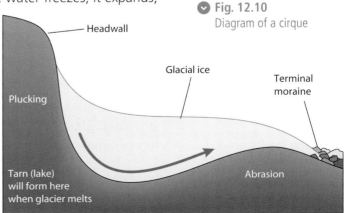

⬇ **Fig. 12.10** Diagram of a cirque

Headwall

Glacial ice

Terminal moraine

Plucking

Tarn (lake) will form here when glacier melts

Abrasion

Fig. 12.11
A U-shaped valley

- In areas of softer rock or deep soil, abrasion creates **deep hollows** along the valley floor. These are known as **rock basins.** After the glacier melted, these basins filled with water to form **ribbon lakes.** When two or more of these lakes are joined together by a stream, they are referred to as **paternoster** lakes.

- Glaciers also **straighten the valley** as they move downslope. Unlike a river, the glacier does not flow around the sides of mountains. Instead, the glacier's power **erodes** through the **interlocking spurs.** All that remains are triangular-shaped cliffs called **truncated spurs.** As a result, the valley is straightened.

- **Hanging valleys** are formed along the valleys smaller tributary valleys. The glaciers that occupy these valleys are smaller and do not have the same erosive power as the main valley. As a result, vertical erosion is not as prominent.

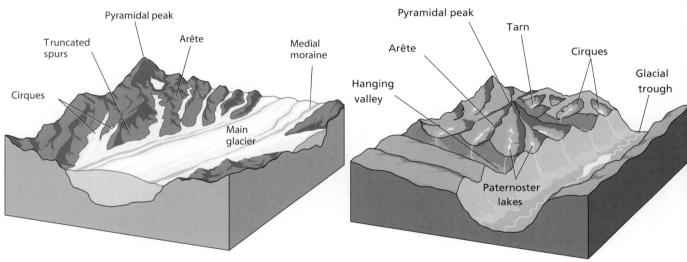

Fig. 12.12 A glacial valley

Fig. 12.13 Glacial valley after glacier has melted

- When the glaciers melt and rivers once again occupy the valley floor, the **main valley** is at a **much lower** level than its tributary valleys. A **waterfall** often marks the point where a hanging valley meets the main valley.

- Due to plucking and abrasion and different resistance of rocks to erosion, the floor of a glaciated valley can descend in a series of steps called **rock steps.** Often, these steps are well **below sea level** due to intense vertical erosion from the glacier.

- When the glacier melts, seawater rushes in to flood the valley. These **drowned glacial valleys** are called **fiords. Killary Harbour** in Co. Mayo is an example of a fiord.

(a)

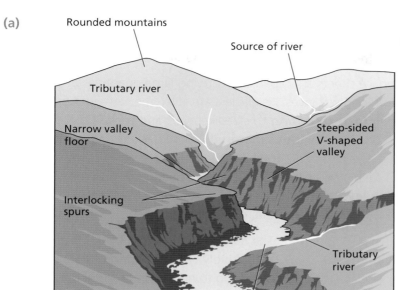

Rounded mountains

Source of river

Tributary river

Narrow valley floor

Steep-sided V-shaped valley

Interlocking spurs

Tributary river

Confluence

◀ **Fig. 12.14** A valley (a) before and (b) after glacial erosion

(b)

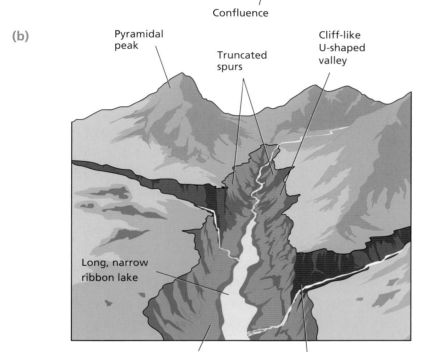

Pyramidal peak

Truncated spurs

Cliff-like U-shaped valley

Long, narrow ribbon lake

Wide, flat valley floor

Tributary in a hanging valley with a waterfall

ACTIVE LEARNING

1. Explain the processes of glacial erosion.
2. Name four features you would expect to find in a glaciated valley.
3. Give two Irish examples of a cirque.
4. Give two Irish examples of a U-shaped valley.
5. How is a pyramidal peak formed?
6. What is a hanging valley and how is it formed?
7. What is a paternoster lake?
8. What is the name given to a drowned glacial valley?
9. What is a bergschrund?
10. Explain fully how a cirque is formed.
11. Draw a labelled diagram of a U-shaped valley and explain how it is formed.

EDUCATE YOURSELF

Glacial Erosion	
Plucking	Cracks and joints, plucks rock away, water freezes around rock
Abrasion	Frozen jagged rock, smooth and polish, striation, deep scratches
Cirque	Corries/cooms, basin-shaped hollows, side of mountain, zone of accumulation, three steep sides, gently sloping side, back wall, side walls, tarn, Devil's Punchbowl, north/north-east, expansion of ice, freeze-thaw action, firn, water freezes in cracks, plucking, crevasses, bergschrund, scree, abrasion, rotational slide, deepens cirque, arête, narrow ridge, steep-sided, pyramidal peak, Carrantouhill
Glaciated valley	U-shaped valley, Glendalough, originally V-shaped valley, change shape, vertical and lateral erosion, shatters loose rock, plucks rock, deepens valley, abrasion, smooth valley floor, deep hollows, rock basin, ribbon lakes, paternoster lakes, interlocking spurs, truncated spurs, hanging valleys, waterfall, rock shapes, drowned glacial valleys, fiords

12.4 Glacial Transportation

<table>
<tr><td>

GEO DICTIONARY

Rock flour: rock that has been ground into powder by the glacier

Unstratified: does not have layers

Moraine: material transported by glaciers

</td></tr>
</table>

Glaciers and ice sheets are capable of carrying large quantities of eroded material over long distances. As glaciers are solid, they are **not capable of sorting their load according to size** like rivers and coasts do. Instead, the glacial load consists of **various material,** from finely ground 'rock flour' to large boulders or blocks of soil. As the material is mixed together in the glacier, it is said to be unsorted. Glaciers can melt quickly, so their loads are not **deposited in layers.** Instead the material is 'dropped' as a glacier retreats. The absence of layers means that the rock is **unstratified.**

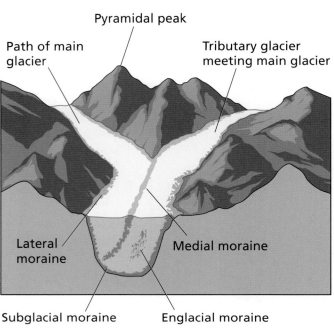

Path of main glacier

Pyramidal peak

Tributary glacier meeting main glacier

Lateral moraine

Medial moraine

Subglacial moraine

Englacial moraine

🔺 **Fig. 12.15** Different types of moraine

The material transported by glaciers is **collectively called moraine.** Moraine is classified according to how it is transported by the glacier.

- **Supraglacial moraine** is carried along on top of the glacier, as if on a slow-moving conveyor belt. Most of this material comes from **weathered material** on the sides of the valley. Freeze-thaw action breaks off fragments of rock from the side of the valley. These fragments of rock (scree) slide down the valley due to the **influence of gravity** before coming to a stop on top of the glacier. As the glacier moves, this material is carried away.

- **Englacial moraine** is carried **within the glacier.** Most englacial material is a result of weathered rock **falling through the crevasses** on the surface of the glacier. It can also occur when large pieces of rock fall on the glacier. The rock is so heavy that its pressure is capable of melting the ice beneath it and sinking into the glacier.

- **Lateral moraine** is carried along the **sides of glaciers.** Scree formed from freeze-thaw action slides down the sides of the valley and gathers at the side of the glacier. As the glacier moves, a ridge of material is created along both sides of the glacier. Lateral moraines also form as a result of plucking of material from the **sides of the valley.**

- **Subglacial moraine** is carried along the ground **beneath a glacier.** Subglacial moraine accumulates from material that was **plucked from the valley floor** or from scree that fell through deep crevasses in the glacier and reached the bottom.

- **Push moraine** is shoved along the **front of the glacier.** The glacier acts like a bulldozer, scraping sediment off the valley floor and pushing it along the valley as it moves.

ACTIVE LEARNING

1. What is the name given to the unsorted material transported by glaciers?
2. What is englacial moraine?
3. What is the difference between supraglacial moraine and englacial moraine?

EDUCATE YOURSELF

Glacial Transportation
Rock flour, deposited in layers, unstratified, supraglacial moraine, englacial moraine, lateral moraine, subglacial moraine, push moraine

12.5 Glacial Deposition

Material carried by a glacier is **deposited when the ice melts.** This melting occurs in the **zone of ablation** at the end point of the glacier. This is usually in lowland areas. The deposited material is called glacial drift. We will look at two types of glacial deposits:

1. **Boulder clay** (also referred to as glacial till) is the material **deposited directly by the glacier.** Boulder clay is **unsorted and unstratified,** consisting of material ranging from **rock flour to large boulders.** Generally the term **'glacial till'** is preferred as material deposited by the glacier does not necessarily include boulders or clay. Boulder clay is unconsolidated, meaning it is easily weathered and eroded.

2. **Fluvioglacial deposits** are similar to materials deposited by rivers. Melt water from the glacier flows beneath or ahead of it, carrying **sand and gravel** as it does so. This material is then sorted according to size before being deposited in layers, meaning it is **stratified.**

⌃ **Fig. 12.16** Boulder clay deposits: mud and pebbles mixed together

Moraines

The term 'moraine' is the collective word to describe material transported and deposited by glacial activity. Moraine consists of **unsorted and unstratified** material, ranging from **fine soil and rock flour to large boulders.** When glaciers melt, the moraine is deposited in ridges along the floor of the glaciated valley. There are four main types of moraine:

1. Lateral moraine
2. Medial moraine
3. Terminal moraine
4. Recessional moraine

Lateral Moraine

- Lateral moraines form when **long ridges of material** are deposited along the **sides of a glaciated valley.** Material from the moraine is collected in two ways.

    1. Fragments of rock are broken off the upper slopes of the valley and roll onto sides of the glacier. As the glacier moves down the valley, the material is carried away at its sides.

    2. Additional debris is added to the glacier as it scrapes along the sides of the valley. As it moves, **plucking and abrasion tears off rock and soil** from both sides of its path.

- When the glacier melts, this material is deposited in ridges along the sides of the valley. As the glacier deposits material along either side of the valley at roughly the same speed, the lateral moraines are usually at similar heights.

(a)

Medial Moraine

- Medial moraines are ridges that run along the **middle of the glaciated floor.** They form when a **tributary glacier** joins the main glacier.

- At this point, two lateral moraines join to form a medial moraine along the middle of the glacier. When the glacier melts, a ridge of **unstratified** material is left running through the middle of the valley.

⬆ **Fig. 12.17** (a) A moraine and (b) a diagram of moraine

(b)

Medial moraines

Lateral moraines

Ground moraine

Outwash

Recessional moraine

Terminal moraine

Terminal Moraine

- A terminal moraine, also known as an end moraine, is a ridge of unsorted, **unstratified material** that forms at the very end of a glacier.

- These moraines are important historical records for scientists as they tell them exactly how far the glacier travelled before it melted.

- As a glacier moves down a valley, it acts like a bulldozer by **scraping rock and soil from the valley floor** in front of it.

- Eventually, the glacier will reach a point of balance. This means that the glacier advances at the same speed at which it melts. As this happens, the glacier does not advance any further as it melts.

- As melting continues, more material is deposited at this point allowing the terminal moraine to build up further. Eventually a large ridge that stretches across the valley is formed. Ireland has a large terminal moraine that stretches across the south of the country from **Wicklow to the mouth of the Shannon River. This marks the most southerly point of the last large glacier to move across Ireland.** Over the last 10 000 years, much of the moraine has been eroded away.

⬆ **Fig. 12.18** Part of terminal moraine that runs from Wicklow to the River Shannon

Recessional Moraine

- As temperatures increased towards the end of the last ice age, glaciers began to melt more quickly. Temporary periods of **colder weather stopped the melting** process and halted glacial retreat, leading to ridges of boulder clay being deposited.

- During this time, materials were carried to the front of the glacier and deposited there. These deposits built up to form ridges called **recessional moraines.**

- One retreating glacier or ice sheet may produce **several recessional moraines** as **temperatures fluctuated.**

A-Z GEO DICTIONARY

Ground moraine: flat or gently sloped areas of moraine deposited by a rapidly retreating glacier

Ground Moraines

- Ground moraines are formed by the **rapid retreat** of glaciers. As the glacier retreats rapidly, the boulder clay or till is deposited evenly along the valley floor.

- As a result, the material does not form ridges. Instead the deposition creates an area of **flat or gently rolling landscape** that is very fertile for agriculture. The Central Plain of Ireland is one such ground moraine that is widely used for agriculture.

- Ground moraines are the **most common type of moraine** and can be found on all continents.

Drumlins

- Drumlins are **oval-shaped mounds** that are formed as a result of glacial deposition.

- Their **elongated shape** comes from a **streamlining action of glacial ice** as it moves over till and scree.

- Drumlins are usually found in lowland regions and plains and vary greatly in size. The largest drumlins are between 1 and 2 km long, 500 m wide and up to 50 m high. The long axis of the drumlin lies **parallel to the movement** of the ice.

- Drumlins have a steep side, known as the **stoss end.** From the stoss end, the drumlin then slopes gently downward. From this shape, scientists can determine the direction the glacier moved in. The stoss end marks the side the glacier came from, while the gently sloping end marks the direction the glacier was travelling to.

- Drumlins are made of boulder clay or till and are usually found in clusters or **swarms,** ranging in number from dozens to thousands. As boulder clay is **impermeable,** drumlins are often surrounded by marshy land. This marshland is due to poor drainage and original saturation from glacial melt water.

- Although geologists do not fully understand the formation of drumlin clusters it is believed they occur in three stages:

  1. As large glaciers and ice sheets advanced across continents, the glacier transported large quantities of **unsorted and unstratified** boulder clay with it.

  2. During an **interglacial period,** temperatures began to rise. As a result, the glaciers began to retreat, depositing large **lumps of material** unevenly across the countryside.

(a)

(b)

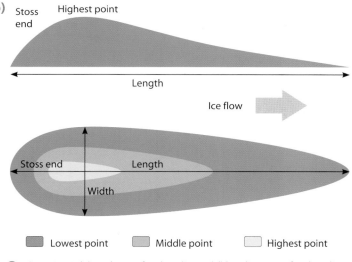

Stoss end   Highest point

Length

Ice flow

Stoss end   Length

Width

■ Lowest point   ■ Middle point   ■ Highest point

⬙ **Fig. 12.19** (a) A photo of a drumlin and (b) a diagram of a drumlin

CORE 1   CHAPTER 12

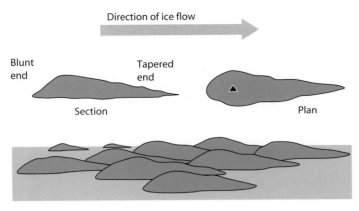

Direction of ice flow

Blunt end

Tapered end

Section

Plan

Fig. 12.20 Basket of eggs topography

Fig. 12.21 Clew Bay in Co. Mayo

ACTIVE LEARNING

1. What is boulder clay?
2. Describe what a drumlin looks like.
3. What are the theories on how drumlins formed?
4. What is meant by the term 'interglacial'?
5. What glacial features are found at Clew Bay, Co. Mayo?
6. With the aid of labelled diagrams, explain how one feature of glacial erosion and one feature of glacial deposition are formed.

3. When temperatures dropped again, the glacier began to advance once more. As the glacier moved over the previously deposited material, it began to **shape and smoothen it.** Eventually, when the ice melted once again, the drumlins were left behind.

- Another possibility is that drumlins were formed when moving glaciers became **overloaded** with debris. As the glacier moved, the **friction between the debris and the ground** became greater than the friction between the glacier and the debris. As a result, the debris was deposited and shaped by the ice moving over it.

- While these theories explain how drumlins are formed, they do not explain why they occur in large numbers and only in certain areas.

- When an ice age ends, large amounts of melt water flow into the sea, causing its level to rise. As drumlins form in lowlands, the rising sea partially submerges or **'drowns' the drumlins.** This can be seen in **Clew Bay, Co. Mayo** where a swarm of drumlins were partially submerged by the sea at the end of the last ice age 10 000 years ago. Swarms of drumlins are also referred as 'basket of eggs topography' due to the appearance they give the landscape.

- As these drumlins are made of boulder clay, and are therefore unconsolidated, they are eroded easily by the sea.

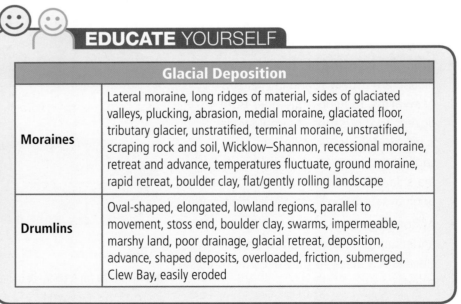

EDUCATE YOURSELF

Glacial Deposition	
Moraines	Lateral moraine, long ridges of material, sides of glaciated valleys, plucking, abrasion, medial moraine, glaciated floor, tributary glacier, unstratified, terminal moraine, unstratified, scraping rock and soil, Wicklow–Shannon, recessional moraine, retreat and advance, temperatures fluctuate, ground moraine, rapid retreat, boulder clay, flat/gently rolling landscape
Drumlins	Oval-shaped, elongated, lowland regions, parallel to movement, stoss end, boulder clay, swarms, impermeable, marshy land, poor drainage, glacial retreat, deposition, advance, shaped deposits, overloaded, friction, submerged, Clew Bay, easily eroded

12.6 Fluvioglacial Landforms

Fluvioglacial landforms are created towards the **end of an ice age,** when glaciers melt and retreat rapidly. Fluvioglacial features are not created by the action of glacial ice, but rather by the **melt water from glacial ice.** As these features are created by flowing water, they resemble landforms created by river processes. The erosional landforms created are **shaped by the processes of hydraulic action, abrasion** and **attrition,** while deposited material is **sorted and stratified.**

A glacial spillway is a common fluvioglacial landform of erosion, and **eskers, erratics** and **outwash plains** are common features of fluvioglacial deposition.

Esker

An esker is a **long, winding ridge** of deposited material that runs along lowland areas. Generally, eskers run parallel to the direction the glacier or ice sheet travelled in. They are mostly composed of **sorted, stratified layers** of sand and gravel. **Eiscir Riada** is an Irish example and runs from Galway to Dublin.

● **Fig. 12.22** An aerial view of an esker

- Eskers formed in **tunnels within glaciers.** Streams of melt water flowed through these tunnels carrying sediment with them.

- As glaciers retreated, they left behind large amounts of water flowing through the narrow tunnel. The restriction of space in the tunnel meant the water flowed rapidly under pressure, making it capable of carrying a greater load.

- When the load became too large to carry, it was deposited in layers along the channel, **raising the level of the river.** During warmer periods or summer months, a greater level of melt water flowed through the tunnels, carrying larger loads.

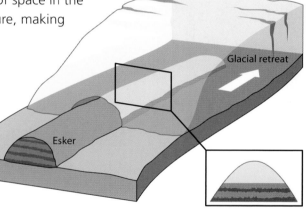

- During colder periods or winter months, the volume of melt water was reduced, causing the stream to deposit its load in **thick layers.** During this time, only fine particles such as sand were transported along the channel and deposited in thin layers.

● **Fig. 12.23** The formation of an esker

- When the glaciers melted, the ridge of deposited materials was left elevated above the surrounding landscape, creating an esker.

- Over thousands of years, the edges of these eskers have become more gently sloping due to **weathering** and **mass movement.**

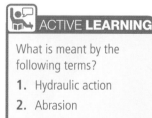

ACTIVE LEARNING

What is meant by the following terms?
1. Hydraulic action
2. Abrasion
3. Attrition
4. Stratified

Outwash Plain

An outwash plain is a **flat or gently sloping** area of land formed by the deposition of sediment from glacial melt water. It forms as a glacier rapidly retreats towards the **end of an ice age.**

The **Curragh** in Co. Kildare is an Irish example of an outwash plain.

- Large amounts of **boulder clay/till** and other sediments carried by glaciers were washed away by melt water. The melt water carried the sediment beyond the **terminal moraine,** before gradually losing energy and slowing down to form lakes known as kettles.

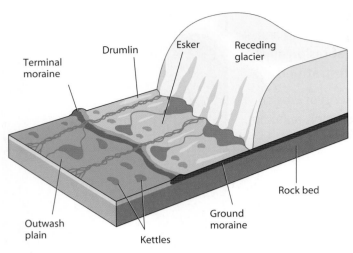

Fig. 12.24 An outwash plain

Fig. 12.25 An erratic carried thousands of kilometres by a glacier

- As the water slowed down, it was unable to continue carrying its load. Heavier material such as gravel and stone was deposited first, close to the terminal moraine.

- **Lighter, finer particles** such as sand and clay were **carried further** before they too were deposited.

Erratic

The word 'erratic' means '**irregular or inconsistent'**. A glacial erratic is a **large boulder** that has been deposited in an area with a **different rock type,** e.g. a large block of granite in a limestone area.

Several glacial erratics, such as **Fionn's Fist,** can be found in Co. Cavan.

Ice sheets and glaciers are capable of carrying these large fragments of rock over very long distances. Eventually the ice melts and the boulder is deposited in a region of different rock type.

Erratics are useful historical records for geologists, as they can be used to identify the direction and path that a glacier travelled.

Glacial Spillway

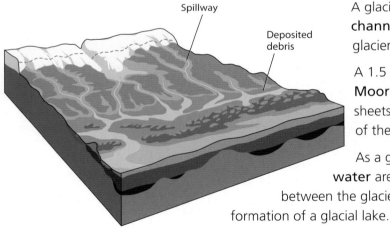

Fig. 12.26 A glacial spillway

A glacial spillway is a **natural drainage channel** that is created by melt water from a glacier eroding into a valley.

A 1.5 km long spillway was formed in **Moorhill,** Kilcullen, Co. Kildare as the ice sheets that covered Ireland melted at the end of the last ice age.

As a glacier retreats, **huge quantities of water** are released. Often this water is trapped in between the glacier and an upland region, leading to the formation of a glacial lake.

- As more water flows into the lake, its level rises. Eventually the water levels rise above the lowest point in the landscape.

- Huge amounts of water flow down the valley, taking on the **characteristics of a youthful river.** The rapidly moving water **cuts into the valley,** causing vertical erosion.

- **Hydraulic action** shatters the bedrock of the valley, carrying a large load of debris with it. Eroded material from the melting glacier is also swept away by the water. This also helps to erode the spillway through the process of **abrasion.**

- Eventually, a V-shaped valley is cut into the landscape. Once the glacier has fully melted, the lake disappears and the **river dries up.**

- Sometimes a small stream occupies the valley but it is too small to have created the spillway.

- Glacial spillways are often surrounded by **marshy or peat soils** formed from prolonged saturation.

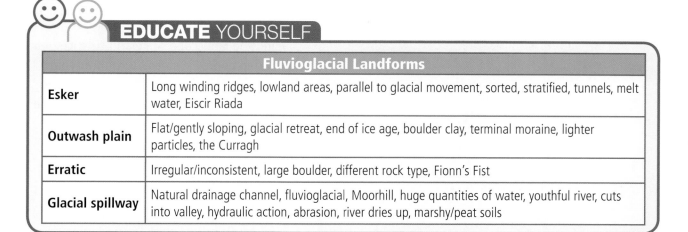

Fluvioglacial Landforms	
Esker	Long winding ridges, lowland areas, parallel to glacial movement, sorted, stratified, tunnels, melt water, Eiscir Riada
Outwash plain	Flat/gently sloping, glacial retreat, end of ice age, boulder clay, terminal moraine, lighter particles, the Curragh
Erratic	Irregular/inconsistent, large boulder, different rock type, Fionn's Fist
Glacial spillway	Natural drainage channel, fluvioglacial, Moorhill, huge quantities of water, youthful river, cuts into valley, hydraulic action, abrasion, river dries up, marshy/peat soils

12.7 Identifying Glacial Features on OS Maps

A = Cirque with tarn	(T 07 98)
B = U-shaped valley	(T 08 96)
C = Hanging valley	(O 11 00)
D = Paternoster lakes	(T 10 96)
E = Pyramidal peak	(T 118 954)
F = Truncated spur	(T 12 98)
G = Arête	(T 10 97)

As part of the exam, students are often asked to identify glacial features of erosion and deposition from an OS map. Here, we will cover the most frequently asked of these features:

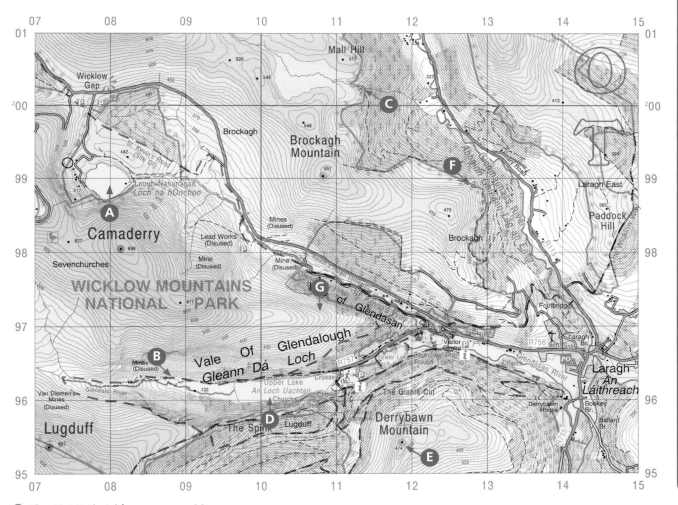

Fig. 12.27 Glacial features on an OS map

12.8 Glaciation and Ireland

The last ice age played a major role in shaping the landscape of Ireland. The ice age began approximately **2.6 million years ago** and **ended roughly 10 000 years ago.** Scientists believe that there were at least **five periods of glacial advance,** with warmer, **interglacial periods** in between. Two of these periods of glacial advance affected Ireland. They were:

- The **Munsterian** glacial period
- The **Midlandian** glacial period

The Munsterian Period

The Munsterian glacial period began roughly **300 000 years ago** and lasted until 130 000 years ago. The vast **majority of Ireland** was covered in a thick ice sheet.

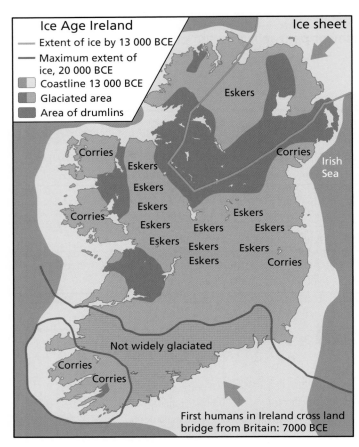

Ice Age Ireland
- —— Extent of ice by 13 000 BCE
- —— Maximum extent of ice, 20 000 BCE
- ☐ Coastline 13 000 BCE
- ▨ Glaciated area
- ▨ Area of drumlins

Ice sheet

Eskers

Corries

Corries
Irish Sea

Eskers

Eskers

Eskers

Corries

Eskers
Eskers
Eskers

Eskers
Eskers

Eskers

Eskers

Corries

Not widely glaciated

Corries
Corries

First humans in Ireland cross land bridge from Britain: 7000 BCE

🔺 **Fig. 12.28** Ice age Ireland

The Scottish ice sheet travelled across the Irish Sea in a south-westerly direction, covering the eastern half of country. Several smaller glaciers formed along the mountains of the west coast. They **joined together** to form a large ice sheet to cover almost all of the country.

Only the peaks of the highest mountains protruded from the glacier. These peaks are called **nunataks.**

As the ice sheet retreated, thick layers of **boulder clay and fluvioglacial** material were deposited along the Irish lowlands.

This warmer interglacial period lasted 60 000 years, before colder temperatures returned.

The Midlandian Period

The Midlandian glacial period began **70 000 years ago** and began to retreat from Ireland roughly 13 000 years ago. During this period, the Scottish ice sheet began to advance again along the eastern coast of Ireland, completely covering the Irish Sea. As this occurred, glacial ice began to accumulate along the upland regions of Donegal, Galway and Wicklow.

The glaciers joined together to form an ice sheet that covered approximately **two-thirds of the country.** A large terminal moraine that runs from the mouth of the **River Shannon to the Wicklow Mountains** in the east marks the **southernmost point** that the ice sheet travelled.

Roughly 13 000 years ago, **temperatures rose once again,** causing the glacier to retreat. As the ice melted, thick layers of glacial and fluvioglacial material were deposited along the midlands. Evidence suggests that small glaciers remained in Wicklow and Antrim until 10 000 years ago.

Effects on Landscape

As well as creating several landforms of erosion and deposition, the ice age impacted greatly on the **Irish coastline, soil formation and animal and plant life.**

During the ice age, sea levels were much lower than they are today. Ireland was connected to Great Britain by a land bridge, and a land bridge also connected Britain to Europe. It is believed that Ireland's first wildlife came to Ireland by crossing these **land bridges** close to the end of the last ice age. The red deer are believed to have arrived during this time.

When the ice fully melted, huge volumes of water were released. This led to a global rise in sea levels, submerging the land bridges that connected Ireland to Britain. The rising water also **submerged much of the low-lying coastline.** Evidence of this can be seen in **Clew Bay,** Co. Mayo.

As the glacial ice advanced across Ireland, **plucking and abrasion** removed a layer of soil and mudstone that covered the **Burren region,** exposing its underlying limestone. The ice also deposited seeds of rare flora in the region, which still grow there today. This rare flora attracts thousands of tourists each year.

Economic Benefits

Ireland's raised **peat bogs also began to form** at the end of the last ice age. As Ireland is bowl shaped, it slopes downwards towards the Central Plain. As the ice retreated, it left behind impermeable boulder clay. This led to a **poor drainage system** in the area, allowing glacial melt water to build up and form marsh lakes. Over thousands of years, the lakes began to fill with poorly decomposed vegetation. Eventually, these lakes completely filled to form the raised bogs of Ireland's midlands which are now commercially harvested by Bórd na Mona.

 EDUCATE YOURSELF

Glaciation in Ireland	
Munsterian Period	300 000 years ago, majority of Ireland, Scottish ice sheet, joined together, nunataks, boulder clay, fluvioglacial
Midlandian Period	70 000–13 000 years ago, temperatures fluctuated
Effects on landscape	Irish coastline, soil formation, animal and plant life, land bridges, submerged, Clew Bay, plucking, abrasion, Burren region, peat bogs, poor drainage

SHORT QUESTIONS

1. (i) Examine the photographs and correctly match each of the letters on the photographs with one of the landforms named in the box.

Landform	Letter
U-shaped valley	
Pyramidal peak	
Erratic	
Corrie lake	

2011 Q7 10M

(i) 2m each
(ii) Benefit named 2m

(ii) Name one way in which glacial landscapes benefit the economy in areas they are found.

LONG QUESTIONS

1. Explain, with the aid of diagrams, the formation of any two landforms.

Two landforms @ 20m each
Landform named 1m
Diagram with two aspects 2m each
Formation explained 5 SRPs @ 3m each

2015 Q3B 40M

2. Explain, with the aid of a diagram(s), the formation of any one Irish landform resulting from glacial processes.

Process named 3m
Explanation 9 SRPs @ 3m each

2010 Q1B 30M

SHORT QUESTIONS

1. Examine the aerial photograph. In the table, match each of the letters A to D with the correct landform from the following list:

    Drumlin   Lateral moraine   Fiord
    Corrie/coom/cirque   Arête   Pyramidal peak

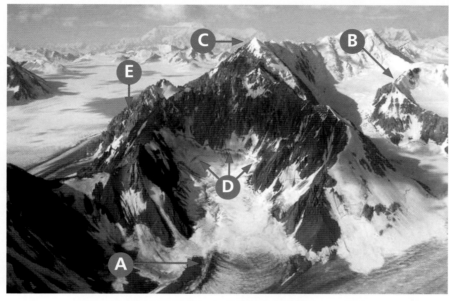

Letter	Landform
A	
B	
C	
D	
E	

2012 Q1 8M

4 x 2m each

LONG QUESTIONS

1. Examine the impact of the processes of erosion on the formation of one glacial landform that you have studied.

Process of erosion 2m + 2m
Landform named 2m
Examination 12 SRPs @ 2m each

2015 Q1B 30M

2. Explain the formation of one landform of erosion and one landform of deposition that you have studied.

Landform of erosion named 2m
Landform of deposition named 2m
Formation of landform of erosion 6/7 SRPs @ 2m each
Formation of landform of deposition 6/7 SRPs @ 2m each

2014 Q2B 30M

Questions on landscape development and surface processes have appeared every year since 2006 at both Higher Level and Ordinary Level, so it is an important topic to be prepared for. In this section, we will look at the formation of landforms by glacial action.

HIGHER LEVEL

EXAM QUESTION

Explain, with the aid of a labelled diagram(s), the formation of one landform of deposition that you have studied.

Marking Scheme
Landform named 2m
Labelled diagram 4m
Explanation 12 SRPs @ 2m each

2011 Q2B 30M

SAMPLE ANSWER

A feature glacial deposition that I have studied is a drumlin [2m].

A drumlin is a low oval-shaped hill of unsorted boulder clay or glacial till that is formed as a result of glacial deposition [2m]. Boulder clay is unsorted material consisting of sand, gravel, clay and pebbles [2m].

Drumlins normally occur in groups called swarms which can be seen in Clew Bay, Co. Mayo [2m].

As large glaciers and ice sheets advanced across continents, they transported large quantities of unsorted and unstratified boulder clay with them [2m]. The largest drumlins are between 1 and 2 km long, 500 m wide and up to 50 m high. The long axis of the drumlin lies parallel to the movement of the ice giving it a steep side, known as the stoss end which slopes gently downwards towards the front [2m]. The stoss end marks the side the glacier came from, while the gently sloping end

Landform named and clearly defined.

An Irish example is clearly provided.

Structure of glacier and two theories of its formation are summarised and explained.

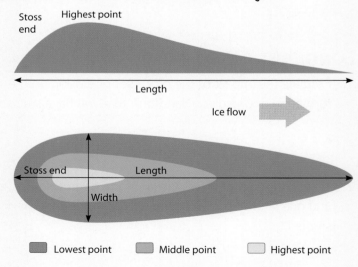

marks the direction the glacier was travelling in [2m]. Drumlins are usually found in clusters or swarms, ranging in number from dozens to thousands, which were deposited under a melting ice sheet laden with boulder clay [2m]. As boulder clay is impermeable, drumlins are often surrounded by marshy land due to poor drainage and its original saturation from glacial melt water [2m].

There are two main ideas as to how drumlins were formed:

1. During the interglacial period, temperatures began to rise, causing glaciers to retreat, depositing large lumps of material across the countryside [2m]. When temperatures fell again, the glacier began to advance again, moving over the deposited material, shaping and smoothing it into its unique shape [2m].

2. Another explanation is that drumlins formed when moving glaciers became overloaded with material which were removed when friction between the material and ground becomes greater than the friction between the glacier and the material [2m]. As the glacier moved over the material, it shaped it into the drumlin shape [2m].

When the ice age ended, large amounts of melt water flowed into the sea, causing its level to rise which submerged the drumlins, e.g. Clew Bay, Co. Mayo [2m]. As the drumlins are made of boulder clay, it is unconsolidated and easily eroded by the sea [2m].

Answer is structured and shows a clear understanding of drumlin formation.

Marks Awarded
Landform named 2m
Labelled diagram 4m
Best 12 SRPs @ 2m each
Total 30/30

TOPIC MAP

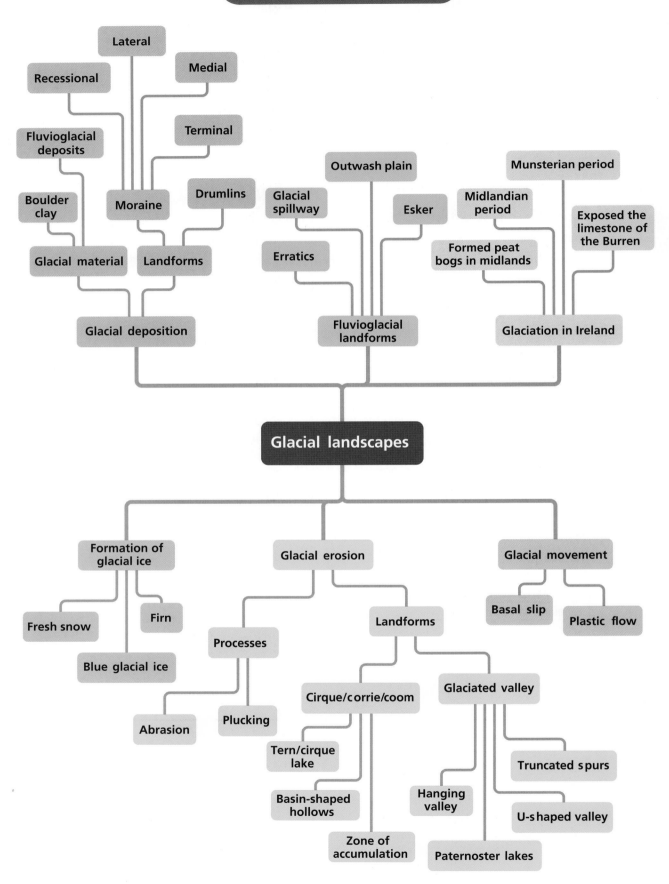

CHAPTER 13

Higher Level only

Isostasy

So far, you have learned about forces from within the crust (endogenic forces) and the surface forces which cause weathering and erosion (exogenic forces). In this chapter, we will look at the balance that exists between the two forces and what happens when these forces are thrown off balance due to the rising and sinking of the Earth's crust. This is known as isostasy. This chapter is for Higher Level students only.

KEY WORDS

- Endogenic forces
- Exogenic forces
- Isostatic movement
- Isostatic equilibrium
- Isostatic rebound
- Fluvial readjustment

- River rejuvenation
- Knickpoint
- Paired terraces
- Incised meanders
- Entrenched meanders
- Coastline of submergence

- Coastline of emergence
- Raised beaches
- Raised cliffs
- Raised wave-cut platforms
- Peneplain

LEARNING OUTCOMES

What you MUST know
- A definition of isostasy
- Coastlines of emergence and submergence
- Adjustment to base level of a river (fluvial readjustment)
- Landscape development and peneplain development

Introduction

From your study of physical geography so far, you know that the Earth's crust is in a **continuous cycle of landform creation and destruction.** Landforms such as volcanoes and fold mountains create vertical rises in the Earth's crust. These are gradually worn down overtime by denudation (weathering and erosion).

- **Forces from within the crust** which form tectonic landscapes, such as fold mountains and volcanic plateaus, are referred to as **endogenic forces.**
- **Forces** which breakdown these landforms **on the surface** (weathering and erosion) are referred to as **exogenic forces.**

 GEO **DICTIONARY**

Endogenic forces: forces from within the Earth. Convection currents cause plates to collide separate and slide past, creating vertical landforms on the surface

Exogenic forces: forces on the surface. Weathering and erosion leads to the breakdown of landforms created by endogenic forces

CORE 1 CHAPTER 13

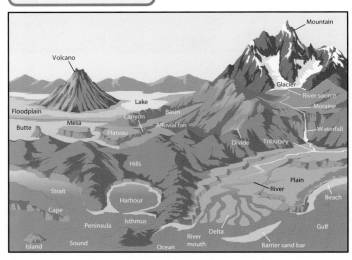

GEO DICTIONARY

Isostatic movement: the vertical movement of the Earth's crust

Isostatic equilibrium: the heavier a piece of crust is (e.g. a mountain range), the further it will sink into the mantle

For much of our planet's history, these forces have been balanced, However, occasionally, the balance between endogenic and exogenic forces is interrupted. This happens when **weight is added to or taken away from the Earth's crust.** This adding or removing of weight can cause the crust to sink further into the asthenosphere or rise upwards from it. This is referred to as **isostatic movement.**

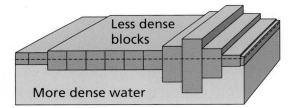

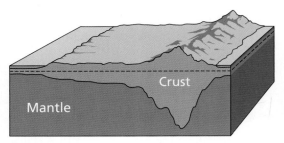

⌃ Fig 13.1 Landscape is a balance between endogenic and exogenic forces. Convection currents cause volcanic and mountain landscapes on the surface through separation and collision, which are then broken down by the external forces of weathering and erosion.

⌃ Fig 13.2 The Earth's crust can move vertically in response to loads on top of it.

Why?

Endogenic forces created the Caledonian fold mountains in Ireland 400 mya as they forced the African and Eurasian Plates together. Over the past 400 million years, these mountains have been worn down by exogenic forces (weathering and erosion), which explains why the mountains are on average just 600 metres high today.

⌄ Fig 13.3 Glacial and interglacial periods

13.1 Isostatic Movement

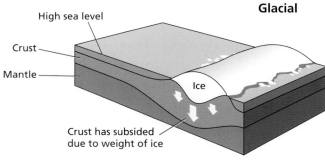

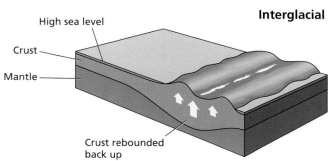

Isostatic movement refers to the **vertical movement** of the Earth's crust. As you already know from your study of plate boundaries, the Earth's **crust floats on top of the asthenosphere.** This is the semi-molten magma of the upper mantle. The heavier the crust is, the more of it will **sink into the asthenosphere.** Therefore, thick parts of the Earth's crust, such as those containing mountain ranges sink further into the asthenosphere than thin crust does. This sinking of the crust is referred to as **isostatic equilibrium.**

From this, we now know that the Earth's crust is **not perfectly rigid** and that it can sink or rise further by the **addition or subtraction of weight.** The most common addition of weight (called loading) occurs during ice ages, when large **glaciers press down on the crust**. This occurred in Europe during the **last ice age** when the additional weight from the ice caused the crust to sink further into the asthenosphere. This is referred to as **isostatic readjustment**. When this occurs, the **sea level** gets **higher by comparison** as the crust sinks downwards. When an ice age ends, the weight of the **glaciers is removed** from the crust, causing it to **rise upwards** once again. This is known as **isostatic rebound**. As the crust rises, the **sea level gets lower** by comparison. This has a major impact on the **profile and processes of rivers**.

ACTIVE LEARNING

1. Explain the term 'isostasy'.
2. What are endogenic forces?
3. What are exogenic forces?

☺ ☺ **EDUCATE** YOURSELF

Isostasy	Vertical movement of crust, crust floating on asthenosphere, pushed down by weight, isostatic equilibrium, glaciers add weight, isostatic readjustment, crust sinks, sea level rises, crust rises, sea level falls, affects river profiles

13.2 Fluvial Readjustment

As you now know, a river's profile typically has three stages: **youthful, mature and old**. Rivers normally flow from their source in upland areas to the sea. Where a river enters the sea is known as its base level. As the crust rebounds upwards after an ice age, the sea level falls relative to the crust. As the sea level is now lower, the **river must erode downwards** once again in order to reach sea level. This is referred to as **fluvial readjustment**. As the river erodes downwards again, it takes on the characteristics of a **youthful river**: flowing rapidly and eroding vertically into the river bed. This moves the river from an old stage to a youthful stage once again. This is known as **river rejuvenation** (meaning 'to make young again'). The River Nore in Co. Kilkenny and the River Moy are examples of Irish rivers which have experienced readjustment and rejuvenation.

Landforms Associated with Rejuvenation

Knickpoints

Rejuvenation **begins at the mouth** of a river, eroding vertically towards sea level. As it does so, a **new V-shaped valley** is created. **Headward erosion** causes the new valley to migrate upstream, gradually **destroying the old river profile**. The point where the new river profile meets the old river profile is called a **knickpoint**. A waterfall may form at a knickpoint as there is a sudden drop in the river's profile. Isostatic rebound may occur repeatedly, or in stages, meaning that there is more than one knickpoint on the river profile. As each new knickpoint **migrates upstream**, it removes the profile of the older one.

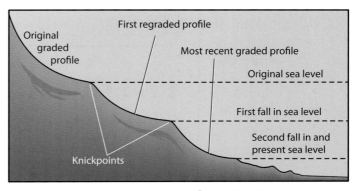

▲ **Fig 13.4** Fluvial readjustment and rejuvenation

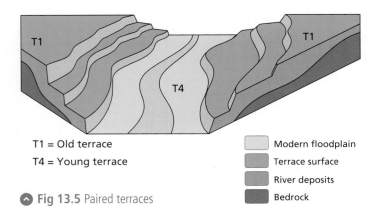

T1 = Old terrace
T4 = Young terrace

Modern floodplain
Terrace surface
River deposits
Bedrock

 **Fig 13.5** Paired terraces

Paired Terraces

River rejuvenation causes the **vertical erosion** of the old river valley. As it does so, it carves a **new valley floor** in its old floodplain. This creates a valley within a valley. This downward erosion leaves the edges of the **old floodplain elevated above** the new valley at both sides. The two sides of the old floodplain are referred to as **paired terraces** as both sides stand at equal heights above the new valley floor.

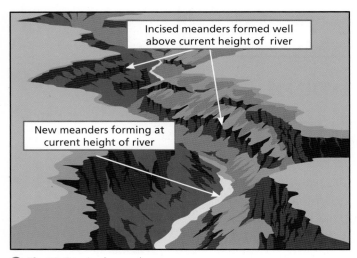

Incised meanders formed well above current height of river

New meanders forming at current height of river

Fig 13.6 Incised meanders

Incised Meanders

As you have already learned, a river develops meanders in its middle and lower stages. When a river is rejuvenated, it has much more erosive power. Although a rejuvenated river will usually maintain its winding course, the **meanders are deepened** by cutting into the old floodplain's floor. As this happens, **steep cliffs are formed** on the outer bends of the meanders. Incised meanders are also referred to as **entrenched meanders.**

ACTIVE **LEARNING**

1. When does fluvial rejuvenation occur?
2. Explain how knickpoints form.
3. What are paired terraces?
4. Explain, with the aid of a diagram, how incised meanders form.
5. Name an Irish river that has experienced rejuvenation.

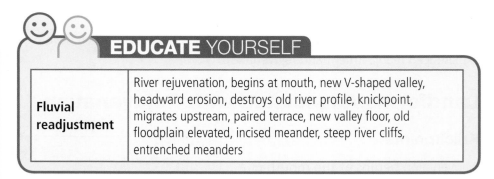

EDUCATE YOURSELF

| **Fluvial readjustment** | River rejuvenation, begins at mouth, new V-shaped valley, headward erosion, destroys old river profile, knickpoint, migrates upstream, paired terrace, new valley floor, old floodplain elevated, incised meander, steep river cliffs, entrenched meanders |

13.3 Coastal Isostasy

Isostatic movement also impacts coastlines. When weight is added to the Earth's crust, the sea level rises relative to the land. When weight is removed from the crust, land rises from the asthenosphere. When this occurs, the sea level falls relative to the land. This rising and sinking is called isostatic movement.

The last period of isostatic movement to affect Ireland occurred during the last **ice age** which began about 2.6 million years ago and ended 10 000 years ago.

- As glaciers developed on the crust, they pushed the crust downwards into the asthenosphere, causing a **rise in sea level.** This is called a **coastline of submergence.**
- When the ice age ended, the weight of the ice was removed from the crust. Slowly, the crust began to rise upwards once again, causing a relative **drop in sea level.** This is called **isostatic rebound,** which leads to a **coastline of emergence.** This rebound process is said to be finished across Ireland with the exception of the north-east of Co. Antrim.

Evidence of Isostasy

Evidence of coastal emergence can be seen by the presence of coastal landforms in areas no longer reached by the sea. Examples of such features include **raised beaches, raised cliffs** and **raised wave-cut platforms.** These were created by the same coastal processes active today, but were formed when the sea level was much higher relative to the coastline. When the ice age ended, the crust began to uplift to its original level. As it did, the landforms were elevated high above sea level.

About 5400 years ago

About 2100 years ago

1855

Present storm beach ridge

⬆ **Fig 13.7** Raised beaches

The landforms created during the ice age are now elevated above the reach of the current sea level. Beneath them, similar landforms are being formed at the height of the new sea level. Evidence of raised landforms can be seen along Antrim's **Coast Road,** were there is a raised beach 40 m above sea level. A raised beach can also be found in Carndonagh in Co. Donegal.

EDUCATE YOURSELF

Coastal isostasy	Ice age, rise in sea level, coast of submergence, drop in sea level, isostatic rebound, coast of emergence, e.g. coast of Antrim
Evidence of isostasy	Raised beaches, raised cliffs, raised wave-cut platforms, Coast Road, Co. Antrim, Carndonagh, Co. Donegal

ACTIVE **LEARNING**

1. Explain how raised cliffs and raised beaches are formed.
2. Name two Irish locations where raised beaches can be found.

13.4 Landscape Cycle and Peneplains

Over the course of hundreds of millions of years, landscapes go through a cycle of development.

Stage 1

Land is created as **magma pours onto the Earth's crust** before cooling rapidly to form high flat plateaux of land. Isostatic rebound can also bring new land to the surface. This generally **flat landscape is largely featureless** as it has not yet been weathered and eroded.

Stage 2

Weathering and **erosion cut vertically into the plateau,** carving out **valleys and hillsides.** For example, a river carves out V-shaped valleys while a glacier carves out U-shaped valleys. Materials broken down here are then **transported downslope and deposited** on the lowlands of the valleys.

Stage 3

Over a long period of time, **hills and steep valleys are broken** down by weathering and erosion. As this occurs, lowland areas become level as layers of eroded material are **deposited by rivers and melting glaciers.**

Stage 4

Eventually, hills and steep valleys are almost completely broken down to create a **flat lowland** referred to as a **peneplain.** A peneplain is not a permanent landscape as isostatic movement, sea level change or tectonic activity can cause the plain to become a **plateau once again.** When this occurs, the process is repeated.

(a)

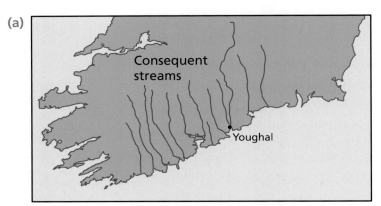

(b)

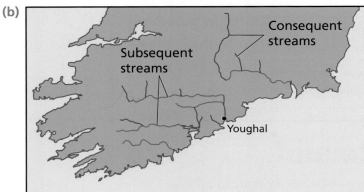

⬆ **Fig 13.8** (a) Rivers of south Munster 60 million years ago (b) rivers of south Munster today

Irish Peneplain

An **example** of an Irish peneplain can be found in **Munster.** At one point, there was a peneplain in Munster that sloped southwards towards the sea. This **gently sloping surface** had formed from an old marine seafloor which was raised above sea level. As the peneplain **sloped gently southwards,** the rivers flowed in that direction. These are called **consequent streams** as they flow in that direction as a consequence of the slope.

Since then, a combination of **vertical erosion** and Earth movements has led to the formation of a series of **west-east flowing rivers** such as the Blackwater, Lee and Bandon. These rivers cut into the peneplain, removing the overlying chalk. When the rivers reached the more-**resistant sandstone anticlines** underneath, they continued to **flow in a west-east direction.** This movement continued, despite moving against the direction of the anticlines, before eventually reaching the **less-resistant limestone anticlines** further east. Here, the rivers **joined the drainage basins** of the originally **south-flowing rivers.** This formed a series of parallel ridges and valleys which created a trellised drainage pattern.

The tributaries of these rivers have divided the peneplain into **isolated hills** of more or less even height separated by small river valleys. In some places the rivers, such as the Blackwater, have cut steep-sided gorges into the landscape as they flow south before entering the sea.

Landscape Cycle and Peneplains	
Stage 1	New land formed or brought to surface
Stage 2	Weathering and erosion, valleys and plateaux
Stage 3	Hills and valleys weathered and eroded, deposition levels lowland
Stage 4	Peneplain; Irish peneplain: Munster, old marine seafloor, slopes gently, Rivers Blackwater, Lee and Bandon

ACTIVE LEARNING

1. What is a peneplain?
2. What are consequent streams?
3. Explain how the drainage patterns of Munster have changed over time.

Note!
This topic has not yet appeared in the short questions section of the Higher Level exam. However, it would be useful to familiarise yourself with the diagrams and images of the different features covered in this chapter in case it is asked in future short questions.

EXAM QUESTIONS

HIGHER LEVEL

LONG QUESTIONS

1. Examine the diagram which shows the stages in the cyclical development of a fluvial landscape and answer each of the following questions:

   (i) Name each of the stages A, B and C.

   (ii) Name one fluvial landform from each of the stages A, B and C.

   (iii) Explain briefly what is meant by peneplain.

   (iv) Explain briefly what is meant by base level.

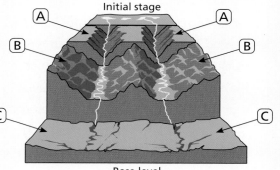

Initial stage

Base level

(i) 3 stages @ 2m each
(ii) 3 features @ 2m each
(iii) Two valid statements @ 2m each
(iv) Two valid statements @ 2m each

2014 Q3A 20M

2. Examine how isostasy has impacted on the Irish landscape.

Impact identified 2m
Examination 14 SRPs @ 2m each

2015 Q2C 30M

3. Explain how isostatic changes have impacted on the Irish landscape, using examples that you have studied.

Impact/feature identified 2m + 2m
Example 2m + 2m
Explanation 11 SRPs @ 2m each

2011 Q3C 30M

Isostasy is a topic which has caused problems for students since it first appeared in 2009. As it is a relatively short topic, appearing at the end of a long physical section, many students do not give it as much attention as they do the tectonic and surface processes chapters. However, isostasy has appeared as a question every second year since 2009. In this section, we will look at the more specific question on fluvial readjustment, which appeared in 2013.

HIGHER LEVEL

EXAM QUESTION

Explain how rivers adjust to a change in base level, with reference to example(s) that you have studied.

2013 Q1C 30M

Marking Scheme
Adjustment identified 2m
Example 2m
Explanation 13 SRPs @ 2m each

SAMPLE ANSWER

The ice age ended in Ireland roughly 10 000 years ago, allowing Ireland's rivers to begin flowing on the landscape once again. As the massive weight of the ice was removed from the continental plate, isostatic rebound caused it to rise upwards, causing the sea level to fall relative to the land [2m]. As the sea level is now lower, the base level of the river erodes downwards once again in order to reach the sea. This is referred to as fluvial readjustment, where the river takes on the characteristics of a youthful river again and erodes vertically into the river bed [2m]. Eroding into the river bed is known as river rejuvenation (meaning to make young again) [2m].

The point where the river becomes rejuvenated is known as a knickpoint [2m]. Rejuvenation begins at the mouth of a river and migrates upstream through headward erosion [2m]. As it does so, it forms a new V-shaped valley and destroys the old river profile [2m]. A waterfall may form at a knickpoint as there is a sudden drop in the river's profile [2m]. Isostatic rebound often occurs in stages, meaning that there may be numerous knickpoints on the river's profile at one time [2m]. As each new knickpoint migrates up the stream, it removes the older one, until the river's profile has become fully adjusted to the new base level [2m].

As the river adjusts to base level, it carves a new valley floor in its old floodplain, creating a valley within a valley [2m]. This leaves the old floodplain elevated above the new valley floor at both sides – creating what is known as paired terraces [2m]. Rejuvenation gives a river much more erosive power in its middle and lower courses, which deepens existing landforms such as meanders [2m]. Although rejuvenated rivers maintain a winding course, their meanders are deepened by cutting into the old floodplains floor. These are referred to as incised meanders [2m]. Features of river rejuvenation can be found in the paired terraces of the River Nore, Co. Kilkenny [2m]. Incised meanders can be found in the River Moy [2m].

Opening paragraph explains how isostasy occurs after an ice age.

The second paragraph clearly discusses rejuvenation and adjustment to base level.

The third paragraph discusses the effects of fluvial readjustment and the landforms it creates.

Examples are provided.

Coastline processes are correctly left out of the answer.

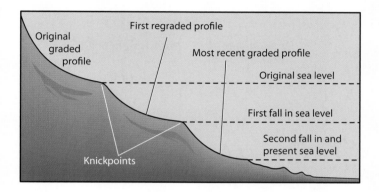

Marks Awarded
Adjustment identified 2m
Example (a river) 2m
Additional example (different river) 2m
Optional diagram 2m
Best 13 SRPs @ 2m each
Total 30/30

Answer is well structured and deals with fluvial readjustment in full detail. Key words related to isostasy and base adjustment are well explained and made relevant to the question asked.

TOPIC MAP

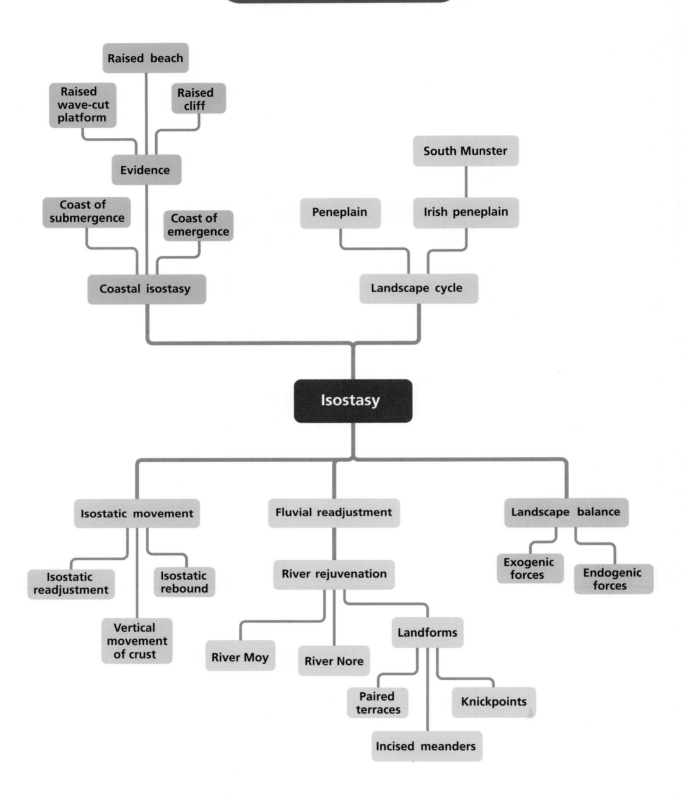

CORE UNIT 2

Geographical Skills

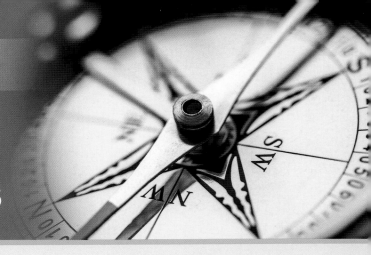

CHAPTER 14
Ordnance Survey Maps

The Discovery Map Series of Ireland is divided into 89 Ordnance Survey maps which provide a large amount of detail for both urban and rural areas. In this chapter, you will learn how to read, sketch and interpret Ordnance Survey maps. Your knowledge of physical landforms and surface processes will help you to interpret maps.

KEY WORDS

- Scale
- Grid referencing
- Subzone
- Easting
- Northing
- Cardinal points
- Straight-line distance
- Curved-line distance

- Contour lines
- Colour height
- Spot heights
- Triangulation stations/pillars
- Even slope
- Concave slope
- Convex slope
- Compound/uneven slope

- Cross-section
- Vertical exaggeration
- Average gradient
- Area of regular and irregular shapes
- Sketching

LEARNING OUTCOMES

What you MUST know

- How to measure scale on a map
- How to read and record four- and six-figure grid references
- How to tell direction on a map
- How to read and construct cross-sections (Higher Level only)
- How to sketch maps and use a legend to explain your sketch

- How to calculate area on a map
- How to interpret symbols, patterns and other map information
- How to recognise physical, human and economic landscapes

What you SHOULD know

- Rural settlement patterns
- Urban functions
- Economic landscape

Introduction

> **Note!**
> These skills are developed further in the Electives on Patterns and Processes in Economic Activities and Patterns and Processes in the Human Environment.

Map work requires being able to recognise and read information shown on Ordnance Survey (OS) maps. There are a number of skills you must learn, or further develop, from your Junior Cycle Geography course. These skills are:

- Measuring scale
- Reading and recording grid references
- Reading map direction
- Measuring distance and height

- Reading and constructing cross-sections
- Calculating area
- Sketching maps

You will also learn some new skills.

Each map has a legend (see Fig. 14.26 on page 282), which is a sheet explaining all the symbols that appear on the map extract. While reading OS maps, you will also learn how to recognise Irish landforms (introduced in Core Unit 1 Physical Geography), as well other physical patterns such as drainage and uplands/lowlands. Human patterns such as the location of settlement and functions of land will also be studied. All of these skills help you to correctly interpret maps, which is an important skill for not only your Leaving Certificate exam, but for your life also.

Skill 1: Measuring Scale

SCALE 1:50 000
SCÁLA 1:50 000

1 KILOMETRES 0 1 2 3 4 5 6 7 KILOMETRES 8
1 STATUTE MILES 0 1 2 3 4 STATUTE MILES 5
2 ceintiméadar sa chiliméadar (taobh chearnóg eangaí) 2 centimetres to 1 Kilometre (grid square side)

⬢ **Fig. 14.1** Scale on an OS map

Scale means the ratio between a distance on a map and the actual distance on the ground. For example, the scale in Fig. 14.1 is 1:50 000. This means that every 1 cm on the map is equal to 50 000 cm on the ground. When we convert this to km, it reads 1 cm is equal to 500 m (half a km). So, 2 cm is equal to 1 km. The Geo Numeracy box shows how to calculate scale in its simplest form.

Maps can be on a small scale or large scale:

- **Small-scale** maps show large areas of land in very little detail. For example, a world map covers a large area but does not have a lot of detail.

- **Large-scale** maps show smaller areas in greater detail. Examples of large-scale maps are street maps or town/city maps.

Skill 2: Reading and Recording Grid References

Grid references are a way of locating places and features on a map. There are three parts (or components) to recording or reading a correct grid reference:

1. **Subzone:** Ireland is divided up into 25 squares known as subzones. These 25 subzones measure 100 km by 100 km and are named by a letter (I is the only letter not used). Collectively, these squares are known as the National Grid. Each subzone is divided into 100 equal parts, numbered 00–99. These are the blue lines that we see on OS maps.

2. **Eastings:** The numbers (coordinates) which run along the bottom and top of a map are called eastings. These form the vertical blue lines which run through an OS map.

3. **Northings:** The numbers (coordinates) running along on the left and right sides of a map are called northings. These form the horizontal blue lines that run across a map.

When we give a grid reference we use the following order:

LEN: **L**etter **E**asting **N**orthing

⬢ **Fig. 14.2** The National Grid

⬢ **Fig. 14.3** Eastings and northings

Four-figure Grid Reference

Four-figure grid references give the location of a full square on a map, or of a larger feature such as a town or village or an island. In order to give a correct four-figure grid reference, we use the LEN method:

* Subzone Letter (L)
* Two-digit easting that forms the left side of the square (E)
* Two-digit northing that forms the base of the square (N)

Six-figure Grid Reference

To give a more precise location for a feature on a map (e.g. a castle), we use a six-figure grid reference. To calculate a six-figure grid reference, you must imagine that each grid square is divided up into 10 equal parts along both the easting and the northing (like graph paper is). Imagine these 10 parts are like decimal places. We can now get a third digit after our easting and northing readings. When we write the six-figure grid reference, the decimal point is not included.

Note!
On a full-size OS map, each grid square is 2 cm x 2 cm. To divide your square into ten even parts divide the square into 2 mm sections.

ACTIVE LEARNING

Use the OS map of Dungarvan (Fig. 14.21 on page 272) to calculate the following four- and six-figure grid references:

1. **Four figure:** parking spot, Ballyknock Lower, area of coniferous forest
2. **Six figure:** castle, standing stone, holy well, cairn, post office, garda station

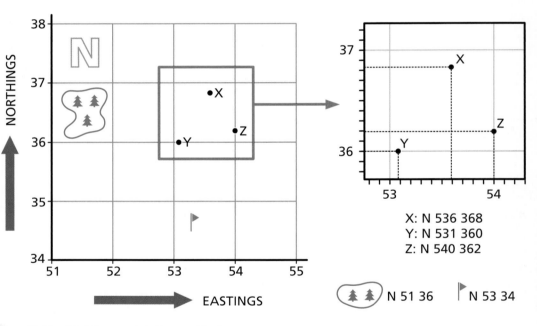

X: N 536 368
Y: N 531 360
Z: N 540 362

🌲🌲 N 51 36   ⚑ N 53 34

🔼 **Fig. 14.4** Four- and six-figure grid references

Note!
Another way to remember the correct order for grid referencing is: 'In the Door and Up the Stairs'

Read the squares along the bottom of the map and then along the side, or read the x-axis first and then the y-axis.

Grid referencing questions are asked every year on both Higher Level and Ordinary Level papers. Therefore, it is important that you know them well.

Looking at Fig. 14.5, we can see the following six-figure grid references:

V 922 709: Golf course

V 891 678: Standing stone

V 862 675: Antique Church

V 884 705: Castle

V 874 689: Illaunnakilla Island

Looking at Fig. 14.5, we can see the following four-figure grid references:

V 85 68: Illaunnakilla Oileán na Cille

V 86 72: Coniferous forestry

V 88 70: Natural woodland

V 90 70: Pier

V 89 66: Gortlicka

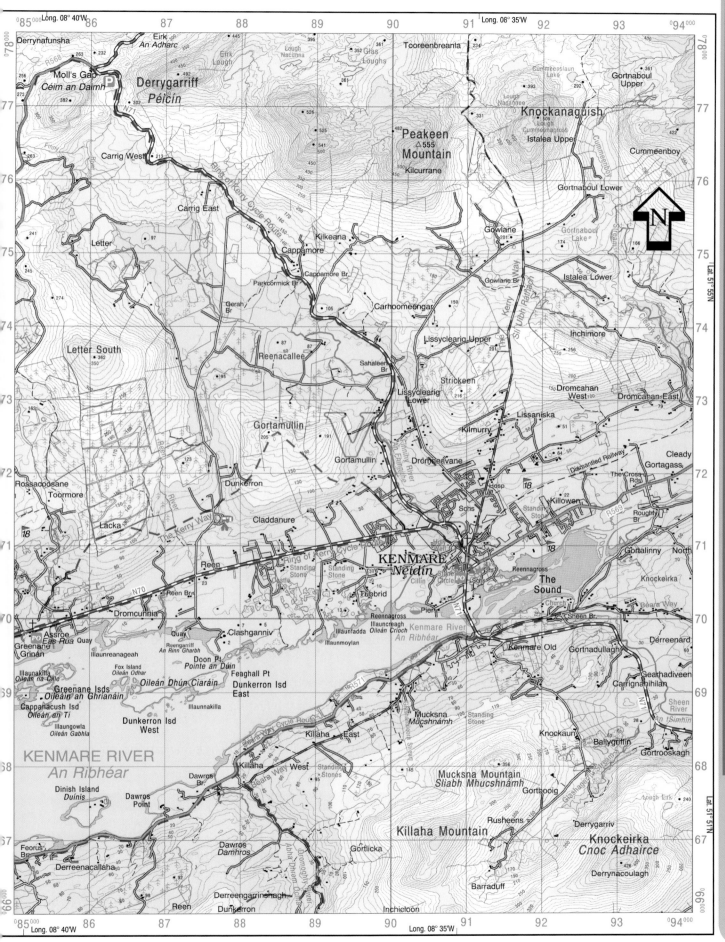

Fig. 14.5 OS map extract of Kenmare

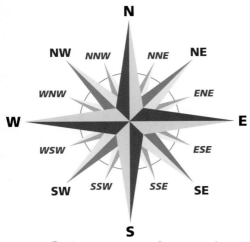

N
NW NNW NNE NE
WNW ENE
W E
WSW ESE
SW SSW SSE SE
S

Fig. 14.6 Can you figure out what each of these points stands for?

Skill 3: Reading Map Direction

Every OS map has a North arrow which allows us to calculate the four main cardinal points on a map (north, south, east and west). When the spaces in between the cardinal points are divided up, we can make a total of 16 different points of direction.

Skill 4: Measuring Distance

In the exam, you may be asked to calculate the straight-line distance between two points or the distance of a curved object such as a river or a road.

Straight-line Distance

- Put a straight edged piece of paper between the two objects to be measured.
- Mark where each point touches the page.
- Remove the sheet and place it against the linear scale at the bottom of the legend (supplied with all map extracts). Make sure you put the first point against the 0 and not at the start of the line.
- Read off the length in km.

ACTIVE LEARNING

Using Fig. 14.5 and Fig. 14.6, calculate the direction you would be travelling from Dinish Island (V 85 67) to:

1. Reen
2. Letter South
3. Kenmare
4. Gortamullín
5. Reenacallee
6. Dawros Point
7. Dunkerron Island
8. Claddanure

Curved-line Distance

Measuring curved line distance is slightly more difficult than measuring straight lines. It must be done carefully to get an accurate reading. Keep in mind that curved lines are made up of a series of straight sections. As in Fig. 14.7:

- Put a mark on a straight-edged piece of paper and place the mark against the starting point on the map.
- Next mark where the line makes its first turn.
- Turn the page until it lines up with the line again and mark it at the next turn.
- Continue this until you reach the end point.
- Remove the sheet and place the first mark at 0 on the linear scale at the bottom of the legend.
- Now read the length of the line from the first mark to the last to get your distance in km.

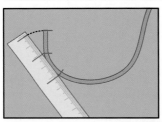

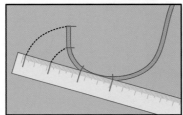

Fig. 14.7 Measuring a curved line

Note!

Usually in the exam, you will be asked to measure the distance of roads, railways or rivers.

Avoid the temptation to leave out tiny sections. If you do, your answer will not be accurate.

You are allowed an error of just 0.1 km either side of the correct answer.

ACTIVE LEARNING

1. Using the Kenmare OS map (Fig. 14.5 on page 259), measure the distance between the following:
   (a) The golf course (V 922 709) to the garda station (V 912 706)
   (b) The standing stones (V 891 678) and the youth hostel (V 911 706)
2. Using the Dungarvan map (Fig. 14.21 on page 272), calculate the length of the N72 up to the point where it joins the N25.
3. Using the Kenmare map (Fig. 14.20 on page 270), measure the distance of the Beara Way Cycle Route until it meets the N71.

Skill 5: Measuring Height

Height is shown in four different ways on a map:

- Contour lines
- Colour
- Spot heights
- Triangulation stations/pillars

Contour Lines

- Contour lines mark areas of equal heights above sea level.
- They are usually drawn at intervals of 10 m.
- Index contours represent 50 m intervals (they are darker and thicker) and are always numbered.

Colour Layers

- Seas are shown in light blue.
- Land that lies between 0 m (sea level) and 100 m is shown in dark green.
- Land between 100 m and 200 m is shown in light green.
- Land between 200 m and 300 m is shown in cream.
- Land above 300 m is shown in brown.
- The higher above 300 m the land is, the darker the shade of brown it is.

> **Note!**
>
> Being able to accurately tell the height of an area also allows you to determine what landscapes can exist in that area, e.g. upland areas are where waterfalls and V-shaped valleys form.

Spot Height

- Round black spots are used tell the exact height of an area in metres.

Triangulation Stations or Pillars

- Triangulation stations or pillars are points on the top of hills and mountains where the exact height has been measured.
- These points are represented by a black triangle with the height written beside it in metres.
- Triangulation points that are not filled with black mark the highest point on the map.

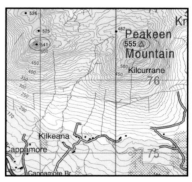

▲ **Fig. 14.8** Spot heights and triangulation pillars on Peakeen Mountain

Skill 6: Identifying Slope

We can identify different slope patterns by looking at contour line patterns. The more tightly packed contour lines are, the steeper the slope. The more widely spaced contour lines are, the more gentle the slope is. If an area of land is flat, there are no contour lines as the height does not change. There are four basic types of contour line:

- **Even slopes** can be identified on a map by their evenly spaced contour lines. They are sometimes referred to as regular slopes.

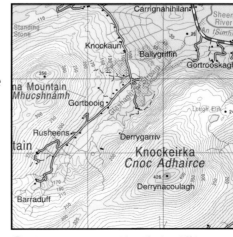

▲ **Fig. 14.9** Can you identify the different slopes visible on this OS map extract?

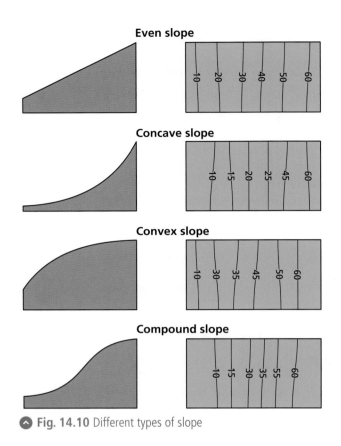

Fig. 14.10 Different types of slope

- **Concave slopes** are gentle at the bottom and steeper towards the top. Contour lines are widely spaced at the bottom, and closer together towards the top.
- **Convex slopes** are steep at the bottom and more gentle towards the top of the slope. Contour lines are close together at the bottom and more widely spaced towards the top.
- **Compound/uneven slopes** are made up of steep and gentle slopes. Spaces between contour lines vary along the slope.

FACT

Contour lines join places of equal height. If contour lines are close together, it means that the height is changing rapidly (i.e. it is a steep slope).

If there is wide space between contour lines, it means that the slop is very gentle.

Skill 7: Drawing a Cross-section of a Map (Higher Level only)

When you look at an OS map, you are viewing the area from above. OS maps show us that the landscape varies in height by using contour lines, colour, spot heights and triangulation stations.

A cross-section is a sideways view of an OS map that shows the relief of the landscape. In an exam, you may be asked to draw a cross-section of the landscape between two points.

To draw a cross-section accurately, use the following steps:

- Place a straight-edged piece of paper along a line that joins the end points of the cross-section (where it starts and where it ends).
- Mark your end points on the piece of paper and also make note of their contour line heights.
- Mark the heights of as many contour lines as you can on the sheet between your start and end points, noting their heights also.
- Mark on your paper where the cross-section (your sheet of paper) cuts across features such as road, lakes and rivers.
- Next, draw an *x*-axis (horizontal line) and a *y*-axis (vertical line) on graph paper.

- Mark the *y*-axis in metres above sea level and write a suitable scale, e.g. 2 cm = 100 m increase in height (one full graph paper box is 100 m up).

- Place your sheet of paper straight along the x-axis and mark in all of your points from start to finish (your starting point is where the *x*-axis and *y*-axis meet).

- Plot your heights on the graph paper and join them in a smooth curve (do not use a ruler to join them).

- Mark in any important features such as roads, rivers and lakes.

- Mark the six-figure grid references of your start and end points on the *x*-axis.

- Add the title of your cross-section (e.g. Cross-section Across Peakeen Mountain).

- Calculate the vertical exaggeration. Because we have to squash such a large area into such a small graph, increases in slope look much bigger than they are in real life. This is called vertical exaggeration. We can figure out by how much slopes have been exaggerated using a simple formula which is shown in the Geo Numeracy box.

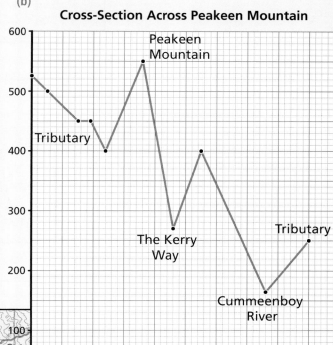

(b)

Cross-Section Across Peakeen Mountain

Vertical exaggeration is l0

(a)

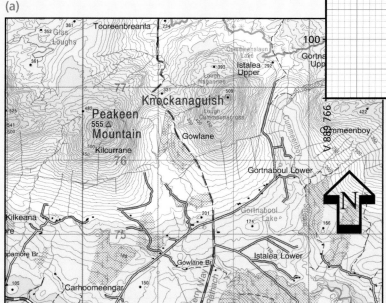

▲ **Fig. 14.11** (a) An extract of the OS map of Kenmare (Fig. 14.20 on page 270) and (b) a cross-section of the map extract

GEO **NUMERACY**

To calculate vertical exaggeration, do the following:

The normal scale for distance on OS maps is 2 cm = 1 km, i.e. 2 cm = 1000 m

The scale written for height (*y*-axis) is up to you, but I suggest making every full graph box equal 100 m, i.e. 2 cm = 100 m.

Therefore, to find out by how much our height is exaggerated on the graph, we divide the *x*-axis scale by the *y*-axis scale:

$$\frac{\text{Horizontal scale (HS)}}{\text{Vertical scale (VS)}} = \frac{2 \text{ cm} = 1000 \text{ m}}{2 \text{ cm} = 100 \text{ m}} \qquad \text{Vertical exaggeration (VE)} = \frac{1000}{100} = 10$$

Therefore the vertical exaggeration is 10.

ACTIVE **LEARNING**

The line X-Y on the map of
the Canary Islands, right,
indicates the line of a
cross-section. An elevation
profile of the line X-Y is
also shown.

1. Name the island at
   A on the elevation
   profile.

2. What is the depth of
   the ocean at B on the
   elevation profile?

3. Calculate the
   difference in elevation
   between point C and
   point D on the profile
   to the nearest 1000 m.

> **Fig. 14.12** (a) A map of the
> Canary Islands and (b) a cross-
> section (0 represents sea level)

Map of Canary Islands

(a)

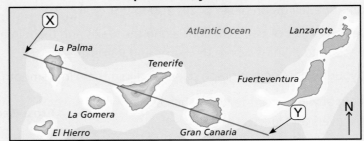

(b)

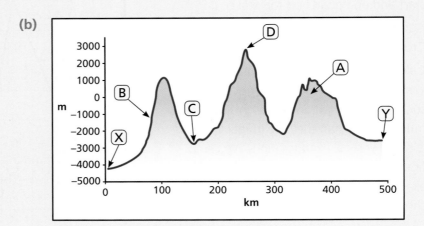

Skill 8: Calculating Average Gradient

Average gradient is the ratio between distance travelled and change in
height. If a person walked for 1 km and the height changed by 10 m, we can
figure out the average change in gradient (slope):

$$\frac{1000 \text{ m}}{10 \text{ m}} = 100 \text{ m}$$

therefore for every 1 m change in height a person has to walk a distance of
100 m. So how do we calculate it?

We use the following formula:

Average gradient (AG) $= \dfrac{\text{Vertical interval (VI) (the difference in height between the two points)}}{\text{Horizontal equivalent (HE) (the distance travelled)}}$

GEO NUMERACY

Using Fig. 14.13, calculate the average gradient
between the triangulation point of Crohaun Mountain
S 275 005 to the spot height at S 298 001.

$$AG = \frac{VI}{HE} = \frac{484 \text{ m} - 154 \text{ m}}{2.4 \text{ km}} = \frac{330 \text{ m}}{2400 \text{ m}} = \frac{1}{7.3} = 1{:}7.3$$

Therefore for every 7.3 m you walk,
the height changes by 1 m.

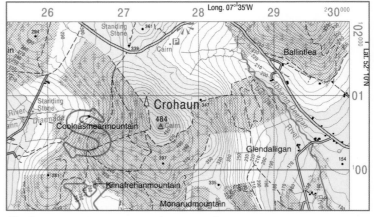

Fig. 14.13 OS map extract showing Crohaun Mountain

Skill 9: Calculating Area

Regular Shape

To calculate the area of a regular shape on an OS map extract:

1. Count the number of squares along the bottom of the map.

2. Count the number of squares along the side of the map.

3. To calculate the area, multiply your answers from step 1 and step 2 to get the area in km².

Irregular Shape

To calculate the area of an irregular shape on an OS map extract:

1. Count the number of squares fully covered (tick them as you go along so you do not count them twice by mistake).

2. Count the number of squares more than half covered. Ignore squares that are less than half covered.

3. Add your answers from step 1 and step 2 to get the area in km².

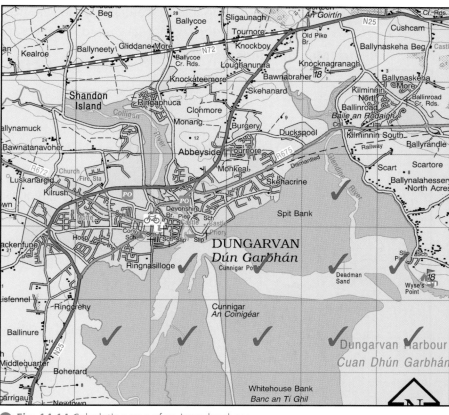

⬆ **Fig. 14.14** Calculating area of an irregular shape

Skill 10: Sketch Mapping

Drawing an accurate sketch map requires a great deal of care. Although many students attempt to draw sketch maps in the exam, they often make careless mistakes that can be avoided by applying these rules:

- Turn the map extract until the north arrow is pointing upwards. This will give you the correct orientation for the map.

- Draw the frame of your map to half-scale. This can be done in three ways:

  1. Measure the width and length of the map with your ruler and divide both by 2.

  2. Count the number of squares along the width and the side. Let each square equal 1 cm (normally each square is 2 cm).

  3. Let each half square of your graph paper represent a full square of the map. If you do this then you can use the graph squares to guide you while inserting the features.

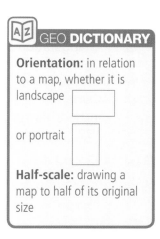

AZ GEO DICTIONARY

Orientation: in relation to a map, whether it is landscape ☐ or portrait ☐

Half-scale: drawing a map to half of its original size

- Write the title of the map along the top of the frame and insert the north arrow inside the frame.
- If there is a coastline visible, insert it.
- Insert the required features. Always begin with large features such as roads or rivers as they will help you to correctly locate the rest of the features.
- Identify each feature with a key and/or label.
- Ensure that all features included are the correct size and proportion (i.e. that they do not take up too much or too little space on your sketch).

Sketch Map of Dungarvan

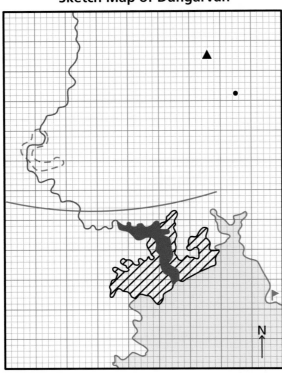

KEY
- Built-up area
- ▲ Triangulation pillar (highest point)
- ▶ Golf course
- ⌒ Colligan River
- • Cairn
- ⌒-- Inchadrislawood Loop
- —— N72

Fig. 14.15 Sketch map of the Dungarvan OS map

SAMPLE **QUESTION**

Examine the OS map extract of Dungarvan (Fig. 14.21 on page 272).
Draw a half-scale map of the extract and show and name the following:

- A named river
- The N72 national secondary road
- The highest point on the map
- A built-up area (Dungarvan town)
- A golf course
- An antiquity
- A named walkway

The sketch map in Fig. 14.15 answers this question.

Skill 11: Identifying Human Processes

Human processes refer to how people use the landscape around them. On maps, we can identify human processes through:

- Communications
- Rural settlement
- Urban functions

Communications

Communications refer to how people connect with one another. The types of communication links that can be identified on an OS map are roads, railways, canals/rivers, ports, ferries and airports. Many factors influence the development of communications:

- **Rivers:** Roads are built away from rivers to avoid flooding. Usually roads cross rivers at their narrowest point, known as the **bridging point** of a river. This can be seen where roads cross the River Shannon in Fig. 14.24.

Note!
When drawing a sketch map, always use a pencil so mistakes can be erased.
Do not waste too much time colouring.
As long as features can be clearly identified, colouring is not necessary.
Do not draw in grid squares.
Always include the north arrow.

- **Mountains and uplands:** Mountains and uplands make the development of communications very difficult and expensive. As a result, very few roads, rail or other means of transport are built along mountains. Roads that are forced to cut through mountains do so at the mountain's lowest point, known as the pass or gap. As a result, upland areas are isolated and difficult to access.

- **Lowlands:** Most people live in low-lying areas. As a result, most communication links are located along them. The flat land or gentle gradient make it much easier and much less expensive to construct roads and rail tracks.

Rural Settlement

Rural settlement refers to housing and villages that occur in the countryside. The density and location of rural settlements are influenced by a number of factors, such as:

1. **Altitude:** People prefer to live in lowland areas that are less than 200 m above sea level. Upland areas are more exposed to winds, making them cold and windy. Upland areas also experience more relief rainfall. These areas also have poorer communication links, making them more isolated,

2. **Aspect:** People tend to build houses on south-facing slopes as these receive more sunshine, making them warmer.

3. **Drainage:** People generally avoid living in areas that are prone to flooding.

4. **Slope/relief:** People choose to live on mainly flat or gently sloping land. Usually this land is more fertile for farming and is closer to services such as telephone, internet, water and sewage.

Rural Settlement Patterns

There are four types of rural settlement that can be identified on an OS map:

1. Linear
2. Nucleated
3. Dispersed
4. Absence

1. *Linear Settlement*

Linear settlement is also referred to as ribbon settlement. Linear settlement occurs when houses are built in a line along a road. People choose to build here as it has easy access to water and electricity. As a result of its popularity, farmers often sell land that is beside a road as it is valuable. Linear housing is most commonly found on the outskirts of towns and villages. Planning authorities do not favour this type of settlement as it contributes to urban sprawl.

GEO **DICTIONARY**

Density: in relation to settlement, this means the number of houses per kilometre squared. This is not the same as population density, which refers to the number of people living per kilometre squared

Relief rain: precipitation that falls when water vapour is forced over mountains and it condenses into water

Urban sprawl: the unplanned growth of an urban area into the surrounding countryside

Fig. 14.16 Linear settlement

Fig. 14.17 Nucleated settlement

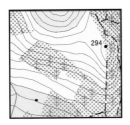

Fig. 14.18 Dispersed settlement

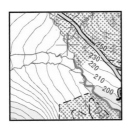

Fig. 14.19 Absence of settlement

2. Nucleated Settlement

Nucleated settlement is also referred to as clustered settlement. As the name suggests, houses are located in groups. This type of settlement can be found at crossroads or in housing estates. It also occurs at bridging points of rivers, which were natural meeting points. Often, bridging points developed further to become small market towns or much larger towns.

3. Dispersed Settlement

Dispersed settlement is also referred to as scattered settlement. Dispersed settlement occurs as 'one-off' houses, which are dotted around the countryside. Usually these are farmhouses which are built on their own and surrounded by farmland. They are often located at the end of a driveway or unmarked road.

4. Absence of Settlement

As the name suggests, these areas show no evidence of settlement on a map. Areas with an absence of settlement normally have issues such as being too mountainous or prone to flooding.

Urban Settlement

Urban settlement refers to towns and cities, commonly known as built-up areas. There are many reasons why towns and cities develop at a certain location:

- When the Normans conquered Ireland in the twelfth century, they built large castles. Settlements began to develop around these castles as they offered protection and a chance to trade. This led to the development of towns.
- The Normans were also very religious, with monasteries built alongside castles. People lived around monasteries as they offered education and charity. Kilkenny City is an example of a Norman settlement.
- Towns developed near rivers, which offered protection and transport.
- Towns also developed at the bridging points of rivers. As people needed to cross rivers at these points, they became natural meeting places. Trade began to develop at these points leading to the establishment of market towns.
- Towns are set up at the nodal point of roads. As roads converge, they become natural places for trade to develop.
- Towns often develop on flat or gently sloping land which is easy to build on.
- Many of Ireland's coastal towns developed at ports in order to allow overseas trade. Beach towns also allow for tourist activities.

Urban Functions

Functions of a town refers to the services it offers to the people who live in or around it. Typical functions include:

- Education: schools, colleges, universities
- Industrial: industrial estates
- Transport: roads, railway, airports, ports, car parks
- Market: shopping
- Port: harbour, quay, pier
- Religious: church, cathedral, graveyard
- Health: hospital
- Recreational: golf course, parks, sports grounds
- Residential: housing estates

Evidence of Tourist Functions

Ordnance Survey maps provide information on tourist attractions and services. Below are the main tourist attractions shown on OS maps.

- **Antiquities:** Given Ireland's history of settlement, there are several pieces of evidence of historic settlement on most OS maps. Tourists visit these areas to see evidence of these cultures and to learn about Irish history. On an OS map, antiquities are marked with a red dot and identified with a label, such as castle or holy well.

- **Recreation:** Ireland offers a range of recreational activities, such as water sports, golfing, hill walking and orienteering.

- **Rivers/lakes:** These attract tourists who are interested in activities such as angling and kayaking and offer attractive areas for picnics.

- **Forestry:** Coillte, which manages Ireland's forests, has promoted the use of forestry and woodland for trails and adventure racing.

- **Nature reserves and national parks:** Ireland has many natural parks and reserves that attract people who wish to observe wildlife in its natural environment.

> **Note!**
> If you are asked questions that require map evidence, you must back up your observations with grid references from a map. Follow the simple SEE guideline: Statement – Evidence – Explanation.

> ### ACTIVE LEARNING
>
> Examine the map extract of Enniscorthy (Fig. 14.22 on page 274) and answer the following questions:
>
> 1. Give a six-figure grid reference for three tourist attractions located on the map.
> 2. Identify three functions of Enniscorthy town, giving grid references.
> 3. Locate examples of three types of rural settlement, giving a four-figure grid reference for each.

OS Map Legend

A legend explains what each of the symbols on a map represents (see the OS map legend Fig. 14.26 on page 282).

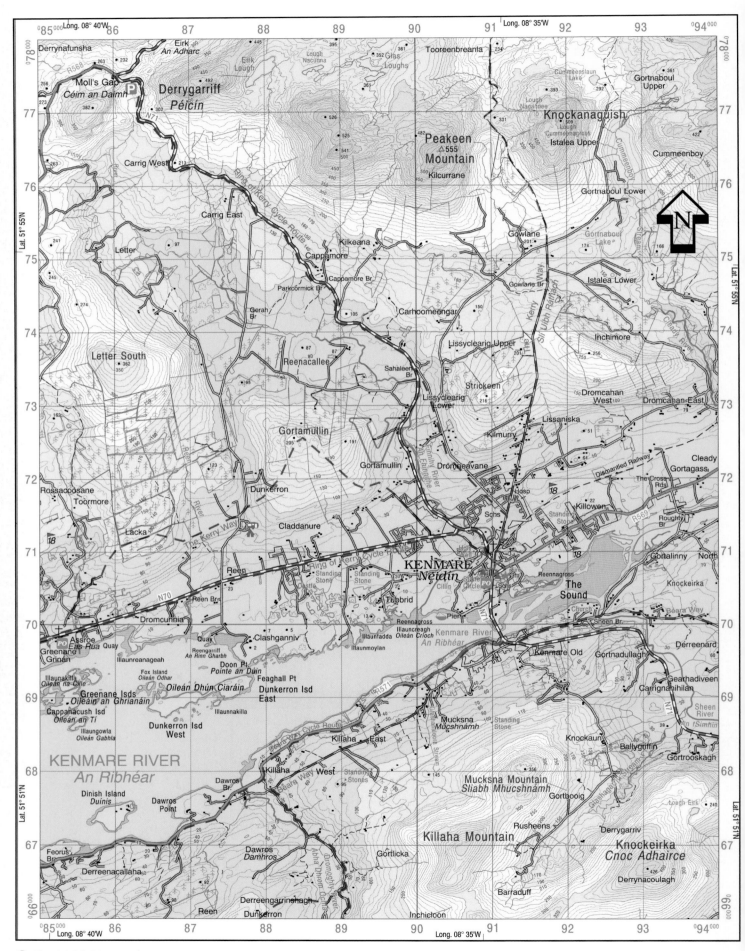

Fig. 14.20 OS map of Kenmare

Use Fig. 14.20 and Fig. 14.26 to answer these questions.

ORDINARY LEVEL

1. Identify the features at the following grid references:
   (i) V 884 704
   (ii) V 852 713
   (iii) V 904 765
   (iv) V 909 686

2. Find a six-figure grid reference for:
   (i) A castle
   (ii) Peak of Letter South Mountain
   (iii) A youth hostel
   (iv) A caravan park

3. Calculate the area of the map in km².

4. Calculate the distance from V 872 665 to V 888 769. Give your answer in km.

5. Locate and give a grid reference for the highest point on the map.

6. Name and locate three tourist attractions on the map.

7. Draw a sketch map of the area and include the following:
   • An area of land over 500 m
   • The N70 national secondary road
   • An antiquity
   • A built-up area

HIGHER LEVEL

1. Give a four-figure grid reference for:
   (i) Linear settlement
   (ii) Nucleated settlement
   (iii) Dispersed settlement
   (iv) Absence of settlement

2. Measure the distance of the following:
   (i) The N70
   (i) The Sheen River

3. Locate each of the following slopes on the map:
   (i) A convex slope
   (ii) A concave slope
   (iii) An even slope
   (iv) A compound slope
   Draw a cross-section of the slope and provide the grid reference of the start point and end point of the slope.

4. Draw a cross-section of the Kenmare map from V 904 765 to V 883 698.

5. Calculate the average gradient from V 931 666 to V 909 686.

6. Calculate the area of land covered by forestry.

7. Draw a sketch map of the area and include the following:
   (i) A V-shaped valley
   (ii) A built-up area
   (iii) An area of natural woodland
   (iv) The complete course of Finnihy River
   (v) The N71 national secondary road

8. Examine the 1:50 000 Ordnance Survey map and legend. Draw a sketch map of the area shown to half-scale. On it, correctly show and label each of the following:
   • The entire route of the waymarked walk called Béara Way shown on the map
   • The entire area of coniferous plantation at V 85 72
   • The entire area of land above 300 m at Letter South Mountain
   • The entire area of Kenmare River shown on the map

   2015 Q2A 20M

Proportion 4m
Four features @ 4m each

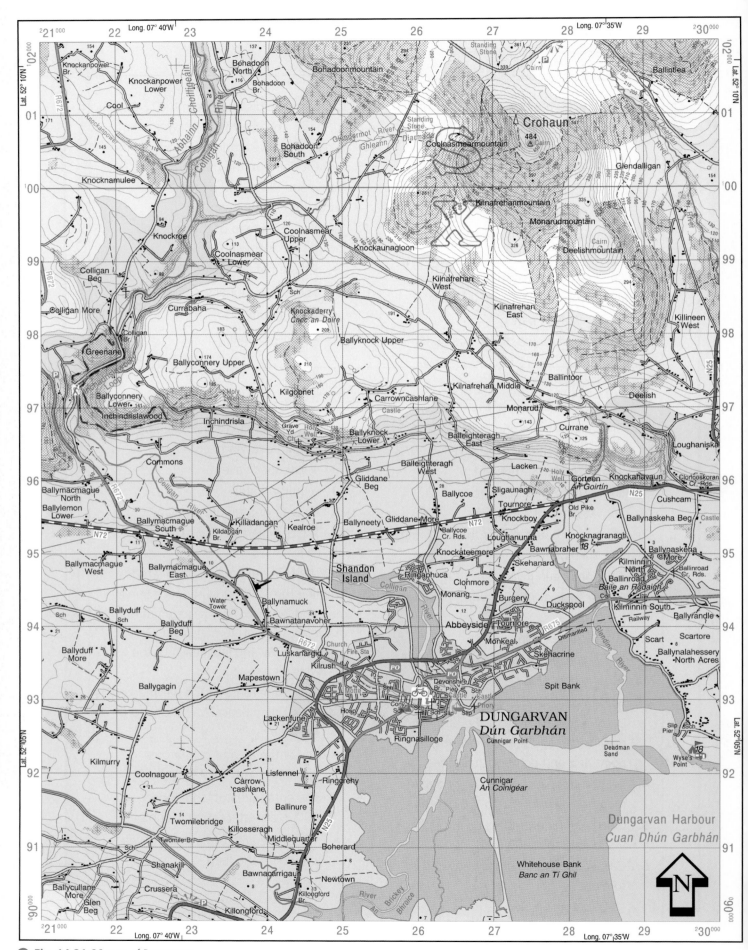

Fig. 14.21 OS map of Dungarvan

Use Fig. 14.21 and Fig. 14.26 to answer these questions.

ORDINARY LEVEL

1. What features can be found at the following grid references?
   - (i) X 258 928
   - (ii) S 275 006
   - (iii) X 297 923
   - (iv) X 267 931
   - (v) X 282 952

2. Find a six-figure grid reference for each of the following:
   - (i) A garda station
   - (ii) A post office
   - (iii) A holy well
   - (iv) A priory
   - (v) A standing stone
   - (vi) A mast

3. Calculate the straight-line distance between:
   - (i) The camping site and the cairn on Deelishmountain
   - (ii) The castle at X 264 931 and X 297 954

4. (i) Give a six-figure grid reference for the highest point on the map.
   - (ii) What is the height of the land at X 274 994?
   - (iii) What height is the cairn at the peak of Deelishmountain?

5. Name two tourist amenities found a Wyse's Point (X 296 923).

6. Examine the 1:50 000 Ordnance Survey map and legend. Draw a sketch map of the area shown. On it, show and label the following:
   - (i) An area of land above 300 m
   - (ii) Two named rivers
   - (iii) The built-up area of Dungarvan
   - (iv) An area of coniferous plantation

Frame 1m
Proportions 2m
Overall impression 2m
Items shown 5 @ 3m each
Items named 5 @ 2m each

2014 Q3 A 30M

HIGHER LEVEL

1. (i) Give a six-figure grid reference for a mast shown on the map.
   - (ii) Calculate the area of the Ordnance Survey map located in subzone X.
   - (iii) What is the aspect of the slope in grid box X 22 90?

2. Give a four-figure grid reference for:
   - (i) A convex slope
   - (ii) An area of mixed woodland
   - (iii) A trellis drainage pattern
   - (iv) A meeting point of roads

3. Measure the length of the following:
   - (i) The N25 from X 243 900 to 300958
   - (ii) The Colligan River

4. Using evidence from the map, suggest one reason why Dungarvan is not suitable for developing as a deep-water port.

5. Draw a sketch map of the area shown to half-scale. On it, correctly show and label each of the following:
   - The complete course of the Colligan River
   - Locate a gorge on the Colligan River and mark it with an X
   - The Cunnigar sand spit
   - An area of land above 300 m

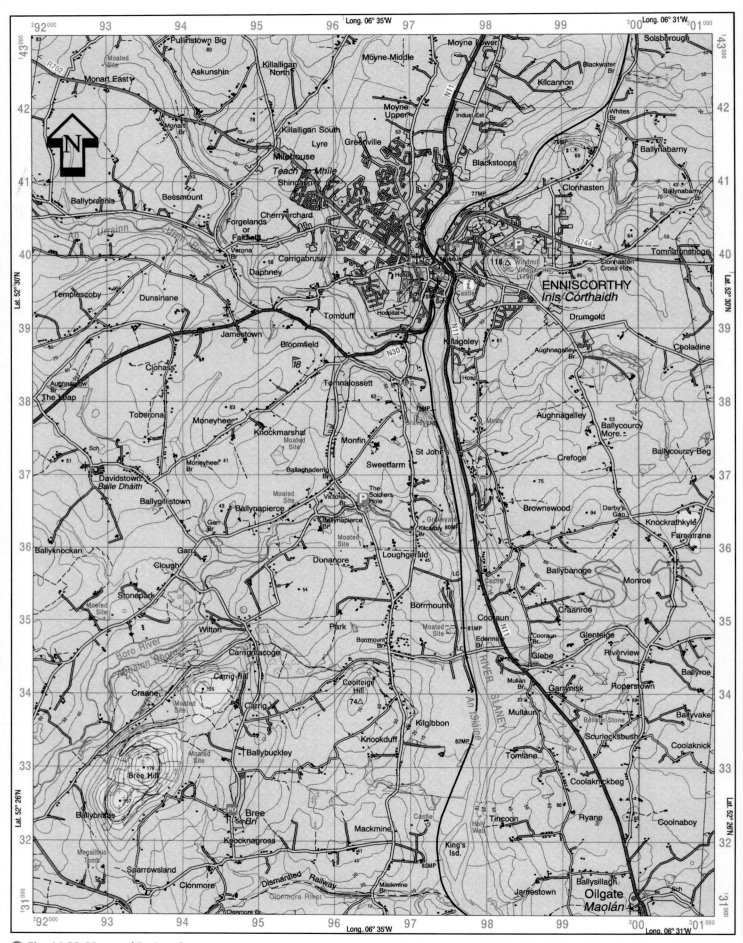

● **Fig. 14.22** OS map of Enniscorthy

Use Fig. 14.22 and Fig. 14.26 to answer these questions.

ORDINARY LEVEL

1. Give a six-figure grid reference for each of the following:
   (i) A moated site
   (ii) A golf course
   (iii) A historic battlefield
   (iv) A railway station
   (v) The peak of Bree Hill

2. Measure the straight-line distance of:
   (i) The post office in Bree to the nearest post office in Enniscorthy
   (ii) The golf course to Vinegar Hill Battlefield
   (iii) The tourist information in Enniscorthy to the castle at S 973 323
   (iv) The garda station in Oilgate to the garda station in Enniscorthy

3. Give a four-figure grid reference for the following:
   (i) A coniferous plantation
   (ii) A river meander
   (iii) Nucleated settlement
   (iv) Linear settlement
   (v) An area of land above 150 m
   (vi) An area of disused railway line

4. Examine the 1:50 000 Ordnance Survey map and legend. Draw a sketch map of the area shown and on it show and name the following:
   - The River Slaney
   - An area of land above 100 m
   - A railway line
   - The N11
   - The built-up area of Enniscorthy

| Frame 1m |
| Proportions 2m |
| Overall impression 2m |
| Items shown 5 @ 3m each |
| Items named 5 @ 2m each |

2013 Q1A 30M

HIGHER LEVEL

1. Examine the 1:50 000 Ordnance Survey map and legend. Draw a sketch map to half-scale of the area shown. On it, correctly show and name each of the following:
   - The complete course of the River Slaney
   - The confluence of the River Slaney and Boro River (mark it with an X on the sketch map)
   - An area of land above 170 m
   - An area of natural woodland

| Proportion 4m |
| Four features @ 4m each |

2013 Q1A 20M

2. Calculate the distance of the following:
   (i) The Slaney River
   (ii) The N11

3. Calculate the general direction you would be travelling in if going from:
   (i) The post office in Bree to the train station in Enniscorthy
   (ii) The megalithic tomb at S 927 316 to the moated site at S 929 426
   (iii) Oilgate to the golf course at Bloomfield

4. Mark the confluence of two rivers with an X.

5. Calculate the area of land to the east of the River Slaney.

6. Suggest three reasons why the town of Enniscorthy developed at its location. Provide evidence from the map for each reason.

7. Draw a cross-section of the landscape from S 935 329 to S 994 365.

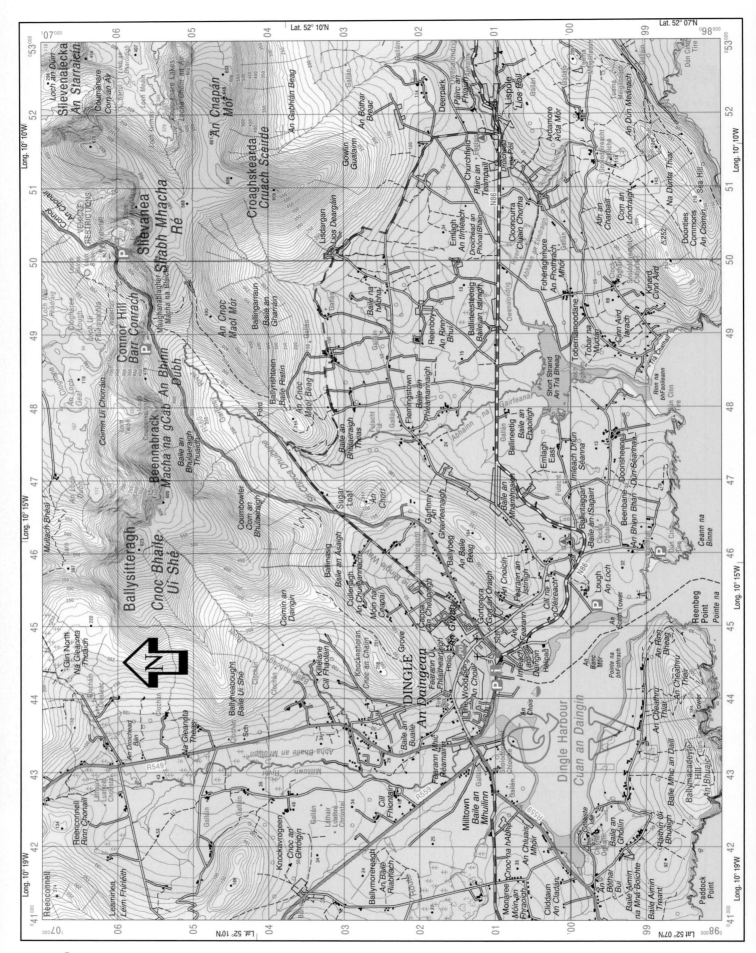

Fig. 14.23 OS map of Dingle/an Daingean

Use Fig. 14.23 and Fig. 14.26 to answer these questions.

ORDINARY LEVEL

1. What features are found at the following grid references?
   (i) V 435 982   (ii) V 462 002   (iii) Q 444 039
   (iv) Q 444 010   (v) V 478 986

2. From what direction would you be travelling if:
   (i) You travelled from the post office in Dingle to the viewpoint at Q 50 06?
   (ii) You travelled from Paddock Point (V4198) to An Cnoc Maol Mor (Q 49 04)?

3. Calculate the area of land in subzone Q.

4. Calculate the straight-line distance (in km) between:
   (i) Dingle post office and the car park at V 460 988
   (ii) The viewpoint at Q 056 491 and Gallán at Q 426 044

5. Give two reasons why there is an absence of roads in large areas north of northing 04.

6. Name the feature of coastal deposition in grid square V 48 98.

7. State one reason why there is no evidence of settlement in the area at Q 50 04.

8. Examine the 1:50 000 Ordnance Survey map and legend. Draw a sketch map of the area shown and on it show and name the following:

   • The coastline
   • The Miltown River
   • A lighthouse
   • A named area of land above 400 m
   • A corrie lake

Frame	1m
Proportions	2m
Overall impression	2m
Items shown	5 @ 3m each
Items named	5 @ 2m each

   2011 Q1A 30M

HIGHER LEVEL

1. Name and give a six-figure grid reference for the following:
   (i) Gallán   (ii) Youth hostel
   (iii) Highest point on the map   (iv) An ogham stone

2. Locate each of the following slopes on the map extract:
   (i) A concave slope   (ii) A convex slope   (iii) An even slope

3. Give a four-figure grid reference for each of the following:
   (i) A landform of river erosion   (ii) A landform of coastal deposition
   (iii) A landform of coastal erosion   (iv) A landform of glacial erosion

4. Provide three reasons why Dingle has developed as a town in its present location.

5. Name and give the location by grid reference of three rural settlement patterns and explain each pattern in detail.

6. Using graph paper, draw a cross-section from Q 526 046 to Q 510 000 inserting all major contour lines and features.

7. Examine the 1:50 000 Ordnance Survey map and legend. Draw a sketch map to half-scale of the area shown. On it, mark and name each of the following:

   • The complete course of the Garfinny River
   • A section of coast with coastal cliffs
   • A beach
   • An area of land over 600 m east of easting 50

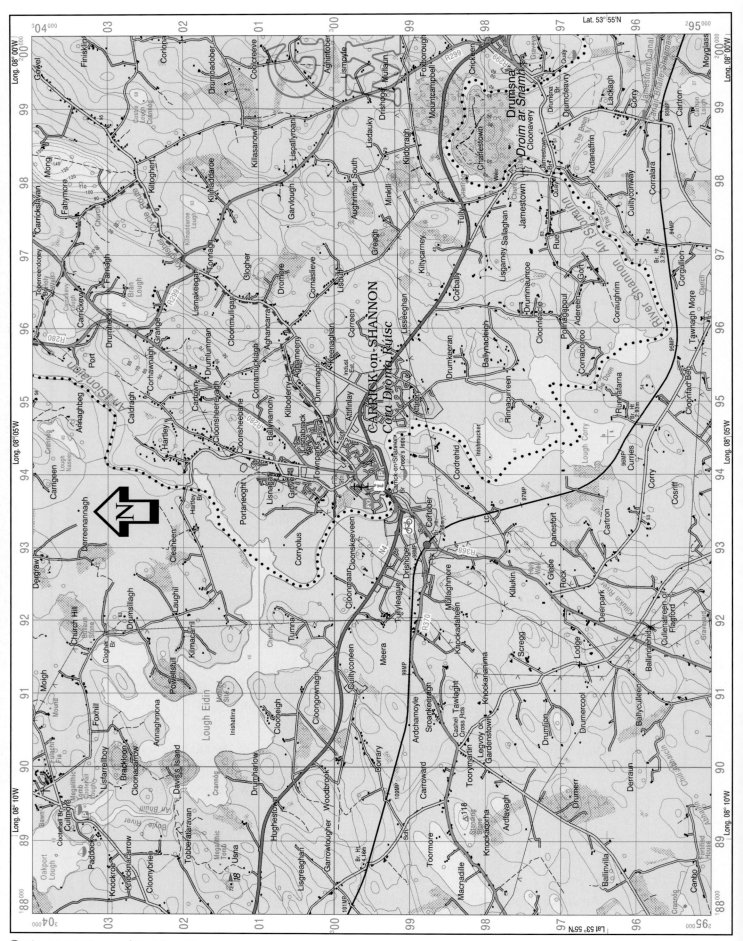

▲ **Fig. 14.24** OS map of Carrick-on-Shannon

Use Fig. 14.24 and Fig. 14.26 to answer these questions.

ORDINARY LEVEL

1. What type of rural settlement pattern is located at G 99 03?

2. Calculate the straight-line distance from the nine-hole golf course to the tourist information office in Carrick-on-Shannon.

3. In what direction would you be travelling if you went from the Fortified House (M 887 952) to the post office in Carrick-on-Shannon?

4. Give six-figure grid references for three antiquities on the map.

5. What is the highest point on the map? (Give your answer in metres.)

6. Why do you think there is an absence of settlement on one side of the third-class road at G 92 01?

7. Calculate the distance between the tourist information centre and the moated site at G 911 014.

8. Calculate the area of land in subzone M.

9. Examine the 1:50 000 Ordnance Survey map and legend. Draw a sketch map of the area and include the following:

- The River Shannon
- An area of mixed woodland
- Oakport Lough
- The Jamestown Canal
- An area of land over 120 m above sea level in the northeast of the map

Frame 1m
Proportions 2m
Overall impression 2m
Items shown 5 @ 3m each
Items named 5 @ 2m each

2012 Q1A 30M

HIGHER LEVEL

1. Examine the Ordnance Survey map and legend. Write the correct answer to each of the following questions:

   (i) Name and give a six-figure grid reference for an antiquity built by the early Christians.

   (ii) Name and give a six-figure grid reference for the highest point on the map.

   (iii) Calculate the area of the map west of the River Shannon.

   (iv) Give a four-figure grid reference for two different types of rural settlement located on the map.

2. Name two tributaries that join the River Shannon on the map and give a six-figure grid reference for the confluence of each.

3. Describe three functions of the town of Carrick-on-Shannon. Provide evidence from the map for each function.

4. Explain three possible reasons for the development of Carrick-on-Shannon as a town in its location.

5. Measure the distance of the following:

   (i) The complete course of the N4

   (ii) The railway line

6. Draw a cross-section of the area from G 983 037 to G 934 001.

7. Name and locate three tourist attractions shown on the map.

8. Examine the 1:50 000 Ordnance Survey map and legend. Draw a sketch map to half-scale of the area shown. On it, correctly show and name each of the following:

- The complete course of the River Shannon
- The N4
- A built-up area
- An artificial waterway

Ordnance Survey map questions appear every year on both the Higher Level and Ordinary Level exam papers. Therefore, it is vital that you repeatedly practise the map skills outlined in this chapter. Those who go on to study the Patterns and Processes in the Human Environment Elective will revise some areas of maps such as settlement patterns and functions of towns. However, it is vital that you practise other key skills here. The sample answer deals with the 2010 Higher Level Q1A, which requires you to sketch a map of the Carrick-on-Suir map.

Although the question does not mention drawing the map at half-scale, it is best to do so as it makes it much easier to correctly locate the features needed.

I suggest drawing in the features in the following order:

- Start by drawing in the Suir River, clearly marking in the river braiding. This is a feature of river deposition.
- Then, draw the course of the Glen River as it connects to the River Suir and helps to further divide up the page. This will help you to accurately locate other features.
- Next, include the trellised drainage as it also connects to the River Suir.
- Finally, draw in the V-shaped valley.

HIGHER LEVEL

Examine the 1:50 000 Ordnance Survey map (Fig. 14.25 on page 281) accompanying this paper. Draw a sketch map of the area shown. On it, mark and include the following:

- One landform created by the processes of river deposition
- A V-shaped valley
- An area with a trellised drainage pattern
- The complete course of the Glen River

Note!
This sketch map is not at half-scale.

2010 Q1A 20M

Marking Scheme
Proportion 4m (correct scale used)
Four features @ 4m each (2m each for sketch, 2m each for naming)

As always, you must draw in a north arrow and put a title on top of the sketch.

Be sure to label features or include a key/legend to identify your features.

Correct proportion and scale is used, meaning features are more likely to be put in the correct place. Features are clearly drawn and labelled making them easy to identify..

SAMPLE **ANSWER**

Sketch Map of Carrick-on-Suir

Marks Awarded
Proportion 4m
Four features @ 4m each
Total 20/20

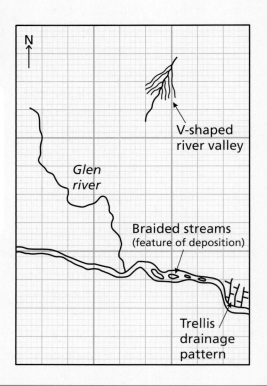

N

V-shaped river valley

Glen river

Braided streams
(feature of deposition)

Trellis drainage pattern

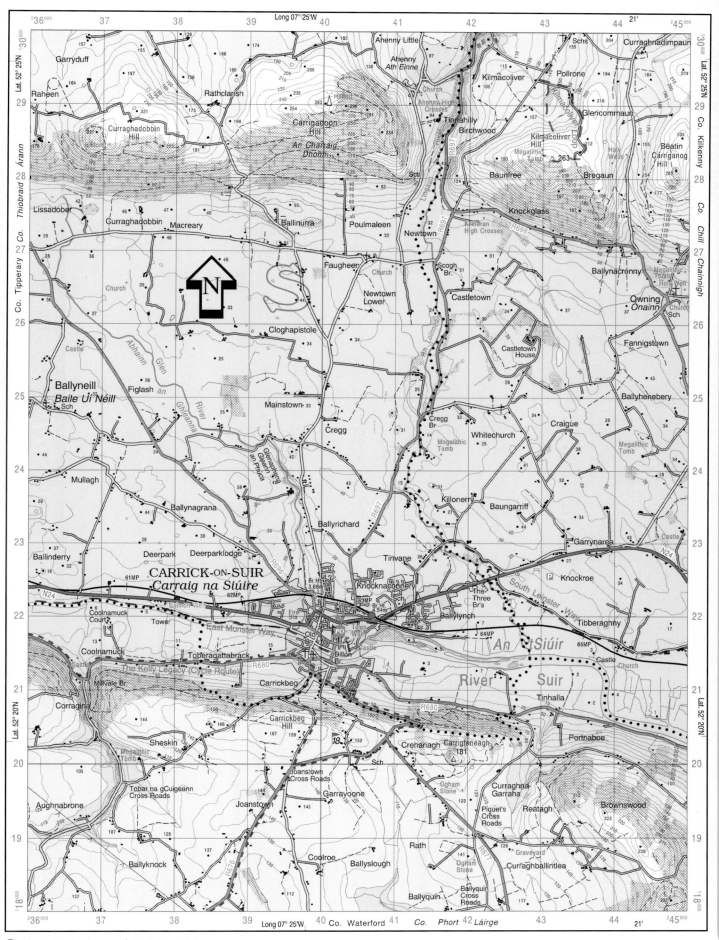

⌄ **Fig. 14.25** OS map of Carrick-on-Suir

Fig. 14.26 OS map legend

Legend
Eochair

Ordnance Survey Ireland
Suirbhéireacht Ordanáis Éireann

DISCOVERY SERIES
SRAITH EOLAIS

Roads

- **M1** Mótarbhealach / Motorway (Junction number)
- **N 11** Bóthar príomha náisiúnta / National Primary Road
- **N 71** Bóthar tánaisteach náisiúnta / National Secondary Road
- Carrbhealach dúbailte / Dual Carriageway
- Bóthar príomha /tánaisteach náisiúnta beartaithe / Proposed Nat. Primary / Secondary Road
- **R 574** Bóthar Réigiúnach / Regional Road
- Bóthar den tríú grád / Third Class Road
- Boithre de chineál eile / Other Roads
- Bealach / Track (4 metres min, 4 metres max)
- Line tarchurtha leictreachais / Electricity Transmission Line

Features

- Stáisiún cumhachta (uisce) / Power Station (Hydro)
- Stáisiún cumhachta (breosla iontaiseach) / Power Station (Fossil)
- Crann / Mast
- Brú de chuid An Óige / Youth Hostel (An Óige)
- Brú saoire Neamhspleách / Independent Holiday Hostel
- Láithreán carbhán (idirthurais) / Caravan site (transit)
- Láithreán campála / Camping site
- Ionad picnici / Picnic site
- Ionad dearctha / Viewpoint
- **P** Ionad páirceála / Parking
- **A T** An Taisce / National Trust
- Tearmann Dúlra / Nature Reserve
- Feirm Ghaoithe / WindFarm
- **i** Ionad eolais turasóireachta (ar oscailt ar feadh na bliana) / Tourist Information centre (regular opening)
- **i** Ionad eolais turasóireachta (ar oscailt le linn an tSéasúir) / Tourist Information centre (restricted opening)
- Foirgnimh le hais a chéile / Built up Area
- Eaglais no séipéal / Church or Chapel
- Ardeaglais / Cathedral
- Garda Síochána / Police
- **PO** Oifig phoist / Post office
- Galfchúrsa, machaire gailf / Golf Course or Links
- Bealach rothar / Cycle route
- Siúlbhealach le comharthaí; Ceann Slí; Waymarked Walks; Trailheads
- Aerphairc / Airfield
- Aerfort / Airport
- Bádóireacht / Boating activities
- Teach Solais in úsáid / as úsáid / Lighthouse in use / disuse
- Bád fartha (paisinéirí) / Ferry (Passenger)
- Bád fartha (feithiclí) / Ferry (Vehicle)
- Trá / Beach
- Line lag trá / Low Water Mark
- Líne bharr láin / High Water Mark
- Abhainn nó sruthán / River or Stream
- Canáil, canáil (thirim) / Canal, Canal (dry)
- Loch / Lake
- shingle, mud sand or loose rock

Railways / Boundaries / Land features

- Staisiún traenach / Railway Station
- **LC** Crosaire comhréidh / Level Crossing
- Tollán / Tunnel
- Iarnród tionscalaíoch / Industrial Line
- Iarnród / Railways
- Séadchomhartha Ainmnithe / Named Antiquities
- Clós, m.sh. Ráth nó Lios / Enclosure, e.g. Ringfort
- Láthair Chatha (le dáta) / Battlefield (with date)
- Foraois mheasctha / Mixed Woodland
- Foraois bhuaircíneach / Coniferous Plantation
- Coillearnach Dhuillsilleach / Deciduous Woodland
- Páirc Foraoise / Forest Park
- Seilbh de chuid an Aire Chosanta / Dept. of Defence Property
- Páirc Náisiúnta / National Park
- Teorainn idirnáisiúnta / International Boundary
- Teorainn chontae / County Boundary
- An Ghaeltacht / Irish speaking area

SUMMIT INFORMATION

- Above 600m
- 599m - 400m
- Below 400m

NOTE Over 600m summits must have a prominence of 15m. Between 400m and 599m a prominence of 30m and from 150 to 399m a prominence of 150m.

The summit classification is courtesy the Mountain Views hillwalking community.
The lists used, updated to 2009, include:
The "Arderins" 500m list.
The "Vandeleur-Lynam" 600m list,
and other lists for smaller tops and county high points.

⊕ Mountain Rescue Base

- Céim imline comhairde 10m / 10m Contour Interval
- Céim imline comhairde 50m / 50m Contour Interval
- Cuaille triantánachta / Triangulation Pillar
- **123** Spota airde / Spot Height
- Trasnú cliathráin / Graticule Intersection

IRISH NATIONAL GRID

A	B	C	D	E
F	G	H	J	K
L	M	N	O	P
Q	R	S	T	U
V	W	X	Y	Z

Irish Transverse Mercator Not used on this extract. (ITM) is a newly derived GPS compatible mapping projection that is associated with the European Terrestrial Reference System 1989 (ETRS89). For further information on ITM and for coordinate conversion visit our website.

CENTRE OF SHEET ITM CO-ORDINATES:
EXAMPLE: ⊕ **499973E 827008N**

www.osi.ie

This is a sample reference only
(Discovery Sheet 23)
Sample reference: G 103 079

Compiled and published by Ordnance Survey Ireland,
Phoenix Park, Dublin 8, Ireland.
Arna thiomsú agus arna fhoilsiú ag Shuirbhéireacht Ordanáis Éireann, Páirc an Fhionnuisce, Baile Átha Cliath 8, Éire.

SCALE 1:50 000
SCÁLA 1:50 000

1 STATUTE MILES 0 1 2 STATUTE MILES
1 KILOMETRES 0 1 2 3 4 5 6 7 8 KILOMETRES

2 ceintiméadar sa chiliméadar (taobh chearnóg eangaí) 2 centimetres to 1 Kilometre (grid square side)

TOPIC MAP

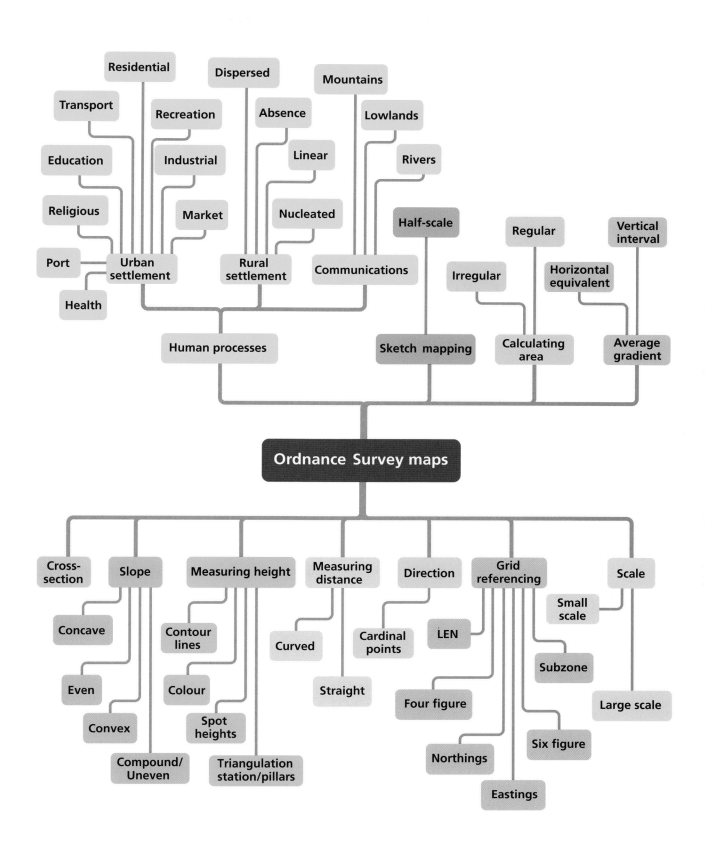

CHAPTER 15

Aerial Photographs

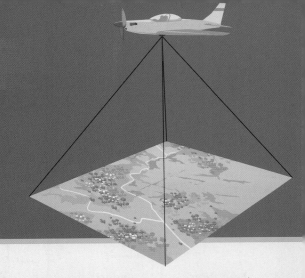

For many students, interpreting aerial photographs proves the most difficult skill to master. Although aerial photographs cover a smaller area than that shown in OS maps, students often struggle with correctly locating and drawing objects when sketching and reading from them. Some students also struggle with using the correct terms for locating objects.

KEY WORDS

- Vertical
- Oblique
- Background
- Middle ground
- Foreground
- Sketch map
- Functions
- Site
- Transport
- Environment

LEARNING OUTCOMES

What you MUST know
- How to identify a vertical or an oblique photograph
- How to give correct location on aerial photographs
- How to tell the time of year on a photograph
- How to tell the direction in which a camera is pointing
- How to accurately sketch a map of an aerial photograph

What you SHOULD know
- Where to locate further developments in an aerial photograph
- How to identify traffic management projects that have been carried out
- How to identify land use and functions from an aerial photograph

Introduction

In this chapter, you will learn how to read and sketch aerial photographs. Aerial photographs are pictures of the ground taken from a plane or helicopter. Aerial photographs provide detailed information on town buildings, land use and traffic management. When they are used with OS maps, they give us a wider understanding of the importance of the photographed town/city to its surrounding area.

15.1 Types of Aerial Photograph

There are three main types of aerial photograph:

- A **vertical photograph** is taken when the camera is **pointing directly downwards** on the area that is being photographed. Only the roofs of buildings are visible, along with roads and fields. All buildings are of the same scale, which is known as a **true scale.**

- A **high oblique** photograph is taken when the **camera is pointing at an angle of 60°** from the ground. As a result, the sides of buildings are also visible. High oblique photographs cover a much **larger area than vertical photographs. Objects at the front** of a high oblique photograph **look larger than objects at the back** of the photograph. This means that the scale is not true on high oblique photographs. Some of the **horizon is visible** in the background of a high oblique photograph.

- A **low oblique** photograph is taken when the **camera is pointing at an angle of 30°** from the ground. Low oblique photographs cover a much **smaller area than high oblique photographs.** As with all oblique photographs, low oblique photographs **do not have a true scale.**

🔼 **Fig. 15.1** A vertical aerial photograph

🔼 **Fig. 15.2** A high oblique aerial photograph

🔽 **Fig. 15.3** A low oblique aerial photograph

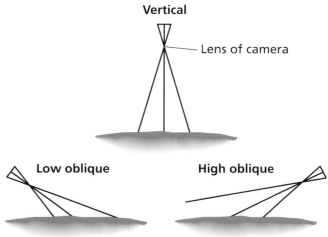

🔽 **Fig. 15.4** The position of the camera for each type of aerial photograph

CORE 2   CHAPTER 15

15.2 Location on an Aerial Photograph

Aerial photographs are divided up into nine boxes.

Vertical Photograph

A north arrow allows you to divide the photograph into nine equal parts. Compass points are used to locate features on a vertical photograph.

Fig. 15.6 shows how to locate compass points when the camera is not facing north.

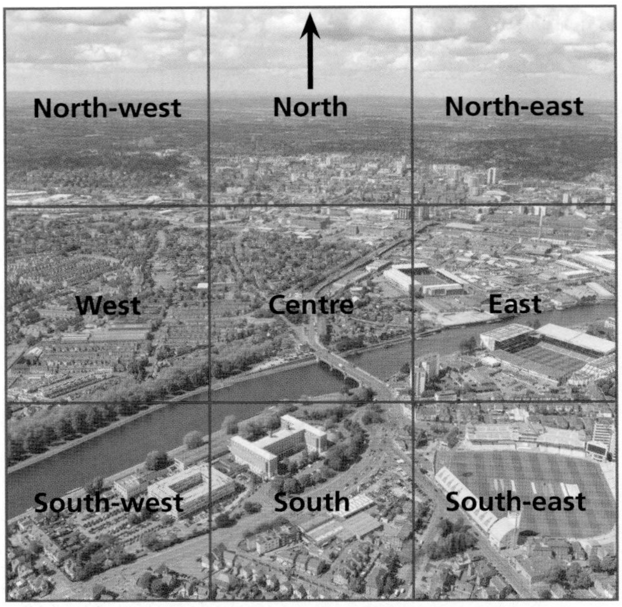

Fig. 15.5 Finding location on a vertical aerial photograph when the camera is facing north

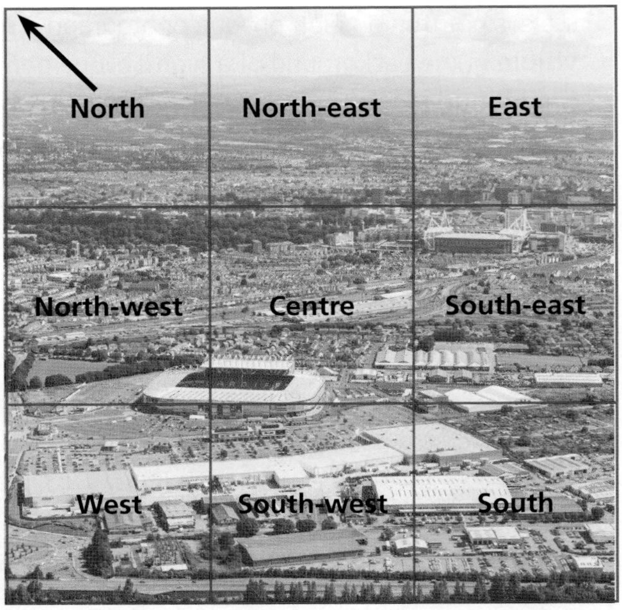

Fig. 15.6 Finding location on a vertical aerial photograph when the camera is not facing north

Left Background	Centre Background	Right Background
Left Middle Ground	Centre Middle Ground	Right Middle Ground
Left Foreground	Centre Foreground	Right Foreground

Oblique Photograph

When finding location on an oblique aerial photograph, compass points cannot be used. Instead, features are located using the nine sections shown on the left.

Time of Year

It is possible to tell the time of the year on a photograph by observing the following:

- **Spring:** ploughed fields are visible, and young animals are visible in fields.
- **Summer:** there are leaves on deciduous trees, fields are freshly cut (so look yellow), there are bales in the fields and shadows are shorter.

- **Autumn:** there are brown, yellow and red leaves on trees, shadows are longer, there are few animals in the fields and smoke rises from house chimneys.
- **Winter:** trees are bare, smoke rises from chimneys and tillage fields are left bare.

Direction of Camera

Students are often asked to find the direction the camera was pointing in when the photograph was taken. Many find this quite difficult, but here is an effective way of doing this:

Fig. 15.7 Time of year on an aerial photograph

- First, pick a distinctive feature at the front (foreground) of the photograph such as a church or bridge. Second, pick a distinctive feature at the back (background) of the photograph and draw a line connecting it to the feature at the front.
- Find the same two features on the OS map and join them up.
- Find the direction of this line using the north arrow on the OS map and you have calculated the direction in which the camera was pointing.

Using the aerial photograph shown in Fig. 15.8 and the OS map of Kenmare (Fig. 14.20 on page 270), we can calculate the direction in which the camera was pointing. Pick out the distinctive triangle shape made from converging roads on the left middle ground.

Join the point of the triangle to the church in the centre background. Repeat this on the OS map of Kenmare and use the north arrow to find out the direction the camera was pointing in.

Answer: south south-west

FACT

During the summer, the sun is higher in the sky, meaning it shines down more directly on the ground. This makes shorter shadows.

15.3 Sketch Maps

To draw a sketch map of an aerial photograph, follow these steps:

- Measure the length and width of the original photograph. You will usually be asked to sketch the photograph at half-scale (half the length and half the breadth), so divide the length and width by 2.
- Draw the frame of the photograph to half-scale, ensuring it is the same shape and orientation as the original.
- Divide the frame of the sketch map and the aerial photograph into nine equal squares.
- Only include a north arrow if one is printed on the aerial photograph.
- Draw in the coastline if it is visible.
- Draw in each of the features asked in the question, ensuring that you draw the outline shape of the features. Label them or explain them in a legend/key at the bottom of the sketch.
- Always label roads and rivers on the sketch map, but remember to draw them to half-scale. Many students insert rivers/roads at too big a size, which means they take up far too much space.

Fig. 15.8 An aerial photograph of Kenmare

Note!

See the sketch map on page 293 (Fig. 15.10).

15.4 Land Use and Functions

Aerial photographs enable us to recognise many land uses and functions.

Primary Activities	
Agriculture	Pastoral farming is easily recognisable by its green fields or grazing animals.
	Arable farming can be recognised through freshly ploughed fields or yellow fields with ripening crops.
Forestry	Coniferous trees are evidence of state forests.
	Native woodlands are usually found in historic parks.
Renewable energy	Wind farms and solar panels are visible in aerial photographs. Wind farms are typically located in rural areas away from housing. Solar panels are located on roof tops of buildings.
Horticulture	Glasshouses are used for growing fruits, vegetables and flowers. Areas of horticulture are typically located close to urban areas to provide easier access to markets.
Secondary Activities	
Industrial	Factories are identified by their flat roofs and rectangular shape. They are built in areas with good transport links and are often located in industrial estates on the outskirts of towns.
Tertiary Activities	
Educational	Educational services are schools, colleges and universities. They can be difficult to identify on aerial photographs. Some schools can be identified as they are surrounded by playing fields or tarmac courts. Many schools in Ireland now have Green Flags flying outside their buildings.
Tourism	Tourist services can be identified by tourist offices, hostels, caravan sites, golf courses and historical sites such as castles.
Transport	Transport services include roads, railway, airports, car parks and bus stations.
Market/ Retail	Typically, markets and retail areas are located in the CBD (Central Business District). The CBD can be identified by colourful shop fronts or higher buildings towards the centre of the town or city.
	Shopping centres can be identified as they are usually located on the outskirts of a town and are surrounded by parking spaces.
Port	Harbours, quays, piers, containers or cranes close to the water indicate the presence of a port.
Ecclesiastical	Churches, cathedrals and graveyards are evidence of religious/ecclesiastical functions.
Medical	Hospitals, clinics and ambulances parked in a row are indicators of medical functions.
Protection	Garda and fire stations are evidence of protection functions in a town.
Residential	There are five main types of housing that can be identified from an aerial photograph: 1. Detached houses are built on their own. Normally they are separated from the next detached house by a hedge or garden. 2. Semi-detached houses are two houses joined together. Typically semi-detached houses are located in housing estates. 3. Terraced houses are joined together in rows. These are normally located on streets close to the town or city centre or in older housing estates. 4. Apartments are normally built in blocks. These are single buildings which are divided into several apartments. They are usually multi-storey and often have balconies. 5. Bungalows are one-storey houses that are built on their own. They are usually located on the outskirts of an urban area.
Recreational	Recreational areas include parks, sports fields and walkways.

> **ACTIVE LEARNING**
>
> 1. Examine the aerial photograph of Kenmare (Fig. 15.11 on page 294). Identify and locate three different land uses/functions on the photograph.
> 2. Draw a sketch map of the Kenmare photograph and include the following:
>   - Two connecting roads
>   - The CBD
>   - A recreational area
>   - A car park
>   - An ecclesiastical land u

15.5 Traffic Management

Observing traffic management on an aerial photograph can be divided into two basic categories: where traffic congestion is likely to occur and measures taken to reduce the traffic congestion.

Congestion Hotspots

Traffic congestion is likely to occur on or near:

- Narrow streets
- Crossroads or where several streets/roads meet
- Main shopping areas
- Schools
- Bridges

 Fig. 15.9 Yellow boxes help to reduce traffic congestion by preventing junctions from becoming blocked with traffic.

Reducing Traffic Congestion

Traffic congestion can be reduced in a number of ways. These are usually visible on aerial photographs.

- Pedestrianised streets in shopping areas divert traffic away from congested areas.
- One-way systems aid traffic flow on narrow streets.
- Roundabouts allow for a more constant flow of traffic.
- Ringroads and bypasses reduce the amount of traffic entering a town.
- Yellow boxes prevent traffic from blocking junctions.
- Off-street parking stops cars from parking at the side of streets and making the streets narrower.
- Double yellow lines prevent cars from parking on streets.

15.6 Future Economic Development

Identifying the location of a particular land use can appear as part of a sketch map question in which you are asked to insert a feature or in short questions in which you are asked to comment on land use.

1. Site

It is cheaper and less difficult to build on flat land on the outskirts of a town. The outskirts of a town also allows for future expansion and services such as parking and loading/unloading areas. Agricultural or unused land that has been rezoned for development is known as a 'greenfield site'.

Brownfield sites already have old buildings which have become vacant. They are more expensive to purchase and more difficult to redevelop, but they can be in areas that are ideal for accessing markets.

2. Transport

New developments should have access to essential transport links such as roads/motorways, rail, ports and airports. This allows for efficient movement of goods and people.

In the exam if you are asked to locate a school, it is best to choose a greenfield site away from busy roads as heavy traffic could be dangerous for schoolchildren crossing roads.

GEO DICTIONARY

Congestion hotspot: areas prone to traffic delays

ACTIVE LEARNING

Use Fig. 15.13 on page 296 to answer these questions.

1. Suppose a new factory is being built in Enniscorthy, Co. Wexford. Choose a site for this development and justify your choice with three pieces of evidence from the photograph.

2. Identify and explain three types of traffic management used in Enniscorthy.

3. Explain three functions of Enniscorthy. Correctly locate each function using the correct terms.

3. Environment

New developments must not be placed next to parks, historic sites or other preserved areas. Factories must not be located too close to residential areas due to noise levels. Avoid locating new developments in areas where there are traffic congestion hotspots.

Comparing OS Maps and Aerial Photographs		
	OS Map	Aerial Photograph
Presentation	Maps show information through symbols, colour, etc.	An actual photograph of the area is shown.
Scale	The OS map has a scale stated on the map, usually 2 cm = 1 km.	Vertical photographs are true to scale while oblique photographs are not.
Area	Maps usually cover a large area, typically 108 km².	Smaller areas are shown on aerial photographs.
Direction	Direction is stated with an arrow indicating north.	Direction is shown on a vertical aerial photograph. Direction is not stated on an oblique photograph.
Distance	It is easy to calculate distance due to a stated scale.	It is difficult to estimate distance due to an absence of scale.
Location	Location is given by four- and six-figure grid references.	Location is given in general terms such as left background, etc., on an oblique photograph and using compass directions on a vertical photograph.
Altitude and gradient	Altitude is clearly shown through contour lines. Gradient can be calculated easily.	Altitude and gradient are difficult to observe.
Transport	Roads can be observed through colour and naming/numbering. In urban/built-up areas, only main streets are shown.	Road can be clearly seen but are not named or numbered. All streets are shown.
Land use and functions	Important public sector buildings are named/labelled. Houses/buildings in rural areas are represented by small, black squares. Only land used for forestry is labelled. Other land uses are not labelled.	Building uses are not labelled but some can be identified. Surrounding land uses can be seen and identified, e.g. agricultural land.

EXAM QUESTIONS

ORDINARY LEVEL

SHORT QUESTIONS

1. Examine the aerial photograph (Fig. 15.11 on page 294) and the sections taken from it on the right. Indicate whether the descriptions of the locations of each of the sections from the aerial photograph are correct, by circling the correct option in each case. One has been done for you.

2015 Q7 10M

| Each @ 2m each |

Centre Background
(True) False

Left Foreground
True False

Centre Middle Ground
True False

Right Middle Ground
True False

Right Background
True False

Left Background
True False

ORDINARY LEVEL

2. (i) Examine the aerial photograph of Dungarvan (Fig. 15.12 on page 295). Using accepted notation (right background, etc.), write the correct location of each of the following:

- A circus
- A roundabout
- A sandy beach

(ii) Was this aerial photograph taken during winter or spring? State one reason for your answer.

2014 Q3 10M

| (i) 3 @ 2m each |
| (ii) 2 @ 2m each |

3. (i) Examine the aerial photograph of Enniscorthy (Fig. 15.13 on page 296). Using accepted notation (right background, etc.) write the correct location of each of the following:

- A meander
- A car park
- A recreational area
- A bridge with cars

(ii) Is the aerial photograph a vertical or an oblique photograph?

2013 Q7 10M

| (i) 4 features correctly located @ 2m each |
| (ii) Photograph type correctly identified 2m |

LONG QUESTIONS

1. Examine the aerial photograph of Kenmare (Fig. 15.11 on page 294). Draw a sketch map of the area shown on the aerial photograph. On it, show and label the following:

- An area of agricultural land
- Two connecting streets
- A roundabout
- A car park
- An area of waste ground

2015 Q7A 30M

| Sketch outline 1m |
| Proportions 2m |
| Overall impression 2m |
| Five items shown @ 3m each |
| Five items labelled @ 2m each |

> **Note!**
> Long questions on aerial photographs are not as frequently asked as OS map questions in the core section of the exam paper. However, they appear almost every year in the Elective sections.

2. Examine the aerial photograph of Carrick-on-Suir (Fig. 15.16 on page 299). Draw a sketch map of the area shown on the aerial photograph. On it show and name the following:

- A church
- A recreational (leisure) area
- The main street (Central Business District)
- A modern residential (housing) area
- A bridge

2010 Q12 30M

| Sketch outline 1m |
| Proportions 2m |
| Overall impression 2m |
| Five items shown @ 3m each |
| Five items labelled @ 2m each |

3. Examine the aerial photograph of Enniscorthy (Fig. 15.13 on page 296). Draw a sketch map of the area shown on the aerial photograph. On it show and name the following:

- Two connecting streets
- An industrial area
- An agricultural area
- A railway bridge
- A river

2013 Q7A 30M

| Sketch outline 1m |
| Proportions 2m |
| Overall impression 2m |
| Five items shown @ 3m each |
| Five items labelled @ 2m each |

HIGHER LEVEL

SHORT QUESTIONS

1. Study the sketch map and the aerial photograph (Fig. 15.16 on page 299). Indicate the location on the aerial photograph of each of the features marked below. Use accepted notation (left background, etc.).

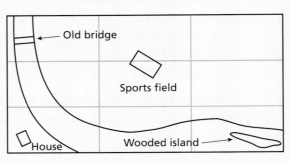

Feature	Location
Old bridge	
House	
Wooded island	
Sports field	

Four features located @ 2m each

2010 Q4 8M

LONG QUESTIONS

1. Examine the aerial photograph of Kenmare (Fig. 15.11 on page 294). Draw a sketch map of the aerial photograph, half the length and half the breadth. On it, correctly show and label each of the following:

   • A car park
   • The triangular street network in the middle ground of the aerial photograph
   • A large commercial/industrial building in the foreground of the aerial photograph
   • An area of waste ground suitable for development

   Sketch outline 4m
   Four features shown @ 3m each
   Four features labelled @ 1m each

   2015 Q8A 20M

2. Examine the aerial photograph of Dungarvan (Fig. 15.12 on page 295). Draw a sketch map of the aerial photograph, half the length and half the breadth. On it, correctly show and label each of the following:

   • A recreational area
   • A large commercial/industrial building
   • A bridge
   • An area of waste ground suitable for development

   Sketch outline 4m
   Four features shown @ 3m each
   Four features labelled @ 1m each

   2014 Q8A 20M

3. Examine the aerial photograph of Dingle/an Daingean (Fig. 15.15 on page 298) accompanying this paper. Draw a sketch of the aerial photograph, half the length and half the breadth. On it show and name each of the following:

   • The harbour area
   • Two connecting roads/streets
   • A commercial area
   • A recreational area

   Sketch outline 4m
   Four features shown @ 3m each
   Four features labelled @ 1m each

   2011 Q8A 20M

Sketch mapping is a question many students find difficult to complete accurately. Here, we will look at the 2012 question from the Higher Level paper.

HIGHER LEVEL

EXAM **QUESTION**

Examine the aerial photograph of Carrick-on-Shannon (Fig. 15.14 on page 297). Draw a sketch map of the aerial photograph, half length and half the breadth. On it label each of the following:

- The complete course of the largest river
- The tributary river in the left background
- The confluence and mark it with an X on the sketch map
- A drumlin

2012 Q1A 20M

At half-scale, this aerial photograph should measure 12.65 cm x 8.45 cm.

Note!
Questions related to aerial photographs also appear in the Economic Elective.

Marking Scheme
Proportion 2m
Frame 2m
Four features @ 4m each

SAMPLE **ANSWER**

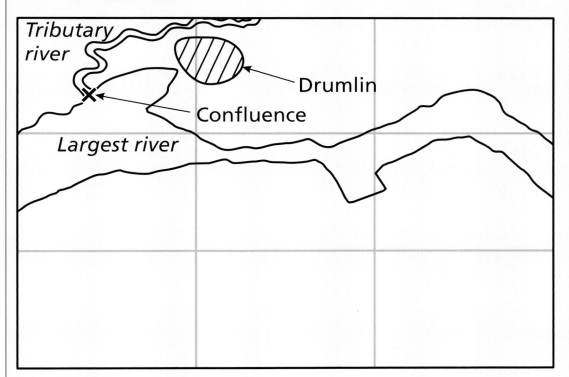

Tributary river

Drumlin

Confluence

Largest river

⌄ **Fig 15.10** Sketch map of Carrick-on-Shannon

Fig. 15.11 Aerial photograph of Kenmare

Fig. 15.12 Aerial photograph of Dungarvan

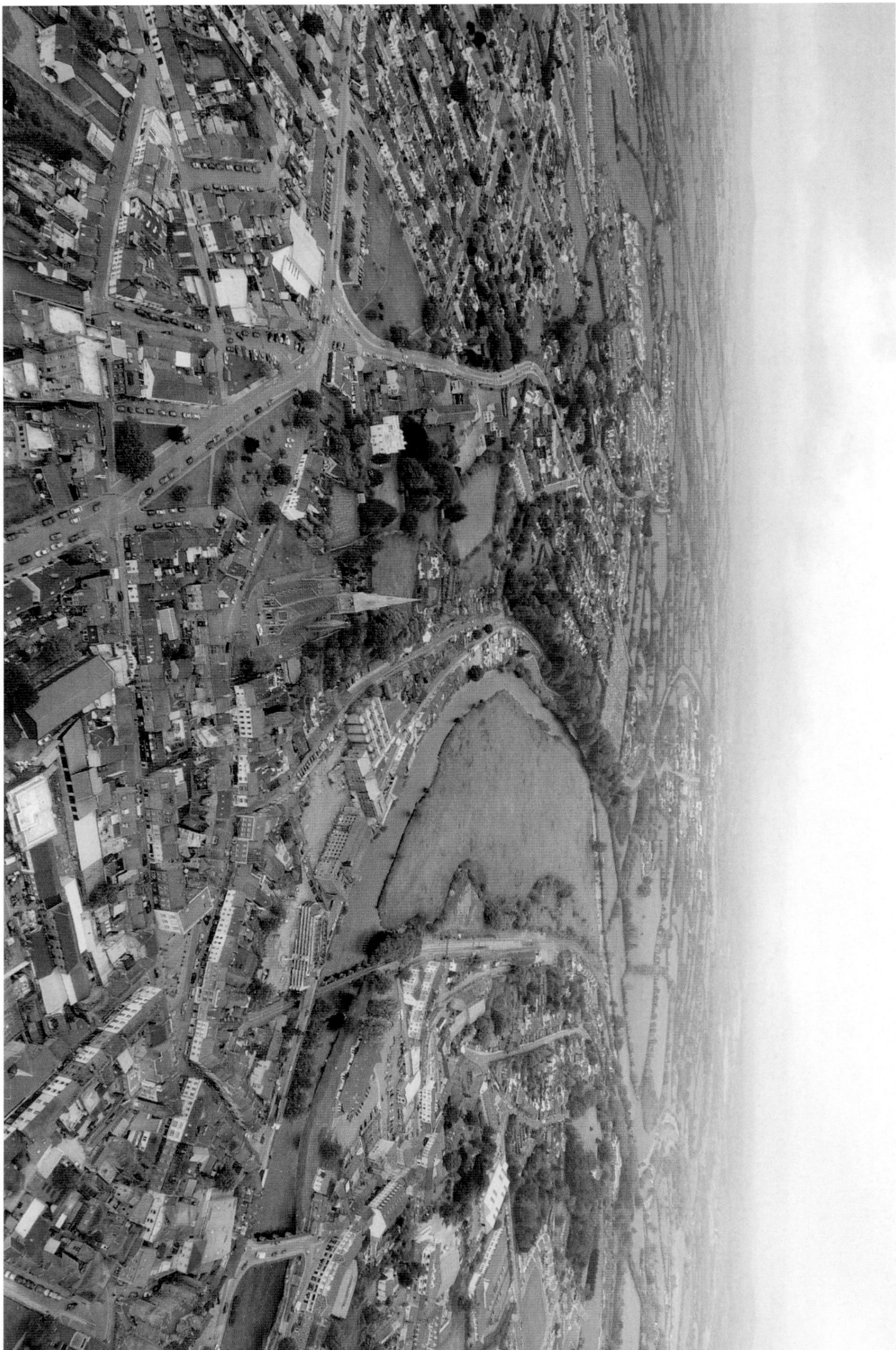

Fig. 15.13 Aerial photograph of Enniscorthy

● Fig. 15.14 Aerial photograph of Carrick-on-Shannon

Fig. 15.15 Aerial photograph of Dingle/an Daingean

◀ **Fig. 15.16** Aerial photograph of Carrick-on-Suir

TOPIC MAP

Off-street parking

Roundabouts

One-way street

Summer

Spring

Environment

Autumn

Transport

Winter

Site

Traffic lights

Yellow box

Time

Traffic management

Future economic development

Aerial photographs

Sketching

Location

Types of photograph

Frame

Divide

Oblique

Oblique

Locate

Label

Vertical

Vertical

High

Title

Background

Foreground

Low

North arrow

Middle ground

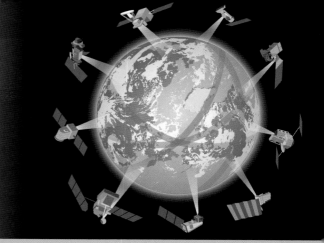

CHAPTER 16

Satellite Images

In this chapter, we will look at the use of satellite images in geography. Satellite imagery is a relatively new tool in the world of geography, allowing us to observe areas that were previously beyond our reach. The only sure way to become fully comfortable with reading satellite images is to practise answering questions on them as often as possible.

KEY WORDS

- Natural disasters
- Human interference
- Coastal features
- Urban sprawl

LEARNING OUTCOMES

What you MUST know
- How to observe and identify features shown in satellite images

Introduction

Satellite images provide a wide view of an area, which helps us to understand a variety of patterns and processes. The most common examples of patterns and processes monitored using satellite images are:

- Natural disasters such as volcanic eruptions, hurricanes and tsunamis
- Deforestation
- Weather patterns
- Changes to coastal features and how to identify them
- Urban sprawl

 GEO **DICTIONARY**

Urban sprawl: the unplanned growth of a town/city into the surrounding countryside

16.1 Natural Disasters

Before and After a Tsunami

(a) (b)

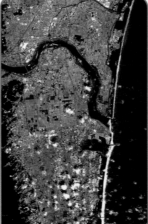 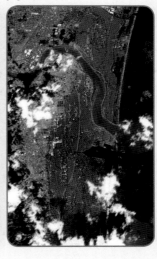

> **Fig. 16.1**
> (a) Before and (b) after satellite images of the 2011 Japanese tsunami

Volcanic Eruption

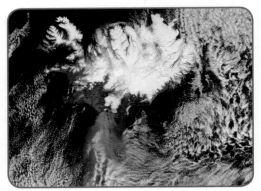

Fig. 16.2 A satellite image captures the ash cloud from Eyjafjallajökull volcano in Iceland in 2010.

Earthquake

Fig. 16.4 A satellite image captures damage caused to the Dharahara Tower in Kathmandu, Nepal after the 2015 earthquake.

Forest Fire

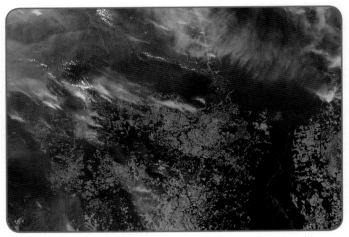

Fig. 16.3 A satellite image captures the devastation caused by forest fires in the Amazon.

16.2 Deforestation

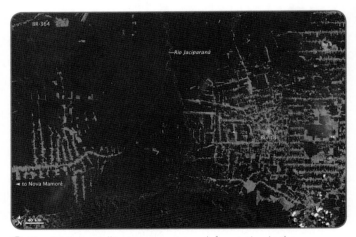

Fig. 16.5 A satellite image captures deforestation in the Amazon Rainforest.

16.3 Weather

Big Freeze

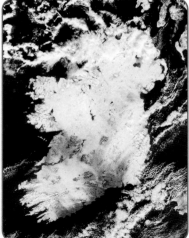

Fig. 16.6 A satellite image shows a snow-covered Ireland on 20 December 2010, when the lowest recorded temperature was −17.2 °C.

Hurricane

Fig. 16.7 A satellite image captures Hurricane Katrina building strength before hitting New Orleans in Louisiana in the US in 2005.

Drought

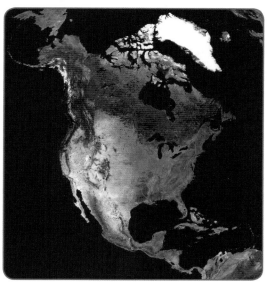

◁ **Fig. 16.8** A satellite image shows the drought-stricken West coast of the US versus the lush green East coast.

16.4 Coastal Features

Reclaimed Land

⬆ **Fig. 16.9** A satellite image of the Netherland's coastline

Nile Delta

⬆ **Fig. 16.10** A satellite image of the famous Nile Delta

16.5 Urban Sprawl

Urban Sprawl Over Time

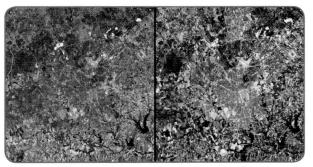

⬆ **Fig. 16.11** A satellite image shows urban sprawl of San Antonio in Texas in the US over time.

Dublin

⬆ **Fig. 16.12** A satellite image shows the extent of Dublin's urban region.

16.6 Human Interference

Oil Spills

⬆ **Fig. 16.13** A satellite image captures an oil slick in the Gulf of Mexico.

Hydroelectric Dam

⬆ **Fig. 16.14** A satellite image shows the Tarbela hydroelectric dam in Pakistan.

Drought

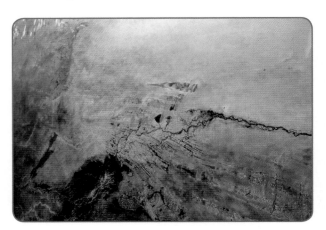

⬆ **Fig. 16.15** A satellite image shows the impact of drought on the Sahel Region in Africa.

Irrigation

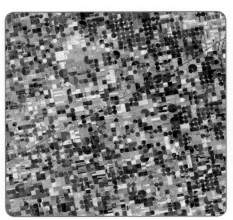

⬆ **Fig. 16.16** A satellite image shows irrigated crop circles in the south-western US.

▶ **Fig. 16.17** Three separate satellite images capture the shrinking of the Aral Sea in Kazakhstan/Uzbekistan over a 20-year period, one of the worst human-made environmental disasters in history.

Note!
The Aral Sea disaster is covered in more detail in the Patterns and Processes in the Human Environment Elective.

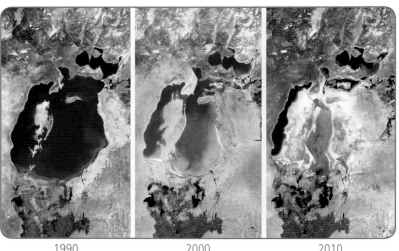

1990　　　　　　　2000　　　　　　　2010

ORDINARY LEVEL

SHORT QUESTIONS

1. (i) Match each satellite image with the most suitable description, by writing the correct letter in each case, in the table below.

Description	Letter
A flowing glacier in Switzerland	
A hydroelectric power station	
Niagara Falls, Canada	
Trim Castle, Co. Meath	

(ii) State **one** use of satellite images.

(i) 4 x 2m
(ii) 2m

2014 Q10 10M

2. Match each satellite image with the most suitable description, by writing the correct letter in each case, in the table below.

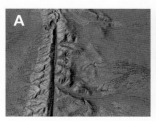  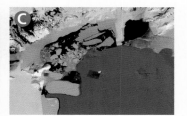

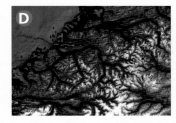 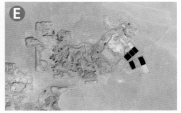

Description	Letter
A factory burning fossil fuels	
Fiord in Norway	
Mining in the desert	
The San Andreas Fault	
Icebergs breaking from an ice sheet	

Five parts @ 2m each

2013 Q10 10M

SHORT QUESTIONS

1. Match each of the letters A, B, C and D with the description that best matches it in the table below.

 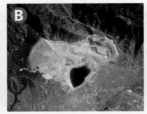 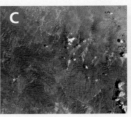 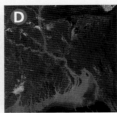

Description	Letter
Delta	
Open-cast mining	
Dust storm	
Forest fire	

Four parts @ 2m each

2015 Q12 8M

2. Match each of the letters A, B, C and D with the description that best matches it in the table below.

  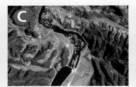 

Description	Letter
Deforestation	
Hydroelectric power station	
Nuclear power station	
River flooding	

2013 Q10 8M

3. Match each of the letters A, B, C and D with the description that best matches it in the table below.

   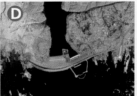

Description	Letter
The Aswan Dam	
A hurricane	
A recent lava flow	
Coastal sediments	

Four parts @ 2m each

2012 Q10 8M

Geographical Information Systems

Note!
This topic for is Higher Level students only. So far it has not appeared on exam papers, but it is only a matter of time before it does!

In this short chapter, we will look briefly at the use of geographical information systems (GIS).

KEY WORDS

- Geographical information systems
- Composite layers

LEARNING OUTCOMES

What you MUST know
- A description of GIS
- The uses of GIS

GIS is a tool which allows geographers to combine a variety of data sources to create a single visual map. GIS maps are more versatile than OS and other printed maps. They are now the preferred way of producing visual data for geographers. GIS is typically used along with maps, statistics, aerial photographs and census information to create a more detailed map. Unlike OS maps, GIS mapping can show social and economic features as well as physical ones.

GIS data is stored digitally on computers, allowing it to be updated as new information becomes available. Information is added in layers. For example, a layer with physical features such as water and mountains is added. Settlement layers such as towns, cities and villages are added next. Then, transport links such as roads and rail are added. Finally, services are added.

The layers are combined into one composite layer, creating a fully detailed map. GIS is very versatile, meaning it can be used in many different areas, such as:

- Map creation
- Urban planning
- Deciding where to locate services
- Rezoning of agricultural land

As this list suggests, GIS is mainly used by governments to assess services needed in an area and where best to locate them. It also allows them to plan for future needs. Private companies can also use GIS in order to establish the best sites for their business.

⌃ **Fig. 17.1** Composite layers

 GEO **DICTIONARY**

Composite layer: when different layers of a GIS file are combined, the full file is referred to as a composite layer

CORE 2 CHAPTER 17

CHAPTER 18

Graph Interpretation

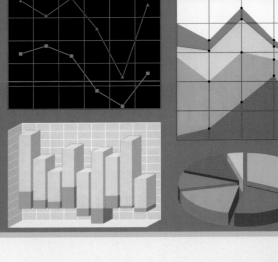

Geographers use graphs to effectively present results. Graphs are a visual representation of data collected. Data presented in graphs can be categorised and explained easily. In this chapter, you will learn how to construct and read basic graphs used by geographers.

KEY WORDS

- Frequency
- Bar chart/graph
- *x*-axis
- *y*-axis
- Basic bar chart
- Multiple bar chart

- Stacked bar chart
- Divided bar chart
- Pie chart
- Trend/line graph
- Climograph
- Triangle graph

- Scatter graph
- Tables
- Population pyramid
- Choropleth map

LEARNING OUTCOMES

What you MUST know
- How to read a variety of different graphs
- How to construct a number of different types of graph
- How to label graphs correctly
- How to turn your data frequencies into percentages

What you SHOULD know
- How to construct tables using the information from graphs (this may be useful for your field trip project)

Introduction

Note!
It is important that you learn how to construct and read a number of graph types, as you will be required to draw them as part of your Geographical Investigation.

Graphs are simple ways of effectively showing statistical information collected in an organised and easy-to-read way. It is important that you become familiar with a variety of different graphs and the types of information they are used to show. In this chapter, we will look at the following:

- Bar charts
- Pie charts
- Trend/line graphs
- Climographs
- Triangle graphs

- Scatter graphs
- Tables
- Population pyramids
- Choropleth maps

Note!
A question on graph interpretation has appeared every year at Higher Level and Ordinary Level.

18.1 Graph Types

Data collected by geographers can be illustrated in several different ways. We will look at many of these in this section.

Bar Charts

A bar chart is probably the easiest way to present statistical information. Bar charts consist of rectangular bars that are drawn to scale to the amount they represent. The horizontal line (*x*-axis) shows what type of data each bar represents, while the vertical line (*y*-axis) shows a value for that type of data.

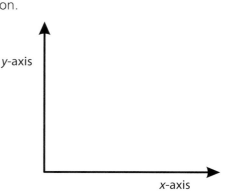

◔ **Fig. 18.1** A bar chart has an *x*-axis and a *y*-axis.

How to Draw a Bar Chart

1. Always draw a bar chart on graph paper and use a ruler.

2. Draw and label the *x*-axis and *y*-axis.

3. Give the bar chart a title, based on information provided.

4. Number the *y*-axis, ensuring that you have equal intervals between each value. For example, 2, 4, 6, 8, 10 and not 2, 6, 8, 12, 14.

5. Ensure that each bar on the graph is the same width (colour code them if you have enough time).

Types of Bar Chart

There are four main types of bar chart:

1. A basic bar chart shows only a single value.

2. In a multiple bar chart, a number of values are grouped together to show comparisons. A population pyramid is an example of a multiple bar chart.

3. In a stacked bar chart, each bar shows more than one set of information or data. This means that information can be compared against the rest of the data shown. As a result, one graph can show several sets of data that would otherwise require several graphs. A stacked bar chart is also known as a compound bar chart.

4. A divided bar chart is typically used to show the results of a simple survey, e.g. sports played by students at a school. A single rectangular bar is divided into blocks/ percentages, with each section representing one of the components.

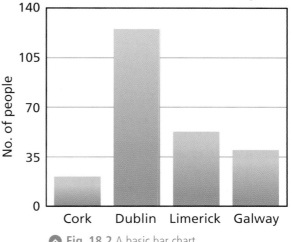

◔ **Fig. 18.2** A basic bar chart

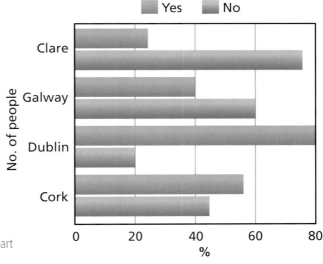

◑ **Fig. 18.3** A multiple bar chart

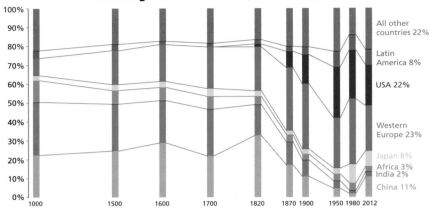

Percentage of world GDP (1000–2012)

All other countries 22%
Latin America 8%
USA 22%
Western Europe 23%
Japan 8%
Africa 3%
India 2%
China 11%

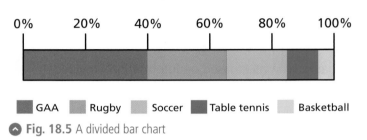

Sports played by students

GAA | Rugby | Soccer | Table tennis | Basketball

⬆ **Fig. 18.5** A divided bar chart

> ⬆ **Fig. 18.4** A stacked bar chart

Note!

Many students choose a graph question in the exam, but mistakes are often made (graph drawn incorrectly, title missing, scale missing, etc.). If a graph question on the Ordinary Level paper is worth a full 30m as a part A, the typical marking scheme is:

Graph paper 4m
Labelled scaled axes 2 @ 3m each
Five items @ 4m each
Total 30/30

If a graph question is worth a full 20m on the Higher Level paper as a part A, the typical marking scheme is:

Title 2m
Graph paper 2m
Scaled axes 2 @ 2m each
Information plotted 2 @ 6m each
Total 20/20

🔢 GEO NUMERACY

There are 360° in a circle.

The total of anything is 100%.

Therefore, 1% = 3.6° on a pie chart.

To find the angle from the percentage, multiply by 3.6.

For example, 15% is calculated as follows:

15 x 3.6 = 54°

To calculate angles from data without percentages, use the following formula:

$$\frac{\text{Frequency}}{\text{Total frequency}} \times 360$$

Frequency is the number in a certain category, e.g. 28 students walk to school.

Total frequency is the total number of components surveyed, e.g. 150 students were asked how they travelled to school.

To find the angle for the number of students who walk to school:

$$\frac{28}{150} \times 360 = \frac{10\ 080}{150} = 67.2°$$

Pie Charts

Geographers use pie charts to show data groups as percentages of the whole.

How to Draw a Pie Chart

- To draw a pie chart, use a compass to draw a full circle and mark in the centre point with a pencil. Draw a radius line from the centre point to one side of the circle. (Do not draw a line straight across the circle.)

- Use a protractor with the radius as the baseline to measure all of the angles and mark them along the circle. Join each of these marks to the centre point to complete your segments.

How students travel to school

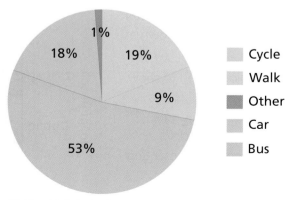

Cycle
Walk
Other
Car
Bus

⬆ **Fig. 18.6** A pie chart

Trend/Line Graphs

A trend graph is a simple way of showing change over time. It can be used to show one set of information (variable), or several sets of information. All data is shown on one graph, meaning it can be easily compared.

How to Draw a Trend Graph

- Make sure that the units on the vertical y-axis are drawn to scale and named.

- Make that the horizontal x-axis is divided equally and named (it does not need to be drawn to scale).

- Mark on each point and then join up the lines.

- Label each line and make each one a different colour.

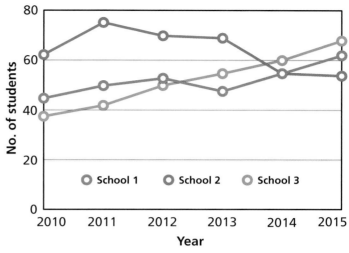

First year school enrolments in different schools

Fig. 18.7 A trend/line graph

Climographs

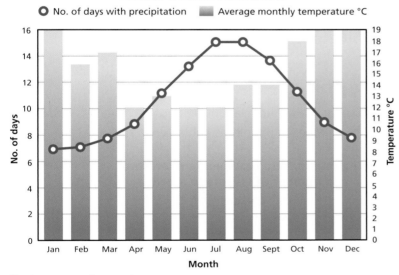

Valencia weather station 2015

Fig. 18.8 A climograph

Climographs combine a bar chart and a line graph to show the monthly precipitation and temperature for a certain area over a certain time. The bar graph shows precipitation, while the line graph depicts temperature. Each vertical axis has a different scale: the left represents precipitation and right represents temperature. These graphs also allow us to work out means and ranges.

ACTIVE LEARNING

Use Fig. 18.8 to answer the following questions.

1. What is the mean number of days per month when precipitation occurred?

2. Which months were the warmest?

3. Which months were the wettest?

4. What is the temperature range?

5. How many dry days were there that year?

ACTIVE LEARNING

1. Use Fig. 18.6 to answer the following questions:

   (a) If the total frequency is 150, calculate the degrees in each segment.

   (b) Calculate the number of students who travel to school by:
   - Car
   - Walking
   - Bus
   - Bicycle

2. Use Fig. 18.7 to answer the following questions:

   (a) Which school had the largest enrolment increase between 2010 and 2011?

   (b) In what year were two of the schools' enrolments the same?

   (c) In what year did school 3 have the largest enrolment?

   (d) Which school had the largest average enrolment from 2010 to 2015?

   (e) In what years did each of the schools have their largest enrolments?

GEO **DICTIONARY**

Mean: the average

Range: the difference between the highest and lowest

Triangle Graphs

Triangle graphs are used to display data from three different sources. The three sides are divided into percentage scales, with each side representing a different variable. The percentages from the three variables must add up to 100 per cent. Triangle graphs are commonly used for determining soil types, as they are made of three components, e.g. sand, silt, clay; or for representing economic activities (primary, secondary, tertiary).

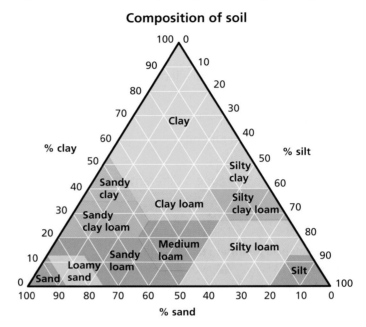

● **Fig. 18.9** A triangle graph

Scatter Graphs

A scatter graph is used to show the relationship between two sets of data, e.g. temperature and number of people visiting a beach for a year.

● **Fig. 18.10** A scatter graph

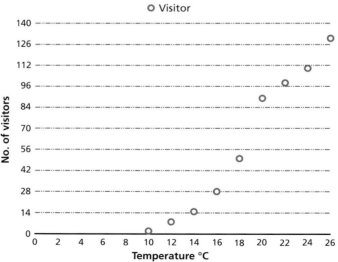

Tables

Tables are used to record and categorise data collected. For example, the following table is recording the number of waves (wave frequency) at three different sites. The wave frequency was recorded four times at each site

Wave Frequency	Site 1	Site 2	Site 3
Minute 1	11	12	11
Minute 2	12	12	10
Minute 3	11	11	11
Minute 4	13	12	9
Average	12	12	10

ACTIVE **LEARNING**

Using graph paper, draw a suitable graph to present the data collected in the table on the left.

Population Pyramids

A population pyramid shows the breakdown of population according to age and gender.

The pyramids are divided into halves (with males on the left and females on the right). The ages are divided into groups of five years: 0–4, 5–9, 10–14 and so on.

Choropleth Maps

A choropleth map is generally used to show the density/relative change of population in an area, e.g. population density or population increase or decline. Values are normally represented by colour, with darker colours representing higher values and lighter colours representing lower values.

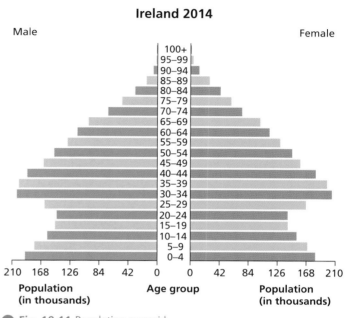

Fig. 18.11 Population pyramid

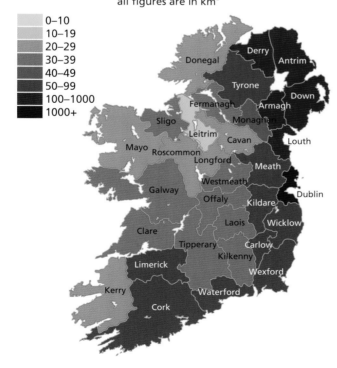

Fig. 18.12 Choropleth map

GEO **DICTIONARY**

Population density: the number of people per square km in an area/ country

Relative change: the difference between two different sets of data, e.g. the relative change between the population density of counties in Ireland in 2011 and 2016

CORE 2

CHAPTER 18

SHORT QUESTIONS

1. (i) Match each statistical chart with the most suitable title in the table below, by writing the correct letter in each case.

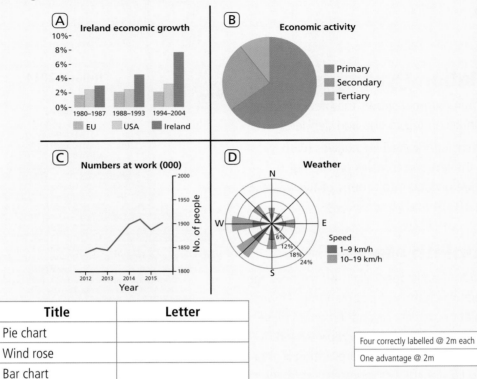

Title	Letter
Pie chart	
Wind rose	
Bar chart	
Trend graph	

Four correctly labelled @ 2m each

One advantage @ 2m

(ii) State one advantage of using a graph to present information.

2015 Q11 10M

2. Examine the graph and indicate whether each of the following statements is true or false by circling the correct option in each case.

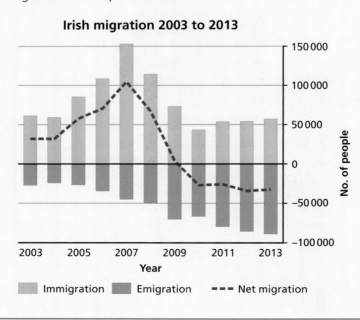

(i)	Immigration was at its highest level in 2005.	True	False
(ii)	Emigration and immigration levels were equal in 2003.	True	False
(iii)	Net migration was at its highest level in 2007.	True	False
(iv)	Immigration is the movement of people into a country.	True	False
(v)	Net migration is the difference between immigration and emigration.	True	False

Each question 2m

2014 Q11 10M

LONG QUESTIONS

1. Examine the pie charts showing the percentage of Ireland's livestock, crops and milk produced in the BMW region and the South and East region in 2011 and answer the following questions.

Percentage of Border, Midlands and West region (BMW) and in the South and East region in 2011

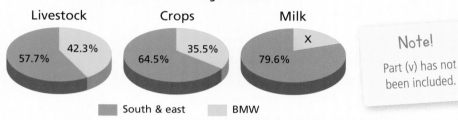

Livestock — 57.7% / 42.3%
Crops — 64.5% / 35.5%
Milk — 79.6% / X

■ South & east   ■ BMW

Note! Part (v) has not been included.

(i) What percentage of Ireland's livestock was produced in the BMW region?

(ii) Which region produced the most crops?

(iii) Calculate X, the percentage of milk produced in the BMW.

(iv) Name any two crops grown in Ireland.

Each part answered @ 6m each

2013 Q5A PARTS I–IV 24M

SHORT QUESTIONS

1. Examine the table showing information regarding afforestation in Ireland in selected years and answer each of the following questions.

Year	1923	1953	1983	2013
Hectares of trees planted privately	0	153	327	6249
Hectares of trees planted by public bodies	388	4199	5698	3
Total	388	X	6025	6252

(i) Calculate the difference between the number of hectares of trees planted privately and the number of hectares of trees planted by public bodies in 1983.

(ii) Calculate X, the total afforestation in 1953.

(iii) What was the trend in private planting between 1923 and 2013?

(iv) Explain briefly one reason for this trend in private planting.

Four parts @ 2m each

2015 Q11 8M

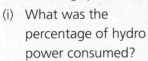

2. Examine the chart, which shows the consumption of renewable energy in the European Union (EU) in 2011 and answer each of the following questions.

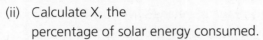

Comparison of renewable energy in the EU, 2011

X 3.6%
9.1%
15.8%
68.0 %
A 20.2%
B

Solar energy
Hydro power
Wind power
Geothermal energy
Biomass:
A Other biomass and waste
B Wood and wood waste

(i) What was the percentage of hydro power consumed?

(ii) Calculate X, the percentage of solar energy consumed.

(iii) Calculate B, the percentage of biomass generated from wood and wood waste.

(iv) Explain briefly what is meant by geothermal energy.

Four parts @ 2m each

2014 Q12 8M

3. Examine the wind rose and answer each of the following questions.

(i) What percentage of wind blowing from the south-west was at a speed of between 1 and 9 km/h?

(ii) What percentage of wind blew from the north-west?

(iii) From what direction did the wind blow most frequently?

(iv) From what direction did the wind blow least frequently?

Wind rose

N
W
E
6%
12%
18%
24%
S

Speed
1–9 km/h
10–19 km/h

Four parts @ 2m each

2013 Q8 PARTS I–IV 8M

LONG QUESTIONS

1. Using the information in the pie chart, answer each of the following questions.

(i) Name the two European Union (EU) member states to which Ireland exported the most seafood in 2012.

(ii) Name the two regions/countries to which Ireland exported the least seafood in 2012.

(iii) Calculate the total percentage of seafood exports to non-EU regions/countries in 2012.

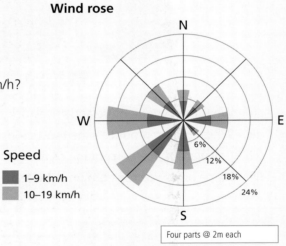

Irish seafood exports in 2012

11%
5%
6%
10%
15%
23%
21%
5%
2%
2%

Region/country
Africa
Asia
Russia
Other non-EU
France
United Kingdom
Spain
Germany
Italy
Other EU

(i) 2 @ 4m each
(ii) 2 @ 4m each
(iii) Total 4m

2015 Q5A 20M

EXAM **FOCUS**

EXAM **QUESTION**

Examine the data in the table showing dependency ratios in a number of Irish regions in 2011.

Region	Dependency Ratio
Galway City	35
Galway County	54
Cork City	42
Cork County	52
Waterford City	49
Waterford County	55

(i) Using graph paper, draw a suitable graph to illustrate this data.

2014 Q12A 20M

Marking Scheme
Title 2m
Vertical axis named 1m
Horizontal axis named 1m
Six items drawn @ 2m each

Note!

This question had a part (ii) worth 4m. Therefore part (i) is worth 16m.

SAMPLE **ANSWER**

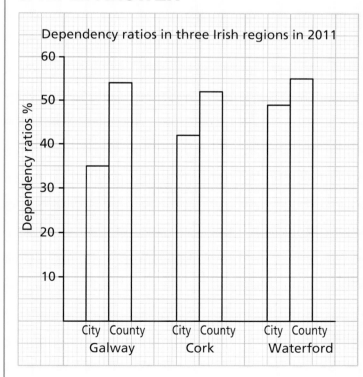

The student has clearly labelled the bar chart and included two correctly drawn axes.

Graph paper is used.

Suitable scale is chosen and all bars are a consistent width.

Marks Awarded
Title 2m
Both axis drawn and labelled 1m + 1m
Six items drawn correctly @ 2m each
Total 16/16

CORE 2 CHAPTER 18

TOPIC MAP

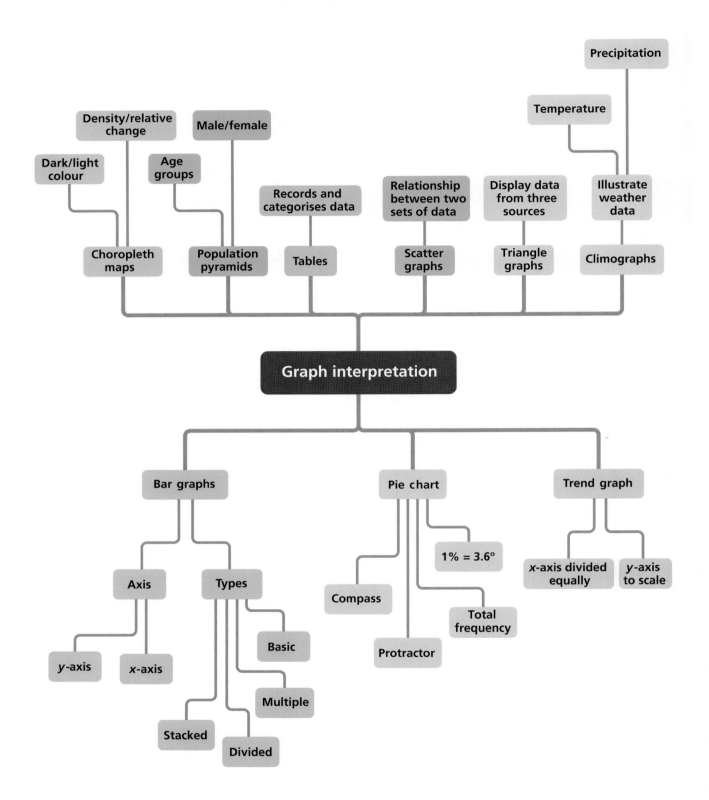

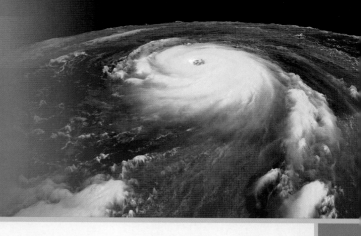

CHAPTER 19

Weather Maps

In this chapter, you will learn how to identify and understand weather maps and their symbols. You will learn how to identify weather systems displayed on weather maps and their associated atmospheric conditions. Reading weather maps is a skill so make sure to practise answering questions on them.

KEY WORDS

- Synoptic chart
- Met Éireann
- Isobar
- Front
- Depression

- Anticyclone
- Millibar
- Warm front
- Cold front
- Occluded front

- Wind chart
- Wind rose diagram
- Isotherms
- Sunshine map

LEARNING OUTCOMES

What you MUST know

- How to identify isobars and read atmospheric pressure
- How to identify a cold front, a warm front and an occluded front
- How to identify a cyclone and an anticyclone on a synoptic chart
- How to read wind radar and wind rose diagrams

What you SHOULD know

- The weather conditions associated with each front type

What is USEFUL to know

- Additional weather maps of Ireland and Europe, which can be obtained on www.met.ie

Introduction

Weather maps illustrate the meteorological conditions over a specific area at a specific time. Met Éireann is Ireland's meteorological organisation. It constructs weather charts by piecing together several weather reports from different weather stations across the country. The overall weather conditions are represented on a synoptic chart through a series of coloured lines and symbols. The following information is included on synoptic charts:

- Isobars
- Fronts
- Depressions
- Anticyclones

GEO DICTIONARY

Meteorology: the study of atmospheric conditions and forecasting of weather conditions

Synoptic chart: a map that represents the overall weather conditions of an area through a series of symbols

CORE 2 CHAPTER 19

19.1 Weather Conditions

Isobars

Isobars are lines on a weather map **that connect areas of equal atmospheric,** or barometric, pressure. The **millibar (mb)** is the **unit of measurement of atmospheric pressure.** Each isobar represents a difference of 4 mb of atmospheric pressure. Millibars are also referred to as hectopascals.

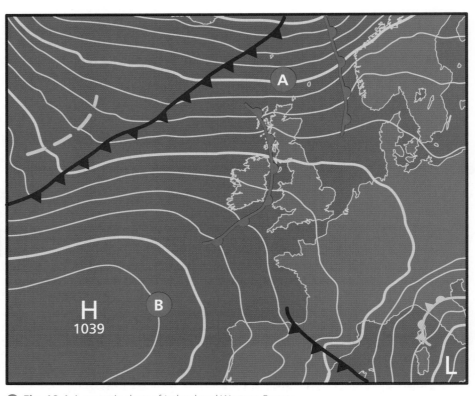

▲ **Fig. 19.1** A synoptic chart of Ireland and Western Europe

A **wind** is caused by air moving from **areas of high pressure to areas of low pressure** and vice versa. There are clear links between wind patterns and isobars.

- Isobars that are **closely grouped together** indicate that there are **strong winds** as a result of rapidly changing atmospheric pressure (*see the area marked A in Fig. 19.1*).

- Isobars that are **spaced widely apart** indicate **that conditions are calm** as there is a slow change in atmospheric conditions (*see the area marked B in Fig. 19.1*). This means winds are light.

- Winds typically blow almost **parallel to isobars,** giving winds a **swirling motion** (think of the shape of hurricanes).

Fronts

A weather front is the **point where two air masses meet.** Fronts move with air masses and bring quickly changing weather conditions. Three types of front can be identified on a weather chart:

- A **warm front** occurs where **warm air meets cold air.** As the **warm air is lighter,** it **rises over the cold air** in front of it. As the warm air rises slowly, it cools forming clouds, which then lead to drizzle and rain.

- A **cold front** occurs where a **cold air mass pushes under a warm air mass** in front of it, forcing the warm air to rise rapidly. This **creates thick clouds and short heavy bursts** of rain.

- An **occluded front** occurs where a cold front **overtakes a warm air mass** and pushes it upwards, forcing it off the ground. As the warm air mass is pushed upwards, it **cools and condenses quickly** leading to **short bursts of heavy rainfall.** An occluded front first takes on the characteristics of a warm front before producing conditions similar to a cold front.

Depressions/Cyclones

A depression or cyclone is an area of **low atmospheric pressure** that forms from warm air rising from the ground. It is **marked 'L' on a weather chart,** which stands for low pressure or depression. Depressions bring unsettled weather conditions. Winds blow toward the low-pressure centre in an anticlockwise direction (*see* Fig. 19.5(b)) and bring unsettled, changeable weather such **as** cloud cover, precipitation and **strong winds.**

⬆ **Fig. 19.2** A warm front

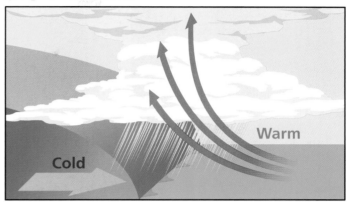

⬆ **Fig. 19.3** A cold front

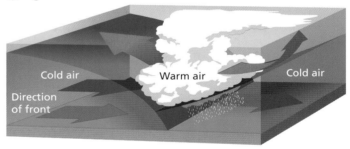

⬆ **Fig. 19.4** An occluded front

(a)

  **Fig. 19.5** (a) A low-pressure system moving across Ireland and (b) a low pressure/cyclone

(b)

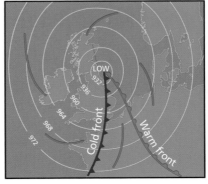
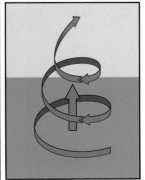

(a)

High/Anticyclones

A high or an anticyclone is an area **of high atmospheric pressure** that forms **as cold air presses down on the Earth**. It is **marked 'H' on a weather chart**, which stands for high pressure or anticyclone. Anticyclones bring **settled weather**. Winds blow **towards the centre in a clockwise direction** (*see* Fig. 19.6(b)) and bring weather conditions such **as clear, cloudless skies, light winds** and **no rain.**

(b)

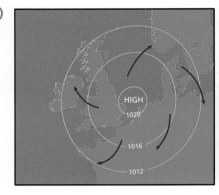 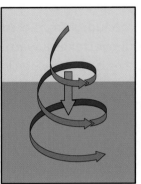

Fig. 19.6 (a) A high-pressure system moving across Ireland (high pressure = clear skies) and (b) a high pressure/anticyclone

ACTIVE **LEARNING**

1. What type of weather is associated with each of the following?
    (a) A cold font
    (b) A warm front
    (c) An occluded front
2. What is a cyclone and how would you identify it on a synoptic chart?
3. What type of weather is associated with an anticyclone?
4. Use Fig. 19.7 to answer the following questions:
    (a) What is the direction of the most common wind to blow across Malin Head?
    (b) In general, are westerly or easterly winds stronger?
    (c) What was the most frequent wind at Dublin Airport?
    (d) Which wind was the least frequent?
    (e) What percentage of weather was calm at Valencia?

19.2 Weather Charts

Wind Radar Charts

Met Éireann uses wind radar charts to show the **most frequent winds blowing** in an area. The charts show:

*   The **direction** from which the wind blows
*   The **percentage of time it blows** from that direction, using a 'Scale of frequency' bar
*   The **percentage of calm weather,** which is read from the figure at the centre of each weather station chart

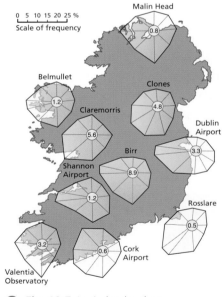

Fig. 19.7 A wind radar chart

Wind Rose Diagrams

Wind rose diagrams are used to show **wind speed and direction** in an area over time. Each 'arm' of the diagram shows the **direction the wind was blowing from,** while the different **colours indicate the different speeds.** In Fig. 19.8, we can see that the most frequent wind direction was southerly, but the strongest winds came from the west and north-east.

Precipitation Maps

Precipitation maps are used to show the **average annual precipitation** across an area. **Darker blue** represents **heavier annual precipitation,** while lighter blue represents lower annual precipitation. **Isohyets** are also used to **show rainfall on a weather map.**

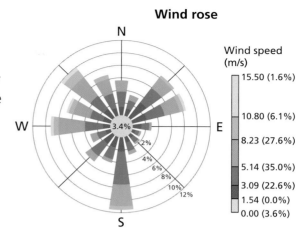

Wind rose

Fig. 19.8 A wind rose diagram showing the speed and direction of winds

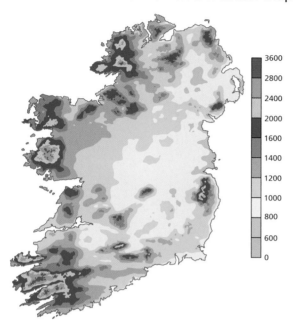

Fig. 19.9 Precipitation map of Ireland (amounts are in mm)

GEO DICTIONARY

Isoyhets: lines or blue shading on a map connecting areas which experience the same levels of precipitation

Isotherms: lines or red shading on a map which connect areas of equal temperature

Temperature Maps

Temperature maps are used to show the **average temperatures** across an area. Darker red represents higher temperatures, while lighter red represents lower temperatures. Isotherms are used to show temperature on a map.

Sunshine Maps

Sunshine maps show average daily sunshine as a fraction of the length of day (sunlight hours).

Note!
Go to Met Éireann's website **www.met.ie** to find daily weather charts.

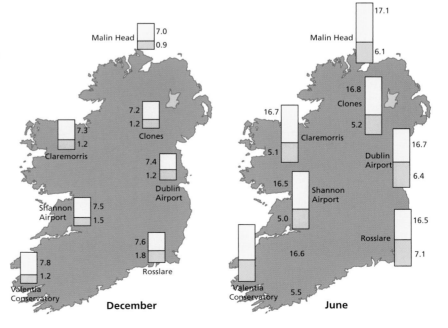

Fig. 19.10 Sunshine maps of Ireland showing the difference between average December and June hours of sunshine

ORDINARY LEVEL

SHORT QUESTIONS

Note!
So far, weather maps have appeared as short questions on both the Ordinary and Higher Level papers.

1. Examine the climate graph showing average temperature and rainfall levels for Dublin and answer each of the following questions.

Climate graph for Dublin

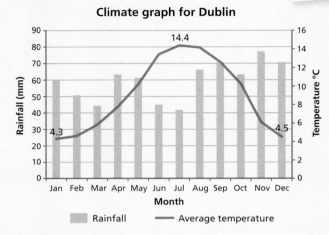

(i) Which month had the highest rainfall levels?

(ii) Which month had the lowest rainfall level?

(iii) In which month was the highest average temperature recorded?

(iv) Did the average temperature fall below 0° in any month?

(v) What was the average temperature range in degrees Celsius (°C)?

Five parts @ 2m each

2014 Q8 10M

2. Examine the weather chart and answer the following questions.

(i) Match the two letters, A and B, on the weather chart with the correct front in the table.

Front	Letter
Cold front	
Warm front	

(ii) What do the letters H and L on the weather chart stand for?

(iii) What is the lowest barometric pressure over the Atlantic to the south-west of Ireland?

(iv) What is the name usually given to Ireland's climate?

(i) 2 @ 2m each

(ii)–(iv) @ 2m each

2012 Q10 10M

SHORT QUESTIONS

1. Examine the weather chart and indicate whether each of the following statements is true or false, by circling the correct option in each case.

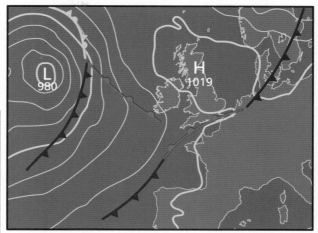

(i) The pressure over the south-west coast of Ireland is 1022 hPa.	True	False
(ii) There is a warm front located on the south coast of England.	True	False
(iii) Ireland is under the influence of a north-easterly airflow.	True	False
(iv) Winds over Ireland are strong to gale force.	True	False

Four parts @ 2m each

2015 Q4 8M

2. Examine the map and answer each of the following questions.

(i) What is the mean daily temperature at A?

(ii) Calculate the approximate mean daily temperature range in Co. Kerry.

(iii) What is the name given to lines on a weather map that join places of equal temperature?

(iv) Explain briefly why temperatures in the West of Ireland are usually higher than temperatures in the midlands in January.

Mean daily January temperature in Ireland

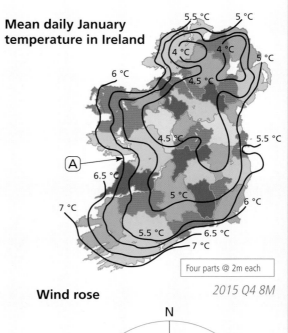

Four parts @ 2m each

2015 Q4 8M

3. Examine the wind rose and answer each of the following questions.

(i) What percentage of wind blowing from the south-west was at a speed of between 1 and 9 km/h?

(ii) What percentage of wind blew from the north-west?

(iii) From what direction did the wind blow most frequently?

(iv) From what direction did the wind blow least frequently?

Wind rose

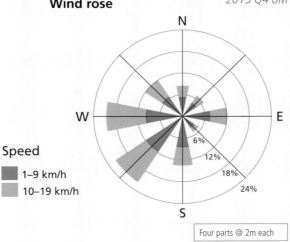

Speed
■ 1–9 km/h
■ 10–19 km/h

Four parts @ 2m each

2015 Q4 8M

TOPIC MAP

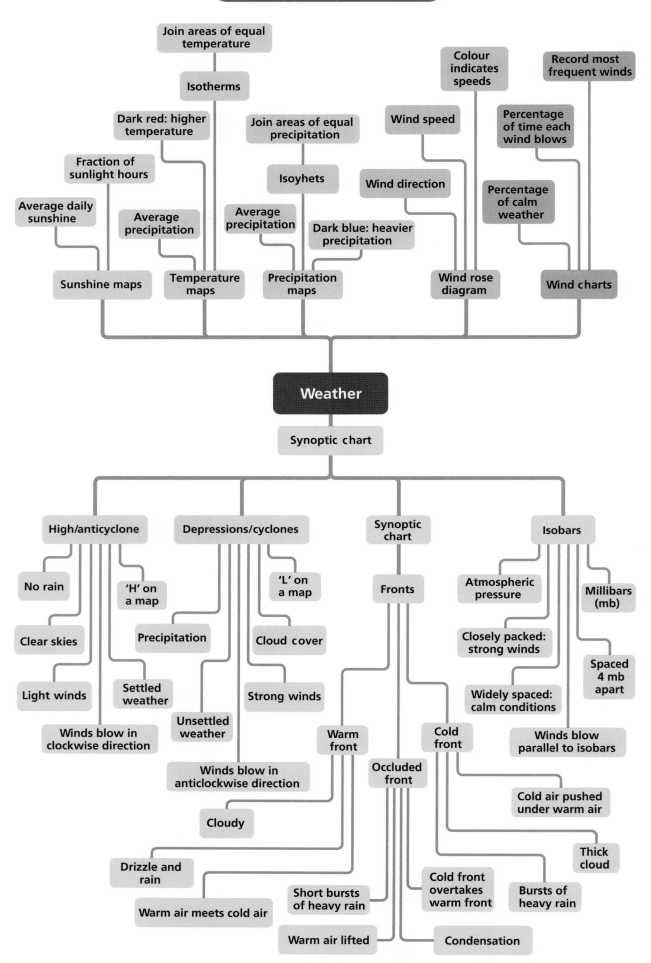

Join areas of equal temperature

Isotherms

Dark red: higher temperature

Join areas of equal precipitation

Wind speed

Colour indicates speeds

Record most frequent winds

Percentage of time each wind blows

Fraction of sunlight hours

Isoyhets

Wind direction

Average daily sunshine

Average precipitation

Average precipitation

Dark blue: heavier precipitation

Percentage of calm weather

Sunshine maps

Temperature maps

Precipitation maps

Wind rose diagram

Wind charts

Weather

Synoptic chart

High/anticyclone

Depressions/cyclones

Synoptic chart

Isobars

No rain

'H' on a map

'L' on a map

Fronts

Atmospheric pressure

Millibars (mb)

Clear skies

Precipitation

Cloud cover

Closely packed: strong winds

Light winds

Settled weather

Strong winds

Widely spaced: calm conditions

Spaced 4 mb apart

Winds blow in clockwise direction

Unsettled weather

Warm front

Cold front

Winds blow parallel to isobars

Winds blow in anticlockwise direction

Cold air pushed under warm air

Cloudy

Occluded front

Thick cloud

Drizzle and rain

Cold front overtakes warm front

Bursts of heavy rain

Warm air meets cold air

Short bursts of heavy rain

Warm air lifted

Condensation

CORE UNIT 3

Regional Geography

CHAPTER 20

The Concept of a Region

In this chapter, you will learn about the concept or idea of regional geography. A region is an area that has particular characteristics which set it apart from other regions. There are several basic indicators of regions that you will learn in this chapter:

- Climate
- Landscape
- Administration
- Language

- Industry
- Economy
- Urban regions

Much of the information you have learned in the physical section of the course becomes relevant throughout this chapter. You will see how physical processes impact on human processes.

KEY WORDS

- Regionalism
- Boundaries
- Climate
- Cool temperate oceanic
- Geomorphological
- Burren
- Carbonation
- North European Plain
- Administrative
- Regional Assemblies

- Gaeltacht
- Wallonia
- Flanders
- Northern Ireland
- Nationalist
- Republican
- Unionist
- Loyalist
- Discrimination
- Protestant

- Catholic
- Civil rights
- Islamic
- Core region
- Peripheral region
- Industrial decline
- Urban regions
- Urban sprawl

LEARNING OUTCOMES

What you MUST know
- How regions can be defined according to their physical characteristics
- How regions can be defined according to their climates
- How administrative regions are defined by their governments
- How cultural regions can be defined by language and religion

- How to define socio-economic regions
- Examples of regions of industrial decline

What you SHOULD know
- Additional statistics about regions

What is USEFUL to know
- How to identify all of these regions on a map

Introduction

Before you begin this chapter, it is important that you discover what you already know about regions. If you have joined your local GAA or other sports club, you will have encountered the concept of regions – even if you were unaware of it. You might have joined a team, worn a jersey with the local colours and crest printed on it, and played teams from other areas who wore their own colours and crests. No matter what sport or other club you join, or what interest you have, once you compete it creates the identity of 'us' and 'them'. This is the basis of regionalism.

There are four general indicators of regions:

1. **Image:** The name of a region often creates a perception or image of that region. For example, if someone mentions Dublin, you almost certainly think of the city rather than of the rural countryside.

2. **Area:** Certain regions can be identified as their landscapes differ from the surrounding areas, e.g. the Burren, the Sahel, the Amazon.

3. **Boundaries:** Boundaries mark the points where one region ends and another begins, e.g. county boundaries. Some boundaries are easily seen, such as mountain ranges, while others are not visible, such as political boundaries, e.g. county and country borders.

4. **Change:** Many regions change over time. Cities and towns get larger, which causes their boundaries to expand over time. For example, as more countries join the European Union (EU), its boundary changes. In contrast, as more people leave the Irish-speaking Gaeltachts of the West of Ireland, their boundaries shrink.

While there is a lot of information to take in, you will become more comfortable with the concepts of regions over the course of this chapter.

Concept 1: Climate Regions

Climate is the **average weather conditions experienced by an area over a long period of time.** There are **six major climate types** in the world:

- Tropical
- Arid
- Temperate
- Continental
- Polar
- Mountain

These major climates can be **divided into subcategories,** e.g. Ireland has a **cool temperate oceanic climate,** while Italy has a warm temperate oceanic climate. Climates differ in terms of **temperature and precipitation.** In turn, climate impacts the soil type and the flora and fauna that exist in an area. Climates also **affect the type of human activity** that takes place in a region.

Note!

The impact of climate on soil, flora and fauna is covered in the Geoecology Option.

ACTIVE LEARNING

Think about the following terms and compile a list of words you associate with each. You will find that many of the words on the list help to create the idea of regionalism in your mind.

Discuss your lists as a class.

1. The West of Ireland and Dublin
2. Northern Ireland
3. Language
4. Accents
5. The Burren
6. GAA clubs
7. Religion

GEO DICTIONARY

Flora: plants
Fauna: animals

ACTIVE LEARNING

To examine how boundaries change, search for the following European maps online:

1. Europe pre-1914
2. Europe pre-1989
3. EU countries

CORE 3 CHAPTER 20

Cool Temperate Oceanic Climate

A cool temperate oceanic climate is found along the western margins of Europe. It is located between **40° and 60° north** of the equator and is experienced by all **areas that touch the northern Atlantic.** As a result, it is also referred to as a **maritime climate.** The Atlantic heavily **regulates the climate,** directly impacting on its temperature and precipitation characteristics. Ireland lies **55° north of the equator** and is the most westerly European country experiencing a cool temperate oceanic climate.

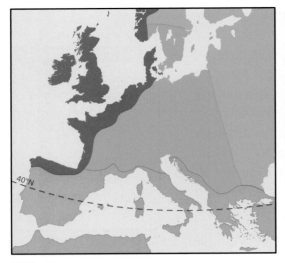

- ■ West European (cool temperate oceanic)
- ■ Mediterranean (warm temperate oceanic)
- ■ Central European (cool temperate transitional)
- ■ East European (cool temperate continental)

Fig. 20.1 Map of European climates

Characteristics of Ireland's Climate

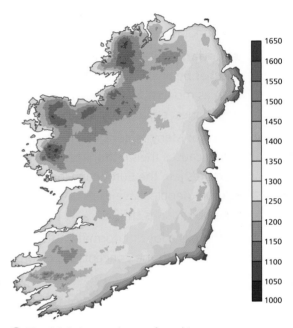

Fig. 20.2 Average hours of sunshine per year

Temperature

- **Summers** in Ireland are warm, averaging between **15 °C and 17 °C.**
- **Winters** in Ireland are mild, averaging **6 °C** due to the warming influence of the **North Atlantic Drift.** This is a warm current of water which flows from the Gulf of Mexico, northwards along the western coast of Europe.
- The annual **temperature range** is **11 °C.**
- **May and June** are the **sunniest months** of the year, with an average of **six hours of sunshine per day.**
- **December** is the **dullest month** of the year, with as little as **1 to 2 hours of sunshine** per day.
- Typically, the west of the country receives **less sunshine** than the rest as **heavy cloud cover** is carried in from the **Atlantic.** The **south-east** is the **sunniest** area of the country.

Precipitation

- Ireland experiences **frequent rainfall** throughout the year, with the heaviest rainfall occurring in the winter.
- Rainfall is **not evenly distributed** throughout the country. The **West receives up to 2500 mm per year,** while the **east** experiences **800 mm per year.**

- The West receives more rainfall due to its **upland relief,** which forces **moisture upwards.** It then **cools and condenses,** leading to heavy rainfall (known as relief rainfall). The West acts as a **rain shadow** for the east, meaning less rainfall occurs in the east.

Impact of the Atlantic on Ireland's Climate

- The **North Atlantic Drift** is a **warm ocean current** that flows north from the Gulf of Mexico.

- Its warming influence **raises the temperature of Ireland's coastal waters** by several degrees during the winter. This keeps **Ireland's ports ice free.**

- Given its location, Ireland would be expected to have cold winters. The North Atlantic Drift is the main reason Ireland experiences **mild winters.** It also has a **cooling effect in Ireland during the summer** as the water takes longer to heat up than the land. This **moderating effect** is the reason for Ireland's **small temperature range.**

- The prevailing **south-westerly winds** also help to moderate temperatures in Ireland. These winds are a warm air mass. As they blow over the Atlantic, they **evaporate large amounts of sea water.**

- When the **moisture-laden winds** reach Ireland, they are forced upwards leading to **relief rainfall.** Ireland's latitude of 55° N coincides with the meeting of the **cold polar front and the warmer south-westerly air mass,** which causes frontal depressions to form.

- Depressions form in the Atlantic and move inland across Ireland, causing **periods of bad weather.** As a result, Ireland's weather is very changeable and difficult to predict.

GEO DICTIONARY

Rain shadow: in Ireland, precipitation occurs along the western coast due to relief rainfall, meaning the east remains drier

ACTIVE LEARNING

1. Define 'climate'.
2. Describe the characteristics of a cool temperate oceanic climate.
3. Explain the effects of the North Atlantic Drift on Ireland's climate.
4. Why does the West of Ireland experience more rainfall than the east?

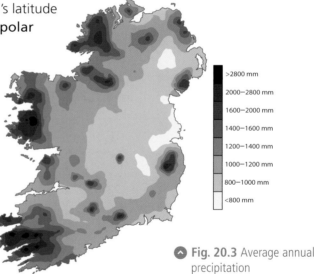

>2800 mm
2000–2800 mm
1600–2000 mm
1400–1600 mm
1200–1400 mm
1000–1200 mm
800–1000 mm
<800 mm

Fig. 20.3 Average annual precipitation

EDUCATE YOURSELF

Climates	6 major climates, divided into subcategories, temperature and precipitation, affects human activity
Cool temperate oceanic climate	40–60° N of equator, areas that touch northern Atlantic, maritime climate, regulates the climate, Ireland 55° N of equator
	Temperatures: summer 15–17 °C, winter 6 °C, North Atlantic Drift, temperature range 11 °C; May and June sunniest months, 6 hours sunshine per day; December dullest month, 1–2 hours sunshine per day; West less sunshine, heavy cloud cover; south-east sunniest, clearer skies
Impact of North Atlantic Drift (NAD) on Ireland's climate	NAD, warm ocean current, raises the temperature of Ireland's coastal waters, keeps ports ice-free, mild winter, cooling effect during summer, moderating effect, small temperature range, south-westerly winds, evaporate large amounts of water, moisture-laden winds, relief rainfall, cold polar front meets warm south-westerly air mass, forms low pressure, causes periods of bad weather, changeable and difficult to predict

Concept 2: Physical/ Geomorphological Region

A|Z GEO **DICTIONARY**

Geomorphological: of or relating to the form or surface features of the Earth

Geomorphological regions are defined by their **unique physical features** such as **relief, rock type and drainage.** There are several unique physical regions in Ireland such as the **Burren**, the **Munster Ridge Valley** and the **Antrim-Derry Plateau.**

The Burren

△ **Fig. 20.4** Poulnabrone Portal Dolmen

- The **Burren in Co. Clare** is a unique physical region of Ireland. The Burren is a **karst region** composed of **limestone** that has been **exposed on the surface.** In total, the region covers **250 km²**, a small section of which is a **protected natural park.**

- The Burren began its formation under water some **350 million years ago,** when most of what is now Ireland was covered by a **shallow tropical sea** (*see* Chapter 6 for limestone formation). The Burren region was raised **above sea level** during the **Armorican folding period** over **250 million years ago.**

- The underlying limestone was covered by **thin layers of silt and mudstone,** which protected it from **weathering and erosion.** Eventually, **glaciers** eroded the overlying layers during the last ice age, **exposing the limestone to the surface.**

△ **Fig. 20.5** Limestone pavement of the Burren

- Once the limestone was exposed to the surface, the processes of **chemical weathering and erosion shaped the limestone,** creating both **surface and underground features. Carbonation, solution and hydraulic action** led to the creation of surface features such as **limestone pavement** with **clints and grikes,** along with **swallow holes and dry valleys.**

- In total, **60 per cent of the Burren** is made up of **limestone pavement,** while the remaining **40 per cent is covered in thin soil** that supports agriculture.

A number of **lakes and rivers appear in dry valleys** during the winter when the water table rises above the level of the swallow holes. However, once the **summer** arrives, these water **features disappear.**

- **Underground features** such as **caves, stalactites, stalagmites and pillars are formed** from solution and dissolution, with many examples dotted throughout the region. The famous **Aillwee Cave** in the Burren contains a range of underground features which can be viewed by the public.

FACT

Aillwee Cave also attracts experienced divers who explore sections of the cave that are closed to the public. Only three people have succeeded in getting to the very end of the cave.

- The Burren region also supports **unique flora and fauna**. A **variety of orchids** grow that are not normally supported by the Irish climate. One type of Arctic-Alpine plant typically found in the valleys of Greenland also grows here.

ACTIVE LEARNING

1. Describe the following physical regions and how they formed: (a) the Munster Ridge Valley (b) the Antrim-Derry Plateau.
2. Explain how the limestone in the Burren formed.
3. Name one surface and one underground feature found in the Burren.
4. Explain how carbonation occurs.

⌃ **Fig. 20.6** The unique landscape of the Burren

EDUCATE YOURSELF

Geomorphological regions	Geomorphological, unique physical features, relief, drainage, rock type, Burren, Munster Ridge Valley, Antrim-Derry Plateau
The Burren	Karst region, limestone, exposed on surface, 250 km², protected national park, 350 mya shallow tropical sea; above sea level; Armorican folding period 250 mya, covered in thin layers of silt and mudstone, weathering and erosion exposing the limestone, chemical weathering, erosion shaped the limestone, surface and underground features, carbonation, solution, hydraulic action, limestone pavement – clints and grikes, swallow holes and dry valleys, 60% of Burren is limestone pavement, 40% covered in thin soil, lakes and valleys appear, disappear in summer, underground features: caves, stalactites, stalagmites, pillars; Aillwee Cave – unique flora and fauna, variety of orchids

The North European Plain

- The **North European Plain** is a lowland region that lies **between the Alps to the south and Scandinavian uplands** to the north.

- The region stretches from northern France and south-west Belgium as far as Bulgaria and the Black Sea. Ireland and Great Britain were once part of the Northern European Plain, but they were left as islands when **rising sea levels cut them off from mainland Europe**.

- Previously, this region was **beneath a shallow sea,** causing sedimentary rocks to form on the sea floor. When the African Plate collided with the Eurasian Plate **40–60 million years ago, the Northern European Plain was uplifted** above sea level.

- As the region uplifted, its **layers of sedimentary rock were slightly warped,** but not folded or faulted like the Alpine region to the south was. This gives the region its **flat or undulating landscape.**

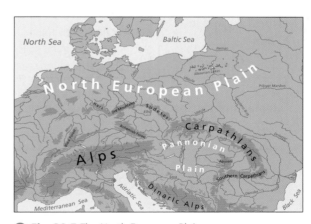

⌃ **Fig. 20.7** The North European Plain

GEO **DICTIONARY**

Undulating: gently sloping landscape

CORE 3 CHAPTER 20

GEO DICTIONARY

Limon: a fertile soil deposited by glaciers. These light, sandy soils are easily transported and deposited by winds

ACTIVE LEARNING

1. Explain how the North European Plain was formed.
2. How do humans interact with the North European Plain?

- The region was largely **shaped by glaciers** which flowed in a **south-westerly direction during the last ice age.** When the ice age ended, fine **glacial deposits were deposited by wind** creating **fertile limon soils** across the region.

- This, combined with **drainage from rivers** such as the **Rhine, Meuse** and **Loire** and their tributaries, has made the region **suitable for agriculture.**

- Along the coast of the North Sea, coastal deposition and longshore drift created a **straightened coastline.** The reclaimed land of the **Netherlands** lie some **4 m below sea level.**

Human Interaction with the North European Plain

Fig. 20.8 Intensive agriculture on the undulating North European Plain

- The North European Plain is one of the **most densely populated regions in the world** due to its **favourable climate, relief and economic resources.** The region has a long **history of intensive agriculture,** with its **flat terrain and fertile soils** suiting large-scale mechanised farming.

- Large **deposits of coal and metals** such as **iron ore** led to the region becoming **highly industrialised.** The flat relief also allowed for the development of some of the best communications links in the world with **excellent road, rail, air and port networks** throughout.

EDUCATE YOURSELF

North European Plain	Between Alps and Scandinavian uplands, rising sea levels cut off Britain and Ireland, formed beneath a shallow sea, uplifted 40–60 mya, layers of sedimentary rock slightly warped, flat/gently rolling landscape, shaped by glaciers in south-westerly direction, glacial deposits limon soils, drainage from Rhine, Loire and Meuse Rivers, suitable for agriculture, deposition created straightened coastline, Netherlands 4 m below sea level
Human interaction	One of most densely populated regions in the world, intensive agriculture, flat terrain and fertile soils, large deposits: coal and iron ores, highly industrialised, excellent transport links

Concept 3: Administrative Regions

- Unlike the previous two concepts, administrative regions are **not related to physical characteristics.** Instead, they are based on political boundaries, where governments **divide countries into smaller sections** which can then be more easily governed.

- Governments are responsible for providing **services to their citizens.** In order to do this most effectively, governments use **councils or departments** to manage each divided areas. Each of these areas is an administrative region.

Ireland

Counties

The Republic of Ireland **consists of 26 counties,** which date back to divisions made by the **Anglo-Normans** in the twelfth century.

Many Irish people have come to **identify strongly with their county,** as it gives them a sense of place. This can be seen at **GAA** matches.

Ireland has a **two-tier system of government: local government** looks after the **individual needs of its citizens** and **national government** is concerned with **running the country.**

Councils

In total, there are **28 county councils** in Ireland: 25 counties in Ireland have one county council each, while Dublin has three. **Cork, Dublin, Galway, Limerick and Waterford also have a city council each.** In 2014, Waterford's and Limerick's city councils amalgamated with their county councils.

Elected **county councils** are responsible for the day-to-day running of their county in areas such as:

- Planning permission
- Waste disposal
- Motor taxation
- Road maintenance

⌃ **Fig. 20.9** Irish counties

County Councils

County councils are also responsible for **representing the views of local people at national level.** Every **five years,** each local authority draws up **development plans** for its county, outlining its plans for **economic and social development.**

However, many councils are **struggling to secure the funds** they need as a result of the economic **recession and austerity budgets.**

City councils were developed in response to the **increasing percentage** of the **population living in urban areas.** As of 2015, **60 per cent of Irish** people live in **urban areas.** City councils serve the **same functions as** county councils.

Regional Assemblies

In **1994, Ireland** was divided into **eight regional authorities** in order to manage the services that councils provide and **to manage the development of each region as a result** of EU funding.

⌃ **Fig. 20.10** The Regional Assemblies of Ireland

In **1999**, two **Regional Assemblies** were established to take over management of the **Structural Funds** the **EU** provided to develop each region. The assemblies represented the poorer **Border Midland and Western (BMW) Region** and the wealthier **Southern and Eastern Region.**

In 2014, the **eight regional authorities were reduced to just three assemblies:**

- The Eastern and Midland Region
- The Northern and Western Region
- The Southern Region

EDUCATE YOURSELF

Administrative	Not related to physical characteristics, governments divide country into smaller sections, provide services to citizens
Ireland	26 counties created by Anglo-Normans, many identify strongly with their county, e.g. GAA, two-tier system of government, local government – individual needs of citizens; national government – running of the country, 28 county councils, 5 city councils
Councils	Planning permission, waste disposal, motor taxation, roads, sewage
County councils	Represent local views at national level, development plans – economic and social; struggle to secure funds – recession and austerity budgets
City councils	Increasing urban population, 60% Irish population in urban areas, same functions as county councils
Assemblies	1994 eight regional authorities, management of development of each region as a result of EU funding; 1999 regional assemblies, manage EU structural funds, BMW and South and Eastern Regions, eight regional authorities reduced to three assemblies: Eastern and Midland, Northern and Western and Southern Regions

● **Fig. 20.11** 13 regions of France (including Corsica)

 GEO **DICTIONARY**

French Revolution: a revolution that began in 1789 and overthrew the ruling French monarchy and established a democratic government

France

- France has a **three-tiered government administration,** consisting of national, **regional and local** bodies. These administrative divisions date back to the French Revolution of 1789.

Regional Government

- There are **13 regions in mainland** France, with **four overseas regions.** Regions are the **largest unit of government** in the country.

- Regional authorities are **responsible for the provision of a large number of public services** such as **school management, health facilities** and **creation of employment.**

- In order to do this, an assembly is **elected by the people of each region.** Each region is made up of a number of **smaller administrative regions called *departments (départements).***

- It is the responsibility of the assembly to **manage any development plans** put forward by the **region's departments.**

Departments

- There are **95 departments in mainland France,** with another **two on the island of Corsica.**

- Departments operate in the **same way as county councils do in Ireland:** they are responsible for **local provision of needs.** Departments are designed to be **roughly equal** in terms of **physical size and population.**

- Departments provide many **social services** such as **social housing, disability services** and the **maintenance of public schools.**

- The citizens of each department **elect their own local council,** which is overseen by a ***Préfet*** (prefect), who is the **chief administrator.**

Communes

- There are **36 680 communes** in France.

- Communes are the **smallest units of local government.** They are roughly **equivalent in size to the parishes** of Ireland. The populations of communes **vary greatly,** with some **rural areas** having **low population densities,** while others are **densely populated urban areas.**

- The citizens of each commune **elect an assembly and a mayor.** Each assembly is responsible for the organisation and **management of local services** such as **water, sewage** and the **maintenance of public parks.**

- Each commune is also responsible for **registering births, deaths and marriages,** as well as **collecting local taxes.** Communes were the first type of government **established after the French Revolution.**

ACTIVE LEARNING

1. Name the three administrative divisions of French government.
2. Explain the role of communes.
3. Describe the functions of departments and regions.
4. Explore the French government website for the latest news and statistics: **www.gouvernement.fr**

Note!
The website in Q4 will prove to be a valuable source of information as you study the Paris Basin in Chapter 24.

EDUCATE YOURSELF

France	Three-tiered government administration: local, regional, national; French Revolution 1789
Regional	13 regions in France, 5 overseas regions, largest unit of government, responsible for provision of public services – school management, health facilities, creation of employment, assembly elected by people of each region, divided into smaller administrative departments, regions manage development plans by departments
Departments	95 in mainland, 2 in Corsica, roughly equal size population and area, operate like Irish county councils, local provision of services – social housing, disability services, maintenance of public schools; elect local council, chief administrator, *préfet*
Communes	36 680 communes, smallest units of local government, equivalent size of Irish parishes, population densities vary greatly, consist of assembly and a mayor, manage local services (water and sewage, register births, deaths, marriages), collect local taxes, oldest type of government, established after French Revolution

Fig. 20.12 There are many indicators of culture.

ACTIVE LEARNING

1. What comes to mind when you think of 'Irish culture'?

2. Visit **www.livescience.com** and search for 'culture'. The website provides many views of culture from many different countries. This gives an excellent perspective on how culture varies from place to place and from people to people.

FACT

At the time of the Great Famine, there were 8 million people living in Ireland, 4 million of whom spoke Irish as their first language.

The Irish language is over 1600 years old and was spoken long before the existence of what we call modern English.

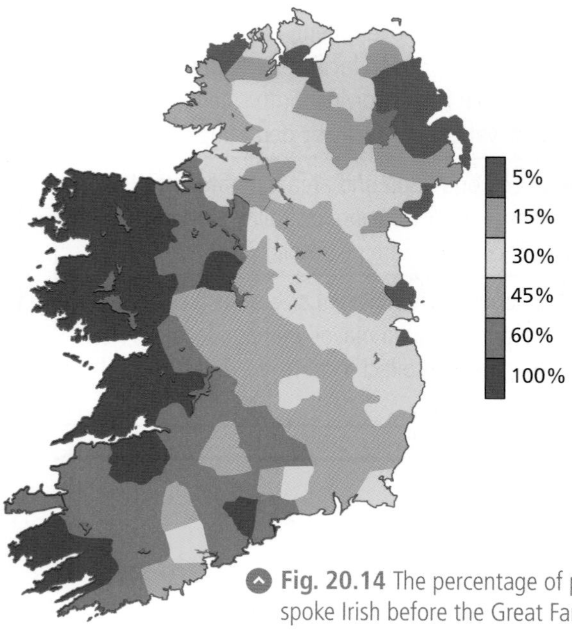

5%
15%
30%
45%
60%
100%

Fig. 20.14 The percentage of people who spoke Irish before the Great Famine

Concept 4: Cultural Regions

Introduction

When you think of the word 'culture', what comes to mind? Even though we are aware of certain aspects of our own culture, it is a diffcult concept to define.

In answering the Active Learning Q1, some of you may have mentioned many positive traits such as traditional music and dance, literature, sport, 'craic', festivals and friendliness. Perhaps Guinness made it onto the list! But what does culture mean? In this section, we will look at two specific cultural indicators: language and religion.

Culture could be defined as the **characteristics, customs, traditions and beliefs of a group of people,** which are handed down from generation to generation. Both **language and religion** are **powerful indicators** of culture as they create a sense of identity among a group of people. There are many different languages on the continent of Europe, and each creates a sense of belonging for the people who speak it. Sharing faith can also create a **sense of belonging.**

Language

The Gaeltacht

The Gaeltacht is the term given to the parts of Ireland where **Irish** is the **main language** spoken.

Fig. 20.13 Crossing the language boundary into the Gaeltacht

FACT

Culture comes from Latin word *cultus*, which means 'to tend, grow, cultivate or nurture'.

History

- Irish was the **native language of Ireland** at the time of the **Norman invasion** in the twelfth century. The invasion led to **the gradual spread of English** over the next 700 years.

- From **1831, the British government** enforced a law that English was to be **taught in schools.**

- Until the **Great Famine** (1845–49), **50 per cent of Ireland's population spoke Irish** as their first language. Irish was **dominant along the West coast** of Ireland – Munster, Connacht and Donegal – and the islands off the West coast.

- The Famine led to a **rapid decline of Irish** as **mass starvation and emigration** occurred, especially along the West **(1 million died, 1 million emigrated).**

- The **USA and Britain** were the **main destinations** of Irish emigrants. As English was spoken in these countries, people felt it was **necessary to learn the English language.**

⌃ **Fig. 20.15** Gaeltacht areas (in green) in 1926

- Even though the Famine ended in 1849, **emigration continued,** which further reduced the number of Irish speakers.

Establishment of Gaeltachts

- Gaeltachts were **established as cultural regions in 1926** as the number of **Irish speakers** had **halved since 1851.**

- The Gaeltachts were **divided into two areas:**

  1. **Fíor Gaeltacht** are areas where **at least 80 per cent of the population speaks Irish in everyday life.**

  2. **Breac Gaeltacht** are areas where **at least 25 per cent of people speak Irish in everyday life.**

- Since the establishment of Gaeltacht regions in 1926, many **Breac Gaeltacht regions** have **disappeared** altogether. The largest Gaeltachts are **located in Kerry, Connemara** and **Donegal,** with each having its own dialect. Each Gaeltacht region is **surrounded by English-speaking areas.**

⌃ **Fig. 20.16** Gaeltacht areas (in green) today

Today

- It is estimated that there are roughly **61 000 people** who live in **Fíor Gaeltacht areas** and speak Irish as their first language. A further **20 000 live in Breac Gaeltacht regions,** where **English is widely spoken.**

- In response to the decline of Irish, the **government has tried to support the Gaeltacht regions.** The **Department of Arts, Heritage and the Gaeltacht** is responsible for assisting organisations such as Údáras na Gaeltachta.

GEO DICTIONARY

Raidió na Gaeltachta: Irish-language radio station which broadcasts nationally

TG4: Irish-language TV station which broadcasts nationally

FACT

Údáras na Gaeltachta is the regional authority responsible for the economic, social and cultural development of the Gaeltacht.

The overall aim is to ensure that the Irish language is preserved and passed on to future generations by making the Gaeltacht regions self-sufficient through:

1. Attracting employment to Gaeltachts by promoting science, ICT, tourism, manufacturing and aquaculture, renewable energy, food marketing and arts and crafts. Currently there are over 7000 people employed full-time in Údáras na Gaeltachta client companies.

2. Supporting community economic developments and social development through social employment schemes, youth clubs, etc.

- Údáras na Gaeltachta is responsible for the economic, social and cultural **development** of the Gaeltacht.
- **Raidió na Gaeltachta and TG4** have also helped to promote the Irish language throughout the country.
- **Ireland** is now recognised as being a **bilingual country:** Irish became an **official language of the EU in 2007.**

EDUCATE YOURSELF

History	Irish language, everyday language, native language, 12th century Norman invasion, gradual spread of English; British rule, 1831 English taught in national school; until Famine 50% spoke Irish, dominant along West coast, starvation and emigration, rapid decline of Irish; USA and Britain main destinations English speaking; emigration continued after Famine
Gaeltachts	Established cultural regions 1926, numbers halved since 1851, Fíor Gaeltacht 80%+ Irish speaking, Breac Gaeltacht 25%+ Irish speaking; since 1926 many Breac Gaeltacht disappeared; largest Gaeltachts Kerry, Connemara, Donegal, surrounded by English-speaking areas
Today	Fíor Gaeltacht 61 000 speakers, Breac Gaeltacht 20 000 speakers, government support, Department of Arts, Heritage and Gaeltacht, Údáras na Gaeltachta, economic, social and cultural development, Raidió na Gaeltachta and TG4, official language of EU

ACTIVE LEARNING

1. What are the official languages of Ireland?
2. Describe the three main events which led to the decline of the Irish language.
3. What are the main functions of Údáras na Gaeltachta?
4. Do you think the preservation of the Irish language is important or do you feel that it is no longer relevant to our society? Discuss your views with your classmates.
5. Visit **www.udaras.ie** to find out more about its role in promoting and protecting the Irish language.

Belgium

- Ideally, we should all embrace difference and accept that other's beliefs, language and practices may be different from our own but are just as important. However, **cultural differences can also lead to tension,** aggression and resentment between different cultural groups.
- This is the case in **Belgium,** where tension exists between the **Flemish-speaking and French-speaking communities.**

History

- Since Belgium gained **independence in 1830,** tension has existed between the **French-speaking region of Wallonia** and the **Flemish-speaking region of Flanders.**

- As well as cultural differences, tensions between the groups exist due to economics. **Until the 1960s, Wallonia was much wealthier than Flanders.** Throughout the nineteenth and early twentieth centuries, the **presence of coal and iron ore** meant that Wallonia was **industrially prosperous** compared to the **poorer agricultural region** of Flanders.
- Due to the wealth of Wallonia, **French** was the **official language of the government** and **education.** People who wished to **pursue a career** in politics, medicine or education were **required to speak French.**
- This requirement meant that **Flemish people were not fully represented at government level,** with very few career opportunities available to them.
- The discovery of **oil and gas off the shores of Flanders** in the **1960s** changed the economics of the country. **Wallonia's economy began to decline** and **Flanders economy began to boom.**
- With growing wealth and power, the Flemish began to assert themselves. They **defeated government plans to make French the official language** of Belgium in the 1960s. This led to **violent clashes between the two groups.**

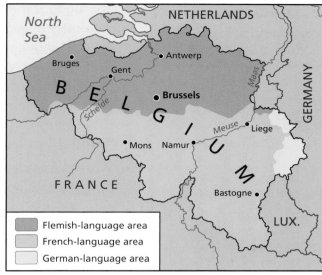

Fig. 20.17 Language regions of Belgium

Flemish-language area
French-language area
German-language area

ACTIVE LEARNING

Can you think of any cultural tensions that exist among any other cultural groups?

Fig. 20.18 The Walloon flag

Fig. 20.19 The Flemish flag

Response to Tension

- Fearing that **tensions could destroy the Belgian state,** the government **established a federation.** This means that the **national parliament sits in Brussels** and controls foreign policy, the national budget and the defence forces, while **Wallonia, Brussels and Flanders** each has its **own regional government** which **manages public services** in their regions.
- As a result, Belgium is divided into three main regions: **Wallonia, Flanders** and bilingual **Brussels. Each region has its own flag,** TV stations and celebrities – all of which highlight the division of the Belgian people due to language. **German is spoken** in the much smaller region of **East Cantons.**

 GEO **DICTIONARY**

Federation: a form of government in which a group of states has a central government but keep control of their own internal affairs

- Throughout the Brussels region, **equality is shown to both cultural groups** with **road signs and advertisements** appearing in **both languages.** Even **libraries** must have an equal amount of **Flemish and Walloon books** on their shelves. In the national parliament, **questions must be asked and answered in both French and Flemish.**

Result

- While these attempts by the government have resulted in some progress, **tensions still exist,** with both regions distrusting each other.

- This distrust can be seen in the recent **difficulty of forming a national government. In 2010, negotiations** began on the formation of a **coalition government.** The negotiations lasted for **541 days.**

- These language and cultural tensions **continue to threaten the future of Belgium.**

Fig. 20.20 Signposts in Brussels must be in both French and Flemish.

Fig. 20.21 Cultural differences divide Belgium

EDUCATE YOURSELF

Belgium	
History	Cultural differences led to tension, Belgium Flemish-speaking and French-speaking communities; independence 1830, French-speaking Wallonia, Flemish-speaking Flanders; until 1960s Wallonia wealthier, coal and iron ore, industrially prosperous, Flanders poorer agricultural land; French official language of government/education, French required to pursue career, Flanders not fully represented at government; 1960s offshore oil and gas in Flanders, Wallonia's economy declined/ Flanders economy boomed, government defeated in making French official Belgian language, violent clashes between groups
Response to tensions	Belgian established as federation: Wallonia, Flanders, Brussels (bilingual), East Cantons (German-speaking); established, own regional governments – manage public services, equality shown, libraries – French and Flemish books, national parliament questions in both French and Flemish
Result	Tensions still exist, difficulty forming national government, 2010 negotiations took 541 days to form government, tensions threaten future of Belgium

Religion

Religion is perhaps the **strongest cultural indicator** in the world. As well as sharing a sense of identity, people who practise the same religion **often have the same attitudes and views** of the world. While religion has the **ability to unite groups** of people, it also has the **power to divide,** with hostile relationships developing between people of different religious beliefs.

In this section we will look at:

- Religious tensions between **Catholics and Protestants** in **Northern Ireland**
- **Unifying characteristics** of the Islamic faith and tensions associated with it

Buddhist	Confucian	Hindu
Confucian/Taoist	Shinto	Bah'i	Sikh
Islamic	Christian	Jewish

⌃ **Fig. 20.22** The major world religions

Northern Ireland

History

- Northern Ireland is a region that is **divided along religious lines.** Northern Ireland was officially established by the **Government of Ireland Act in 1920,** but divisions date back as far as the 1600s.

- In **1609, King James I** carried out the **Ulster Plantation.** This involved removing **native Irish Catholics** from their land and giving it to **loyal English and Scottish settlers** who practised the Protestant religion.

- Before the plantation, the Ulster Chieftains had strongly resisted English rule. It was hoped that the plantation would **spread the Protestant religion throughout the province** and help to stop the native Irish from rebelling. However, **rebellion and violent clashes** continued between cultural groups.

- After the **War of Independence,** the **26 counties of the south** became the Irish Free State (now the Republic of Ireland). The **six counties of Northern Ireland** remained under British control as it was **majority Protestant.**

Divisions

- Most of Northern Ireland's **Protestants are loyalist or unionist,** meaning they align themselves with **British views and traditions.**

- Catholics are mainly nationalist or republican, aligning themselves with the **views and traditions** of the **Irish Republic.**

- As a result, religion has become a **dividing force** and means of **displaying identity in Northern Ireland.** This can even be seen in **geographical**

⌃ **Fig. 20.23** King James I carried out the Ulster Plantation in the hope of spreading the Protestant religion and customs.

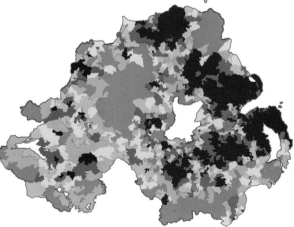

- ■ >60% more Protestant than Catholic
- ■ 30% to 60% more Protestant than Catholic
- □ 0% to 30% more Protestant than Catholic
- □ 0% to 30% more Catholic than Protestant
- ■ 30% to 60% more Catholic than Protestant
- ■ >60% more Catholic than Protestant

⌃ **Fig. 20.24** Religious divides in Northern Ireland

War of Independence:
the war between Ireland
and Britain

**Government of Ireland
Act 1920:** the act which
led to the formation
separate states within
Ireland

Segregated: separated
or set apart

segregation, with **unionist culture generally strongest** in **large urban
areas** and **nationalist culture generally dominant in rural areas.**

- Some city areas are **predominantly Catholic or Protestant** and these are
often the sites of the strongest division. For example, in Belfast, **the Falls
Road is Catholic and nationalist,** while the **Shankill Road is Protestant
and unionist.**

- After the **1921** election, a **majority unionist government formed** and
established a **Protestant state for Protestant people.** Nationalists
became **mistrusted** because of their desire to be part of a united Ireland
and, as a result, were **discriminated against.**

- Such discrimination was seen in the **allocation of jobs, housing and
policing.** This resulted in the region being **segregated,** with most young
people **attending segregated schools,** playing **different sports** and
socialising only within their own religious group.

Fig. 20.25 The British Army on patrol in
Belfast in 1972

Civil Rights, Troubles and Progress

- In the **1960s,** a **civil rights campaign** was organised by
the **nationalists.** The government's refusal to negotiate
with the campaigners and a strong military suppression of
protests led to the led to **violent conflicts** between the
two communities.

- This conflict, known as **'the Troubles',** lasted over **30
years** and led to over **3600 deaths.** It was not until the
Good Friday Agreement of 1998 that political power was
successfully shared by both communities.

- While progress has been made through **integration of
schools, sports** and other **traditions,** it has been slow and
difficult.

- Only a **minority of schools are integrated** despite the
fact that schools are the most powerful means of **breaking
down barriers of mistrust.**

- **Continued divisions** can be seen in occasional outbreaks
of violence, **Orange Order marches** and even in the
decisions of sports stars James McClean and Rory McIlroy to
play for Ireland in their respective sports.

 GEO **DICTIONARY**

The Troubles: a period of violence between republican and loyalist organisations. Many
acts of terrorism were carried out by paramilitary organisations on both sides, e.g. IRA,
UVF, UDA

Good Friday Agreement: a political agreement in 1998 which brought about a peace
process in Northern Ireland

Orange Order: a Protestant organisation. The orange colour comes from William of
Orange, the Protestant King who defeated the Catholic King James at the Battle of the
Boyne in1690

EDUCATE YOURSELF

Religion	Strong cultural indicator, same religion, same attitudes and views, ability to unite/divide groups, Catholics and Protestants in Northern Ireland
History	Divided along religious lines, Government Of Ireland Act 1920, 1609 King James, Ulster Plantation, native Irish Catholics removed, loyal English and Scottish settlers given land, spread Protestant religion, rebellion and violent clashes, War of Independence, 26 counties of south, 6 counties of north, majority Protestant
Discrimination	Protestants loyalist or unionist, British views and traditions, Catholics nationalist, Irish views and traditions, religion as a dividing force, displaying identity in Northern Ireland, geographical segregation, unionist culture stronger in urban areas, nationalist culture stronger in rural areas, predominantly Catholic or Protestant neighbourhoods, Falls Road in Belfast Catholic and nationalist, Shankill Road majority Protestant and unionist; 1921 election majority unionist government formed, Protestant state for Protestant people, nationalists became mistrusted, discriminated against, allocation of jobs, housing and policing, segregated schools, different sports and traditions
Civil rights/ Troubles	Civil Rights campaign, nationalists 1960, violent conflicts, the Troubles, 30 years, over 3600 deaths, Good Friday Agreement 1998, integration of schools/traditions, minority of schools integrated, breaking barriers of mistrust, continued divisions

> **Note!**
> Political, cultural and economic interaction in Northern Ireland will be examined in more detail in Chapter 26 The Complexities of Regions.

ACTIVE LEARNING

1. What was the Ulster Plantation?
2. Explain how religion has been a divisive force in Northern Ireland.
3. In what decade did the Troubles begin?
4. Why do you think the integration of schools is so important for removing barriers?
5. Search for 'the Troubles' on **www.bbc.co.uk/history** for further information on the history of Northern Ireland.

Islamic World

History

 GEO DICTIONARY

Pilgrimage: a journey made to a holy place as an act of religious devotion

- Islam is religion which began in the **seventh century** from the teachings of **the prophet Muhammad. People who practise Islam** are called **Muslims.** Muslims believe that Muhammad received divine messages from God (Allah) and these were written down in the **Qur'an,** which is Islam's holy book. In 2010, there were more than **1.6 billion Muslims in the world,** representing **22 per cent of the world's population.**

- Following the **death of Muhammad in 632 CE, Islam** spread rapidly as Muslim armies and traders spread the religion throughout the **Middle East and North Africa,** as well as parts of southern Asia.

- Modern-day migration and people converting have also led to **Muslim communities existing in many European countries** and in the **US.** For example, there are more than **49 000 Muslims living in Ireland.**

- Many people embraced Islam due to its progressive views that they are all equal before Allah, that the **rich must help the poor** and that Muslims **treat each other as family.**

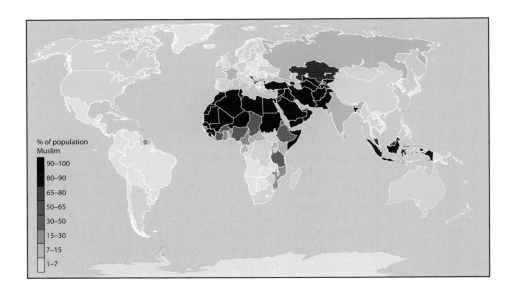

Fig. 20.26 Muslim populations across the globe

% of population Muslim
- 90–100
- 80–90
- 65–80
- 50–65
- 30–50
- 15–30
- 7–15
- 1–7

Beliefs

- Muslims follow the Qur'an (Koran) which lays down the main teachings of Islam. The main teachings are called the **Five Pillars of Islam:**

    1. Believe in one God – Allah.

    2. Pray five times a day.

    3. Provide alms (charity) to the poor.

    4. Fast from dawn until dusk during the month of Ramadan, with some exceptions.

    5. If possible, visit **Mecca,** the **holy city** in Saudi Arabia. This pilgrimage is **called Hajj.**

- Islam also has **strict rules of behaviour.** Examples include:

    1. Muslims must **dress modestly.** When in public, many women **wear a hijab,** which covers their hair, or a **niqab,** which also covers their face.

    2. Alcohol and gambling are forbidden.

- Muslims **worship in places called mosques,** which are identified by their **large domes and narrow towers, called minarets.** An Irish example can be seen in **Clonskeagh, Co. Dublin.**

Family

- **Family** is at the **heart of the Islamic faith,** with Muslims believing that the peace and security provided by family are necessary for **personal and spiritual development.**

- Families **encourage love and charity,** which can be seen in the way **young members are encouraged to look after the older generations** in their family.

Fig. 20.27 The niqab covers a woman's face while in public.

Fig. 20.28 Clonskeagh Mosque in Co. Dublin: the large dome and narrow tower make it easily identifiable

Negative Views

- Over the past decade in particular, some people have linked the Islamic faith to **negative acts committed by extremists.**

- Terrorist acts – such as the **attacks in Paris in November 2015, the bombings in Istanbul in January 2016 and the attacks in Brussels in March 2016** – carried out by an extremist group that calls itself Islamic State have led to a **negative view** of the religion among a minority of people in Western European countries and in the US.

- However, these acts are **condemned by the vast majority of Muslims.**

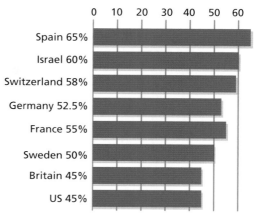

% of respondents who think Islam is not compatible with the West

Spain 65%	
Israel 60%	
Switzerland 58%	
Germany 52.5%	
France 55%	
Sweden 50%	
Britain 45%	
US 45%	

Fig. 20.29 Opinions of Islam in the Western World from a survey taken in the aftermath of the November 2015 Paris attacks

EDUCATE YOURSELF

Islamic world	7th century, Qur'an, Prophet Muhammad, 1.6 billion followers (22% world population), death of Muhammad 632 CE, rapid spread of Islam, Middle East, North Africa and southern Asia; 49 000 Muslims in Ireland, rich help poor, treat others as family
Beliefs	Five Pillars of Islam, pilgrimage to Holy City of Mecca; strict rules of behaviour, alcohol and gambling forbidden, worship in mosques, large domes, narrow towers, Clonskeagh, Co. Dublin
Family	Heart of Islam, personal and spiritual development, encourage love and charity, young look after older generations,
Negative views	Acts of terrorism, negative view of religion for some in the West, e.g. Paris attacks 2015, acts condemned by Muslim communities

ACTIVE LEARNING

1. How many Muslims are living in Ireland?
2. What are the five main teachings of Islam?
3. Describe one strict rule of behaviour in the Islamic faith.
4. Why do some people have negative views of Islam?
5. Search for 'Islam' on the following websites for more information on the Islamic faith:
   www.bbc.co.uk/religion
   www.religionfacts.com

Concept 5: Socio-economic Regions

Some regions are **more economically developed than others.** These are known as **core regions.** Typically this occurs due to **natural advantages** such as **fertile soils, a favourable climate, a flat terrain** and an abundance of **raw materials.**

Other regions are **less developed** because they **lack these resources.** As a result, **standards of living** tend to be **lower** in these areas. These are known as **peripheral regions.**

Some regions were **once economically rich** but **declined** as their **raw materials were used up.** These are known as regions of **industrial decline.** In this section, we will examine these three regions.

Core Regions

Fig. 20.30 The central core of Europe

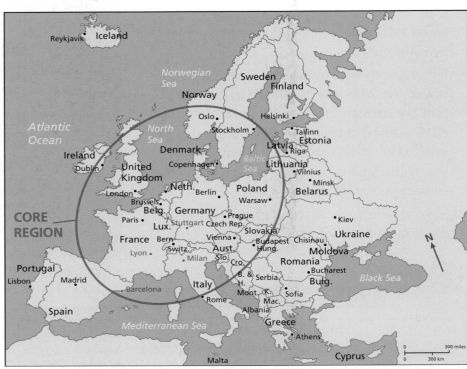

GEO DICTIONARY

Core: an area which is more economically developed than its surrounding areas, usually due to natural advantages

Raw materials: the materials needed for the production of a finished good

Peripheral: an area which is less economically developed compared to the core. It usually lacks the natural advantages of the core

Inward migration: when people move into a region

Inward investment: investment in a region from MNCs

Multinational company: a company with branches in several countries

Central Business District: the centre of trade in a city, usually located in the city centre

- Core regions are areas of **high economic development.** They can occur at both **national and international levels.** Core regions **dominate trade, industry, government** and **communications.**

- As a result, **standards of living** tend to be **higher** in core regions compared to the surrounding areas. Typically, the region **experiences inward migration.**

- An international core region exists **across several countries in Europe,** stretching from **London to Milan** and from **Paris to Stockholm.** It includes several individual core regions such as the **Paris Basin** and the **North Italian Plain.**

- **National** cores are the **most developed areas of a country.** Usually, these cores are located in and **around capital cities,** e.g. the **Greater Dublin Area.** These are also referred to as **secondary cores.**

- Core regions generally have similar characteristics such as:

  - **Plentiful deposits of natural resources,** such as **iron ore,** as well as **fertile soils** and **flat, accessible terrain**

  - High levels of **inward investment** from manufacturing companies and multinational companies (MNCs)

  - A **young and educated workforce** due to a high level of educational services and inward migration

  - A **highly urbanised** region with a high population density

  - A majority of people **employed** in the **tertiary (services) sector**

  - A large number of **banking and MNC headquarters** located close to the Central Business District (CBD)

We will study the core regions of the **Greater Dublin Area** (Chapter 22) and the **Paris Basin** (Chapter 24).

Peripheral Regions

In simple terms, **peripheral regions** are the **opposite of core regions**. They **lack industrial** and **economic development**. Typically, the region **experiences outward migration**. Peripheral regions tend to be **isolated** from the core, such as the **West of Ireland, Northern Scandinavia** or **Southern Italy** (Mezzogiorno). Peripheral areas have similar characteristics such as:

- **Unfavourable physical landscape** such as **mountains** and other terrain that make it **difficult to build good communications** and transport networks

- **Thin and infertile soils,** leading to **subsistence** agriculture

- A higher than average **percentage** of people **employed** in the **primary sector**

- A **less urbanised** region, with a **low population density**

- A population that tends to be **older and less skilled** due to outward migration of young people to the core region. This is known as a **'brain drain'**.

We will study the peripheral regions of the **West region** of Ireland (Chapter 21) and the **Mezzogiorno region** of Italy (Chapter 23).

In 2004 and 2007, the **European Union expanded** to include several Central and **Eastern European countries, e.g. Lithuania.** These countries were **under communist rule until 1991** and are **less developed**. These countries **share** many of the same **characteristics as peripheral regions**.

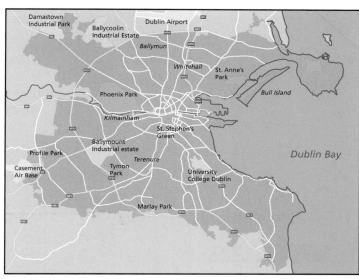

⊙ **Fig. 20.31** Dublin and its surrounding regions have well-developed communications and a large urban population.

⊙ **Fig. 20.32** The West of Ireland has limited transport development and few large urban areas.

📖 GEO **DICTIONARY**

Outward migration: when people leave a region

Subsistence agriculture: farming that provides just enough to survive

Brain drain: caused by the outward migration of a region's youngest and most skilled workers. As a result the region's population is aged and unskilled

Communist rule: Communists took control of Russia after a revolution in 1917, and spread their system of government to surrounding states after World War II. It was a system of government based on the holding of all property in common, by the state

Economic regions	Varying levels of development
Core regions	High economic development, national and international level, dominate trade, industry, government and communications, higher standard of living, inward migration, international core in Europe; national core Greater Dublin Area, plentiful natural resources, iron ore and fertile soils, inward investment from MNCs, young and educated workforce, highly urbanised, high level tertiary employment, banking and MNC headquarters, e.g. Greater Dublin Area and Paris Basin
Peripheral regions	Opposite of core, lack industrial and economic development, outward migration, isolated, unfavourable physical landscape, mountainous, difficult to build communications and transport, soils thin and infertile, subsistence farming, above average employment in primary sector, less urbanised, low population density, population older and less skilled, brain drain, e.g. West of Ireland, Mezzogiorno, Eastern and Central European countries

ACTIVE LEARNING

1. Name three types of economic region.
2. Name two core regions.
3. Name two peripheral regions.
4. Explain the differences between core and peripheral regions.

Industrial Decline

- Industrial decline occurs when a region that was **once industrially prosperous** is **no longer able** to sustain its level of economic development.

- Industrial decline normally occurs when **raw materials** such as coal or iron ore **run out,** or when **technology or products become outdated.** Most examples of regions in industrial decline rose to power during the **Industrial Revolution** at the end of the **eighteenth century and the beginning of the nineteenth century.**

Industry growth stages

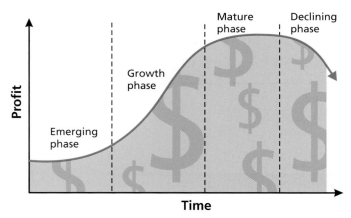

⌵ **Fig. 20.33** Industry typically follows a growth–maturity–decline pattern.

- As **coal was the main energy source** at this time, areas with coal deposits boomed. Examples of these regions include **South Wales, the Sambre Meuse Valley** in Wallonia, **Sheffield** in Northern England and the **Nord** in France. These once-prosperous regions have **since become industrial wastelands.**

- Industrial decline can **also occur** when **manufacturing industries decline.** In this section we will look at:
  - **Limerick** in Ireland
  - **The Sambre Meuse Valley** in Wallonia, Belgium

CASE STUDY

Limerick

- Limerick City is a region which has undergone **industrial decline** over the past number of decades. It is an unusual case study as its decline was **not based on exhausted coal deposits or a lack of inward investment,** but rather on its overreliance on traditional manufacturing industries.
- In the 1950s, the Irish government responded to the **economic recession** by developing the **Programme for Economic Expansion.** This aimed to attract industry to Irish cities.

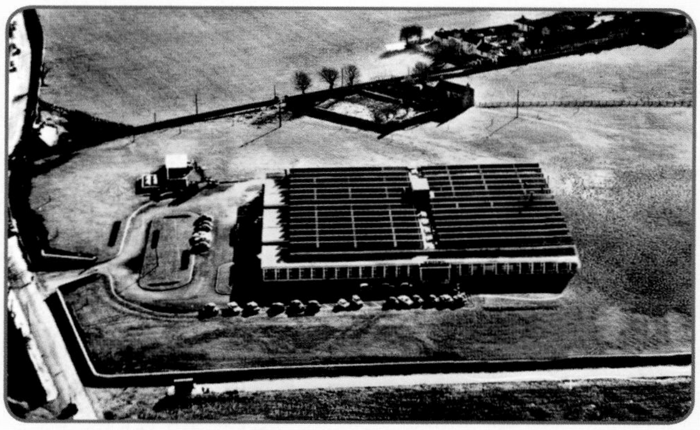

Fig. 20.34 Krups Engineering Plant closed in 1999.

- The programme led to a **large increase in the number of MNCs** setting up in Limerick as **foreign direct investment increased. Between 1961 and 1971,** the population grew by **21 per cent** due to **inward migration of workers** from rural areas.
- **Manufacturing industry,** which employed **28 per cent of the region's workforce,** was the engine for **growth in the city.** One of the major attractions for manufacturing companies was the **high number of manual workers** available, along with the region's access to the **Shannon Estuary** and **Shannon Airport.**
- As more people entered the city, the **construction industry boomed** as **new housing estates** were built along the **west of the city.**

GEO DICTIONARY

Foreign direct investment: investment in an area from foreign companies

Manual workers: people who do physical work

Decline

- **Despite** the **initial positive effects** of economic investment from MNCs, the **traditional industries (food processing, machinery, textiles, footwear),** which formed the industrial economic base for the city, began to **decline.**
- As of 1971, three sectors accounted for **75 per cent of the region's industrial employment.** These were:
  1. **Food processing:** dairy products, flour milling, bacon curing, etc.
  2. **Machinery/electrics**: Krups, Irish Wire Products, etc.
  3. **Textiles/footwear**: clothing, leather, etc.
- Once Ireland **joined the EU in 1973,** many **traditional industries were forced to close** as they were **unable to compete** with MNCs. The main industries to suffer from EU membership were **textiles, timber and food processing,** which led to a large **increase in unemployment** across the city.
- **The Limerick Clothing Factory** and **Limerick Shoes** closed with a loss of nearly **1000 jobs,** marking the beginning of the end of the textile industry in the region.
- The **decline** in Limerick's industries **increased in the 1980s** due to global **recession,** particularly in areas around the **docks.** Companies such as **Ranks** (flour millers), the **Bacon Company of Ireland and Condensed Milk of Ireland** all closed in the 1980s.
- The **Ferenka Steel** factory closed in 1977, leading to the **loss of 1400 jobs.**
- **Rationalisation and technology improvements** led to further job losses as **MNCs were much more labour efficient** than traditional Irish companies.

GEO DICTIONARY

Rationalisation: when more efficient and less labour-intensive ways of operating a business are implemented. This typically leads to job losses

CORE 3 CHAPTER 20

Revival

- Throughout the 1980s and 1990s, **job losses** were **offset by new employment opportunities**, in companies such as **Dell Computers and Analog Devices.** However, these companies mainly employed **third-level graduates.** Therefore, many of **those who lost their jobs** throughout the 1970s and 1980s were **unable to take advantage** of these opportunities.

- As a result, **employment and industrial activity are unevenly spread** throughout the city, with **areas of high unemployment.**

- In 1999, at the peak of Dell's employment in the city, **7500 people were permanently unemployed** in the city.

- The **loss of 900 jobs** with the closure of **Krups in 1999** and the **loss of 2500 jobs** following the closure of **Dell** in **2009** greatly **damaged industrial recovery** in the city.

- **Modern industrial estates** have developed around the city, which have attracted further inward investment, while the completion of the **M7 motorway** has linked Limerick to city to Dublin.

EDUCATE YOURSELF

Limerick	
Growth	Industrial decline not based on loss of raw materials; recession, Programme for Economic Expansion, increase of MNCs, direct investment increased, population grew by 21 per cent 1961–71; manufacturing 28% of workforce, labour intensive, Shannon Estuary and Shannon Airport, new housing estates
Decline	Traditional industries declined, food processing, machinery/electronics, textiles, EU 1973, traditional industries closed, textiles, timbers and food processing worst affected, Limerick Clothing factory and Limerick Shoes 1000 job losses; decline of docks; Ranks, Bacon Company of Ireland and Condensed Milk closed; Ferenka Steel 1400 job losses, rationalisation and technology, labour efficient
Revival	Losses balanced by new employment from MNCs, Dell and Analog Devices, required third-level graduates, many unemployed unable to take advantage; 1999 – 7500 permanently unemployed, Krups closed 1999 – 900 job losses; Dell closed 2009 – 2500 job losses; damaged industrial recovery, modern industrial estates, M7 motorway connects to Dublin

CASE STUDY

The Sambre Meuse Valley

- The Sambre Meuse Valley is located in the **Wallonia region of Belgium.**

- At the **height of the Industrial Revolution,** the Sambre Meuse Valley was the economic core of **Belgium.** The region **prospered due to its large reserves of coal and iron ore.**

- **Steelworks, engineering and chemical industries located in the valley** as its nearby **deposits of coal** made it **suitable for heavy industry.**

GEO DICTIONARY

Heavy industry: an industry which uses heavy or bulky raw materials to manufacture its product

- During its peak, the valley had over **120 mines** and employed over **122 000 people**. More than **30 million tonnes of coal** were mined **each year.** As the valley is located in the south of Belgium, **Wallonia** became the **core region of the country.**

- Industrial growth **lasted for over 150 years** in the valley until **1960,** when **rapid decline** began.

- From 1960, a **number of factors combined** to turn the **region into an industrial wasteland.** By the 1960s, the region's **main coal deposits** were **used up,** causing many factories **to move to Poland** which had large deposits of cheap coal.

- Second, **oil and gas** deposits were **discovered** off the coast of **northern Belgium** in the **Flanders** region. Oil is far **more efficient** and a cleaner power source **than coal.**

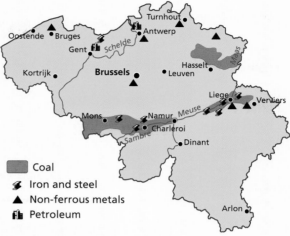

Basic resources and processing

- Coal
- Iron and steel
- Non-ferrous metals
- Petroleum

Fig. 20.35 The Sambre Meuse Rivers draw a line across Belgium. Grey shows where coal deposits were located along with associated industries.

- This caused many of the **factories** in the Sambre Meuse Valley to **relocate to the Flanders** region. Between **1960 and 1973,** over **50 000 people lost their jobs** in the Wallonia region. As the region's **unemployment rate soared, outward migration** of Walloon workers occurred as they searched for employment in Brussels and the newly emerging industries in Flanders.

- The last coal mine in the Sambre Meuse Valley closed in 1992. **Unemployment rates peaked at just under 20 per cent.** The region **struggled to attract new industries** as its **outdated** factories and **industrial waste** made the region unattractive for investors.

- As **Flanders** grew to become the **economic core of Belgium,** both the country's government and the EU invested in **redeveloping the Sambre Meuse Valley** and the whole Wallonia region.

- **Unemployed workers** were provided with **training** in order to give them the **skills** necessary to work in **modern manufacturing industries.**

- **Slag heaps** and other **industrial wastes** were **cleaned up** to make the region more attractive for new investors.

- **Communication links** were **improved** to make the region **more accessible** from other major cities.

- **Charleroi Airport** was **upgraded** to offer more international routes.

- Modern, serviced **industrial estates** were built to attract new MNCs to the region.

- Despite bringing some economic recovery to the region, the **standard of living** is far **below that of the Flanders** region to the north.

ACTIVE LEARNING

1. What is industrial decline?

2. Give two reasons why industrial decline occurs.

3. Explain how industrial decline occurred in Limerick.

4. Search for 'Dell's Limerick closure' on **www.independent.ie** to read an article on the true impact of Dell's closure in Limerick.

Fig. 20.36 Slag heaps overlooking houses in Wallonia

GEO DICTIONARY

Slag heap: a hill made from mining waste

Sambre Meuse	Wallonia region, height of Industrial Revolution, economic core of the country, large coal and iron ore deposits, steelworks, engineering and chemical industries located here, suitable for heavy industry, at peak 120 mines and 122 000 people employed, 30 million tonnes of coal per year, 150 years of industrial growth
Causes of decline	1960 rapid industrial decline, coal deposits used up, factories moved to Poland for cheaper coal, oil and gas found in Flanders
Effects	1960–73 – 50 000 become unemployed, outward migration, unemployment rates peaked at 20%, struggled to attract new investment, outdated factories and industrial waste, unattractive to investors, Flanders became economic core
Response	Government and EU investment, unemployed received training, slag heaps and industrial waste cleaned, communication links improved, Charleroi Airport upgraded, modern industrial estates, standard of living still below Flanders

Note!
We will look at urban regions in more detail at the end of each of the next five chapters. You will also study urbanisation in more detail if doing the Patterns and Processes in the Human Environment Elective.

 ACTIVE LEARNING

1. Why did Wallonia prosper during the Industrial Revolution?
2. What industries were attracted to Wallonia and why?
3. Describe three factors which led to industrial decline in Wallonia.
4. What discovery led to Flanders becoming the economic core?
5. Describe the effects of the decline on employment in Wallonia.
6. Why did Wallonia struggle to attract new industry?
7. What measures did the government and the EU take to improve Wallonia?

Concept 6: Urban Regions

 **GEO DICTIONARY**

Hinterland: the area that a city services

Nodal point: the meeting point of transport routes

- An urban region refers to a **city or large town** and its **zone of influence.** The zone of influence is also known as the **hinterland,** and refers to the **area surrounding an urban region that is serviced by a city.**

- Normally, cities are **important nodal points,** meaning they are **meeting points of roads, railways and other transport routes.**

- Cities are very **important economic regions** as they provide **employment, education, recreational** and **commercial** services.

Origin of Cities

⊙ **Fig. 20.37** In the 80 years of the Industrial Revolution, the population of Britain tripled as cities developed, creating a much more dense population. Towns such as Liverpool, Manchester and Sheffield grew rapidly to become huge industrial cities.

- The origins of modern cities date back to the **Industrial Revolution in Britain** over **200 years ago.**

- **Prior** to the Industrial Revolution, most people **lived in rural areas** where they worked as farmers. When **factories were built,** they **attracted people from** the **countryside** to work in them.

- **Houses** were **built close to the factories** for workers to live in. As workers were **now earning a wage,** they were able to buy products. This **attracted service industries** such as shops and banks.

- Over time, further employment, services and residential areas were built to create the cities we have today. As the towns grew and technology developed, **transport links developed** and changed.

Urban Sprawl

- As **towns and cities became bigger,** they **spread out into the surrounding countryside.** This process is called urban sprawl.

- Often, **urban sprawl** is **unplanned** as agricultural land is built on and **former small villages become large** commuter towns, e.g. **Tallaght** in Dublin.

- In some instances, large **towns and cities can join together** into urban regions known as **conurbations,** e.g. the **Randstad** in the Netherlands.

Irish Urban Regions

- **Ireland** is one of the **least urbanised countries** in Europe, with just over **60 per cent** of its population living in **urban areas.**

- Ireland's larger urban areas are **located along the coast,** having **origins as ports** during British rule.

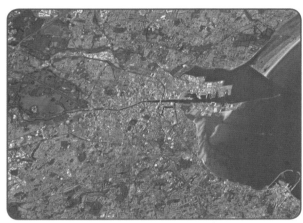

Fig. 20.38 Dublin is a primate city and has expanded into surrounding counties

- **Dublin** (the capital) is a **primate city,** meaning it is at least twice the size of Cork (the second biggest city). It is the **centre of trade in Ireland,** with its hinterland spreading into surrounding counties. It is referred to as the **Greater Dublin Area** (GDA).

ACTIVE LEARNING

1. Explain briefly how modern industrial cities developed during the Industrial Revolution.

2. What is a primate city?

3. Search for 'Industrial Revolution' on **www.historyworld.net** for more information on the Industrial Revolution and the development of modern industrial cities.

GEO DICTIONARY

Conurbation: when two or more urban areas join together, e.g. Randstad

Primate city: a city which is at least twice as large as the second biggest city in a country

 EDUCATE YOURSELF

Urban region	City or large town, zone of influence/hinterland areas surrounding an urban region, serviced by a city, roads, railways and other transport links, important economic regions – employment, education, recreational and commercial services
Origins	Industrial Revolution >200 years ago; prior lived in rural areas; factories built attracted people from countryside; houses built close to factories, now earning a wage, attracted service industries, e.g. shops, banks, led to industrial cities of today, transport links developed and changed
Urban sprawl	Towns and cities became bigger, spread out into surrounding countryside, urban sprawl, can be unplanned, former small villages became large, e.g. Tallaght, towns and cities join together, conurbation, e.g. Ranstad
Ireland	One of least urbanised, 60% living in urban areas, located along coast, origins as ports, Dublin primate city, centre of trade in Ireland, Greater Dublin Area

SHORT QUESTIONS

1. Match the description of a region with the example of the region most associated with it, by writing the correct letter in each case, in the table.

Letter	Description of Region
A	A region of industrial decline
B	A peripheral region
C	A physical region
D	An administrative region in Ireland
E	An urban region

Example of Region	Letter
Paris	
Antrim-Derry Plateau	
Sambre Meuse, Belgium	
Mezzogiorno	
Longford County Council	

Five correctly matched @ 2m each

2015 Q8 10M

LONG QUESTIONS

1. The culture of a region is often defined by its religion, language, music, dance and games. Describe and explain the importance of culture in any region that you have studied.

Naming the region 3m

Description/explanation 9 SRPs @ 3m each

2014 Q4A 30M

SHORT QUESTIONS

1. The table contains information on regions, regarding their type, specific example and general location. Complete the table by inserting the most appropriate terms from the list, in their correct position in the table.

One row of the table is completed for you.

Mediterranean   Ireland   Paris Basin   Basque Lands

Berlin   Northern Spain   Southern Europe

North European Plain   Germany   County Meath

Type of Region	Specific Example	General Location
Geomorphological	Paris Basin	North European Plain
Urban		
Climate		
Administrative		
Cultural		

Four correctly matched @ 2m each

2014 Q8 8M

2. (i) Examine the table. Match the region type with the example in Europe that best matches it, by writing the correct letter in each case, in the space provided.

Letter	Region Type
A	Climatic region
B	Urban capital
C	Geomorphological region
D	Language region

Example in Europe	Letter
The Central Plain of Ireland	
Wallonia	
Mediterranean	
Berlin	

(ii) Briefly define each type of region listed below:

Peripheral region

Administrative region

Four correctly matched @ 1m each
Two definitions @ 2m each

2012 Q6 8M

LONG QUESTIONS

1. Examine the cause and impacts of industrial decline with reference to any regions that you have studied.

Cause identified 2m
Impact identified 2m
Examination 13 SRPs @ 2m each
Award valid sketch with SRP

2015 Q4B 30M

2. Examine how socio-economic factors can be used to define regions, with reference to examples that you have studied.

Socio-economic factors named 2m + 2m
Examples of regions named 2m + 2m
Examination 11 SRPs @ 2m each

2013 Q4C 30M

Up until now, all questions you have answered have related to the physical and geographical skills sections of the geography course. From this chapter onwards, we look at regional geography: how areas can be distinguished and defined by their different characteristics.

The processes that affect physical geography are for the most part constant – sedimentary rock is formed in the same way and waterfalls are formed in the same way – regardless of when they occur.

In contrast, regional geography is always changing. For example, areas which were once core economic regions can decline and become peripheral; the violence seen in Northern Ireland has greatly reduced since the times of the Troubles and the focus is now largely on peace. It is important that you realise this when looking at past exam papers. One of the major changes that has occurred during your lifetime was the global economic recession, which began in 2008. This has had a large impact on the core and peripheral regions of Europe.

When answering a Regional Geography question:

- Make sure that you have a named example of each aspect you are asked to discuss. These examples must be appropriate for the question asked.

- There are many figures and statistics to remember in the Regional Geography section. However, there are only a limited amount of SRPs awarded for statistics alone. Instead, focus on full explanations to show your understanding.

- Underline the key words of the question.

- Think of Regional Geography as 'causes' and 'effects', i.e. what caused this to happen and how did it affect the region? By doing this, you are more likely to give a balanced answer that follows a logical order.

The following exam question appeared on the 2012 Higher Level paper. While relatively straightforward, the question was answered incorrectly by the majority of students who answered it.

The State Examiner Report stated:

> A significant number of candidates **presented answers dealing with economic and socio-economic factors that define regions** rather than how the physical landscape can be used to define regions as the question required. Successful candidates discussed physical regions such as the Paris Basin and karst regions.

HIGHER LEVEL

EXAM QUESTION

Examine, with reference to examples that you have studied, how the physical landscape can be used to define regions.

2012 Q5B 30M

Marking Scheme
Named specific locations 2 + 2m
Examination 13 SRPs @ 2m each

SAMPLE ANSWER

The karst region of the Burren in Co. Clare and the North European Plain are two regions which are defined by their physical landscape [2m + 2m]

The Burren

A karst region is one which is covered in limestone rock that has been exposed to the surface [2m]. The Burren is one such karst region which covers a total area of 250 km², some of which is a designated national park, with many surface and underground karst features [2m]. The limestone of the Burren formed 350 mya when most of Ireland was submerged by a shallow tropical sea [2m]. It was raised above sea level during the Armorican folding period 250 mya, with its limestone covered in a thin layer of silt and mudstone [2m]. This thin layer of silt/mudstone protected the underlying limestone from weathering and erosion until glaciers eroded them away during the last ice age, exposing the limestone to the surface [2m]. Once the limestone was exposed, erosion from rivers and the chemical process of carbonation shaped the limestone, creating surface and underground features, e.g. limestone pavement which makes up 60% of the Burren [2m]. Underground features such as caves, stalagmites and stalactites have formed, which attract tourists from all over the world, e.g Aillwee Cave [2m]. A number of lakes and temporary rivers appear on the surface during winter, before disappearing again in the drier months of the summer. These temporary lakes are known as turloughs [2m].

North European Plain

The North European Plain is a lowland region which lies between the Alps and Scandinavian uplands [2m]. The lowland region stretches from northern France as far as Bulgaria and the Black Sea, making it distinct from its surrounding upland regions [2m]. This region began to form underneath a shallow sea as layers of sedimentary rock formed on its floor [2m]. When the African Plate collided with the Eurasian Plate 40-60 mya, the NEP was uplifted above sea level [2m]. Unlike the surrounding regions, the NEP was not folded, instead it became gently warped forming its undulating landscape [2m]. The region was shaped by glaciers, while wind later covered the region in limon soil from glacial deposits to form fertile farming land [2m]. As a result, the NEP is one of the most densely populated regions in the world, which is aided by its favourable climate [2m].

This answer is clearly linked to distinctive physical regions which are named as examples. The answer is written logically, fully examining each example given.

Marks Awarded
Two examples named @ 2m each
Best 13 SRPs @ 2m each
Total 30/30

TOPIC MAP

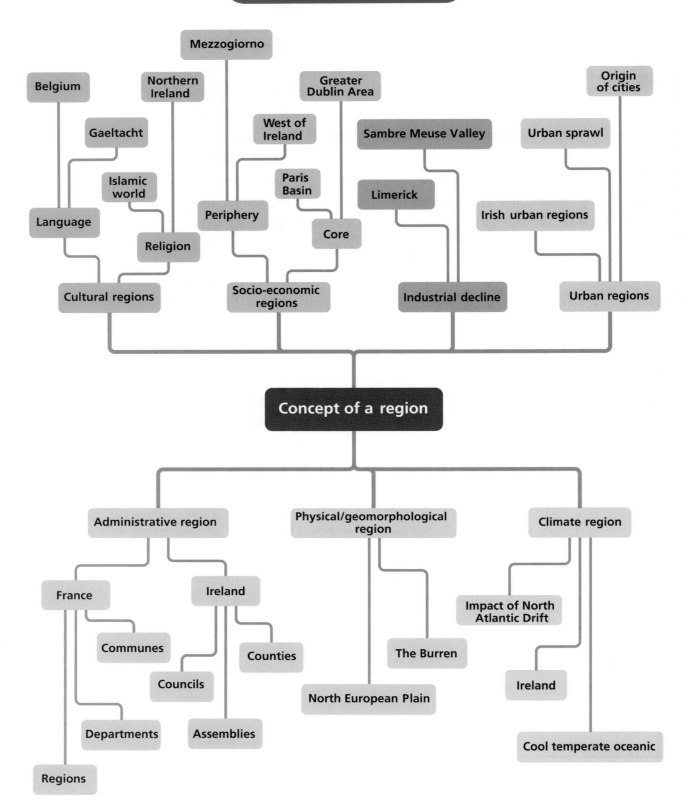

- Mezzogiorno
- Belgium
- Northern Ireland
- Greater Dublin Area
- Origin of cities
- Gaeltacht
- West of Ireland
- Sambre Meuse Valley
- Urban sprawl
- Islamic world
- Paris Basin
- Limerick
- Irish urban regions
- Language
- Periphery
- Religion
- Core
- Cultural regions
- Socio-economic regions
- Industrial decline
- Urban regions

Concept of a region

- Administrative region
  - France
    - Communes
    - Councils
    - Departments
    - Regions
  - Ireland
    - Counties
    - Assemblies
- Physical/geomorphological region
  - The Burren
  - North European Plain
- Climate region
  - Impact of North Atlantic Drift
  - Ireland
  - Cool temperate oceanic

CHAPTER 21

Irish Regions 1:
Peripheral Socio-economic Region (The West of Ireland)

In this chapter, we will look at the economic development of the West of Ireland. Although Ireland is a highly developed country, large gaps exist between its core and peripheral regions. The West of Ireland is a peripheral region, which has a number of physical and social disadvantages that have hindered its development.

KEY WORDS

- Cool temperate oceanic
- Upland
- Gley
- Podzols
- Peaty soil
- Boulder clay
- Agriculture
- Forestry
- Fishing
- Oil and gas exploitation
- Manufacturing
- Tourism
- Transport
- Rural depopulation
- Population density
- Rural-urban migration

LEARNING OUTCOMES

What you MUST know
- Physical characteristics of the West region
- Climate characteristics of the region
- How to draw the Irish map and fill in the main features (physical, transport and urban) of the West
- The development of primary, secondary and tertiary activities in the West
- Human processes of the region
- Urban development in the region

What you SHOULD know
- Galway CASE STUDY 📁
- Statistics that show the contrast between regions

What is USEFUL to know
- How to understand information provided in graphs as a means to contrast regions

21.1 The West Region

Although Ireland is a small country, of just over **72 000 km²**, its physical, economic and human processes vary greatly. As you have learned from studying administrative regions, Ireland was divided into eight regional authorities. As of 2014, the **old regional authorities** were replaced by larger Regional Assemblies. The **West region** consists of Galway, Mayo and Roscommon. It **is now part of the Northern and Western Regional Assembly.**

> **Note!**
> Keep in mind that many of the disadvantages that exist in the West, when reversed, are the advantages of the east. For example, much of the West region is dominated by upland mountainous land which makes agriculture difficult.
> In contrast, one of the advantages of the east region is that much of it is dominated by flat, low-lying land which is easily cultivated.

North West
Donegal
Northern and Western Region
Sligo
Monaghan
West
Mayo
Leitrim
Cavan
Midlands East
Roscommon
Longford
Louth
Galway
Westmeath
Meath
Dublin
Offaly
Dublin
Shannon
Clare
Laois
Kildare
Eastern and Midland Region
Wicklow
Kilkenny
Carlow
Limerick
Tipperary
Wexford
Kerry
Waterford
South East
Cork
Southern Region
Cork/Kerry

⊙ **Fig. 21.1** The new Regional Assemblies.

However, the West remains a region on its own in the context of its **unique landscape, poor economic development** and **cultural heritage**. Its lack of development can also be linked to the devastating impact of the **Great Famine (1845–49)**. In this chapter, we will examine the West under the following headings:

- Physical processes: relief, climate, soils, vegetation
- Economic activities: primary, secondary and tertiary activities
- Human processes: cultural, population, urban regions

The West of Ireland is a **peripheral region** of Ireland. It is a sub-region of the Northern and Western Regional Assembly (and formerly of the Borders, Midlands and West (BMW) Assembly). The Northern and Western Regional Assembly is a **Category One** region of Europe. This means it receives the maximum level of assistance through grants.

The West region typifies the economic difficulties experienced throughout the larger assembly as a result of physical and economic disadvantages.

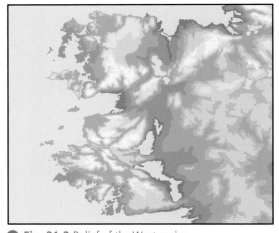

⊙ **Fig. 21.2** Relief of the West region

21.2 Physical Processes

In this section, we will look at the following physical factors that influence the region:

- Relief
- Soil
- Climate
- Drainage
- Vegetation

Relief

The relief of the West region has been shaped by three main processes:

1. Folding
2. Glaciation processes
3. Coastal processes

1. Folding

The West region can be split into an **upland western section** and a **low-lying eastern** section. Fold mountains dominate the western coastline. These were formed during the **Caledonian folding** period over **400 million years** ago as the North American and Eurasian Plates collided. Large amounts of **quartzite and shale** were folded upwards, creating a chain of mountain ranges. Over time, weathering and erosion have worn these mountains down to their current height. Examples include the Twelve Pins and Maumturk Mountains in Connemara, Co. Galway, and **Croagh Patrick** in Co. Mayo.

⊙ **Fig. 21.3** Quartzite cap of Croagh Patrick

2. Glaciation

During the last ice age, known as the **Pleistocene,** many of the mountains along the West region were eroded by glacial processes. Cirques and deep glacial valleys were carved out of the rock as glaciers moved downslope.

The low-lying, eastern half of the region is part of the **Irish Central Plain.** The **underlying limestone** bedrock is covered by thick **layers of boulder clay,** which was deposited at the end of the Pleistocene. As boulder clay is impermeable, it **affects the drainage** of the region.

In areas such as **Clew Bay in Co. Mayo,** boulder clay deposits have been shaped by glacial movement to form swarms of **drumlins.** These drumlins are **partly submerged** by seawater, giving the landscape a **gently rolling appearance.** The rise in sea level at the end of the Pleistocene drowned several glacial and river valleys. An example of a drowned glacial feature is the fiord at **Killary Harbour in Co. Mayo.**

3. Coastal Processes

Due to its exposure to the Atlantic Ocean, the coastline of the West region has been greatly **shaped by coastal processes** of erosion and deposition. Coastal erosion has formed many headlands and cliffs, while beaches and bays have been formed by coastal deposition. Due to the direction of the prevailing winds, cliffs and bays have a **south-westerly aspect.**

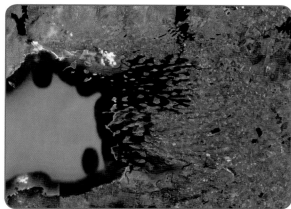

▲ **Fig. 21.4** Satellite image of Clew Bay

Marsh lakes: also known as wetlands, these lakes form in low-lying areas that flood frequently

Drainage

There are several rivers and lakes in this region. The main rivers are:

- The **River Moy** in Co. Mayo
- The **River Corrib** in Co. Galway
- The River Clare in Co. Galway
- The River Suck in Co. Roscommon
- The **River Shannon,** which runs along the eastern border of the region

The main lakes are:

- **Lough Corrib** in Co. Galway
- Lough Mask in Co. Mayo
- Lough Conn in Co. Mayo

Much of the region is **poorly drained** and **prone to waterlogging.** A large part of the region is covered with impermeable boulder clay. At the end of the Pleistocene, large amounts of glacial meltwater were unable to drain away, leading to the formation of **marsh lakes.**

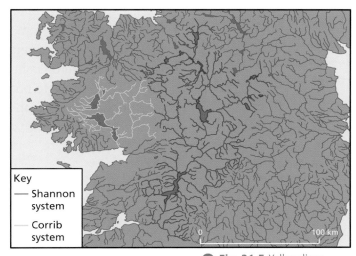

Key
— Shannon system
— Corrib system

▲ **Fig. 21.5** Yellow lines show deranged drainage of West

Blanket bog: areas covered by a thin layer of peat, typically found along upland regions

Raised bogs: deep, basin-shaped areas of peat which formed in former lakes or hollows

Drumlin swarms also interrupt drainage, causing streams to flow around them and changing their direction repeatedly. This led to the formation of **deranged drainage** in many areas.

The River Shannon drains much of the eastern fringe of the West region. The Shannon has a **gentle profile,** meaning that it flows slowly. In many parts, the water's velocity is so slow that it **floods regularly.** As a result, much of the land along its western bank is poorly drained. Evidence of this can be seen by the number of **lakes along the river's course,** e.g. Lough Allen and Lough Ree.

- Brown earths
- Peat soils
- Podzol soils
- Gley soils

Fig. 21.6 Soil map of Ireland

Soil

Soils vary throughout the West due to differences in relief, drainage and climate. However, they are generally of poor quality. The main soils of the region are:

- Peat soils
- Podzols
- Gleys
- Brown earths
- Boulder clays

Peat Soils

Peat soils exist along the upland areas in Mayo and Galway, forming expanses of **shallow blanket bogs.** These soils are **infertile** and often **waterlogged,** making them **unproductive.** Blanket bogs are normally **3–4 m deep.** Their poor mineral content and **inaccessibility to machinery** means they are useless for agriculture. In some poorly drained, marshy areas, deeper raised bogs have formed.

Leaching: the washing of nutrients from the A horizon to the B horizon, beyond the reach of plant roots

Hardpan: a layer of impermeable minerals which forms in the B horizon as a result of leaching

Rough grazing: uncultivated land used for the grazing of livestock

Podzols

Podzols form as a result of heavy rainfall and leaching. As heavy rain falls, minerals in the soil are washed from the A horizon to the B horizon. The minerals form an impermeable hardpan between the horizons, which leads to poor drainage. **Waterlogging is common** throughout the year, and especially in the winter months.

Fig. 21.7 Marsh lands of the West

Gleys

Gley soils form as a result of **severe saturation of clay soils.** Glacial deposits and drumlins lead to poorly drained areas. As the movement of water is slow here, it is absorbed by the soil, leading to saturation. **Water fills the pores in the soil,** removing all air. Due to the lack of oxygen, very **little vegetation survives. Rushes thrive** on gley soils. As a result, this soil is used for rough grazing in agriculture.

Brown Earths

Brown earths make up **64 per cent of all soils in Ireland,** but are **limited to parts of south Galway** and other **low-lying areas** in the West region. In the West, these soils are not deep and are often referred to as **shallow brown earths.** The soils formed as a result of the **deciduous forests** that covered the lowlands of the region. The humus from annually decaying leaves built up in the soil making them fertile. These soils are normally **fertile and well drained,** making them **valuable for agriculture.** Brown earths in this region tend to be **slightly acidic,** due to leaching caused by year-round rainfall. This makes them less suitable for agriculture.

▲ **Fig. 21.8** Rushes growing on gley soil

Vegetation

The natural vegetation of the West varies according to soil type. Bog cotton, heather and scrub grasses cover the blanket bogs of the mountainous regions. Rough grassland covers the podzolic and gley soils, with rushes often being the main vegetation. Brown earths were originally covered by thick deciduous grasslands, but are now used for agricultural grasslands.

EDUCATE YOURSELF

Physical Processes	
Relief	Upland in west section, lowland in east section
	Folding: Caledonian, 400 mya, quartzite and shale, Croagh Patrick
	Glaciation: Pleistocene, Central Plain, boulder clay, affects drainage, drumlin swarms, Clew Bay, rolling landscape
	Coastal processes: south-westerly aspect
Drainage	River Moy, River Corrib, Lough Corrib, poorly drained, prone to waterlogging, marsh lakes, deranged drainage, River Shannon, gentle profile, floods regularly, lakes along course
Soil	Vary throughout West
	Peat: shallow blanket bogs, infertile, unproductive, 3–4 m deep, inaccessible for machinery
	Podzols: heavy rainfall, leaching, hardpan, waterlogging
	Gleys: severe saturation of clay, water fills pores of soil, little vegetation survives, rushes thrive
	Brown earths: limited to south Galway, low-lying areas, shallow, deciduous forests, fertile, well drained, valuable for agriculture, slightly acidic
Vegetation	Natural vegetation depends on soil type, heather, scrub grasses, blanket bog in mountainous areas, rough grassland on podzols and gley, grassland on brown earths

Climate

Like the rest of Ireland, the West region has a **cool temperate oceanic** climate. However, due to its closeness to the Atlantic, its temperatures are more **moderate,** and its precipitation levels are higher.

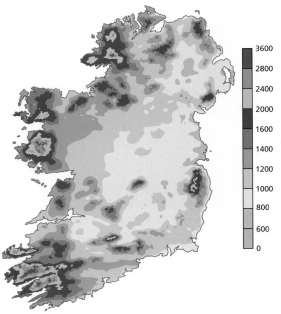

Fig. 21.9 Average annual rainfalls (in mm) of Ireland for the past 20 years

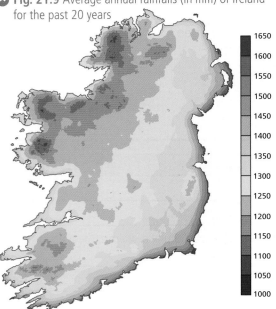

Fig. 21.10 Annual hours of sunshine of Ireland for the past 20 years

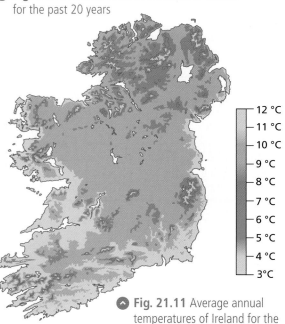

Fig. 21.11 Average annual temperatures of Ireland for the past 20 years

Precipitation

Precipitation levels are higher in the West than in any other region in Ireland. There are a number of reasons for this. Ireland's latitude lies at the meeting of the warm **south-westerly and cold polar fronts.** As a result, **cyclones or depressions form** and blow inland from the Atlantic. This leads to **heavy rainfall.**

Relief rainfall occurs in the upland areas of the West. The warm, prevailing south-westerly winds **absorb moisture from the warm currents** they blow over. When the warm air mass reaches the mountain ranges of the West coastline, it is forced to rise upwards over the mountains. As the warm air rises upwards, it cools and **condenses into rain clouds,** leading to heavy precipitation.

Some upland regions receive over **2500 mm** of precipitation per year, while lowland regions receive over **1100 mm per year.** This is well above the average of 800 mm in the east. Most precipitation falls in the form of rain, with **snowfall rarely occurring.** Snow that does fall is usually limited to the peaks of mountains during winter and early spring.

Temperatures

The West has a small temperature range that is **regulated by the Atlantic Ocean. Winters are mild,** with average temperatures of **6 °C. Summers** are relatively **cool,** with average temperatures of **15 °C.** This gives an **annual temperature range** of just **9 °C.** There are a number of factors that influence the temperature of the region:

- The **North Atlantic Drift** is a warm ocean current that increases air temperatures during the winter. This current keeps the coastline **free from ice** and extreme weather conditions experienced by other countries at Ireland's latitude.

- The prevailing south-westerly winds help to **moderate temperatures,** keeping them mild during the winter months and driving the North Atlantic Drift.

- Altitude affects temperatures due to **'lapse rate'.** This basically means that they higher up you go, the colder it gets. For every 150 m increase in altitude, the temperature drops by 1 °C. The mountainous regions of the West are much colder than the low-lying regions. **Upland regions** are also **exposed to winds,** which lower temperatures further. This is known as **wind chill.**

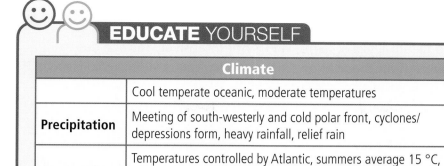

EDUCATE YOURSELF

Climate	
	Cool temperate oceanic, moderate temperatures
Precipitation	Meeting of south-westerly and cold polar front, cyclones/depressions form, heavy rainfall, relief rain
Temperature	Temperatures controlled by Atlantic, summers average 15 °C, winters average 6 °C, small temperature range, North Atlantic Drift, lapse rate, uplands exposed, wind chill

GEO DICTIONARY

Lapse rate: for every 150 m increase in altitude, the temperature drops by 1 °C

ACTIVE LEARNING

1. In what ways do you think physical processes could affect the development of agriculture in the West?

2. Visit **www.met.ie** and compare the weather forecasts for the West and the east or Dublin region.

3. For more detailed information on soils, visit **gis.teagasc.ie/soils**

21.3 Primary Activities

Agriculture

Characteristics

Agriculture is **vital to the economy** of the West, with **13.6 per cent** of the region's population earning their living through farming. In Roscommon, 20 per cent of the population is dependent on agriculture. However, this is mainly as a result of **traditional family practices** rather than because of farming's profitability.

Agriculture in the West is **subsistent** and **underdeveloped,** meaning that farming is less prosperous in this region than in other regions in Ireland. Farms in the West are dependent on less-profitable farming practices such as **sheep** and **dry stock cattle** rearing. This is because the land is **unsuitable for** more intensive farming such as **tillage** and dairy. Only **0.5 per cent** of productive farmland in the West is used for **growing cereals.** Some 72.8 per cent of land is used for pastoral farming. Before the Great Famine of 1845–49, families **divided farms between their (usually male) children.** As a result, farm sizes are smaller in the West than in most other regions in Ireland. **Average farm sizes** in the West are just over **25 hectares,** which is too small to produce a large income. Fig. 21.12 shows average farm size in the West region.

Note!

Be sure to learn the name of a river and mountain of each region you study and where they are located. You may need to include them in the map you draw of the region.

GEO DICTIONARY

Tillage: growing crops

Dry stock cattle rearing: grazing cattle to fatten them for beef

Counties	No. of Farms	Total Farm Area (ha)	Average Farm Size (ha)
Galway	13 445	347 123	25.82
Mayo	12 458	278 997	22.41
Roscommon	6313	171 293	27.13
Total	32 216	797 413	25.12

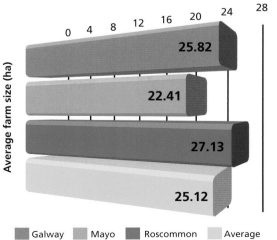

Fig. 21.12 Average farm size county by county

CORE 3

CHAPTER 21

REGIONAL GEOGRAPHY **367**

Despite the small size of farms, land is **not intensively farmed** due to **low levels of mechanisation.** This makes agriculture in the region labour intensive. The age profile of farmers in the West is continually rising, with **60 per cent of farmers over the age of 55** in 2014. This was a 5 per cent increase since 2010. Many older farmers are **reluctant to spend money to modernise their farms,** preferring to use their **traditional methods.** A lot of money is needed to modernise farms, which has made **younger family members reluctant to take over farming** the land. Many **farms have been abandoned** as young people leave the region for third-level education, employment and a better standard of living.

Agriculture in the West is **highly subsidised by the EU,** with grants known as **Direct Payments** issued each year. Without these payments, farming in the West would decline rapidly, as only **14 per cent of farms are economically viable** without them. As agriculture in the West is generally not profitable, over **50 per cent of farmers are part-time** or 'hobby' farmers. This means that they have jobs outside of the farm. Usually these farms are small in scale. **Hobby farming** is typically carried out to **maintain a family's tradition of farming** rather than for income.

Changing Farming Practices

Younger farmers in the West often change from traditional practices to avail of **niche markets.** As a result, many of the farms in the West are becoming **multifunctional.** Common examples of additional functions of agricultural land include:

- Using the farmhouse as a **bed and breakfast** during the summer months
- **Hillwalking** paths through the farmland
- **Craft foods** such as jams and baking
- **Pet farms**

This multifunctionality **changes the traditional views of farming** in the West, allowing it to become more **commercial.** As the EU will reduce its support for the West in the future, farmers must expand and change in order to survive.

Fig. 21.13 A path for hillwalkers runs through farmland

Factors Affecting Agriculture in the West

There are a number of factors that affect agriculture in the West. These include:

- Climate
- Relief and drainage
- Soils
- Lack of urban markets
- Rural depopulation

Note!
The two most common questions on agriculture ask you to either discuss its development or to describe the factors that influence it.

Factor 1: Climate

- The climate of the West influences all other physical factors.
- High levels of precipitation and **lower temperatures limit tillage farming.**
- **Heavy rainfall** has led to the development of less fertile soils due to leaching, erosion and waterlogging.
- **Cooler temperatures** have led to a **shorter growing season.**
- Cattle must be housed for longer periods.
- **Large amounts of silage** and other feeds must be given to the animals for many months of the year. This **adds to farm expenditure** and reduces income for the farmer.

⌃ **Fig. 21.14** High levels of rainfall restrict farming in the region.

Factor 2: Relief and Drainage

- Due to the **upland terrain,** much of the land is **unsuitable for agriculture.**
- Access by machinery is more difficult.
- Rainfall is **heaviest along upland areas,** leading to waterlogging.
- **Waterlogging** has led to the formation of blanket bogs along the slopes of mountains.
- Glaciers moved across the landscape and scraped away much of the overlying soil, leaving them **bare and infertile.**
- The soil is **thin and stony,** making it difficult to cultivate.
- Glacial deposits disrupted drainage.
- Boulder clay is **impermeable,** causing waterlogging and marshland to develop, which is unsuited to intensive agriculture.
- Many of the breeds of sheep kept are suited for mountainous landscape.
- The **upland relief shortens** the **growing season.**

⌃ **Fig. 21.15** Upland relief makes access difficult.

Factor 3: Soils

- Upland areas are covered in **infertile peat soils,** which are prone to waterlogging.
- Infertile soils limit most agriculture to sheep and cattle rearing.

Fig. 21.16 Unproductive podzol soil

- **Severe leaching** has formed infertile podzols, e.g. in east Mayo. This leads to the growth of **stronger weed grasses** such as rushes.
- **Hardpans** disrupt drainage, causing frequent waterlogging.
- **Arable farming** is very **difficult**.
- Many farmers **do not earn enough money to be able to invest in machinery.** This means they cannot cultivate soils to their full benefit.

Factor 4: Markets/ Infrastructure

- The West is in a peripheral location and is **isolated from the main Irish and EU markets.**
- Transport infrastructure is **poorly developed.**
- **The cost of transporting goods** to markets are **high.**
- **Galway** is the **only large urban area,** which results in a limited market for produce.
- **Galway** is the **only port** in the region, meaning goods must first be transported to the east before reaching EU markets.
- Cattle farmers **sell their reared animals to farmers in the Greater Dublin Area (GDA)** and south-east regions where they are fattened for factories.
- This **provides little income** for farmers in the West, but they do it because it is convenient.

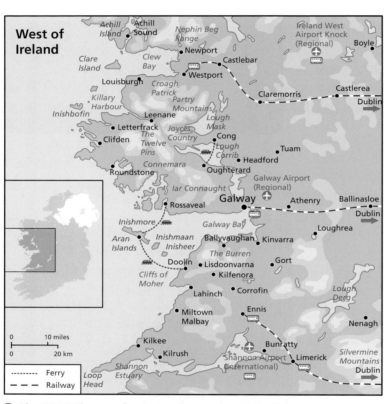

Fig. 21.17 There are few large urban markets in the West region.

Factor 5: Rural Depopulation

- **Traditionally, land passed from generation to generation** (typically from father to son). The son who inherited the land was expected to operate the farm in the same way as his father had.
- As Ireland developed, agriculture was **no longer seen as the only means of earning a living.** Younger generations chose not to take up farming, instead opting for careers that paid better and had more security.
- The introduction of free post-primary education in the 1960s and free third-level education in the 1990s meant that young Irish people in the West had opportunities that were not available to their parents. Younger generations spent more time in school and college and **pursued better-paid careers.**

- Young people are **more likely to gain employment close to where they attended college.** This led to a large reduction in the number of farms in the West, as older farmers retired and were not replaced.

- **Rural-urban migration is continuing** to cause a greater level of land abandonment throughout the West.

- Continued **rural depopulation** means that **services** for farmers such as marts and veterinary offices are **shutting down**.

⬆ **Fig. 21.18** What do you think is the message of this cartoon?

 EDUCATE YOURSELF

Agriculture
Vital to economy, employs 13.6%, traditional family practices, subsistence, underdeveloped, sheep rearing, dry stock cattle, unsuitable for tillage, less than 0.5% cereals, subdividing land prior to famine, average size 25 hectares, not intensively farmed, low levels of mechanisation, 60% of farmers over 55 years, many reluctant to modernise, conventional farming, young people reluctant to farm, land abandoned, highly subsidised by EU, 14% economically viable, 50% farmers are part-time, hobby farming for sentimental reasons; niche markets, multifunctional (B&B, hillwalking, craft foods, pet farms), changes traditional farming, commercial

Forestry

Under the **National Development Plan,** the Irish government aims to increase the area of Irish land covered by forestry to **15 per cent** (it is currently 10 per cent). Much of the **afforestation** is happening in the **West region,** as much of the **upland** soils are poor and unproductive for agriculture but support the growth of trees. Many farmers also feel that **marginal land** used for rough grazing could be used more profitably for forestry. In order to encourage this, both the EU and the Irish government **offer grants to farmers** in the West to grow forests on their marginal land.

Much of these plantations are of **coniferous forests,** which are managed by the **state-sponsored** company **Coillte.** In total, Coillte has overseen the plantation of more than **50 000 hectares** of coniferous forests in the West. So far, Coillte has mainly planted on upland and marsh areas, but the increasing level of land abandonment in the West may lead to further afforestation on less marginal land.

The very exposed upland areas in the West **do not allow for afforestation** due to **cold temperatures,** but many parts of the region are suitable for planting forests. Forestry is suited to the West for a number of reasons:

- A mild, **wet climate** and relatively **long growing season** favour the rapid growth of coniferous trees such as Sitka spruce and Scots pine, which grow twice as fast in the West as in the east.

 **GEO DICTIONARY**

Marginal land: unproductive agricultural land

ACTIVE LEARNING

Look at Fig. 21.19. Why is there no forestry in the right background of this photo?

⬆ **Fig. 21.19** Marginal land and upland areas can be used for coniferous plantations.

- Trees grow well in the gleys, podzols and peaty soils of the West and provide a **long-term alternative** to unproductive farming of marginal land.
- Trees can be planted on **cutaway bogs,** making use of isolated or inaccessible land.

Fishing

The West **is suitable for the development of a strong fishing industry.** Although it is not as economically important to the region as agriculture, the fishing industry provides **employment** for over **2000 people.** These people are employed in:

- Fishing
- Fish processing
- Aquaculture

Ireland's western coastline is **indented** as a result of the erosion from the Atlantic Ocean. These coastal indentations provide plenty of **locations for fishing ports** and are ideal locations for **fish farming.** The North Atlantic Drift is a **warm current** that keeps the ports of the West ice-free throughout the winter. The warm waters also promote a great **diversity of fish;** cod, herring and mackerel thrive in it.

Ireland lies on a wide and shallow **continental shelf** that is ideal for fish breeding. The sun's light can penetrate the water and encourages the growth of **plankton.** The abundance of plankton provides a **plentiful supply of food for the fish,** encouraging them to breed there.

Due to the relatively **low levels of pollution** entering the sea along the West, the waters are clean and free from harmful **biotoxins.** This encourages the development of shellfish farming, e.g. oyster farming in Galway Bay or mussel farming in **Killary Harbour, Co. Mayo.**

Attempts to further develop fishing in the West region have been hindered by restrictions introduced by the EU. The **Common Fisheries Policy** (CFP) was introduced in 1983 to **combat overfishing,** which threatened the future of the industry and the survival of certain fish species. The CFP was introduced to manage and **conserve fish stocks** throughout EU waters.

Quotas, embargoes and **restrictions** in fishing vessel **size and equipment** were implemented to prevent overfishing. Despite the introduction of the CFP, fish stocks along the West kept declining leading to further restrictions. One of the main rules was the **total allowable catch** (TAC), which sets the amount of fish each country can catch in a year. Further restrictions to **net and vessel size** were also introduced. The TAC allows Ireland just **19.5 per cent** of the total amount of fish caught in a season in the EU. Only **20 per cent of the fish caught in Irish waters is caught by Irish-registered boats.** This reduces the impact of fishing as an economically beneficial industry to the West.

Rossaveal in Co. Galway is the largest fishing port in the West. In total, the harbour accommodates **438 vessels,** although the owners of just 62 of these live in the Rossaveal area. Fishing is a **vital employer for the people who**

GEO DICTIONARY

Aquaculture: the farming of aquatic animals and plants

Cutaway bog: an area of bog that has had its peat harvested

Continental shelf: edges of a continental crust that are submerged by shallow waters

Plankton: microscopic organisms that are eaten by many fish. They can be animal or plant based

Biotoxins: poisons produced by a living organism

Overfishing: catching fish at a greater rate than they can breed, which causes their numbers to decline

Quota: limit on the number of fish that can be caught each fishing season

Embargo: a ban on fishing at certain times/in certain areas

Total allowable catch: the amount of fish that can be caught by EU countries in a year

live in the town, even though only **1690 tonnes** of fish are landed at Rossaveal.

In response to the EU restrictions, aquaculture expanded rapidly during the first decade of the 2000s. In 2010, the aquaculture industry generated over 150 000 tonnes of produce. Three aquaculture companies have set up in Rossaveal. These are:

- An Crompan
- Kilcummin
- Connemara Abalone

These firms allow for long-term development of the fishing industry **without impacting on the environment** or contributing to overfishing. Currently, Ireland's fish production through aquaculture is **fifth highest in the EU** and is expected to **grow by a further 61 per cent by 2020.**

Overall, in order to make fishing a more profitable industry in the West, further investment is needed by the Irish government to **upgrade ports** and further develop the aquaculture industry.

Oil and Gas

There has been **limited success** in the development of oil and gas off the western coast. The largest find was in 1996 where a new gas field was discovered 70 km off the coast of Mayo.

The **Corrib Gas Field** was discovered to have over 28 million cubic metres of natural gas. This would be enough to meet Ireland's **gas supply for the next 18 years.** Despite the obvious advantages of the find, the discovery has caused much controversy for a number of reasons:

- The Corrib gas project is operated by a private company, Shell and E&P Ireland Ltd.
- Legislation introduced in the late 1980s reduced the benefit of oil and gas finds to the Irish government. This means that Ireland is ranked as the **second lowest globally,** in terms of revenue earned by the government from the discovery of hydrocarbons (fossil fuels). This means that Shell are **selling gas to Bord Gáis Energy at normal market prices** rather than at a reduced rate.
- Controversy occurred in Co. Mayo as a result of Shell's decision to **pump raw gas ashore** rather than refining it beforehand. **Refined gas** is much **less volatile** that raw gas, which is piped ashore under high pressure. Shell chose the village of **Bellnaboy** as the location of its refinery.

⊙ **Fig. 21.20** Aquaculture along a sheltered bay

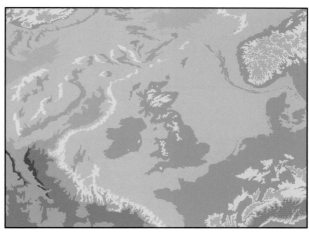

⊙ **Fig. 21.21** Light blue showing Ireland's continental shelf

⊙ **Fig, 21.22** Plenty more fish in the sea?

ACTIVE LEARNING
Look at Fig. 21.22. What is the message of this cartoon

The building of the refinery went ahead despite **strong local opposition** due to safety concerns. In March 2013, Exxon Mobil carried out further drills in the area. While early signs were promising, they have **not led to any further oil or gas finds.**

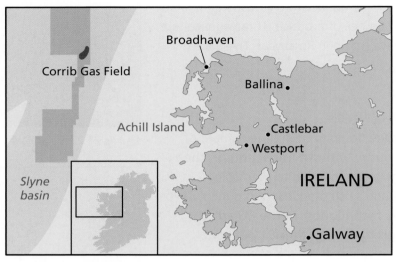

⬆ **Fig. 21.23** The site of the Corrib Gas Field

EDUCATE YOURSELF

Other Primary Activities	
Forestry	National Development Plan Aim: 15% forestry coverage nationally (currently 10%), afforestation in West, upland, marginal lands, grants offered, coniferous forestry, Coillte, 50 000 hectares, exposed uplands unsuitable, suits West, wet climate, long growing season, long-term alternative to unproductive land, cutaway bog
Fishing	Coast favours fishing development, employs 2000 people, indented coastline, sheltered bays, locations for fishing ports and fish farms, warm currents (NAD), diversity of fish, continental shelf, plankton, plentiful supply of fish, low levels of pollution, free of biotoxins, aquaculture, e.g. Killary Harbour, Co. Mayo, CFP, combat overfishing, conserve fish stocks, quotas, embargoes, restrictions, size and equipment, TAC, 11% EU fish caught in Ireland, 16% of EU waters, Rossaveal, Co. Galway, vital employer for people in town, fifth-highest aquaculture producer in EU, 61% growth by 2020
Oil and gas	Limited success, Corrib Gas Field, gas supply for 18 years, sold to Bord Gáis at normal price (no reduction), second lowest benefits globally, pump raw gas ashore, refined gas less volatile, Bellnaboy, strong local opposition, no further finds

21.4 Secondary Activities

Secondary economic activities refer to the **processing of raw materials** by manufacturing them into finished or semi-finished products. Manufacturing in the West region is **underdeveloped** in comparison to the GDA. There are a number of **physical and social factors** that **have hindered the development** of secondary activities. As a result, the region relies on more **traditional secondary industries** such as **food processing, timber processing** and **textiles.**

Factors Influencing Manufacturing in the West

The four **main factors** that affect secondary activities in the West are:

1. Infrastructure
2. Labour force
3. Traditional industries
4. Government intervention

1. Infrastructure

The infrastructure of the West is poorly developed and lacks the needed investment. Its upland terrain and poor drainage makes the development of modern road and rail links both difficult and expensive. The region is serviced by only one motorway (the M6) which was completed in 2009. The motorway connects **Galway to Dublin,** while Mayo and Roscommon are connected to the east only through a national primary route (N5), much of which is in need of repair. This lack of primary route is a **deterrent for industries** that might want to locate in the West. The **transport of goods can be expensive** and often **slow** compared to the well-serviced urban areas in the east. The **lack of efficient routes** adds to the West's peripheral location and **isolates it from the larger Dublin and EU markets.** The location of **Ireland West Airport** (IWA) at **Knock in Co. Mayo** provides access to the West. However, the **small number of flights** departing from the airport means it provides **little incentive** for companies to locate there.

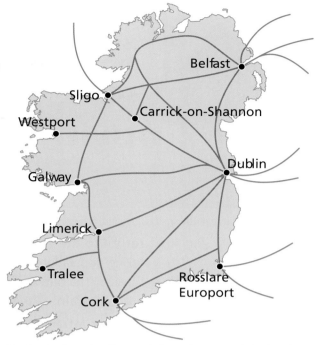

Fig. 21.24 Ireland's main industrial transport links (purple lines = road links; blue lines = shipping links)

GEO DICTIONARY

Incentive: something that encourages a company to locate in an area

Telecommunications: telephone, radio, television and internet services

Telecommunications such as broadband access are **limited** in the West. This is a deterrent to any **modern business** as they **rely on high broadband speeds.** Many parts of the West are broadband 'blackspots' where no internet signal is available. While significant improvements have been made over the past number of years, average broadband speeds are much **lower than in the east** and are well **below the EU average.**

The West **lacks well-serviced industrial estates,** which are the **preferred locations for MNCs** and other companies. As industrial estates tend to locate along **developed road links** on the outskirts of urban areas, the **West is not considered a suitable location** for them. Industrial estates provide **electricity and water,** which are necessary for large machines. Industrial estates also allow companies to link together and **establish beneficial relationships.**

2. Labour Force

The West has a **low population density of just 25 per km².** Only **30 per cent** of the West's population **lives in urban areas.** Galway City is the **largest urban centre,** with **a population of 70 000.** A lack of urban centres means **MNCs find it difficult to choose a location** where they will

Fig. 21.25 National University of Ireland, Galway

have an adequate supply of a skilled workers or large enough local markets to sell their goods.

The West suffers from **outward migration** to other regions due to a number of factors. The main cause is a **lack of third-level colleges and universities.** The West has only **one university** and two Institutes of Technology, meaning that many students **attend colleges in the south and east** of the country. Students are **more likely to gain employment** in their chosen fields in areas **close to where they attended college.** As a result, many **do not return to the West.** This can lead to **several social problems,** such as a falling population density, an ageing population and the closing down of services. The outward migration of young people from the West is known as a **'brain drain'** as the region loses its most educated and skilled people.

Colleges attract MNCs because they can carry out **research and development** and they provide an educated and skilled workforce. MNCs can invest in college courses and fund PhD research. After graduation, students have the expertise to work for the company. **Galway** is the **only area** in the West with a **university,** meaning most **MNCs are concentrated near the city.**

3. Traditional Industries

Outside of Galway, industries tend to be **labour intensive** and on a much **smaller scale.** Labour-intensive jobs are **prone to job losses** due to **rationalisation** and **mechanisation.** The **collapse of the construction sector** since the 2008 recession is an example of the **insecurity** of labour-intensive industry. Until 2008, building and construction accounted for over **50 per cent of secondary activities** in the West.

The West has a much **higher level of unskilled employment** than the GDA, meaning annual **wages are also lower.** On average, manufacturing wages are **15 per cent lower in the West.**

Some **57 per cent of Roscommon's workforce** is employed in the **food processing industry.** This industry can also suffer from **sudden job losses** due to unstable markets or increased production costs. The meat-processing plant **Kepak Ltd** operates in Athleague, Co. Roscommon. The company cut 50 jobs in February 2014 **due to the economic downturn.** This could have a knock-on effect on companies that supply Kepak, such as **FDK Engineering** which specialises in the production of **food processing machinery** for dairy and meat.

4. Government Intervention

Government intervention has greatly influenced industry in the West region. In the 1930s, the Irish government introduced legislation to **protect domestic industry** from foreign competition. This discouraged foreign companies from setting up in Ireland and particularly in the West. This has contributed to the region's **overreliance on traditional, labour-intensive industries**. During the 1950s, Ireland passed new laws to attract more industry. A **low corporation tax** was introduced to attract MNCs to the country. However, very few companies set up in the West due to poor communication links and its distance from urban and EU markets.

Since Ireland joined the EU in 1973, the West (which is now part of the Northern and Western Assembly) has been designated a **Category One** region. This means that the region receives **high levels of grant support** in order to develop communications and other infrastructure. **Structural funds** are also given to the region for **education and training** in order to establish a skilled workforce. The **Industrial Development Agency** (IDA) also offers grants and tax breaks in order to attract companies to the West and other peripheral locations. **Údarás na Gaeltachta** was set up in order to **promote employment** in the **Gaeltacht regions** of the West such as Connemara. Grants paying up to **€14 000 of each employee's wage** are offered to companies setting up in Gaeltacht regions.

Under the **National Development Plan (NDP),** the **National Spatial Strategy** (NSS) 2002–2020 aimed to develop several gateways (e.g. Galway) and hubs (e.g. Tuam, Athenry). Hubs are centres of economic development, e.g. Dublin. Gateways are areas which are linked to hubs to help promote economic development. The aim was to make these areas more **attractive to industries.** The NSS helped to **improve communication links** and **industrial infrastructure** such as industrial estates. The NSS also established guidelines for rural and residential development in the West. Despite the NSS being scrapped in 2014, the designated **hubs and gateways** have become more attractive for industry. For example, in 2015 **Apple Inc.** announced an **€850 million investment** to develop a new data centre in Athenry.

● **Fig. 21.26** The sign translates as: The sea spends its day ebbing and flowing.

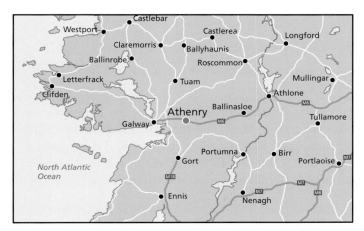

● **Fig. 21.27** Athenry has experienced growth as a result of its proximity to Galway.

Examples of Industries in the West

Industry in Westport

Fig. 21.28 Allergan Ireland has located in Westport.

The town of Westport has seen a growth in industrial investment. This is partly due to its designation as a hub under the National Spatial Strategy.

The pharmaceuticals company Allergan Ireland is a subdivision of an American cosmetics company. It began operating in Westport in 1977 with just 25 employees. Today, it employs over 800 people and accounts for over half of the company's worldwide revenue.

Allergan produces a variety of pharmaceutical products but is now best known for manufacturing Botox. You may think Botox is used only to make ageing celebrities look younger. However, it is also an effective treatment from cerebral palsy, multiple sclerosis and spinal injuries.

Fig. 21.29 The Boston Scientific Campus

Over the last decade, the company has become more involved in research and development. It now employs 250 highly experienced scientists to develop new products.

Allergan's campus covers over 30 acres, but any further plans to develop the site have been shelved since the recession began.

Industry in Galway City

Galway City has many advantages for manufacturing, such as:

- A population of over 75 000, providing a large labour pool and a large local market
- Developed transport links (M6, railway, port, airport)
- Good telecommunications, with much higher broadband speeds than the average in the West and several serviced industrial estates
- A university (NUIG), with nearly 20 000 students, providing a constant supply of skilled graduates

As a result of this, the city has been chosen by many IT, medical device and pharmaceutical companies such as:

- Hewlett Packard
- Boston Scientific
- MedTech
- Ingersoll Rand
- Medtronic

We will look at Boston Scientific and Medtronic in more detail:

> **GEO DICTIONARY**
>
> **Indirect jobs:** jobs created to provide additional services to existing business sectors, e.g. hotels, restaurants and B&Bs are examples of indirect employment from tourism; also known as spin-off jobs

CASE STUDY 📁

Boston Scientific

Boston Scientific is one of the world's largest medical device manufacturers. The company employs over 2600 people in Galway, which is the site of its largest manufacturing plant. The company produces specialist cardiovascular devices such as stents and catheters. The company established its research and development and manufacturing plant in 1994, which has now grown to over 37 000 m². Boston Scientific is now the largest single industrial supplier in the West and the largest medical device employer in Ireland.

Medtronic

Medtronic is another large medical device company. It invested in Galway in 1999. Galway is now the site of its largest research and development and manufacturing plant in the world. Employing over 2000 people, the company also encourages many indirect jobs, with a further 1300 semi-skilled workers employed in assembly, packaging, transport, etc. After the recession began in 2008, pay freezes were introduced with many fearing job losses in the future.

Factors Influencing Manufacturing in the West	
Infrastructure	Lacks investment, development is difficult and expensive, one motorway (M6 Galway–Dublin), lack of routes a deterrent to industry, transport of goods expensive, slow, isolates region from Dublin and Eu markets, IWA, limited flights, telecommunications limited, modern business needs broadband – lower than EU average, lacks serviced industrial estates, locate along modern transport links
Labour force	Low population density, 25 per km², difficult for industry to choose location, 30% of population lives in urban areas, Galway City 70,000 people, outward migration, one university (NUIG), migrate east for education, employed near college attended, brain drain, colleges attract MNCs, research and development, West's MNCs concentrated around Galway City
Traditional industry	Labour intensive, small scale, prone to job losses, rationalisation, mechanisation, insecurity, e.g. construction industry, higher level of unskilled employment, wages are lower, 57% of Roscommon workforce in food processing, Kepak Ltd, forced to downsize, FDK engineering, food processing machinery
Government intervention	Government 1920–1950s protected domestic industry, overreliance on traditional industry, 1950s new laws to discourage outward migration, low corporation tax, Category One, high level grant support, structural funds, education and training, IDA, Údarás na Gaeltachta promoted employment in Gaeltacht, up to €14 000 of each employee's wage, NDP, NSS, improve communications and industrial infrastructure, hubs and gateways (scrapped 2014), Apple Inc. Athenry €850 million

21.5 Tertiary Activities

Tertiary economic activities involve the **provision of services.** For example, teachers provide education, which is a service rather than a physical product. Regions with **more tertiary industries** are considered to be **wealthier** than regions with mainly primary and secondary industries. In the West region, **fewer people are employed in the tertiary sector** than elsewhere in the country. In this section, we will look at the development of **transport** and **tourism** in the West.

Transport

Developed transport links such as roads, rail, ports and airports are **necessary** for the **movement of people** and the **delivery of the goods** in a **quick and efficient** manner. Transport links in Ireland are seen as vital in attracting industry and further development. As Ireland is geographically small and many areas of the West are sparsely populated, **road links are the main means** of moving people and products.

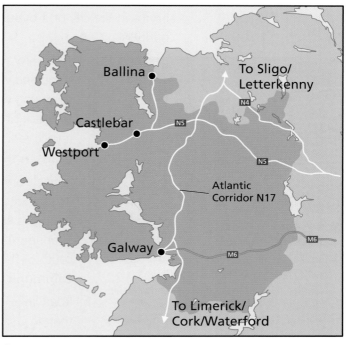

⊙ **Fig. 21.30** Major road links in the West

In the West region, transport infrastructure is **underdeveloped** despite efforts to modernise it over the past two decades. Due to the relief of the region, **roads are winding** as they **loop around mountains**. Many of the West's primary roads **follow the paths carved through mountains** by river valleys. Due to the unsuitable relief, **road construction is expensive** and often very difficult due to areas of **bog and marsh** which cause **foundations to sink**.

As the **region** is **mainly rural,** it makes the development of **central road and rail links** difficult, and a well-developed **public transport service** is **not cost-effective** due to **low population densities**. Therefore, the movement of people is mainly through **privately owned cars,** while most goods are transported by heavy goods vehicles (HGVs).

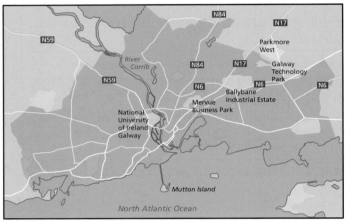

Fig. 21.31 The convergence of so many roads in Galway City has created traffic congestion.

Roads

Galway was chosen as a **gateway** for development, meaning that it became the **focus of transport development**. The modernisation of transport in Galway is seen as vital in **connecting it to Dublin's** large urban market. The completion of the **M6 motorway** has greatly reduced the travel time between Dublin and Galway (it is currently equal to travel time by train).

However, Galway's City's **centralised population** has caused **traffic congestion** for many parts of the day, resulting in **delays for people travelling to and from work** and for HGVs delivering goods. In response to this, roundabouts leading into the city were replaced by traffic lights and modernised traffic lanes, which aided traffic flow around the city. Despite the improvements, traffic within the urban area remains an issue due to the lack of a **light rail service** in the city or **a bypass** for traffic wishing to access the west of the county.

Fig. 21.32 The Quincentennial Bridge was built to reduce the amount of traffic entering Galway City centre. However, as car ownership increased during the economic boom of the 1990s and early 2000s, the bridge also became congested.

The **Galway City Bypass Project** is currently at its planning stage and will be designed to ensure that only traffic operating within the city will have to enter it. However, due to a lack of funding and disagreement as to whether or not it will work, it is **unlikely to be built**. Further **upgrades to roads in towns surrounding the city** are also planned.

Projects are also taking place along the Clifden-Oughterard (N59), Gort **(N18)** and Tuam **(N17)** routes. These road upgrades are important as they **shorten travel times** to Shannon Airport, Limerick and other major cities in the south of the country. It is believed that these improved **communication links** will help **economic growth**.

Road links in **Roscommon and Mayo are less developed** than in Galway. The N5 is the only national primary route to Dublin from these counties. Many sections of the **N5** are in poor condition, especially throughout the Roscommon section. Poor roads lead to **longer travel times** and **higher transport costs**. While upgrades to the road were planned, the economic **recession** has led to a **withdrawal of funding**.

Railway

With the gradual improvement in road networks in the region, the **number of people choosing to travel by rail has fallen.** With the **completion of the M6,** travelling by rail to Dublin is no longer more **time efficient or cheaper.** The reopening of **passenger services between Limerick and Galway** has become a more realistic option for commuters in the area, as it also **serves commuter towns** along the way. This can encourage shopper and tourist traffic to the region, as well as commuters.

The development of **freight lines** is seen as an important measure in **developing industrial links** between the region and the rest of the country. A freight line has been constructed between **Ballina** and the **Dublin** and **Waterford ports**. This line enables the **importing and exporting** of materials.

Southern line to Clare, Limerick, Waterford, Cork and Kerry

⌃ **Fig. 21.33** Rail links of the West (the green lines shows the proposed WRC)

A campaign organisation called **West=On=Track** was established in **2003** to petition for the reopening of the **Western Rail Corridor (WRC)**. The WRC is a freight line that is seen as having the **potential to develop economic activity** throughout the West region. The organisation's main belief is that more balanced infrastructural development between the east and West of the country will in turn lead to more evenly **balanced economic development**.

 GEO **DICTIONARY**

Commuter: a person who travels between home and work

Air

The IWA at Knock, Co. Mayo is the only **international airport** in the region, meaning that there is limited access to air travel. The IWA provides **access to business and tourist markets** in the UK and other EU cities. Since the opening of the airport at Knock in 1986, it has become an important transport link in the region. The airport has nearly **1 million arrival passengers** each year. It employs over 1000 people. The **Department of Finance** continues to **provide aid** for the development of the airport and will do so until **2023**. At that stage, it is hoped that the airport will have become **financially independent**.

⌃ **Fig. 21.34** Ireland West Airport at Knock

GEO DICTIONARY

Liquidation: when a company ceases trading and uses any remaining assets to pay debt or divide among its shareholders

In **2007, Galway Airport** was the **fastest-growing airport in Ireland** in terms of passenger numbers. The Government gave €6.3 million to aid development. However, the economic recession greatly affected the airport, leading to an **80 per cent reduction** in the number of passengers between 2007 and 2011. The airport **closed in November 2011** due to the liquidation of its main business partner, Aer Arann. Over **250 direct and indirect jobs** were lost as a result.

The airport reopened in **January 2015,** but only on a temporary basis for **freight.** It is unlikely that the airport will be used as a major passenger airport anytime in the future.

▲ **Fig. 21.35** Aerial view of Galway Harbour

Port

The West **lacks major cargo or passenger ports.** Galway has the only port capable of dealing with cargo, although it is too **outdated** to attract any major industrial traffic. It also **does not cater for international passenger services.** A new proposal to develop the port in Galway has been made, which would include the following:

- Harbour warehousing
- Coal yard
- Waste export
- Steel import yard
- Roll-on/roll-off yard
- Container yard
- Parklands
- Promenade

If this development is completed, it will provide more incentive for heavy industries to locate in areas surrounding the city.

EDUCATE YOURSELF

Transport	Movement of people and goods, roads main mode of transport, underdeveloped, roads are winding, loop around mountains, follow paths carved through mountains, road construction expensive, region mainly rural, central transport links difficult, public transport is impossible, low population densities, privately owned cars
Roads	Galway chosen as gateway, focus of transport development, connecting to Dublin, M6 motorway, Galway City centralised population, traffic congestion, delayed commuting times, lack of bypass or light rail, Galway City Bypass Project, unlikely to be built, upgrades to roads in surrounding towns, e.g. N17/N18, shorten travel times, high cost of travel, recession, withdrawal of funding
Railway	Declining numbers using rail, completion of M6 motorway, rail no longer time efficient, passenger service Limerick to Galway, serves commuter towns, freight lines encourage industrial links, Ballina to Dublin/Waterford port, importing/exporting goods, West=On=Track, Western Rail Corridor (WRC), potential to develop balanced economic activity
Air	IWA, international airport, access to business and tourist markets in UK/EU, 1 million arrival passengers per annum, Department of Finance provides aid, financially independent 2023, Galway Airport – 2007 fastest growing in Ireland, €6.3 million in aid, 2008 recession 80% reduction in passengers by 2011, closed November 2011, reopened January 2015, unlikely to carry passengers
Port	Galway, cargo port, no international passenger services, new port development, could attract heavy industry

ACTIVE **LEARNING**

1. How have the physical processes impacted on the development of transport links of the West region?

2. Name one major road link in the West and name the city it connects to.

3. Why is it not possible to develop cost-effective public transport in the West?

4. Why does traffic congestion occur in Galway City?

5. What measures have been taken to upgrade roads in the West?

6. Why has the number of people choosing to travel by rail declined?

7. What is the Western Rail Corridor?

8. What is the importance of an airport to the development of the West?

9. What facilities are proposed with the redevelopment of the port in Galway?

Tourism

Nearly **66 per cent** of people in the West region are employed in the **tertiary sector.** Most of this employment is **directly or indirectly** in the **tourism sector.** Tourism in the region has changed over the past two decades, with the development of **more widespread tourist facilities.** Hotels, guesthouses, B&Bs, youth hostels and spas/leisure centres have developed and modernised to give tourists more choice. Of the three counties, **Galway** receives the **majority of tourists,** due to its developed **transport links** and its reputation as a **cultural city.** Tourism in the West region can be divided broadly into four categories:

- Natural attractions
- Cultural attractions
- Religious pilgrimages
- Sporting occasions

Natural Attractions

The West has a reputation for having wild, **natural and unspoilt scenery.** The West's **coastline** has been **shaped by the Atlantic,** which has created **unique coastal landforms** such as the cliffs carved out along the edges of **Croaghaun Mountain in Co. Mayo. Surfing schools** have set up along many of the region's bays as surfers from all over the world are attracted by the large Atlantic waves. Tourists can travel the Wild Atlantic Way to explore the region's dramatic coastline.

⬆ **Fig. 21.36** Croaghaun Mountain, Achill Island, Co. Mayo

Connemara National Park covers 2957 hectares of scenic mountains, bogs, woodlands, heaths and grasslands. Four of the mountains in the park make up part of the famous Twelve Pins peaks. The park attracts a **wide range of tourists** with interests in activities such as hillwalking, photography, geology and horticulture.

The West markets itself to tourists as a region to be discovered or explored. Such initiatives include the **Great Western Greenway,** a former railway which was converted into a walking/cycling trail that runs along the coast between Westport and Achill Island. **Boating trips** are also offered along the River Shannon for tourists looking to experience its natural ecosystem.

⬆ **Fig. 21.37** Céide Fields coast road, Co. Mayo

▶ **Fig. 21.38** A traditional Irish cottage in Connemara, Co. Galway

Cultural Attractions

The region is home to the **largest Gaeltacht** in the country. **Each summer,** the Connemara Gaeltacht attracts over **20 000 students** to its Irish colleges. While there, students also take part in other traditional Irish activities such as céilís and storytelling.

GEO DICTIONARY

Megalithic tomb: a stone burial tomb, dating from prehistory

The **Céide Fields of Co. Mayo** are regarded as the bast-preserved Stone Age settlements in the world. At over **5000 years old** and covering 10 km², the fields are home to **megalithic tombs** and dwellings and offer tourists a chance to see how the country's first farmers lived.

The West is also home to a number of **heritage towns** such as **Westport in Co. Mayo,** which was built during the Georgian Period (1714–1830). **Strokestown** in Co. Roscommon is home to the **Famine Museum,** which attracts tourists from all over the world, especially Irish-Americans whose ancestors emigrated to the US during the Famine.

▲ **Fig. 21.39** Knock Shrine, Co. Mayo

GEO DICTIONARY

Marian Shrine: a shrine marking the spot where a person claims to have seen the Virgin Mary

Religious Pilgrimages

Knock in Co. Mayo is a major **Marian Shrine** which attracts **Catholic pilgrims** from all over the world. The shrine's popularity eventually led to the building of **Knock International Airport** (now Ireland West Airport, Knock) in 1985.

Croagh Patrick in Co. Mayo is referred to as 'Ireland's holiest mountain' and has been a place of worship for over 5000 years. Pilgrims believe that St Patrick stayed there for 40 days during his Lenten fast. On the last Sunday in July, thousands of people climb the mountain to mark their devotion to Ireland's patron saint.

Sporting Occasions

As well as **surfing,** the West has become popular for many other **water sports** such as cliff diving, kayaking, angling and triathlons.

Gaelforce West is a tough endurance race that attracts thousands of competitors each year. The **race** takes competitors along some of the region's best sights.

The region has many **outdoor adventure resorts** such as **Delphi Mountain Resort** and Petersburg Outdoor Activity Centre, both of which are in Co. Mayo.

The **Galway Races** attract tens of thousands over the week-long festival and generate over **€70 million annually** for the local economy. The **Volvo Ocean Race** has been held in Galway twice, attracting sailing enthusiasts from different countries.

There are several **golf courses** dotted along the coast of the West, which offer tourists the chance to play golf in the breezy Atlantic conditions.

Challenges Facing Tourism in the West

Despite the West's many attractions, tourism in is limited by a number of factors, including:

- Tourism in the West is **seasonal and peaks from June to September** and declines greatly throughout the winter and spring months. The only **exception is Galway,** which manages to attract **tourists throughout the year. Outside of Galway,** many facilities close during winter, meaning that **employment in the sector is part-time.** This particularly affects rural enterprises such as B&Bs and hillwalking.

- **Access** to the **Galway** has **improved** with the completion of the **M6 motorway, but other areas** remain **difficult to reach,** with long travel times. Most of Ireland's tourists fly into Dublin Airport and most often do not travel far outside the city. As a result, **less than 15 per cent** of tourists **travel to the West region.**

- Until as recently as 2005, **planes travelling from the US** to Dublin were required to **stop over at Shannon.** Due to Shannon's closeness to the West, many tourists travelled to the region. However, more fuel-efficient planes and an 'open skies' policy by the EU put an **end to stopovers** at the airport, leading to a **decline in tourists visiting the region.**

- Many European tourists prefer **to take city** or **weekend breaks,** which have **boosted tourism in Dublin** but has caused a **decline in the less** accessible West.

Solutions to Tourism Challenges

- **Discover Ireland** and **Fáilte Ireland** are tourist agencies set up by the government to **promote tourism in Irish regions.** Each agency runs **advertising campaigns** to highlight the unique experience each Irish region has to offer. For the West, both agencies have highlighted the **scenic attractions and adventure opportunities.**

- Despite the cutbacks to transport and tourism development due to the recession, the West was made **more accessible due to the completion of the M6 motorway.** In the past, **Shannon,** Dublin and Cork **airports** were run as a **single enterprise.** Shannon is now **independent, making it free to lobby for flight** and airline contracts. As a result, the **number of passengers** flying into Shannon has **risen by 8 per cent annually.**

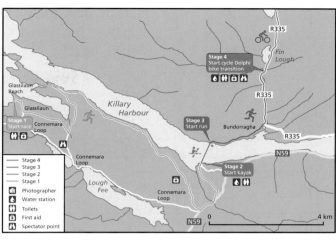

⌃ **Fig. 21.40** Gaelforce West race stages

ACTIVE LEARNING

1. Why would tourists wish to visit the West?

2. What factors prevent the further development of tourism in the West?

3. Describe the main challenges facing the development of tourism in the West.

4. Describe three potential solutions to the challenges facing tourism in the region.

FACT

The number of tourists visiting Ireland grew by 12.5% between 2014 and 2015.

- **Plans to develop Galway port** could attract European **cruise ships** to stop over. This would lead to a large increase in the number of tourists visiting the city.
- Apps and websites such as **booking.com** and **tripadvisor.com** allow small tourist businesses to advertise to a much wider market than they would normally have access to.

EDUCATE YOURSELF

Tourism	66% employed in tertiary sector, most directly or indirectly in tourism, more widespread tourist facilities, Galway attracts majority of tourists, transport links, cultural city
Natural attractions	Natural/unspoilt scenery, coastline shaped by Atlantic, unique coastal landforms, Croaghaun Mountain in Mayo, surfing schools, Connemara National Park, wide range of tourists, Great Western Greenway, boating trips
Cultural attractions	Largest Gaeltacht, 20 000 students each summer, Céide Fields, heritage towns, Westport, Strokestown, Famine Museum
Religious pilgrimages	Knock, Co. Mayo, Marian Shrine, Catholic pilgrimage, IWA, Croagh Patrick, Co. Mayo
Sporting occasions	Surfing, water sports, Gaelforce West, outdoor adventure centres, Delphi Mountain Resort, Galway Races (€70 million annually), Volvo Ocean Race, golf links courses
Challenges to tourism	Seasonal peaks (June–September), Galway an exception, outside of Galway employment is part-time, access to Galway improved (M6), other areas difficult to reach, less than 15% of tourists travel to West, planes travelling from US previously stopped at Shannon, end of stopovers led to decline in tourists, many tourists prefer city breaks, boosted tourism in Dublin, decline in less-accessible West
Solutions	Discover Ireland, Fáilte Ireland promote tourism in Irish regions, advertisement campaigns, scenic attractions and adventure opportunities, more accessible, M6, Shannon Airport now separated from Dublin and Cork airports, free to lobby for flights, number of passengers increasing by 8% annually, plans to develop Galway port, cruise ships, booking.com and tripadvisor.com

21.6 Human Processes

Human processes refer to the **behaviour of people** and **how they relate to their physical surroundings.** As you now know, the physical landscape of the West restricts economic development, which in turn affects human processes such as:

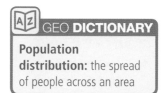

GEO DICTIONARY

Population distribution: the spread of people across an area

- Population change
- Population distribution and density
- Urban development

Population Change

The population of the West region has **changed greatly over time.** In 1841, before the **Great Famine,** there were **850 000 people living in the West region.** The majority of this population were **rural dwellers** and **subsistence farmers,** most of whom grew potatoes as their main food source. The Great Famine (1845–49) led to a **rapid decline in the population** as it affected the West of the country much more than the east.

GEO **NUMERACY**

Look at the table below. To calculate the percentage increase in population from 2006 to 2011:

- Subtract the 2006 figure from the 2011 figure:
  445 356 − 414 277 = 31 079

- So there was a 31 079 increase since 2006. In order to turn this into a percentage, divide the increase by the original number of people, i.e. the 2006 figure. We then multiply this answer by 100/1.

$$\frac{31\ 079}{414\ 277} \times \frac{100}{1} = 7.5\%$$

Therefore, there was a 7.5% increase between 2006 and 2011.

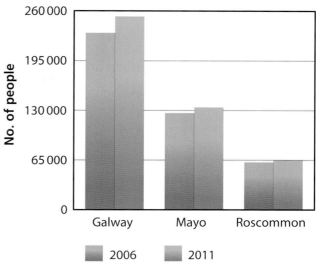

■ 2006   ■ 2011

⌃ **Fig. 21.41** Population growth of the West

County	2006	2008	Population Change	Percentage Change
Galway	231 670	250 653	18 983	8.2%
Mayo	123 839	130 638	6799	5.5%
Roscommon	58 768	64 065	5297	8.9%
Total	414 277	445 356	31 079	7.5%

GEO **DICTIONARY**

Vacancy rate: the percentage of houses that are not occupied in a region

Celtic Tiger: the name given to the period of economic boom in Ireland from 1995 to 2008

Census: an official count and survey of a population

After the Famine, **mass emigration continued** as younger people sought a better standard of living in Britain and the United States. **By 1971**, the population of the West region had fallen by **over half a million people** to 312 000.

Ireland **joined the EU in 1973,** which led to **population increase** for the first time since the Famine. Population declined once again in the **1980s** a **global recession** led to **206 000 people** leaving Ireland, many of whom were from the West. The economy recovered again in the 1990s in the **Celtic Tiger era,** in which the West's **population grew quickly.** The **2011 census** showed that the West's population had grown to **445 356** – over half of the pre-Famine population. Despite the economic recession that began in 2008, the population grew rapidly between the 2006 and 2011 censuses. However, the **population of the West is still susceptible to outward migration during an economic downturn.** In many parts of the West, there is a greater than **25 per cent vacancy rate of houses,** with west Mayo and Connemara the worst affected.

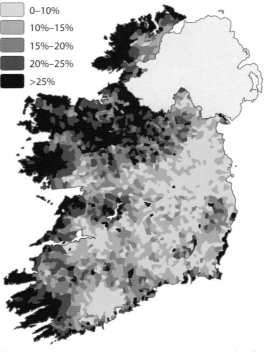

0–10%
10%–15%
15%–20%
20%–25%
>25%

⌃ **Fig. 21.42** Percentage of houses vacant in Ireland

CORE 3 CHAPTER 21

Population Density and Distribution

The **population distribution** of the West region is **not even,** as areas such as the **Connemara Mountains and West Mayo are sparsely populated.** Urban areas such as Galway City, Ballina and Castlebar are **more densely populated.** The **rough terrain** of Connemara and other parts of the West means that many areas are **unsuitable to build on,** while **poor peat and gley soils** have contributed to **farmland being abandoned.** This has led to a **population density** of **less than half** that of the **national average** (25 per km² compared to 66 per km²).

Rural depopulation has been an issue for the West since the Famine, with population densities now **as low as 3 per km²** in parts of Connemara. As **younger people (18–30) are more likely to migrate** from the region, the West is robbed of its future generations. This contributes to **low marriage and birth rates,** as well as a lack of **skills and talents.** This fact is proven by a number of statistics from the last census:

- Some **20.3% of all houses** in the West are **vacant.**
- Almost one in ten (9.8%) people in the West **live alone.**
- Some **26%** of the West's population is **over the age of 65.**
- The West has the **lowest number of primary schools** but also has **the lowest average student-to-teacher ratio.**

Despite ongoing rural depopulation, **urban areas** in the West have **shown strong growth,** e.g. Galway City, Westport and Ballina. This is mainly due to **foreign direct investment,** which has created employment, and **improved access to the region.**

Human Processes	
Population change	Changed greatly over time, before Great Famine 850 000 living in the West region, rural dwellers, subsistence farming, Famine – rapid decline in population, mass emigration continued after Famine, 1971 decline of over half a million, joined EU in 1973, population increase, 1980s – global recession, 206 000 emigrated, Celtic Tiger era, population grew quickly, 2011 census – 445 356, still susceptible to recession, rural-urban migration, 25% vacancy rate of houses
Population density	Population not even, Connemara Mountains and west Mayo sparsely populated, urban areas more densely populated, rough terrain unsuitable to build on, poor peat and gley soils, farmland abandoned, population density – less than half national, rural depopulation, density as low as 3 per km² in parts of Connemara, younger people (18–30) more likely to migrate, low marriage and birth rates, 20.3% of houses vacant, 9.8% live alone, 26% over the age of 65, lowest number of primary schools, lowest average student-to-teacher ratio, urban areas shown strong growth, e.g. Galway City, foreign direct investment, improved access to the region

Urban Development

Some **54.2%** of the West's population are **rural dwellers,** while nearly **65% of all houses in the West are detached.** With the **exception of** Galway City, **urban regions are small.** Outside of Galway, only **Ballina** and **Castlebar** have populations of more than **10 000,** while **Loughrea** and **Ballinasloe** have populations of **5000.**

Despite their small size, these urban areas **provide vital services** and income for their populations, e.g. market services. Towns such as **Tuam** and **Athenry** have **benefitted from their relatively close proximity to Galway City,** with companies and workers choosing to locate there. An example of this is the building of a **new Apple Inc. data centre** in **Athenry,** which will employ over 150 people and most likely attract further investment to the town.

Immigration has also led to **urban growth** in the West, with **11.5%** of the region's population being **foreign nationals.** For example, many Brazilians moved to **Gort** during the Celtic Tiger era.

FACT

The word 'boycott' originated in Ireland. In 1880, the inhabitants of Ballinrobe, Co. Mayo started a campaign against Charles Cunningham Boycott, a land agent who worked for Lord Erne. All local shops refused to serve him, and the boy who delivered his post was threatened.

CASE STUDY

Galway City

Galway is the **largest urban area** in the **West region,** and is the **fourth-largest** and **fastest-growing** city in **Ireland.** Galway is built on a flat site between the **banks of the River Corrib** and Galway Bay. Currently, the city's population is just over **75 000,** with significant growth occurring over the past number of years, despite the recession.

Origins

Galway's origins date back to **1124 CE,** when the O'Connor clan built **forts** there as they warred with the O'Flahertys. The city was **captured by the Normans** after a siege in **1240,** with the Norman Lord Richard de Burgo building a castle there. He also **built a wall around the city** to protect it from invasion. Over time, the city **grew as a merchant and port city** as trade developed with **France and Spain.**

The city was **under siege** once again between **1651 and 1652** by Oliver Cromwell's forces, which led to **widespread starvation and disease.** The city was eventually captured and the majority of the **ruling families had their wealth confiscated,** causing the city to go into decline.

Revival

The city briefly **recovered during the early nineteenth century** until the Famine. A **railway terminal** was **opened** which **connected the city to Dublin,** allowing for increased trade. The city also became a **nodal point on the River Corrib.** In **1845,** the university, now known as **NUIG, was built,** which **provided employment and education** for the region. As a result, the **population of the city increased.** As the **Famine** took hold, the city began to **decline** again.

Fig. 21.43 An aerial photograph of Galway City

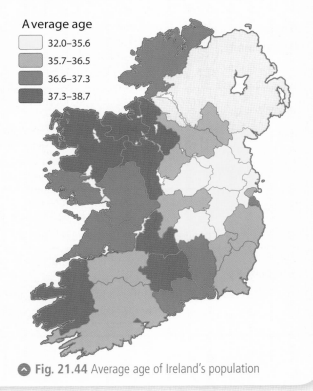

Average age

32.0–35.6
35.7–36.5
36.6–37.3
37.3–38.7

Fig. 21.44 Average age of Ireland's population

CORE 3 CHAPTER 21

Fig. 21.45 The Spanish Arch is a remnant of the original Norman wall that surrounded Galway City.

Fig. 21.46 Eyre Square after its redevelopment

20th Century Onwards

In **1911,** the **population** of Galway City had fallen to just **13 000.** It was not until the city's **manufacturing industries** began to develop that the **population began to grow again.** In the last number of decades, MNCs, such as **Medtronic and Boston Scientific,** have located in the city, along with other medical, IT and financial companies. The **IDA** played an important role in **attracting these industries,** as did the **skilled employment** and **research and development services** supplied by **NUIG.** The opening of the **M6 motorway** to Dublin has led to development due to **cheaper and faster transport** to the city. A significant amount of **urban redevelopment** has also occurred along **Eyre Square** and Shop Street. Galway has also developed into a **major tourist centre.** The city is now known as **Ireland's cultural heart,** with a variety of attractions such as:

- **Festivals**
- **Celebrations**
- **Music**
- **Film**

Galway City is currently ranked as the **14th best holiday destination in Europe.** As the population increases, the **city's limits have now sprawled** into the seaside town of **Salthill** and the **Claddagh.**

EDUCATE YOURSELF

Urban development	54.2% rural dwellers, 65% of all houses detached, except for Galway urban regions small, Ballina and Castlebar >10 000 people, Loughrea and Ballinasloe >5000, provide vital services, Tuam and Athenry benefitted from proximity to Galway, Apple Inc. data centre Athenry, immigration – urban growth, e.g. Gort, 11.5% foreign nationals in region
Galway	Largest urban area in West, fourth-largest and fastest-growing city in Ireland, banks of the Corrib, 75 000 people
Origins	1124 CE – fort, captured by Normans 1240 CE, built a wall around the city, grew as a merchant and port city, trade with France and Spain, under siege 1651–52, widespread starvation and disease, ruling families ruined
Revival	Revived during the early 19th century, railway terminal opened, connected the city to Dublin, nodal point on the River Corrib; 1845 NUIG built, provided employment and education, population of city increased, Famine led to decline
20th century	1911 population 13 000, manufacturing industries, population grew, MNCs Medtronic and Boston Scientific, IDA attracted further industry, skilled employment and R&D services, NUIG; M6 cheaper and faster transport, urban redevelopment Eyre Square, major tourist centre, Ireland's cultural heart, 14th best destination in Europe, city's limits have sprawled – Salthill and Claddagh

A long question on Irish Regional Geography has appeared every year on both the Higher Level and Ordinary Level papers, so it is vital that you practise answering exam questions on this topic. In this section, we will look at two question types:

- Drawing a map of the region

- An answer on human processes/population dynamics

Note!
The exam questions for this chapter are at the end of Chapter 22.

Map Skills

Each year, the Higher Level paper requires you to draw a map of a region you have studied. This question may ask you to draw an Irish, a European or a subcontinental region. Generally, students find Irish regions the most difficult to draw as they have a very indented coastline due to coastal processes. While there are many suggested tips on how to draw Ireland, the best advice is to practise!

Here we will focus on a question from the Higher Level 2007 Regional Geography section.

HIGHER LEVEL

EXAM QUESTION

Draw an outline map of Ireland. On it, show and name different examples of each of the following:

- Any one Irish region that you have studied

- One urban centre in the region

- One relief feature in the region

- One drainage feature in the region

2007 Q4A 20M

Marking Scheme
Map outline 4m
Region shown and named 2m + 2m
Urban centre shown and named 2m + 2m
Relief feature shown and named 2m + 2m
Drainage feature shown and named 2m + 2m

SAMPLE ANSWER

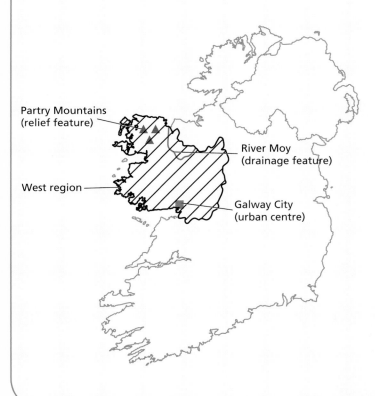

Partry Mountains (relief feature)

River Moy (drainage feature)

West region

Galway City (urban centre)

The outline of Ireland is a difficult one to draw due to its indented coastline, so it is very much a case of practice making perfect. First, draw a rectangle that is 10 cm across and 12 cm high. Then using this sketch as reference, measure Ireland from the peninsulas on the bottom left to the furthest headland on the top right. Then measure the peninsula to the left of the Partry Mountains across to Co. Dublin. By keeping these measurements in your mind, you will know if your sketch is in proportion. The outline of Ireland in your OS Map legend should help you with the overall shape.

Marks Awarded
Map outline 4m
Region shown and named 2m + 2m
Urban centre shown and named 2m + 2m
Relief feature shown and named 2m + 2m
Drainage feature shown and named 2m + 2m
Total 20/20

TOPIC MAP

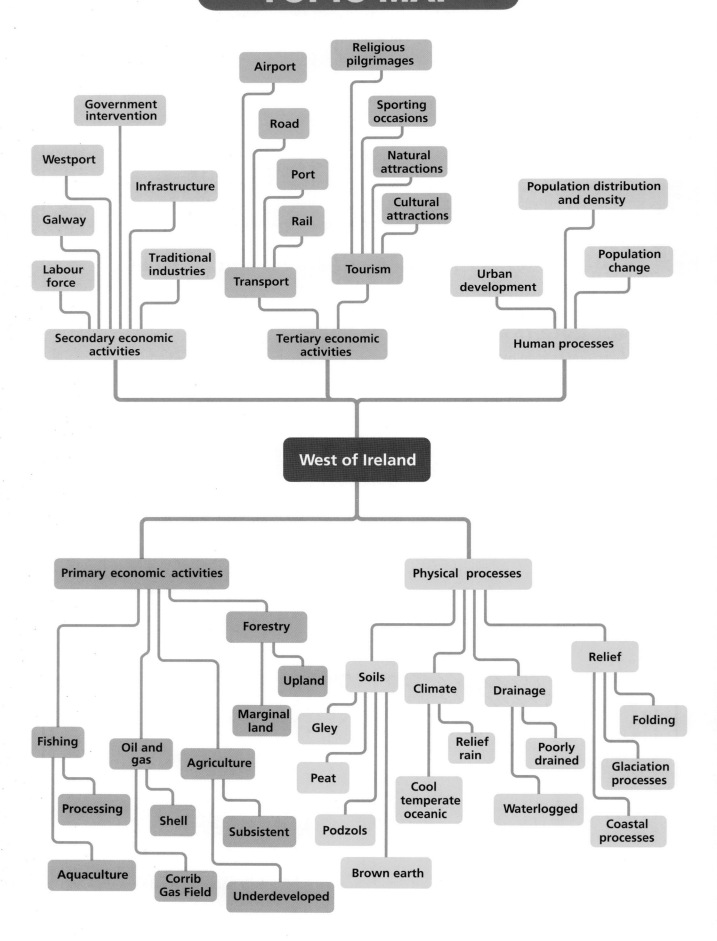

West of Ireland

Government intervention

Westport

Galway

Labour force

Infrastructure

Traditional industries

Secondary economic activities

Airport

Road

Port

Rail

Transport

Religious pilgrimages

Sporting occasions

Natural attractions

Cultural attractions

Tourism

Tertiary economic activities

Population distribution and density

Population change

Urban development

Human processes

Primary economic activities

Forestry

Upland

Soils

Climate

Drainage

Relief

Marginal land

Gley

Relief rain

Poorly drained

Folding

Fishing

Oil and gas

Agriculture

Peat

Cool temperate oceanic

Waterlogged

Glaciation processes

Processing

Shell

Subsistent

Podzols

Coastal processes

Aquaculture

Corrib Gas Field

Underdeveloped

Brown earth

Physical processes

CHAPTER 22

Irish Regions 2:
Core Socio-economic Region
(The Greater Dublin Area)

GDA
Dublin City
River Liffey
M50 motorway
Wicklow Mountains

In this chapter, we will look at the economic development of the Greater Dublin Area. Unlike the West region, the GDA is a highly developed core region. The GDA has a number of physical and social advantages that have aided its development.

KEY WORDS

- Primate city
- Undulating relief
- Brown earths
- Cool temperate oceanic climate
- Intensive agriculture
- Commercial
- Developed
- Industry
- Transport links
- Tourism
- Financial services
- Inward migration
- Rural-urban migration
- Urban sprawl

LEARNING OUTCOMES

What you MUST know
- Physical characteristics of the GDA
- Climate characteristics of the region
- How to draw the Irish map and fill in the main features of the GDA
- The development of primary, secondary and tertiary activities in the GDA
- Human processes of the region
- Urban development in the region

What you SHOULD know
- Intel and Pfizer CASE STUDIES
- Statistics that show contrast between regions

What is USEFUL to know
- How to understand information provided in graphs as a means to contrast regions

22.1 The Greater Dublin Area

The Greater Dublin Area is the **core socio-economic region** of Ireland and includes the counties of **Dublin, Meath, Kildare and Wicklow**. As of 2015, it is part of the new Eastern and Midlands Region, but remains a distinct region of its own due to its strong economy and favourable physical characteristics. It is the **wealthiest** and most **highly developed** region in the country. The region's economy is **centred in Dublin City**, which is the **primate city**. The GDA has Ireland's **highest population**

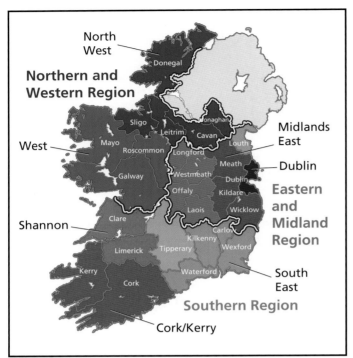

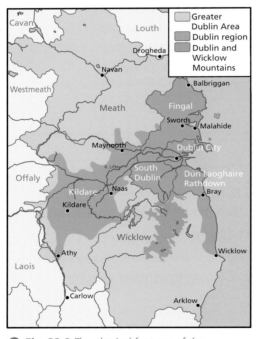

Fig. 22.1 The Regional Assemblies of Ireland

density, which **promotes employment** and a **higher standard of living** than in the rest of the country. As you study this chapter, pay particular attention to the contrast between the GDA and the West region.

Note!

Questions asking you to discuss contrasting regions are becoming much more frequent in the exam, so it is not enough to learn just one Irish region. You must know the characteristics of both **and** how they differ.

Fig. 22.2 The physical features of the Greater Dublin Area

22.2 Physical Processes

In this section, we will look at the following physical factors that influence the region:

- Relief and drainage
- Climate
- Soil

Relief and Drainage

The majority of the GDA consists of **undulating lowland relief.** The exceptions are the **Dublin and Wicklow Mountains** to the south, which formed during the **Caledonian folding period 400 million years ago.** The mountains provide **shelter to the southern section** of the region. Unlike the West, the region is not **severely indented by coastal processes** as the Irish Sea is sheltered, meaning its currents are much weaker than the Atlantic's. In some areas, **resistant metamorphic rock** forms **headlands,** e.g. **Wicklow Head.** In lowland coastal areas, deposition forms **beaches,** e.g. **Portmarnock.**

As **limestone** is the **main bedrock** of the region, **drainage is good.** The permeable limestone allows water to drain freely from the soil which prevents waterlogging during wetter months. The **Rivers Liffey,** Tolka, Vartry and Boyne drain the region before flowing into the Irish Sea.

Fig. 22.3 The Dublin and Wicklow Mountains

Climate

The GDA has a **cool temperate oceanic climate** similar to the rest of Ireland. However, due to the GDA's **distance from the Atlantic Ocean,** its climate differs from that of the West.

The GDA receives roughly **four hours of sunshine** per day compared to just 2.3 hours of sunshine in the West. Winter **temperatures average 5 °C,** which is **slightly colder than the average** winter temperatures of the West.

Summer temperatures are **slightly warmer** than in the West, **averaging 16 °C in July.** These differences are explained by the region's **distance from the moderating effect of the Atlantic Ocean.** During the winter, the Atlantic Ocean **loses heat slowly,** which has a **warming effect on the West.** The GDA is too far from the Atlantic to be affected by it, while the Irish Sea is too small to have a moderating effect.

Annual precipitation averages **750 mm,** which is less than half of the West region's average of 1500–2500 mm. The main reason for this difference is that the **West region is dominated by mountain ranges** along its coast. Moisture moving in from the Atlantic is forced upwards, leading to relief rainfall. As the **GDA is lowland** and on the **sheltered side of the West region's mountains,** it receives less rainfall. This is known as the **rain-shadow effect.** The position of the **Dublin and Wicklow Mountains** to the south **reduces** the **effect** of the **prevailing south-westerly winds.** As a result, the Dublin and Wicklow Mountains receive higher levels of relief rainfall. This further contributes the rain-shadow effect on the rest of the region.

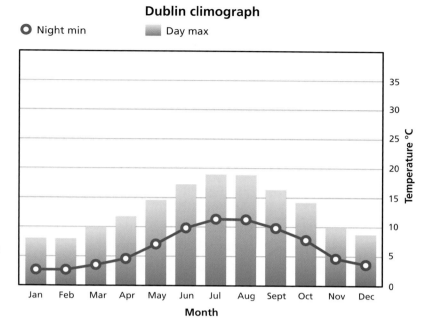

Dublin climograph

○ Night min　　▨ Day max

Fig. 22.4 Climograph of Dublin City

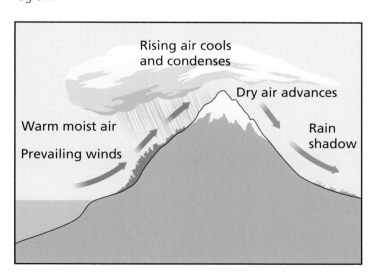

Rising air cools and condenses

Dry air advances

Warm moist air

Prevailing winds

Rain shadow

Fig. 22.5 The rain-shadow effect

Soil

The soil of the GDA is **typically fertile** as a result of the **thick deciduous forest** that once covered the region. **Brown earth soils** developed underneath these deciduous forests as **decaying leaves provided humus.** This humus built up over time to **form fertile soils. Alluvial deposits** from the region's main rivers have **developed productive soils** in areas such as the **Boyne Valley in Co. Meath,** which is one of the most fertile areas in Ireland. Marine deposition has led to the **formation of light sand soils** along **North Co. Dublin.** These soils are **free draining and fertile,** which has made them **suitable for market gardening and horticulture.** The underlying **limestone bedrock** along parts of Meath and Kildare have led to a **high calcium content** in their brown earth soils.

Along the south of the region, **infertile peat soils** have developed over the slopes of the **Dublin and Wicklow Mountains.**

Fig. 22.6 When deciduous leaves rot into the ground, they form humus, which leads to brown earths.

EDUCATE YOURSELF

	Physical Processes
Relief	Undulating lowland relief, Dublin and Wicklow Mountains, Caledonian mountains 400 mya, shelters southern section of region, coastline not severely indented by coastal processes, resistant metamorphic rock, e.g. Wicklow Head, beaches, e.g. Portmarnock, limestone bedrock, good drainage, River Liffey
Climate	Cool temperate oceanic, distance from the Atlantic, 4 hours of sunshine, winter temperatures 5 °C, slightly colder than average of West, summer slightly warmer, 16 °C in July, distance from moderating effect of Atlantic, loses heat slowly, warming effect on West but GDA too far away, annual precipitation 750 mm, West upland, GDA lowland, on sheltered side of Western mountains; rain-shadow effect, Dublin and Wicklow Mountains, reduce effect of prevailing south-westerly winds
Soil	Typically fertile, thick deciduous forest, brown earth soils, decaying leaves provide humus, forms fertile soils, alluvial deposits, productive soils, e.g. Boyne Valley, Co. Meath, formation of light sandy soils in North Co. Dublin, free draining and fertile, suitable for market gardening and horticulture, limestone bedrock, high calcium content, infertile peat soils along Dublin and Wicklow Mountains

 ACTIVE **LEARNING**

1. Describe the relief of the GDA.
2. Write a paragraph contrasting the climate of the GDA with the climate of the West region.
3. Explain how a rain-shadow effect reduces rainfall in the GDA.
4. Briefly explain how brown earths formed in the GDA and why this soil is so fertile.

22.3 Primary Activities

The GDA has a much **smaller percentage** of people **employed in the primary economic sector than the West does**. Despite this, activities such as **agriculture** are much **more productive** in the GDA due to a range of favourable conditions.

1. Agriculture

Characteristics

Only **3 per cent of people living in the GDA** make their living from agriculture. Despite this, agriculture in the region is **highly productive and specialised,** averaging **40 per cent higher incomes than the national average.** Unlike farming in the West, agriculture in the GDA is **commercial and intensive,** ensuring **high yields** and **maximum output.** The GDA also contains **50 per cent** of all the **country's greenhouses.** This has led to a thriving market-gardening sector in **Lusk,** North Co. Dublin.

Factors Affecting Agriculture in the GDA

Unlike the West region, where natural and social factors hinder agricultural development, the **physical and social advantages** of the GDA **aid its development.** Such factors include:

- Climate
- Relief
- Soil
- Markets

Factor 1: Climate

Climatic conditions **favour farming** in the region. Summers **average 16 °C,** which is warmer than in the West, while the region also receives nearly **two hours more sunshine each day.** This allows for **arable farming** such as wheat, barley and oats. Some **15 per cent of Ireland's wheat** is grown in the region. The warmer temperatures mean a **longer growing season** of 280 days. The long growing season is particularly **important for market gardening** and the growth of **potatoes; 20 per cent of the national potato crop** is produced here. The proximity to the **Irish Sea lowers** the risk of **severe frost,** which **reduces damage** to salad, flower and root crops.

Factor 2: Relief

The **lowland relief** of the GDA means that it is easily **accessible by machinery** leading to **high levels of modern mechanisation.** Due to its **accessibility,** all areas of land are **intensely farmed.** As a result of its lowland relief, the **region is not exposed,** meaning **soil temperatures are warmer,** which **promotes plant growth.** It also means **less soil erosion** occurs from wind or relief rain. The only exceptions are the **Dublin and Wicklow Mountains.** This area is **not suited to intensive agriculture.** Instead **sheep rearing** and **forestry** are carried out.

Fig. 22.7 Cheviot sheep grazing the Wicklow Mountains: the marks on their wool are so that farmers can distinguish their flocks from other flocks grazing the same mountain range.

Rainfall is low, averaging **750 mm** per year, and is distributed relatively **evenly throughout the year.** The dry weather **aids the ripening of wheat,** other arable crops and winter fodder for animals. The GDA is **not as damp** as the West, which **lowers the risk of crop diseases** such as **potato blight.**

Fig. 22.8 The drier, sunnier climate allows for the growth of arable crops.

Factor 3: Soils

The **highly fertile brown earths** allow for **intensive farming of arable crops** without making it less fertile. The soils are **stone-less and easily worked,** making them **less labour intensive.** The soils are **calcium rich,** which produce **rich grasses** that promote **healthy bone growth in animals.** This is one of the leading factors in the successful horse breeding in Co. Kildare.

Fig. 22.9 An aerial view of farms surrounding Dublin City, showing their proximity to markets

FACT

Tayto Crisps is a very successful business. It was started by John 'Spud' Murphy, with just £500. The company's mascot, Mr Tayto, released a fictional autobiography in 2009 entitled *The Man Inside The Jacket.*

Factor 4: Markets

The presence of **Dublin City** means the region has **easy access to a large urban market.** The **standard of living in the GDA is higher** than in the rest of the country, meaning there is more disposable income to spend on both **basic** and more **specialised foodstuffs.**

Transport links are **well developed,** which combined with the GDA's farms' proximity to the city, make **transport costs much lower** than in the West. Due to the commercial nature of farming in the region, problems such as **ageing farmers, land abandonment** and **outdated farm practices** are **not as much of an issue** as they are in the West. Instead **farmers** are **younger** than in the West, with an **age average of 37.**

Many farmers in the GDA are **highly educated** in both farm and business practices. They adopt a **market-oriented and scientific approach to farming.** The **subdivision of land that reduced farm size in the West did not occur in GDA.** As a result, **farm sizes are much larger** than those in the West, averaging **42 hectares.**

Food processing in the GDA is on a much **larger scale** than in the West. Companies such as **Largo Foods (Tayto)** buy **10 per cent of the national potato crop** and **Guinness** use local suppliers of **wheat and barley** for their manufacturing plants in the region.

Dublin City has a market of **1.2 million people.** A number of larger **satellite towns** which grew during the Celtic Tiger provide **other big markets for agricultural produce.**

EDUCATE YOURSELF

Agriculture	
Removal of natural resources, harvesting of raw materials, smaller percentage employed in primary sector than in West, primary activities in the GDA much more productive than in the West, 3% of GDA employed in agriculture, highly productive and specialised, 40% higher incomes than national average, commercial and intensive, high yields and maximum output, physical and social factor aid development	
Relief	Lowland relief, accessible by machinery, high levels of modern mechanisation, accessibility, all areas intensely farmed, region is not exposed, soil temperatures warmer, promotes plant growth, less soil erosion, exceptions Dublin and Wicklow Mountains – not suited to intensive agriculture, sheep rearing and forestry
Climate	Favour farming, averages 16 °C, two more hours sunshine per day, arable farming – wheat, barley and oats, 15% of Ireland's wheat grown in region; longer growing season, important for market gardening, early potatoes, 20% of national potato crop, Irish Sea reduces risk of severe frost, lessens damage to crops, GDA not as damp – lowers risk of diseases, e.g. blight
Soils	Highly fertile brown earths, intensive farming of arable crops, stone-less and easily worked, less labour intensive, calcium rich, rich grasses promote healthy animal bone growth
Markets	Access to a large urban market, standard of living higher, demand for basic and specialised foods, 50% of Ireland's greenhouses, thriving market-gardening sector in Lusk, transport links well developed, transport costs lower, ageing farmers, land abandonment and outdated practices not an issue; farmers young – average age 37, highly educated, market orientated and scientific approach; family enterprises – land not subdivided, farms larger (42 hectares) than in West, food processing larger scale than in West, Largo Foods (Tayto) –10% national potato crop, Guinness – wheat and barley; satellite towns provide other big markets

2. Forestry

Due to the **majority of land** being **highly productive** for agriculture, very **little forestry exists**. Compared to the West where forestry is planted on marginalised land to boost income, forestry in GDA is **limited to the Dublin and Wicklow Mountains**. The acidic **peat soils** of the mountains and **mild winters** promote the growth of **coniferous forests**. Many of these forests are used as parks rather than for timber production.

3. Fishing

Fishing was **once an important economic activity** in the GDA, but has **declined in recent decades**. Today, just **2 per cent of Ireland's total catch** is landed in the GDA. This is down from **35 per cent in 1960**. **Howth** is the **largest fishing port** in the GDA and the **sixth largest in Ireland**. Fishing declined in the region due to a **rapid decline in fish stocks** as a result of **overfishing**.

In an attempt to conserve fish in the Irish Sea, the **EU introduced quotas, fishing seasons** and **conservation areas**. These led to even **less fish being caught**. Upgrades to western ports meant the **GDA was unable to compete**. The **West region developed aquaculture** as a means of compensating for EU restrictions and depleting

ACTIVE LEARNING

1. How have physical factors affected the development of agriculture in the GDA?

2. 'The GDA has access to a larger local market than the West region does.' Describe the ways in which agriculture in the GDA has benefited from this.

⬆ **Fig. 22.10** Howth fishing port

fish stocks. This industry is **more limited in the GDA. The Irish Sea is more polluted** than the Atlantic Ocean, meaning **fish farming is not as productive.** This **pollution** also **affects shellfish farming.** This is of major concern to the **Dublin Bay** area, which produces **40 per cent of Ireland's exported prawns.**

 EDUCATE YOURSELF

Other Primary Activities	
Forestry	Majority of land highly productive, little forestry exists, limited to Dublin and Wicklow Mountains, mild winters, coniferous forestry
Fishing	Once an important economic activity, declined in recent decades, 2% Ireland's total catch, 35% in 1960, Howth largest fishing port, sixth largest in Ireland, rapid decline in fish stocks due to overfishing, EU quotas, fishing seasons and conservation areas, less fish being caught, upgrades to western seaports, GDA could not compete; West region developed aquaculture, more limited in GDA, Irish Sea more polluted, fish farming not as productive, pollution affecting shellfish farming, Dublin Bay – 40% of Ireland's exported prawns

ACTIVE **LEARNING**

1. Search online for 'Irish fishing quotas' and 'Dublin Bay prawns' for more information on the quotas and produce in Ireland's fishing industry .
2. Why was the fishing industry in the GDA unable to compete with the fishing industry of the West?

Why?

As the EU expands, companies might leave Ireland to set up in newly joined countries whose economies are not as developed. This occurs for a number of reasons such as access to cheaper materials and labour and EU incentives. An MNC's duty is to make profit, so it has no loyalty to a country. For example, Dell left Ireland in 2009 to avail of cheaper labour and materials in Poland.

It is important that the GDA develops home-grown industries, i.e. industries set up and developed in Ireland.

22.4 Secondary Activities

Manufacturing in the GDA is **highly developed** compared to in the peripheral West region. There are a number of **physical and social factors** that **have aided the development** of secondary activities. As a result, the region has modern and technologically advanced industries.

The GDA is Ireland's **largest and most developed manufacturing region. Some 25 per cent of all manufacturing plants** are located in the region, which employs **40 per cent of Ireland's industrial workforce.** The GDA's industry **grew rapidly in the 1990s** (during the Celtic Tiger), with **60 per cent of all new industry** locating in the region. A downside to this is that the region is now **heavily dependent on foreign direct investment (FDI)** and could suffer as a result of EU expansion.

This dependency was highlighted throughout the latest recession: **30 000 manufacturing jobs were lost in 2009** (one year after the recession began). A further **30 000 manufacturing jobs were lost in the region over the next four years** of recession before a slight recovery began. In 2013, FDI led to the creation of 13 000 jobs with the aid of state sponsorship.

Factors Influencing Manufacturing in the GDA

There are six main factors why companies choose to locate in the GDA:

1. Strong agricultural sector
2. Developed transport links
3. Well-serviced industrial estates
4. Educated workforce
5. Government intervention
6. Distribution of industry

Fig. 22.11 Locally grown barley is used to produce Guinness.

1. Strong Agricultural Sector

Due to a highly **intensive agricultural sector** in the region, there is a **large food processing industry. Much of the barley** grown in the region is used for the **brewing and distilling** industry in Dublin City by companies such as **Guinness,** and **protein-rich barley** is used for **animal feed.** North Dublin's **horticultural farms** produce **vegetables for Green Isle Foods. Kepak Group in Co. Meath** employs over **900 people** in its meat production plant, with much of **the beef, lamb and pork** produced supplied to the local Dublin City market of **1.2 million.**

2. Developed Transport Links

The GDA is a **major transport hub,** with all of Ireland's **major road and rail links** connected to Dublin City. This has made the GDA **attractive for companies** as it operates as a **centre for distribution** to the rest of the country. The GDA also has **Ireland's biggest port,** which attracts companies to **export their finished goods to the UK** and other larger **EU markets.** It also allows for easy **import of raw materials. Dublin Airport** has connections to hundreds of destinations all over the world, which attracts **footloose industries** such as **IT companies.**

Intel uses **Dublin Airport to export processor chips** to overseas markets. The building and completion of **Terminal 2** has seen an **increase in flights** and traffic passing through the region, which further promotes growth. **Motorways** now **link the GDA to all major cities** in Ireland, i.e. Cork, Limerick, Galway and Belfast, which allows for fast and efficient distribution of goods. For example, **Irish News Media** uses the **motorways** to **transport their newspapers** to the rest of the country.

> **GEO DICTIONARY**
>
> **Transport hub:** the focal point of roads and rail, which acts as a centre for distribution of goods and people
>
> **Footloose industry:** an industry that is not tied to a location because of a need for raw materials. They are free to locate in areas where there is a strong market, large labour pool or cheap assembly costs

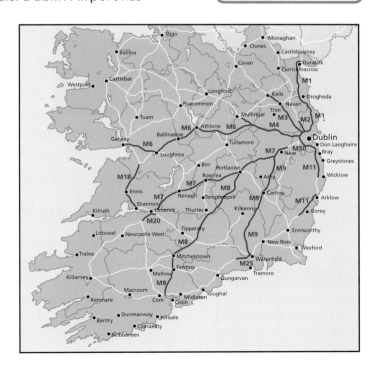

Fig. 22.12 All major motorways radiate from the GDA.

3. Well-serviced Industrial Estates

Previously, the GDA's **industries** were **located** near the centre of **Dublin City,** close to where workers lived. Over the past number of decades, industry has **moved to well-serviced industrial estates** on the **outskirts** of the city, e.g. **Sandyford, Coolock** and **Clondalkin.** These industrial estates are **linked to transport networks,** such as the **M50,** which **prevent** the need to bring **HGVs** through the **city centre.** The industrial estates are well **serviced with water, electricity** and **broadband,** which attracts industry.

'Forward factories' are also supplied, where companies can move into ready-to-use factories. Most of these **newly built industrial estates** are located in **West Dublin,** in towns such as **Tallaght.** Many of the people employed in these industrial estates live in the nearby suburbs.

4. Educated Workforce

Dublin has a **young, highly educated workforce** with skills that make them attractive for knowledge-based industries such as IT and medical supply companies. The GDA is the **focus of Irish education,** with **80 per cent of all college graduates** based here.

Trinity College Dublin, University College Dublin, Dublin City University, St Patrick's College, NUI Maynooth and several Institutes of Technology attract manufacturers of healthcare, software and biotechnology. These companies avail of **skilled graduates and R&D** to help with **innovation and product development. Some 45 per cent** of the region's workforce is **under the age of 25,** with **three of every four PhDs** in Ireland being awarded from the region's universities.

⌂ **Fig. 22.13** Trinity College Dublin

5. Government Intervention

The Irish government has also **attracted industry** to the region by offering several **incentives.** Possibly the biggest incentive is Ireland's **low corporation tax of 12.5 per cent,** which allows companies to keep a larger percentage of their profits. The **IDA** also provided **grants** to companies wishing to set up in the region. As a result the region now has:

- Five of the world's top-10 IT companies
- 10 of the world's top-10 ICT companies
- Nine of the world's top-10 software companies

6. Distribution of Industry

The **distribution of industry** in the GDA has **changed greatly over the past century.** The **oldest industries** in the region located **close to** Dublin's inner city, e.g. **Guinness,** textile, **food processing** and **printing companies.** As industry **modernised,** it **moved to industrial estates on the outskirts,** which had modern factories, cheaper land and **less traffic congestion.** During the Celtic Tiger era, over 900 MNCs set up in the region. These MNCs are from diverse areas, e.g:

- Medical/pharmaceutical industries such as Wyeth Pharmaceuticals, GlaxoSmithKline
- Knowledge-based industries such as Google

These **industries are widely dispersed,** with many located close to the M50, while others moved further from the city, e.g. Intel is based in Leixlip, Co. Kildare.

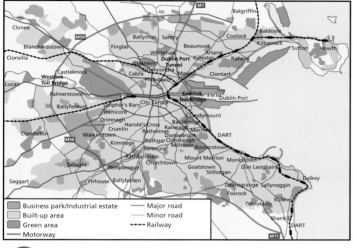

Business park/Industrial estate — Major road
Built-up area — Minor road
Green area ···· Railway
Motorway

ACTIVE LEARNING

1. Based on your knowledge of the factors which have led to the successful development of industry in the GDA, discuss which factors you think are vital to attract industry in other areas of Ireland.

2. Describe how the distribution of industry has changed over time and explain why industrial estates are attractive locations for industries.

3. Discuss how education and a large labour pool have influenced the development of industry in the GDA.

4. Carry out a quick survey. How many of your classmates are considering attending a college or university in Dublin?

Fig. 22.14 Distribution of industry around Dublin City

EDUCATE YOURSELF

Factors Influencing Manufacturing in the GDA	
Processing of raw materials, highly developed, physical and social factors have aided development, largest and most developed manufacturing region, 25% of all manufacturing plants, 40% of Ireland's industrial workforce, grew rapidly in 1990s, 60% of all new industry locate here, heavily dependent on FDI	
Strong agricultural sector	Intensive agricultural sector, large food processing industry, brewing and distilling, barley – brewing and distilling, Guinness; protein-rich barley for animal feed; horticultural farms, vegetables for Green Isle Foods, Kepak Group in Co. Meath, 900 people process beef, lamb and pork, Dublin City market of 1.2 million
Developed transport links	Major transport hub, major road and rail links, attractive for companies, centre for distribution, Ireland's biggest port, export finished goods to the UK and EU markets, import of raw materials, Dublin Airport attracts footloose industries and IT companies, Intel uses Dublin Airport to export processor chips; Terminal 2 increase in flights, motorways link GDA to all major cities, Irish News Media uses motorways to transport papers
Well-serviced industrial estates	Previously industries located in Dublin City Centre, moved into well-serviced industrial estates on outskirts, e.g. Sandyford, Coolock, Clondalkin, linked to transport networks – M50 prevents HGVs going through city centre, industrial estates – serviced with water, electricity and broadband, forward factories, newly built industrial estates in West Dublin, e.g. Tallaght
Educated workforce	Young and highly educated workforce, focus of Irish education, 80% of all college places, skilled graduates and R&D, 45% under the age of 25, 3/4 of all PhDs awarded here
Government intervention	Attracted industry, incentives, low corporation tax of 12.5%, IDA grants aid, 5/10 top IT companies, 10/10 top ICT companies, 9/10 top software companies
Distribution of industry	Changed over past century, oldest industries closest to inner city, e.g. Guinness, food processing and printing companies, moved to urban fringes, modern factories, cheaper land and less traffic congestion, medical/pharmaceutical industries e.g. Wyeth Pharmaceuticals, knowledge-based industry, e.g. Google, industries widely dispersed

Fig. 22.15 Intel Campus in Leixlip, Co. Kildare

Intel

Intel produces **microprocessors,** which are the **'brain' of a computer** and are needed for all computer functions. The company moved to Ireland in **1989,** where they converted a **360-acre site** in Leixlip, Co. Kildare into a **€12.5 billion technologically advanced manufacturing plant.** The site at **Collinstown Industrial Park** employs **4500 workers,** most of whom have a **third-level degree.**

Intel is **closely linked to UCD and TCD** and sponsors many masters programmes. In March **2014,** Intel announced a **€5 billion campus upgrade,** which will provide **further employment** opportunities. As with all companies who locate in Ireland, Intel benefits from our **12.5 per cent corporation tax,** which is much lower than our European counterparts, e.g. Great Britain has a 28 per cent corporation tax. In 2016, Intel announced that it would be reducing its global workforce by 12 000 (11 per cent of its total). Some 10 per cent of these jobs are to be cut in Ireland.

Pfizer

Pfizer is a **biotechnology company** that produces **medicines and vaccines.** Located in **Grange Castle,** Clondalkin, the company employs more than **1200 people** in the GDA, **97 per cent** of whom **have a third-level degree.** In 2012, the company invested **€145 million,** which generated **400 new jobs.** It is now one of the **largest biotechnological manufacturing plants** in the world.

Pfizer produces:

- **Prevnar 13:** a vaccine which is used to treat childhood viruses

- **Enbrel:** a treatment for rheumatoid arthritis

Fig. 22.16 Pfizer Campus at Grange Castle, Co. Dublin

22.5 Tertiary Activities

In the GDA, **80 per cent of workeers are employed in the tertiary sector,** which is more than elsewhere in the country. In this section, we will look at the development of:

- Transport
- Tourism
- Financial services

Transport

As the GDA is the **core economic region of the country,** it is the **focal point of all road and rail links.** All motorways (**M1–M11**) **connect to the GDA,** meaning it is **linked to all other major urban areas** in Ireland. The **M50** motorway runs in a **semicircle around the city** and connects to a major national routes.

The **transport infrastructure of the GDA** has **benefitted** greatly from the **Government's National Development Plan** (NDP). Until the early 2000s, Dublin City's **transport infrastructure was poor and undeveloped.** The **economic boom** of the Celtic Tiger led to a **significant increase in car usage** in and around the city. As the region's **roads were not designed to cater for such large volumes of traffic, congestion** became a **major issue.** With average speeds through the city dropping from **22 km/h in 1991** to **14 km/h by 1997,** the Government decided to invest in the **development** of a **modern public transport system.** Improvements included:

- **The DART commuter rail line** was expanded to **increase services and upgrade trains** and carriages.
- **Intercity train services** were improved.
- **Two Luas tram lines** were built to connect Dublin's suburbs to the city centre.
- The **M50** was upgraded to a **six-lane motorway** with an **automated toll bridge** to aid traffic flow.
- **The Port Tunnel** was completed and connected to the **M50,** meaning **HGVs** no longer have to pass through the city.
- **Quality bus corridors** (QBCs) were introduced, which have reduced travel times on **Dublin Bus.** Dublin Bus now carries **120 million passengers per year,** although numbers are falling due to the **increasing popularity of the Luas.**

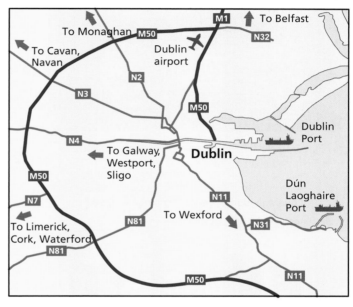

● **Fig. 22.17** Dublin is the focal point of all transport in Ireland.

GEO DICTIONARY

Quality bus corridors: lanes of roads used exclusively by buses and taxis, which allow quick and congestion-free travel around the city

● **Fig. 22.18** QBCs make public transport a more attractive option.

- The city's **12 000 taxis** can also use the **QBCs,** which has led to faster commutes and lower fares.
- A successful **bike sharing scheme** was developed in Dublin. Each bike is used an average of 10 times per day.

Despite the improvements, **travel speeds** through Dublin dropped to just **8 km/h in 2015.** This is due to the fact that **90 per cent of commercial transport** in Ireland is still carried out on roads, while increasing **rural-urban migration** means that the number of cars commuting to and from the city will continue to increase.

Dublin Airport handles over **21 million passengers per year** and operates over 160 routes with 57 airlines now flying from there.

⌃ **Fig. 22.19** Dublin's bike sharing scheme has over 100 stations dotted across city.

(a)
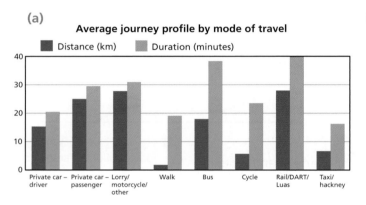

(b)
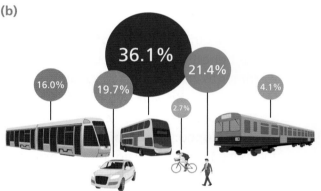

⌃ **22.20** (a) The average distance:time ratio by different mode of transport across Dublin (b) the popularity of different modes of transport in Dublin

Tourism

The GDA receives **more tourists than any other region in Ireland.** The region has benefitted from being the **main point of entry into the country,** with **90 per cent of all scheduled flights** landing in Dublin Airport. In 2015, Dublin Airport carried **21 million passengers,** earning **€7.6 billion** for the GDA region.

Unlike the West, the GDA has **year-round tourism.** Over **6 million domestic tourists** visit the region each year, meaning that it **does not rely solely on visitors** from outside the country. **Tourism** in the region, **declined** greatly during the **global recession** which began in 2008. As families throughout the EU had less money, tourists looked for better value when choosing their holiday destinations. As Ireland is the **fifth most expensive EU state to live in,** the number of **overseas tourists declined** rapidly. However, as the economy recovers, tourist numbers are **increasing once again.** In **2014,** Dublin City had **occupancy rates of 80 per cent,** the highest since 2007.

The GDA offers a **wide range of tourist attractions,** which has led to the industry thriving in the region.

- Kildare attracts **sport and recreation** tourists who visit for horse racing at the **Curragh** and golf in the **K Club,** which hosted the Ryder Cup in 2006.

- **Newgrange** in Co. Meath attracts tourists interested in **history and archaeology.**

- Wicklow attracts tourists interested in **natural beauty** due to its mountainous and glaciated landscape, e.g. **Powerscourt** and **Glendalough.**

⌃ **Fig. 22.21** Newgrange, Co. Meath

- Dublin offers the perfect **city break** with tourists attracted to the Guinness Brewery (>1 million visitors per year), Dublin Zoo (950 000 visitors), Dublin Castle (170 000 visitors) and National Gallery (590 000 visitors).

Financial Services

The **International Financial Services Centre** (IFSC) is located in **Dublin's North inner city** on the former docklands. This is home to the **headquarters of Ireland's main banks.** The IFSC deals with **international trade of finance.** The IFSC was set up in 1987 to **boost investment and employment** in the Irish economy. The Government established a special **10 per cent corporation tax** for companies which **set up in the IFSC.** This special rate ended in 2002 but by then it had already attracted many companies.

The IFSC has been a major success in **reversing the emigration and unemployment of the 1980s.** Many graduates from the GDA's colleges and universities could find employment with the **international companies** in the IFSC. Today, the IFSC **employs over 35 000 people** and pays approximately **€1 billion in corporation tax** and a further **€1 billion** through **tax on employees' wages.**

Some 450 international companies have offices in the IFSC, including 25 of the world's top-50 banks. Half of the world's **top-20 insurance companies** also have offices there.

⌃ **Fig. 22.22** The IFSC

EDUCATE YOURSELF

Tertiary Activities	
GDA 80% employed in the tertiary sector	
Transport	Core economic region of the country, focal point of all road and rail links, M1–M11 connect to the GDA, linked to all other major urban areas, M50 semicircle around the city, transport infrastructure of the GDA benefitted from NDP, transport infrastructure was poor and undeveloped, economic boom, increased car ownership, roads unable to cope with traffic volume, congestion became a major issue, speeds of 22 km/h in 1991 and 14 km/h in 1997, investment in development of modern transport system, DART commuter rail line, Luas tram lines, M50 six-lane motorway around Dublin, Port Tunnel, QBCs, Dublin Bus 120 million passengers a year, 12 000 taxis access to QBCs, bike-sharing scheme, 2015 travel speed of 8 km/h, 90% of commercial traffic by road, rural-urban migration, Dublin Airport 21 million passengers per year
Tourism	More tourists than any other region in Ireland, main point of entry into the country, 90% of all scheduled flights, 21 million passengers, €7.6 billion per annum, year-round tourism, 6 million domestic tourists, does not rely solely on overseas visitors, global recession, fifth most expensive state to live in, overseas tourism declined, increasing once again, 2014 80% occupancy rates, wide range of tourist attractions, sport and recreation, e.g. Curragh and K Club; history and archaeology, e.g. Newgrange; natural beauty, e.g. Powerscourt and Glendalough, Dublin city break
Financial services	IFSC, Dublin's north inner city, headquarters of Ireland's main banks, international trade of finance, boost investment and employment, 10% corporation tax for businesses setting up in IFSC, reversed emigration and unemployment of 1980s, attracted international companies, employs 35 000 people, €1 billion in corporation tax, €1 billion in tax on wages, 25/50 world's top banks located here, half of world's top 20 insurance companies

 ACTIVE **LEARNING**

1. Describe the measures taken to develop and modernise the transport network of the GDA region.
2. Why has the average travelling speed through Dublin continued to decline?
3. Explain why the GDA receives the majority of tourists visiting Ireland.
4. What attractions are available in the region?
5. Describe the important role played by the IFSC in providing employment and attracting international companies to the region.

22.6 Human Processes

Roughly **1.8 million** people live in GDA, which is **40 per cent of the country's population. Since 1946,** the region's **population has doubled** due to high levels of **inward migration** from **other parts of Ireland,** especially from the peripheral region of the West. **Most growth** in the region took place from the **1960s onwards** as Ireland's economy developed, leading to **increased employment** in the region.

Population Change and Distribution

In the 1960s, Dublin City was relatively small, with most of the **population living close to the city centre.** Population distribution changed as **inner city residential areas** were **replaced by newer housing** on the **urban fringes** of the city, in regions such as **Ballymun** and Tallaght. As the city was

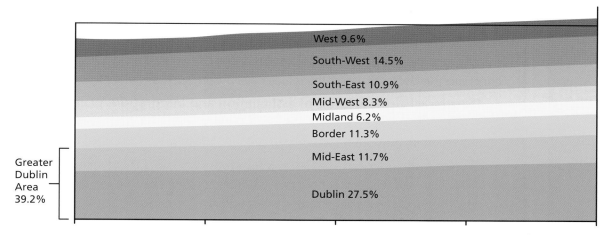

West 9.6%

South-West 14.5%

South-East 10.9%

Mid-West 8.3%

Midland 6.2%

Border 11.3%

Mid-East 11.7%

Greater Dublin Area 39.2%

Dublin 27.5%

⌃ **Fig. 22.23** Population distribution in Ireland

prevented from growing eastward by the Irish Sea and **southward by the Dublin Mountains**, the city **sprawled westward**, transforming villages and small towns into **large, urbanised commuter towns**. Examples of these transformed areas include **Tallaght**, Lucan, Clondalkin and **Blanchardstown**, which have a combined population of over **200 000**.

Inward Migration

Due to its **higher levels of employment** and **better education opportunities**, the GDA has always **attracted migrants** from **other parts of the country**. Today, **33 per cent of the GDA's population** was **born outside the region** (in other parts of Ireland or in other countries). Areas such as **nursing, teaching and the civil service** have attracted young, educated workers from all over Ireland. The **IFSC has also attracted workers** to the private sector, where **wages are 10 per cent higher** than in other regions in the country.

Dublin is now a **multicultural city** with **people born outside Ireland accounting for 8 per cent** of its **population**. This has introduced a wide range of **cultures**,

⌄ **Fig. 22.24** Predicted population growth of Dublin in comparison to other parts of Ireland

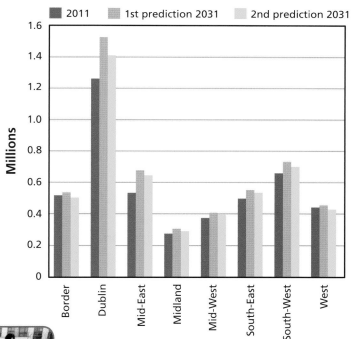

■ 2011   ▨ 1st prediction 2031   □ 2nd prediction 2031

Millions

◄ **Fig. 22.25** Cultural diversity can be seen in schools.

GEO **DICTIONARY**

Assimilation: when migrants take on the customs, attitudes of the country they have moved to. Many migrants are unable to assimilate, which leads to segregation or division within areas of a city

Integration: as assimilation is the adoption of the new country's values, some would argue against it, preferring instead integration, which is coming together without loss of identity

FACT

Italian and Chinese migrants settled areas in New York City, creating Little Italy and Chinatown in New York. These originated due to a lack of integration of immigrants.

Dublin now has its own Chinatown!

languages, religions and **foods.** Evidence of this can be seen from the **large range of ethnic shops, restaurants** and **religious buildings** in the city, e.g. the **mosque at Clonskeagh** is one of two in the city. Despite enriching the city's culture, some issues have arisen, such as:

- There have been **low levels of assimilation and integration.** While some immigrants have assimilated into parts of the city, many live in groups away from the native Irish population.

- For older immigrants, there are often **language barriers** that make it difficult to gain employment. While younger children are able to learn English quickly, older generations often find it more difficult.

- Many **foreign nationals gain employment** in retail, construction, tourism and catering industries, which are **prone to job losses.** This was seen in 2008, when the recession led to a large number of the then-**150 000 foreign nationals** in the city returning to their native countries.

 EDUCATE YOURSELF

Human Processes	
Population	1.8 million people, 40% of the country's population, since 1946 population has doubled, inward migration from other parts of Ireland, e.g. the West, most growth 1960s onwards, increased employment in the region, 1960s population living close to city centre, inner residential areas replaced by newer housing urban fringes, e.g. Ballymun, forced to sprawl westward, large urbanised commuter towns, e.g Tallaght, Blanchardstown, Lucan and Clondalkin – 200 000 people
Inward migration	Higher levels of development, better education opportunities, attracted migrants from other parts of the country, 33% of GDA's population born outside of the region, nursing, teaching and civil service attract young workers, IFSC attracted workers – wages 10% higher than national average, multicultural city, foreign nationals make up 8% of region's population, wide range of cultures, languages, religions and foods, ethnic shops, restaurants and religious buildings, e.g. mosque at Clonskeagh, low levels of assimilation, language barriers, many foreign nationals gain employment in areas prone to job losses, 150 000 migrants in city

ACTIVE **LEARNING**

1. Why does the GDA experience large levels of inward migration?
2. What barriers prevent integration of migrants into Dublin City?
3. What suggestions could you make to increase integration of migrants into Dublin City?
4. The Syrian civil war and Paris and Brussels terror attacks have led to a lot of media coverage regarding the 'why we should' and 'why we should not' welcome refugees. This has also led to some ill feeling about immigration. Do you think large-scale immigration causes problems or is the media scaremongering?

Urban Development: Dublin City

Dublin is the **primate city of Ireland. Its population has continued to rise** as inward migration to the region continues. Including its suburbs, **the city** now has a population of over **1.1 million people**, totalling **61 per cent of the GDA's total population.**

Origins

Dublin's **growth** has taken place **over many centuries.** Originally developing as a Viking trading town (*Dubh Linn* meaning 'black pool'), the city **expanded during Norman times** as its walls ran between Dublin Castle and the Liberties, south of the Liffey. Dublin was very important to the English rulers in Ireland as it was the **centre of all Irish trade** and was made Ireland's capital. The colony was **ruled from Dublin Castle** with **major landmarks** such as the **GPO** and the **Four Courts** being built during the colonial era.

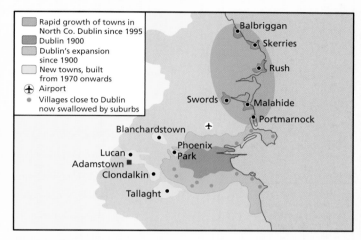

Key:
- Rapid growth of towns in North Co. Dublin since 1995
- Dublin 1900
- Dublin's expansion since 1900
- New towns, built from 1970 onwards
- ✈ Airport
- ● Villages close to Dublin now swallowed by suburbs

Balbriggan, Skerries, Rush, Swords, Malahide, Portmarnock, Blanchardstown, Phoenix Park, Lucan, Adamstown, Clondalkin, Tallaght

Fig. 22.26 Growth of Dublin over time

Eighteenth and Nineteenth Centuries

During the **eighteenth century,** trade links were developed by creating the **Grand Canal and Royal Canal** and the **construction of the Bull Wall and the South Wall** to shelter Dublin Port. **Textile and brewing industries** thrived in the old part of the city, the Liberties. As the **seat of the Irish parliament,** Dublin developed as the **political centre** of the country.

In **1800,** the **Act of Union abolished** the Irish parliament, leading to a **decline of the inner city** as the wealthy began to move away from the city centre. **During and after the Famine, rural-urban migration** saw large amounts of **poorer people migrate** to the **inner city.**

During this time, Dublin also became the **hub of all road and rail routes** as it became the most important port for **supplying Britain's markets.**

Twentieth Century

By the beginning of the twentieth century, the inner city slums were considered among the worst in the world. The life expectancy in Ireland at the time was just 56 years for both males and females. From the **1960s onwards, improved technology** such as **containers and roll-on/roll-off vehicles** have caused **large-scale unemployment in Dublin Port** leading to **inner city decline.** This decline resulted in a **high rise in crime** and drug use in Dublin's **inner city.** The Dublin council devised a plan to **rehouse many inner city residents in Ballymun. Badly built apartment blocks,** a **lack of services** and a **high dropout rate from schools** increased levels of **crime and poverty** in Ballymun and throughout the city. These also contributed to the city's growing drug problem.

A Z GEO DICTIONARY

Colony: a country or region under political control of a different country

Seat of parliament: where government ministers meet to discuss the politics of the country

Act of Union: an act introduced by the British government in 1800 in response to the 1798 rebellion. It shut down the Irish parliament. From then on, Irish MPs would have to travel to Westminster. Ireland officially became part of the United Kingdom of Great Britain and Ireland

Abolish: to put an end to

Life expectancy: the average amount of time a person is expected to live

CORE 3   CHAPTER 22

Fig. 22.27 Greater Dublin Area development

Manufacturing industry developed along what is now the M50. This led to further **inward migration,** leading to **rapid urban sprawl** as the **suburbs expanded** into the countryside.

Small villages to the west of the city were transformed into **new satellite towns,** e.g. Tallaght. These villages began to grow to accommodate the increasing population. With the development of satellite towns, people began to **commute to and from the city centre.** Improvements to transport systems such as the **Luas** and the introduction of **quality bus corridors** have been added to the city's infrastructure to ease traffic congestion.

Urban Regeneration and Development

Poorer people tended to live in poorer quality housing in the city centre, where rents were cheaper. This led to **social stratification** as the city's housing became divided according to wealth. The Government decided to **renovate Dublin's inner city** during the 1980s and 1990s. This is known as urban regeneration. **Dublin's Docklands** and the **IFSC were redeveloped.** More recent developments include the **Convention Centre** and the **3 Arena. Ballymun** was **redeveloped** with **modern housing, shopping centres, offices, community centres, schools** and other public amenities being built.

Fig. 22.28 The disastrous-high rise accommodation of Ballymun before redevelopment

(a)

(b)

Fig. 22.29 Dublin Docklands (a) before and (b) after regeneration

Celtic Tiger and Beyond

During the 1990s, the **demand for housing** saw increasing **urban sprawl,** as more residential areas were built beyond Tallaght and other satellite towns. This **urban sprawl broke the county's limit,** with Maynooth and Leixlip in Co. Kildare experiencing rapid growth. The Celtic Tiger led to **increased car ownership,** as the **cost of city housing** forced people to **commute from counties surrounding the city,** e.g. Meath, Kildare and Wicklow.

In order to control the growth of Dublin, the **Local Government Act** was established in 1993. **Three more councils – Dún Laoghaire-Rathdown, Fingal and South Dublin** – were created to provide more efficient waste, water, sewage and other public services.

However, **poorly planned housing** led to uncontrolled urban sprawl continuing. With the collapse of the housing market in 2008, many housing estates were left unfinished as **'ghost estates'.** Due to the halt in housing construction since 2008, there is now a **housing shortage** in Dublin which has greatly **increased rent and house prices** across the city.

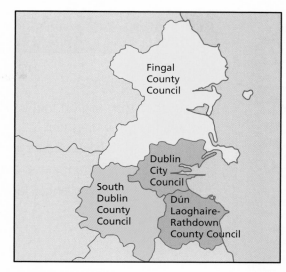

Fig. 22.30 Dublin is divided into four separate councils, which are in charge of managing the provision of services.

EDUCATE YOURSELF

Urban Development: Dublin City	
Primate city of Ireland, population has continued to rise, 1.1 million people in city, 61% GDA's total population	
Origins	Growth over many centuries, expanded during Norman times, centre of all trade for English in Ireland, ruled from Dublin Castle, landmarks GPO and Four Courts built during colonial era
18th and 19th centuries	Trade links developed, Grand Canal and Royal Canal, textile and brewing industries, seat of parliament, political centre, 1800 Act of Union abolished parliament, decline of inner city, during/after Famine rural-urban migration, poorer people migrated to inner city, hub of all road and rail routes, supplying Britain's markets
20th century	1960s onwards improved technology in docks (containers and roll-on/roll-off vehicles), large-scale unemployment, inner city decline, high rise in crime, rehoused inner city residents in Ballymun, badly built apartment blocks, lack of services, high dropout rates from schools, increased crime and poverty, manufacturing developed along M50, inward migration and urban sprawl, suburbs expanded, new satellite towns, e.g. Tallaght, commute to and from city, Luas and QBCs
Urban regeneration and redevelopment	Social stratification, renovate Dublin's inner city, Dublin Docklands redeveloped, IFSC, Convention Centre and 3 Arena, urban redevelopment Ballymun, modern housing, shopping centres, offices and schools, increasing demand for housing, urban sprawl into other counties, increased car ownership, increasing cost of city housing, commute from surrounding counties, e.g. Meath, Local Government Act – three more councils, poorly planned housing, 'ghost estates', housing shortage, increased rent prices

ACTIVE LEARNING

1. Explain why some parts of Dublin experienced increased levels of poverty, unemployment and crime.

2. What measures were taken to address the problems of Dublin City?

3. Search for 'ten steps to solving Dublin's housing crisis' on **www.independent.ie** to read a guide to solving the housing crisis in Dublin. Can you think of any more suggestions?

Note!
These exam questions cover Chapters 21 and 22.

LONG QUESTIONS

1. Name one **Irish region** that you have studied and answer each of the following questions.
   - (i) Name **two** types of agriculture practised in the region.
   - (ii) Explain the advantages that this region has for the development of agriculture.
   - (iii) Describe the challenges faced by agriculture in this region.

Region named 3m
Description/Explanation 9 SRPs @ 3m each

   2014 Q6B 30M

2. (i) Describe the advantages of European Union expansion for Ireland.
   (ii) Describe the disadvantages of European Union expansion for Ireland.

(i)	At least one advantage named 2m
	Advantages explained 6 SRPs @ 3m each
(ii)	At least one disadvantage named 2m
	Disadvantages explained 6 SRPs @ 3m each

   2013 Q4B 40M

3. Name an **Irish region** you have studied and explain any two of the following:
   - The reasons why **tourists** are attracted to this region
   - The type of **farming** practised in this region
   - The importance of **transport** in this region

Region named 1m
Activity 1 explained 7 SRPs @ 3m each
Activity 2 explained 6 SRPs @ 3m each

   2011 Q4B 40M

4. Explain how any **two** of the following influence the development of agriculture in an **Irish region** you have studied:
   - Relief and soils
   - Climate
   - EU policies
   - Markets

   Clearly state the name of the region in your answer.

Irish region named 4m
Factor 1 explained 6 SRPs @ 3m each
Factor 2 explained 6 SRPs @ 3m each

   2010 Q4B 40M

5. Discuss how any **two** of the following factors influence the development of manufacturing industry in an **Irish region** that you have studied:
   - Availability of transport networks
   - Access to raw materials
   - Markets
   - Government and European Union policies

Region named 1m
Factor 1 explained 7 SRPs @ 3m each
Factor 2 explained 6 SRPs @ 3m each

   2015 Q5B 40M

6. Describe the importance of any **two** of the below activities in an **Irish region** that you have studied:
   - Tourism
   - Transport
   - Manufacturing

Region named 1m
Activity 1 described 7 SRPs @ 3m each
Activity 2 described 6 SRPs @ 3m each

   2012 Q4C 40M

HIGHER LEVEL

LONG QUESTIONS

1. Account for the development of agriculture in an **Irish region** that you have studied, with reference to any **two** of the following factors:

   - Relief
   - Climate
   - Markets

   | Account of factor 1 7/8 SRPs @ 2m each |
   | Account of factor 2 7/8 SRPs @ 2m each |

   2014 Q6C 30M

2. Contrast the development of agriculture in **two Irish regions** that you have studied.

   | Clearly stated contrasts 2m + 2m |
   | Discussion 13 SRPs @ 2m each |

   2011 Q4B 30M

3. Examine the factors that influence the development secondary economic activity in an **Irish region** that you have studied.

   | Named example 2m |
   | Factors named 2m + 2m |
   | Examination 12 SRPs @ 2m each |

   2013 Q4B 30M

4. Account for the development of transport **or** tourism in an **Irish region** that you have studied.

   | Challenges identified 2m + 2m |
   | Description/explanation 13 SRPs @ 2m each |

   2015 Q6C 30M

5. Discuss the factors that influence the development of **one** tertiary economic activity in an **Irish region** that you have studied.

   | Named tertiary economic activity 2m |
   | Factors 2m + 2m |
   | Discussion 12 SRPs @ 2m each |

   2012 Q6B 30M

6. Account for the distribution of population throughout an **Irish region** that you have studied.

   | Examination 15 SRPs @ 2m each |

   2012 Q4C 30M

As you know, a question on Irish Regional Geography has appeared every year at both Higher Level and Ordinary Level. So the more you practise answering questions on this topic, the better prepared you will be for the exam.

In this section, I have included a question on the development of secondary activities in an Irish region from the 2013 Higher Level paper. Although the answer is for a Higher Level question, most of the information given would also be required to answer an Ordinary Level question.

Looking at the question, we can see that:

- 'Factors' is plural, which means at least two factors must be discussed.
- The region you discuss must be Irish. Naming a European or a subcontinental region will result in 0 marks.

HIGHER LEVEL

EXAM QUESTION

Examine the factors that influence the development of a secondary economic activity in an **Irish region** that you have studied.

Marking Scheme
Named example 2m
Factors named 2m + 2m
Examination 12 SRPs @ 2m each

2013 Q4B 30M

EXAM FOCUS

SAMPLE ANSWER

An Irish region in which I have studied the development of secondary economic activity is the Greater Dublin Area (GDA) [2m]. Two factors which have influenced the development of secondary economic activities in the GDA are developed transport links [2m] and a highly educated workforce [2m].

The GDA is the major transport hub of Ireland, meaning it is the focal point of all transport links and connects to all other main cities through motorway and rail [2m]. These developed transport links have made the GDA attractive for manufacturing companies as it provides a centre for distribution to the rest of the country [2m]. Motorways now link the GDA to all major cities in Ireland, e.g. Cork, Limerick, Galway and Belfast, which allows for fast and efficient distribution of goods [2m]. For example, Irish News Media uses the motorways to transport its papers to the rest of the country [2m]. As well as road and rail, the GDA has Ireland's biggest port, which allows manufacturing industries to import raw materials and export goods to the UK and other EU markets [2m]. Dublin Airport allows companies such as Intel to export their processor chips to overseas markets, with flights to hundreds of destinations all over the world [2m].

The GDA is the focus of Ireland's education services, offering 80 per cent of the country's total college places [2m]. Young students move to Dublin to take college places in TCD, UCD, DCU, St Patrick's, NUI Maynooth and several Institutes of Technology, creating a constant supply of skilled workers for Dublin-based industries [2m]. The presence of these third-level institutions also attracts manufacturers of healthcare, software and biotechnology, who invest in research and development and handpick the best graduates [2m]. Some 45 per cent of the region's workforce is under the age of 25. With so many college graduates, this young workforce is trained in the latest technologies and innovations [2m]. The GDA also leads the way in expert graduates, with 3 out of every 4 PhDs being awarded by colleges in the region [2m]. While education has attracted MNCs, it means that we are now heavily dependent on foreign direct investment. As a result, the GDA will have to compete against newly joined EU members to protect employment in the region [2m].

The opening statement quickly establishes the region being discussed and the two factors which have influenced it. In just two sentences, you have secured 6/30m (20%). Be careful: many students forget to write the name of the region before they begin. Sitting exams is stressful and it is easy to overlook the small things. It is always a good idea to highlight the key words of the question to serve as a reminder.

Each factor is discussed separately to avoid potential confusion or repetition within a paragraph.

Marks Awarded	
Region named 2m	
Factors named 2m + 2m	
Discussion best 12 SRPs @ 2m each	
Total 30/30	

TOPIC MAP

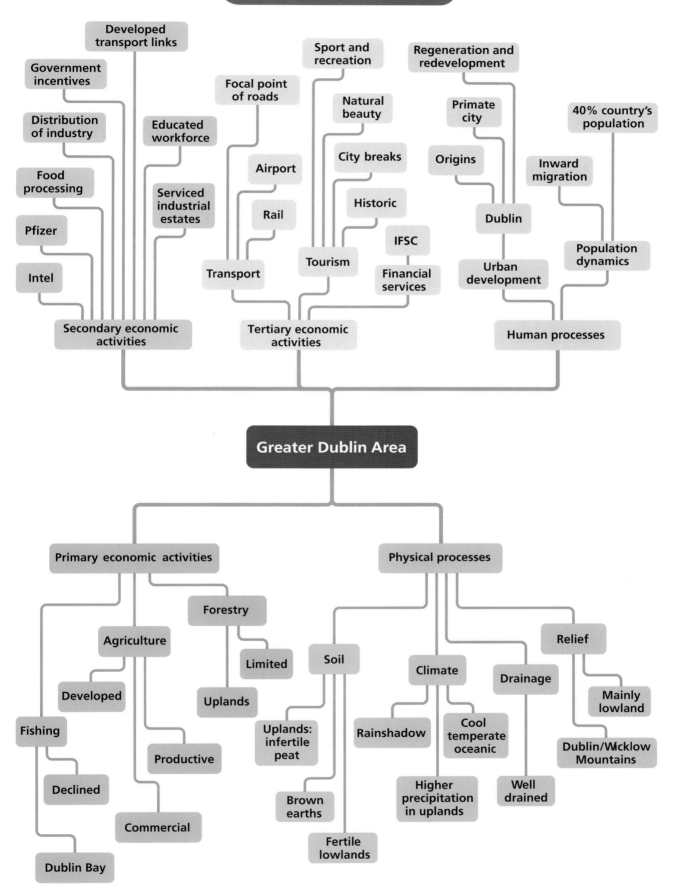

CHAPTER 23

European Regions 1:
Peripheral Socio-economic Region (The Mezzogiorno)

In this chapter, we will look at the economic development of the Mezzogiorno in Italy. Although Italy is a highly developed country, large gaps exist between its core and peripheral regions. The Mezzogiorno is a peripheral region, which has a number of physical and social disadvantages that have hindered its development.

KEY WORDS

- Relief
- Apennine Mountains
- Drainage
- Mediterranean climate
- Soils
- Agriculture

- Cassa per il Mezzogiorno Scheme
- Forestry
- Fishing
- Heavy industry
- Autostrada del Sole
- Outward migration

- Brain drain
- Drought
- Finsider Steelworks
- Seasonal tourism
- Taranto
- Camorra
- Fiat

LEARNING OUTCOMES

What you MUST know
- Physical characteristics of the Mezzogiorno
- Climate characteristics of the region
- How to draw a map and fill in the main features of the Mezzogiorno
- The development of primary, secondary and tertiary activities in the Mezzogiorno
- Human processes of the region
- Urban development in the region

What you SHOULD know
- Naples CASE STUDY 📁
- Statistics that show contrast between the Mezzogiorno and the Paris Basin (covered in Chapter 24)

What is USEFUL to know
- How to understand information provided in graphs as a means to contrast regions

23.1 The Mezzogiorno

The Mezzogiorno is the name given to the **Italian Peninsula south of Rome**, and the islands of Sicily and Sardinia. Mezzogiorno means 'midday', when the sun is at its hottest. The region is so-called as it receives **large amounts of sunshine**. In many ways, the issues facing the Mezzogiorno are **similar to** those of the **West region in Ireland**. The Mezzogiorno is **one of the poorest regions in the EU,** with an **unemployment rate** of **over 20 per cent.**

Despite accounting for **40 per cent of Italy's landmass,** the Mezzogiorno generates just **25 per cent of the country's gross national product (GNP).** Much like in the West of Ireland, there has been large-scale **outward migration of young people.** Over 9 million emigrated from the region in a 20-year period between 1953 and 1973 alone. The majority of these were 18–30-year-olds. In 1954, 49 per cent of the population was classified as illiterate, while 85 per cent of families in the region were considered to be living in poverty. Despite improvements due to government and EU investment, the region **remains economically underdeveloped** due to several disadvantages.

23.2 Physical Processes

In this section, we will look at the following physical factors that influence the region:

- Relief
- Drainage
- Climate
- Soil

Relief

Some **85 per cent** of the Mezzogiorno is characterised as being **upland or hilly.** The **Apennine Mountain range** runs like a spine through the centre of the peninsula for roughly **2000 km.** The mountains are an **extension of the Alps,** which began forming 60 million years ago, when the African Plate began to collide and subduct underneath the Eurasian Plate. The collision caused the **uplifting and folding of limestone** to form the Apennine range, whose tallest peak is the at 2912 m Corno Grande. Unlike the West region of Ireland, the Mezzogiorno receives **little rainfall,** meaning the limestone folds have **not been weathered as quickly** by carbonation.

Along the African and Eurasian destructive boundary, the subducting African Plate has led to the formation of **active volcanic peaks** such as **Mount Vesuvius (1281 m), Mount Etna (3350 m)** and **Mount Vulture (1326 m).**

Due to the dominance of the Apennines, **lowland areas are confined to narrow coastal plains** such as the **Bay of Naples.** Traditionally, many of these lowlands were swamps of marshland and were infested with mosquitoes carrying malaria. As part of government investment in the region, these **swamps were drained and** are now used for **agriculture.**

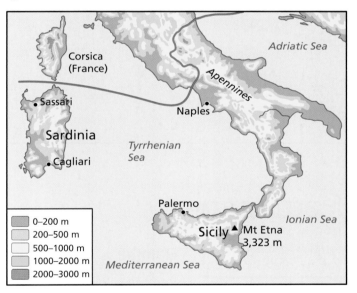

▲ **Fig. 23.1** Relief map of Italy

Drainage

A combination of little rainfall and limestone bedrock means there is **little surface water** flowing throughout the Mezzogiorno. As limestone is **permeable,** the water disappears into swallow holes. As a result, many karst

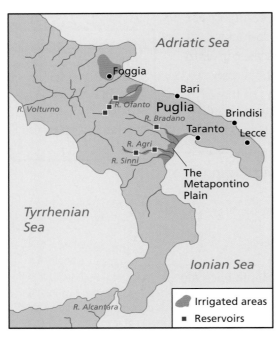

Fig. 23.2 Main rivers of the Mezzogiorno

regions, similar to those in the Burren in Co. Clare, exist in the region. The **Volturno, Brandano** and **Agri** are the largest rivers in the region. The Volturno's source is in the central Apennines. It runs south-west for 175 km and enters the Tyrrhenian Sea north of Naples. The Brandano River flows east for 170 km before entering the Caspian Sea. The **Agri** flows south-east for 136 km into the Ionian Sea. The **Ofanto** flows east for 170 km through Campania into the Adriatic Sea. Due to little rainfall and **high evaporation rates** during the **summer months,** the volume of water in these rivers is greatly reduced.

Climate

The Mezzogiorno has a **Mediterranean climate,** which is also known as a **warm temperate climate.** The climate is characterised by **hot, dry summers** and **warm, moist winters.**

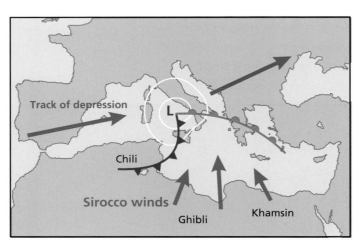

Fig. 23.3 Dry Sirocco winds blow in from Africa towards the Mezzogiorno.

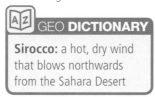

Sirocco: a hot, dry wind that blows northwards from the Sahara Desert

Temperature

During **July,** the region experiences high temperatures, averaging **25 °C.** These high temperatures are due to the region's **low latitude** and the affect of the **Sirocco.** The Sirocco is a **hot, dry wind** that blows northwards from the Sahara Desert. The winds **carry huge amounts of sand and dust** and often reach speeds of 100 km/h and peak in March and November. The winds can **destroy crops** such as vines and fruits and damage trees and foliage.

Winter temperatures are mild, averaging **9 °C.** However, due to the **varying relief** of the region, **temperatures vary.** Upland areas are **cooler than low-lying areas.**

Rainfall

Rainfall is low throughout the summer months, which often leads to **prolonged periods of drought.** The **Azores High** is an **anticyclone** which dominates the Mediterranean during the summer months. The high pressure brings settled weather with **little cloud** and **warm sunshine.** Often just **20–40 mm of rain falls** in the three months of May, June and July. Any rainfall that does occur is in the form of **convectional rain,** which leads to **torrential showers** and flash flooding.

During **winter,** the high pressure retreats south, allowing **cyclones** from the mid-Atlantic to reach the Mezzogiorno. This low pressure brings **unsettled weather** conditions to the region. **Cyclonic rain** occurs due to the low pressure, but it is **not evenly distributed** due to the dominance of the Apennine Mountains. As the moisture-laden air mass rises over the mountain range, it condenses, causing **relief rain.** The mountains act as a **rain shadow to the east,** meaning it receives less rainfall. Rainfall during the **winter** averages 600–800 mm.

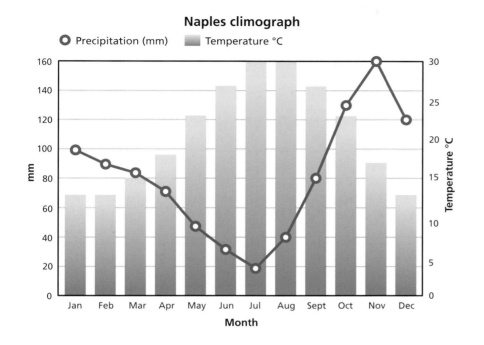

Naples climograph

○ Precipitation (mm) ▭ Temperature °C

◀ **Fig. 23.4** Precipitation and temperature of Naples

Soil

Soils in the Mezzogiorno are **heavily influenced by physical processes** such as climate, relief and underlying bedrock. Throughout the region, soils vary from **fertile to infertile.** In the areas surrounding volcanic mountains such as **Mount Vesuvius** and **Mount Etna, soils** are rich in minerals and can be used to **grow a variety of crops.**

Along the Brandano, Agri and Volturno river valleys, **alluvial soils** have been deposited, leading to **fertile floodplains.** However, as these rivers have low volumes of water, the floodplains are **small and narrow,** so cover a small area. Deep red soils, known as **terra rossa,** have developed in areas of the southern peninsula and Sicily. These soils formed from **weathered limestone** with a **high iron content.**

Limestone is common throughout the region, but unlike Ireland, a lack of rainfall means it is not weathered easily. As a result, soils in limestone regions, such as Apulia, are **thin and infertile.** This is worsened by **high levels of erosion** on slopes and hillsides. This is typically triggered by the **sudden torrential downpours** during the summer and **poor farming practices** such as **overgrazing.** In the southern 'toe' of the region (**Calabria**), underlying granite breaks down into **infertile soil** that is useless for agriculture. The limitation of the soil for use in agriculture has been a **contributing factor** to the **peripheral economy** of the region.

GEO DICTIONARY

Terra rossa: fertile red soil formed from the weathering of limestone, which has a high iron content. It is extremely fertile and can be used for the intensive growth of cash crops

FACT

Terra rossa soils are also known as Mediterranean red soils. As well as using these soils for agriculture, the Romans used terra rossa soil to make bricks for building houses, as its clay texture allowed it to stick together.

⬆ **Fig. 23.5** Fertile soils at the foot of Mount Vesuvius

Physical Processes	
Relief	85% upland/hilly, Apennine Mountains, 2000 km, extension of Alps, limestone folds not weathered quickly, active volcanic peaks, e.g. Mount Vesuvius, lowlands confined to narrow coastal plains, e.g. Bay of Naples, swamps drained for agriculture
Drainage	Little water, limestone bedrock, little surface water, permeable, Volturno, Brandano, Agri, high evaporation rates, volume of water reduced
Climate	Temperature: Mediterranean climate, hot and dry summers, warm and moist winters, July temperatures average 25 °C, low latitude; Sirocco – hot and dry winds, destructive to crop, carry dust, winters are mild, average 9 °C, varying relief = varying temperatures, uplands cooler than lowlands
	Precipitation: rainfall low in summer, prolonged periods of drought, Azores High, anticyclones, 20–40 mm rainfall in summer, settled weather, convectional rainfall, torrential downpours, flash flooding, high pressure retreats in winter, cyclones from mid-Atlantic, unsettled weather, moisture-laden air mass, condenses, relief rainfall, mountains – rain shadow to east, less rainfall, average 600–800 mm in winter
Soil	Influenced by physical processes, climate, relief and underlying bedrock, soil varies fertile to infertile, Mounts Vesuvius and Etna soils fertile, rich in minerals, variety of crops, alluvial soils, fertile floodplains, low volumes of water – small and thin floodplains; terra rossa – weathered limestone with high iron content, lack of rainfall, Apulia thin and infertile, erosion on hillsides and mountains, torrential downpours and poor human management, overgrazing; Calabria – infertile soil; contributing factor to peripheral economy of region

ACTIVE **LEARNING**

1. What percentage of the Mezzogiorno is upland?
2. Why do low levels of rainfall lead to slower weathering of limestone?
3. Using your knowledge of volcanic formation, explain with the aid of a labelled diagram how Mount Vesuvius formed.
4. What is meant by the term 'permeable'?
5. Name the three main rivers of the Mezzogiorno region.
6. Explain the term 'Sirocco' and its impact on agriculture in the region.
7. Why is rainfall low during the summer in the Mezzogiorno?
8. Why is rainfall unevenly distributed throughout the region?
9. Where are the most fertile soils of the Mezzogiorno?
10. Why are there high levels of soil erosion along hillsides and mountains?

23.3 Primary Activities

Primary activities in the Mezzogiorno are limited due to a **lack of natural resources.** Therefore, primary activities tend to be **subsistence** rather than profitable. The two main primary activities in the region are agriculture and fishing. There are low levels of forestry in some inland areas.

Agriculture

Although important to the economy of the Mezzogiorno, agriculture is generally **unproductive and subsistent.** Both physical and social factors have hindered the development of an efficient and profitable agricultural sector in the region.

Physical Factors Affecting Agriculture in the Mezzogiorno

Physical factors which hinder its development include:

- Relief
- Climate

Relief

As **85 per cent of the region** is dominated by the **Apennines** and other slopes, agriculture is **limited by relief.** Due to a **lack of rainfall or moisture,** limestone is not broken down as easily as it is in Ireland. This leads to **thin and generally unproductive soils.** As a result, upland areas are **unable to support arable farming.** Instead, **tree crops,** such as **olive trees,** are cultivated along the **steep slopes.** The **roots of these trees** are able to **anchor** themselves in the relatively thin soils, which binds the soil together and **prevents soil erosion.**

⌃ **Fig. 23.6** Thin soils form on the slopes of the Apennines.

During summer months, **traditional goat and sheep farmers** used to move their herds further up mountains where temperatures are cooler. When winter arrived, they moved their herd to lowlands again. This practice, known as **transhumance,** died out during the 1950s and 1960s. **Goats and sheep** rather than cattle are still farmed in **upland** areas. This is due to **poor grass growth** in these regions, which means only **rough grazing** is available. Goats and sheep are also better adapted to upland regions and have better balance for grazing on steep slopes.

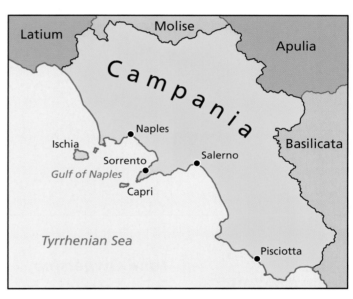

⌃ **Fig. 23.7** Lowland fertile Plain of Campania

The steep slopes of the Mezzogiorno have made the **mechanisation of farms difficult** as machines cannot access the steep land. As a result, farming in the region remains **labour intensive.** In lowland plains such as the **Plain of Campania,** farming is much **more productive** as soils are **deep and fertile.** This allows for a large **variety of crops** to be grown and much easier cultivation of land.

Climate

The climate of the Mezzogiorno provides a **constant challenge** for farmers in the region, as **water supply is a constant worry.** The **Azores High** brings constant **high pressure** to the region over the **summer** months, which means **very little rain falls. High temperatures** lead to **high evaporation rates** of water both in rivers and in soil. As a result, the region suffers from **drought and lower crop yields** due to stunted growth. In response to this, **irrigation schemes are necessary** to prevent crops from wilting. Over **1 million hectares of land are irrigated** in the region, mainly for the growth of **olives, grapes** and **citrus fruits.** Despite government investment in irrigation, high evaporation rates and **decreases in river volume**

Fig. 23.8 Irrigation schemes are necessary but limited in the Mezzogiorno.

Fig. 23.9 The range of crops grown in Sicily

Typical Sicilian foods
- Melons
- Blood oranges
- Lemons
- Almonds
- Tomatoes
- Grapes
- Couscous
- Red onions
- Extra virgin olive oil
- Black bread
- Cheese

during the summer months mean it is **not sustainable** for the future.

Olives are grown throughout the summer as they are **drought resistant.** The trees have **thick barks** and **waxy leaves** that help them retain moisture, while their **deep taproots** are capable of reaching water at large depths.

As summer temperatures are so high, **most farming is carried out during the winter** as it is still mild, with more rainfall.

The high summer temperatures have led to **intensive growth of citrus fruits** as **cash crops.** The hot temperatures allow for **early ripening of fruits,** which are then sold to the wealthier markets in north Italy and the EU. **Sicily** produces nearly **two-thirds of Italy's citrus fruits.** However, the growing of citrus fruits is **limited** to **lowland areas** where more **fertile soil** and **irrigation are available.**

Human Factors Affecting Agriculture in the Mezzogiorno

Human/social factors have also impacted on the development of agriculture in the Mezzogiorno. These factors are:

- Land ownership
- Government Intervention

Land Ownership

Until the **1950s,** over **70 per cent** of the Mezzogiorno's population **worked in agriculture.** During this time, only **25 per cent of farmers owned their own land,** while the remaining **75 per cent worked as braccianti** on large **landlord estates** called **'latifundia'.** These latifundia estates were **subdivided** into small plots called **'minifundia' and rented to tenants.**

Minifundia were typically between **3 and 5 hectares,** making it difficult for farmers to produce enough to pay rents and also support their own families. As a result, farmers **overgrazed and overcropped** their land in order to **pay landlords rent of up to 60 per cent** of their total produce. The majority of landlords lived in the north of Italy, and many did not manage the land correctly or ensure its productivity. These **absentee landlords** rarely reinvested capital in their estates, meaning farm practices were **labour intensive, outdated** and **extensive.** Farmers who rented the small plots did not try to improve their plots as they had **no land security** from one year to the next. As a result, agriculture developed on a **subsistence basis.**

Government Intervention

As a result of **increasing poverty** and **social unrest** in the region, the Government attempted to **reform agriculture** through the **Cassa per il Mezzogiorno Scheme.**

The Cassa Scheme transferred over **10 per cent of all land** in the region from **landlords to tenant farmers.** Some **100 000 former braccianti** families were **given farms** of between **5 and 50 hectares,** depending on the quality of the land.

These farmers were then **trained** in more **profitable farming methods,** such as growing **cash crops** and a greater variety of **crops** (olives, vines, citrus fruits, winter wheat). This allowed farmers to move **from extensive and subsistence** farming **to more intensive commercial farming.**

In order to support the **intensive production of crops** in an areas **prone to drought, irrigation schemes were developed.** Wells were dug and water was piped from rivers and reservoirs.

GEO DICTIONARY

Cooperative: a jointly owned enterprise that is owned and run by its members for their mutual benefit; cooperatives usually involve the production or distribution of goods, such as farm produce

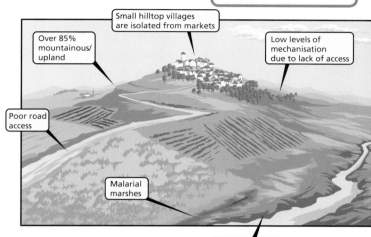

Fig. 23.10 Challenges facing agriculture in the Mezzogiorno

The **Autostrada del Sole** motorway was built to allow **easy transport of goods** from the region **to the larger markets in the north.** This meant that **perishable products** such as **fruits and vegetables** could now be exported more easily.

New urban centres were developed in the region to **give farmers access to necessary farm materials** and **markets.** This helped to **prevent outward migration** from rural areas.

New farm houses were built, allowing the farmers to live on their land. Previously, many had **commuted** from remote hillside homes to their land.

The Cassa Scheme **ended in 1984.** It was **replaced by the EU Regional Development Fund,** which now supports farms in peripheral locations. By 1984, the Cassa Scheme had spent **€20 billion,** of which **70 per cent was on agricultural reform.**

Positive Impacts

- **Cooperatives were formed** to help farmers sell goods to the north. This meant the region had access to a much larger and wealthier market in the north and throughout the EU.

- **Malarial swamps were drained** in the Metapontino, allowing the land to be reclaimed for agricultural use. Wheat is now intensively grown there.

- The Mezzogiorno is now the **biggest producer** of **olive oil** in the world.

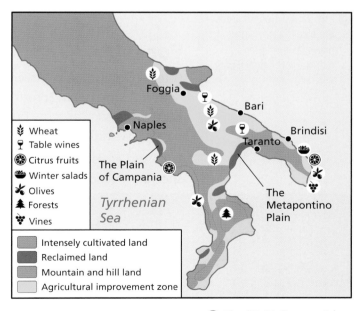

Fig. 23.11 Commercial farming in the Mezzogiorno

- Along the **Plain of Campania, mixed cultivation** now takes place. The **deep, fertile soils** along Mount Vesuvius support a wide variety of crops. Previously, farmers had grown single crops, which depleted the soil of nutrients.

- **Mechanisation of farms** and **increasing use of technology** have aided the development of more **intensive farming.**

Negative Impacts

- Government intervention has mainly **benefitted lowland areas. Upland** areas have been **largely unaffected** by the developments, meaning their farming practices are still less developed than the wealthier north of the country. This has **widened the income gap** between the upland and lowland areas.

- The **intensive growth of cash crops** such as tomatoes has led to **seasonal overproduction.** Over the past three decades, the number of tomatoes being produced in the region has increased tenfold (1000 per cent). With more cash crops being grown, supply far outweighs demand. This greatly **reduces the market price.**

- The use of **irrigation is expensive and unsustainable.** With the region suffering from regular periods of drought, irrigation schemes drain further water from the ground and rivers.

- **Arable farming is still limited to lowland regions,** with extensive pastoral farming dominating in upland areas.

⬀ **Fig. 23.12** Upland areas are ideal for growing olives, as they can withstand the dry climate.

Forestry

Forestry production is **extremely limited** in the Mezzogiorno as the climate does **not support** it. Forestry grown in the region tends to be **mixed hardwood** such as oak, cork, cypress and olive trees. Most of the region's **natural woodland** was **cleared for settlement and farms.**

In upland areas, the thin **soils do not support growth of most tree species,** meaning dense patches of forests do not grow. Some trees, such as olive, have **adapted to growing in the climate conditions** of the region: they have **waxy leaves** to protect from the **intense sunshine** and **deep taproots** to reach water deep in the soil.

Fishing

Fishing is **not a significant economic activity** in the Mezzogiorno. Despite this, fishing remains **an important source of income** in **small town ports** along the coast of the region. In **coastal areas with**

⬀ **Fig. 23.13** The fishing port at Naples

infertile land, fishing is the **only source of employment.** Much of the fish caught is **supplied to the local tourist markets** along the Amalfi Coast, just south of Naples.

A couple of factors limit the fishing industry in the region. The Mediterranean Sea's **high salt content prevents plankton** from building up and **reduces the amount of fish breeding** due to a lack of food. Tourist regions around Mediterranean pollute the water, leading to **algal blooms,** which kill large numbers of fish.

GEO DICTIONARY

Algal blooms: occur when nutrients and run-off in water promote the rapid growth of the microorganism algae. Algae cover the surface of the water in a thick green scum

EDUCATE YOURSELF

Primary Activities		
Lack of natural resources, subsistent living, agriculture unproductive and subsistent		
Physical factors affecting agriculture	Relief: 85% upland Apennines, limited by relief, lack of moisture, thin and unproductive soils, unable to support arable farming, cultivate tree crops – olive trees, roots of trees anchor on thin soils, prevent soil erosion; traditional goat and sheep farmers, transhumance, goats and sheep farmed upland, poor grass growth, rough grazing, mechanisation is difficult, labour intensive, Plain of Campania, productive soils deep and fertile, variety of crops	
	Climate constant challenge, water supply a constant worry, Azores High, high pressure summer months, very little rainfall, high temperatures, high evaporation rates, drought and lower crop yields, irrigation schemes are necessary, 1 million hectares of land are irrigated, olives, grapes and citrus fruits; decreases in river volume, not sustainable; olives drought resistant, thick bark and waxy leaves, deep tap roots; most farming carried out in winter, intensive growth of citrus fruits in summer, early ripening, Sicily grows two-thirds of Italy's citrus fruits, limited to lowlands fertile soil and irrigation available	
Human factors affecting agriculture	Land ownership: before 1950s 70% worked in agriculture, 25% owned their own land, 75% worked as landless labourers (braccianti), landlord estates latifundia, overgrazed and overcropped, pay landlords up to 60% of produce, absentee landlords, labour intensive, outdated and extensive, no land security, subsistence basis; subdivided into smaller plots to tenants – minifundia (3–5 hectares),	
	Government investment: increasing poverty and social unrest, agricultural reform, Cassa per il Mezzogiorno scheme, 10% of all land transferred to peasants, 100 000 former braccianti given farms (5–50 hectares), upskilled and trained, profitable farming methods – cash crops and vegetables, extensive/subsistent farming to intensive/commercial farming, intensive production of crops, prone to drought, irrigation schemes developed, Autostrada del Sole, easy transport of goods to northern markets, perishable fruits and vegetables exported, new urban centres for markets and materials, prevent outward migration, new farm houses on land, stopped need for commuting, abolished in 1984 replaced by EU Regional Development Fund, €20 billion 70% on agricultural reform	
	Positive impacts: cooperatives formed, malarial swamps drained, mixed cultivation in Plain of Campania, mechanisation of farms	
	Negative impacts: benefitted lowlands areas, upland largely unaffected, widened income gap, seasonal overproduction of cash crops, reduced market price, irrigation expensive and unpredictable, arable farming limited to lowlands	
Forestry	Extremely limited, not supported by climate, mixed hardwood, natural woodland cleared for settlement and farms, thin soil does not support most species, olive tree has adapted to harsh climate – waxy leaves and deep taproots	
Fishing	Not a significant economic activity, important source of income for small town ports, only source of income, supplied to local tourist markets, Amalfi Coast, high salt content of Mediterranean prevents plankton and lowers fish breeding, algal blooms	

23.4 Secondary Activities

Manufacturing in the Mezzogiorno is **heavily controlled by the state,** which owns or has **control over the majority of industries** operating in the region. Roughly **one-quarter** of the **population** of the region is **employed in the secondary sector,** a **large percentage** of whom are **unskilled.** A number of **factors have prevented manufacturing from becoming well developed** in the region. These include:

- A poor primary sector
- Peripheral location
- Limited labour force

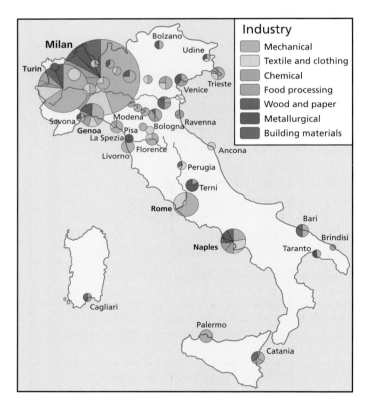

Fig. 23.14 Distribution of industry in Italy is uneven.

Poor Primary Sector

The Mezzogiorno **lacks natural resources** such as oil, gas, minerals and even water. Only small deposits of oil and gas are found in the region, which means all **industry must import raw materials** from abroad. Most of the region's **gas is imported from Algeria** via large networks of pipeline. Renewable energy such as **hydroelectric power is very limited,** as prolonged periods of **drought** throughout the summer means reservoirs and river levels drop significantly due to evaporation. Since the beginning of the 2000s, there has been investment in solar power but it is still not widely used as it is expensive. Combined with this, the region is covered by **limestone bedrock** which is **permeable.** This means there is a **lack of surface water** that is necessary to cool machinery in heavy industry, e.g. steelworks.

A **lack of agricultural diversity** also **limits** industries such as **food processing.** Olive oil and wine are produced from locally grown olives and grapes, while citrus fruits are used to produce vitamins. However, apart from these, food production is limited.

Peripheral Location

The Mezzogiorno is located **far away from the larger urban markets** of the EU; the southern tip of the region is **1100 km from the country's capital.** As **85 per cent of the region is steep or upland,** it is both **expensive and difficult to develop high-quality road and rail links.**

Until the **1950s,** delivery of goods was **hindered by winding mountain roads** and **narrow tunnels through mountains.** Rail links were often disrupted in the winter, as snowfall in upland areas blocked routes.

The building of the **Autostrada del Sole** in 1964 finally **connected the Mezzogiorno to the north of Italy.** Despite the modern motorway link, the **long distance means that transport costs are still high.** Due to this added cost, it is **difficult for the region to compete with goods produced closer to the economic core** of the EU.

The Mezzogiorno's peripheral location has proved to be a **major barrier to MNCs** locating there. As well as being unable to attract capital from MNCs, the region is **isolated from its own government's influence.** With little local capital, the region is also **unable to modernise** and develop homegrown industry.

The **standard of living** in the Mezzogiorno is **much lower than in the northern part of the country.** This means that **local markets do not have the wealth** to support industrial products. There is a **lack of capital to invest** in start-up businesses.

▲ **Fig. 23.15** Narrow winding roads have added to the region's peripheral location.

▲ **Fig. 23.16** The Autostrada del Sole has made the region more accessible.

Limited Labour Force

With the exception of Naples and Palermo, there are very **few large cities** in the Mezzogiorno, which would provide a large labour pool or local market. This makes **choosing a location for industry difficult** and unattractive.

Twenty-three per cent of families in the Mezzogiorno are still classed as **living in poverty.** They are **seven times less likely to go to college** than the those living in the wealthier north. Only three of the region's universities rank in Italy's top 20. As a result, **there is large-scale outward migration** as young people **travel north for education, a better standard of living and employment opportunities.** This outward migration leads to a 'brain drain', as the region loses its future workforce and their skills. It also leads to a **smaller tax base** within the region.

Fig. 23.17 Growth poles (in yellow) selected by the government

Government Investment

In **1957**, the **Cassa per il Mezzogiorno** aimed to **improve manufacturing** in the region by investing **€2.3 billion in industrial development** over 25 years. The **Vanoni Plan** began in 1965 and created over **300 000 jobs** in the region between 1965 and 1970.

'Growth poles', which included **Pescara, Naples** and the **Bari-Brindisi-Taranto** triangle, were selected by the government as **centres of economic activity** within the region. These centres were chosen as they had **higher populations and access to port facilities.** It was hoped that success in these regions would lead to further industrial growth in surrounding areas.

The Vanoni Plan

The Vanoni Plan aimed to attract inward investment to the region by making it more **suitable for MNCs.**

- **Well-serviced industrial estates, tax exemptions** and **transport subsidies** were offered for MNCs who set up in the region or for companies who wished to relocate from the north to the Mezzogiorno.

- **Funds were allocated for businesses** to **educate and upskill** the local workforce, creating a larger labour pool.

- Large amounts of **investment in infrastructure** led to the completion of the Autostrada del Sole. This meant industries, such as food processing, could transport goods more efficiently.

- A **new airport was built at Calabria,** reducing the isolation of the region from large EU markets.

Unemployment rate %

	0
	4
	6
	8
	10
	15
	>20

Fig. 23.18 Despite improvements, unemployment remains high in the Mezzogiorno.

The government invested in **improving ports** to develop heavy industries such as **oil refining, petrochemical production** and **gas distribution.** This investment in ports accounted for **60 per cent of all investment** in the region during this time.

The **Act of Parliament** required all **state-owned companies** to invest at least **60 per cent of all new investments** in the Mezzogiorno. Large, **state-owned factories** such as the steelworks at Taranto provided **75 per cent of all new jobs.**

Finsider Steelworks was set up in Taranto in **1964,** leading to **increased activity at the port.** This has made Taranto the **most important port in the Mediterranean** and the third most important in Italy. The port handles over **35 million tonnes of freight,** making it a centre of economic activity in the region. However, companies such as Finsider produce much more steel than they can sell. The surplus is sold at reduced rates.

Industrial employment has tripled in the region to **1.4 million people** as a result of the Cassa Scheme.

Lasting Problems

Although the Cassa per il Mezzogiorno brought improvements, several difficulties still exist in the region:

- The **large steelworks,** which were the focus for nearly **75 per cent of new industrial employment** in the region, were far **more capital intensive than labour intensive.** This means that the industries **cost a lot of money to build,** but did not **generate many jobs.** Furthermore, these industries are **prone to job losses** due to rationalisation and mechanisation.

- **Outward migration,** although declining, continues as young workers are attracted to better-paying jobs in the north.

- The Cassa caused **uneven development in the region** as coastal areas attracted far more investment than those further inland. This has led to an increase in the income gap within the region.

- The economic recession that began in 2008 resulted in **higher numbers of workers in the Mezzogiorno losing their jobs than in the north of Italy.** This is due to the lack of employment flexibility in the region where workers are trained for one job only.

Prevailing Issues in the Mezzogiorno

- The government is continuing its efforts to **decentralise some of the industries** to areas further inland in an attempt to develop industry more evenly throughout the region.

- Since the Cassa Scheme ended in 1984, the EU has part-funded infrastructural improvements in port regions such as Naples and Taranto. The **Regional Development Fund** also aims to further improve transport links in the region.

The government must tackle the continuing high levels of poverty in the region.

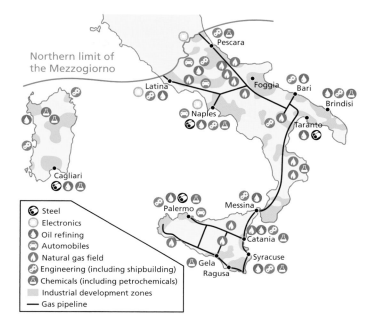

Fig. 23.19 Distribution of industry across the Mezzogiorno: note the absence of industry south of Naples along the western half of the region.

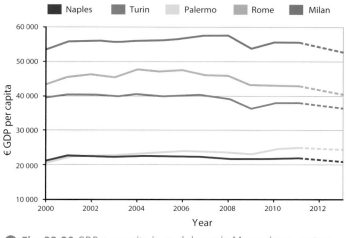

Fig. 23.20 GDP per capita is much lower in Mezzogiorno centres.

 **GEO DICTIONARY**

Decentralise: to spread out industry to several areas rather than concentrating it in a single location

Employment flexibility: when workers are trained and able to carry out more than one role or job

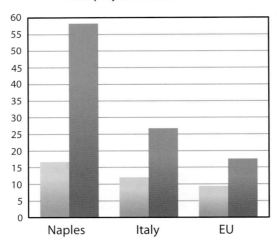

Unemployment rates 2015

% Unemployment

% Unemployment among 18–25 year olds

- Twenty-three per cent live in poverty.
- The unemployment rate is 20 per cent.
- The infant mortality rate is four times higher than in northern Italy and twice as high as the EU average.
- One-quarter of children drop out of education after primary school.
- Infrastructure is still far less developed than in the North.

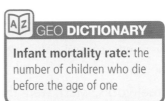

GEO **DICTIONARY**

Infant mortality rate: the number of children who die before the age of one

◀ **Fig. 23.21** Unemployment rates in Naples compared to Italy's and the EU's average

EDUCATE YOURSELF

Secondary Activities	
Heavily controlled by the state, control over majority of industries, quarter of population employed in secondary, large percentage unskilled, factors have prevented manufacturing from becoming well developed	
Poor primary sector	Lacks natural resources, must import raw materials, gas imported from Algeria, hydroelectric power limited, drought, limestone bedrock is permeable, lack of surface water, lack of agricultural diversity, limits food processing
Peripheral location	Far away from larger EU markets, 1100 km from country's capital, 85% of region is upland, expensive and difficult to develop high-quality road and rail links, until 1950s hindered by twisted mountains roads, narrow tunnels through mountains; Cassa, Autostrada del Sole connected region to north, long-distance transport costs high, difficult to compete with goods produced closer to economic core, major barrier preventing MNC investment, isolated from government influence, unable to modernise
Limited labour force	Few large cities, choosing a location for industry difficult, 23% living in poverty, seven times less likely to go to college, large-scale outward migration, travel north for a better standard of living, employment opportunities and education, brain drain, smaller tax base, standard of living much lower than north, local markets not wealthy, lack of capital to invest
Government investment	1957 Cassa Scheme improve manufacturing, €2.3bn industrial development, Vanoni Plan, 300 000 jobs, growth poles generate centres of economic activity – Pescara, Naples and Bari-Brindisi-Taranto, higher populations and port facilities
Vanoni Plan	Well-serviced industrial estates, tax exemptions and transport subsidies, funds allocated for businesses, educate and upskill, investment in infrastructure, new airport at Calabria, improving ports, oil refining, petrochemical production, gas distribution, 60% of all investments, state-owned factories, 75% of all new jobs, Finsider Steelworks 1964, increased activity at Taranto port, most important port in Mediterranean, 35 million tonnes of freight, industrial employment has tripled, employs 1.4 million people
Lasting problems	Large steelworks, 75% of new industrial employment, more capital intensive than labour intensive, cost a lot but few jobs, prone to job losses, outward migration, uneven development in the region, higher numbers of workers in Mezzogiorno lost jobs than the north
Prevailing issues	Decentralise some of the industries, Regional Development Fund

23.5 Tertiary Economic Activities

In general, tertiary activities in the Mezzogiorno are underdeveloped due to the region's heavy dependency on seasonal tourism. Some **67 per cent of the Mezzogiorno's population is employed in the tertiary sector,** but these jobs are **largely seasonal and dependent on the 17 million tourists** who arrive annually. We will look at the two areas of tertiary activities:

- Transport
- Tourism

Transport

A major issue for the Mezzogiorno is its **peripheral location** as its **lack of developed transport links** made it difficult to travel to. Its **steep terrain** makes the development of **communication links** both difficult and expensive. Before the Cassa Scheme, the **region's roads were narrow,** winding and of poor surface quality, making them **slow and dangerous to travel on.** Newer, wider roads only began to be built under the Cassa Scheme. The region also **lacked railway and port facilities,** which made it inaccessible.

Transport was **hindered by the mountainous terrain** which is covered in snow throughout winter and **prone to landslides due to flash flooding.** Earthquakes also occur along these routes. The old roads were **unable to support larger container trucks,** which limited the amount of goods they could transport.

The Cassa Scheme invested **€2.5 billion** to improve transport infrastructure in the region in order to **decrease transport costs** and **journey times.** The largest project was the construction of the **Autostrada del Sole** (A1 in Fig. 23.22), which linked **Naples in the south-east to Milan in the north.** This opened a vital **arterial link to the richer markets of the north.** The Autostrada stretches for over **754 km.**

Modern bridges were also built across valleys and **tunnels through mountains.** This allowed for more **direct transport routes. Deep-water ports** were developed at **Naples,** Augusta, **Calabria** and **Taranto** to allow for the development of **steel manufacturing, petrochemical production and oil and gas refining.**

Taranto and Gioia Tauro are now the **two busiest ports in the Mediterranean.** As a result, the region plays a **major role in container traffic in the Mediterranean.** Since the end of the Cassa Scheme, the **EU Regional Development Fund** and the **EU Structural Fund** have invested in the development of transport in the region. Between **2007 and 2013,**

ACTIVE LEARNING

1. Prior to the 1950s, what factors discouraged companies from locating in the Mezzogiorno?

2. How did the Cassa Scheme make the region more attractive for industry?

3. Explain fully what is meant by the term 'growth pole'.

4. What is a 'brain drain' and why does it occur in the Mezzogiorno?

5. Why might a company still be unwilling to locate in the region?

Fig. 23.22 Motorways of Italy

GEO DICTIONARY

Arterial link: an important transport route

€10 billion was spent on developing transport and communication links in the region. This funding is given to all EU regions whose Gross Domestic Product (GDP) is 75 per cent of the EU average or lower.

After Italy's telecommunications company Telecom Italia was privatised in 2013, broadband speeds and access have improved in the region.

Fig. 23.23 Lines of containers at Gioia Tauro Port, which is the second busiest port in the Mediterranean

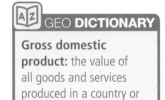

GEO DICTIONARY

Gross domestic product: the value of all goods and services produced in a country or region each year

Tourism

Tourism is of **vital importance to the economy** of the Mezzogiorno, with over **17 million tourists** visiting the region annually. Of this, only **6 million are international tourists,** with the remaining **11 million being domestic tourists.** There are many **natural advantages** which allow for tourism in the region:

1. Climate
2. Landscape
3. History and culture

1. Climate

The region has a Mediterranean climate, which has long, **hot dry summers** averaging 25 °C. This has made the region ideal for **sun and beach holidays. Winter temperatures rarely drop below 11 °C** in lowland areas, making conditions perfect for **walking and cycling tours.** In upland areas, winter snowfalls have led to a **growing skiing sector** in areas such as Mount Etna.

Fig. 23.24 The Amalfi Coast lies south of Naples and attracts sun-seekers each summer.

2. Landscape

The Mezzogiorno has many areas of **unspoilt beauty** as its coastlines are **less commercialised than in the north.** The region has over **800 km of coastline** which have been **shaped by the Mediterranean and Adriatic Seas.** Along the west coast, the **Bay of Naples** and **Amalfi Coast** provide beautiful scenery and **long stretches of beaches.** On the east coast, tourist sites have developed at beaches such as **Pescara** and **Puglia. Volcanic mountains** attract walkers, sightseers and nature lovers to climb its slopes each year. Mount Vesuvius attracts **2.5 million tourists per year.**

3. History and Culture

The Mezzogiorno is rich in both historical and cultural heritage. The **ruins of the Roman city** of **Pompeii** attract tourists who wish to walk along the ancient streets and find out more about **Roman culture.** Greek temples at **Agrigento in Sicily** also attract tourists.

Tourists also visit the region to eat the famous southern **Italian cuisine** such as pizza, pasta and fish. Restaurants in the Mezzogiorno are **less influenced by EU culture** and tend to be family run or specialise in specific dishes.

Although they harm the region in many ways, the **Mafia** have become a tourist attraction as visitors want to find out more about their **history and origins in Sicily.** In places such as **Palermo, Corleone and Syracuse,** tourists can **stay overnight in the former estate of a Mafia don** (the head or boss of a Mafia family). Students from abroad can study at the Mediterranean Centre in Syracuse.

Development of Tourism

Despite the region's many attractions, **only 13 per cent of foreign tourists visiting Italy travel to the Mezzogiorno.** The main barrier to increasing tourism is the region's **peripheral location.** The **lack of a well-developed transport service** has limited tourism to coastal areas such as Naples. Also the **driving distance** of the Mezzogiorno from the rest of the EU is a deterrent.

In the 1950s, the **Cassa** Scheme **allocated 15 per cent of its total fund to the development of tourism.** It aimed to generate both **direct and indirect employment.** It was hoped the increase in tourism would provide larger **local markets for farm produce.** The funds **improved** services such as **accommodation and catering** through building **modern hotels and apartments.** The scheme made the region more accessible through the building of a **new airport at Calabria.** Airlines such as Ryanair fly to the region, opening it up to tourists from many European countries. **Ferry links between Calabria and Sicily** and Sardinia were also set up.

Problems

The development of tourism in the Mezzogiorno faces a number of obstacles:

- **Seasonal tourism:** Although tourist numbers to the region have increased as a result of investment, tourism remains a **seasonal industry** in the south. This is despite the mild climate in winter months. This means that employment in hotels and restaurants lasts for the summer and autumn, with many returning to agriculture in the off season. It is important that ski holidays in areas such as Mount Etna are developed fully.

- **Noise pollution:** With increased tourism comes **increased noise** from holiday makers, nightclubs, etc. Often tourist development can occur quickly in small villages, meaning locals face increased noise disruption throughout the tourist season.

- **Coastal damage:** The Mediterranean Sea does not have strong tides to carry away pollution, such as sewage, from coastal resorts. This has led to **many areas becoming polluted,** which destroys both tourist and fishing industries.

- **Inflated land prices:** As areas become more attractive for tourists, investors drive up the **price of land.** Demand for hotels and holiday homes often means **locals cannot afford to live there.** This generally leads to **outward migration.**

▲ **Fig. 23.25** The Agrigento is the ancient ruins of a Greek temple, attracting tourists interested in history and culture.

▲ **Fig. 23.26** A pipe pumps a polluted substance into the sea in the Bay of Naples.

- **Limited water supplies:** Water supplies are low in the region throughout the summer. Tourism leads to increased **demands for water for swimming pools** and hotels.
- **Unequal development:** Most tourist development has occurred **along coastal regions,** while areas further inland remain inaccessible and unattractive for tourists. This contributes to the income gap in the region.

EDUCATE YOURSELF

Tertiary Activities	
67% of Mezzogiorno employed in tertiary, seasonal, dependent on tourism	
Transport	Decrease transport costs, make journeys shorter, Autostrada del Sole, Naples to Milan, arterial link to richer markets in north, 754 km, construction of modern bridges, tunnels through mountains, direct transport routes, development of deep-water ports in Naples, Calabria and Taranto, steel manufacturing, petrochemical production, oil and gas refining, two busiest ports in Mediterranean, EU Regional Development Fund, EU Structural Fund, €10 bn 2007–2013, allocated to EU regions with GDP below 75% EU average, Telecom Italia privatised in 2013, faster broadband speeds
Tourism	Vital to economy, 6 million international tourists, 11 million domestic tourists, natural advantages
	Climate: hot, dry summers, 24–27 °C, sun and beach holidays, winter temperatures rarely drop below 11 °C, walking and cycling tour, growing skiing sector
	Landscape: unspoilt beauty, less commercialised, 800 km of coastline, shaped by Mediterranean and Adriatic Seas, Bay of Naples, Amalfi Coast, large stretches of beaches, Pescara, Puglia, volcanic mountains, 2.5 million tourists per year
	History and culture: ancient ruins of Roman city of Pompeii, Roman culture, Agrigento in Sicily, Italian cuisine, less influenced by EU culture, Mafia history and origins in Sicily, Palermo, Corleone and Syracuse, stay overnight in former don's estate
	Development: only 13% of foreign tourists visit here, peripheral location, lack of well-developed transport, long distance to drive, Cassa – 15% of total fund to development of tourism, direct and indirect employment, local markets for farm produce, improved accommodation and catering, modern hotels and apartments, new airport at Calabria, ferry links between Calabria and Sicily
	Problems: seasonal tourism, noise pollution, coastal damage, inflated land prices, limited water supplies, unequal development

 ACTIVE **LEARNING**

1. What is meant by the term 'peripheral location'?
2. What are the main difficulties in developing efficient transport links in the Mezzogiorno?
3. How has the government tried to improve transport infrastructure in the region?
4. What natural advantages does the region have that aid the development of tourism?
5. What is meant by the term 'seasonal employment'?
6. What are the negative effects of tourism in the region?

23.6 Human Processes

 GEO **DICTIONARY**

Dialect: a variety of a language spoken in a particular area

The Mezzogiorno has an **ethnically diverse population** which dates back to invasions of the region throughout history. These invading forces included the Greeks, Romans, Normans and Arabs. Most people are **Catholic,** but there is a small but growing number of Muslims in the region. **Italian is the national language,** but there are a **variety of local dialects**.

Population Dynamics

The Mezzogiorno makes up **40 per cent of the land area of Italy,** but has only **35 per cent of the population. Population distribution is uneven,** with the coastal lowlands being much **more densely populated** than the mountainous areas inland. The region's population density is **140 per km²,** which is **30 per cent lower than the national average.** In **lowland coastal regions** such as Campania, population density is **400 per km²,** whereas **Basilicata** in the upland regions has a population density of just **50 per km².**

Birth/Death Rates

Italy has reached **Stage 5 of the Demographic Transitional Model** (DTM). Stage 5 is also known as the **'senile stage'** as there are very **low birth rates,** which leads to an **ageing population.** An ageing population occurs when there are fewer births, so the age profile of the population increases. This means that there are more older people. Stage 5 is associated with developed regions. However, **birth rates in the Mezzogiorno are higher than the EU average.** The **average birth rate of Italy is 9.4 per 1000,** but areas of the Mezzogiorno, such as **Campania** have a birth rate of **13.2 per 1000.** This is mainly due to the strong **Catholic** ethos in the region and the fact that less-developed regions tend to have higher birth rates.

Nonetheless, **family sizes have begun to decrease** across the Mezzogiorno as women are staying in education longer and pursuing careers. As a result, the **population has begun to age.** The **lower birth rate** had a **positive effect** on the Mezzogiorno as it **reduced outward migration.** With fewer births, there **were fewer people competing for jobs.** This improvement is **mainly seen around urban areas** in the region, with **rural areas still experiencing outward migration.** With birth rates just above death rates, the **population growth of the region is low.**

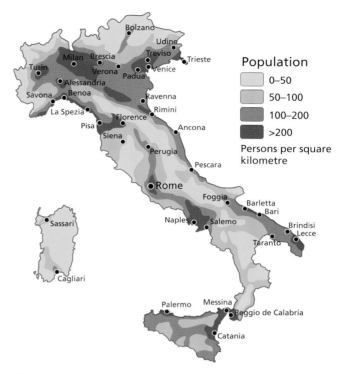

Fig. 23.27 Population density of Italy

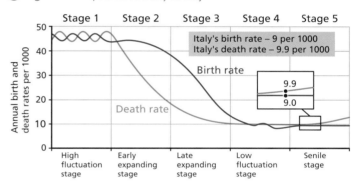

Italy's birth rate – 9 per 1000
Italy's death rate – 9.9 per 1000

Fig. 23.28 Birth and death rates in the Mezzogiorno are higher than the national average.

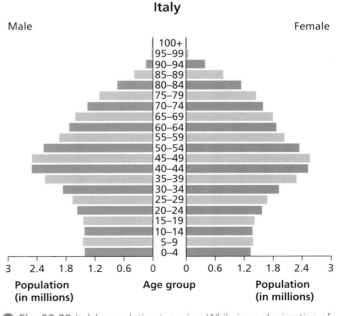

Fig. 23.29 Italy's population is ageing. While inward migration of young people from the Mezzogiorno fills the labour gaps of the north, the Mezzogiorno is robbed of all its future skills and talents.

Life Expectancy

Life expectancy has **improved in the region over the past 50 years,** with **women** living **to an average of 82 and men to an average of 76.** This increased life expectancy has **coincided with an increased standard of living** in the region. Despite these improvements, **health care remains underdeveloped** in the region, which has led to a **higher child mortality rate** than the EU average.

Migration

Roughly **2 per cent of the Mezzogiorno's population are foreign nationals.** With decreasing outward migration, some areas have experienced **net immigration** over the past decade. Inward migration has mainly occurred from **refugees crossing the Mediterranean from war-torn North African and Middle Eastern countries.** Currently, many refugees from Syria are seeking refuge in Sicily and other areas of the region. Approximately **50 000 migrants enter the country illegally each year.** Many migrants take up **seasonal work picking fruit and vegetables** during the harvest season. With increasing numbers of people seeking refuge, the **government has introduced a quota on the number of migrants** entering the region and has increased patrols to prevent people entering illegally.

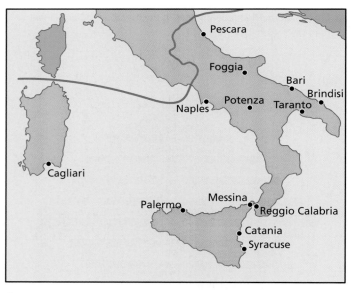

🔼 **Fig. 23.30** Detections of illegal migrations into Italy in 2015

Urban Development

As of 2015, **70 per cent of the region's population lives in towns and cities.** Most of these urban regions are located along the **lowland coastal areas.** Naples, Bari and Taranto are the **largest urban centres,** with only small 'hilltop' towns and villages existing inland. Most of these **hilltop towns experience outward migration** to the larger urban regions of Naples and Bari.

🔼 **Fig. 23.31** Urban centres of the Mezzogiorno

Naples

Naples was founded in **600 BCE by the Greeks.** Naples' city centre streets are a UNESCO world heritage site. With a **population of 3 million**, Naples is the **third largest city in Italy** after Milan and Rome.

The city's economy is driven by its many **craft industries** such as leather work, clothes and shoe manufacturing. Naples also has a large port which **provides employment** and has attracted oil **refining, petrochemical production** and **other heavy industries.** The Cassa Scheme aided the development of the city by attracting industry and **improving its communication links** to the north, e.g. the Autostrada. Fiat has a car assembly plant in Naples which has attracted further investment from electronic and engineering companies.

▲ **Fig. 23.32** An aerial view of Naples

A|Z GEO **DICTIONARY**

BCE: means Before Common Era and is the same as BC, but non-religious

World heritage site: an area or region that has been identified as having specific cultural or physical significance

Urban Decay and Regeneration

Naples has gained a reputation as being an **unsafe and a dirty city.** This is due to its **crowded narrow streets, traffic congestion, poor rubbish collection, high crime rate** and the influence of the **Camorra (the name of the Mafia in the region).**

In response to the ongoing issues, both **government and EU funding** invested in modernising the city. The funding **improved water and sewage systems,** as the water supply was frequently polluted. In order to reduce traffic congestion, **new tram lines** were developed, while existing tram lines were **extended** and modernised.

Despite improvements, the **regeneration of the city will take many years.** The poorer residential districts are in need of renewal as their accommodation and services are outdated and basic.

Rubbish collection remains an issue as the city struggles to find landfill sites. **Less than 20 per cent of the city's waste is recycled,** meaning landfill sites are quickly filled to capacity. The Camorra runs **illegal dumping services** which has greatly damaged the local environment. Much of the rubbish is dumped or burned at illegal sites which **increases air pollution.**

There is a **high level of unemployment** throughout the city, especially among young men. Some of these young men turn to crime, with the Camorra operating protection rackets and other criminal activities. There are frequent **feuds between rival gangs**, leading to gun violence and a **high number of murders** each year.

▲ **Fig. 23.33** Rubbish left uncollected on a street in Naples

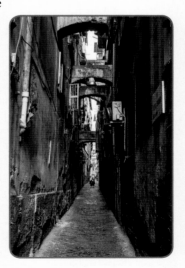

▲ **Fig. 23.34** Narrow streets of Naples

Tourism

Despite the city's many problems, it remains a **popular tourist destination.** Tourism is **vital to the city's economy** and provides much-needed employment. The city operates as a **gateway** to famous sites such as **Pompeii and Herculaneum.** Many tourists stay overnight in the city or use it as a base during their travels. There are many other attractions.

- The **National Archaeology Museum** is home to thousands of Ancient Roman artefacts.
- The **Teatro di San Carlo** attracts opera goers from all over Europe.
- Tourists can avail of **several transport links** to the city. The Autostrada connects to the wealthier north Italian market, while **budget airlines,** such as Ryanair, at Naples Airport connect to Northern Europe.
- Naples is believed to be home to the original pizza and is well-known for its local cuisine and family restaurants.

EDUCATE YOURSELF

Human Processes		
Catholicism, Italian national language, variety of local dialects		
Population dynamics	40% of the land area, 35% of Italy's population, population distribution uneven, lowlands densely populated, density of 140 per km², lower than national average, lowland coastal region Campania has 400 per km², upland Basilicata has 50 per km²	
	Birth rate/death rates: stage 5 demographic transitional model, senile stage, low birth rates, Mezzogiorno higher than EU average, Italy 9.4 per 1000, Mezzogiorno 13.2 per 1000, Catholic practices, family sizes have begun to decrease, population has begun to age, lower birth rates, positive effect reduced outward migration, fewer births means fewer people looking for jobs, urban areas, rural areas outward migration, population growth in the region is low	
	Life expectancy: improved in region over past 50 years, women 82 years and men 76 years, increased standard of living, healthcare remains underdeveloped, higher than EU average child mortality	
	Prevailing issues: outward migration, GDP 24% of national total, >20% unemployment rate, 22% part-time, lower than average literacy rates, low levels of income, political corruption, Mafia/organised crime	
	Migration: 2% of the Mezzogiorno's population are of foreign origin, net immigration, refugees crossing Mediterranean from North Africa and Middle East, 50 000 illegal migrants per year, seasonal work picking fruit and vegetables, government quota on migrants entering country	
Urban development	70% of region's population live in towns and cities, lowland coastal areas, Naples, Bari and Taranto, largest urban centres, hilltop towns experience outward migration	
Naples	600 BCE, 3 million people, third largest city, craft industries, provides employment, oil refining, petrochemical production, other heavy industries, improving communication links	
	Urban decay and regeneration: unsafe and dirty, crowded narrow streets, traffic congestion, poor rubbish collection, high crime rate, Camorra, government and EU funding, improved water and sewage, new and extended tram lines, regeneration will take time, less than 20% of waste recycled, illegal dumping services, increases air pollution, high levels of unemployment, feuds between gangs, high number of murders	
	Popular tourist destination, vital to city's economy, gateway to Pompeii and Herculaneum, National Archaeology Museum, Teatro di San Carlo, several transport links, budget airlines	

ACTIVE LEARNING

1. Explain why birth rates are higher in the Mezzogiorno than in the rest of Italy.
2. Describe how outward migration and immigration impact on human processes in the region.
3. Describe two problems experienced by the city of Naples.
4. Despite its ongoing problems, Naples is a popular tourist destination. Would you visit the city regardless of the high crime rate or would you avoid it?

EXAM FOCUS

Questions on European regions are extremely common at both Higher Level and Ordinary Level, so it is important that you have a full understanding of all topics covered in this chapter. In this section, we will answer a question from the 2010 Higher Level paper. Much of the information is relevant for Ordinary Level students.

HIGHER LEVEL

EXAM QUESTION

Examine the factors that influence the development of one tertiary economic activity in a **European region (not in Ireland)** that you have studied.

Marking Scheme
Tertiary activity named 2m
Region named 2m
Two factors identified 2m + 2m
Examination 11 SRPs @ 2m each

SAMPLE ANSWER

2010 Q4B 30M

I have studied the development of transport links [2m] in the Mezzogiorno region of Italy [2m]. One factor which has had a negative influence on the development of transport is the region's upland relief [2m].

The steep, upland terrain of the Mezzogiorno makes the development of communication links difficult and expensive [2m]. Traditionally, the region's roads were narrow and had a poor surface, making them slow and dangerous to travel on [2m]. During the winter months, the mountainous terrain is often covered in snow, which blocks roadways and railway lines. In times of heavy rain, landslides can occur due to flash flooding [2m]. Many of the old roads were not strong enough to support larger container trucks, which limited the amount of goods they could transport [2m]. The upland terrain greatly increased travel times as roads were forced to wind around mountains and valleys, with a lack of modern bridges and tunnels to allow a more direct route [2m].

A second factor which has influenced transport in the region is government investment [2m]. The Cassa per il Mezzogiorno Scheme invested €2.5 billion in improving transport infrastructure in the region [2m]. This was carried out in order to decrease transport costs and make journey times shorter [2m]. The largest project was the building of the Autostrada del Sole, a 754 km motorway that links Naples to Milan [2m]. Major investment was also given to the construction of modern bridges across valleys and tunnels through mountains. to allow for direct transport routes [2m]. Deep-water ports were also developed at Naples, Augusta, Calabria and Taranto [2m]. Since the end of the Cassa Scheme, the EU Regional Development Fund and the EU Structural Fund have invested in the development of transport in the region [2m].

While this seems like a very straightforward question, you must be careful. Although you can choose two factors, you must discuss only **one** tertiary economic activity. Many students misread this question and wrote about two tertiary activities.

This answer is quite short, but it shows you the importance of providing clear and precise information. Each sentence contains an SRP which builds on the previous one.

As already mentioned, the key here was not to fall into the trap of answering on tourism and transport!

Marks Awarded	
Tertiary activity named 2m	
Region named 2m	
Two factors identified 2m + 2m	
Examination 11 SRPs @ 2m each	
Total 30/30	

TOPIC MAP

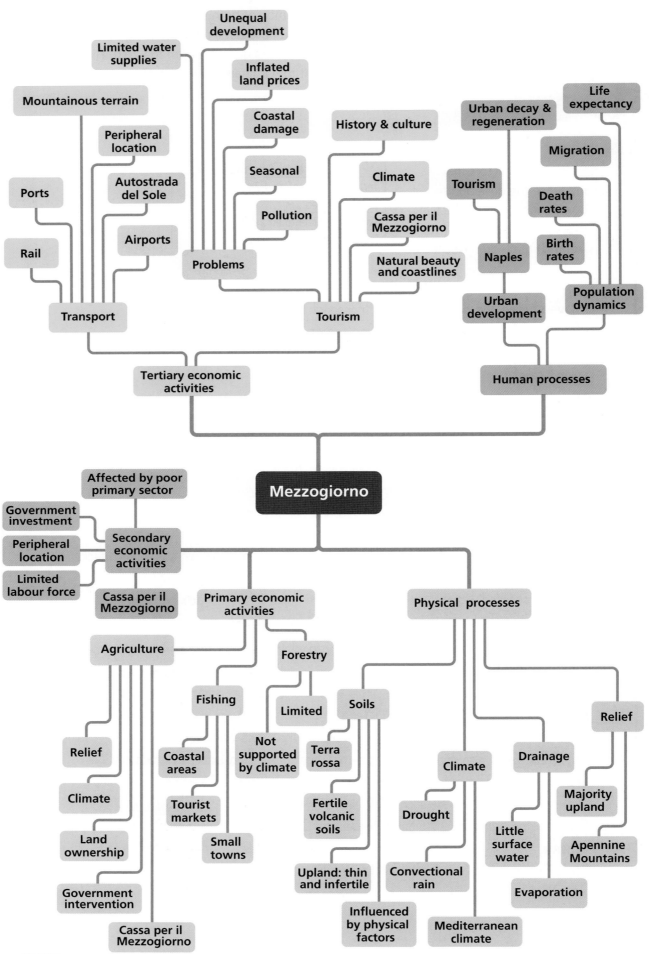

CHAPTER 24

European Regions 2:
Core Socio-economic Region (The Paris Basin)

In this chapter, we will look at the economic development of the Paris Basin. The Paris Basin is a core region, and the centre of all economic activity in France. The region has a number of physical and social factors which have aided its development.

KEY WORDS

- Relief
- Drainage
- Climate
- Transitional climate
- Soil
- Agriculture
- Markets
- Specialist
- Beauce

- Normandy
- Brie
- Champagne
- Forestry
- Fishing
- Communications
- Decentralisation
- Cosmetic Valley
- TGV

- Metro
- Le Havre
- Boulevard Périphérique
- Demographic Transitional Model
- Migration
- Schéma Directeur
- Nodes

LEARNING OUTCOMES

What you MUST know
- Physical characteristics of the Paris Basin
- Climate characteristics of the region
- How to draw a map and fill in the main features of the Paris Basin
- The development of primary, secondary and tertiary activities in the Paris Basin
- Human processes of the region
- Migration and cultural tensions in the region
- Urban development over time: Paris

What you SHOULD know
- Cosmetic Valley CASE STUDY 📁
- Statistics that show contrast between the Paris Basin and the Mezzogiorno (covered in Chapter 23)

What is USEFUL to know
- How to understand information provided in graphs as a means to contrast regions

24.1 Physical Processes

The Paris Basin is the core region of France and one of the most important core areas in the EU. The region is characterised by natural advantages such as a temperate climate, fertile soils and gently sloping relief. The Paris Basin is highly economically developed, with the large domestic market of Paris at its centre.

In this section, we will look at the following physical factors that influence the region:

- Relief
- Drainage
- Climate
- Soil

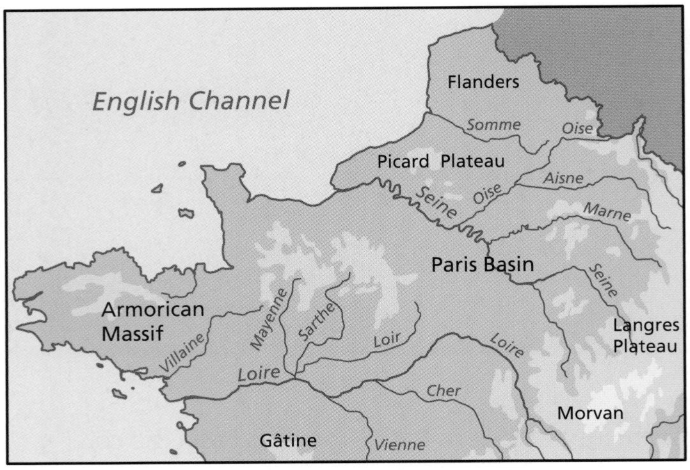

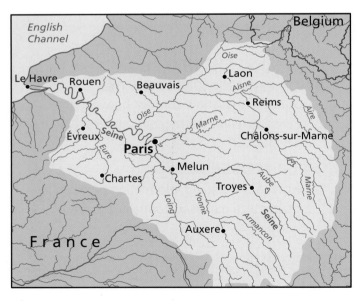

Fig. 24.1 Relief of the Paris Basin

Relief

The Paris Basin is in the north of France. It covers 25 per cent of the country, stretching over **500 km from east to west and 300 km from north to south.** It is made up of **layers of sedimentary** rock – mainly **chalk** and **limestone.** These layers were **folded downwards** 400 million years ago to form the gentle, **basin-shaped syncline** that characterises the region. Around the edges of the basin, the folded sedimentary rock was exposed by weathering to form **escarpments**. These escarpments form **natural borders** and give the region its **basin shape**. The **Île-de-France** lies at the flat, centre of the basin while the relief **rises toward the edges.**

FACT

The Somme was the setting for a deadly battle in World War I, which saw over 1 million soldiers killed or wounded. Farmers in the region still dig up barbed wire and weapons from the battle. This is referred to as the 'iron harvest'.

GEO DICTIONARY

Escarpment: a steep slope at the edge of a plateau or separating lands of different heights

Transitional climate: the climate where two climates meet, i.e. where one climate merges into another

Drainage

The Paris Basin has a **good drainage system** made up of three main rivers: **the Seine, Somme and Loire.** The Seine and its tributaries flow 776 km northwards into the English Channel at the deep-water port of Le Havre. It drains over **78 000 km^2 of the region.** The Seine and its alluvial floodplains have made much of the region fertile for agriculture. The **Somme flows 245 km** from its source in the **upland forests of Picardy,** draining the northern section of the region. The Loire flows from **east to west** and **drains** the **southern section** of the region.

Fig. 24.2 The River Seine drainage basin

Climate

The Paris Basin is characterised by **two main climate** types: a **cool temperate oceanic climate** in the **west** of the region and a **continental climate** towards the **east** of the region. A **transitional climate** exists between where the **two climates meet.** As the west of the Paris Basin is **close to the sea,** it is **heavily influenced** by the **North Atlantic,** meaning it has a **maritime climate.** Due to the influence of the sea, **temperatures are moderate** throughout the year. **Winters are mild,** with temperatures averaging **5 °C** as the sea has a **warming influence on the land. Summers are warm,** with temperatures ranging between **16 and 24 °C (averaging 18 °C).** Due to the influence of **Atlantic depressions,** the region receives **rainfall throughout the year,** averaging **800 mm per year.**

Further inland, the region experiences a **cool, continental climate.** Beyond the influence of the sea, the eastern region experiences **colder winters and warmer summers.** Winters average just **2 °C**, leading to nearly **three months** (an average of 83 days) of **snow and frost.** Temperatures rise to **24 °C** in July and average **19 °C** through the summer months. **Precipitation** is slightly **lower than** in the **west**, averaging **700 mm per year.**

The centre of the Paris Basin is characterised by a transitional climate: its **characteristics are between** the cool temperate of the west and the continental of the east.

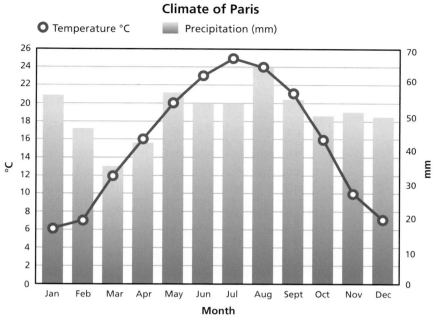

Climate of Paris

○ Temperature °C   ▨ Precipitation (mm)

Fig. 24.3 Precipitation and temperature of Paris

Soil

The **soil** of the Paris Basin is **varied** due to the many **different sedimentary rocks** that lie across the region. This variation has led to regions being **divided into *pays*** according to soil. Each *pay* has **developed different agricultural activities.** Much of the Paris Basin is covered by **thick limon soils** (also called loess soils), which were carried by winds to the region from a **periglacial environment** and deposited in thick layers. Limon soils (found in **Beauce**) are **deep and stoneless,** making them **ideal for agricultural activity.** To the **east** of the region, **clay soils** cover areas such as **Wet Champagne.** The underlying **bedrock** of Wet Champagne is **impermeable,** meaning the clay soils **retain moisture,** making them **damp.**

The Dry Champagne area is covered in **infertile, stony and dry soil** that formed from the **weathering of underlying chalk.** The **Seine, Loire** and **Somme** Rivers provide **fertile alluvial soils** along their banks, which are deposited by **annual floods.** In the southern Paris Basin, the area of **Sologne** is covered by **infertile soils and gravels.**

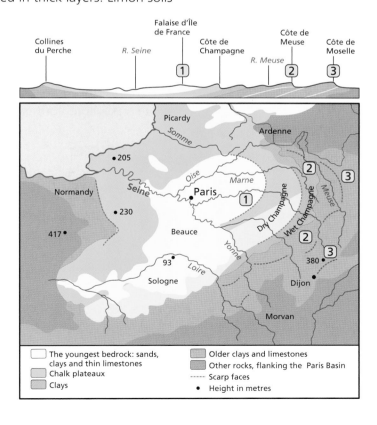

Fig. 24.4 Relief, composition and drainage of the Paris Basin

☐ The youngest bedrock: sands, clays and thin limestones
☐ Chalk plateaux
☐ Clays
▨ Older clays and limestones
▨ Other rocks, flanking the Paris Basin
---- Scarp faces
• Height in metres

Physical Processes	
Relief	500 km east-west, 300 km north-south, layers of chalk and limestone, folded downwards, basin-shaped syncline, escarpments, natural borders, Île-de-France – flat, rises towards edges
Drainage	Good drainage system, Seine drains 78 000 km² of region, Somme drains north section, Loire drains south section
Climate	Two climate types: cool temperate oceanic and continental climate
	Cool temperate oceanic: west, heavily influenced by Atlantic, maritime climate, temperatures are moderate, winters mild (5 °C), warming influence on land, summers warm (16–24 °C), average summer 18 °C, Atlantic depressions, rainfall throughout, 800 mm per annum
	Continental climate: east, cool climate, colder winters (2 °C), warmer summers (19 °C), precipitation 700 mm per year, lower than west, transitional climate where both meet, characteristics of both
Soil	Varied, different sedimentary rocks, divided into pays, each pay has different agricultural practices, thick limon/loess soils, periglacial environment, deep and stoneless, ideal for agriculture, e.g. in Beauce; east clay soils, e.g. Wet Champagne, bedrock impermeable, damp soils; Dry Champagne infertile, stony, dry, weathering of chalk; rivers fertile alluvial soils along bank, annual floods, infertile soils and gravels

 ACTIVE **LEARNING**

1. What are synclines? How are they formed?
2. How might the climate of the Paris Basin influence agriculture across the region?
3. Where would be the better place to grow cereal crops, east or west? Explain your answer.
4. Where would be the better place to practise pastoral farming, east or west? Explain your answer.
5. Why are limon soils suitable for agriculture?
6. What does 'impermeable' mean and why does it cause soil to be damp?

24.2 Primary Activities

Only a **small percentage of the Paris Basin's economy is based on primary economic activities.** Examples of such primary activities in the Paris Basin are agriculture, forestry and fishing.

Agriculture

The Paris Basin is one of the most **intensely farmed regions in the EU.** Due to **natural advantages,** agriculture in the region is both **productive, intensive and diverse.** Relief, climate and soil are suitable for farming and heavily influence agriculture in the region. **Variations in relief, climate and soil** have led to **a wide range of agricultural activities** in different locations. Farmers also have access to a large market.

Factors Affecting Agriculture in the Paris Basin
Relief

The **gently sloping lowlands** of the Paris Basin are **ideal for cultivation** as the elevation **rarely goes over 200 m** above sea level. The gentle slopes allow **easy access** for **machinery,** meaning farms are **highly mechanised.**

 GEO **DICTIONARY**

Diverse: varied; in relation to agriculture to produce more than one crop

This means agriculture is quick and **intensive**. The **gentle slopes** create an **effective drainage network** with run-off carried away by rivers, such as the Seine and Somme.

In Dry Champagne, the **gently, south-facing escarpments** are ideal for **viticulture,** as they are **well drained** and **receive plenty of sunlight.** The grapes grown here are used to produce **Champagne**. In **Wet Champagne,** the gently sloping fields have allowed for **widespread arable farming,** e.g. in Picardy, and **pastoral farming,** e.g. in Artois.

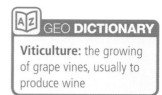

GEO **DICTIONARY**

Viticulture: the growing of grape vines, usually to produce wine

Climate

The climate of the Paris Basin has allowed the development of **specialised agriculture,** such as **cereal farming** in Beauce. **Moderate rainfall** in **spring** and **early summer** promotes the **growth of cereals** such as wheat and barley, while **warm summer temperatures** allow **crops** to **ripen.**

In the **western half** of the region, the slightly **wetter oceanic climate** is ideal for growing grass, which has promoted **intensive dairy farming.** The mild winter temperatures, combined with **evenly distributed rainfall** throughout the year, allow for a **long growing season.** This grass growth allows for **high stocking rates.**

Soil

The **variation in soils** throughout the Paris Basin **impacts on the type of farming** carried out in each region. Large parts of the region are covered in **limon soils,** which are **fertile and easily worked.** Île-de-France is covered in limon soils, allowing for the **intensive growth of wheat.**

The **clay soils** of Wet Champagne are **ideal for growing grass,** which has led to the development of **productive dairy cooperatives.** Dairy farming is also carried out along the **floodplains of the region's main rivers** as fertile **alluvium soil** suits the growth of **grassland.** In Dry Champagne, the **soil** is formed from the **weathering of underlying chalk,** meaning it is dry and infertile. The soil is **suitable for viticulture,** although it needs to be irrigated at times during summer. In areas of Dry Champagne where it is not suitable to plant vines, **extensive sheep farming** is carried out. In the southern region of **Sologne,** gravelly soils are infertile and **not suited to agriculture.**

▲ **Fig. 24.5** Vineyards on the gentle slopes of Dry Champagne

FACT

The bubbles which make Champagne so famous were actually a mistake and were considered a fault in the wine. As a result, the Benedictine monks who made it spent a lot of time trying to stop the wine from becoming fizzy.

Over 85 000 hectares of land in the Dry Champagne area are planted with the grapes which produce over 200 million bottles of Champagne annually.

▲ **Fig. 24.6** The climate in Beauce allows for the intensive harvesting of wheat.

CORE 3 CHAPTER 24

REGIONAL GEOGRAPHY **447**

Markets

Markets are a **human factor** that have influenced agriculture in the Paris Basin. The region has a population of **22 million people,** which means farmers have **access to a large market.** The population is highly urbanised, so there is a constant **demand for fresh milk, bread** and **vegetables. Horticulture** and **milk production** occur **close to the edge of the city** in order to provide for this **wealthy** market.

Market gardening of **fruit, vegetables and flowers** is carried out on agricultural land **close to the city.** As the region's **transport links are well developed,** farmers can **transport** their goods to the nearby market **cheaply and efficiently.**

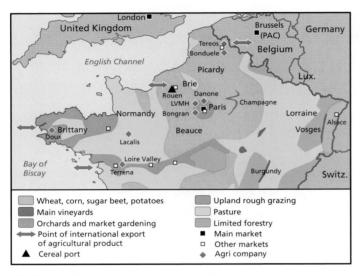

Fig. 24.7 Agricultural produce of the Paris Basin

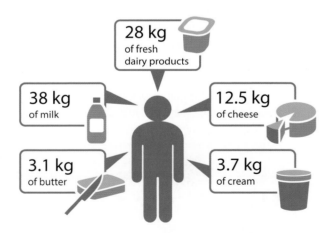

Fig. 24.8 The amount of dairy products the average French person consumes each year

---

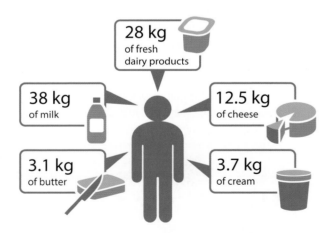

GEO DICTIONARY

Bloodstock: breeding of thoroughbred (pedigree) horses, usually to be used for horse racing

---

Agricultural Areas of the Paris Basin

As you have already learned, the Paris Basin has a variety of soils and landscapes, meaning certain areas specialise in particular crops or animals. These specialist areas are:

- Brie
- Normandy
- Beauce
- Champagne

Brie

Brie lies east of Paris and has **heavy, damp soils** that promote grass growth. Therefore, Brie is dominated by intensive **dairy farming** with high stocking rates. The **high milk yields** are used to supply the nearby urban market and to produce **Brie cheese.** Farming in Brie is **profitable** and large-scale.

Normandy

Normandy is close to the west coast. It has a **damp and mild climate** due to the influence of the Atlantic, which allows grass to grow quickly. This has promoted dairy farming, with **high stocking rates** and **intensive practices.** Cheese making, e.g. **Camembert,** is important in Normandy. The food company **Danone** is located here, which needs a **constant supply of milk.**

The **limestone bedrock** of the area has led to **calcium-rich pasture,** which **promotes bloodstock** as horses develop **strong bones.** Normandy also specialises in **apple orchards. Golden Delicious** apples are grown in this area.

Beauce

Beauce specialises in **cereal production**, such as **wheat, canola** and **barley**. The area has the **highest cereal yields** in the EU and is referred to as the 'granary of France'. Much of the **wheat** produced here is used for **milling** and **animal feed**. Most of the **barley** grown is used in **brewing industries**.

Beauce's flat, fertile and **treeless landscape** allows for **intensive production**. Farms in the area are **highly mechanised. Sugar beet** is grown as a **rotation crop** to allow soils to recover. **Overproduction and pollution** have become a major concern in Beauce. Overproduction has led to **a wider range of crops**, such as **potatoes and vegetables**, being grown there.

Champagne

Champagne wine is the most **famous product** of this area. The sparkling wine is produced in vineyards on the gently south-sloping, chalk escarpment (Falaise d'Île-de-France). These are the **most northerly vineyards in France**.

Forestry

Natural forestry has been **removed** from the Paris Basin over the past number of centuries **to clear land for agriculture**. Forestry is limited to the **scarp and vale landscape** along the **south-eastern border** of the Paris Basin. Soils here are **gravelly and infertile**, making them **unsuitable for agriculture**. Mixed farming and **forestry** also **occur in Sologne** along the south of the region.

Fishing

Commercial fishing is **limited to the coastal areas** along the **English Channel** in ports such as **Cherbourg** in Normandy, **Le Havre** and **Dieppe**. These ports have **large fishing fleets**, which vary from **deep-sea fishing** boats to **coastal trawlers**. Over the past number of decades, fishing has **declined** in the region as **overfishing of cod** has **depleted stocks**. **EU quotas** and **restrictions** have also **affected** the **income** of fishers.

Aquaculture is becoming **increasing popular** along **inlets and bays** on the coast. **Forty per cent** of French oysters are farmed along the **coast of Normandy**. These are mainly sold to the Parisian market.

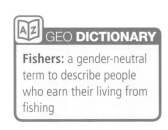

GEO DICTIONARY

Fishers: a gender-neutral term to describe people who earn their living from fishing

◀ **Fig. 24.9** Main fishing ports of the Paris Basin

Primary Activities	
Small percentage of Paris Basin's economy	
Agriculture	Intensively farmed, natural advantages, productive and diverse, variations in climate
Factors affecting agriculture	Relief: gently sloping lowlands, ideal for cultivation, easy machinery access, rarely exceeds 200 m, highly mechanised, gentle slopes, effective drainage network, Rivers Seine and Somme, Dry Champagne – gently sloping south-facing escarpments, viticulture, well drained, plentiful sunlight, Wet Champagne – gently sloping fields, widespread arable farming, pastoral farming, Artois
	Climate: specialised agriculture, cereal farming – Beauce/Île-de-France, moderate rainfall, spring/early summer, growth of cereals, wheat and barley, warm temperatures, crops ripen, wetter oceanic climate (western half), intensive dairy farming, evenly distributed rainfall, long growing season, high stocking rates, e.g. Brie
	Soil: variations in soil, impacts on farming type, fertile limon soils Île-de-France, easily worked, intensive growth of wheat, Wet Champagne clay soils, ideal for grass growth, highly productive dairy cooperatives, alluvium floodplains of main rivers, lush grassland, Dry Champagne weathered chalk, infertile, suitable viticulture, Sologne not suited to agriculture
	Markets: human factor, 22 million people, access to large and wealthy market, demand for fresh milk, bread and vegetables, horticulture and milk production close to the city, market gardening close to city, transport links well developed, cheap and efficient transport
Agricultural areas	Brie: east of Paris, heavy, damp soils, dairy farming, high milk yields, Brie cheese, profitable
	Normandy: damp and mild climate, high stocking rates, intensive practices, Camembert, Danone, constant demand and supply of milk, limestone bedrock, calcium-rich pasture, promotes bloodstock – strong bones
	Beauce: cereal production – wheat, canola and barley, 'granary of France', highest cereal yields in EU, soft wheat – milling and production of animal feed, barley – brewing industry, highly mechanised, flat fertile and treeless, sugar beet – rotation crop, overproduction and pollution, diversification of crops, potatoes and vegetables
	Champagne: Champagne wine, Falaise d'Île-de-France, most northerly vineyards in France, market centre
Forestry	Natural forestry removed, cleared for agricultural land, scarp and vale landscape, south-eastern border, gravelly and infertile soil, unproductive for agriculture, mixed farming and forestry in Sologne
Fishing	Limited to coastal areas along English Channel; ports Cherbourg, Le Havre, Dieppe; large fishing fleets, deep-sea fishing and coastal trawlers, overfishing of cod, depleted stocks, EU quotas, aquaculture increasingly popular, inlets and bays, 40% of French oysters coast of Normandy

Note!

A question on primary activities in a European region frequently appears on both Higher Level and Ordinary Level papers. They appear almost annually on the Ordinary Level paper. Remember, it is not just enough to know statistics or general knowledge on farming in a region. You must also be able to discuss the factors affecting agriculture in the region.

ACTIVE LEARNING

1. Explain how one physical factor and one human factor have influenced the development of agriculture in the Paris Basin.
2. How does climate affect the agriculture of the Paris Basin?
3. What is viticulture? Why is Dry Champagne suitable for viticulture?
4. Describe the characteristics of agriculture in the following areas:
   (a) Beauce (b) Normandy (c) Brie (d) Champagne
5. Discuss the development of forestry in the region.
6. Why do you think forestry is so limited in the Paris Basin?
7. Explain two challenges facing the fishing industry in the Paris Basin?

24.3 Secondary Activities

Many different **manufacturing activities** take place in the Paris Basin, the majority of which are carried out by **MNCs**. There are many **advantages that attract industry** to the Paris Basin such as:

- A strong agricultural sector
- Availability of labour force and education opportunities
- Well-developed communications
- A large market
- Raw materials

Industry in the region has also undergone decentralisation.

Strong Agricultural Sector

The **intensive and productive agricultural sector** surrounding the Paris Basin means that there is a good **supply of fruits, vegetables** and **grains**. This has led to the development of **large food processing industries**. **Dairy food processing** is an important industry, with **five French dairy companies located in the Paris Basin ranking in the top 25** globally.

Dairy products, such as milk protein, are also used in the **chemical and pharmaceutical industries**. The local market also provides a **constant demand** as France is the **largest consumer of milk and cheese** in the world. Some **67 per cent of dairy products** are exported to the **EU market**. **Cereals** supply the **boulangeries** in Paris. Wheat, barley and other grains grown in the region are **transported** to Paris for making **pastries, chocolate,** etc.

French Dairy Companies World Rankings
Lactalis (No. 1)
Danone (No. 4)
Sodiaal (No. 17)
Bongrain (No. 18)
Bel (No. 24)

GEO DICTIONARY

Boulangeries: Parisian bakeries which are known for the quality of their breads and pastries

Availability of Labour Force and Education Opportunities

Over **11 million people** live in the **Greater Paris Area**, with over **22 million people** in the **Paris Basin**. This provides a **large labour force**. The presence of **17 universities** in the region **attracts industries**. High-tech industries can invest in **research and development at the universities,** and also have a supply of **high-quality graduates**. Some **85 per cent of research and development** carried out in France takes place in the **Paris Basin region,** with **technological parks** and industrial estates integrated in order to **develop new products**. Due to this innovation, **manufacturing companies** locate their headquarters in the Paris Basin, making the region the **focus of decision making** for the country.

PSA Peugeot Citroen, the largest car manufacturer in France, has its main headquarters in the Paris Basin.

PSA Peugeot Citroen
2.8 million sales
83 930 employees
14 500 researchers
4 research and development centres

Well-developed Communications

Communications are well developed throughout the region with **efficient road, rail, port, airport** and **broadband infrastructure**.

The **deep-water port of Le Havre** enables ships to **access the region from the English Channel**. Modern docking facilities and warehouses

GEO DICTIONARY

Docking facilities: facilities which allow for loading and unloading of ships

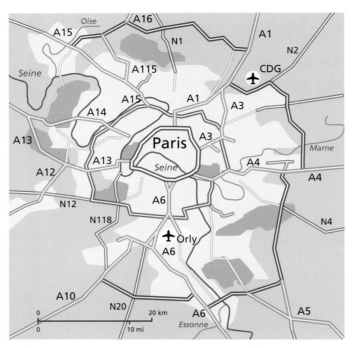

Fig. 24.10 All transport routes radiate from Paris.

have been built along the river. These are specifically designed to **store large, bulky goods** for heavy industry. Due to this, heavy industries such as steel, **oil refining, petrochemical** and **textiles** have located along the Seine.

The **flat relief** of the region means that **communication links** are **easily constructed** as they do not have to tunnel through mountains. **Straight roads** can be built that **link to** the **capital**, Paris. This has made Paris a **nodal point for communications.** It has also allowed for **efficient distribution of produce** throughout the region.

The region has one of the **best rail networks** in the world, which provides an excellent public transport system. The **Trains à Grande Vitesse (TGV)** is a high-speed rail service. It **connects** to the **major urban hubs** of France and also extends into neighbouring countries, including Switzerland and Germany. A high-speed rail called the Eurostar connects France to the UK. This makes large **EU markets easily accessible for passengers and freight.**

Freight trains can reach speeds of **270 km/h**. Since 2015, all trains have 'swap bodies', meaning the **carriage containers can be lifted directly off the train and placed on the back of lorries.** This makes **transporting of goods** from manufacturing areas **fast and efficient.**

The **Metro** is a mostly **underground** subway which enables workers to travel quickly around the city. **Charles de Gaulle** and **Orly airports** allow for **import and export of light materials.**

Large Market

With over **22 million people** living in the Paris Basin, there is a **constant demand for local produce. Standards of living are high,** meaning there is large **wealthy market** that can afford luxury goods. This has led to the development of **niche markets** for high-end goods produced by companies such as **Chanel** (clothing and perfume) and **Cartier** (jewellery).

Paris has become world famous for designer goods. Many designer brands **locate around the city. Cosmetic Valley** is less than **100 km** from the city in the **Chartres** area and is home to world-famous brands such as **L'Oréal** and **Guerlain.**

Raw Materials

The Paris Basin is **rich in natural resources,** as are the **former colonies of France** from which it imports goods. The region has deposits of **iron ore,** which are used in the **steel and engineering sectors.** France's former colony of **Cameroon supplies timber** to the region.

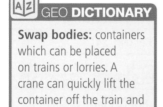

Swap bodies: containers which can be placed on trains or lorries. A crane can quickly lift the container off the train and place it directly on the back of the lorry

Although the region has **limited deposits of fossil fuels,** pipelines have been constructed to bring **natural gas from the Pyrenees in the south of the country** to the Paris Basin. **Pipelines** also link **Le Havre** and Marseille to **oil fields in the Netherlands**. This infrastructure has led to the development of important **textile and petrochemical industries.**

Decentralisation of Industry

Paris grew rapidly from 1800 onwards. By 1950, the government had begun the process of **decentralisation. Industries** were encouraged **to move away from the Greater Paris Region** and locate in other urban areas throughout the Paris Basin. In 1963, the Agency for **Spatial Planning and Regional Attractiveness** (DATAR) was put in charge of **developing infrastructure** and other supports to **convince industries to relocate** from Paris to elsewhere in the region.

Decentralisation has played a major role in strengthening the economy of other parts of the Paris Basin, while **reducing the rate of urban sprawl** in Paris. Since the 1970s, **industrial decline has occurred** as the high cost of land and labour and traffic congestion encouraged companies to leave the Paris Basin and **relocate to peripheral parts** of the country. This has led to the **number of people employed in manufacturing halving** between 1975 and 2005. The region is still prosperous, but **unemployment has increased.**

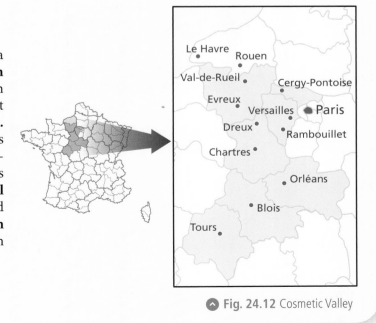

⌃ **Fig. 24.11** Manufacturing centres in the Paris Basin

Employment in the Paris Basin in 2013
3.32 million unemployed
1.6 million are part-time workers

CASE STUDY 🗀

Cosmetic Valley

Cosmetic Valley is the name given to the area of France that **specialises** in the **production of cosmetics** and perfumes. It was founded in 1994 and is now a **technopole,** meaning that it is a **centre of high-tech manufacturing.** Since it was founded, Cosmetic Valley has grown across seven departments in Île-de-France and Normandy. Cosmetic companies such as **L'Oréal, Guerlain, Jean Paul Gautier, Dior** and **Maybelline** have located there. The area has **high levels of research and development** and **education,** which specialise in innovations and new products.

⌃ **Fig. 24.12** Cosmetic Valley

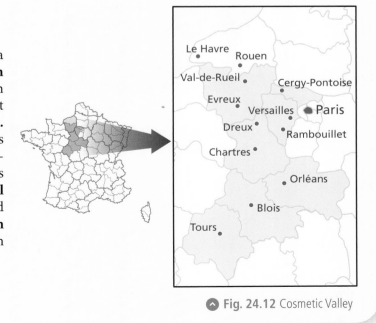

Employment and Research and Development

Cosmetic Valley creates much employment in areas such as:

- Growing aromatic plants
- Creating and formulating products
- Manufacturing perfumes and cosmetics
- Control testing and analysis laboratories
- Advertising, design and packaging

In total, the region hosts **800 companies** which **employ over 70 000 people**. In order to guarantee a constant supply of **high-quality graduates,** companies fund and sponsor PhD programmes. There are **seven universities,** 136 colleges and 200 public research centres which guarantee a **skilled workforce.**

Over **8600 researchers** are employed in Cosmetic Valley. They carry out over **100 research projects** with a **budget of €200 million per year.** As a result of this investment, the area has become one of the countries most important manufacturing centres in the country, generating over **€11 billion in revenue annually.**

EDUCATE YOURSELF

Secondary Activities	
Large variety of manufacturing industries, MNCs, advantages attract industry	
Strong agricultural sector	Intensive and productive agricultural sector, supply fruit, vegetables and grains, large food-processing industry, dairy food processing, 5 of top-25 dairy companies in the world, chemical and petrochemical industries, constant demand, largest consumers of milk and cheese in the world, 67% dairy products exported to EU markets, cereals supply boulangeries, goods easily transported
Availability of labour and education opportunities	27.5% employed in manufacturing, 22 million people in region, large labour force, 17 universities attract industry, high-tech industries, high-quality research and development, high-quality graduates, 85% of country's research and development, new innovations in pharmaceuticals, focus of decision making
Well-developed communications	Efficient road, rail, port and airport networks, River Seine – development of heavy industry, deep-water port at Le Havre, access to English Channel, modern docking facilities, store large bulky goods, oil refining, petrochemical, textiles, flat relief, easily constructed links, straight roads link to capital, nodal point for communications, quick and easy access for agricultural produce, efficient distribution of produce, best rail networks, TGV, connects major urban hubs, EU markets easily accessible for passengers, freight trains – 270 km/h, 'swap bodies' and carriage containers placed on back of lorries, Metro; Charles de Gaulle and Orly airports, import and export light materials
Large market	22 million people, constant demand for local produce, standards of living are high, wealthy market, high-end goods, locally produced goods, Chanel, Cartier, located around city, fashion designers, Cosmetic Valley – L'Oréal and Guerlain
Raw materials	Rich in natural resources, former French colonies, agricultural produce, iron ore – steel and engineering companies, Cameroon supplies timber – limited deposits of fossil fuels, natural gas piped from Pyrenees to region, oil from Netherlands to Le Havre, textile and petrochemical industries
Decentralisation of industry	Decentralisation in Paris, industries move away from Greater Paris Area, DATAR, developing infrastructure, encourage industries to relocate, reducing rate of urban sprawl, industrial decline, relocate to peripheral areas, number of manufacturing workers halved between 1975 and 2005, unemployment figures increased

1. What is a heavy industry?

2. How has the Paris Basin's agricultural sector aided the development of manufacturing?

3. Explain how the region's communications have aided the development of manufacturing in the region.

4. How has France's former colonisation of African countries contributed to manufacturing in the region?

5. How does the Paris Basin overcome its shortage of fossil fuels?

6. What is meant by the term 'decentralisation'? Why did it occur in Paris?

7. What is industrial decline?

8. Briefly describe the development of Cosmetic Valley.

24.4 Tertiary Activities

Approximately **70 per cent of the Paris Basin's workforce** is employed in the tertiary sector. This sector is hugely important to the economy. The two tertiary services we will focus on are:

- Transport
- Tourism

Transport

As a core region of Europe, the Paris Basin has **well-developed transport links.** The region's **low-lying relief** has allowed for **easy construction of road and rail links.** All transport links connect to the city of **Paris**, making it the **nodal point of the national transport network.**

Roads

All **motorways radiate out from Paris** like the **spokes of a wheel,** connecting the city to all other regions of France. The **Boulevard Périphérique** is a **ring road around Paris,** allowing access to various parts of the city without the need to travel through it. The road is **one of the busiest in Europe.** Although it was originally meant to **reduce traffic congestion,** its popularity has led to widespread traffic delays. As Boulevard Périphérique is **surrounded by the city** and its suburbs, the road cannot be **widened.** Between **1.1 and 1.2 million** vehicles use the road every day, with average speeds of **40 km/h.**

 **Fig. 24.13** Traffic congestion on Boulevard Périphérique

Airports

The Paris Basin has **well-developed airports,** such as **Charles de Gaulle, Beauvais** and **Orly.** These airports promote **tourism** and international **trade for light industry.** Charles de Gaulle is the second busiest airport in Europe, handling approximately **200 000 passengers per day.**

Rail

The **SNCF** is the national railway company. Its rail lines **mainly run parallel to the country's motorways,** meaning they radiate out from Paris to other regions of France. The **TGV** is France's **high-speed rail system,**

> **GEO DICTIONARY**
>
> **Light industry:** industries that use or produce small or light materials, e.g. electronics, medical devices

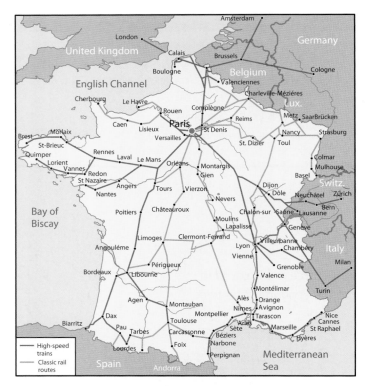

Fig. 24.14 SNCF rail lines

Fig. 24.15 Le Havre is the largest port in France and a centre for distribution.

Fig. 24.16 The Palace of Versailles

which **transports passengers from Paris to destinations** all over the country. The TGV can travel at speeds of up to 300 km/h, although its normal travel speeds are much lower than this. The TGV also **connects to other major cities in Europe** such as Cologne, Brussels, Amsterdam and London (via the Channel Tunnel). Its popularity has greatly **reduced the need for air travel** within France and between France and the UK.

Ports

Located in the north of the Paris Basin, **Le Havre** is one of Europe's **busiest ports**. Modern **roll-on/roll-off container** ships and ferries have allowed the export of French produce such as **wine, food and clothing to its main export market in the UK**. There are many ferry crossings to Britain and Ireland, which have **aided tourism**. The **River Seine** is an important transport feature, with **canals connecting the river** to other parts of the region. This allows for the **transport of bulky goods**.

Tourism

The Paris Basin benefits from Paris being the **main point of entry** into the country. The region receives **15 per cent of national tourism,** with **45 million people** visiting **each year.** Tourism is a major contributor to the economy, generating **€20 billion per year. Eleven per cent of all employment** in Paris is in the tourist industry.

The main tourist attractions are:

- Historic sites
- Theme parks
- City breaks

Historic Sites

Many of the region's **city centres** date back to **medieval times,** with most now **preserved and pedestrianised.** This allows tourists to freely explore and enjoy them. **Gothic cathedrals** such as **Notre Dame,** which receives **13 million tourists per year,** and cathedrals in Reims and Chartres attract many visitors. Other historic sites include:

- **The Palace of Versailles** was the former home of the royal family prior to the French Revolution.

- **The Louvre Museum** is home to over 35 000 priceless artefacts, such as the *Mona Lisa.* Over 9.3 million tourists visit the museum, 70 per cent of whom are from overseas.

- **The Arc de Triomphe** is a monument commissioned by Napoleon after his army's victory at Austerlitz in 1806. Visitors can access the monument by Metro lines.

Theme Parks

Disneyland Paris is located at **Marne-la-Valée,** 32 km east of Paris. The resort was built in 1992 **near Charles de Gaulle airport,** for ease of access. Despite initially struggling to attract visitors, the resort has become the **number one visitor attraction in Europe,** with over **15 million visitors** each year. As well as having generated nearly **€40 billion in revenue** since it opened, the resort also employs roughly **55 000 people each year.**

▶ **Fig. 24.17** Disneyland Paris attracts over 15 million tourists per year.

City Breaks

Paris is the most visited city in the world, with **33 million people visiting** annually. Tourism generates **240 000 jobs in the city,** accounting for 11 per cent of total employment. Paris offers a wide range of attractions, with famous sites such as the **Eiffel Tower,** which is visited by over **12 million people each year.** The city has also become known for its fine dining and romantic setting. Paris attracts tourists from all over Europe for weekend breaks.

Factors Which Benefit Tourism

As well as its diverse range of attractions, Paris Basin tourism has benefitted from:

- Well-developed transport links
- A large domestic market
- **Low-cost air travel** from companies such as **Ryanair**
- **Longer annual holidays** and shorter working days which have led to longer stays
- New markets, as **Central and Eastern European countries joined the EU, more tourists travelled from these countries.** The Asian market also grew by **10 per cent** between **2014 and 2015.**

FACT

For the first time in its history, Disneyland Paris closed from 14–17 November 2015 as a mark of respect to those killed in the terrorist attacks in Paris.

The top five resorts in the Paris Basin are:

- Disneyland Paris
- Notre Dame Cathedral
- Eiffel Tower
- Louvre Museum
- Palace of Versailles

Tertiary Activities		
Well developed, 70% of region's workforce		
Transport	Well developed, low-lying relief – easy construction of roads/rail, Paris – nodal point of national transport network	
	Roads: motorways radiate out from Paris, spokes of a wheel, Boulevard Périphérique, ring road around Paris, one of busiest in Europe, aimed to reduce traffic congestion, surrounded by city, unable to expand, 1.1–1.2 million vehicles per day, average speed 40 km/h, movement of goods and people	
	Airports: well developed and busy airports, Charles de Gaulle, Orly, Beauvais, trade for light industry and tourism, 200 000 passengers per day	
	Rail: SNCF, rail runs parallel to motorways, TGV, Paris to several destinations, connects to other major cities in Europe, 115 million passengers per year, reduced need for internal flights	
	Ports: Le Havre, roll-on/roll-off containers, export wine, food and clothing to UK, aided tourism, River Seine, canals connect to rivers, transport of bulky goods	
Tourism	Main point of entry, 15% national tourism, 45 million per year, €20 billion per year, 11% of employment	
Historic sites, theme parks and city breaks	Medieval city centres, preserved and pedestrianised, gothic cathedrals – Notre Dame (13 million tourists per year), Palace of Versailles, Louvre Museum (9.3 million tourists per year), Arc de Triomphe, Disneyland Paris, Marne-la-Vallée, near Charles de Gaulle Airport, no. 1 visitor attraction in Europe, 15 million visitors per year, €40 billion revenue since opening, 55 000 employed	
Factors which benefit tourism	Well-developed transport links, large domestic market, package holidays, e.g. Ryanair, longer annual holidays = longer stays, new markets: EU enlargement countries, Asian market 10% increase 2014–2015	

ACTIVE LEARNING

1. What percentage of the region's workforce is employed in the tertiary sector?
2. What is meant by 'nodal point'?
3. Explain the importance of the Boulevard Périphérique.
4. What is the TGV?
5. Why is Le Havre such an important port for the region?
6. Find three statistics which highlight the importance of tourism to the region's economy.
7. Describe three tourist attractions in the region.
8. List five factors which have benefitted tourism.
9. What is meant by the term 'domestic tourism'?

24.5 Human Processes

Population Dynamics

The **population** of the Paris Basin is roughly **22 million,** double the number of people living there in 1921. However, both the **density and distribution varies greatly** throughout the region. The **Île-de-France** is far **more densely populated** than the rest of the Paris Basin, containing more than **half of the region's population.** The **Seine Valley** between Paris and **Le Havre** is also **densely populated.** The **southern and eastern edges** of the Paris Basin are **more sparsely populated** due to the **unproductive soils** and **unfavourable climate.** These lead to **rural-urban migration.**

Birth Rates

The **Paris Basin is in Stage 4** of the **Demographic Transitional Model (DTM)**, but this is **due to migration. Without migration,** the region would be **in the senile stage** of the DTM. Throughout France, the birth rate is low, at just **1.9 children per woman.** Despite this, the population of the Paris Basin is **increasing by 0.8 per cent annually.** This increase is due to **migrant families** who come from countries with **traditionally larger families.**

The government has introduced a number of incentives to encourage an increase in birth rates to at least replacement rate. These include:

- **170 weeks maternity** and parental leave
- **High children's allowances** (nearly €300 per month for families with three children)
- **Subsidised crèche and preschool places**
- Working mothers who take **time off** to have a **third child** receive **€750 per month for one year**

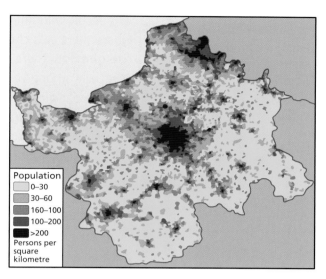

⌃ **Fig. 24.18** Population density of the Paris Basin

Population
- 0–30
- 30–60
- 160–100
- 100–200
- >200

Persons per square kilometre

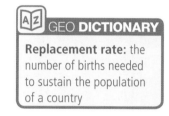

GEO DICTIONARY

Replacement rate: the number of births needed to sustain the population of a country

Death Rates

Death rates are low in the Paris Basin, as you would expect for one of the most developed countries in the world. **Life expectancy is high** in both males and females and there is a **low child mortality rate.** As birth rates are low, the **population** of the Paris Basin has **begun to age,** moving towards the senile stage of the DTM.

Migration

The Paris Basin is the most popular destination for immigrants to France, as it is for French migrants.

Three main factors have affected migration patterns to the Paris Basin:

- Colonisation
- Rural-urban migration
- EU enlargement and the collapse of communism

After the end of the World War II, migrants from the **former French colonies** in West and North Africa moved to the region. They **filled labour shortages** as France's economy grew. Many migrants **experienced discrimination** and were able to secure only the **lowest-paying jobs.**

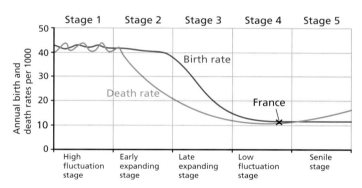

⌃ **Fig. 24.19** The population of France is in Stage 4 of the DTM but this is largely due to immigration.

⌃ **Fig. 24.20** High-rise ghettos have led to the segregation of migrants.

As a result, migrant communities were established in the Paris suburbs, where there was **cheaper accommodation.** This has resulted in **high-rise ghettos.** There are **high levels of poverty and unemployment,** especially among younger generations who were born in France. In the most recent **global recession,** many of those who were the first to **lose their jobs** were migrants and ethnic minorities. This leads to **tensions with the government.** Cultural tensions have developed as a result. Many African migrants remain on the **fringes of French society.**

There has been frequent conflict between the police and people living in the ghettos. For example, in **2005, rioting occurred** after two young men of North African descent were electrocuted in a power station while hiding from the police. In the aftermath of the rioting, **migrant integration** became an **important issue.**

● **Fig. 24.21** Muslims at prayer in Paris

There has been increased tension between some French people and Muslim communities. Controversy arose in **2010 when the government introduced a law banning the wearing of the niqab in public places.**

The collapse of **communism** and **EU enlargement** led to an increase of **Polish, Russian and other Central and Eastern European migrants.** In general, these migrants have **assimilated** into French society.

Forty per cent of all internal migrants come from the **'empty diagonal',** a **peripheral area** in the south-eastern part of the country, e.g. the Massif Central. Most of these migrants are from rural areas and move to the city in search of **employment** and a **higher standard of living.**

EDUCATE YOURSELF

Human Processes	
Population dynamics	Population 22 million, density and distribution varies greatly – Île-de-France most densely populated, half region's population, Seine valley and Le Havre also densely populated; south-eastern edges sparsely populated, unproductive soil, unfavourable climate, rural-urban migration
Birth rates	Stage 4 of DTM, only due to migration; without migration in senile stage, government incentives encourage growth, 170 weeks maternity leave, high children's allowance, subsidised crèche and preschool, €750 per month work leave for one year for third child
Death rates	Death rates low, life expectancy high, low child mortality, population ageing, moving to senile stage
Migration	Popular destination for immigrants, colonisation, rural-urban migration, EU enlargement and collapse of communism, migrants from former colonies after WWII, filled labour shortage, experienced discrimination, secured lowest-paying jobs, areas of cheap accommodation, high-rise ghettos, high levels of unemployment and poverty, global recession, increased tension, cultural tensions, e.g. riots 2005, violent clashes, migrants and police; integration an important issue, tension between some French people and Muslim communities, 2010 banning of niqab, collapse of communism and EU enlargement – Polish, Russian and Eastern European migrants, assimilated into French society, 40% empty diagonal, peripheral area in south-eastern France, move to city for employment and better standard of living

24.6 Urban Development

Paris is a **primate city** and has grown rapidly over the past two centuries. The population of the **Greater Paris Area** is more than **11 million,** with its inner-city population exceeding **2.2 million.** The city centre has a **population density of 20 000 per km².**

Today, Paris is a **multifunctional city,** meaning it has political, administrative, retail, educational, research and tourist functions. The majority of its workforce is employed in the tertiary sector. Most French banking, insurance and other major company headquarters are located in the city. The world-famous **University of Sorbonne** is one of 17 universities located in the city of Paris.

Despite the city's important functions and relative prosperity, it is not without problems. **Tensions and inequality between ethnic groups still exist,** which has led to **social stratification.**

△ **Fig. 24.22** The Greater Paris Area has a population of 11 million.

GEO DICTIONARY

Multifunctional city: a city which provides many services, e.g. education, employment, banking

Growth

The city grew rapidly, mainly because of **high levels of rural–urban migration** after World War II. **Increased mechanisation** reduced the need for the **agricultural workers,** causing many to move to the city in search of work. As **inward migration occurred,** the city's **suburbs grew outward.** The **high levels of immigration** also put **pressure** on transport, water and sewage **services.**

The **1960s** saw an **economic boom** across Western Europe, prompting many French employers to look for cheap labour in former North African colonies such as Algeria. This further increased the stress on services. **Urban sprawl** became an increasing concern.

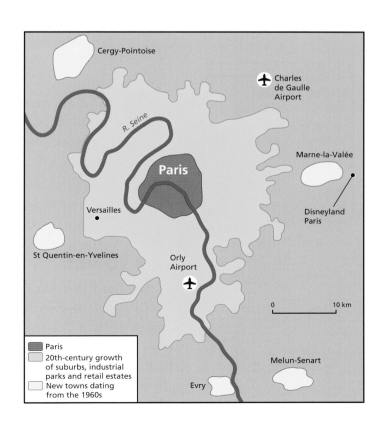

Cergy-Pointoise

Charles de Gaulle Airport

R. Seine

Paris

Marne-la-Valée

Versailles

Disneyland Paris

St Quentin-en-Yvelines

Orly Airport

0   10 km

Melun-Senart

Evry

Paris
20th-century growth of suburbs, industrial parks and retail estates
New towns dating from the 1960s

❯ **Fig. 24.23** The growth of Paris over time

Decentralisation

In order to **reduce** the **pressure** on services, city planners encouraged **decentralisation** of manufacturing industries away from Paris. **Renault** was a manufacturing company which availed of decentralisation incentives to set up in Flins, north of Paris. Many cosmetic companies also moved away from the city, creating the now-famous **Cosmetic Valley** in the Chartres area.

Urban Regeneration

By 1960, urban regeneration was necessary in order to manage and control the growth of the city and the lack of services.

The government introduced the Schéma Directeur project, which aimed to:

- **Conserve old and historic buildings**
- **Develop modern transport links** throughout the city
- **Redevelop the city centre**
- Construct **new towns** in Île-de-France to contain urban sprawl

(a)

(b)

 **Fig. 24.24** Paris (a) before and (b) after redevelopment

Eight suburban areas were chosen for special development to become **nodes**, e.g. Saint-Denis and La Défense. These **nodes** were provided with **modern office blocks, housing, shopping centres** and **transport links.** These areas have thrived, becoming **self-sufficient** centres.

The Schéma was successful as many **old and historic buildings,** such as the Louvre, **were repaired and modernised. Employment** was created and **improved transport links reduced traffic congestion.**

New Towns

Five new towns were built outside of Paris to **reduce urban sprawl.** Each town contained **residential areas, leisure parks, technological parks** and **research centres.** The towns were also connected to Paris via rail. **Marne-la-Vallée** is an example of one of these towns. It has a population of **280 000** spread out over **15 km².** It attracts many tourists each year to its main attraction – **Disneyland Paris.**

EDUCATE YOURSELF

Urban Development: Paris

Primate city, Greater Paris Area 11 million, inner city 2.2 million, density 20 000 per km², multifunctional city, University of Sorbonne, tensions and inequality, social stratification, rural-urban migration, increased mechanisation of farms, inward migration, suburbs grew, low-quality migrant accommodation, pressure on services, decentralisation to reduce pressure, Renault, Cosmetic Valley, 1960s economic boom, lacking necessary modern services, Schéma Directeur, eight nodes chosen, modern facilities, conserve old and historic buildings, repaired and modernised, employment, improved transport five new towns, reduce urban sprawl, e.g. Marne-la-Vallée , population 280 000, 15 km², Disneyland Paris

ACTIVE LEARNING

1. What is meant by the term 'decentralisation'?
2. List three aims of the Schéma Directeur.

Note!
These exam questions cover Chapters 23 and 24.

EXAM QUESTIONS

ORDINARY LEVEL

LONG QUESTIONS

1. Name a **European region (not in Ireland)** that you have studied and explain any **two** of the following:

   - The importance of **transport** to this region
   - The reasons why **tourists** are attracted to this region
   - The type of **farming** practised in this region
   - The reason for the development of **industry** in this region

Naming the region 1m
Activity 1 explained 7 SRPs @ 3m each
Activity 2 explained 6 SRPs @ 3m each

   2014 Q4B 40M

2. Explain how any **two** of the following influence the development of agriculture in a **European region (not in Ireland)** that you have studied:

   - Relief and soils
   - Climate
   - Markets

Naming the region 4m
Description/Explanation 12 SRPs @ 3m each

   2014 Q5B 40M

3. Explain how any two of the following influence the development of manufacturing industry in a **European region (not Ireland)** that you have studied:

   - Transport
   - Raw materials
   - Markets
   - Government and European Union policies

Region named 1m
Influence 1 explained 7 SRPs @ 3m each
Influence 2 explained 6 SRPs @ 3m each

   2012 Q6B 40M

4. Describe the development of manufacturing industry in a **European region (not in Ireland)** that you have studied. Clearly state the name of the region in your answer.

Region named 4m
Description of development 12 SRPs @ 3m each

   2010 Q5B 40M

CORE 3 CHAPTER 24

5. Name **a European region (not in Ireland)** that you have studied and answer each of the following questions.
   (i) Name **two** tourist attractions in this region.
   (ii) Explain the reasons why tourists are attracted to this region.
   (iii) Describe **one** problem associated with tourism in this region.

| Region named 1m |
| (i) One tourist attraction named @ 2m
One tourist attraction named @ 1m |
| (ii) Explanation 9 SRPs @ 3m each |
| (iii) One problem 3 SRPs @ 3m each |

2015 4B 40M

6. Describe the development of transport in any one **European region (not in Ireland)** which you have studied. Clearly state the name of the region in your answer.

| Naming the region 1m |
| Describing the development of transport
13 SRPs @ 3m each |

2011 Q6B 40M

7. Explain two advantages of tourism for the economy of a **European region (not in Ireland)** that you have studied. Clearly state the name of the region in your answer.

| Region named 3m |
| Advantage 1 stated 3m
Explaining the advantage for the economy 4 SRPs @ 3m each |
| Advantage 2 stated 3m
Explaining the advantage for the economy 3 SRPs @ 3m each |

2010 Q4C 30M

LONG QUESTIONS

1. Account for the development of agriculture in a **European region (not in Ireland)** that you have studied, with reference to any two of the factors listed below:
   • Relief
   • Markets
   • Climate

| Discussion of factor 1 8 SRPs @ 2m each |
| Discussion of factor 2 7 SRPs @ 2m each |

2012 Q4B 30M

2. Examine the development of primary activities in one **non-Irish European region** of your choice.

| Region named 2m |
| Primary activities named 2m + 2m |
| Explanation 12 SRPs @ 2m each |

2006 Q5B 30M

3. Account for the development of manufacturing in a **European region (not in Ireland)** that you have studied.

| Examination 15 SRPs @ 2m each |

2015 Q5B 30M

4. Describe and explain any **two** factors that influence the development of secondary economic activities in a **European region (not in Ireland)** that you have studied.

| Region named 2m |
| Two named factors 2m + 2m |
| Examination 12 SRPs (6 SRPs per factor) @ 2m each |

2010 Q6C 30M

HIGHER LEVEL

5. Examine the factors that influence the development of **one** tertiary economic activity in a **European region (not in Ireland)** that you have studied.

| Named tertiary economic activity 2m |
| Two factors identified 2m + 2m |
| Region named 2m |
| Examination 11 SRPs @ 2m each |

2010 Q4B 30M

6. Account for the distribution of population throughout a **European region (not in Ireland)** that you have studied.

| Examination 15 SRPs @ 2m each |

2013 Q5C 30M

So far, the Exam Focus has provided model answers to aid you in your exam preparation. But what about your note-taking and studying skills? The Educate Yourself tables are a useful revision tool after studying a chapter in class. We will now look at another effective way of cutting down on study times for the Regional Geography section. You will have to do some of the work too!

Often, a Regional Geography exam question will ask you to compare/contrast the difference in economic activities in two regions you have studied, e.g. the West and the GDA in Ireland and the Mezzogiorno and the Paris Basin in Europe. We will look at a sample Higher Level question.

HIGHER LEVEL

SAMPLE QUESTION

Describe the differences in the development of secondary economic activities in two European regions that you have studied.

Marking Scheme		
Two named region 2m + 2m		
Secondary activity named 2m		
Discussion 12 SRPs @ 2m each		

30M

Creating Notes for your Answer

While this may seem like a lot of work, it is a useful study tool and is great practice for how to structure answers in exam.

- Divide a sheet of paper in two with a vertical line. Write the name of one region in the left-hand column and the name of the other region in the right-hand column.

- Fill in the information relating to the development of secondary economic activities in the first region, using Chapter 23 or the Educate Yourself tables to help you.
- When you have written 15 pieces of information, switch your attention to the other region.

When you are done, you have notes to answer the question – and enough information to answer a question on each region independently. An example is shown below.
(Note: you can choose any relevant information.)

Mezzogiorno (Peripheral)	Paris Basin (Core)
17% industrial workforce	27.5% industrial workforce, majority of French industry
Unskilled and uneducated; only 3 of top 20 Italian universities	Educated workforce; 21 million in Paris Basin; 17 universities, e.g. University of Sorbonne
Rural dwellers, few urban areas to sell goods	Large urban market, luxury goods – jewellery/perfume/fashion, e.g. Chanel
Undeveloped agriculture, poor local markets, limited food processing	Highly productive agricultural sector has encouraged large-scale food processing and food co-ops, e.g. Danone
Lacks natural resources, e.g. energy, water	Plentiful supply of natural resources, oil pipelines supply energy
Autostrada del Sole, construction of communications difficult due to upland relief, long distance from EU markets	Developed communication links, transport is cheap – airport, rail, shipping, motorway. Flat relief makes construction easier; nodal point of communication, public transport, TGV/Metro
Isolated from government influence, outward migration of young skilled workers – brain drain	Centre of all economic trade; young workforce due to inward migration
Cassa per il Mezzogiorno – €2.3 billion to promote employment (1957), currently 18% unemployed	20% national workforce with a high number of MNCs
Ports such as Taranto developed to promote heavy industry, petrochemicals and steel industry	River Seine – deep-water port, importing/modern warehouses, modernised heavy industry
Very few homegrown businesses as there is a lack of local capital for investment	L'Oréal – cosmetics company and worldwide brand; Cosmetic Valley is a large homegrown industrial centre
Car assembly in Naples	Car manufacturing – Renault and Peugeot Citroen
Bari-Brindisi-Taranto industrial triangle, companies encouraged to locate in region	Several growth centres, decentralisation encouraged
Growth poles selected for economic development and growth, EU Regional Development Fund to promote industrial development	Technological and industrial parks allow MNCs to set up alongside colleges/universities
Workforce has tripled, produces just 25% of national GDP	Region produces most of the country's GDP

TOPIC MAP

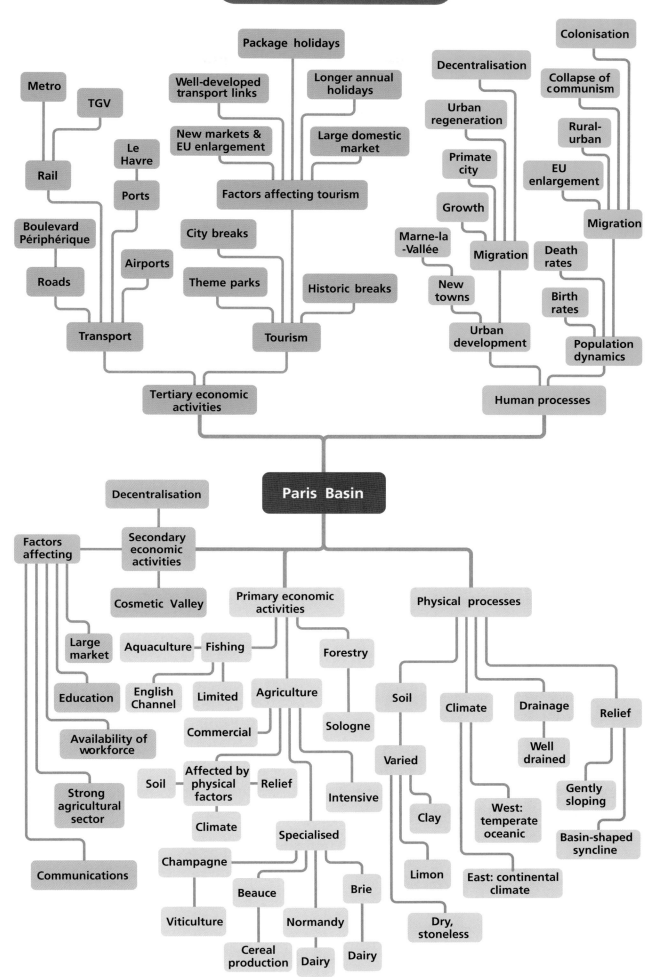

Package holidays

Metro

TGV

Well-developed transport links

Longer annual holidays

Decentralisation

Colonisation

Collapse of communism

Urban regeneration

New markets & EU enlargement

Large domestic market

Rail

Le Havre

Primate city

Rural-urban

Ports

Factors affecting tourism

Growth

EU enlargement

Boulevard Périphérique

Marne-la -Vallée

Migration

Migration

Death rates

City breaks

Airports

New towns

Birth rates

Roads

Theme parks

Historic breaks

Transport

Tourism

Urban development

Population dynamics

Tertiary economic activities

Human processes

Paris Basin

Decentralisation

Factors affecting

Secondary economic activities

Cosmetic Valley

Primary economic activities

Physical processes

Large market

Aquaculture

Fishing

Forestry

Soil

Climate

Drainage

Relief

Education

English Channel

Limited

Agriculture

Sologne

Well drained

Availability of workforce

Commercial

Varied

West: temperate oceanic

Gently sloping

Soil

Affected by physical factors

Relief

Intensive

Strong agricultural sector

Clay

Basin-shaped syncline

Climate

Specialised

Communications

Champagne

Limon

East: continental climate

Beauce

Brie

Viticulture

Normandy

Dry, stoneless

Cereal production

Dairy

Dairy

CHAPTER 25

Subcontinental Geography: Brazil

In this chapter, we will examine the subcontinental region of Brazil. You will learn about the physical landscape and economic and human processes of Brazil, as well as its cultures and traditions. While much detail of the country is given in this chapter, it is a good idea to explore the country further online. Many questions in the Regional Geography section of the exam ask you to discuss a subcontinental region under specific headings. Therefore, it is vital that you gain a good understanding of this chapter.

KEY WORDS

- Relief and drainage
- Brazilian Highlands
- Guiana Highlands
- Pantanal
- Amazon Basin
- Coastal Lowlands
- Amazon River
- Tropical/subtropical climate
- Semi-arid
- Terra rossa
- Tropical soil
- Agriculture
- Mining
- Iron ore and steel
- Automotive industry
- Distribution of industry
- Trans-Amazonian Highway
- Ecotourism
- Multicultural
- Colonialism
- Rural-urban migration
- Carnival
- Air pollution
- Favelas

LEARNING OUTCOMES

What you MUST know
- Physical characteristics of Brazil
- Climate characteristics of the region
- How to draw a map and fill in the main features of Brazil
- The development of primary, secondary and tertiary activities in Brazil
- Race relations and tensions in Brazil
- Human processes of the region
- Urban development over time: São Paulo
- Cultural processes of Brazil

What you SHOULD know
- Statistics about economic activity or population dynamics in Brazil
- Additional information provided in the case study on the growth of São Paulo

What is USEFUL to know
- Statistics and information related to Brazil's economy and development

Introduction

 ACTIVE LEARNING

Before we begin, let's examine what you and your classmates already know about this country. Think about the following in relation to Brazil and have a class discussion:

1. The rainforest
2. Climate
3. Cities
4. Sport
5. Music and festivals
6. Religion (use city names to help you)

Can you think of any foodstuffs that come from Brazil?

Subcontinental refers to a part of a continent that is distinguishable from the rest of the continent. For example, Brazilians speak Portuguese whereas the majority of countries in South America speak Spanish.

Brazil accounts for over 50 per cent of the South American continent's landmass. It is the fourth largest country in the world. With a population of 203 million, it is also the fifth most populated country in the world. Brazil is home to some of the most unique natural landscapes and features in the world such as the Brazilian Highlands and the Amazon Rainforest. The people of Brazil are from rich and diverse cultures, ranging from native Amerindians to descendants of African slaves and ancestors of Portuguese colonists and migrants from countries all over the world.

25.1 Physical Processes

In this section, we will look at the following physical factors that influence the region:

- Relief
- Climate
- Vegetation
- Drainage
- Soil

Relief

The relief of Brazil is divided into almost **half upland and half lowland.**
The upland regions can be divided into two main areas:

- The Brazilian Highlands
- The Guiana Highlands

The lowlands of Brazil can also be divided into three main areas:

- The Amazon Basin
- The Pantanal
- Coastal Lowlands

Brazilian Highlands

The Brazilian Highlands make up **just over half** of the country's landmass, **encompassing the south, east and centre of Brazil.** The highlands consist of **rugged terrain** of **steep cliffs, rolling hills** and **rock outcrops.** Despite the **undulating landscape,** the highest areas **do not exceed 2800 m above sea level.** The Brazilian Highlands form a natural wall behind most of Brazil's major cities, which are located along the coastline.

⬆ **Fig. 25.1** Relief and drainage of Brazil

Rock outcrop: exposed bedrock

Guiana Highlands

The Guiana Highlands are located **north of the Amazon Basin,** and are very similar to the Brazilian Highlands. They consist of **gently rolling hills.** Brazil's highest mountain Pico da Neblina, standing at almost **3000 m,** is located here.

Amazon Basin

The Amazon Basin accounts for **40 per cent of the country's landmass,** covering most of **northern and western Brazil.** The basin has a **gently sloping relief,** consisting of small **undulating hills** called **terra firma** (meaning 'dry land'). These small hills formed from **alluvial deposits** from the Amazon River. The **floodplains** of the Amazon River are up to **100 km wide** in places, creating a relatively flat landscape.

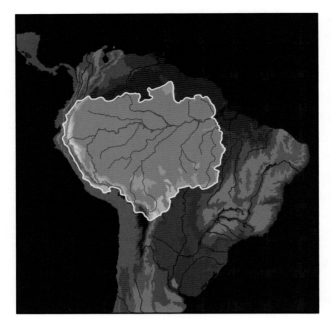

▲ **Fig. 25.2** The Amazon Basin

Pantanal

The Pantanal is a lowland region on the **western edge of Brazil.** Although it is much smaller than the Amazon Basin, it is one of the **largest wetlands in the world.**

ACTIVE LEARNING

1. What season do you think is shown in Fig. 25.3? Why?
2. Search for 'the Pantanal' on www.goodnature.nathab.com to discover more facts about the Pantanal. If possible, present your findings to the class.
3. Why do you think regions such as the Pantanal and the Amazon have low population densities?

GEO DICTIONARY

Wetlands: saturated land consisting of marshes and swamps

▲ **Fig. 25.3** The Pantanal wetlands in western Brazil

Coastal Lowlands

A **narrow coastal plain,** which is up to **200 km wide in some places,** runs along the **eastern coastline.** Most of Brazil's **major cities** are built along this coastal lowland. The lowlands **widen in the south** to form **grassy plains** along Brazil's border with Uruguay.

EDUCATE YOURSELF

Relief	
Brazilian Highlands	Half of the country's landmass, south-east-centre of Brazil, rugged terrain, steep cliffs, rolling hills, rock outcrops, undulating landscape, highest point of 2800 m
Guiana Highlands	North of Amazon Basin, rolling hills, Pico da Neblina almost 3000 m
Amazon Basin	40% of the country's landmass, northern and western Brazil, gently sloping relief, undulating hills (terra firma), alluvial deposits, floodplains of 100 km wide
Pantanal	Western edge of Brazil, one of the largest wetlands in the world
Coastal Lowlands	Narrow coastal plain along eastern coastline, 200 km wide in places, major cities built here, widens in the south, grassy plains

Drainage

The **Amazon River drains** nearly **60 per cent of Brazil** and is the most voluminous river in the world. It flows in a **west-to-east direction** before emptying into the Atlantic Ocean. The river's **current is so strong** that it carries sediment as far as 20 km out to sea, so **deltas do not form.** In total, the Amazon carries **20 per cent of all fresh water** reaching the world's oceans.

Fig. 25.4 Drainage network of Brazil

Fig. 25.5 The Amazon River

The **north-east is drained by the San Francisco and Parnaíba Rivers,** which cover **645 000 km².** In the Brazilian Highlands, the Xingu and Tocantins Rivers flow north-east before joining the Amazon. The **south-east is drained by the Paraguay-Paraná and Uruguay Rivers.**

Climate

The majority of Brazil has a **tropical** or **subtropical climate.** The north-east has a **semi-arid** climate, with drought and flood cycles. The majority of Brazil (90 per cent) lies in the tropical zone, where **June to September** is the **coolest** time of year and **December to March** is the **warmest** time of the year.

Tropical Climate

Most of Brazil has a tropical climate, with the following characteristics:

- **Average rainfall** is 1000–1800 mm per year, but this is often higher. In the **Amazon lowlands,** for example, precipitation averages over **2000 mm** per year.

- **Temperatures average 27 °C** throughout the year, meaning **climate conditions do not change** significantly from season to season.

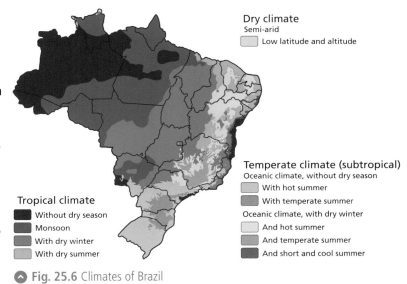

Dry climate
Semi-arid
☐ Low latitude and altitude

Temperate climate (subtropical)
Oceanic climate, without dry season
☐ With hot summer
☐ With temperate summer
Oceanic climate, with dry winter
☐ And hot summer
☐ And temperate summer
☐ And short and cool summer

Tropical climate
■ Without dry season
■ Monsoon
☐ With dry winter
☐ With dry summer

Fig. 25.6 Climates of Brazil

- Along the **east coast,** the **cooling influence of the Atlantic Ocean** means that temperatures are slightly lower. **Rio de Janeiro averages 23 °C** due to the influence of warm ocean currents.

Zonal Differences

The **Brazilian Highlands** have **greater variations** of temperature and precipitation, depending on **distance from the equator** and **altitude.**

- Unlike the Amazon, which receives rainfall throughout the year, the central highlands receive **most rainfall** in the **summer months** (November–April).

- This precipitation occurs in **torrential downpours.**

- **Temperatures** in the Brazilian Highlands **average** roughly **20 °C** but can drop as low as **14 °C in June/July.**

Semi-Arid Climate

The **north-east of Brazil** has a **semi-arid climate.**

- **Rainfall is scarce,** with only **350–750 mm of rainfall** per year. The north-east experiences a dry season that lasts from May to December. Drought is common, with a **severe drought** occurring on average **every seven years.** When rainfall does occur, it is often in **downpours,** which cause flooding and soil erosion.

- Due to the **intense heat,** the water is quickly evaporated, causing the soil to dry. **Temperatures** in the north-east average **29 °C,** with **daytime temperatures** reaching **38 °C.** However, due to the low amount of rainfall, **humidity levels are low.**

GEO DICTIONARY

Zonal differences:
90 per cent of Brazil has a tropical/subtropical climate. Differences in the physical landscape, distance from the sea, etc. create small variations in climate characteristics. These are referred to as zonal differences

 EDUCATE YOURSELF

Climate	
Tropical climate	Average precipitation 1000–1800 mm per year, Amazon lowlands >2000 mm per year, average temperatures 27 °C, cooler on east coast due to Atlantic, Rio de Janeiro 23 °C, climate conditions do not vary greatly throughout the year
Zonal differences	Brazilian Highlands greater variations, most rainfall in summer months, torrential downpours, average temperatures 20 °C, can drop to 14 °C in winter
Semi-arid	North-east of Brazil, rainfall is scarce at 350–750 mm per year, dry season May–December, drought every seven years, rain falls in downpours, average temperatures of 29 °C, daily temperatures of up to 38 °C, low humidity levels

Soil

Soils in Brazil are varied, ranging from fertile terra rossa and alluvial soils to less fertile tropical red soils. This variation in soil quality impacts the distribution of agriculture throughout Brazil.

Tropical Red Soil

- Brazil's tropical red soils support vast rainforests.

- The soils are **not very fertile.**

- Forests are sustained by humus from **decaying leaves of deciduous trees.**

(a)

(b)

(c)

Fig. 25.7 Soils of the Amazon:
(a) terra rossa soil, (b) tropical red soil,
(c) alluvial soil

- Leaves are quickly broken down by fungi and bacteria, which thrive in the warm, humid conditions.

- **Humus is quickly absorbed by the roots** of plants, so it does not accumulate in the soil.

- When land is cleared for agriculture, the soil loses its source of humus.

- Without trees, the soil is no longer shielded from the heavy rain or intense sunlight.

- The **heavy rain leaches the soil,** washing minerals beyond the reach of plant roots.

- The **soil becomes infertile** and useless for agriculture.

- The constant sunshine then bakes the soil into **impermeable layers** called **laterite.** Laterite is impossible to cultivate.

Terra Rossa and Alluvial Soils

- **Terra rossa,** meaning 'red soil', is the **most fertile soil** in Brazil.

- It is named after its **dark red colour.**

- It is found along the **south-eastern state** of São Paulo.

- It is rich in minerals and contains a large amount of **humus.**

- **It is highly productive** for agriculture.

- **Alluvial soils** form along floodplains of rivers. They are found along all major rivers in Brazil – especially the Amazon.

- Rivers **deposit thick layers** of alluvial soil during floods.

- The soil is fertile and **agriculturally productive.**

Vegetation

Vegetation in Brazil is dominated by **tropical rainforest** (jungle), which covers almost **half of the country.** The rainforest grows in response to the **high levels of rainfall** and **warm temperatures,** which create **humid**

Fig. 25.8 Tropical rainforest

conditions for growing plants. In the drought-ridden **north-east** of the country, **semi-arid scrub and cactus** grow, although the **vegetation cover is sparse.**

Note!

A common question in the exam is how physical processes impact economic activities, especially primary activities.

ACTIVE LEARNING

1. Describe the relief of Brazil under the following headings:
   - Amazon Basin
   - Brazilian Highlands
   - Coastal Lowlands

2. Describe the climate characteristics of the Amazon Basin, Brazilian Highlands and north-east Brazil.

3. Using your knowledge of soils in Brazil, suggest which soil you feel is most suitable for the development of agriculture. Explain your choice.

FACT

Brazil has 13.5 per cent of the world's arable land.

15.2 per cent of the world's fresh water is in Brazil's rivers and lakes.

25.2 Primary Activities

Brazil has a **large amount of natural resources,** which makes primary activities the driving force behind much of its economic development. Agriculture and mining are huge employers in the country.

Agriculture

Since the 1970s, agriculture in Brazil has become **increasingly modernised and intensive.** Brazil is now one of the **largest food producers and exporters** in the world. The government invested heavily in farming to start a 'Green Revolution' in the country. Over **800 000 farmers** were **given loans** to modernise their farms and increase productivity. This led to the large-scale **commercialisation** of agriculture, which was aided by foreign investment.

More than **38 million people (19 per cent of the population) are employed in the agricultural sector,** making it vital to the economy of Brazil. The agriculture of Brazil is affected by a combination of physical and human factors.

Physical Factors Affecting Agriculture in Brazil

Physical factors that affect agriculture in Brazil are:

1. Climate **2.** Soil

● **Fig. 25.9** Intensive corn production

1. Climate

Due to Brazil's tropical climate, it has year-round rainfall and warm temperatures that allow for a **continual growing season.** As a result, farmers can grow a **wide range of crops. Corn, soya bean** and **wheat** are grown throughout **central and southern Brazil.** Because of the climate, most of Brazil's **commercial farming** occurs in the south and central regions. Mechanisation has allowed people to farm much larger areas of land with less work. As a result, commercial farming has begun to move north-west to the **Amazon Rainforest.**

With temperatures averaging between **16 and 24 °C** and well-defined **wet and dry seasons,** the **subtropical climate** of the **east and south-east** of Brazil are ideal for **coffee cultivation.** The **São Paulo** and **Minas Gerais** regions produce most of the country's coffee.

North-east Brazil has a **semi-arid climate,** which is **unable to sustain arable farming** or intensive **beef production.** Farming is **subsistent** and **extensive** in this region, with herds of cattle **grazing the sparse vegetation. Drought** occurs regularly, which leads to **large losses of herds.** Many farming families **abandon their land** to seek a **better standard of**

● **Fig. 25.10** Coffee growing on the slopes of Minas Gerais mountain

living in the major cities on the east coast. When rain falls, it is in **heavy downpours** that loosen and **wash away soil.** The **Sertão** region is the worst affected, with **famine** and **poverty common** among subsistence farmers.

2. Soil

The terra rossa soils of the south-east are **extremely fertile** and allow for intensive cultivation of crops. Coffee is grown on the terra rossa soils along the east and south-east of Brazil.

⬆ **Fig. 25.11** Subsistence farming in Pernambuco in Brazil

In the Amazon, tropical soils are **difficult to cultivate** over long periods. When the rainforest vegetation is first cleared, humus in the soil allows for **intensive growing of cash crops** such as soya bean. With the soil's natural source of humus removed, **nutrients are not replenished** each year. With each harvest the **soil loses fertility** until it is no longer usable for agriculture. The intense heat **bakes the soil into a laterite,** which is impossible to cultivate.

In order to keep soils fertile, farmers use huge amounts of **artificial fertilisers.** The rainforest is so large that many farmers feel that they do not need to use expensive fertilisers as there is **plenty of land** to cultivate. Farmers just abandon infertile areas and clear more of the rainforest through **slash and burn. Ranching** is increasingly carried out along the **Amazon Basin,** as the more fertile lands of the south and east are used for arable farming.

Along the floodplains of rivers such as the Paraguay and Amazon, **alluvial** soils promote the growth of **rich grasses.** This has allowed for the development of ranching in Brazil. Farmers here are increasingly changing to cereal crops such as **corn and wheat** along these floodplains. This has pushed ranching further towards the Amazon Basin in the north-west.

Human Factors Affecting Agriculture in Brazil

Human factors that affect agriculture in Brazil are:

1. Colonialism **2.** Markets

1. Colonialism

Brazil was colonised by the **Portuguese** in the **fifteenth century.** The Portuguese set up **sugar plantations** along the **eastern coast,** as they found both the **climate** and the **soils ideal.** As the plantations grew in size, more people were needed to work on them. Some **100 000 slaves** were brought from West Africa to Brazil to plant and harvest sugar cane. As sugar supply became more plentiful, the Portuguese also began growing **coffee.** The effects of this are seen today, as Brazil is the largest coffee-producer in the world.

After gaining **independence in 1822,** Brazil still relied heavily on exporting sugar and coffee to the Portuguese market. This is referred to as **neo-colonialism.** The overreliance on a single market led to a farming monoculture in Brazil.

> **FACT**
>
> In 1877–79, a famine caused by drought in Sertão killed half of the region's population.

> **A-Z** **GEO DICTIONARY**
>
> **Slash and burn:** the cutting down and burning of natural vegetation to clear land for agriculture

⬆ **Fig. 25.12** Slash and burn along the edge of the Amazon Rainforest

> **A-Z** **GEO DICTIONARY**
>
> **Neo-colonialism:** relying on a country's former colonists for economic trade. Despite Brazil gaining independence from Portugal, it relied heavily on Portugal for the sale of sugar and coffee as Portugal was its only developed market

> **ACTIVE LEARNING**
>
> Research online whether coffee and sugar prices are rising or falling this year. Try to find out why this rise/fall is occurring. If possible, present your findings to the class.

2. Markets

With a population of over 200 million people, Brazil has a **huge domestic market.** Brazil has **17 cities** with populations of **over 1 million,** most of which are located along the **eastern coastline.** This means there is a **constant demand** for farm produce. Brazilians are the fourth-largest consumers of beef in the world. MNCs like McDonald's and Burger King use Brazilian beef for their US market. Brazil is a member of the **Mercosur,** which is a political and economic agreement between a number of countries in South America. By joining the Mercosur, Brazil has access to a market of a further **187.5 million people.** MNCs such as Nestlé have located in Brazil to produce coffee. Brazil accounts for **30 per cent of the world's coffee** produced.

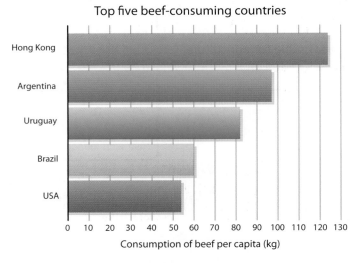

Top five beef-consuming countries

Consumption of beef per capita (kg)

⊙ **Fig. 25.13** Three of the top five beef-consuming countries are members of the Mercosur. The US and Hong Kong are the first and second largest importers of Brazilian beef.

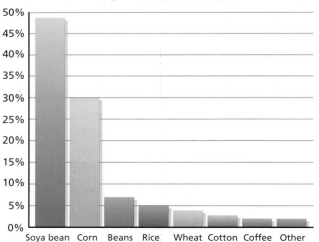

Percentage of crops produced in Brazil

⊙ **Fig. 25.14** Variety of crops grown in Brazil

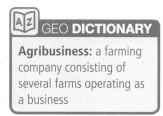

What Is Produced?

Some **30 per cent of Brazil's landmass is agricultural land.** Three-quarters of this land is used for cattle ranching and pastoral farming, while the remaining 25 per cent is used for arable farming. Over the last two decades, the Brazilian **government has invested heavily** to address the problem of farming monoculture. Since then, a wider **range of goods is grown on farms.**

Arable

Intensive arable farming has led to Brazil becoming one of the world's major food producers. The main arable foods grown are:

- Soya bean
- Corn
- Rice
- Wheat
- Cotton
- Coffee
- Fruits

Soya Bean

Nearly half of all arable farmland is now used for growing soya bean. Soya bean became increasingly popular as **feed for cattle, poultry and pigs in the US** and the **EU.** This increased global demand and led to Brazil becoming the **second-largest producer** in the world. Soya bean production is **highly mechanised,** with only **one farmer** needed to work every **200 hectares of land.**

Soya bean farms are large, ranging between **1000 and 15 000 hectares,** and are mostly owned by **agribusinesses.** In 2014, Brazil produced 68 million tonnes of soya. This generated a total of **€17 billion,** making it the country's most important agricultural export.

Soya production is most **intensive in the south** of the country as the climate is suitable to **two harvests per year,** without the need for irrigation. However, as global demand increases, soya production has begun **moving northwards** towards the edges of the Amazon Rainforest.

Sugar Cane

Brazil is the **largest producer and exporter** of sugar cane in the world. It is now grown throughout the country for food and for the production of **ethanol.** Ethanol is a biofuel which is produced from crushed sugar cane. Ethanol production began in the 1970s as a means of **reducing fossil fuel** imports. Today, Brazil produces almost one-third of the world supply of ethanol. Over **50 per cent of all cars** in the country now use it.

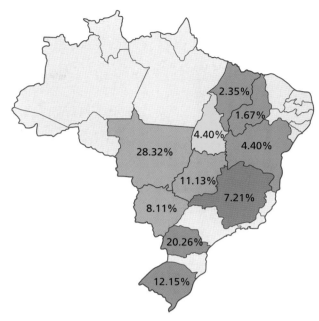

Fig. 25.15 Soya bean production in Brazilian states

Coffee

Brazil is the largest producer of coffee in the world. Coffee once accounted for 60 per cent of Brazil's exports but this has fallen to just **2 per cent.** Coffee is grown mainly on the **terra rossa soils** of the **São Paulo, Minas Gerais** and **Paraná** states at altitudes of 1000 m as temperatures are cooler.

Cattle Ranching

Brazil is one of the largest beef producers in the world, with the **second largest cattle herd** in the world (after India). Ranching occupies **75 per cent of agricultural land** in the country. Beef production employs approximately **360 000 people.** Cattle ranching is carried out in many parts of the country and is **continually spreading** to new areas. Originally, cattle were reared on the **rich grassy plains** in the south. It has now spread **north and west** to Brazil's interior and Amazon Basin. The government aims to **double beef production over the next 10 years,** but there is major concern over how this will happen without further destruction to the rainforest.

Brazilian beef accounts for just under **half of all EU beef imports** (131 000 tonnes). The Brazilian beef industry is worth just under **€4 billion per year.**

Fig. 25.16 All fuel stations are required to sell ethanol as well as fossil fuels.

Fig. 25.17 Livestock herds in the Amazon Basin

(partial) — fuel prices:
Etanol Comum 2.179
Gasolina Comum 2.849
Gasolina Aditivada 2.949
Diesel Comum 2.089

(legend):
0 – 0.4 M
0.4 – 1.6 M
1.6 – 4.5 M
4.5 – 11 M
11 – 20 M
(M = millions)

Poultry

Brazil is the **largest producer of chicken** in the world, producing over 13 million tonnes. Poultry production accounts for 1.5 per cent of the country's GDP. Some **69 per cent of the chicken is sold directly to the domestic market,** with the average Brazilian consuming 39 kg of chicken per year. The remaining 31 per cent is exported to more than **150 countries** worldwide.

 Fig. 25.18 Poultry farm in Brazil

EDUCATE YOURSELF

Agriculture		
Increasingly modernised, intensive, among largest food producers and exporters, 800 000 farmers given loans – Green Revolution, commercialisation, cost to environment, 38 million/19% of population employed in agriculture		
Physical factors	Climate: continual growing season, variety of crops – corn, soya bean, wheat, central/southern Brazil; commercial farming, subtropical climate east and south-east, suits coffee growing, 16–24 °C, wet and dry seasons, São Paulo and Minas Gerais main coffee regions; semi-arid region north-east, no arable farming, subsistent and extensive, grazing sparse vegetation, regular drought, famine and loss of herds, Sertão – land abandoned, severe downpours, soil erosion	
	Soil: terra rossa fertile, suits coffee growth, east and south-east; tropical soils difficult to cultivate, depletion of minerals, monoculture and leaching, intense cash crops, nutrients not replenished, soil loses fertility, bakes into laterite, artificial fertilisers needed, fertilisers not used as land is cheap, slash and burn, ranching; alluvial soils rich grasses, corn and wheat	
Human factors	Colonialism: Portuguese 15th century, sugar plantations on eastern coast, climate and soils ideal, 100 000 slaves from West Africa, coffee plantations, independence 1822, neo-colonialism	
	Markets: huge domestic market, 17 cities population >1 million, eastern coastline, constant demand, Mercosur additional 187.5 million people, MNCs e.g. Nestlé, 30% world's coffee produced	
What is produced?	Soya bean: 50% arable land, feed for cattle, poultry and pigs, second largest producer, highly mechanised, one farmer per 200 hectares, €17 billion per year, most intensive in south – two harvests per year, moving northwards	
	Sugar cane: largest producer in world, ethanol, reduces fossil fuels, 50% of Brazilian cars use ethanol	
	Coffee: terra rossa, São Paulo, Minas Gerais, Paraná, dry season (June–September)	
	Cattle ranching: second largest herd, 75% agricultural land, 360 000 employed, rich grassy plains of south, continually spreading north and west, slash and burn, doubling production in next 10 years, half of EU beef imports, €4 billion per year	
	Poultry: largest producer, 69% domestic market, 31% exported	

 ACTIVE **LEARNING**

Explain how one physical factor and one human factor have affected the development of agriculture in Brazil.

2. Mining

Brazil is rich in mineral resources, with valuable metals and ores such as:

- Platinum
- **Gold**
- **Iron ore**
- Pewter (a tin and lead alloy)
- Bauxite
- Coal
- **Oil**

A total of **175 000** people are employed in the mining sector in Brazil. It is estimated that for every mining job created, 13 more jobs are created along the supply chain.

⌃ **Fig. 25.19** An open cast mine in the Amazon Basin

Gold

Gold is the most valuable metal in the world and gold mining was **once Brazil's most important economic activity.** When the Portuguese and Spanish colonists arrived in South America during the sixteenth and seventeenth centuries, they mined large quantities of gold.

In the twentieth century, new mines were located in the states of **Pará and Eldorado do Juma** in the Amazon Basin. These discoveries led to a **gold rush** as people moved to these areas in the hopes of making their fortune. **Makeshift towns** were built by miners. Successful miners earned over **€500 per gram** of gold.

⌃ **Fig. 25.20** Gold panning along rivers destroys river banks.

Today, the largest gold mining operations are run by **MNCs.** In 2013, Brazil produced **75 million tonnes of gold,** making it the 11th-biggest producer in the world. It is expected that Brazil will become the seventh-largest gold producer by 2017. Brazilian gold producers have benefitted from the global recession – gold came to be seen as a safe investment.

FACT

Gold did not have monetary value to the native Amerindians. When the colonists arrived, they were amazed to find gold being used as an everyday metal.

Oil

Brazil extracts the majority of its petroleum from **offshore oil fields** along its continental shelf. When oil became very expensive in the 1970s, the Brazilian government invested heavily in offshore exploration. Numerous oil fields were discovered, the largest of which is the **Campos offshore field.** Brazil now produces over **2.5 million barrels of oil per day.** Brazil is **self-sufficient in oil,** which **reduces the cost of manufacturing** in the country.

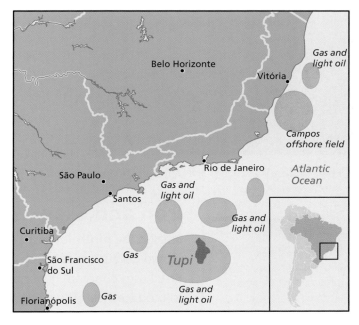

⊙ **Fig. 25.21** Major oil and gas fields in Brazil

Iron Ore

Brazil has a huge quantity of iron ore, which is used in its manufacturing industry. The largest deposits of iron ore are found in the Minas Gerais state in the south-east and along the fringes of the Amazon Basin.

EDUCATE YOURSELF

Mining		
175 000 employed in mining, 1 mining job = 13 more in associated industries		
Gold	Gold most valuable metal in the world, €500 per gram of gold, largest gold mining operations run by MNCs 2013 — 75 million tonnes of gold, 11th biggest, seventh largest by 2017	
Oil	Offshore oil, Campos offshore field, 2.5 million barrels of oil per day, self-sufficient in oil, reduces the cost of manufacturing	
Iron ore	Huge quantity of iron ore, manufacturing industry, largest deposits in Minas Gerais, fringes of the Amazon Basin	

25.3 Secondary Activities

Roughly **15 per cent** of Brazil's workforce is employed in secondary economic activities. A higher percentage is employed in both the primary and tertiary sectors. Until **World War II,** Brazil's industry relied heavily on agricultural exports to Portugal. Some **80 per cent of all exports were agricultural produce,** such as sugar, coffee and cotton. The war hugely **disrupted international trade,** which meant that Brazil was not able to import many of the goods it needed. This, combined with a **rapidly growing population,** forced Brazil to focus on developing its own manufacturing base.

As Brazil had a lot of mineral resources, the government invested heavily in **iron and steel manufacturing.** The **Volta Redonda Steel Mill** was set up in the **Rio de Janeiro** state in the 1940s.

It took until the 1970s for the secondary sector to begin to grow rapidly. This growth in manufacturing led to increased **rural-urban migration** as people moved to the larger cities to find work in the new factories. The **Real Plan of 1994** further increased Brazil's manufacturing sector by **reducing inflation** and **improving the value of its currency.**

Brazil's GDP rose from less than $50 billion in 1970 to $2.4 trillion in 2014.

⊙ **Fig. 25.22** Volta Redonda Steel Mill

Iron and Steel Manufacturing

Brazil is the **ninth-largest steel producer** in the world. The industry has grown because of **large deposits** of iron ore and government investment. Brazil uses **charcoal** generated from the burning of the **Amazon Rainforest** to produce steel. The development of the steel industry was based in the **Minas Gerais** and **Rio de Janeiro** states as they had a rich supply of **iron ore and carbon.**

GEO DICTIONARY

Inflation: a rise in the cost of goods. This reduces the buying power of money, meaning people can buy less with their money

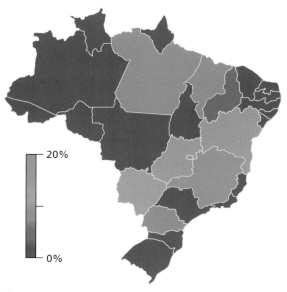

 Fig. 25.23 Each region's percentage of total charcoal production in Brazil

 Fig. 25.24 Extracting iron ore in the Minas Gerais region

As Brazil looked to reduce imports, several state-owned or **semi-state steel mills** were set up. Government-led steel production continued until the 1990s, when **privatisation** of steel mills began. Today, Brazil has **29 steel mills,** owner by 11 different company groups. Since the 1940s, Brazil has changed from a major importer of steel to a **major exporter.**

The country produces approximately **35 million tonnes** of steel annually, generating **€12.5 billion** per year.

Automotive Industry

In 1991, Brazil became a founding member of the **Mercosur,** a **trade agreement** between the South American countries which joined. The opening up of the Mercosur market also **attracted investment** from **MNCs,** especially European and Asian **car manufacturers. Rio de Janeiro** and **Santos** were chosen as the main centres for automotive manufacturing due to their **large labour pool** and **developed infrastructure.**

Until this time, car manufacturing was not possible in Brazil due to **high production costs, a lack of highly skilled workers** and a **lack of technology.** However, inward investment from MNCs such as **Toyota** and **Fiat** led to Brazil to becoming a major car manufacturing country. The government introduced a number of steps to aid and protect the industry:

1. Protectionism: Any cars not produced in Brazil or other Mercosur countries are subjected to a **30 per cent extra tax.** This is to protect the market from cheaper Chinese imports. By 2017, **10 out of the 12 steps** in car production must occur in Brazil or other Mercosur countries for cars to be exempt from this tax.

2. Investment: The government has begun to **invest in research and development** (R&D) to develop new car models with more energy efficient engines. **Inmetro** is the organisation responsible for setting standards for engines and electrical appliances. By 2017, all cars will have to reach a certain standard on CO_2 emissions in order to be certified by Inmetro. There has been heavy investment in making **engines more**

GEO DICTIONARY

State-owned/semi-state: industries owned or part-owned by the government

Privatisation: when a government-owned company is sold off to private industry

ACTIVE LEARNING

1. Research the Real Plan of 1994 and the effects it had on Brazil.

2. Search for 'Mercosur profile' on www.news.bbc.co.uk for more information on Mercosur.

GEO DICTIONARY

Protectionism: taxing imported goods to make them more expensive. This protects the importing country's domestic industries

Flex-fuel engines: engines that can run on fossil fuels or ethanol

CORE 3 CHAPTER 25

Fig. 25.25 Flex-fuel engines reduce CO_2 levels.

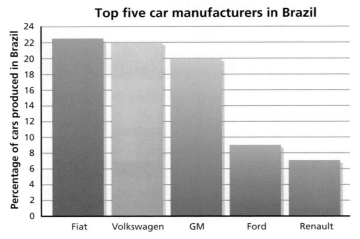

Fig. 25.26 Top five car brands in Brazil

> **Note!**
> You can also use information about primary activities when answering questions on secondary activities. For example, the mining industry fuels manufacturing or intensive agriculture impacts food processing.

Fig. 25.27 Location of plants and distribution centres in Brazil

environmentally friendly. Brazilian companies have developed '**flex-fuel engines**', which can run on fuel made from ethanol and petrol. **Ethanol** is produced from sugar cane.

As Brazil continues to develop, its citizens' **standard of living continues to rise**. As a result, **car ownership is increasing**. For example, 1000 new cars are bought in São Paulo each day.

Some 65 per cent of all cars bought in South America are **produced in Brazil**. It is one of the top-10 car manufacturers in the world, with **3 million cars produced annually**. Further employment is created through the manufacture of car parts such as **tyres and brakes**.

Food Processing

Brazil has an intensive food processing industry, which is based on the country's large agricultural sector.

- With a population of over 200 million people, the country has a large domestic market.
- There are 45 000 food processing companies across Brazil.
- Food processing generates €195.4 billion per year.
- MNCs such as Néstle, Cadbury and Kraft have invested in Brazil because of the availability of cheap raw materials, its large labour force and its large domestic market.

Textiles

- An increase in the standard of living among Brazil's growing middle class has led to an increased demand for clothes.
- Brazil produces 9.5 million garments per year, making it the fourth-largest manufacturer of textiles in the world.
- With 1.9 million workers, the textile industry is the second-largest employer in the country.
- Only 15 per cent of textiles produced are exported due to the large domestic market.

Distribution of Industry

Industry in Brazil is **not evenly distributed** throughout the country. Most manufacturing is concentrated in the **south-east industrial triangle** of **São Paulo-Rio de Janeiro-Belo Horizonte**. Manufacturing developed in this region for a number of reasons:

1. The south-east is **rich in natural resources** such as iron ore and bauxite. This attracted iron and steel mills to states such as Minas Gerais.

2. There were already **large cities** developed along the south-east coast, providing a large **labour pool** and large **local market,** e.g. Rio de Janeiro and São Paulo.

3. **Telecommunications** in the south-east are well developed, with **modern road and rail links.** The government has also invested heavily in broadband infrastructure.

4. **Oil and gas deposits** were found off the coast of Rio de Janeiro, which led to the development of **refining and petrochemical industries.**

5. **Ports** were already developed along the **south-east in Rio de Janeiro and Santos,** which meant it was easier to move goods.

As a result, the **standard of living is much higher in the south-east.** The **wealthier population** also provides a market for expensive goods. In the past, the **north-east's poor agricultural economy** did not develop due to an unsuitable climate. This meant that **food processing and textile manufacturing did not develop.** Manufacturing is beginning to develop in the north-east due to inward investment.

▲ **Fig. 25.28** Major road links in South America

EDUCATE YOURSELF

Secondary Activities		
15% employed in sector, prior to WWII 80% exports agricultural produce, war disrupted international trade, unable to import, developed iron and steel manufacturing, Volta Redonda Steel Mill, Rio de Janeiro; Real Plan 1994 reduced inflation, increased value of currency		
Iron and steel	9th largest producer, large deposits of iron ore, charcoal – Amazon, Minas Gerais, Rio de Janeiro, state/semi-state steel mills, privatisation (1990s), 29 steel mills, major exporter, 35 million tonnes per annum, €12.5 billion per annum, 110 000 jobs, development of other industries	
Automotive industry	Mercosur, free trade, attracted MNCs, car manufacturers, Rio de Janeiro and Santos, large labour pool, developed infrastructure, previous limitations – high production costs, lack of skilled workers, lack of technology; government investment – Toyota and Fiat, protectionism, 30% added tax on imports, R&D, Inmetro – ethanol, market increasing car ownership, €88 billion annually, produces 65% cars bought in South America, 3 million cars annually	
Distribution of industry	Not evenly distributed, south-east industrial triangle, São Paulo-Rio de Janeiro-Belo Horizonte, rich in natural resources, large cities, large labour pool, local markets, telecommunications, modern road and rail, oil and gas deposits, refining and petrochemicals, ports	
	Standard of living higher in south, wealthier population, north-east is poorer, poor agriculture – no food processing/textiles	

ACTIVE LEARNING

1. Discuss the ways in which the Brazilian government promoted industrial growth from 1940 onwards.

2. Why would industries choose to locate in the south-east of Brazil rather than further inland?

3. In what ways does being a member of the Mercosur help Brazil's economy?

25.4 Tertiary Activities

Despite Brazil being considered a developing country:

- **Some 60 per cent of Brazil's workforce** is employed in the tertiary sector.

- There is a **high standard of living along the south-east** where services are concentrated.

- In the last decade, Brazil has increased its market share in both the **domestic and international market.**

- The tourism sector has increased, with the **2014 Fifa World Cup** and the **2016 Olympic Games** in Rio de Janeiro.

In this section, we will focus on transport and tourism.

Transport

Transport links in Brazil **vary greatly** from region to region, as the construction of an extensive transport network throughout such a large country is a **major challenge.** Around the major cities of the **south-east, transport links** are **well developed.** In contrast, there is a **lack of transport** infrastructure throughout the country's **interior.** Away from the coast, construction of roads is made difficult by **mountainous landscape, marshland** and **dense forest.** Added to this, the **low population densities** away from the coastal cities make the planning of routes difficult.

Fig. 25.29 The Trans-Amazonian Highway is a major transport link.

Roads

Roads are the **most important mode of transport** in Brazil, with over **60 per cent of all transport** taking place on roads. Modern, well-developed **motorways** link the **major cities** of the south-east such as Rio de Janeiro, Belo Horizonte and São Paulo. The core industrial region of Brazil has long-developed transport networks, but it was not until the **1950s and 1960s** that the **government** began to **develop road networks** further **inland.** Cities such as Brasília were developed in order to **reduce the strain on coastal cities** as a result of population growth.

Major roadways were built to allow for the **movement of goods to and from the interior.** The building of the **Trans-Amazonian Highway** began in 1972. It now stretches for over **4000 km from the most eastern point** of Brazil as far as the **Amazon Basin.** One of the main aims of this road was to **allow people in the drought-stricken north-east to migrate** further inland. These motorways also give miners, loggers and ranchers easier access to new lands.

Since the establishment of the **Mercosur** in 1991, Brazil has invested in developing extensive motorways **to link with** other member states such as **Argentina and Uruguay**. The development of road links between these countries **encourages trade.**

Rail

Much like the road network, Brazil has well-developed railway links along its **south-eastern coast**. With the exception of tourist lines along the south of the country, **passenger services are of little importance.** Most rail lines are used for **transporting minerals and ores** to the coast for processing or export. Freight lines are **vital to the agricultural economy** as they carry bulky produce to large domestic markets and shipping ports in the east.

In São Paulo and Rio de Janeiro, the issue of **traffic congestion was addressed** by constructing modern underground **Metrô systems.** These allow for the efficient movement of people throughout the cities. Over **600 000 people use the Metrô in São Paulo each day,** and the Metrô in Rio de Janeiro carries over 500 000 people each day.

A **high-speed rail link between Rio de Janeiro and São Paulo** is planned to be constructed by 2017. The train will travel at speeds of up to 300 km/h, completing the journey in 90 minutes. Over **11 000 km of track will be built** to connect more **remote areas to the industrial and market cities** of the east. This will further develop the country's agricultural **freight** network.

Airports

Although most Brazilians cannot afford it, air travel is becoming increasingly important and **demand for it is growing** because of tourism. It also connects inland areas to cities on the east coast.

International airports are limited mainly to the **south-east.** São Paulo, Rio de Janeiro and Manaus have the largest airports. Over **30 million passengers** pass through **São Paulo Airport** each year.

⌃ **Fig. 25.30** Unequal development of rail links in Brazil

⌃ **Fig. 25.31** Airports of Brazil

Fig. 25.32 Inland port at Manaus, Amazon

Waterways

In the **1960s,** the government began investing in the development of **modern port facilities** in order to **encourage heavy industry along the eastern coast.** Roads were also linked to the ports to allow for the efficient export of goods to European and US markets. The **port of Santo,** near São Paulo, is the country's busiest port, handling **28 per cent of all of Brazil's exported goods. Some 90 per cent of all industry in** the **São Paulo** state is **located within 200 km of the port.**

Rio de Janeiro Port is one of the busiest ports in Brazil and handles the majority of the country's heavy raw materials such as oil, gas, coal and iron ore. Some **90 per cent of Brazil's exports** go through the country's **ports.**

The inland **city of Manaus** is the main transport hub for the entire Amazon Basin region. It relies heavily on water transport. **Electrical and IT companies have located manufacturing plants in the region,** which has helped it to become a modern urban centre.

Tourism

Brazil has a wide range of both **natural and cultural attractions** that could provide the basis for a large tourist industry. Although Brazil is far away **from the large wealthy markets** of the US and EU, its tourist sector has grown rapidly over the last decade. Today, tourism accounts for over **6 per cent of the country's GDP** and **6 per cent of the country's employment.** The growth has occurred as a result of the **improved political image** of Brazil abroad and a growing domestic middle class with better working conditions.

By securing the **2014 Fifa World Cup,** Brazil created **new markets.** Tourists from all participating countries visited for the four-week-long tournament, while the matches were **broadcast to over 3 billion people worldwide.** Over **1 million people visited** the country for the tournament, **60 per cent of whom were visiting for the first time.** The World Cup attracted some negative publicity, especially because of the **€11 billion cost of building** stadiums in a country where many people live in poverty. Hosting the 2016 Olympic Games in Rio futher boosted the country's tourism industry.

(a)

(b)

Fig. 25.33 (a) Favelas overlooking the newly built multimillion-euro stadium and (b) protests ahead of the 2016 World Cup.

Domestic tourism has **grown from 19 million people in 2004 to 69 million in 2014.** The rise is linked to strong **economic growth** and **increasing urbanisation.** More people have **disposable income** and **better working conditions** so they have more money and time off to go on holiday.

Physical Attractions

The **Amazon Rainforest** contains over **half of all the plants, animals and insects** in the world. This makes it attractive to tourists who want to study and observe its unique habitat. Although the Amazon is **remote and difficult to access,** increasing numbers of operators are offering guided tours. Tourists can take part in activities such as fishing for piranhas, swimming with pink dolphins and **visiting native tribe settlements.** Rainforest used for **ecotourism is many times more profitable** than rainforest that is cleared for agriculture.

Although increasing in popularity, ecotourism still accounts for only a **small percentage of tourism income in Brazil.**

▲ **Fig. 25.34** Unique sights of the Amazon

ACTIVE **LEARNING**

1. Find the cost of a return flight to Brazil from an Irish airport.
2. Find the cost of a flight from Rio de Janeiro to Brasília.
3. Go to **www.guardian.com** and search for 'brazil-world-cup-people-amazon-fifa-manaus'. Read the article and discuss the arguments for and against the staging of the 2014 World Cup in Brazil.
4. What potential positives and negatives are there of developing ecotourism?

GEO DICTIONARY

Ecotourism: tourism in natural environments, intended to support conservation efforts and observe wildlife, e.g. guided tours in the Amazon Rainforest

Sun Holidays

Brazil has over **9000 km** of **eastern coastline** with many **long and sandy beaches.** This, combined with its warm **tropical and subtropical climate,** promotes more **traditional sun holidays.** **Copacabana beach** in Rio de Janeiro is one of the most famous beaches in the world.

Heritage and Culture

Due to Brazil's history, it has many cultural attractions from its native population and **European colonists.** The city of Olinda is a **heritage** site dating back to the Portuguese colonisation. Preservation of the site began in 1930. It is one of the best examples of a Portuguese colonial town in the world.

Brazil is famous for its **Carnival festival,** which takes place in the four days leading up to Ash Wednesday.

▲ **Fig. 25.35** Copacabana beach

▲ **Fig. 25.36** The crowded streets of Rio Carnival

The largest Carnival takes place in Rio de Janeiro, with over 2 million people visiting each day. Over 250 000 people are employed part-time for the Rio festival. It generates **€590 million** for local hotels, restaurants and bars.

EDUCATE YOURSELF

Tertiary Activities	
60% Brazil's workforce, concentrated along south-east, higher standard of living, domestic and international market, 2014 Fifa World Cup, 2016 Olympics	
Transport	Varies greatly, major challenge, well developed in south-east, lack of transport in interior, mountainous landscape, marshland, dense forest, low population densities
	Roads: most important mode of transport, 60% of all transport, motorways link major cities, government investment 1950/1960s, road networks inland, reduce strain on coastal cities, movement of goods from interior to coast, Trans-Amazonian Highway, 4000 km, Amazon Basin, east coast, allowed migration inland, encouraged new settlements, Mercosur, links to Argentina and Uruguay
	Rail: south-east coast, few passenger services, freight, transports, minerals and ores, vital to agricultural economy, Metrô systems ease traffic congestion, São Paulo >600 000 passengers per day, high-speed rail connecting Rio and São Paulo, 11 000 km of new freight line, connect remote areas to cities/markets
	Airports: demand growing, connects inland to cities on east, São Paulo Airport 30 million passengers per year
	Waterways: 1960s investment, modern port facilities, encourage heavy industry, port of Santo, 28% of exported goods, 90% of São Paulo industry within 200 km of port, ports account for 90% of exports, Amazon River, Manaus, electrical and IT companies located there
Tourism	Natural and cultural attractions, distance from large wealthy markets, 6% of GDP, 6% country's employment, increasing with improved political image, 2014 Fifa World Cup, broadcast to over 3 billion, 1 million people visited – 60% for first time, €11 billion cost of building stadiums; domestic tourism growing – risen by 50 million in 10 years, strong economic growth, increasing urbanisation, better working conditions
	Physical attractions: Amazon Rainforest, half of plants, animals and insects, remote and difficult to access, visiting native tribe settlements, ecotourism
	Sun holidays: 9000 km eastern coastline, long and sandy beaches, tropical and subtropical climate, traditional sun holidays, Copacabana beach
	Heritage and culture: European colonists, natural heritage, Carnival festival, Rio Carnival 2 million per day, 250 000 people employed for festival, €590 million for services

25.5 Human Processes

Race and Race Relations in Brazil

Brazil is a **mixed race** and **multicultural** society because of its **colonial history.** The country was originally populated by **nomadic tribes** until the arrival of the **Portuguese colonists** in the sixteenth century. **Slaves** were brought from **West Africa** to Brazil and forced to work on sugar plantations. People worked as slaves until as recently as 1888. As a result of the large number of African slaves, Brazil has more people of African origin (called Afro-Brazilian) than any other country outside the African continent. The largest percentage of **Afro-Brazilians** is found in the **north-east** region, especially in the city of **Salvador.** The largest concentration of people of Portuguese and other European descent are found in the south and south-east of the country. Many people are of mixed ancestry, but are generally considered either white or Afro-Brazilian depending on the colour of their skin.

Race relations in Brazil are **poor,** especially between white Brazilians and Afro-Brazilians. Despite being in the majority, **Afro-Brazilians** are far **more likely to live in poverty** than white Brazilians. In major cities, **white Brazilians** earn an average of **2.4 times** more than Afro-Brazilians. In the former slave port of **Salvador,** this figure rises to **3.2 times** more. In response to this, the government has ordered its national universities to **reserve half of their places** for the **poorest students** from **public schools.**

A favela is a town consisting of make-shift shelters made from scrap materials. They are also referred to as shanty towns or slums. In Rio de Janeiro, over **half of the population** living in favelas is **Afro-Brazilian.** In the **richer parts** of the city, only **7 per cent are Afro-Brazilian.** This highlights the level of poverty faced by the Afro-Brazilians. **Standards of living** for **white Brazilians have increased greatly over the past 20 years.**

Fig. 25.37 Brazil is a multicultural society.

Fig. 25.38 Evidence of the wealth gap in São Paulo.

Native Brazilians

Some 500 years ago, there were an estimated **2 to 6 million native Brazilians.** Today only an estimated **350 000 remain** due the devastating influence of colonists. Many native Brazilians were forced into **slavery** and **had their lands confiscated,** which led to many dying from **exhaustion** and **starvation.** European colonists carried **diseases** such as **influenza** and **smallpox,** which killed many natives as their **immune systems had never encountered European diseases and were unable to fight them.**

Today, **deforestation** remains a threat to native Brazilians as the Amazon Rainforest is cleared to make way for agriculture. Due to this threat, the Brazilian government has **reserved 20 per cent of the Amazon** for Brazil's native tribes. Today, Brazilian natives are divided into about **200 cultural groups** with roughly **120 different languages.**

Fig. 25.39 Native tribe populations are dwindling.

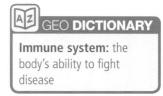
GEO DICTIONARY

Immune system: the body's ability to fight disease

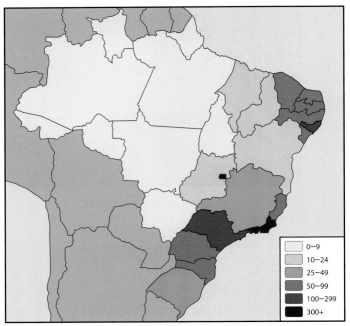

 Fig. 25.40 Population density of Brazil in km²

Population Dynamics

Brazil has more than **half of the total population** of all of South America. **In 1900, Brazil's population was 17 million.** As of July 2014, it is approximately **203 million.** A number of factors led to this rapid increase, including **rural-urban migration** and **increased standards of living,** all leading to higher birth rates. Over the past two decades, population growth has slowed. In 1900, the country was in **Stage 2** of the DTM; by 2005 it was in **Stage 4.**

Density and Distribution

The **population density** of Brazil is estimated to be **22 per km².** The population of Brazil is very unevenly distributed, with over **80 per cent of the population** living **within 320 km of the east coast.**

When Portuguese colonists first arrived in Brazil, they founded cities and towns along the eastern coast as it had a **more tolerable climate** than further inland. In the 1950s, the government attempted to move the population away from the overcrowded cities of the east. Between 1954 and 1956, the capital city of **Brasília** was built over **1200 km inland** to **attract migrants.** Today, Brasília is the **fourth-largest city** in the country, with a population of **2.9 million.** Migrants were also attracted to move west to **exploit** the country's **natural resources.** This has led to the destruction of the **Amazon Rainforest,** which is home to many of Brazil's native tribes. The harsh climate of the **north-east** means it **does not attract settlement.** The exception is along coastal ports where **temperatures are cooler.**

 Fig. 25.41 The developed CBD of São Paulo

The **south-east** is the **most densely populated** part of the country because it has a **high concentration of industry.** The industrial triangle of São Paulo-Belo Horizonte-Rio de Janeiro **attracts millions of economic migrants** who abandon their rural lands in search of a **better standard of living** in the cities. This migration has placed **pressure on services** in these cities, especially housing. The shortage of housing has led to the development of favelas. There are over **8 million** people living in **favelas in São Paulo,** and **1.6 million** living in favelas in **Rio de Janeiro.**

ACTIVE LEARNING

1. Explain why the population of Brazil rose rapidly from 1900 onwards.
2. Describe the population density and distribution of Brazil.

Fertility Rates

In 2015, Brazil's fertility rate was **1.79 per woman** down from **6.2 in 1960**. The declining fertility rate is due to the **increasing standard of living, better education** and the improved **status of women** in Brazilian society. As women are staying in education longer, they are pursuing careers and delaying having children. **Lower infant mortality** rates mean that mothers are having fewer children.

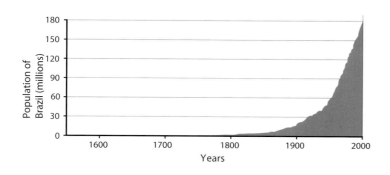

Fig. 25.42 Population growth in Brazil

Life Expectancy

Brazil's life expectancy is **68 years for males** and **76 years for females**, which is **typical of a middle income country**. **Male** life expectancy is still **significantly lower** than in countries in Western Europe.

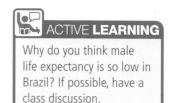

ACTIVE LEARNING

Why do you think male life expectancy is so low in Brazil? If possible, have a class discussion.

EDUCATE YOURSELF

Human Processes	
Race and race relations	Mixed race, multicultural, colonial history, nomadic native tribes, Portuguese colonists, West African slaves, Afro-Brazilians – north-east, Salvador; Portuguese/European settlers – south-east; race relations are poor, Afro-Brazilians more likely to live poverty, white Brazilians earn 2.3 times more; Rio >50% people living in favelas are Afro-Brazilians, < 7% in rich areas
Native Brazilians	500 years ago 2–6 million natives, 350 000 today, slavery and confiscation of land, starvation and exhaustion, diseases – smallpox and influenza, immune systems unable to cope, deforestation, 20% of Amazon reserved, 200 cultural groups, 120 languages
Population dynamics	Half South American population, 203 million, 17 million in 1900, rural-urban migration, increased standard of living, stage 2 to stage 4 of DTM
Density and distribution	22 per km², 80% living within 320 km of east coast, more tolerate climate, Brasília, 1200 km inland, attracted migrants, fourth-largest city, 2.9 million people, inland migration – exploitation of natural resources and destruction of rainforest, north-east unattractive for settlement, coastal ports cooler, south-east most densely populated, high concentration of industry, attract migrant workers, pressure on services, favelas – 8 million São Paulo, 1.6 million in Rio
Fertility rates	1.79 per woman, 6.2 in 1960, increased standard of living, education, status of women, lower infant mortality
Life expectancy	Typical middle income country, 68 males, 76 females, male life expectancy much lower than in Western European countries

Growth of an Urban Area: São Paulo

São Paulo is the **largest and most economically important** city in Brazil. The population of Greater São Paulo is **22 million** and it is continually increasing. Despite lying on the Tropic of Capricorn, which has a tropical or subtropical climate, São Paulo has a **cooler climate** due to its **altitude of 760 m.**

Historic Development

São Paulo was founded by Jesuits in **1554** when **Portuguese colonists** settled along the eastern coast. The Portuguese developed São Paulo as a **centre** for exporting raw materials. In the **eighteenth century, gold was discovered** in the São Paulo state, causing it to **grow in economic importance.** The population of the city grew as the gold trade attracted fortune hunters. At this time, the city also became the **core market** for the sale and export of **sugar.**

In **1934,** São Paulo became a **university city** which created a more skilled workforce. The city also became a **financial centre,** which encouraged **wealthy plantation owners** to live on the outskirts of the city. **Railway lines** were built to link the city to the nearby port of Santos, which made it easier to export goods. **Roadways** were also built to connect the city to the coffee plantations further inland.

Fig. 25.43 The remains of the sixteenth-century St Paul's Church in São Paulo

Industrial Development

Industrial development was slow until the start of World War II. In wartime, Brazil was unable to import the goods it needed. The Brazilian government invested in producing its own goods. São Paulo was chosen as the **main city for manufacturing** due to its developed transport links, large population and availability of raw materials. Today, over **50 per cent of Brazil's industrial production** occurs in the city of São Paulo. Petrochemicals, agrichemicals, fertilisers and iron ore are some of the main products of the city.

While industrial development has made the city much wealthier, it has come at a cost. **Air pollution** caused by manufacturing and traffic congestion has led to São Paulo being nicknamed 'Cough City'. There are approximately **7 million cars** in the city and over **2000 industrial plants**. As air pollution increases, so too do the levels of **respiratory diseases.**

Fig. 25.44 Increased car ownership damaged air quality and put pressure on transport networks.

The government has implemented several policies to reduce air pollution in the city. **Policies** were introduced to restrict driving and reduce emissions from vehicles and to reduce industrial pollution. These policies have helped **reduce the level of air pollution by 21 per cent** over a four-year period.

Inward Migration

With the **abolition of slavery** in 1888, large numbers of former slaves moved to the São Paulo state in **search of work on sugar and coffee plantations.** Many of their descendants live in the city today. As industry developed in the city, large numbers of migrants moved there in search of employment. The **rapidly growing population** placed huge **pressure on services** in the city, leading to many families living in terrible conditions.

Roughly **20 per cent** of São Paulo's population lives in **favelas,** which lack services such as sanitation, water and health care, and have a **high crime rate.** Rubbish collections are not possible in favelas due to their **narrow streets,** leading to a **high risk of fire** and the **spread of disease.**

São Paulo's favelas are constantly growing because housing is cheap and close to many of the inhabitants' places of work. The authorities have developed a method of **burning methane** gas emitted from landfill sites to provide **power to the homes in the favelas.**

Fig. 25.45 Fire sweeps through a favela in São Paulo

 EDUCATE YOURSELF

Growth of an Urban Area: São Paulo

Largest city, most economically important, 22 million, cooler climate 760 m altitude, founded in 1554, port, gold discovered in 18th century, growth of economic importance, core market for sugar, 1934 university city, financial centre, railway and transport links; industrial development – main city of manufacturing, 50% of all industrial production, air pollution, 7 million cars owned, 2000 industrial plants, respiratory diseases, transportation policies, reduced air pollution by 21%; inward migration – abolition of slavery, pressure on services, 20% population in favelas, high crime rate, narrow streets, high risk of fire and disease, burning methane to power favela homes

25.6 Brazilian Culture

Due to the number of ethnic groups living in Brazil, it is no surprise that it has a rich cultural heritage.

Religion

The Portuguese **colonists** brought **Catholicism** to Brazil in the sixteenth century. During the colonial period, **African slaves and native peoples were forbidden** from **practising their own religions.** This was a way of spreading the Catholic religion. Slave masters also felt that **denying these people their beliefs** helped to **strip them of their identities** as a 'group'. In **1824,** Catholicism became the **official religion of Brazil,** although it was also stated that people were free to practise the religion of their choice.

Fig. 25.46 The Christ the Redeemer Statue is world famous.

Today, Brazil has more Catholics than any other country in the world. Some **65 per cent** of the population identifies as Roman Catholic. Of these, approximately **20 per cent** attend mass or **participate in the religion.** The explanation for this is that Brazilians regard themselves as Catholic more by **tradition than by belief.**

Brazil is now a republic, meaning that the Catholic Church should have no influence on government policy. However, politicians are still careful not to take any action which may offend the Church. This shows the influence the religion still has on the culture of the country.

Other **minority religions** survive in Brazil. African slaves found ways of continuing their worship without their owners' realising. Slaves gave **Catholic names to their gods in order to hide and protect their beliefs.** As a result, many of their descendants continue to practise these religions, which include Candomblé, Umbanda and Batuque.

Language

From your study of the Gaeltacht and Belgium, you know that language is an **important cultural indicator. Portuguese** is the official language of Brazil, which dates back to colonial times. Due to the influence of African descendants, Brazilian Portuguese is full of expressions that are borrowed from **African languages.**

Several other **native languages** exist, but they are spoken only by a small number of people. With **120 different languages** spread across 350 000 native Brazilians, many of these languages are in danger of disappearing. The most common native language is **Guarani,** which is spoken by 35 000 tribal people close to the Paraguayan border.

Music and Sport

Both music and sport are **strong cultural indicators** in Brazil. The country has become world famous for its **carnivals,** which are celebrated with traditional music and dance. Samba, which is derived from **traditional African music,** is Brazil's most famous musical style. Brought to Brazil by slaves, the fast-paced music has survived and evolved throughout the centuries.

Brazil is famous for its world-class **soccer** players such as **Pelé,** who is regarded as the greatest player of all time. With **five World Cup titles,** Brazil is the most successful international team of all time.

Soccer is the most popular sport in the country and plays such an important part in Brazilian lives that some **employees are given time off** to watch World Cup matches. **Samba soccer** is played on the streets by children and adults of all ages.

> **Fig. 25.47** The Brazilian football team

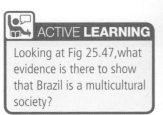
ACTIVE **LEARNING**
Looking at Fig 25.47, what evidence is there to show that Brazil is a multicultural society?

Brazilian Culture	
Religion	Portuguese in 16th century, 65% Catholic, 20% practising, tradition rather than belief, slaves' and natives' religions forbidden, stripped them of identities as a group, 1824 Catholicism became official language, minority religions
Language	Important cultural indicators, Portuguese, African languages, samba, 120 native languages, Guarani
Music and sport	Strong cultural indicators, carnivals, traditional African music, soccer – Pelé, five World Cups, samba soccer, employees given time off to watch tournament

EXAM QUESTIONS

ORDINARY LEVEL

LONG QUESTIONS

1. Name a **continental/subcontinental region (not in Europe)** that you have studied and answer each of the following questions.

   (i) Name **one** primary economic activity that contributes to the economy of this region.

   (ii) Explain the advantages that this region has for the development of the primary economic activity named in part (i) above.

   (iii) Describe **one** problem faced by this primary economic activity in this region.

Region named 1m
(i) Primary activity named 3m
(ii) Advantages explained 9 SRPs @ 3m
(iii) Problem described 3 SRPs @ 3m each

   2015 Q6C 40M

2. Explain how any **two** of the following influence the development of agriculture in a **continental/subcontinental region (not in Europe)** that you have studied:

   • Relief **and** soils

   • Climate

   • Markets

Influence 1 explained 5 SRPs @ 3m each
Influence 2 explained 5 SRPs @ 3m each

   2012 Q4B 30M

3. Describe and explain the development of manufacturing industry in a **continental/subcontinental region (not in Europe)** that you have studied.

Naming the region 3m
Description/explanation 9 SRPs @ 3m each

   2014 Q5B AND 2011 Q5C 30M

HIGHER LEVEL

1. Examine the factors that influence the development of **one** primary economic activity in a **continental/subcontinental region (not in Europe)** that you have studied.

Factors identified 2m + 2m
Examination 13 SRPs @ 2m each

   2015 Q6B 30M

2. Explain the development of agriculture in a **continental/subcontinental region (not in Europe)** that you have studied, with reference to any two of the following factors:

   • Soils   • Markets   • Relief

Discussion of factor 1 8 SRPs @ 2m each
Discussion of factor 2 7 SRPs @ 2m each

   2013 Q5B 30M

HIGHER LEVEL

3. Discuss the factors that influence the development of secondary economic activity in a **continental/ subcontinental region (not in Europe)** that you have studied.

| Factors identified 2m + 2m |
| Discussion 13 SRPs @ 2m each |

2014 Q5C 30M

4. Examine the influence of any two of the human processes in the table, on the development of a **continental/subcontinental region (not in Europe)** that you have studied.

Population dynamics	Language	Religion
Urban development	Rural development	

| Challenges identified 2m + 2m |
| Description/explanation 13 SRPs @ 2m each |

2015 Q5C AND 2012 Q6C 30M

5. Account for the growth **and** distribution of population in a **continental/subcontinental region (not in Europe)** that you have studied.

| Examination 15 SRPs @ 2m each |

2014 4C 30M

In this section we will look at a Higher Level question on how to draw a sketch map of Brazil.

HIGHER LEVEL

EXAM QUESTION

Draw an outline map of a **continental/subcontinental region (not in Europe)** that you have studied.

On it show and label the following:

- A named feature of relief
- A named river
- A named urban centre
- A major road or rail link

Marking Scheme
Map outline 4m
Four features @ 4m each
Shown 2m each
Named 2m each

2012 Q4 A 20M

SAMPLE ANSWER

Sketch map of Brazil

Amazon River

The Brazilian Highlands

Brasília

São Paulo–Brasília motorway

Rio de Janeiro

São Paulo

Marks Awarded	
Map outline 4m	
Four features shown and named @ 4m each	
Total 20/20	

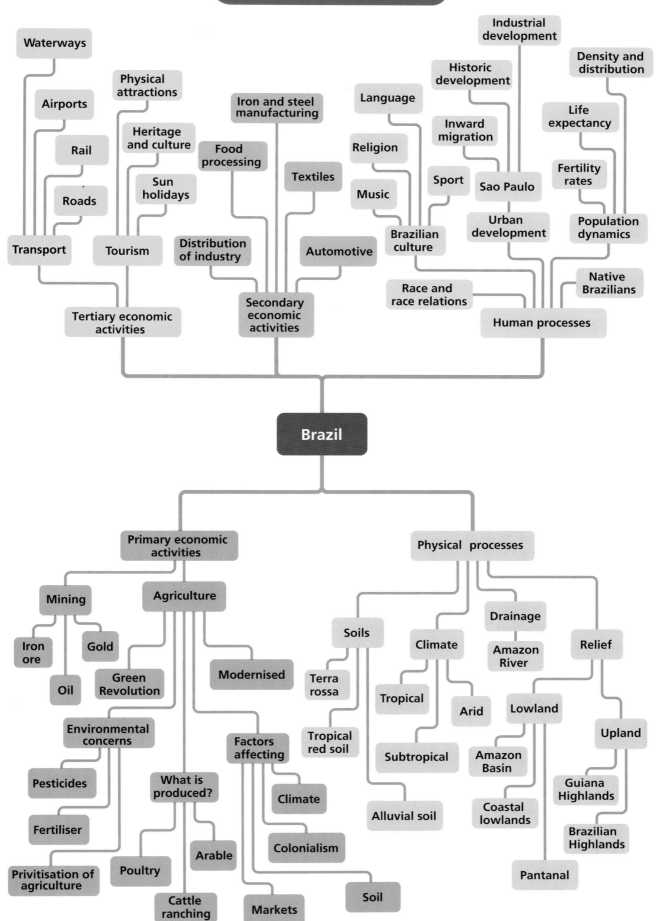

TOPIC MAP

Waterways

Physical attractions

Airports

Iron and steel manufacturing

Language

Industrial development

Historic development

Density and distribution

Rail

Heritage and culture

Food processing

Textiles

Religion

Inward migration

Life expectancy

Roads

Sun holidays

Music

Sport

Sao Paulo

Fertility rates

Transport

Tourism

Distribution of industry

Automotive

Brazilian culture

Urban development

Population dynamics

Tertiary economic activities

Secondary economic activities

Race and race relations

Native Brazilians

Human processes

Brazil

Primary economic activities

Physical processes

Mining

Agriculture

Soils

Drainage

Relief

Iron ore

Gold

Climate

Amazon River

Terra rossa

Oil

Green Revolution

Modernised

Tropical

Arid

Lowland

Upland

Environmental concerns

Factors affecting

Tropical red soil

Subtropical

Amazon Basin

Guiana Highlands

Pesticides

What is produced?

Climate

Alluvial soil

Coastal lowlands

Brazilian Highlands

Fertiliser

Arable

Colonialism

Privitisation of agriculture

Poultry

Pantanal

Cattle ranching

Markets

Soil

CHAPTER 26

The Complexities of Regions

In this chapter, we will examine the complexities of regions. In Chapter 20, you learned how regions are created and defined. In this chapter, you will learn how political, economic and cultural relationships develop and change over time.

KEY WORDS

- Northern Ireland
- Good Friday Agreement
- Economic interdependence
- Basque Country
- EU development
- EU enlargement
- Gaeltacht
- Fíor Gaeltacht
- Breac Gaeltacht
- Urban sprawl
- Commuter
- Reunification

LEARNING OUTCOMES

What you MUST know
- The political, economic and cultural interactions in Northern Ireland
- The political, economic and cultural interactions in the Basque Country
- The origins and expansion of the European Union
- Future challenges in the European Union
- The impact of EU enlargement on Ireland
- Shrinking boundaries of Ireland's Gaeltachts
- Expanding boundaries of Dublin City
- Changing political boundaries: unification of Germany

What you SHOULD know
- How to understand information provided in graphs and illustrations

What is USEFUL to know
- Additional information from current affairs events on developments in Ireland and the EU

Why?

When trying to understand the complexity of regions, think small. Imagine your home as a metaphor for political interaction. Think of your room or your belongings. If somebody enters your room without knocking or uses one of your belongings without permission, you might get angry. This is the basis of difficulties caused by 'political' boundaries (this is **my** room). As we scale this up to real regions, the level of complexity grows hugely.

Introduction

The term 'complex' means complicated, which is a perfect way to describe the regions of the world today. Although most regions have clearly defined boundaries, their **interaction with neighbouring regions** can lead to **complex political, economic and cultural relationships**. These relationships also affect the physical boundaries of regions. As **some cultures grow or shrink** in size, the **region gets bigger or smaller** as a result.

Political boundaries have changed throughout history and will **continue to change in the future.** In this chapter, we will look at a number of examples that highlight the complexity of regions.

26.1 Political, Economic and Cultural Interactions in a Divided Ireland

Northern Ireland

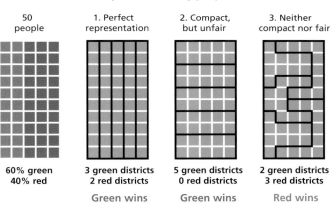

As you have already learned, Northern Ireland is a region with diverse cultural groups – nationalist and unionist. In this section, we will look at Northern Ireland's interactions with the Republic of Ireland.

Republic of Ireland

▲ **Fig. 26.1** Northern Ireland

Northern Ireland

In **1920,** the British government passed the **Government of Ireland Act.** This act divided the island in two: the **six counties** of Northern Ireland and the **26 counties** of the Irish Free State. The partition created **two separate states within the island** of Ireland. A mainly **unionist majority ruled Northern Ireland,** while the Irish Free State (now the **Republic of Ireland)** was ruled by a **nationalist majority.** A complex relationship developed between the two regions.

GEO DICTIONARY

Gerrymandering: the unfair manipulation of electoral boundaries to favour one party over others

Political Interactions

After the formation of the **Irish Free State in 1922, political interaction** between the two states was largely **negative** with a relationship of **mistrust developing.** Several factors combined to increase the political divide.

Unionist and **nationalist politicians** had different political outlooks. Unionists consolidated their **power in Northern Ireland** through **gerrymandering.** Gerrymandering is a system of **rigging electoral boundaries.** In Northern Ireland, **areas** which were **majority nationalist** had their **electoral boundaries changed** so that unionists would be elected.

This system **prevented the Nationalist Party** and other smaller parties from **gaining power.** The unionist grip on power in the North **stopped** any **political cooperation** with **the Republic.**

Three different ways to divide fifty people into five districts

50 people	1. Perfect representation	2. Compact, but unfair	3. Neither compact nor fair
60% green 40% red	3 green districts 2 red districts	5 green districts 0 red districts	2 green districts 3 red districts
	Green wins	Green wins	Red wins

▲ **Fig. 26.2** How gerrymandering can fix elections

As a result of discrimination, nationalists organised a series of **civil rights marches in the 1960s,** which were largely **supported by the politicians in the Republic.** These protests often turned violent, when protesters were attacked by the police and army. This started a virtual civil war between the two sides, which reinforced the divide between them. The period of unrest, known as **'The Troubles',** lasted for more than 30 years. Many acts of terrorism were carried out by both sides. There was **little or no political interaction** between **Northern Irish and Republic of Ireland politicians** during this time.

It was not until the **Good Friday Agreement in 1998** that significant **progress** was made towards peace. The agreement brought about

GEO DICTIONARY

Civil war: a war between groups within the same country

Northern Ireland general election, 1965

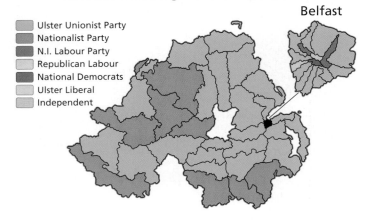

Legend:
- Ulster Unionist Party
- Nationalist Party
- N.I. Labour Party
- Republican Labour
- National Democrats
- Ulster Liberal
- Independent

Belfast

Fig. 26.3 Northern Ireland election results, 1965

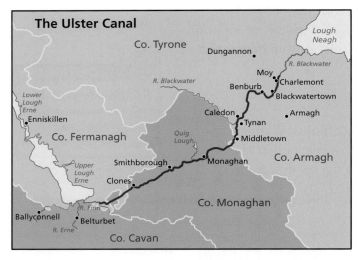

Fig. 26.4 The Ulster Canal passes through both the Republic and the North.

GEO **DICTIONARY**

Economic interdependence: when the economies of two different countries or regions depend on each other for provision of goods and services (with each specialising in certain areas)

power-sharing between **unionists and nationalists** and a new era of **political cooperation between the North and the Republic.** The Good Friday Agreement set up the **North-South Ministerial Council,** which is composed of **government ministers from both sides** of the border. The council deals with areas such as:

- **Waterways: Waterways Ireland** deals with the development and maintenance of over 1000 km of inland waterways North and South for recreation and tourism. It also monitors and maintains fisheries in the border areas.

- **Transport: Strategic Transport Planning** reviews and **updates transport networks** in the island of Ireland, especially **along the borders,** e.g. cross-border **bus services.**

- **Trade: InterTradeIreland** coordinates **trade and business** between North and South.

Economic Interactions

Between **1922 and 1973,** there was **little or no economic interaction** between the North and the Republic. There were several factors which contributed to this:

- **Protectionist policies** were introduced in the South in the 1930s and lasted until the 1950s. These **taxed imports** in order to protect a country's own industry from **competition.**

- The **North** had **strong traditional industries,** such as **textiles and shipbuilding,** which made it **economically self-sufficient.** Therefore, it did not **need to trade with the South.** By contrast, the **Republic** had a mainly rural economy, without much **industry.** It produced little to export.

Both regions' economies changed in the **1950s and 1960s.** The **Republic's economy grew rapidly** and the **North's economy went into decline.** The **Republic of Ireland** introduced a low **corporation tax (currently just 12.5 per cent),** which **attracted** foreign **investment.** By 1969, **Northern Ireland** was the **poorest region in the UK.**

When Ireland and Britain **joined the EU** (then the EEC) in **1973,** economic interaction between North and South began to develop. Ireland and Britain's **economic interdependence** grew. **Trade** between the North and South also **grew** and now exceeds **€3 billion per annum.**

The **Good Friday Agreement** brought peace and economic stability. The construction of the **M1 Dublin-Belfast motorway** links the South to the North. Both of these developments helped to further enhance trade between the two parts of the island.

Other economic interactions include:

- The **Irish government invested over €15 million in the development of Derry Airport** as it is used regularly by the people of Donegal.

- Thousands of **shoppers travel to the North** when sterling loses value relative to the euro, and Northern shoppers travel South when the euro loses value.

Cultural Interactions

Cultural interactions between the North and South were limited due to longstanding **cultural barriers.** This is particularly evident in the cultural indicators of **sport** and **education.**

Sport

The **GAA** is prominent in all 32 counties of Ireland. In the North, the GAA has been embraced by **Catholic nationalists** rather than by the unionist community. In **2001,** the **GAA lifted its ban** on **British armed forces** and members of the Police Service of Northern Ireland (**PSNI**) playing GAA.

Since the **Good Friday Agreement,** more emphasis has been placed on **integrating both cultures' traditions.** For example, the **GAA has run Cúl Camps** in unionist communities. **Children** and **volunteers** from **both communities** attend and help out.

At national level, **Ireland's rugby and boxing teams** are composed of athletes from the **whole island** which has encouraged inclusivity. The Irish rugby team's anthem **'Ireland's Call',** which refers to the **'four proud provinces of Ireland',** is played before each match.

⌃ **Fig. 26.5** The M1 motorway from Dublin to Belfast has allowed for borderless movement of people and trade between the North and South.

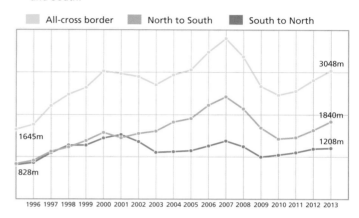

| All-cross border | North to South | South to North |

1996 1997 1998 1999 2000 2001 2002 2003 2004 2005 2006 2007 2008 2009 2010 2011 2012 2013

3048m
1840m
1208m
1645m
828m

⌃ **Fig. 26.6** Cross-border trade between the North and South

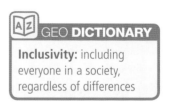

GEO DICTIONARY

Inclusivity: including everyone in a society, regardless of differences

⌃ **Fig. 26.7** 'Four Provinces. One Team' was the Irish rugby team's motto for the 2015 World Cup.

FACT

Sport can cause divisions. The Republic of Ireland and Northern Ireland have separate soccer teams, and the decision of some Northern players to play for the Republic has caused tension. For example, James McClean received death threats when he declared for the Republic of Ireland.

Rory McIlroy was also put under pressure to declare for either Ireland or Great Britain for the Rio Olympics in 2016. The decision was so stressful that McIlroy considered not competing at all. In the end, he decided to play for Ireland.

How important do you see non-segregated education for the future of NI?

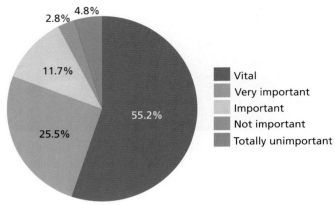

- Vital — 55.2%
- Very important — 25.5%
- Important — 11.7%
- Not important — 2.8%
- Totally unimportant — 4.8%

Religion breakdown of people responding Vital/Very important

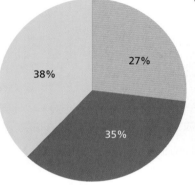

- Protestant — 27%
- Catholic — 35%
- None/Other — 38%

🔵 **Fig. 26.8** Parental views on integrated schools in Northern Ireland

ACTIVE LEARNING

1. What act led to the formation of Northern Ireland?
2. Name the two main political views that exist in Northern Ireland.
3. What agreement led to peace in Northern Ireland?
4. Why was there so little economic activity between the Republic and Northern Ireland prior to 1973?
5. How has the M1 benefitted trade between the two regions?
6. Name two strong indicators of culture in Northern Ireland.

Education

The Republic and the North have **separate education systems.** Northern Ireland post-primary schools study for **GCSE** and **A Levels,** while students in the Republic sit **Junior Cycle and Leaving Certificate** examinations.

Within the North, the **nationalist community** is more likely to attend **Catholic schools** run by religious orders. **Unionist families** are more likely to attend schools with a **Protestant tradition. Integrating schools** is seen as a key way to **knock down cultural barriers.** If **younger generations** attend the same schools, they form **friendships with people from different traditions.** This also forces **interaction between parents.**

EDUCATE YOURSELF

Northern Ireland
1920 Government of Ireland Act, six counties remained under British rule, 26 counties gained independence in 1922, two separate states, unionist majority in North, nationalist majority in Republic, complex relationship developed

Political interactions	Irish Free State 1922, political interaction negative, mistrust developed, unionist and nationalist politicians different political outlook; unionists in power – gerrymandering, unionist majority, prevented Nationalist Party gaining power, stopped political cooperation between North and Republic, civil rights marches, supported by politicians in South, the Troubles, little or no political cooperation, Good Friday Agreement, political progress, power-sharing, political cooperation, North-South Ministerial Council, government ministers from both sides, Waterways Ireland, Strategic Transport Planning, InterTradeIreland
Economic interactions	1922–73 little or no economic interaction, protectionist policies, taxed each other's imports, 1950s–1960s Republic's economy grew rapidly, North's economy in decline, Republic low corporation tax attracted investment, 1969 Northern Ireland poorest region in UK; 1973 joined EU, economic interdependence, trade grew, €3 billion per annum, Good Friday Agreement, M1 Dublin-Belfast motorway
Cultural interactions	Sport: GAA nationalist, 2001 lifted ban on PSNI and armed forces, Good Friday Agreement, integrating both cultures' traditions, GAA Cúl Camps, children and volunteers from both communities, Irish rugby and boxing teams – whole island
	Education: separate education systems, GCSE and A Levels, Junior Cycle and Leaving Certificate; nationalist community – Catholic schools, unionist families – Protestant schools, integration of schools, knocks down cultural barriers, younger generations, interaction between parents

26.2 Conflict in a Culturally and Politically Diverse Region: The Basque Country

The **Basque Country** (sometimes referred to as the Basque Region) is located in northern Spain and is separated from the rest of Spain by the Pyrenees Mountains. The Pyrenees are a natural border between the Basque of **north-west Spain** and south-west France.

As of 2014, the **population** in the Basque Country was **2.2 million people.** The majority of the population live in urban areas such as **Bilbao,** which is the **economic heart** of the region. People of **Basque descent** have **lived in the region** for over **10 000 years,** which has had an **impact on their sense of culture** and their pride of place. The Basque people are considered to be among the **oldest ethnic groups in Europe.** Most Basque people **feel the region is a country** in its own right and wish to **separate from Spain.**

Fig. 26.9 The Basque Country

This desire for **political separation** stems from the oppression of the Basque people during the **regime of General Franco of Spain** (1939–75). At this time, all **expressions of Basque culture,** including its language, were **banned.** This led to the **foundation of resistance groups,** such as Euskadi Ta Askatasuna (**ETA**) which was set up in 1959.

ETA used **violence** in its campaign for Basque independence. ETA planted many **bombs in Spain,** and have killed **over 850 people.** Following the death of Franco in 1975 and the **granting of autonomy** to the Basque Country, ETA **continued to commit terrorist acts.**

In 1979, **three Spanish Basque provinces** (Vizcaya, Guipuzcoa and Navarra) **joined together.** They were given **limited autonomy by the Spanish government.** This included **control of their schools** and **police force.** The Spanish government also **recognised the Basques' culture** and **language** as being **distinct from that of Spain.** The Basque people now **elect their own president and parliament,** but are still under the **international control of Spain.** The **Basque regional government** now has most of the **power** in the region.

Fig. 26.10 The Basque people are extremely proud of their culture.

Fig. 26.11 ETA wants to establish an independent Basque State.

GEO DICTIONARY

Autonomy: independence or freedom, self-government

Basque Country

North-west Spain, population 2.2 million, Bilbao economic heartland, Basque descent lived in region over 10 000 years, impacted sense of culture, among oldest ethnic groups in Europe, feel they are a country separate from Spain, political separation, General Franco, banned expression of Basque culture, foundation of resistance groups, ETA, violence – 850 dead, Basque autonomy; ETA violence continued, 1979 – autonomous region, control schools and police force, elect president and parliament, political and cultural changes weakened ETA, 2011 permanent ceasefire

These political and cultural changes have weakened ETA. As the Basque Country has its own regional government, most people turned away from supporting **violence as a way** to gain independence. Consequently, in March 2006, ETA announced a ceasefire. They launched an attack on Madrid Airport in December 2006, in which two people were killed. In January **2011, ETA** declared a **permanent ceasefire**.

▲ **Fig. 26.12** The EU flag

26.3 The Origins and Expansion of the European Union

The **origins** of the EU came in the **aftermath of World War II**. To **prevent further conflict** and to ensure economic progress, in 1950 French Foreign Minister **Robert Schuman** presented a plan for **cooperation between European states**. This plan led to the Treaty of Paris in 1951, which set up the European Coal and Steel Community (ECSC). Initially, six countries joined:

- Belgium
- France
- Italy
- Luxembourg
- Netherlands
- West Germany

The treaty allowed for **free trade of coal and iron** across member states' borders. As the free trade proved successful, they signed the **Treaty of Rome in 1957** to form the **European Economic Community (EEC)**. The treaty set up a **common market,** which allowed the free movement of all goods between the six EEC states. As the prosperity of the six states grew, more countries applied to join.

In **1965,** the EEC changed its name to the **European Community (EC),** which emphasised the idea of a **community rather than** focusing on **financial cooperation**. The **European Parliament** was also set up to **discuss political issues and introduce laws.**

In 1986, the **Single European Act** was signed which **eliminated** any remaining **trade barriers.** It also meant that laws passed become law in all EC member states.

In 1992, the **Maastricht Treaty** set out the aim of having a **single currency** (euro). The euro was introduced in 2002. Member states which have adopted the euro as their currency are collectively called the **Eurozone**.

The Maastricht Treaty also established a European **defence force of 60 000.** At this time, the EC changed its name to today's European Union (EU).

Enlargement Over Time

The number of EU member states has grown:

- 1957: original six members of ECSC
- 1973: Denmark, Britain and Ireland join
- 1981: Greece joins
- 1986: Portugal and Spain join
- 1995: Austria, Sweden and Finland join
- 2004: Cyprus, the Czech Republic, Estonia, Hungary, Latvia, Lithuania, Malta, Poland, Slovakia and Slovenia join
- 2007: Romania and Bulgaria join
- 2013: Croatia joins

As of 2016, the **EU has 28 member states,** with the likelihood that more will join in the future.

Fig. 26.13 EU enlargement over time

Note!

Can you identify all of the EU member states on a map? If not, it may be a good idea to practise this as it can often appear as a short question or part of a 20m question (Part A). While most students can identify Western European countries, many struggle to identify countries that have joined since 2004.

26.4 Issues and Concerns: Future of the EU

While it is clear that the EU has brought about **stability and prosperity** for its members, a number of questions remain as to how it will develop in the future. In this section, we will examine the future of the EU in terms of:

- Political union
- Economic union
- Sovereignty

Political Union

A strong **political union between member states** is vital for the future of the EU. However, there are concerns over the idea of **drafting common laws** on tax rates and other issues and policies about the environment, defence and other international affairs. The **Common Foreign and Security Policy** (CFSP) was established with the aim of **outlining common political goals.** The EU parliament has also elected a **Foreign Minister** to **represent**

ACTIVE LEARNING

1. In what year did Ireland join the EU?
2. What change did the Single European Act bring about?
3. Visit the official EU website on **ec.europa. eu** to find out about EU developments that affect Ireland.

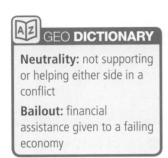

Fig. 26.14 EU military staff coat of arms

the EU's views on a global level. Sections of the treaties have tried to unify the political aims and views of the member states. Examples of such treaties are:

Maastricht Treaty (1992)	The formation of a **60 000 strong EU army**
	Concern: Ireland's **neutrality is threatened** by the notion of an EU army. Ireland has been neutral since World War II. An EU army could draw Ireland and other neutral countries **into conflicts.**
Amsterdam Treaty (1997)	Introducing common immigration laws for EU member states and also paving the way for further EU enlargement
	Concern: As the EU becomes larger, more and more **political points of view must be addressed.** This makes it increasingly **difficult to create unified political goals.** One of the most famous differing political views was on involvement in the Gulf War in 2003. Further disagreement has developed on **'bailout' packages** for countries such as Portugal and Greece.
Unified in Diversity (2005)	Member states rejected an EU constitution of **'Unified in Diversity'**, which aimed to present the EU as a single trading block. The **EU constitution differed from many of its member constitutions**, leading to it being scrapped. Instead it was replaced by the **Lisbon Treaty in 2009** which established a **President of the European Council.** It was argued that the **Lisbon Treaty** would make the **EU more efficient**, but it was rejected by Ireland in the first referendum due to a number of concerns.
	Concerns: Ireland's **neutrality, taxes** (especially our low corporation tax), workers' rights

With some changes, the Lisbon Treaty was passed in a second Irish referendum. This unified approach has made the EU a **strong political force** when voting on global issues.

Economic Union

The EU offers **free movement of both people and goods** between its member states. With Croatia joining as the **28th member state,** the union has grown by 13 members in just 10 years. Enlargement has had positive and negative effects on the EU's economy.

Positives

- Increased prosperity: With each new member state, the **size of the market and labour force** is **increased,** making the EU a heavyweight in world trade. Also, as new members join, their **raw materials become available** for industry throughout the EU. Many MNCs invest in new member states due to their **lower cost of labour** and availability of resources.

- Sharing of skills: Labour shortages in one member state can be **filled by migrant workers** from another. For example, Ireland has had a shortage of science and engineering graduates. These shortages can be filled by workers from the EU.

- **Development:** Many new states that join the EU are heavily dependent on primary economic activities. **Modern technologies** from existing EU members greatly **develop agriculture and industrial output.**

Negatives

- **Cost:** Most new members have less developed economies than existing members. The **EU Structural and Cohesion Funds** must **invest large amounts of money** to develop these economies. The 2004 enlargement cost €25 billion.

- **Outward migration:** As **poorer countries** join the EU, they often **experience outward migration** as their people move in **search of employment** in countries with a **higher standard of living.** This was particularly evident after the 2004 enlargement when people from newly joined countries migrated to the more developed economies in Western Europe. These workers typically gained low-paid employment which in some cases reduced local salary rates.

- **Availability of funds:** EU Structural Funds are mainly **invested in new member states.** This reduces the money available to other areas.

- **Debt crisis: Uncontrolled lending and borrowing** led to countries such as Ireland, Italy and Greece accumulating huge debts. Countries in the Eurozone faced **economic instability** that threatened the currency and the unity of the EU. Billions of euro were lent to indebted countries as 'bailout' packages. Countries receiving bailouts had to give up economic independence as the EU and the International Monetary Fund **(IMF)** carefully monitored their finances. The bailout also highlighted different political views within the EU, with many countries opposing or disagreeing with the terms of the bailouts.

GEO DICTIONARY

IMF: an international organisation which promotes global monetary cooperation and financial stability

Sovereignty: a country's right to govern itself

Sovereignty

Sovereignty refers to a **country's right to make its own laws.** In other words, it is the ability of a country to rule itself. However, with increasing EU political and economic unity, **national sovereignty** of member states **has been weakened**. Member states must now abide by EU legislation in several areas such as the environment and family law. In the past, national governments had the power to veto, or block, new laws and policies. This process has become much more difficult since the **Single European Act of 1987.** In response to national concerns, four organisations were established to oversee the EU and manage future enlargement:

🔺 **Fig. 26.15** With increased EU control, there is a fear of reduced sovereignty for its member countries.

- The **European Commission** is made up of 28 commissioners (one for each member state) who are responsible for **proposing new EU laws.** Although commissioners are allocated by member states, they are not supposed to represent their country. They are expected to **act in the best interest of the EU.** It has been proposed that the number of commissioners be **reduced to 18** which means some member states will **lose some of their influence on** EU policy and development. One of the

Fig. 26.16 The European Parliament debates newly drafted legislation.

conditions of Ireland accepting the Lisbon Treaty was that it retains its commissioner.

- The **Council of the EU** is responsible for **decision making in the EU**. It is the council's responsibility to **adopt EU laws** and **coordinate new policies**. The council is also responsible for negotiating agreements with other countries and international organisations.

- The **European Parliament** allows **debate** between the 751 members of the European Parliament (MEPs). MEPs **debate newly drafted legislation**. The parliament has become increasingly powerful.

- The **European Council** offers **political guidance to the EU**. Its members are the government leaders of the 28 member states. The European Council meets at least four times a year, in meetings commonly referred to as 'EU summits'. **Most decisions are made by consensus.**

 GEO **DICTIONARY**

Consensus: when everyone is in agreement

Although political unity and economic unity have been achieved on some fronts, many EU member states have strong individual senses of nationalism. For example, many Irish people see themselves as being Irish first, and then European.

 **EDUCATE** YOURSELF

Future of the EU	
Political union	Political union between member states, drafting common laws, CFSP outlining political goals, foreign minister represent the EU's views on a global level, singular political view, Maastricht Treaty – neutrality is threatened, may be drawn into conflicts; Amsterdam Treaty – political agendas of all countries must be addressed, difficult to create unified political goals, bailout packages; Lisbon Treaty – President of European Council, concerns – Ireland's neutrality, taxes, strong political force in the UN
Economic union	Positives: free movement of people and goods, 28th member states in EU, increased prosperity, size of market and labour force increased, raw materials made available, lower cost of labour, sharing of skills, labour shortages filled by migrant workers, development of modern technologies, develop agriculture and industrial output
	Negatives: large amounts of money must be invested from structural and cohesion funds; outward migration experienced by poor countries, search employment, higher standard of living; availability of funds – invested in new member states; debt crisis – uncontrolled borrowing
Sovereignty	Country's right to make its own laws, national sovereignty has been weakened, Single European Act 1987
	European Commission: proposing new EU laws, act in the best interest of EU, proposed reduction to 18, lose some of their decision making influence
	Council of EU: decision making in the EU, adopt new laws, coordinate new policy
	European Parliament: democratic debate of new laws
	European Council: political guidance to EU

 FACT

According to John Bruton, who was Taoiseach from 1994 to 1997, 'The European Union is the world's most successful invention for advancing peace.'

 ACTIVE **LEARNING**

1. What are the two main concerns for Ireland regarding the Maastricht Treaty and the Amsterdam Treaty?
2. What are the positives associated with economic union?
3. Explain two negatives associated with economic union.
4. How has Ireland's sovereignty been affected by its membership of the EU?

26.5 The Effects of EU Enlargement on Ireland

In 1973, Ireland became a **member of the EU** (then called the EEC), as did Britain and Denmark. We became one of 15 member states. Membership allowed for the **free movement of people and goods** across the EU. The Schengen Agreement allows for the **free movement of workers** from one EU country to another.

In July 2013, Croatia became the 28th member state to join the EU. This was the sixth **expansion** since Ireland's membership, with each one having both **social and economic implications for Ireland.**

Share of EU mobile workers in % of total labour force

- 25–50
- 10–15
- 5–10
- 3–5
- 0–3
- 0

Fig. 26.17 Percentage of foreign national EU workers as a percentage of total workforce

Economic Implications

Positive

At the time of joining, Ireland's economy relied heavily on **poorly developed agriculture.** Thanks to EU funding and **foreign direct investment attracted by Ireland's membership,** the economy has **developed** into one based on **modern, high-tech industry.** During the Celtic Tiger, there was a **labour shortage of 420 000** workers. In 2007, at the peak of the Celtic Tiger, Ireland had one of the **lowest unemployment rates in Europe at 4.5 per cent,** which made it attractive for migrant workers from other EU countries. Migrants from other countries helped to **fill labour shortages** in areas such as the services industry, and their taxes **contributed to government income.** These taxes helped to pay for the **provision of services such as health and education.**

Negative

Ireland's reliance on foreign direct investment and exports to the EU and international markets makes us **vulnerable to global economic downturns.** Since the 2008 recession, Irish workers have benefitted from the **Schengen Agreement** as many looked for **employment in other EU countries.** By **2012,** our **unemployment rate** had peaked at **14.8 per cent,** not including the tens of thousands who had emigrated. As of January 2016, **unemployment remains high at 8.6 per cent.** More than 20 000 of those who emigrated during this time were foreign nationals. **Foreign nationals** currently make up roughly **15 per cent** of the **Irish workforce.**

A **negative** of having a large number of foreign nationals working in Ireland is **remittance money.** This is when workers send money back home to their families, meaning it is not spent in Ireland.

Some migrants were taken advantage of by employers, being poorly paid and working very long hours. Racism and bullying were also issues in some workplaces.

Fig. 26.18 Polish supporters sporting Ireland/Poland scarves.

Fig. 26.19 A Polish shop in Ireland

FACT

More than half of Ireland's current population was not born when Ireland voted to join the EU in 1972.

Social Implications

Positive

Since joining the EU, Ireland has become a **multicultural society,** which has had a positive impact on Irish culture. By 2014, **11.8 per cent of the Irish population** was made up of foreign nationals, with the largest proportion coming from **Poland (20.6 per cent of all foreign nationals** in Ireland).

The effects of multiculturalism can be clearly seen in **primary schools** with children often being **bilingual,** speaking **English** as well as their **parents' native language.** Many schools have introduced policies to help **integrate students** of **different nationalities** to the community. Extra English classes are offered to children.

Many European languages have been introduced and students can take their **native language,** e.g. Polish, as one of the Leaving Certificate subjects. Schools are a great way of breaking down cultural barriers, as children forge lasting friendships with children of different cultural backgrounds.

Multiculturalism is also evident on most streets in Irish towns and cities, with **restaurants and shops specialising in produce from a wide range of countries.** Many Polish shops have opened, which are also used by Irish nationals who want to try different foods. This is reflected in the **supermarket chains,** where shelves are now **dedicated to the foods and products of different nationalities.** This helps break down barriers and promotes integration.

In some counties, mass is offered in Polish to cater for large numbers of Polish migrants living in surrounding areas.

Emigration is Ireland's pressure release in times of economic crisis. Since 2008, 250 000 people have emigrated from Ireland, most of whom are young, educated people aged 18–30. This represents 5 per cent of the country's population. If they did not emigrate, there would be higher levels of unemployment and higher social welfare payment costs for job seekers.

Italian foods such as pasta, pizza and lasagne are widely eaten in Irish homes. In fact, these foods have only become commonplace in Ireland over the past 25 years. This is an example of multiculturalism.

Negative

While this level of integration is positive, there are concerns about the racist attitudes of some people towards foreign nationals living in Ireland. While Ireland has not experienced issues such as the race riots seen in other EU countries such as France and the UK, there are issues which need to be addressed. One major issue will be the **integration of foreign nationals into neighbourhoods.** Already, some areas of Dublin, Cork, Limerick and other cities are experiencing **social stratification,** where foreign nationals are living together in certain areas of these cities. When this occurs, foreign nationals are separated from Irish nationals and **integration is impossible.** This can lead to what is referred to as **segregation.** As the EU will continue to expand, it is important that the country is capable of **integrating** many different groups.

EDUCATE YOURSELF

The Effects of EU Enlargement on Ireland

Member of the EU since 1973, free movement of people and goods, movement of workers, expansion – social and economic implications for Ireland

Economic	Poorly developed agriculture, developed modern, high-tech industry, FDI, labour shortage of 420 000, lowest unemployment rates in Europe at 4.5%, fill labour shortages, contributed to government income, provision of services such as health and education, vulnerable to global economic downturns, Schengen Agreement, employment in other EU countries, 2012 unemployment rate = 14.8%, unemployment remains high 8.6%, foreign nationals 15% Irish workforce; negative – remittance money
Social	11.8% of the Irish population, Poland 0.6% of all foreign nationals, primary schools – bilingual, English and parents' native language, Integrate students of different nationalities, native language Leaving Certificate exam, restaurants and shops specialising in various cultural produce, supermarkets dedicated shelves to foods/products of different nationalities, integration of foreign nationals into neighbourhoods, social stratification, integration is impossible, segregation, increasingly varied cultures

ACTIVE LEARNING

1. How has Ireland benefitted from the free movement of labour throughout the EU?
2. Explain the term 'remittance money'.
3. In what way has Ireland changed culturally since joining the EU?
4. Class discussion: List the aspects of non-Irish cultures that you enjoy. Think about food, music, sport and film.

26.6 Changing Boundaries: Shrinking of the Gaeltacht

As you learned in Chapter 20, the **Gaeltacht is a cultural region** that is **defined by its language.** In 1926, the Gaeltachts were officially defined as a cultural region, with a defined boundary. The **boundary of the Gaeltacht has shrunk in size** due to **historic and economic factors:**

- The Great Famine and British colonial rule contributed to the decline of Irish-speaking regions.

- The lack of **employment opportunities** in the Gaeltacht regions has led **to widespread outward migration.**

Until the **Normans invaded in the twelfth century,** Irish was the language of the whole of Ireland. The invasion of the Normans led to the **gradual spread of the English**

Fig. 26.20 The extent of the Gaeltacht (in green) in 1926

Fig. 26.21 Extent of the Gaeltacht (in green) in 1956

Note!

There is more information on Gaeltachts in Chapter 20.

Fig. 26.22 The extent of the Gaeltacht (in green) today

language, especially throughout the east of the country. In the western half of the country, Irish remained the dominant language, spoken by the people of Munster, Connacht, Donegal and the islands.

The Great Famine

By the time of the **Great Famine (1845–49),** Irish was the **main language** spoken by **50 per cent (4 million) of the population,** most of whom lived in along the West coast. The Famine caused Irish-speaking regions to shrink rapidly for two main reasons:

1. Of the **1 million** people who died of **starvation** during this time, almost all were in Irish-speaking regions in the West. A further **1 million people emigrated** during this time, the majority of whom again came from **Irish-speaking regions.**

2. As the **US and Great Britain** were the main destinations, Irish emigrants realised it was **necessary to learn English** to find a job.

Colonial Rule

British colonial rule also contributed to the decline of Irish. In **1831,** the British enforced a rule whereby **English** had to be **taught in primary schools,** while banning Irish.

Emigration

Emigration continued throughout the late nineteenth and early twentieth centuries, as Irish people searched for a better life abroad. By 1926, the Irish-speaking regions of Ireland had shrunk to half of their size just after the Famine.

The Gaeltachts were **established as a cultural region** in **1926** in an attempt to protect the language. Gaeltacht regions were limited to small areas in:

- Galway
- Donegal
- Cork
- Mayo
- Kerry
- Waterford

In the 1930s, the Fianna Fáil government also tried to restore language in parts of the east, establishing Gaeltachts in **Baile Ghib** and **Ráth Cairn** in Co. Meath. Irish speakers from Connemara were given land to relocate to these areas.

Shrinking

The size of the Gaeltacht boundaries was greatly **reduced** after a **review in 1956.** This was largely due to **poverty** as a result of global recession, which caused many Irish speakers to leave these areas. By this time, Ireland's population had reached a record low of just 2.6 million.

Today, many of the **Breac Gaeltacht regions** have **disappeared**, while **Fíor Gaeltacht** regions are **continually shrinking**. Today, only seven Gaeltacht areas remain in Ireland, most of which exist along the west coast of counties Kerry, Galway, Mayo and Donegal. Other smaller Gaeltachts exist in Waterford, Cork and Meath. In total, there are just over **95 000 people living in Gaeltacht regions**, with many of these people speaking English on a daily basis. Added to this, approximately just **7000 people** are **directly employed** in the Gaeltacht.

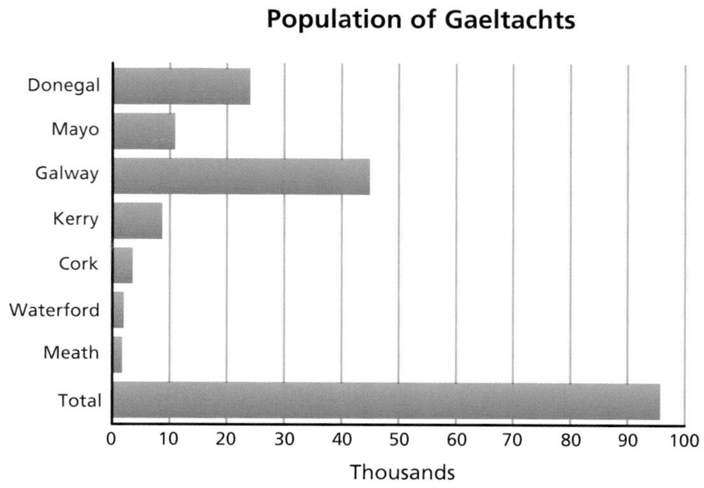

Population of Gaeltachts

Fig. 26.23 The population of the Gaeltachts

Protection

In order to halt the decline of Gaeltachts, a number of measures have been put in place:

- The **Department of Community, Equality and Gaeltacht Affairs** was set up to administrate and develop the region.

- **Údarás na Gaeltachta** promotes the cultural, social, physical and economic development of Gaeltacht regions.

- **Strict planning laws** determine who can build or buy a house in a Gaeltacht region. This is largely aimed at preserving the Irish-speaking communities in Fíor Gaeltacht regions.

- **Raidió na Gaeltachta** and **TG4** broadcast programmes in Irish.

- Irish became an **official language of the EU** in 2005.

EDUCATE YOURSELF

Shrinking of the Gaeltacht	
Gaeltacht a cultural region, defined by language, shrank, historic and economic factors, employment opportunity, widespread outward migration, Normans invaded 12th century, gradual spread of English	
The Great Famine	Great Famine (1845–49), main language, 50% of population, 1 million died + 1 million emigrated from Irish-speaking regions, US and Great Britain, necessary to learn English
Colonial rule	1831 English taught in primary schools
Emigration	Established as a cultural region 1926, Baile Ghib and Ráth Cairn
Shrinking	Reduced – government review in 1956, economic poverty, 7000 people directly employed in Gaeltacht
Protection	Department of Community, Equality and Gaeltacht Affairs, Údarás na Gaeltachta, strict planning laws, Raidió na Gaeltachta and TG4, official language of the EU

ACTIVE LEARNING

1. Describe one historic reason and one economic reason for the shrinking of Irish-speaking regions in Ireland.

2. What is meant by the terms 'Fíor Gaeltacht' and 'Breac Gaeltacht'?

3. What measures have been taken to protect Gaeltacht regions from further decline?

26.7 Urban Growth: Expanding Boundaries in Dublin City

With the global population increasing by roughly 80 million people each year, cities all across the world are getting bigger. Cities in the developing world, such as São Paulo in Brazil or Kolkata in India, are experiencing most of this growth. Modern cities in the developed world originally formed during the Industrial Revolution. These cities are centres for population and economic activity. As **cities develop,** they grow outwards, using up agricultural land, villages and towns located in their hinterland.

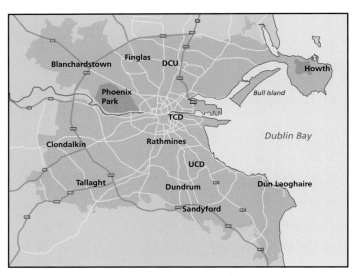

Fig. 26.24 The extent of Dublin today

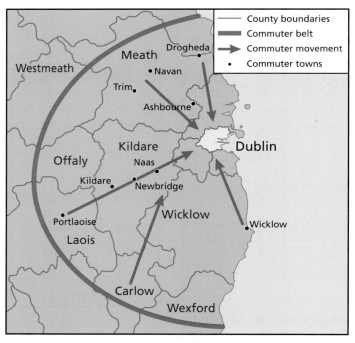

Fig. 26.25 Commuter activity in Dublin

Dublin

Dublin is Ireland's **primate city** and **centre of population and industry in Ireland.** At the beginning of the last century, Dublin was a small city that lay mainly between the **Royal and Grand Canals.** However, **rural-urban migration** brought migrants from the West to the city in search of work. This resulted in the **rapid expansion of the city,** with wealthier families moving to **suburbs** with **low population densities.**

As you have already learned in Chapter 22, in the 1970s **new towns were created** along the western edge of the city in order to accommodate the growing population. These included **Tallaght, Clondalkin** and **Blanchardstown.**

The **Celtic Tiger** saw the built-up area spread further westward into counties surrounding Dublin. As **property prices in Dublin soared,** many **workers** were **unable to afford to buy or rent property** in the city. They moved to 'commuter towns' within driving distance of the city. Surrounding counties' towns became increasingly built-up, leading to the formation of the **Greater Dublin Area.** The construction of **modern motorways** also encouraged **increasing numbers of people to commute** to and from the city each day. Some commute from **as far away as 80 km** each day.

In response to the **uncontrolled urban sprawl,** the Dublin region was spilt into **four separate local councils.** These councils are in charge of providing services to local people and ensuring further growth of the city is **better planned.**

EDUCATE YOURSELF

Urban Growth: Expanding Boundaries in Dublin City

Primate city, centre of population and industry, between Grand and Royal Canals, rural-urban migration, rapid expansion of city, suburbs – low population density, new towns created, Tallaght, Clondalkin, Blanchardstown, Celtic Tiger – property prices rose, workers unable to afford property, commuter towns, Greater Dublin Area, modern motorways, increasing numbers of people who commuted, 80 km commutes, uncontrolled urban sprawl, four separate local councils, better planned in the future

ACTIVE LEARNING

How did rising house prices impact on the growth of Dublin City?

FACT

Yugoslavia was formed in the aftermath of WWI and included several states which had been part of the former Austro-Hungarian Empire.

26.8 Changing Political Boundaries and Impact on Cultural Groups

Political boundaries are not permanent. Throughout history, many political boundaries have changed. For example, you may not have heard of the Kingdom of Naples, which is now the Mezzogiorno region of Italy. More recent examples include:

- The splitting up of Yugoslavia in 1992 into six different countries (Croatia, Slovenia, Bosnia and Herzegovina, Macedonia, Serbia and Montenegro)

- The splitting up of Czechoslovakia into two countries in 1993 (Czech Republic and Slovakia)

One of the best-known examples of the changing of political boundaries is the reunification of Germany in 1990. This reunification had a major economic and cultural impact on the German population.

Reunification of Germany

Fig. 26.26 The division of Germany

In **1945**, after Hitler's Reich had been defeated in World War II, **Germany was divided into four separate zones,** which would be controlled by:

- Britain
- The US
- France
- The Soviet Union (USSR)

Initially, it was intended that the four powers would govern Germany together. However, the development of the **Cold War** between the USSR and the US led to the formation of the **Federal Republic of Germany** (FRG) from the British, French and American zones in 1949. The USSR formed the **German Democratic Republic** (GDR) the same year. The two German states were divided by a heavily guarded border. The political, economical and social divide between east and west was symbolised by the **Berlin Wall,** which the USSR built in 1961.

GEO DICTIONARY

Cold War: political and military tension between two or more countries characterised by threats of warfare but in which no fighting takes place

Federal Republic (West Germany)

West Germany became a **democratic country.** Its **economy developed rapidly** through trade with Britain and the US and **investment in modern industry.** The FRG quickly became the most **prosperous economy in Europe** with its population enjoying a **high standard of living**. The FRG was one of the **founding members of the EEC** (now EU) in 1957. The FRG also experienced population growth during this time, rising from 51 million to 62 million.

GEO DICTIONARY

Collectivisation: an agricultural system where the state owns the land and everything the farm produces. Food is then rationed out by the state

▲ **Fig. 26.27** The Berlin Wall

ACTIVE LEARNING

1. Why did the West experience economic growth and the East experience economic decline after World War II?

2. What were the main obstacles faced by East Germans after reunification?

Democratic Republic (East Germany)

In contrast to the FRG, East Germany experienced **poor economic growth** under the communist system. Instead of modernising, the USSR invested mainly in the **development of heavy industries** that used large amounts of raw materials, energy and labour. **Agriculture** was developed on the basis of **collectivisation,** meaning that farmers were not rewarded for increasing their output. Farmers did not try to improve production or modernise their methods. Overall, economic growth was slow, with people having little money to spend.

The government created a 'police state', in which political opposition was severely dealt with. Spying on the public was normal. Much of the GDR's population wanted to flee the communist regime, with many attempting to escape over or under the Berlin Wall.

Unification

Between **1989 and 1992, communism collapsed** in Eastern Europe and the USSR. On 9 November 1989, the Berlin Wall was opened. On 3 October 1990, Germany officially **reunited** into a single state.

Despite its people having similar cultural traits, language and religion, the unification of Germany was not straightforward. East Germans' expectations were very high in terms of the prosperity reunification would bring. Hundreds of **thousands of migrants from East Germany** moved to the West in search of better-paid jobs. However, their **lack of skills and training** made it **difficult** for them to **gain employment** in modern companies of the West.

Due to the **significant outward migration** of its **younger population,** the former **East Germany** began to experience **population decline.** With an ageing society, it is becoming more and more dependent on government support. Some people in the West resented having to subsidise services in the East.

Huge sums of money were spent on **modernising the East's industrial infrastructure** such as roads, airports and power plants. Despite this, unemployment in the East rose to 3 million as the older companies of the **East were unable to compete with the modern industries** of the West. Today, **none of the top 100 industries** in Germany has headquarters in the East.

In 1990, East Germany's GDP per person was only 30 per cent of the **GDP** of West Germany. As of **2015,** this has grown to **70 per cent. Incomes** in the **East** are currently **84 per cent** of those in similar employment of the **West.** Despite these difficulties, Germany has **regained its economic dominance** within the EU.

😊 😊 EDUCATE YOURSELF

Reunification of Germany	
1945 Germany divided into 4 zones, Cold War, FRG, GDR, heavily guarded border, Berlin Wall	
Federal Republic	Democratic country, economy developed rapidly, investment in modern industry, most prosperous economy in Europe, high standard of living, founding member of EEC
Democratic Republic	Poor economic growth, development of heavy industry, agriculture – collectivisation, consumer income was low
Unification	1989 communism collapsed, reunification of Germany, hundreds of thousands of migrants from East Germany, poor skills and lack of training, difficult to gain employment, significant outward migration of younger population, population decline, unable to compete with modern industries of the West, 0/100 industries headquarters located in East, 2015 70% West's GDP per person, 84% income of West, Germany has regained economic dominance

ORDINARY LEVEL

LONG QUESTIONS

1. Examine the map showing the member states of the European Union and answer each of the following questions.

   (i) Name any two of the founding member states.

   (ii) In what year did Ireland join the European Union and name one other country that joined in the same year?

   (iii) Name the country labelled X, that joined the European Union in 2013.

   (iv) Explain briefly one advantage for member states of the enlargement of the European Union.

   (v) Explain briefly one disadvantage for member states of the enlargement of the European Union.

The European Union

Year of entry:
- 1957
- 1973
- 1981
- 1986
- 1995
- 2004
- 2007
- 2013

| (i) Any 2 @ 3m each |
| (ii) 2 @ 3m each |
| (iii) 6m |
| (iv) 2 SRPs @ 3m each |
| (v) 2 SRPs @ 3m each |

2014 Q5A 30M

HIGHER LEVEL

LONG QUESTIONS

1. Examine how enlargement of the EU impacts on existing member states.

   | Impact identified 2m |
   | Examination 14 SRPs @ 2m each |

   2014 Q4B 30M

2. Examine the interaction between economic, political and/or cultural activities in any region that you have studied.

   | Examination @ 15 SRPs @ 2m each |

   2013 Q6C 30M

A question on Ireland and the EU appears almost every year on either the Higher Level or Ordinary Level Papers. These are normally straightforward questions, with a marking scheme that awards marks for any relevant 15 SRPs.

Try to answer the following question, which is the most commonly asked one in the exam:

HIGHER LEVEL

EXAM QUESTION

Explain the impact of EU enlargement on Ireland.

| **Marking Scheme** |
| 15 SRPs @ 2m each |

2014 Q4 30M

TOPIC MAP

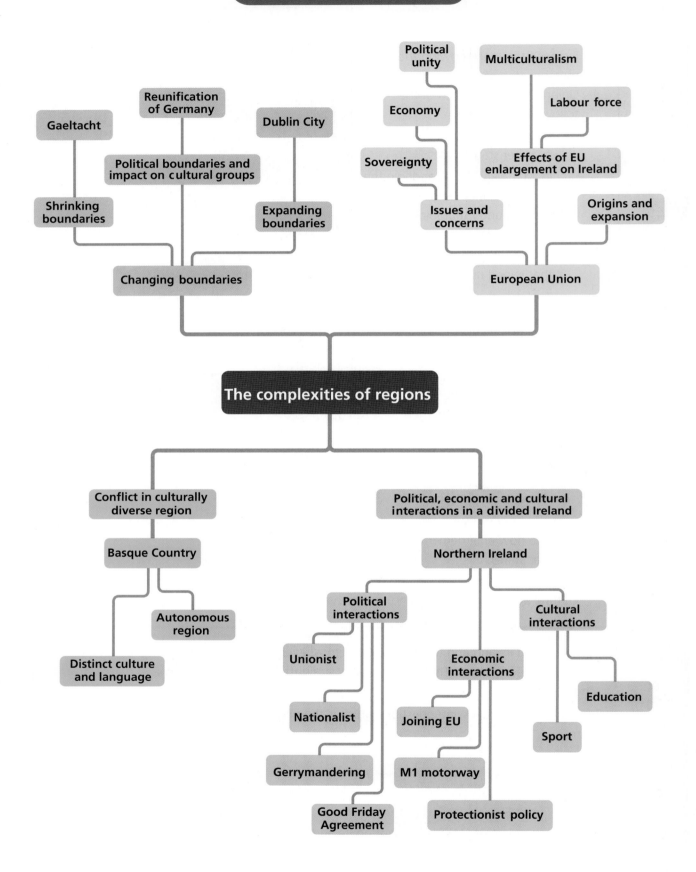

OPTION 7
(HIGHER LEVEL ONLY)

Geoecology

CHAPTER 27

Soils

Higher Level only

In this chapter, you will learn how soil is formed, the characteristics of different soils types and how it is used and misused by humans. Soil is one of two sections in the Geoecology Option and has appeared every year on the exam paper. It is vital that you understand all sections of this chapter.

KEY WORDS

- Composition
- Mineral matter
- Organic matter
- Living organisms
- Air and water
- Horizons
- Humus
- Texture
- Structure
- pH value
- Moisture/water retention

- Topography
- Weathering
- Erosion
- Humification
- Leaching
- Podzolisation
- Laterisation
- Salinisation
- Calcification
- Zonal
- Brown earths

- Latosols
- Sahel
- Desertification
- Overgrazing
- Overcropping
- Deforestation
- Soil conservation
- Stone lines
- Zaï holes
- Contour ploughing

LEARNING OUTCOMES

What you MUST know
- The composition of soil
- The soil profile and the functions of each horizon
- The characteristics of soil
- The factors affecting soil formation
- The natural processes which affect soil formation
- How to classify a soil
- The characteristics of a soil: Irish brown earths
- Human interaction with the Sahel region

- The methods used to conserve soil in the Sahel region

What you SHOULD know
- How to link some of the information about soils in the regions you studied in Regional Geography Unit 3

What is USEFUL to know
- Additional information about drought and desertification from the news and other media

Introduction

Soil is a thin layer of natural material **formed from weathering and erosion.** Soil covers the Earth's land surface, with the exception of the summits of the highest mountains and the most extreme deserts. Most soils are a mixture of crumbling, **broken pieces of rock** and **decomposing organic materials.** Soil is one of our most important natural resources as it contains the **nutrients** necessary **for plants to grow.** Since the majority of plants cannot grow without soil and most animals cannot survive without plants, soil is vital to life on land. **Climate** is the **most important factor** in the **formation of soil.**

27.1 Composition of Soil

All soils are made up of four main components:

- Mineral matter
- Organic matter
- Air
- Water

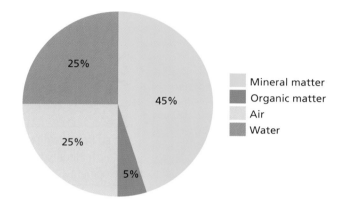

Fig. 27.1 Composition of soil

Mineral Matter

Mineral matter mainly consists of **sand, silt, stones and clay** derived from the **parent rock** that has been broken down by **weathering and erosion.** Mineral matter typically makes up **45 per cent** of the soil's **total volume.** The **size** of the mineral matter **depends on the parent material** the soil is derived from. Some minerals are **soluble,** meaning they dissolve in water. These dissolved minerals can be **absorbed by plant roots,** providing nourishment. For example, limestone produces calcium-rich soil, which in turn produces calcium-rich vegetation.

Fig. 27.2 Earthworms help to mix humus into the soil.

Organic Matter

Organic matter consists of **living creatures,** as well as the **remains of plants and animals.** Although organic matter makes up roughly only **5 per cent** of soil, it plays a **vital role in** determining the **fertility of the soil.** When plant material such as leaves, twigs, needles and bark fall to the ground, it is referred to as **plant litter.** As plant litter and dead creatures decay, they are **broken down further by microorganisms** to form a dark, jelly-like substance called **humus.** Humus is rich in nutrients and **increases a soil's fertility.** It also **binds the soil** together. Humus is found **near the surface,** and gives soil a darker appearance. Larger **living organisms,** such as **earthworms,** help to **mix the humus into the soil** particles, while also **loosening the soil.** This also allows **water and air** to **pass through more easily.**

GEO DICTIONARY

Plant litter: dead plant material, such as leaves, that has fallen to the ground

Parent material: the rock from which a soil is formed

Microorganisms: microscopic living things not visible to the human eye; usually a bacteria, fungus or virus

Air and Water

Air and water are located in the **pores** (spaces) between the mineral particles of the soil. Air usually makes up **25 per cent of the soil's volume** but this percentage can vary. Air **supplies oxygen and nitrogen** to the soil, which are **essential for plant growth.**

Ideally, water should make up **25 per cent of the soil's volume.** The amount of water contained in soil **varies** greatly **according to climatic conditions.** In **desert regions,** the **percentage of water** is very **low,** while soils have a much **higher percentage of water** in areas that experience **heavy rainfall,** e.g. the West of Ireland. Water is **essential for plant growth** as it **dissolves soluble nutrients,** which can then be **absorbed by plant roots.**

Fig. 27.3 Water is essential for plant growth.

EDUCATE YOURSELF

Composition of Soil	
Formed from weathering and erosion, broken pieces of rock and decomposing organic material, nutrients for plants to grow, climate most important factor in soil development	
Mineral matter	Sand, silt, stones, clay from parent rock, weathering and erosion, 45% of total volume, size depends on parent material, soluble minerals
Organic matter	Living creatures, remains of plants and animals, 5% of soil, vital role in fertility of soil, plant litter, broken down by microorganisms, humus, increases soil fertility, binds soil, near surface, living organisms, e.g. earthworms mix humus into soil, loosen soil, water and air pass through more easily
Air and water	Air: pores, 25% of soil's volume, supplies oxygen and nitrogen, essential for plant growth
	Water: ideally 25% of soil's volume, varies according to climatic conditions, low in desert regions, higher in areas with heavy rainfall, essential for plant growth, dissolves soluble nutrients, absorbed by plant roots

27.2 Soil Formation

Soil formation is an incredibly slow process, with four main stages that repeat in a cycle:

1. Bedrock is **broken down by mechanical weathering** to form small soil grains. These make up the 'skeleton' of the soil.
2. **Chemical weathering releases important nutrients** from the rock grains, e.g. phosphorous, potassium and calcium.
3. **Seeds are blown or carried onto the soil** grains and may grow into plants, which **provide humus** for the soil when they die. Early plants that grow on or in the rocks include mosses and lichens.

4. **Microorganisms decompose the remains of plants,** forming humus. This further enriches the soil and helps to bind it together. The humus improves the fertility of the soil, allowing a greater variety of plants to grow.

The cycle continues until the soil reaches its maximum fertility, given the climate it is in.

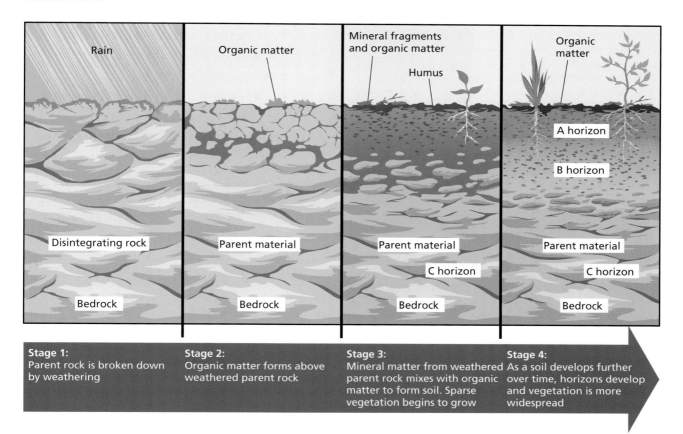

Stage 1:
Parent rock is broken down by weathering

Stage 2:
Organic matter forms above weathered parent rock

Stage 3:
Mineral matter from weathered parent rock mixes with organic matter to form soil. Sparse vegetation begins to grow

Stage 4:
As a soil develops further over time, horizons develop and vegetation is more widespread

Fig. 27.4 The processes of soil formation

27.3 Soil Profile

A vertical cross-section of soil shows that it is made up of several different layers known as horizons. These **horizons** are collectively known as a **soil profile.** From the top down, these horizons are as follows:

- The **O (organic) horizon** is located on the **surface of the soil profile** and consists mainly of **plant litter.** Fresh litter is found at the top, while the litter underneath is at different stages of decomposition.

- The **A horizon** is referred to as **topsoil** as it is the top layer of soil in the profile. It is characterised by **organic matter/humus** mixed with soft particles of soil. The A horizon is typically **darker in colour** due to the presence of humus. The A horizon can be **altered by burrowing animals** and the use of artificial fertilisers. It is the most **biologically active layer,** with most plant roots and soil organisms found here. While the A horizon is the most fertile layer, it can **suffer from leaching** in climates with heavy rainfall.

- The **B horizon** is referred to as **subsoil** and is **lighter in colour** than the A horizon. The B horizon is a **'zone of accumulation'**, meaning that

GEO DICTIONARY

Soil profile: a vertical cross-section of a soil

Horizons: different layers within soil

Biologically active: a biologically active layer in soil is one which has living organisms within it

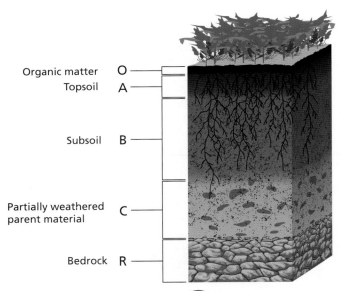

Organic matter O
Topsoil A

Subsoil B

Partially weathered
parent material C

Bedrock R

Fig. 27.5 Soil profile

all minerals washed from the A horizon by rainwater accumulate in the B horizon. Often, these minerals create a **layer of impermeable material** called a **hardpan**. As rainwater cannot pass through the hardpan, the soil's drainage is affected, leading to **waterlogging**.

- The **C horizon** is composed mainly of **partially weathered parent material** that is being slowly broken down.

- The **R horizon** is solid rock and is more commonly known as **bedrock**. **It is undisturbed by the weathering process.**

Fig. 27.6 Visible layers on a soil profile

EDUCATE YOURSELF

Soil Profile	
Vertical cross-section, horizons, soil profile	
O horizon	Surface of soil profile, plant litter
A horizon	Topsoil, organic matter/humus, darker in colour, altered by burrowing animals, biologically active, can suffer from leaching
B horizon	Subsoil, lighter in colour, zone of accumulation, layer of impermeable material, hardpan, waterlogging
C horizon	Partially weathered parent material
R horizon	Bedrock, undisturbed by the weathering process

27.4 Soil Characteristics

Soils can be described by their characteristics, which **combine to form different soil types**. These characteristics **affect the fertility** and productivity of the soil. The main characteristics are:

- Texture
- Structure
- pH value
- Organic matter
- Moisture content and water retention
- Colour

Texture

Texture describes **how a soil feels to touch** and is **determined by** the **amount of sand, silt and clay** particles in it. Texture affects the soil's **ability to absorb water** and **retain nutrients**. It also determines the **ease** with which plants can **penetrate the soil.**

The four main types of texture are:

- Clay
- Sandy
- Silty
- Loam

Clay

Clay consists of **small, tightly packed particles**. Clay soils typically contain more than **50 per cent clay particles** and have a **smooth texture** as they tend to **stick together**. This **stops air and water from moving** through. Clay soils tend to **retain water** during times of heavy rainfall and often become **waterlogged**. The higher water content makes clay soils **sticky. This makes it difficult to cultivate and** for plant roots to penetrate clay soils.

During **dry periods**, clay soils **shrink and crack**, making it almost **impossible for plant roots to penetrate** the surface of the soil. Clay soils are more **suited to grassland** rather than arable farming.

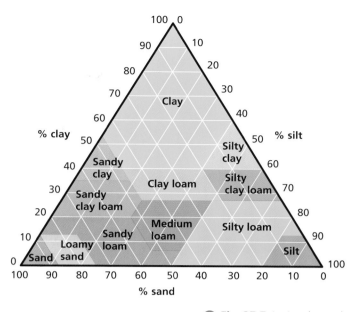

Fig. 27.7 A triangle graph showing the composition of soil

Sandy

Sandy soils have a **loose, coarse texture** due to their **large particles**. Sandy soils **do not stick together,** even when wet. The loose texture **allows air and water to pass** through easily. As the soil **does not retain water**, it may need **irrigation** during **dry weather**. Leaching is a problem as **minerals and nutrients are washed away. As a result,** sandy soils often **need added fertiliser.**

Silty

Silty soils are in **between sand and clay** in terms of **particle size.** They are generally quite **fertile** and support a **wide range of plant growth. Small pores** allow the soil to **retain moisture** and can lead to **waterlogging** during times of **heavy rainfall** as the **particles stick together.** When **dry,** the soil is **powdery** and **easily cultivated.**

Loam

Loam soils are considered the **perfect soil for agriculture.** Loam soils contain roughly **equal parts of clay, sand and silt.** Loam has a **crumb texture** that allows it to **retain moisture,** while also being **free draining** and **easy to cultivate.** As loam retains moisture, it is **not leached,** giving it a naturally **high humus content.**

Structure

Soil **structure** refers to **the way soil grains are held together.** Small **clumps of soil** that have bound together are **called peds.** The **structure of a soil is determined** by the **shape of its peds,** which **vary greatly.** This shape controls the amount of air and water contained in a soil. It also determines the **space available** for **roots, seeds and living organisms.** The most common soil structures are:

Granular

Platy

Blocky

 Fig. 27.8 Varying structures of soil

 Fig. 27.10 Plant litter in soil

- **Crumb** or **granular peds**, which are **small, rounded** clumps of soil, similar **in size** to **breadcrumbs**. This structure is **excellent for drainage** and the **movement of air**. Crumb peds are found in **loam soils**.
- **Blocky peds**, which are **cube-shaped** particles of soil that are **tightly packed** together. Although **naturally good for drainage**, these peds can be **compacted easily**, making it **difficult for roots, air** and **water** to pass through, e.g. sandy soils.
- **Platy peds**, which are **thin, flat particles** that are found in **compacted soils** such as **clay**. Plants have **difficulty growing** in this type of structure as there are **few pore spaces** for air and roots to pass through.

pH Value

A soil's pH indicates **how acidic or alkaline** it is. The pH **controls the type of plants** and **living organisms** that **live in the soil.** Soils with a **pH of 7** are called **neutral.** Soils with a pH **below 7** are **acidic**, while soils with a pH **above 7** are **alkaline.**

Most fertile soils are slightly acidic, with a **pH of 6.5. Severely acidic** soils have been **heavily leached** and **lack minerals.** Soils with a **low pH** have very **few living organisms** or **plants. Lime** is often **added to acidic soils** to **raise their pH.**

Alkaline soils contain **high levels of calcium** and develop in areas with **chalk or limestone bedrock.** They are commonly found in **desert or drought-ridden areas** with permeable bedrock.

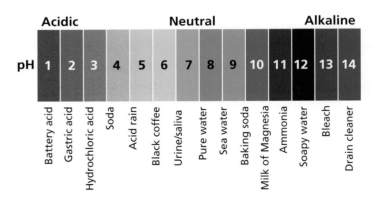

 Fig. 27.9 pH scale

Organic Matter

The organic content of soil is **derived from the remains of plants and animals. Plant litter** and **dead animals** are **broken down** into organic matter by **bacteria** and **fungi.** Living organisms **digest the organic matter** to **form humus.** They help to **mix the humus** into the soil, **aerating** it as they do so. When they die, their **decaying remains** add **more humus** to the soil.

Humus plays an **important role** in making soil fertile. It increases soil fertility in the following ways:

- It is high in plant **nutrients** such as **carbon and nitrogen**.
- It helps to **bind soil particles together** and **reduces the risk of soil erosion**.
- It **helps** the soil to **retain moisture**.
- It **absorbs nutrients**, which **prevents** them from being **leached away**.

The more humus in a soil, the more fertile it will be. **Irish brown earths** are rich in humus as they formed when Ireland was covered by a **thick layer of deciduous forest**. The **more humus** a soil contains, the **darker** it will be.

Moisture Content and Water Retention

The **amount of water** that a **soil can retain** depends on its **structure, humus content and texture**. **Clay** and other platy structured soils are able to **retain large quantities of water**, which can lead to **waterlogging**.

Crumb structures allow **water to pass through** them and are **relatively dry**. Soils with a **high humus content** bind together, allowing the soil to **retain more moisture**.

Coarse, sandy soils retain very little water as they have **large pores** in between their particles. As a result, **sandy soils suffer** from **drought in dry climates**.

Loam soils have a perfect mix of clay and sand, meaning they are **well drained**, while also holding on to **enough moisture** to remain **highly fertile**.

The amount of moisture is influenced by:

- Precipitation: Soils in areas that have **high levels of precipitation** will have a **higher moisture content** than soils in drier areas.
- Underlying rock: Underlying permeable rocks, such as limestone, **hold onto less moisture** than impermeable rocks.
- Hardpan: **Heavily leached soils** may develop a **hardpan**, which is impermeable and leads to waterlogging.

Moisture is **vital to the formation of fertile soil** as it:

- Allows plants to **absorb suitable minerals**
- Allows horizons to develop
- Binds the soil together to prevent erosion

Colour

Colour is the **most identifiable feature** of a soil. A soil's colour can also **indicate its fertility**. Dark brown or black soils are typically **very fertile** as they have a **high humus content**. Due to their **colour, darker soils** tend to be warmer as they **retain heat**, which **promotes seed germination**.

Grey soils tend to be **infertile** as they have been **heavily leached**. Grey soils are said to have a **'washed out' appearance** due to the **lack of humus** and other nutrients. Grey soils, such as **gleys**, have **poor drainage** and **suffer from waterlogging**.

ACTIVE LEARNING

1. What function do microorganisms have in creating organic matter?
2. How do earthworms improve soil fertility?
3. Explain three ways in which humus makes soil more fertile.

FACT

There are more microorganisms in a handful of most soils than there are humans on the planet.

ACTIVE LEARNING

1. Name three soil structures and how they affect moisture content.
2. How do precipitation, underlying bedrock and hardpan affect moisture content?
3. Name three vital functions of moisture in soil.

GEO DICTIONARY

Germination: beginning to grow (shoots)

Gley: sticky, waterlogged soil that is lacking in nutrients. It is typically grey or blue in colour

Fig. 27.11 Red soils have a high iron oxide content.

Red soils are found in **warm and moist tropical** or **equatorial climates**. The red colour forms due to a **high iron oxide content**. The combination of **warm temperatures** and **high levels of rainfall** means the soil undergoes **high levels of chemical weathering**. Red soils are typically **low in nutrients** and **organic matter**.

EDUCATE YOURSELF

Soil Characteristics	
Texture	Clay: small, tightly packed particles, 50% clay particles, smooth texture, stick together, stop air and water from moving, retain water, waterlogged, sticky and difficult to cultivate, difficult for plant roots to penetrate
	Sand: loose, coarse texture, large particles, do not stick together, allows air and water to pass, does not retain water, drains away, irrigation, dry weather, leaching is a problem – minerals and nutrients are washed away, need fertiliser regularly
	Silt: between sand and clay particle size, fertile – wide range of plant growth, small pores, retain moisture, heavy rainfall – waterlogged, particles stick together; dry – powdery and easily cultivated
	Loam: perfect soil for agriculture, equal parts of clay, sand and silt, crumby texture, retain moisture, free draining, easy to cultivate, not leached, high humus content
Structure	The way soil grains are held together, clumps of soil, called peds, structure, determined by shape of peds, vary greatly, amount of air and water, space available for roots, seeds and living organisms
	Crumb: granular peds, small, rounded, breadcrumb size, excellent drainage, movement of air, loam soils
	Blocky: cube-shaped, tightly packed, naturally good drainage, compacted easily, difficult for roots, air and water, sandy soils
	Platy: thin, flat particles, compacted soils, clay, plants difficulty growing, few pore spaces, clay soils
pH value	How acidic or alkaline a soil is, controls plants and living organisms that live in soil, pH 7 neutral, below 7 acidic, above 7 alkaline, most fertile soils slightly acidic pH 6.5; severely acidic, heavily leached and lack minerals, few living organisms and plants, lime added to acidic soils to raise pH; alkaline, high levels of calcium, chalk or limestone bedrock, desert or drought-stricken areas, permeable bedrock
Organic matter	From the remains of plants and animals, plant litter and dead animals broken down by bacteria and fungi, living organisms – earthworms and insects digest the organic matter, form humus, mix the humus, aerating, decaying remains more humus, important role – makes soil fertile, increases soil fertility, nutrients carbon and nitrogen, bind soil particles together, reduces the risk of soil erosion, helps retain moisture, absorbs nutrients, preventing, leached away, Irish brown earths, thick layer of deciduous forest, more humus – darker soil
Moisture content and water retention	Amount of water soil can retain – structure, humus content and texture; clay retains large quantities of water, waterlogging; crumb structures, allows water to pass through, relatively dry, high humus content, retain more moisture, coarse and sandy soils, retain very little water, large pores, sandy soils suffer, drought in dry climates; loam soils, well drained, enough moisture – highly fertile, influenced by precipitation, underlying rock and hardpan; moisture vital to formation of fertile soil, absorb suitable minerals, allows horizons to develop, binds the soil together to prevent erosion
Colour	Most identifiable feature, indicate its fertility, dark brown or black soils, very fertile, high humus content, colour, darker soils retain heat, promotes seed germination; grey soils infertile, heavy leaching, 'washed out' appearance, lack of humus, gleys, poor drainage, suffer from waterlogging; red soils warm and moist tropical or equatorial climates, high iron oxide content, warm temperatures and high levels of rainfall, high levels of chemical weathering, low in nutrients and organic matter

27.5 Factors Affecting Soil Formation

The type of soil that develops in a region is dependent on a number of factors. The most important factors are:

- Climate
- Parent material
- Topography
- Organisms
- Time

Climate

Climate is the **most important factor** that affects the formation of soil. Temperature and precipitation **determine the rate of weathering,** the rate of **biological activity occurring** in soil and what other **soil-forming processes** are in operation.

- In **hot climates, rapid chemical weathering** occurs, as does the **decomposition of organic matter.** This leads to the formation of **deep fertile soils.**

- In regions with **cold climates,** there is very little **biological activity,** which reduces or **halts the formation of humus.** Weathering is **limited to freeze-thaw action** producing thin, **infertile soils.**

- In **wet climates, heavy rainfall leaches nutrients** from the **A to the B horizon.** Many **soils in wet climates** develop a **hardpan,** making them prone to **waterlogging.**

- In regions with **dry climates, drought** leads to the upward movement of water due to **evaporation.** As the **water moves upwards,** it draws **salt and calcium** to the surface. This is referred to as **salinisation and calcification.** Salt can make the soil toxic for plants. When calcium builds up and hardens, it is impermeable and difficult for plants to grow in.

Parent Material

Parent material refers to the **original bedrock** from which the **mineral matter** in soil **develops** as a result of **weathering** or deposition **of sediments. Different parent rocks** develop **different soil characteristics:**

- **Igneous rocks** tend to develop **acidic soils** (low pH).

- **Sedimentary rocks** can develop a **variety of soils,** e.g. **sandstone** produces **slightly acidic,** well-drained **sandy soils. Limestone** produces **calcium-rich** dark-coloured soils, e.g. **terra rossa. Shale** tends to produce **dark-grey, wet, clay soils,** with **poor drainage.**

Not **all parent material is rock.** Many Irish soils developed from **glacial deposits** of boulder clay, sand and gravels. These soils are **deep, fertile and well drained.**

Topography

Soil formation is **affected by gradient, altitude and aspect, which all influence the depth** and **drainage** of a soil. **Flat upland areas** tend to be **cold and wet,** which leads to **waterlogging** and the formation

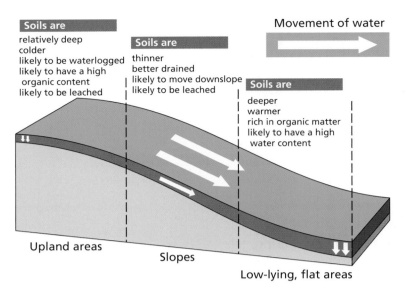

Soils are
relatively deep
colder
likely to be waterlogged
likely to have a high
organic content
likely to be leached

Soils are
thinner
better drained
likely to move downslope
likely to be leached

Movement of water

Soils are
deeper
warmer
rich in organic matter
likely to have a high
water content

Upland areas

Slopes

Low-lying, flat areas

⬆ **Fig. 27.12** The effects of topography on soil formation

of **gley soils**. As **temperatures are low**, **biological activity** of **plants and animals** is slowed, leading to an **accumulation of organic material**, e.g. **peat**.

On **sloping land**, **soil erosion** is usually **faster than the formation of soil underneath**. As a result, **soils are much thinner**. Slopes also encourage **faster run-off**, so these soils are **well drained**.

Soils tend to **accumulate on low-lying, flat areas**. As the weather is **warmer than in upland areas**, there is a higher level of **biological activity** which **converts organic matter** into **humus**.

Organisms

Living organisms can **determine the fertility of soil** as they have a **direct impact on** the **decomposition** of organic material. Typical living organisms found in soil are:

- Plant roots
- Burrowing animals
- Insects and earthworms
- Fungi and micbrobes/bacteria

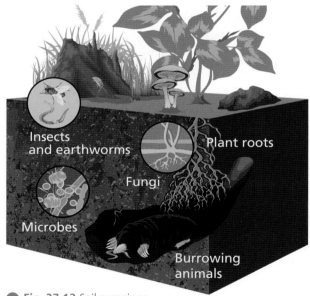

⬆ **Fig. 27.13** Soil organisms

Plant roots are capable of **breaking up and loosening compacted soil** when they penetrate through the surface. Roots also help to **prevent soil erosion** by binding the soil together. The plants cover the soil, **protecting it from rainfall** and other weather conditions. Decaying leaves and **roots supply humus** to the soil.

Larger animals, such as rabbits, **burrow into the soil,** helping it to **aerate and mix** the soil in the **A and B horizons**. Earthworms and insects are **far more numerous** and play an **important role** in aerating and mixing the soil. When they die, their **bodies decompose** and **add nutrients** to the soil. **Fungi and bacteria** help to break down **organic matter into humus,** a process called **humification**.

Time

Soil takes a **long time to form**. The **age of the soil affects** its **properties**. The **older a soil** is, the **longer the soil-forming processes** have been **in operation**. The soil profile of a **young soil** is **not well developed**, while **older soils** have **well-developed profiles**. Older soils tend to be strongly weathered. Most of **Ireland's soils** are **less than 10 000 years old**, as the glaciers from the last ice age removed previous soil cover. This means they are **postglacial**. This is young in geological terms.

EDUCATE YOURSELF

Factors Affecting Soil Formation	
Climate	Most important factor, determines rate of weathering, biological activity occurring, soil-forming processes in operation, hot climates – rapid chemical weathering and decomposition of organic matter, deep fertile soils, cold climates – little biological activity, halts formation of humus, limited to freeze-thaw action, infertile soils, wet climates, heavy rainfall – leaching of nutrients A to the B horizon, soils in wet climates, hardpan, prone to waterlogging, dry climates, drought, increased evaporation, water moves upwards, salt and calcium, salinisation and calcification
Parent material	Original bedrock – mineral matter, weathering of sediments, different parent rocks – different characteristics, igneous rocks – acidic soils, sedimentary rocks – variety of soils, sandstone – slightly acidic, sandy soils, limestone – calcium-rich, terra rossa, shale – dark-grey, wet, clay soils, poorly drained, not all parent material is rock, glacial deposits, deep, fertile and well drained
Topography	Affected by gradient, altitude and aspect, influence the depth and drainage, flat upland areas – cold and wet, waterlogging and gley soils, temperatures low, biological activity plants and animals slow, accumulation of organic material, e.g. peat, sloping land, soil erosion faster than formation of soil underneath, soils much thinner, faster run-off – well drained, accumulate on flat, low-lying areas, warmer than in upland areas, higher level of biological activity, converts organic matter into humus
Organisms	Determine the fertility of soil, direct impact on decomposition, plant roots, animals, insects, fungi and bacteria, plant roots breaking up and loosening compacted soil, prevent soil erosion, protect soil from rainfall, decaying roots supply humus, larger animals, burrow into the soil, aerate and mix A and B horizons, earthworms and insects far more numerous, more important role, bodies decompose and add nutrients, fungi and bacteria, organic matter into humus – humification
Time	Long time to form, age of the soil affects properties, older a soil longer soil-forming processes in operation, young soil not well developed, older soils well-developed profiles, strongly weathered, Ireland's soils less than 10 000 years old, postglacial

27.6 Natural Soil-forming Processes

In order to explain differences in soil, we must examine the variety of physical processes that occur within soil as well as the environmental factors that control these processes. There are eight main processes:

- Weathering
- Erosion
- Humification
- Leaching
- Podzolisation
- Laterisation
- Calcification
- Salinisation

Weathering

The small **particles** that make up **soils** were **originally solid rock,** until they was **broken down by weathering and erosion.** Parent materials make up roughly **45 per cent of most soil types.** Physical/mechanical and chemical weathering processes are active in breaking parent rock into mineral matter.

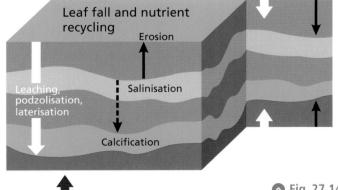

▲ Fig. 27.14 Natural soil-forming processes

Mechanical weathering refers to **freeze-thaw action** and **exfoliation**. These processes eventually break down the rock into **scree**. This scree is further **weathered** into small **particles of mineral matter**.

Exfoliation occurs in areas where there is a **large diurnal temperature range**, e.g. **deserts**.

Fig. 27.15 Scree eventually forms soil particles.

Chemical weathering causes **rock** to **decompose** and changes the **chemical properties** of the minerals. Carbonation causes **limestone and chalk** to dissolve as **carbonic acid in rainwater** reacts with the rocks' **calcium carbonate. Hydrolysis** is also caused by rainwater, which **breaks down granite**. The process turns **feldspar in granite** into **kaolin clay. Oxidation** occurs when **iron in rock** is exposed to oxygen in the atmosphere. Iron in the rock is oxidised (rusted), causing it to **crumble. Soils** formed from oxidation have a **reddish-brown colour**.

Erosion

Erosion refers to the **breaking down and transportation of rock** by water, ice and wind. Rivers deposit **fertile alluvial soils** along their **floodplains. Alluvial soils** consist of particles of **silt and clay** with some **larger particles of sand**. These soils are **extremely fertile** for **agriculture**.

Winds can **erode rock** that is **exposed** to the surface and **carry the material over larger distances** before depositing it. Winds have deposited **fertile limon soil** along the North European Plain, e.g. the **Paris Basin**.

Boulder clay soil formed from glacial deposition. Boulder clay soils are **poorly drained** with a high moisture content. This makes them **sticky and difficult to cultivate**. They are more suited to **pastoral farming**.

Humification

Humification is the **breakdown and decomposition of organic matter into humus**. Humification is important as it **increases soil fertility**.

Humification occurs at a much **faster rate** in areas that **experience high temperatures** and **frequent rainfall**, e.g. **tropical regions**. The **colder a region** is, the slower the **humification process will be**. Where soil is **permanently frozen**, humification does not occur.

Fig. 27.16 Podzolisation occurs due to severe leaching.

Leaching

Leaching is the **washing away and removal of nutrients** from soil by water. **Small amounts** of leaching **increase soil fertility** as water dissolves nutrients close to the surface and carries them downwards to plant roots. Severe leaching **washes the minerals down from the A horizon, well beyond the reach of plant roots, making** the **soil infertile**.

Podzolisation

Podzolisation is an **extreme form of leaching** that occurs as a result of **acidic water percolating through the soil.** It is most common in areas covered in **coniferous forest** or **peat soils** and where there are **high levels of precipitation.** As **water passes through the plant litter** of coniferous forests or other organic matter, it **becomes more acidic.** The **acidic water** is capable of **dissolving and washing away** almost all the **minerals and nutrients** in the soil. This leaves the **A horizon 'bleached' and infertile.** **Quartz** is the only mineral that can **resist the acidic water,** giving the quartz a **grey colour.** The minerals washed from the A horizon accumulate in the B horizon before forming a **hardpan.** Hardpans **make the soil prone to waterlogging.**

Laterisation

Laterisation is another **extreme form of leaching** that is common in **tropical and equatorial regions.** High amounts of **plant litter are rapidly broken** down by **chemical weathering** due to high temperatures and heavy rainfall. The **humus** produced is **dissolved by the rainwater** and **leached deep into the soil.** This leaching **prevents the soil** from **developing horizons** and causes it to become **infertile.** Only **iron oxide** and **aluminium oxide resist** the leaching process. When the iron is **exposed to the atmosphere,** it is oxidized giving the soil its **rusty appearance.** These tropical red soils are known as **latosols.**

Calcification

Calcification is the **accumulation of calcium carbonate** near the soil's surface. It occurs in areas that experience **low levels of rainfall,** where **evaporation rates are higher** than **precipitation rates.** As **evaporation rates are higher,** water is **drawn up through the soil** through **capillary action.**

The upwards-moving water carries calcium carbonate towards the surface. As the water evaporates, the calcium carbonate **accumulates in the A horizon,** creating fertile, calcium-rich soil that is **ideal for grassland.**

Salinisation

Salinisation is the accumulation of **soluble salts** close to the soil's surface. It occurs in **hot desert or semi-desert regions** where **precipitation is low** and **evaporation rates are high.** Capillary action draws **groundwater up through the soil.** Groundwater naturally **contains salt,** which is **left behind** after the **water** has been **evaporated.** Salt accumulates in the soil, which eventually **solidifies to form a hard, toxic crust. Irrigation** can cause salinisation as it **raises the level of groundwater,** bringing the **salt closer to the surface.** Soils with high **salt levels poison plants.**

GEO DICTIONARY

Capillary action: the upwards movement of water due to evaporation

ACTIVE LEARNING

1. Explain fully how freeze-thaw action and carbonation occur.
2. Why does humification occur at a faster rate in equatorial regions?
3. What is the difference between calcification and salinisation?
4. Explain fully how podzolisation occurs.

Natural Soil-forming Processes	
Weathering	Particles of soils originally solid rock, broken down by weathering and erosion, 45% of most soil types, physical/mechanical and chemical weathering processes, freeze-thaw action and exfoliation, rocks decompose, chemical properties, limestone and chalk, carbonic acid in rainwater, calcium carbonate, hydrolysis – breaks down feldspar in granite to kaolin clay, oxidation – iron in rock rusted, crumbles, soils, reddish-brown colour
Erosion	Breaking down and transportation of rock, fertile alluvial soils – floodplains, silt and clay, larger particles of sand, extremely fertile, intense agricultural cultivation, winds, eroding rock exposed, carry the material over larger distances, Paris Basin, boulder clay soil, transported a mixture of stones, poorly drained, sticky and difficult to cultivate, pastoral farming
Humification	Breakdown and decomposition of organic matter into humus, increases soil fertility, colder regions slower humification process, permanently frozen
Leaching	Washing away and removal of nutrients, small amounts, increases soil fertility, washes the minerals down from the A horizon, beyond the reach of plant roots, soil becomes infertile
Podzolisation	Extreme form of leaching, acidic water percolating through the soil, coniferous forest and peat soils, high levels of precipitation, water passes through plant litter, becomes more acidic, acidic water – dissolving and washing away, minerals and nutrients, A horizon 'bleached' and infertile, quartz resists acidic water – grey colour, hardpan – impermeable and prone to waterlogging
Laterisation	Extreme form of leaching in tropical and equatorial regions, plant litter rapidly broken, chemical weathering, humus dissolved by the rainwater, leached deep into the soil, prevents soil from developing horizons, infertile, iron oxide and aluminium oxide resist leaching, exposed to the atmosphere, rusty appearance, latosols
Calcification	Accumulation of calcium carbonate, low levels of rainfall, evaporation rates are higher than precipitation rates, water drawn up through the soil – capillary action, accumulates in the A horizon, ideal for grassland
Salinisation	Soluble salts, hot desert or semi-desert regions, precipitation low and evaporation rates high, capillary action draws groundwater up through the soil, groundwater contains salt, left behind after water evaporated, salt accumulates and solidifies to form a hard, toxic crust, irrigation raises the level of groundwater, salt closer to surface, high salt levels poison the plants

27.7 Soil Classification

Climate has a major influence on the **formation of soil.** Different soils are created in different climate zones across the world. All these soils can be classified into **three general groups:**

1. Zonal soils   **2.** Intrazonal soils   **3.** Azonal soils

1. Zonal Soils

Soils are **classified according to the climate types** that help to form them. They are referred to as **zonal soils** as they occupy **large climatic zones.** For example, **brown soils** are **zonal soils** for areas that experience a **cool maritime oceanic climate,** such as **Ireland. Latosols** are the zonal soils of **equatorial regions,** such as **Brazil.**

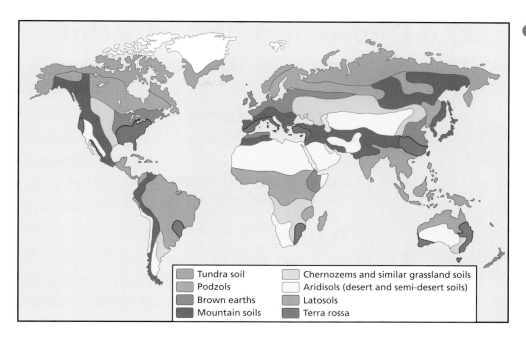

◀ **Fig. 27.17** Global soil map

Legend:
- Tundra soil
- Podzols
- Brown earths
- Mountain soils
- Chernozems and similar grassland soils
- Aridisols (desert and semi-desert soils)
- Latosols
- Terra rossa

2. Intrazonal Soils

Intrazonal soils develop in certain areas due to **local factors** such as **relief, drainage** and **parent material**. These factors are influential enough to change the characteristics of the zonal soil. Examples include **gley soils**, which form in **high clay soils** that are **prone to waterlogging**.

3. Azonal Soils

Azonal soils are younger and have **not developed a full soil profile**. **Regosols** are an example of an **azonal soil** which develops from **deposited materials** from wind, rivers or ice. **Lithosols** consist of partially **weathered material** that typically forms on **steep slopes**.

EDUCATE YOURSELF

Soil Classification	
Climate – formation of soil, three general groups: zonal soils, intrazonal soils and azonal soils	
Zonal soils	Classified according to the climate types, zonal soils – occupy large climatic zones, brown soils, cool maritime oceanic climate, e.g. Ireland, latosols, equatorial regions e.g. Brazil
Intrazonal soils	Intrazonal soils, local factors – relief, drainage and parent material, change the characteristics of the zonal soil, gley soils, high clay soils – prone to waterlogging
Azonal soils	Not developed a full soil profile, regosols, deposited materials, lithosols, weathered material, steep slopes

ACTIVE LEARNING

1. Explain, giving an example, what is meant by the term 'zonal soils'.
2. What is the main difference between zonal and intrazonal soils?

27.8 Characteristics of a Soil: Irish Brown Earths

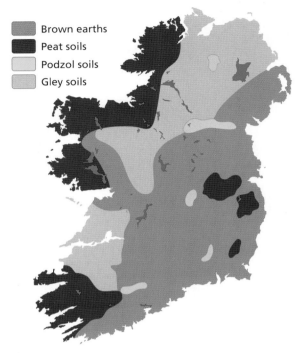

Brown earths
Peat soils
Podzol soils
Gley soils

Fig. 27.18 Soil map of Ireland

Parent Material

Mineral matter accounts for roughly **45 per cent of brown earth's** volume. Most of the soil's **parent material is derived from glacial boulder clay** deposited at the end of the **last ice age**.

Texture

Brown soils tend to be **loamy, meaning they have a crumb structure**, with **loosely packed particles**. This means that **air and water** can **move easily through the soil**, leading to a **free-draining soil**. Brown earths formed underneath **thick deciduous forest**, which provided an **abundance of plant litter**. The high **humus content** gives **brown earth** its **dark colour** and **crumby texture**.

The **high level of rainfall** in Ireland means that **brown earths** are **slightly leached**. Along the **midlands and the east of Ireland**, where **brown earths are common**, rainfall averages **800–1000 mm per annum**, which **limits levels of leaching**. This leaching has given most Irish brown earths a **pH of between 5 and 7**. This pH range allows a **wide variety of plant life** and bacterial activity to occur. A combination of the **slight leaching of nutrients** and the **burrowing activity of living organisms** means that the soil's horizons are **not easily distinguishable**. This gives a **uniform profile**. Brown earths are **naturally fertile** and **easily worked**, making them ideal for either **arable or pastoral farming**.

Local conditions also impact on the characteristics of brown earth soils, creating varied **intrazonal soils**.

- **Acidic brown earths** have developed on land that is over **500 m above sea level**, with **sandstone or granite bedrock**. These rocks are **naturally low in calcium**, which combined with **increased leaching** due to **higher rainfall, lowers their pH**. Acidic brown earths need the addition of lime to make them **fertile for agriculture**.

- **Podzol brown earths** formed in areas where **boulder clay was deposited** over **limestone bedrock**. Due to the underlying bedrock, **water drains away freely**, causing the soil to be **slightly leached and paler in colour**. Podzol brown earths cover **22 per cent of Ireland**.

- **Shallow brown earths** are just **50 cm in depth** and are typically found in **limestone regions** such as the **Burren**. Although they are **extremely fertile**, their **shallow depth limits agriculture**.

Soil Profile of a Brown Earth Soil

Ireland's **natural vegetation** was originally **deciduous forest**, which provided an annual layer of **plant litter**.

1. The **O horizon** is the **upper layers** and consist of **plant litter, leaves and twigs**. Underneath the fresh plant litter, **partially decomposed humus, insects** and **microorganisms** such as **bacteria and fungi** can be found.

2. The **A horizon** is commonly known as the **topsoil**. Most **biological activity** takes place in this horizon, because of the **plant roots, bacteria and animals**. The A horizon consists of **mainly mineral matter** and **humus**, giving the soil a **dark colour**.

3. The **B horizon** is commonly referred to as **subsoil**. The **burrowing activity** of **living organisms**, combined with **slight leaching**, make the A and B horizons **uniform in colour**.

4. The **C horizon** lies just above the **bedrock**, and consists of **partially weathered material**. The bedrock underneath the **C horizon** is **unaltered by weathering processes**.

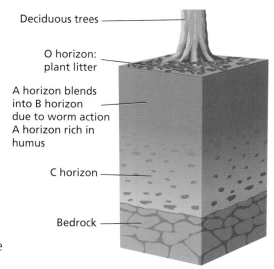

Deciduous trees

O horizon: plant litter

A horizon blends into B horizon due to worm action A horizon rich in humus

C horizon

Bedrock

⬆ **Fig. 27.19** Brown earth soil profile

EDUCATE YOURSELF

Characteristics of a Soil: Irish Brown Earths	
Parent material	Mineral matter 45% of brown soils, parent material is derived from glacial boulder clay, last ice age
Texture	Loamy, crumb structure, loosely packed particles, air and water, move through the soil easily, free-draining, thick deciduous forest, abundance of plant litter, dark colour, crumby texture; high level of rainfall, slightly leached, midlands and east of Ireland, rainfall 800–1000 mm per annum, limited levels of leaching, pH between 5 and 7, wide variety of plant life, slight leaching of nutrients, burrowing activity, living organisms, uniform profile, deciduous woodland, naturally fertile, easily worked, arable or pastoral farming; local conditions, intrazonal soils, acidic brown earths, 500 m above sea level, sandstone or granite bedrock, naturally low in calcium, increased leaching, higher rainfall, lowers pH, addition of lime, fertile for agriculture, podzol brown earths, boulder clay was deposited, limestone bedrock, water drains away freely, slightly leached, paler in colour, podzol 22% of Ireland, shallow brown earths, 50 cm in depth, limestone regions, e.g. Burren, extremely fertile, shallow depth hinders agriculture
Soil profile of a brown earth soil	Natural vegetation, deciduous forest, plant litter, O horizon upper layers, plant litter, leaves and twigs, partially decomposed humus, insects and microorganisms – bacteria and fungi; A horizon topsoil, biological activity, plant roots, bacteria and animals, mainly mineral matter and humus, dark colour; B horizon subsoil, burrowing activity, living organisms, slight leaching, uniform in colour, C horizon above bedrock, partially weathered material, unaltered by weathering

ACTIVE LEARNING

1. List four characteristics of a brown earth soil.
2. What is meant by the term 'soil profile'?
3. How has the process of humification aided brown earth's fertility?
4. Name and explain three intrazonal soils which can form from brown earths.
5. Describe, with the aid of a diagram, the typical soil profile of a brown earth.

27.9 Human Interference with Soil

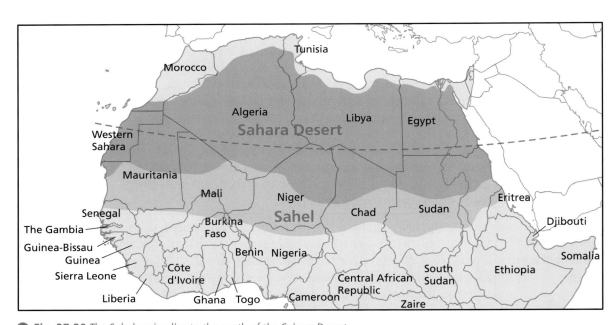
Soil erosion is one of the most **serious environmental problems** facing humans. Some **99.7 per cent of our food** is produced on **land**, with just **0.03 per cent produced in oceans** or other aquatic ecosystems. Each year, over **10 million hectares of land loses its fertility**, which **reduces the amount of land available** for food production. The World Health Organisation estimates that over **3.7 billion people** are **malnourished worldwide** as a result of **soil degradation**. According to current estimates, the amount of **soil being lost** is between **10 to 40 times faster than the rate of soil creation**. This level of **soil loss is unsustainable** and is now a **major concern** in many parts of the world. It is typically as a result of **environmental problems** and **human interference**. These problems are particularly obvious in the **Sahel region**.

The Sahel

The Sahel is a belt of **semi-arid land** of roughly **3 million km²** that runs for 4000 km west to east across Africa. The Sahel acts as a **transitional boundary** between the Sahara Desert to the north and the grasslands and tropical areas of Central Africa to the south.

Originally a grassland savanna biome, the Sahel is being **converted** into a **hot desert biome** which supports a **nomadic, pastoral-based society.**

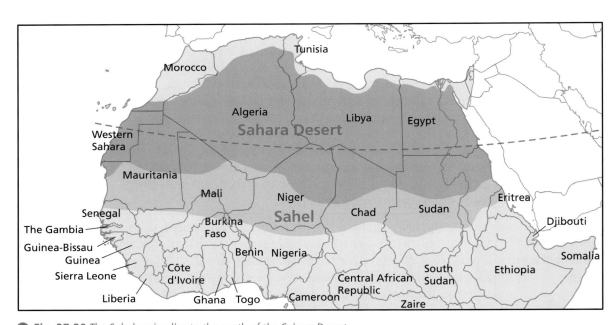

● **Fig. 27.20** The Sahel region lies to the south of the Sahara Desert

Climate

Climate change has **greatly impacted rainfall** in the last 20 years, reducing it by **33 per cent worldwide**. The climate of the **Sahel ranges** between **hot and temperate conditions**, with **rainfall** falling **for four to five months**, typically between May and October.

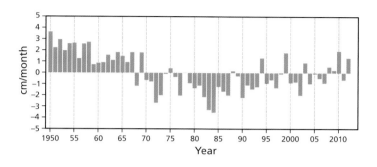

◀ **Fig. 27.21** Rainfall patterns in the Sahel, 1950–2013 (0 is the average rainfall)

Population

Currently, the Sahel's **population** is growing by up to **3 per cent per year**. As a result of this rapid population growth, the Sahel is now **overpopulated**, with a lack of basic resources such as food and fuel.

◀ **Fig. 27.22** Population pyramid for two countries in the Sahel region

Population by age group and gender
(percentage of total population)

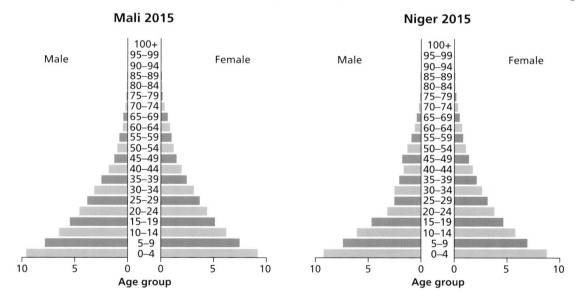

Desertification

Desertification refers to the **uncontrolled spread of desert** into new lands, turning it into **unproductive wasteland**. Currently, **deserts** are **advancing** into the Sahel region at a rate of **5–10 km per year**.

Desertification is **not just limited to the spread of existing desert**, but also refers to areas where the **fertility of soil and vegetation cover** have been **damaged. This leaves soil unprotected** and **prone to soil erosion**.

GEO DICTIONARY

Sedentary farming: farming the same plots of land all of the time, not moving around

Fig. 27.23 Overgrazing in the Sahel

 GEO DICTIONARY

Boreholes: holes dug in the ground to reach the water table

Fig. 27.24 Sedentary farming in the Sahel

Desertification occurs due to a combination of **climate change and human activities.** Typical human activities include:

- Overgrazing
- Overcropping
- Deforestation

Overgrazing

Between the **1930s and 1970s,** the Sahel region received **more rainfall than usual,** which **attracted more people** to live there. The **number of cattle** in the region **doubled,** which put an increased **strain on the soil.** Ownership of **cattle** is seen as a **sign of wealth** in the Sahel. The **number of farmers** also **increased.** This has led to **increased competition for land** among nomadic farmers. With increased herd size, the **land was grazed continually,** until the soil's **nutrients** were **depleted.**

With **grass scarce,** many farmers moved their cattle onto **marginal land,** which led to the **destruction of young trees and shrubs. Farming practices** in the Sahel have also changed. **Sedentary farming** has led to the **fencing in of animals,** meaning land is constantly grazed. **Soils are not left fallow,** leading to the **depletion of nutrients.** Large numbers of **cattle trampling** the soil damages its **structure.** Cattle **hooves compact** the soil, making it **difficult for plant roots** to penetrate it.

With **cattle fenced in,** farmers dug **boreholes** and sank **wells** to provide water for their animals. The groundwater became **rapidly depleted** as it was **not being replenished** as fast as it was being used. The **water table dropped** and many **wells dried up,** leading to a much drier soil. **Rainfall is unable to soak** through the soil due to **compaction** from animals. As a result, **water is evaporated** at a greater rate than precipitation occurs, leading to **capillary action.** This **promotes soil salinisation,** making soil **toxic** for plants.

With **vegetation removed,** soil erosion occurs due to wind and rain. The dry soil is very light, and an **absence of humus** to bind it together means it is easily carried by wind. When rainfall occurs in the Sahel it is in **torrential downpours,** which washes away the topsoil, leaving only the harder, rocky subsoil.

Overcropping

Due to the **rapid increase in population** since the 1960s, the **demand for food** has **also risen while** the area of **land** in the Sahel used for **growing crops has trebled.** The high demand for food means farmers are **unable to leave the land fallow** for a year meaning the land does not recover its lost nutrients, as farmers **do not use artificial fertilisers.**

As there is a **shortage of wood** in the Sahel, **dried manure is used as fuel instead of as a fertiliser.** Artificial fertilisers are **too expensive** for most farmers. Farmers who **borrowed money to pay for fertilisers** were forced to use all the money they made from their **crops** to **pay off their debts.**

As the soil became less fertile, farmers began to **clear marginal land** for agriculture. Marginal land is **naturally less fertile,** and the **removal of its vegetation increases soil erosion.** The soil quickly becomes **infertile.**

Much of the problem began in the 1960s, when governments in the Sahel region **received cheap loans** which they are now **unable to repay.** This has led to many of the countries in the Sahel being classified as **HIPC** (highly indebted poor countries). In order to **qualify for debt relief,** Western governments encourage farmers to **grow cash crops** in large plantations, e.g. **cotton, millet** and **groundnuts.** These crops are then **sold on the international market** to pay off **national debt.** The growth of these cash crops has led to **monoculture,** meaning the **same crop is grown** on soil year after year. Monoculture **rapidly depletes the soil of its nutrients,** causing it to become **infertile.**

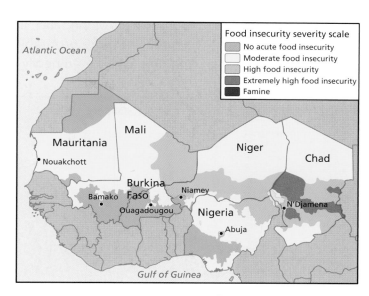

Fig. 27.25 Food insecurity map of the Sahel region

Deforestation

In the Sahel, farmers **clear the natural woodland** to make extra **land for agriculture** and for **fuel and building shelters.** Since the 1960s in **Mali** alone, over **500 000 acres of forestry** have been **cleared. Slash and burn** is the main method used for deforestation, which removes all vegetation from the soil. Currently, trees are being **cut down 30 times faster** than they are **being replaced.**

Forestry is vital in the Sahel, as it **prevents soil erosion.** The trees act as a **barrier to the wind, preventing** the **topsoil** from **being eroded** away. The **intense sun quickly dries out the soil,** making it **light and loosely bound.** As winds now **blow freely across the land,** it **strips away** the **topsoil,** rendering the soil useless. Deforestation has led to more **frequent dust storms** blowing across the Sahel.

Fig. 27.26 Deforestation in the Sahel

In many parts of the Sahel, the **cutting down and selling of trees** for fuel has become **more profitable than agriculture**. This has given rise to **illegal logging**, where even **newly planted trees** have been **cut down** and sold.

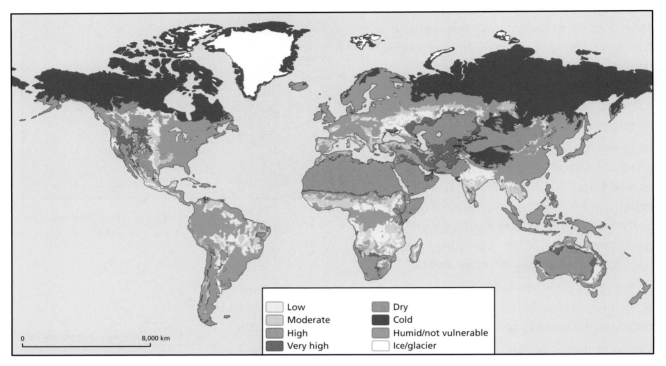

	Low		Dry
	Moderate		Cold
	High		Humid/not vulnerable
	Very high		Ice/glacier

Fig. 27.27 Vulnerability to desertification

EDUCATE YOURSELF

Human Interference with Soil		
Soil erosion, serious environmental problem, 99.7% of food from land, 0.03% produced by oceans, 10 million hectares lose fertility each year, reducing amount of land available, soil degradation, 3.7 billion people malnourished worldwide, soil being lost 10–40 times faster than rate of soil creation, soil loss unsustainable, environmental problems and human interference, Sahel region		
The Sahel	Semi-arid land 3 million km², transitional boundary, originally a grassland savanna biome, converted to hot desert biome, nomadic pastoral-based society	
	Climate greatly impacts rainfall, reduced 33% worldwide, Sahel ranges hot and temperate conditions, rainfall every 4–5 months	
	Population growing 3% per annum, overpopulated, desperate to produce enough food, environmental degradation	
	Desertification: uncontrolled spread of desert, unproductive wasteland, overuse and bad management, deserts advancing into Sahel 5–10 km per year, not just limited to spread of existing desert, fertility of soil and vegetation cover damaged, soil left unprotected, prone to soil erosion, climate change and human activities	
	Overgrazing: 1930s and 1970s more rainfall than usual, attracted more people, number of cattle doubled, strain on the soil, cattle sign of wealth in Sahel, number of farmers increasing, increased competition for land, land grazed continually – nutrients depleted, grass scarce – used marginal land, destruction of young trees and shrubs, settle in one area, sedentary farming, soils not left fallow, depletion of nutrients, cattle trampling – structure damaged, hooves compact soil, difficult for vegetation roots; boreholes and wells, groundwater rapidly depleted, water table dropped, wells dried up, rainfall unable to soak due to compaction, water evaporated, capillary action, soil salinisation, vegetation removed, absence of humus, torrential downpours, topsoil stripped away	

	Overcropping: rapid increase in population, demand for food risen, area of land used for growing crops trebled, grow crops rather than herd animals, unable to leave the land fallow, do not use artificial fertilisers, animal manure, shortage of wood, dried manure for fuel, artificial fertilisers too expensive, loans to pay for fertilisers – produced crops to pay off debts, clear marginal land – naturally less fertile, removal of vegetation increases soil erosion, crops using nutrients, soil becomes infertile and useless, received cheap loans, unable to repay, HIPC, qualify for debt relief – grow cash crops, sold on international market to pay off national debt, monoculture, rapidly depletes soil nutrients
	Deforestation: clear natural woodland for agriculture, fuel and building of shelters, e.g. Mali 500 000 acres, slash and burn, cut down 30 times faster than replaced, forestry prevents soil erosion, barrier to wind, preventing topsoil being eroded, intense sun quickly dries out soil, light and loosely bound, winds blow freely across the land, strips away topsoil, cutting down and selling of trees more profitable than agriculture, newly planted trees cut down

ACTIVE LEARNING

1. Why is the degradation of soil such a serious issue for the population of the Sahel?
2. Why did the population of the Sahel grow so rapidly over the past 50 years?
3. Describe the negative impacts of overgrazing and overcropping.
4. How has deforestation impacted on the soil of the Sahel?

GEO DICTIONARY

Conservation: protection of and restoration of the natural environment

27.10 Soil Conservation in the Sahel

When managed properly, soil is a **sustainable resource.** In order to **prevent further soil erosion**, a number of **affordable techniques** have been developed in the Sahel. There are also **methods to reclaim land** that has already been eroded.

Stone Lines (Bunds)

Stone lines (also called bunds) involve placing lines of small stones across sloping land in order to prevent or reduce run-off. When rain falls, the rainwater becomes trapped behind the stones, allowing it to soak into the soil. This prevents erosion of soil and helps to replenish the water table. Stone lines are very effective on gently sloping land. They take up less than 2 per cent of the ground space but can increase yields by over 50 per cent. This also makes the soil more drought resistant, which is vital when rains fail

Run-off is slowed by the bund, giving more time for water to soak into the soil.

Rainwater increases soil moisture.

Bunds are placed 10 to 25 m apart.

Any soil that has been eroded by run-off is trapped by the bund. Topsoil and organic matter (e.g. leaf litter) is deposited here.

● **Fig. 27.28** Stone lines are a cheap, low-technology method of soil conservation.

to arrive. The bunds also trap seeds, soil and organic matter, preventing the wind from eroding them away. Stone lines are cheap and easy to build, with the materials needed freely available. As this method of conservation is not costly, all farmers can use it. Generally stone lines are constructed during the dry season when farmers are not busy growing crops.

Fig. 27.29 Zaï holes in the Sahel

Zaï Holes

Zaï holes are **planting pits** dug through **hard, crusted soil** during the dry season (November–May). This **farming technique** has been in use for centuries in **semi-arid regions** and has since been adapted to the Sahel. Most Zaï holes are **20–40 cm in diameter** and dug to a **depth of 10–20 cm,** although the depth depends on the soil type. One major advantage of Zaï pits is that they require only a spade and **no high-tech machinery.** After the pits have been dug, they are **filled with compost/plant litter** and **animal manure** if it is available.

The mixture is covered by a **thin layer of soil,** with the remainder of the **dug-up soil forming a ridge around the pit** to **improve water retention.** Termites and other **living organisms are attracted** to the compost and **break it down into humus.** When the first rainfall of the season arrives, **water runs into the pits** and soaks into the ground. **Seeds or saplings** are then **planted in the pit,** which is in turn filled with soil. A wide **variety of crops** can be grown in Zaï holes, from **cereals and vegetables to trees.** The number of Zaï holes planted **per hectare** ranges from **12 000 to 25 000,** depending on the size of the crop.

Zaï holes offer soil conservation, **water retention** and **erosion control.** The main advantages of Zaï holes include:

- **They capture rain** and run-off water.
- **They protect seeds and organic matter** from being washed away.
- **They increase yields** and **biological activity** in the soil, making it more fertile.
- **They concentrate nutrients** and water where they are most needed.
- They lead to an **improvement in soil fertility.**

Fig 27.30 Contour ploughing

Contour Ploughing and Terracing

As you know from the Ordnance Survey chapter, **contours are lines that connect areas of equal height** on a map. **Traditionally,** fields are **ploughed in straight lines** running **up and down** the slope. However, this method **allows water to flow freely** down the slope, which leads to **poor water retention.** Soil erosion also occurs as **loose topsoil is washed down the slope.** Contour ploughing prevents this.

Furrows **follow the contours** of the slope and are **ploughed across the slope,** rather than up and down it. As a result, each **furrow acts like a barrier** which **traps water** as it moves downslope. This slowing of flow gives the water time **to soak through the soil.** This moisture allows the soil to **bind together** and gives it a **crumbly texture.** With a **higher moisture content** and better structure, the **soil is more fertile** leading to **increased yields** and **reduced soil erosion.** Contour ploughing is usually **not carried out during the dry season** as **loosening** the **dry soil** leaves it **prone to wind erosion.**

Terracing is another method which **follows the natural contours of a slope.** Terracing is typically carried out on **slopes** that are **too steep for contour ploughing.** A series of steep walls or **bunds** are **built across a hillside** – one above another. Behind each wall a wide 'step' or flat **terrace** is created. The terrace is just below the level of the bund, which acts as a **barrier to trap water,** which would otherwise flow downslope. Bunds allow water to soak into the soil. Although terracing is an effective form of **soil conservation,** it is **not** particularly **suited** to the mainly **flat Sahel.** Instead, this method is more commonly used in China and **South-east Asia.**

ACTIVE LEARNING

1. Why must techniques be low technology and low cost in the Sahel?
2. Explain fully how stone lines increase soil fertility.
3. Explain the benefits of Zaï holes.
4. How does contour ploughing increase soil fertility?

EDUCATE YOURSELF

Soil Conservation in the Sahel	
Sustainable resource, prevent further soil erosion, affordable techniques, methods to reclaim land	
Stone lines (bunds)	Lines of small stones, sloping land, prevent/reduce run-off, rainwater trapped, soaks into the soil, prevents erosion of soil and replenishes water table, gently sloping land, 2% of the ground space, increase yields by over 50%, soil more drought resistant, trap seeds, soil and organic matter, cheap and easy to build, built during the dry season
Zaï holes	Planting pits – hard, crusted soil, farming technique – semi-arid regions, combat soil erosion, poor farming practices and increased drought, 20–40 cm in diameter, depth 10–20 cm, do not require high-tech machinery, filled with compost/plant litter and animal manure, thin layer of soil, dug-up soil forming a ridge around the pit, improves water retention, termites and other living organisms attracted to compost, break down into humus, seeds or saplings planted in the pit, variety of crops, e.g. cereals, vegetables and trees, captures rain, protects seeds and organic matter, increases yields and biological activity, concentrates nutrients, increases in soil fertility
Contour ploughing and terracing	Traditionally ploughed in straight lines up and down the slope, allows the water to flow freely, poor water retention, contour ploughing prevents loose topsoil being washed down slope, ploughed across slope, furrows follow contours, act like barrier, water soaks through soil, binds together – crumbly texture, higher moisture content, soil more fertile, increases yields and reduces soil erosion, not carried out during dry season – loosening dry soil, prone to wind erosion
	Terracing follows the natural contours of a slope, slopes too steep for contour ploughing, bunds built across a hillside, terrace – barrier to trap water, soil conservation – not suited to flat Sahel, e.g. South-east Asia

HIGHER LEVEL

1. Examine the influence of mineral matter, air, water and organic matter on soil development.

2015 Q16 80M

2. Explain how soil characteristics impact on soil development.

2014 Q16 80M

3. Soil profiles are the result of the operation of soil-forming processes. Discuss.

2014 Q17 80M

4. Examine how desertification and conservation have impacted on soil characteristics.

2013 Q16 80M

5. Discuss how soil development is influenced by any three of the following factors:
   • Mineral matter   • Air   • Water   • Organic matter

2013 Q18 80M

Common Marking Scheme for Geoecology Questions		
Marks awarded	Discussing 3 aspects	Discussing 4 aspects
Total marks for each aspect	27m + 27m + 26m	20m + 20m + 20m + 20m
Identifying an aspect	4m each	4m each
Examination of each aspect	8 SRPs @ 2m each	6 SRPs @ 2m each
Overall coherence	7/6m per aspect	4m per aspect

> **Note!**
> An aspect is an area of discussion that is relevant to the topic being examined. For example, if you are asked a question on the characterisics of a soil, a relevant aspect for brown soils might be 'Texture of Irish brown earths'.

The Geoecology Option is worth 80 marks, or 20 per cent of the Higher Level paper (16 per cent of total exam), so it is vital that you practise answering these questions as often possible. It is the only section in the paper where the overall cohesion of your answer is marked. This means that your answer must be written in a logical order and well structured. In other words, you should discuss three or four aspects relating to the question in detail, rather than giving minute detail on more topics. Furthermore, you must discuss one aspect fully before moving onto the next one. If your answer moves back and forth between different aspects, you will lose overall cohesion marks.

A common mistake students make is to overload their answer with every single fact they can remember about a topic. Much of this may be irrelevant to the question asked. Instead, it is better to write only information that directly relates to the question.

In this section, we will look at a question from the 2012 paper. According to the Chief Examiner's report for that year's paper:

> Candidates' answers lacked focus and in many cases did not deal with each of the terms within their answer. The standard of answering relating to podzolisation was poor in many cases.

This is a problem many students have when answering the Geoecology Option every year. Many students struggle to write answers that are relevant to the question asked. A common approach to the Options section of the course has been to learn off four or five answers and to 'hope for the best'. If you look at the questions which have appeared since 2006, you will find that questions are rarely repeated. The topics may be similar, but the manner in which the questions are asked is rarely the same.

Explain how weathering, leaching and podzolisation have impacted on the characteristics of soil.

2012 Q16 80M

Marking Scheme
3 aspects 27m + 27m + 26m
Aspect named 3 @ 4m each
Each aspect 8 SRPs @ 2m each
Overall cohesion 7m/7m/6m

SAMPLE ANSWER

The Impact of Weathering on Soil Characteristics

Weathering refers to the breaking up and decay of rocks on the Earth's surface through natural, mechanical and chemical processes [2m]. The type of weathering which takes place in a region is largely controlled by the climate and the parent rock [2m]. In temperate climates, such as that in Ireland, freeze-thaw action is the dominant form of weathering due to fluctuating temperatures, while regions covered in limestone or chalk will be mainly weathered through carbonation [2m]. When a soil is formed from weathered limestone, it will be rich in calcium, which will also give the soil an alkaline (low) pH [2m]. These broken pieces of scree, formed from mechanical weathering, are eventually broken down into tiny particles which make up soil [2m].

Latosol soils form in equatorial climates as a result of rapid chemical weathering, which occurs as a result of the hot and humid climate [2m]. The climate allows dead plant matter to be broken down quickly by microorganisms, another form of chemical weathering, making the soil acidic [2m]. Heavy rainfall in equatorial regions, such as the Amazon Rainforest, leads to the leaching away of nutrients through laterisation, leaving only iron in the soil. Oxidation rusts the iron in the soil, giving the latosol soil its characteristic dark red colour [2m].

Hydrolysis is also caused by rainwater, which breaks down granite by turning the mineral feldspar into kaolin clay [2m]. As a result of this, soils which form from the chemical weathering of granite have poor drainage and a clay texture [2m]. If a soil develops from weathered sandstone, it will have good drainage as it is composed of large particles which allow water and air to pass freely through it [2m]. As the large particles do not bind together like clay, sandy soils do not retain water, which can be a problem in times of drought [2m]. As water passes through the soil freely, its minerals can be leached away, making it light brown in colour due to an absence of humus [2m].

Remember, there are other types of weathering you can discuss, e.g. exfoliation affects the characteristics of desert soils.

This answer deals with three aspects, as it suits the question that has been asked.

Your knowledge of the physical processes of Ireland in the Physical Geography unit can help you here, especially the West of Ireland, as it deals with the formation of infertile soils in upland areas. This is also true of Chapter 25 on Brazil in the Regional Geography unit, as the characteristics of the tropical red soils are discussed.

Leaching and podzolisation are very similar, so it is important that you are able to distinguish between the two. If you cannot, you may find yourself repeating information for both sections.

Like in this answer, you must keep referring to how the soil-forming processes affect the soil characteristics, rather than simply describing each process.

EXAM FOCUS

The Impact of Leaching on Soil Characteristics:

Leaching refers to the washing of nutrients from the O and A horizons to the B horizon of a soil, typically from the percolation of rainwater down through the soil [2m]. While small amounts of leaching can increase soil fertility, e.g. brown earths, severe leaching leads to the formation of infertile soils, e.g. latosols [2m]. As minerals are washed downwards from the A horizon, they tend to accumulate and solidify in the B horizon to form a hardpan [2m]. The hardpan is an impermeable layer of minerals that disrupts the drainage of soil, leading to waterlogging [2m]. Many upland soils in the West of Ireland have poor, wet, infertile soils due to leaching from heavy rainfall [2m]. As leaching removes humus from the soil, it also loses its dark brown colour to form a pale, grey soil [2m].

Laterisation is an extreme form of leaching that is common to tropical and equatorial regions [2m]. It occurs as large amounts of plant litter are quickly broken down by chemical weathering due to high temperatures and heavy rainfall [2m]. As rainwater percolates through the soil, the humus is dissolved and leached deep into the soil, away from the reach of plant roots [2m]. This rapid leaching prevents the soil from developing horizons and causes it to become infertile [2m]. The iron oxide in the soil gives latosols their red colour.

The Impact of Podzolisation on Soil Characteristics

Podzolisation is the most extreme form of leaching which occurs as a result of acidic water percolating through the soil [2m]. Podzolisation is most common in areas that are covered by coniferous forest or peat soils and where there are high levels of precipitation [2m]. As water passes through plant litter of coniferous forests, or other organic matter, it becomes much more acidic [2m]. The acidic water is capable of dissolving and washing away almost all of the minerals and nutrients in the soil, leaving the A horizon bleached and infertile [2m]. Quartz is the only mineral which can resist the acidic water, which gives it a grey colour [2m]. Podzolisation also leads to the formation of a hardpan, meaning podzolised soils become waterlogged quite easily [2m].

In upland areas of the West of Ireland, podzolisation has occurred leading to the formation of infertile peat soils [2m]. Podzol brown earths have also formed in Ireland, particularly in areas where boulder clay was deposited over limestone bedrock [2m]. Due to the underlying limestone, water drains freely away, causing the soil to be slightly leached and paler in colour [2m]. Podzol brown earths cover approximately 22 per cent of Ireland [2m].

Marks Awarded			
Aspect 1 4m	Aspect 2 4m	Aspect 3 4m	Total 80/80
8 SRPs @ 2m each	8 SRPs @ 2m each	8 SRPs @ 2m each	
Overall cohesion 7m	Overall cohesion 7m	Overall cohesion 6m	

TOPIC MAP

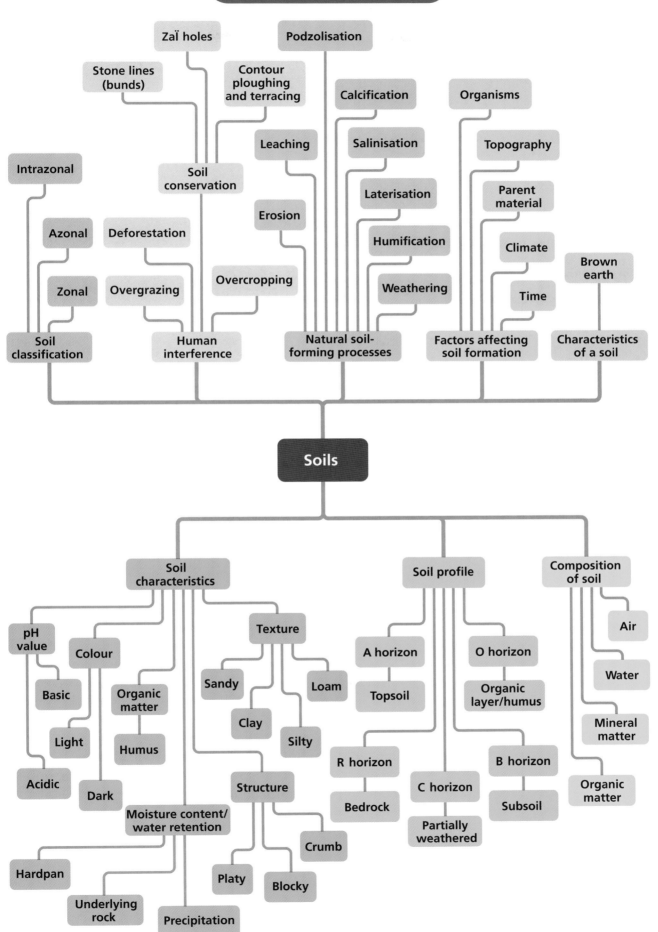

Zaï holes

Stone lines (bunds)

Contour ploughing and terracing

Podzolisation

Calcification

Organisms

Intrazonal

Soil conservation

Leaching

Salinisation

Topography

Azonal

Deforestation

Erosion

Laterisation

Parent material

Zonal

Overgrazing

Overcropping

Humification

Climate

Brown earth

Weathering

Time

Soil classification

Human interference

Natural soil-forming processes

Factors affecting soil formation

Characteristics of a soil

Soils

Soil characteristics

pH value

Colour

Texture

Basic

Organic matter

Sandy

Loam

Light

Humus

Clay

Silty

Acidic

Dark

Structure

Moisture content/water retention

Crumb

Hardpan

Platy

Blocky

Underlying rock

Precipitation

Soil profile

A horizon

O horizon

Topsoil

Organic layer/humus

R horizon

B horizon

C horizon

Bedrock

Subsoil

Partially weathered

Composition of soil

Air

Water

Mineral matter

Organic matter

CHAPTER 28

Higher Level only

Hot Desert Biome

In this chapter, we will look at the hot desert biome – a unique natural world feature that is distinct due to its climate, flora, fauna and soil. It is important that you fully understand how the climate controls the development of the biome and how human activities have influenced it.

> **Note!**
> You must study either this chapter or Chapter 29 Tropical Rainforest Biome.

KEY WORDS

- Biome
- Hot desert
- The Sahel
- Interdependent
- Climate
- Drought
- Evaporation

- Trade winds
- Aridisols
- Calcification
- Salinisation
- Flora
- Cactus
- Adaptation

- Fauna
- Camel
- Poor agricultural practices
- Deforestation
- Economic activity and climate change

LEARNING OUTCOMES

What you MUST know
- The four main characteristics of the hot desert biome
- How climate controls the development of soil, flora and fauna
- How all characteristics of a biome are interdependent

- Human interaction with desert biomes

What you SHOULD know
- Additional examples of flora and fauna adaptations in desert biomes

What is USEFUL to know
- Up-to-date information regarding drought in the Sahel

28.1 Biomes

Biomes are **unique natural world regions**, which are **controlled by climate**. All biomes can be divided into four main components: **climate, soil, flora** and **fauna**. These are all **interdependent**, meaning that they all rely on and are influenced by each other. Climate is the most important factor controlling the characteristics of a biome. Climate determines:

- What soil develops
- What plants grow
- What animals live there

The term 'desert' means a **dry/arid region** which is characterised by **little or no precipitation**, leading to an **absence or scarcity of vegetation**. Deserts cover one-seventh of the Earth's land area. Only **20 per cent of the world's deserts are sandy**; the majority are composed of bare, rocky landscapes. In this chapter, we will focus on the world's **hot, mid-latitude deserts**.

GEO DICTIONARY

Trade winds: hot, dry winds which blow towards the equator from the high pressure horse latitudes

Location

Hot deserts are generally located between **15° and 30° north and south of the equator.** Most hot deserts tend to lie on the **western margins** or in the **centre of continents**. Deserts can be divided into three categories according to their precipitation:

- Extremely arid: almost **no precipitation** per annum
- Arid: **less than 250 mm per annum**
- Semi-arid: **250–500 mm per annum**

The **type of desert** that **develops depends on its location** in relation to **trade winds, high-pressure belts, rain shadows, ocean currents** and **distance from the sea (continentality).** We will discuss these factors in detail under the heading of climate.

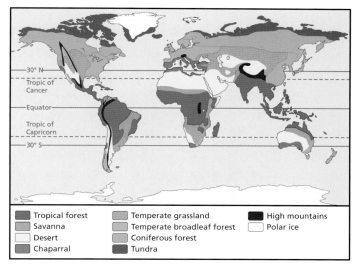

Fig. 28.1 A map of the world's biomes

EDUCATE YOURSELF

Biomes
Unique natural world regions, controlled by climate, soil, flora and fauna, interdependent, dry/arid region, little or no precipitation, absence/scarcity of vegetation, cover 1/7 of Earth's land area, 20% of world's deserts sandy, majority composed of bare, rocky landscapes, hot, mid-latitude deserts

Location	15–30° north and south of equator, western margins, centre of continents, extremely arid no precipitation, arid < 250 mm per annum, semi-arid 250–500 mm per annum, type of desert depends on location to trade winds, high-pressure belts, rain shadows, ocean currents and distance from sea

ACTIVE LEARNING

1. Define the term 'desert'.
2. Name three different types of desert.
3. List the five factors which influence the type of desert that forms.

28.2 Hot Desert Climate

Hot deserts experience a **dry climate**, with **annual rainfall** of between **0 and 250 mm**. Rainfall is **unpredictable** and usually occurs in **short, torrential downpours**. The rainfall is **quickly evaporated** by the **intense sunlight** as the water is **unable to percolate** through the soil. Instead, these downpours aid the soil erosion process as **topsoil is washed away.** At night-time, when **temperatures are lower**, limited amounts of **fog and dew** can fall. When temperatures fall, moisture in the air condenses and

OPTION 7 CHAPTER 28

covers the ground in a **thin layer of water.** In areas such as the **Namib Desert** on the west coast of Africa, moisture from cool ocean currents reaches coastal areas causing precipitation in the form of fog.

Why Deserts Are Dry

Deserts are dry due to one, or a combination, of four factors:

1. The rain-shadow effect

2. Trade winds and high-pressure belts

3. The influence of cold ocean currents

4. Continentality

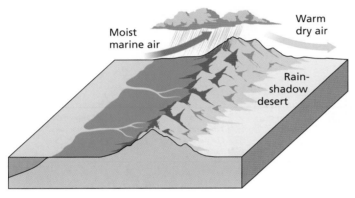

Moist marine air

Warm dry air

Rain-shadow desert

🔺 **Fig. 28.2** The rain-shadow effect

FACT

Some parts of the Atacama Desert in Chile have not had rainfall in over 400 years.

More than 1 billion people live in desert regions – one-seventh of the world's population.

1. The Rain-shadow Effect

Many of the world's hot deserts occur along the **western edges of continents.** As **moisture-laden winds** are carried inland, they are **forced to rise upwards over coastal mountain** ranges. The **moisture is cooled and condensed,** forming cloud. Further condensation **leads to rainfall** on the western slope of the mountain – known as the **windward side.** The **air,** now **shed of its moisture, blows** as dry winds **over the leeward side. When the air reaches the other side,** it sinks to the ground and heats up as it blows across the land, making it **hotter and drier.** This is commonly referred to as the rain-shadow effect.

The **Atacama Desert in Chile** is the driest hot desert on Earth as the Andes Mountains **prevent rain from moving inland** from the west. Similarly, the **Sahara** is made **increasingly drier** due to the rain-shadow effect caused by the Atlas Mountains in the north-west and the Ethiopian Highlands along the west coast.

2. Trade Winds and High-pressure Belts

Most hot deserts are located **15–30 °C north and south of the equator** due to the effects of the **global wind patterns** at these latitudes. **Air is heated** at the **equator, increasing its ability to hold moisture** and causing it to rise. The **warm air continues to rise** as it moves away from the equator, causing **convectional rainfall** along **equatorial regions.** The air is **now much drier** and cooler, **causing it to sink downwards** at 30° north and south of the equator. This area is known as the **horse latitudes.** As the heavy cold air descends, it **presses down on the Earth** forming a **high-pressure belt.** The cool air moves back towards the equator, becoming warmer as it does so. As **warm air holds more moisture, rainfall does not occur** until the air rises again at the equator. The dry winds that blow towards the equator are **called trade winds.** It is due to this high pressure that **hot desert regions** experience **clear, cloudless skies** with constant sunshine throughout the day.

3. The Influence of Cold Ocean Currents

Cold ocean currents influence the distribution of deserts as they lead to **dry air systems** moving inland. As the **moisture-laden winds** blow across cold ocean currents they are **cooled**. As cold air is **unable to hold moisture,** it is **lost at sea,** normally in the form of fog. By the time the **air reaches land,** it is **dry.** Air blowing across the land is warmed, **increasing its ability to hold moisture.** Therefore, **precipitation does not occur.**

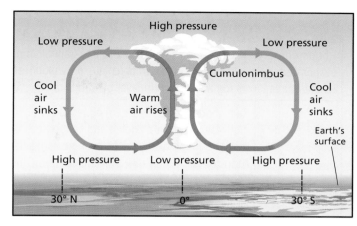

Fig. 28.3 Low-pressure belt formation

4. Continentality

Deserts located in the centre (interior) of continents **do not receive rainfall** as **moisture-laden winds are dried** by the time they **reach inland.** As winds blow across the continents, they are warmed, **increasing the air's ability to hold moisture.** Precipitation almost **never occurs along the interior of deserts,** while the warm winds evaporate any moisture in the soil, e.g. **the Great Australian Desert.**

Temperature of the Desert

The **temperatures** of these deserts are **high,** especially in the summer, when they **exceed 45 °C.** By night, temperatures plummet within an hour of sunset. During the summer, temperatures **drop by roughly 15–30 °C at night,** giving a **large diurnal range.** Winter temperatures are **lower** at 25 °C during the day, but fall **close to freezing point (0 °C)** at **night.**

[A|Z] **GEO DICTIONARY**

Radiates: emits heat

Why the Temperature Range Is so Large

Hot deserts are **located in the tropics,** where the **sun shines down from almost vertically overhead in the summer.** This means that the **sun's rays are concentrated** over a small area, **creating high temperatures** on the surface. As there is **little moisture,** there are **no clouds** to block the sun's rays. As the soil has **little or no vegetation cover,** the ground absorbs all of the heat. The **heat then radiates from the ground,** leading to **high atmospheric temperatures.** Once the **sun sets, the temperatures drop rapidly. Cloudless skies,** while leading to higher temperatures by day, allow the **heat to escape at night.** This explains why there is a large diurnal range.

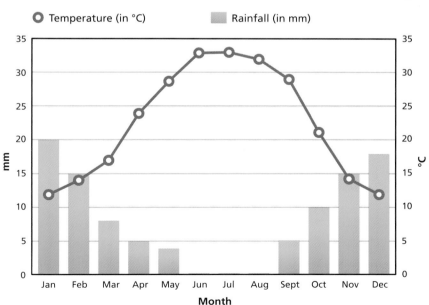

Fig. 28.4 Climograph of the Sahara Desert

Hot Desert Climate

Hot deserts, dry climate, annual rainfall 0–250 mm, rainfall unpredictable – short, torrential downpours, quickly evaporated; intense sunlight, unable to percolate, downpours aid soil erosion, topsoil washed away, night-time temperatures lower, fog and dew, thin layer of water

Why deserts are dry	Rain-shadow effect: western edges of continents – moisture-laden winds, forced to rise over coastal mountains, moisture cooled and condensed, leads to rainfall on windward side, air now shed of moisture blows as dry winds over leeward side, sinks to the ground and heats up, hotter and drier, Atacama Desert in Chile, prevents rain from moving inland, Sahara – increasingly drier
	Trade winds and high-pressure belts: 15–30° north and south of the equator, global wind patterns, air heated – equator, increasing ability to hold moisture, warm air continues to rise, convectional rainfall equatorial regions, now much drier and cooler, sink downwards at 30° – horse latitudes, presses down on the Earth – high-pressure belt, warm air holds more moisture, rainfall does not occur – trade winds, hot desert regions – clear, cloudless skies
	Cold ocean current: dry air systems, moisture-laden winds – cooled, unable to hold moisture, lost at sea, air reaches land – dry, increasing ability to hold moisture, precipitation does not occur
	Continentality: deserts in centre of contintents do not receive rainfall, moisture-laden winds dried, increasing air's ability to hold moisture, precipitation almost never occurs along interior of deserts, e.g. Great Australian Desert
Temperature of the desert	Day 45 °C, night drop by roughly 15–30 °C, large diurnal range, winter, temperatures 25 °C during the day, freezing point at night (0 °C)
	Why temperature range is so large: located in the tropics, sun shines vertically overhead, sun's rays concentrated, creating high temperatures, little moisture, no clouds, soil little or no vegetation cover, heat then radiates from ground, high atmospheric temperatures, when sun sets temperatures drop rapidly, cloudless skies – heat escapes at night

ACTIVE LEARNING

1. Explain two reasons why desert climates do not experience high levels of precipitation.
2. Explain why hot deserts have such a large diurnal range.
3. Name two deserts which experience very little rainfall.

 **Fig. 28.5** Arid soil of the desert

GEO DICTIONARY

Aridisols: soils that form with very low or no organic matter. They are typically alkaline or saline (salty)

28.3 Hot Desert Soils

Aridisols are the main soil type that form in hot desert biomes. These soils **form in direct response to climate** conditions of **low precipitation levels** and **high daytime temperatures.** Due to the coarse texture and poor development of aridisols, most are **incapable of supporting widespread vegetation growth.** Some aridisols have the **potential to be productive** if **water is added.** This is proven by the growth of **oases in the Sahara Desert** or where **irrigation schemes** have led to the support of agriculture, e.g. in **Libya.**

Most aridisols are **coarse and stony/gravelly.** Due to the lack of rainfall, there is **little or no chemical weathering.** Due to the large diurnal range and extreme temperatures, **mechanical weathering is dominant.** Exfoliation breaks down rock due to repeated **expansion/contraction cycles,** which form **coarse, angular pieces of scree.** Any **fine particles of sand** are quickly **blown away** by the **strong winds** in the region. This leads to the **heavier, coarse-grained particles remaining. Low levels of precipitation** and **sparse vegetation growth** have developed soils with a **high mineral content** but **little organic matter.**

Aridisols **do not have a well-developed A horizon** due to a **lack of humus**. This gives the soil a **light grey colour.** The absence of organic matter occurs due to **lack of vegetation**, which **restricts** the **soil-building activities of microorganisms.** This **absence of organic matter** also **prevents water retention** as the gravelly soil has a **poor water carrying capacity.**

Relief also impacts on the development of aridisol soils as **valleys provide pathways for flash floods** which occur during torrential downpours. **Water flowing off slopes deposits mud, gravel and sand** at the base of the valley.

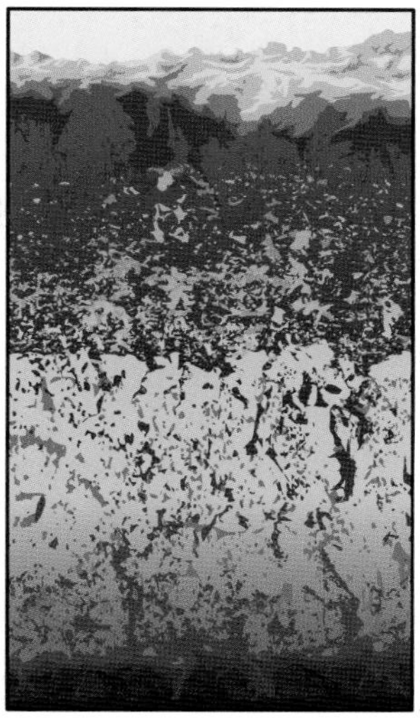

Soil Processes

As **evaporation rates** are far higher than precipitation rates, **capillary action occurs** as **groundwater is drawn up** through the soil. When the water reaches the surface, it is rapidly evaporated, leaving a **layer of minerals behind on the surface.**

Large **salt pans develop** on the surface, with **salinisation poisoning the land** and making it **toxic to most plants.**

A layer of **calcite may form** on the surface if calcification occurs. As calcium builds up on the surface it can **form a hardpan**, which **roots are unable to penetrate.**

▲ **Fig. 28.6** Desert soil profile

A horizon

B horizon

C horizon

EDUCATE YOURSELF

Hot desert soils	Aridisols form in direct response to climate, low precipitation levels and high daytime temperatures, do not support plant life, coarse texture and poor development, potential to be productive, only water needed, oases in the Sahara Desert, irrigation schemes, e.g. Libya, most aridisols incapable of supporting widespread vegetation growth; coarse and stony/gravelly, little or no chemical weathering, mechanical weathering dominant, expansion/contraction cycles, coarse, angular pieces of scree, fine particles blown away – strong winds, heavier coarse particles remain, low levels of precipitation and sparse vegetation growth, high mineral content, low level of organic matter
	Does not have well-developed A horizon, lack of humus, light grey colour, low vegetation productivity, restricts soil-building activities of microorganisms, absence of organic matter and prevents water retention, poor water carrying capacity
	Relief: valleys provide pathways for flash floods, water off slopes deposit mud, gravel, sand, not able to support a wide range of crops
Soil processes	Evaporation rates higher than precipitation rates, capillary action, groundwater drawn up, reaches the surface, evaporated, layer of minerals left behind, salt pans develop, salinisation, poisons land, toxic to most plants, calcite may form, calcification, calcium builds up, form a hardpan, roots unable to penetrate

ACTIVE LEARNING

1. What is the name of the main soil found in desert biomes?
2. Describe how this soil forms.
3. Explain how relief impacts on soil development in the desert.

OPTION 7   CHAPTER 28

28.4 Flora

Vegetation is **sparse** in hot desert regions due to a **shortage of water, high levels of evaporation, lack of humus** and **shallow, stony soils**. Despite these **unfavourable conditions**, some **plant species** have **adapted to the extreme heat and drought**. Vegetation is **spread out to avoid competition** for very limited resources.

Adaptations

These adaptations include:

- Root systems
- Ephemerals
- Succulents
- Fruit growth
- Defence systems

Root Systems

> **Fig. 28.7** Root systems of desert flora

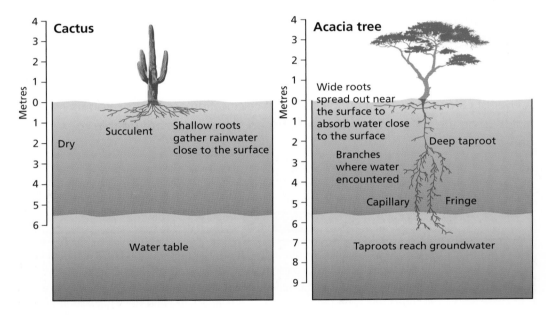

As water is scarce, plants must develop an efficient root system. Hot desert vegetation has one of two types of roots:

1. Some plants have developed **shallow roots** which **spread outwards over a large area** to collect moisture during times of rainfall. Shallow roots are also effective at **collecting dew that forms on the surface** at night. Most **cacti** have shallow roots, as does the **creosote bush**. By drawing water and any organic matter from close to the surface, the roots **avoid having to penetrate calcium hardpans** where calcification has occurred.

2. Some plants have developed **deep taproots** to **allow them to reach groundwater** deep in the soil. For example, the **acacia tree's** taproots can reach water **6–7 metres beneath the surface.**

Ephemerals

Some plants have **adapted their life cycle** to take advantage of the unpredictable desert rains. These plants are known as ephemerals. The **seeds of ephemerals** have **waxy coats** which allows them to **retain their**

GEO DICTIONARY

Ephemerals: plants which have short life cycles; desert ephemerals have adapted to take advantage of short wet periods

moisture for a long period of time. The **seeds lie dormant** in the ground, sometimes for years, **until rainfall occurs**. When rainfall occurs, the **seeds burst into life** by **germinating, growing, flowering** and **producing new seeds**. The new seeds then lie dormant in the soil until the next period of rainfall, e.g. **mouse-ear cress**.

Succulents

Succulents are **plants that have developed ways to store water**. The **cactus** is the best-known example of this. Its **fleshy interior acts as a sponge**. The **deep grooves** on the exterior of the cactus **allow it to expand** when **water is more plentiful**, as well as **channelling water directly towards its roots**. Other succulents can **store water in their roots** or **underground bulbs**. Many succulents have also developed a **waxy exterior to prevent moisture loss**, e.g. the **giant saguaro**.

Fig. 28.8 Ephemerals in bloom

📖 **GEO DICTIONARY**

Succulents: plants which have developed fat, fleshy parts to store water in dry climates

Dormant: alive, but not actively growing

Cactus

The cactus has adapted to the desert climate in a number of ways:

- **Vertical grooves** along the side of the cactus **allow it to expand when water is plentiful**. These grooves also **channel rainwater to the plant's roots** by acting like a drainpipe.

- **Thorns** on the cactus **protect it from being eaten**. These narrow needles also **prevent moisture loss** from the intense heat.

- The **waxy skin** of the cactus prevents loss of moisture and **prevents the cactus** from being **burned by the sun**.

- The inside of the cactus is like a sponge. This **enables the cactus to store** large amounts of **moisture**, which can be used in **times of drought**.

- **Shallow radial roots spread out** over a wide area to gather as much moisture as possible. Much of the **moisture** is gathered from **dew**.

Fruit Growth

Some plants grow fruits, which are **eaten by animals**, especially **birds**. The **seeds** contained in the fruit **pass through the birds undigested** and then **spread over the desert** in bird droppings.

Defence Systems

Many shrubs have poisonous or foul-tasting bark and leaves which **prevent animals from eating them**, e.g. **the oleander plant**. Other plants **avoid blooming during the day** in order to **prevent their leaves drying out** in the intense heat. Instead they **bloom at night**, when temperatures are lower.

Fig. 28.9 A cactus

FACT

A cactus produces and releases over 1 million seeds per year and can live for over 250 years.

Flora		
Sparse – shortage of water and high levels of evaporation, lack of humus and shallow, stony soils, unfavourable conditions, plant species adapted to extreme heat and drought, spread out to avoid competition		
Root systems	Efficient root system, shallow roots, spread outwards over a large area, collecting dew that forms on surface, cactus, creosote bush, avoid having to penetrate calcium hardpans, deep taproots, allow them to reach groundwater, acacia tree, 6–7 m beneath the surface	
Ephemerals	Adapted life cycle, seeds – waxy coats, retain moisture, lie dormant until rainfall occurs, burst into life – germinating, growing, flowering, producing new seeds, e.g. mouse-ear cress	
Succulents	Plants that have developed ways to store water, cactus – fleshy interior acts as sponge, deep grooves exterior expand when water more plentiful, channelling water towards roots, store water in roots or underground bulbs, waxy exterior to prevent moisture loss, e.g. giant saguaro	
Cactus	Vertical grooves, allow it to expand when water in plentiful supply, channel rainwater to roots, thorns protect it from being eaten, prevent moisture loss, waxy skin prevents it from being burned by sun, spongy interior stores moisture in times of drought, shallow radial roots spread out, moisture in form of dew	
Fruit growth	Eaten by animals – birds, seeds contained in fruit, undigested, spread over desert	
Defence systems	Shrubs, poisonous or foul-tasting bark, prevent animals eating them, e.g. oleander plant, avoid blooming during the day, prevent their leaves drying, bloom at night, temperatures lower	

 ACTIVE LEARNING

1. Describe how ephemerals have adapted to the hot desert climate and soil.
2. Explain fully how succulents have adapted to survive in drought conditions.
3. Describe how the cactus has adapted to survive in the desert climate.

 GEO DICTIONARY

Venomous: poisonous

Hibernate: to spend time (usually winter) in a dormant state

28.5 Fauna

Despite hot deserts' incredibly harsh climates, **a number of animals have adapted** ways to survive. There are **few large animals** in deserts as they are **unable to survive without drinking water** for long or to withstand the extreme temperatures. A few large mammals, such as **camels, donkeys and gazelles,** have **developed ways to adapt to these extreme conditions.**

 **Fig. 28.10** A scorpion

Adaptations

Insects, scorpions and spiders are by far the **most numerous** animals living in hot deserts. They can **survive on very little food,** making them well adapted to desert conditions. Many scorpions and spiders are **extremely venomous,** meaning they can **kill their prey with a single sting or bite.** Scorpions can survive for up to a **year without food** as they can **slow down their metabolism and hibernate.** They **can come out of hibernation instantly** if prey passes by.

Many animals have **adapted to avoid the hot daytime temperatures.** These **nocturnal animals hunt and eat at night.** Other animals choose to stay in the shade. For example, **jackrabbits follow the shadows of larger objects** such as cacti and shrubs.

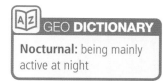
Physical Evolution

In order to withstand the **harsh climate,** many animals have **evolved body parts** which are key to their survival.

Kangaroo Rats

The kangaroo rat has evolved in the following ways:

- Its colour allows it to **camouflage itself** in its surroundings.

- It has **smaller front feet** that allow it to **handle food and dig burrows** with its sharp claws.

- Its **longer back feet** allow it to **leap away** quickly **from predators.** As it leaps away, it often **flicks sand behind it** to blind predators.

⬆ **Fig. 28.11** A kangaroo rat

- Its **long tail acts as a balance** while jumping and allows it to **quickly change direction** by using it as a brake in the sand.

Camels

The camel is the best-known example of an animal that has adapted to suit the desert environment. Its suitability for such a climate has earned it the name of **'Ship of the Desert'.**

- Camels have **two rows of long eyelashes,** which **prevent sand** from getting in their eyes. They also have an **inner eyelid to protect their eyes** during sandstorms.

- Camels can **tighten their nostrils** during sandstorms to **'filter' out the sand** as they breathes.

- Camels have **thick coarse fur** which protects their backs from the **intense sunlight.** Their under belly is **covered in wool** which protects it from the **scorching sand beneath it.**

- Camels **store fat in their hump(s),** which **acts as an effective food reserve.** This fat can be **converted into water** during times of **drought.**

(a)

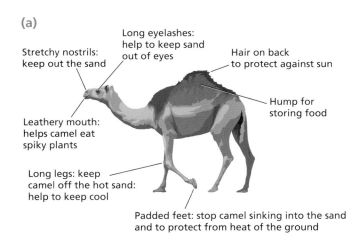

Long eyelashes: help to keep sand out of eyes

Stretchy nostrils: keep out the sand

Hair on back to protect against sun

Leathery mouth: helps camel eat spiky plants

Hump for storing food

Long legs: keep camel off the hot sand: help to keep cool

Padded feet: stop camel sinking into the sand and to protect from heat of the ground

(b)

⬆ **Fig. 28.12** (a) Camel adaptations and (b) a herd of camels

Fig. 28.13 A roadrunner

- Camels have **tough-skinned or 'leathery' mouths** that enable them to **eat cactus** and other **prickly/thorny plants.**
- Camels have **wide, padded feet** which act like snowshoes. This allows them to **walk across loose sand** without sinking or burning their feet.
- Camels can drink over **100 litres of water** at a time. They are able to store this water, meaning they do **not need to drink water again** for several months.
- Camels **conserve body fluids** by **not sweating.** If necessary, **camels' urine can become solid** to avoid water loss when water is running low.

Other Desert Animals	
Roadrunners	Birds that can fly but generally do not to conserve energy; cry excess salt through tears to avoid sweating and water loss; large tail acts as a fan
African meerkats	Have a black ring of fur around their eyes which acts as a natural pair of sunglasses, absorbing sunlight and preventing it from reflecting into their eyes
Dorcas gazelles	Do not need to drink water and do not urinate

EDUCATE YOURSELF

Fauna	
Several animals have adapted, few large animals, unable to survive without drinking water, camels, donkeys and gazelles	
Adaptations	Insects, scorpions, spiders most numerous, survive on very little food, extremely venomous, kill prey with single sting or bite, can slow down metabolism and hibernate, can leave hibernation instantly, nocturnal animals adapted to avoid hot daytime temperatures, jackrabbits follow shadows of cactus and shrubs
Physical evolution	Harsh climate, animals have evolved body parts
	Kangaroo rats: camouflage themselves, smaller front feet, handle food and dig burrows, longer back feet, leap away from predators, flick sand behind, long tail acts as a balance, change direction
	Camels: 'Ship of the Desert', two rows of long eyelashes, trap sand, inner eyelid protects eyes, tighten nostrils, 'filter' out sand, thick coarse fur, intense sunlight, covered in wool, scorching sand beneath it, store fat in hump(s), effective food reserve, converted into water in drought, tough-skinned or 'leathery' mouth, eat cactus, prickly/thorny plants, wide, padded feet, walk across loose sand, 100 litres of water, no need to drink water again for several months, conserve body fluids by not sweating, urine can become solid
	Other: roadrunner does not fly, large tail acts as a fan; African meerkats have black ring of fur around their eyes, natural sunglasses, absorbs sunlight; dorcas gazelle do not need to drink water and do not urinate

ACTIVE LEARNING

1. Which animals are the most numerous in the hot desert biome?
2. Name three ways in which animals have adapted to the desert biome.
3. Describe the ways in which camels have adapted to the desert climate.
4. Using the internet or reference books, research other animals of the desert and how they have adapted.

Human Interference in the Sahel

Hot deserts are **extremely sensitive biomes** as the interdependency between plants and animals is finely balanced. Any interference from humans has an immediate and often devastating impact on the biome's ecosystem. Living conditions in hot desert biome regions are harsh and largely unsuitable for humans. Despite this, close to **100 million people's lives depend on the natural resources** along the fringes of the Sahara Desert, i.e. Sahel region.

In this section we will look at the impact of:

- Poor agricultural practices
- Deforestation
- Economic activity and climate change

Poor Agricultural Practices

The majority of the workforce in the Sahel is employed in agriculture. Agriculture accounts for up to 45 per cent of the region's GDP. It is dominant in the region for two main reasons:

- **Food security:** The region's agriculture is highly undeveloped. Food security is dependent on rain, which falls over four to five months per year. When this rainfall is delayed or does not arrive, starvation becomes a risk for millions of people living in the region. With an increasing population, growing food is a priority for all living there.
- **High levels of debt:** Many countries of the Sahel are highly indebted due to loans obtained in the 1960s. In order to repay these loans and get debt relief, farmers are forced to grow cash crops. As a result, farmers plant as much as possible to repay debt and to have enough food for their families. This leads to overcropping.

Overgrazing

As you have already learned, **poor agricultural practices** can lead to soil degradation. This is particularly true along the **fringes of the Sahara Desert** in the Sahel region. Between the 1930s and 1970s, the Sahel had more rainfall than usual, which **attracted more nomadic farmers** to the region. During this period, the number of cattle being farmed in the area doubled. This put an **ever-increasing strain on the already environmentally sensitive region.** The increase in the number of cattle grazing in the Sahel led to increased competition for land among nomadic farmers. This meant that land was **continually grazed** throughout the year, which led to a **rapid depletion of nutrients** in the soil. As a result, the soil's **fertility was greatly reduced,** leading to **vegetation cover becoming more sparse.** In response to this, farmers began to **graze marginal lands,** which are naturally infertile.

Nomadic farmers began fencing in their cattle on fertile land, to engage in **sedentary farming.** Due to the number of cattle trampling it, the soil's **structure was damaged** as the animals' hooves compacted it. Compacted soil does not allow water to pass through it. This leads to the **soil becoming drier and finer,** while any rainwater that does fall flows along the surface leading to **soil erosion.**

In order to supply water for their animals, farmers **sunk boreholes and wells** which rapidly depleted the water table. The lack of water in the soil leads to **capillary action** which, in turn, leads to **salinisation and calcification.** The increased salt or calcium carbonate in the soil makes it **toxic for vegetation.** With little vegetation now growing, the soil is **exposed to the intense heat of**

Fig. 28.14 Wilting crops of the the Sahel

the sun, causing it to dry further into fine dust. **Winds** blow across the region **removing the topsoil,** leaving the area barren and useless for agriculture. Instead, the land is abandoned and **merges into the Sahara Desert.**

Overcropping

Due to the **rapid increase in population** in the Sahel since the 1960s, the demand for food has also risen. The region is struggling to cope, with between **10 and 20 million people at risk of starvation,** 2 million of whom are children under the age of four. With an ever-growing population and food insecurity a constant threat, the area of land being used to grow crops has trebled over the past 50 years. More farmers are **choosing to grow crops rather than to herd animals.**

With such a high demand for food, farmers are **unable to leave the land fallow** for a year, meaning the soil is **unable to recover its lost nutrients.** Most farmers in the region are **unable to afford artificial fertilisers** to replenish the soil's lost nutrients. Cattle dung, traditionally used as a fertiliser, is used as a substitute for fuel. This means that the **soil becomes less fertile** with each passing growing season. Farmers who used **loans to pay for fertilisers** were forced to use all the **money earned from growing crops** to **repay their debts.**

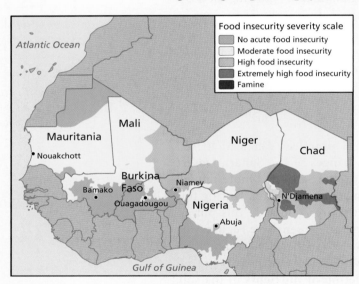

Food insecurity severity scale
- No acute food insecurity
- Moderate food insecurity
- High food insecurity
- Extremely high food insecurity
- Famine

Fig. 28.15 Food insecurity in the Sahel

The growth of cash crops has led to **monoculture developing,** which rapidly depletes the same nutrients from soil. Eventually the soil becomes **useless and barren.** The exposed topsoil is carried away by winds, leading to **desertification.**

Economic Activity and Climate Change

Manufacturing industry can damage biomes in a number of ways, such as by causing acid rain, air and water pollution and altering the climate through the release of **greenhouse gases. Climate change** is a serious threat to the hot desert biomes. High levels of **fossil fuel use,** especially from industrially developed countries, have been linked to **increased drought in the Sahel.** Climate change has caused a **rise in the temperature** of the atmosphere, which has **changed the pattern of rainfall** in the Sahel. As a result of the increased temperature, the air can **hold more water vapour,** meaning **precipitation is less likely** to occur. The seasonal rains are becoming less reliable, meaning that **droughts** are becoming **more frequent and lasting longer.** Rainfall levels in the Sahel have **decreased** by as much as **30 per cent** over the past 25 years (from 720 mm to 440 mm per year). Even in years where the rains do arrive, it is not uncommon for them to arrive over a month late or to last a shorter period of time.

Increased drought has led to increased **food shortages, loss of livestock** and increased use of **contaminated water.** Higher temperatures lead to increased evaporation and reduced condensation, causing a **drop in the water table** as wells, rivers and lakes dry up. The summer of **2012** saw one of the most **severe droughts** in the history of the Sahel. The drought mainly affected the west of the region. **Cereal harvests fell** by over **25 per cent,** which left over 15 million people facing starvation. As of 2016, drought continues to devastate the region. The rate of desertification continues to increase, with over **80 per cent of the region's soils** now experiencing **degradation.** One of the most devastating impacts of this has been the **shrinking of Lake Chad,** which is a vital water source for the surrounding countries. As climate change continues to raise temperatures and reduce rainfall in the region, it is likely that **increased desertification** will occur.

The disappearance of Lake Chad

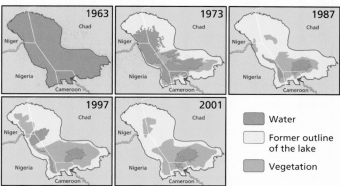

Fig. 28.16 The disappearance of Lake Chad

Deforestation

Much of the Sahel was **once covered in trees and bushes,** most of which have now been removed to make way for settlement, agricultural land or to be used as firewood.

Firewood is an important resource in the Sahel, as it is used for cooking and heat. It is the **only fuel source** as there are no fossil fuels such as oil and gas. High **population growth of over 3 per cent per annum** means that there is an ever-**growing demand for fuel,** which has led to widespread deforestation. This can be particularly seen in expanding cities such as Khartoum in Sudan, which has cleared all its forests within 100 km of the city. In **Mali** alone, over **500 000 acres of forestry have been cleared,** at a rate 30 times faster than they

Fig. 28.17 Deforestation damages soil structure.

can be replaced. In many parts of the Sahel, cutting down and selling trees has become **more profitable than agriculture,** which leads to illegal logging. As a result of deforestation, the frequency of dust storms has greatly increased. The **Sahara advances** into the region at a rate of 5–10 km per year.

FACT

The city of Las Vegas is located in the Nevada Desert in the US. It is now famous for tourism, sporting events and casinos. However, during the 1950s and 1960s tourists flocked to the town to watch the military testing of nuclear weapons from a 'safe' distance.

Human Interference in the Sahel	
Poor agricultural practices	Overgrazing: fringes of Sahara Desert, attracted more nomadic farmers, increasing strain on environmentally sensitive region, continually grazed, rapid depletion of nutrients, fertility greatly reduced, vegetation cover more sparse, graze marginal lands, sedentary farming, structure damaged, soil becoming drier and finer, soil erosion, capillary action – salinisation and calcification, toxic for vegetation, exposed to intense heat of sun, winds remove topsoil, merges into the Sahara Desert
	Overcropping: rapid increase in population, 10–20 million at risk of starvation, choosing to grow crops rather than herd animals, unable to leave the land fallow, unable to recover lost nutrients, unable to afford artificial fertilisers, soil becomes less fertile, loans to pay for fertilisers, money earned from growing crops repay debts, grow cash crops, monoculture developing, useless and barren, desertification
Economic activity and climate change	Manufacturing industry, greenhouse gases, climate change, fossil fuel use, increased drought in Sahel, changed pattern of rainfall, rise in temperature, hold more water vapour, precipitation less likely, droughts more frequent and lasting longer, rainfall decreased by 30%, food shortages, loss of livestock, contaminated water, drop in water table, 2012 severe drought, cereal harvests fell 25%, 80% of the region's soils degraded, shrinking of Lake Chad, increased desertification
Deforestation	Once covered in trees and bushes, firewood only fuel supply, high population growth 3% per annum, growing demand for fuel, widespread deforestation, Mali 500 000 acres of forestry, more profitable than agriculture, Sahara advances 5–10 km per year

ACTIVE LEARNING

1. What is meant by the term 'monoculture'?
2. Why were nomadic farmers attracted to the Sahel during the 1930s–60s?
3. How does overcropping lead to desertification?
4. Why does such a high level of deforestation occur in the Sahel?
5. How has the industrial use of fossil fuels led to increased desertification?
6. Search online for 'the disappearance of Lake Chad' for more information on desertification caused by human interference.

EXAM QUESTIONS

HIGHER LEVEL

1. Examine, with reference to one biome that you have studied, how plants and animals have adapted to specific climatic and soil conditions.

   2015 Q18 80M

2. With reference to one biome that you have studied, account for the type of climate experienced in this biome and explain how this climate impacts on soils and vegetation within the biome.

   2014 Q17 80M

3. The development of economic activities can alter biomes. Discuss this statement with reference to appropriate examples that you have studied.

   2011 Q18 80M

Common Marking Scheme for Geoecology Questions		
Marks awarded	Discussing 3 aspects	Discussing 4 aspects
Total marks for each aspect	27m + 27m + 26m	20m + 20m + 20m + 20m
Identifying an aspect	4m each	4m each
Examination of each aspect	8 SRPs @ 2m each	6 SRPs @ 2m each
Overall coherence	7/6m per aspect	4m per aspect

The section deals with human interaction with the desert biome. I have included a 'structure sheet' which will help you to plan your Geoecology answers. Many students try to learn off sample answers. This can take a long time and forgetting one sentence can lead to a person forgetting all of the sentences that follow it. It is always better to focus on understanding key words. Try using the structure sheet to write your own answer to the question.

HIGHER LEVEL

EXAM QUESTION

Biomes are altered by human activity. Discuss.

2014 Q18 80M

Marking Scheme
3 aspects 27 + 27 + 26
Aspect named 3 @ 4m each
Each aspect 8 SRPs @ 2m each
Overall cohesion 7m/7m/6m

Remember, you can also discuss the positive impacts of human interaction with biomes. This structure sheet deals with three aspects, but you can also include soil conservation methods as a fourth aspect.

Your knowledge of human interaction with the Sahel region in the final section of Chapter 9 Mass Movement and in Chapter 27 Soils will help here.

It is not merely enough to describe how humans interact, but also the effects of their interaction.

The aspects discussed for this structure sheet follow a logical order:

1. Deforestation to make way for agricultural land
2. Overgrazing as the population of the Sahel and its herd size increased
3. Farmers securing loans and growing crops which led to further soil degradation

While it is not necessary to write in this specific order, it does make sense to do so as one leads on to the other.

Structure Sheet		
Aspect 1: Deforestation	**Aspect 2: Overgrazing**	**Aspect 3: Overcropping**
Cutting down and clearing forestry	1930–1970s increased rainfall	Increased population – demand for food
Firewood for cooking and heat	Cattle herds doubled – increased strain	Land used for crops trebled in 50 years
3% population growth per annum	Competition for land – depletion of nutrients	Land not left fallow
Khartoum in Sudan – 100 km radius	Loss of soil fertility – grass scarce	Soils become infertile
Mali – 500 000 acres – 30 times faster than replaced	Sedentary farming – continually grazed	Fertilisers not used – dung for fuel
Prevents soil erosion	Soil structure damaged – compaction from hooves	Debt relief – cash crops
Deciduous leaves – plant litter	Boreholes and wells sunk – water depletion	Monoculture
Dust storms and loss of fertility	Salinisation and calcification – increased dust storms	

Note that these are not SRPs, but act as SRP 'cues'. This method should improve your understanding of the topic. When you have chosen your key points, practise writing your answer with the aid of your notes and this book. You will gradually become more comfortable with the topic and eventually find that you need only these cues to write the answer.

TOPIC MAP

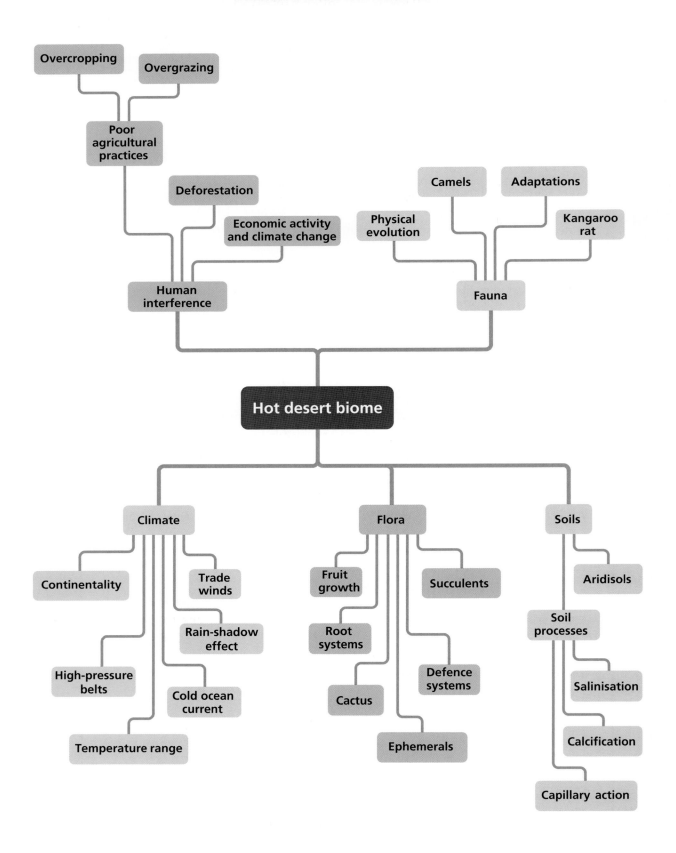

Tropical Rainforest Biome

In this chapter, we will look at the tropical rainforest biome – a unique natural world feature that is distinct due to its climate, flora, fauna and soil. It is important that you fully understand how the climate controls the development of the biome and how human activities have influenced it.

> **Note!**
> You must study either this chapter or Chapter 28 Hot Desert Biome.

KEY WORDS

- Biome
- Amazon Rainforest
- Interdependent
- Climate
- Convectional rain
- Humidity
- Evaporation
- Trade winds
- Tropical red soils
- Latosols

- Leaching
- Nutrient cycle
- Laterite
- Flora
- Fauna
- Emergent layer
- Canopy layer
- Understorey layer
- Shrub layer
- Forest floor layer

- Adaptation
- Deforestation
- Ranching
- Cash crops
- Mining
- Hydroelectric power
- Blast furnaces
- Yanomami

LEARNING OUTCOMES

What you MUST know
- The four main characteristics of the tropical rainforest biome
- How climate controls the development of soil, flora and fauna
- How all characteristics of a biome are interdependent
- Human interaction with the Amazon

What you SHOULD know
- The details of the chart indicating the interdependency of the tropical rainforest biome

What is USEFUL to know
- Up-to-date information regarding conservation efforts in the Amazon

Introduction

Biomes are **unique natural world regions**, which are **controlled by climate**. All biomes can be divided into four main components: **climate, soil, flora** and **fauna**. These are all **interdependent**, meaning that they all rely on and are influenced by each other.

The Interdependency of Biomes

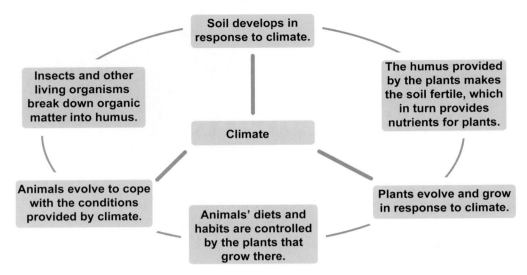

Soil develops in response to climate.

Insects and other living organisms break down organic matter into humus.

The humus provided by the plants makes the soil fertile, which in turn provides nutrients for plants.

Climate

Animals evolve to cope with the conditions provided by climate.

Animals' diets and habits are controlled by the plants that grow there.

Plants evolve and grow in response to climate.

Climograph for Manaus

○ Temperature in °C   ▬ Rainfall (in mm)

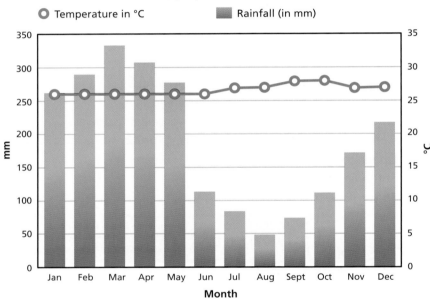

Fig. 29.1 Using the graph, identify the wet and dry seasons

Climate is the most important factor controlling the characteristics of a biome. Climate determines:

- What soil develops
- What plant grows
- What animals live there

The **tropical rainforest biome** lies in the tropics (the Tropic of Cancer to the Tropic of Capricorn). Tropical rainforests can be found in **Central America, South America, Africa** and **Australasia**.

The **largest tropical rainforest** is located in South America in the **Amazon Basin**. In Africa, tropical rainforests are found along the west and centre of the continent. A dense tropical rainforest lies in the eastern half of Madagascar, which has the world's most diverse range of animals and plant life. This **diversity of life** is accredited to the island's remoteness. This has allowed new plants and animals to evolve on the island which have not evolved elsewhere in the world.

Due to the continued felling of rainforest trees, they now only cover 6 per cent of the Earth's land surface.

In this chapter, we will look at the characteristics of the Amazon Rainforest and the impact human interference has had on the rainforest.

Fig. 29.2 Heavy rainfall in the Amazon

29.1 Characteristics of the Amazon Rainforest

Climate

The climate of the Amazon, like all rainforests, is **wet, humid and hot** all year round. Temperatures average **27 °C per annum** and there is a very **small annual temperature range** of just **2 °C**. Therefore, the Amazon does not experience any notable seasonal change. The difference between daytime and night-time temperatures (diurnal range) is greater than seasonal change.

Daytime temperatures occasionally reach **more than 35 °C. Night-time temperatures rarely drop below 24 °C**. This gives the Amazon a **diurnal temperature range** of approximately **11 °C**.

The hot temperatures are caused by the **direct angle of the sun,** which **concentrates its heat** over a small area. As the sun is directly overhead, days are long, with the sun shining for **12 hours for all 365 days of the year**. Due to the **humidity,** the region often seems even hotter. Relative humidity often reaches **77–88 per cent**. This humidity comes from **intense rainfall, evaporation** and **transpiration**. There is constant **cloud cover,** which **acts** as a **blanket,** keeping conditions humid throughout the night also.

Rainfall is frequent in the Amazon, with approximately **200 rainy days per year**. Rain usually falls in **torrential convectional downpours**. Over **2000 mm** of **precipitation** occurs in the region each year. More than half of this precipitation is formed due to the **intense heat which evaporates water** from the soil and vegetation.

The **north-east** and **south-east trade winds meet** at the equator and rise upwards, creating a **low-pressure belt**. As the sun's heat causes the **moisture-laden air** to rise, it **condenses,** leading to the **formation of thick clouds**. Convectional **thunderstorms** form, leading to **torrential rainfall**.

Soil

Latosols, commonly known as **tropical red soils,** are the **zonal soil** that develops throughout tropical rainforests. Due to the **hot, humid conditions** of the Amazon, **chemical weathering of parent material is rapid,** leading to **deep soils forming**. In some areas, latosols are in excess of 30 m deep. Despite the vast amount of vegetation that covers

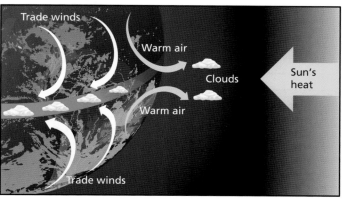

Fig. 29.3 Low pressure forms at the equator leading to high levels of condensation, resulting in torrential rainfall.

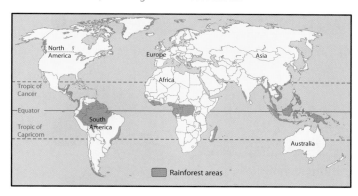

Fig. 29.4 Distribution of tropical rainforests

ACTIVE LEARNING

1. What is meant by the term 'interdependent'?
2. Why are temperatures in the Amazon so high throughout the year?
3. What two winds are responsible for low pressure at the equator?
4. Explain how rainfall forms at the equator.

tropical rainforest, **latosols are generally infertile** if they do not have a supply of plant litter.

As **heavy rainfall** filters down from the canopy to the floor of the rainforest, **leaching occurs**. The rainwater **washes away nutrients** from the A horizon to the B/C horizons, beyond the reach of most plant roots. Only **iron oxide and aluminium oxide** escape the leaching process and build up in the soil over time. The presence of these two minerals gives the soil a **red colour**.

The **texture** of latosols **depends on the parent rock** it is derived from. The formation of a hardpan also leads to marshy areas and swamp developing over time.

The soil's ability to support such a wide diversity of vegetation is due to the **large supply of humus** from **decaying plant and animal litter** on the floor. Due to the warm, humid conditions, microorganisms, such as **bacteria and fungi**, thrive and **quickly break down organic matter into humus**. The humus is **quickly absorbed by the roots of plants** so it **does not accumulate in the soil**. This quick recycling of plant litter means that there is a 'short' nutrient cycle as it only takes a few days for organic matter to be converted into humus and absorbed. This self-sufficient system is very **delicately balanced**. If the **vegetation** that covers it is **removed**, the soil loses its supply of humus and **quickly becomes infertile**. The removal of vegetation exposes the soil to the intense heat from the sunlight directly overhead and causes the soil to bake into **laterite**.

Fig. 29.5 Laterite is so hard it can be used for building houses and roads.

Fig. 29.6 Latosol soil profile

ACTIVE **LEARNING**

1. What is a zonal soil?
2. Describe any three characteristics of latosols.
3. Why is chemical weathering so rapid in the Amazon?
4. What is meant by the term 'short nutrient cycle'?
5. What factors would cause laterite to form?

Flora

The natural vegetation of the Amazon is **rainforest or 'jungle'**. The climate of the Amazon is ideal for **rapid plant growth**. The constant **high temperature** and the **frequent rainfall** create **humid conditions** in which plants thrive. As a result, the rainforest has a **larger biodiversity** than all other biomes in the world. Mahogany, teak and palm oil are just some of the **highly specialised plants** and trees that grow there. The climate accommodates **plant growth throughout the year**, which means that fruit and flowers are present all year.

To avoid competition with each other for sunlight, moisture and nutrients, plants have adapted to the climate by developing a unique **five-layered structure** shown in the table.

Emergent layer	This is the highest layer of rainforest vegetation, containing tall trees such as mahogany. This layer is usually between 40 and 70 m high, and receives the most sunlight.
	Adaptations: The trees in this layer do not sprout leaves until they are 30 m high as there is little sunlight for photosynthesis below that height. As it is exposed to direct sunlight and breezes, there is less humidity in this layer, so their leaves are smaller and waxy. This prevents them from drying out due to intense heat and warm winds. Emergent trees have shallow buttress roots which fan out over a wide area to absorb as much water and nutrients as possible.
Canopy layer	The canopy layer is underneath the emergent layer and is between 30 and 40 m high. Growing in this layer are vines and epiphytes, which are tree-living plants, i.e. plants that grow off other plants.
	Adaptations: Leaves in this layer are large to trap as much light as possible. Like the emergent trees, canopy trees have shallow buttress roots so that they can quickly absorb nutrients from the O horizon. In order to support tall tree growth, the roots fan out over the surface to cover as wide an area as possible. This root system also acts as an anchor and prevents the trees from being blown down. Canopy leaves have 'drip tips' to shed heavy rainfall, which could otherwise break their branches.
Understorey layer	The understorey layer is the middle layer, which grow to heights of 15–30 m.
	Adaptations: The trees have very large leaves to capture as much sunlight as possible as it is quite dark.
Shrub layer	The layer has tall non-flowering shrubs, ferns, small trees and vines that grow to heights of between 5 and 15 m.
	Adaptations: The area receives very little sunlight so plants have very large leaves to capture as much light as possible. Some young trees 'lie in waiting' here. When a larger canopy or understorey tree falls or dies, the young tree quickly grows in order to take advantage of the space and light.
Forest floor layer	The forest floor rises from the floor to 5 m high. Only 1–3% of sunlight reaches this layer. As a result of this darkness, very few plants grow here unless a tree falls and makes a clearing. Where this occurs, sunlight can reach the floor clearly and encourage rapid growth.
	Adaptations: The plants have large leaves to capture as much sunlight as possible.

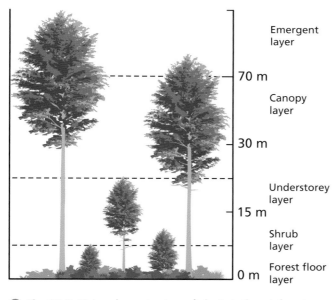

Fig. 29.7 Unique layer structure of plants in the rainforest

Fig. 29.8 Buttress roots spread out over a wide area, providing nutrients and support.

Fig. 29.9 Drip tip leaves are designed to shed water.

Fig. 29.10 The forest floor receives only 1–3 per cent of the sunlight.

ACTIVE LEARNING

1. Why is the climate of the tropical rainforest so suited to the growth of thick vegetation?
2. Describe fully how flora/vegetation has adapted to the climate of the tropical rainforest.
3. Explain the following terms: (a) buttress roots (b) drip tips.

Fig. 29.11 The toucan's strong beak allows it to break the shells of nuts that grow on canopy trees.

Fauna

The tropical rainforest is home to a **diverse range of animal life.** In the Amazon Rainforest alone, there are nearly 30 million species of insect, 1600 species of bird and 2500 species of fish.

Different tropical rainforests contain different species of animal that have become **specialised in their environment.** For example:

- Gorillas are found in the African Rainforest only.
- Orangutans are found in Indonesian Rainforest only.
- Jaguars are found in South American Rainforests only.

Each animal in the rainforest has **adapted to its environment** through **diet, living habits** and **body structure. The canopy layer** attracts **birds** due to its wide variety of **fruit, seeds and flowers.** The birds eat the seeds, before dispersing them throughout the rainforest. The most common birds found in the Amazon are **parrots, toucans** and **eagles.** Birds nest in the trees of the **canopy** and emergent layers due to the plentiful supply of fruit and **protection against predators.**

Fig. 29.12 The flying squirrel has flaps of skin that allow it to glide from tree to tree.

Like birds, many other animals in tropical rainforest **live in specific layers,** eating the specific food that grows there. By living, eating and breeding in these layers only, animals **avoid coming into competition** with each other. Other animals that live in the canopy layers of the forest are **monkeys and squirrels.** Many plants depend on **animals eating their fruit** in order to **pollinate.**

Monkeys have adapted to the canopy by developing **muscular tails** which allow them to **hang off branches** while they reach for food. Their **arms are long,** which allow them to **reach out and grab branches** as they move from tree to tree. The **flying squirrel** is an animal that has evolved to its **arboreal life.** It has evolved **flaps of skin** between its front and back legs, allowing it to **glide for long distances** between trees. This helps it to **escape predators** such as tree snakes. Most flying squirrels never touch the ground during their whole lifetime.

Sloths are one of the best-known animals found in the canopy of the rainforest. Sloths **eat fruits, leaves and twigs** and spend years hanging upside-down on the same tree. Sloths are so slow moving that algae grow on them, giving them a green camouflage. They have a very **slow metabolism** and **need** very **little food** to survive. Sloths are **nocturnal,** and spend most of the day **curled up to disguise themselves** from predators such as the jaguar.

Larger animals, such as the **jaguar,** live on the **forest floor.** The jaguar has adapted to the rainforest environment to become one of the biome's deadliest **hunters.** The jaguar has **long retractable claws** that allow it to 'run' up trees and make escape difficult for its prey. Its long **tail provides balance** for climbing up trees and **acts as a brake** to help it to quickly change direction. The jaguar has a **spotted coat,** which allows it to **blend**

FACT

It is estimated that each 6 km² of rainforest contains 400 species of bird, 150 species of butterfly, 100 species of reptile and 60 species of amphibian.

GEO DICTIONARY

Arboreal: living in trees

Metabolism: the chemical processes that keep things alive, e.g. digestion

Camouflage: the ability to disguise or blend into surroundings

Nocturnal: being mainly active at night

Predator: an animal that hunts and eats other animals

into the vegetation of the dark shadows of the forest floor. This effective **camouflage** makes it easier to stalk prey.

Animals also inhabit the **swamp, marshland and rivers** of the Amazon. The most famous examples include **crocodiles and piranhas,** both of which are vicious predators.

The Amazon is also home to a diverse collection of **amphibians** (frogs and toads), **reptiles** (snakes and lizards), **insects** (ants, beetles, butterflies) and **arachnids** (spiders). Many of these species have developed unique ways to protect themselves from predators. **Camouflage** is the **most common adaptation.** Many spiders, frogs and insects are **green or brown** to blend in with vegetation. Some frogs use the opposite approach and are **brightly coloured** to inform potential predators that they are **venomous.** Some **butterflies** have developed **large 'eye' patterns** on their wings to **fool predators** into thinking they are looking at the head of a large animal rather than a defenceless insect.

Leafcutter ants are capable of climbing tall trees and cutting out small **pieces of leaves** that are roughly **50 times their own weight,** before carrying them back to their nest. The ants bury the leaves in the ground and cover them with their saliva, causing them to grow a **fungus** which is the **sole food** for these ants.

▲ **Fig. 29.13** Camouflage is the most common adaptation in the rainforest. Can you spot the insect, which is the shape and colour of a leaf?

GEO DICTIONARY

Venomous: poisonous

 ACTIVE LEARNING

1. What is meant by the term 'arboreal'?
2. In what way have sloths and monkeys adapted to the tropical biome?
3. What adaptations have made the jaguar an effective hunter?
4. Describe how animals disguise themselves in the vegetation of the rainforest. What is this called?

▲ **Fig. 29.14** The blue dart poison frog is one of the most venomous animals in the world.

 EDUCATE YOURSELF

	Characteristics of the Amazon Rainforest
Climate	Wet, humid, hot, average 27 °C per annum, low annual temperature range 2 °C, night-time temperatures rarely below 24 °C, daytime temperatures occasionally exceed 35 °C, diurnal temperature range 11 °C, direct angle of sun, concentrated heat, 12 hours, 365 days of the year, humidity and 77–88%, intense rainfall, evaporation, transpiration, cloud cover acts as blanket, 200 rainy days a year, torrential convectional downpours, 2000 mm of precipitation, intense heat evaporates water, north-east and south-east trade winds meet, low-pressure belt, moisture-laden air, condenses, formation of thick clouds, thunderstorms, torrential rainfall
Soil	Tropical red soil, zonal soil, hot humid conditions, rapid chemical weathering of parent material, deep soils forming, latosols generally infertile, heavy rainfall, leaching occurs, washes away nutrients, iron oxide and aluminium oxide, red/yellow, texture depends on parent material, large supply of humus, decaying plant and animal litter, bacteria and fungi, quickly breaks down organic matter into humus, quickly absorbed by plant roots, does not accumulate in soil, short nutrient cycle, delicately balanced, if vegetation removed quickly becomes infertile, baked into laterite

	Rainforest or jungle, rapid plant growth, high temperature, frequent rainfall, humid conditions, larger biodiversity, highly specialised plants, plant growth throughout the year, five-layered structure
Flora	Emergent layer: highest layer, tall trees, 40–70 m, do not sprout leaves below 30 m as little sunlight for photosynthesis, exposed to direct sunlight, less humidity, leaves small and waxy, prevents them from drying, shallow buttress roots
	Canopy layer: underneath emergent layer, 30–40 m, leaves large, trap light, shallow buttress roots, absorb nutrients from O horizon, cover wide areas, 'drip tips'
	Understorey layer: 15–30 m, very large leaves, capture as much sunlight as possible
	Shrub layer: non-flowering shrubs, 5–15 m, very little sunlight, large leaves
	Forest floor layer: floor to 5 m, 1–3% of sunlight, very few plants grow here
Fauna	Wide diversity of animal life, specialised in environment, adapted diet, living habits and body structure, canopy layer – birds, fruit, seeds and flowers, animals eat fruit seeds – pollination, parrots, toucans and eagles, canopy – protection against predators, animals live in specific layer, avoid competition
	Monkeys – muscular tails, hang off branches, long arms, reach out and grab branches, flying squirrel – flaps of skin, glides from tree to tree, escape predators
	Sloths: eat fruits, leaves and twigs, slow metabolism, very little food, nocturnal, curl up to disguise themselves
	Jaguar: larger animal, forest floor, hunter, long retractable claws, tail provides balance and acts as brake, spotted coat, blends into vegetation, camouflage
	Swamp, marshland and rivers: crocodiles, piranhas, amphibians, reptiles, insects, arachnids, camouflage most common adaptation, green or brown, brightly coloured – venomous, butterflies large 'eye' patterns fool predators, leafcutter ants, pieces of leaves 50 times their weight, fungus – sole food

29.2 Human Interference

Fig. 29.15 Slash and burn in the Amazon

During the **1970s,** the Brazilian government was desperately **trying to attract industry.** The Government allowed **MNCs** to **exploit** the Amazon's vast bank of **natural resources.** Rapid population growth in Brazil has also interfered with the Amazon as **areas** were **cleared for settlement.** As a result, there are very few parts of the rainforest that remain unaltered by human activity. The Amazon is considered to be the 'lungs' of our planet.

Roughly **20 per cent of the world's oxygen** is supplied by the Amazon Rainforest. Trees **absorb carbon dioxide** (CO_2) and release oxygen. The destruction of rainforests not only destroys this oxygen, but also allows CO_2 into the atmosphere. The removal of the forest destroys an important **carbon sink.**

A-Z GEO **DICTIONARY**

Carbon sink: a forest, ocean or natural environment that absorbs more carbon than it releases

Trees absorb CO_2, which means it is not released into the atmosphere. Deforestation means there are fewer, if any, trees to absorb the CO_2. Instead the gas stays in the atmosphere, which contributes to climate change.

Any major changes to the biome impact, not only the Brazilian people, but the entire world. The major impacts of human activity on the rainforests include:

- Deforestation
- Intensive agriculture practices
- Industrial activity
- Settlement

Deforestation

Since the Brazilian government opened up the rainforest for exploitation, roughly **20 per cent of the Amazon has been felled.** It is now about 5.5 million km². In the **short term,** the destruction of rainforests is **economically beneficial,** but the **long-term** effects of deforestation are **overwhelmingly negative. Logging** is the **main form** of **deforestation** in Brazil. Despite improved techniques and a **greater international awareness** of the need to protect rainforests, unsustainable logging continues. The Brazilian government estimates that **75 per cent of all logging** in the Amazon is **illegal.**

⊙ **Fig. 29.16** Deforestation in the Amazon has had devastating effects.

In the late 1990s, the growing **Asian economies** had depleted most of their own timber supplies. Asian logging companies **bought large areas** of the **Amazon** for a low price. Further **deforestation** occurred to **supply timber** for the global **construction** boom of the 1990s and 2000s. Valuable timbers are felled for wood and unwanted trees are also cleared.

Effects of Logging/Deforestation

Deforestation leads to the **loss of plants and animals** and insect species as their habitats are destroyed. This is referred to as a **loss of biodiversity.** All aspects of the rainforest are **interdependent,** meaning that the removal of one aspect destroys the remaining parts of the biome. When trees are cut down, birds lose their home and source of food. This leads to the decline, and in some cases, extinction of species. As the birds helped to pollinate the trees by eating their seeds, the trees decline even further.

⊙ **Fig. 29.17** Areas of deforestation in the Amazon

Deforestation leads to a **loss of soil fertility** and an **increase in soil erosion.** When the canopy of the rainforest is removed, the soil is **exposed to the climate.** Torrential **rainfall removes topsoil** in rivers of mud. As the water percolates through the soil, **intense leaching** occurs (known as **laterisation**). The **lack of plant litter,** which was once supplied by the trees, means that **humus is no longer formed** in the O horizon, reducing the soil's fertility. The **intense sunlight** evaporates the water from the ground, leading to the **baking of the soil** into a hard, impermeable **laterite** soil during the dry season.

Evapotranspiration:
water that is evaporated
from the soil and vegetation
into the atmosphere

The Amazon produces roughly **half of its own rainfall,** as plant transpiration is evaporated into the atmosphere. This is known as **evapotranspiration.** When the number of **trees** in the Amazon is greatly **reduced,** there is not enough moisture evaporated to produce heavy rainfall. Instead, **trees dries out and die.**

Rainforests contain over **50 per cent of the world's plant species,** much of which may have **medicinal benefits.** Roughly **25 per cent of the world's medicine** is derived from plants that grow in tropical rainforests such as the Amazon. Less than **1 per cent of all plant species** in the world have been **tested** for their medicinal value. As more and more species of plants become extinct, so too are possible cures for serious diseases.

ACTIVE **LEARNING**

1. Why did logging increase in the Amazon from the 1970s onwards?
2. What is meant by the term 'laterisation'?
3. Describe three negative effects of deforestation in the Amazon.

EDUCATE YOURSELF

Deforestation		
1970s Brazil, trying to attract industry, MNCs exploit natural resources, areas cleared for settlement, Amazon 5.5 million km²; 20% world's oxygen, absorb CO_2, carbon sink		
Logging	20% of Amazon felled, short term economically beneficial, long term overwhelmingly negative, logging main form of deforestation, greater international awareness, 75% of logging illegal, Asian companies bought large areas of Amazon, deforestation – supply timber, construction boom	
Effects	Loss of soil fertility, increase in soil erosion, exposed to climate, rainfall removes topsoil, intense leaching, laterisation, lack of plant litter, humus no longer formed, intense sunlight, baking of soil, laterite; half its own rainfall, evapotranspiration, trees reduced, no longer enough, trees dry out and die; 50% world's plant species, medicinal benefits, 25% of medicine, 1% of plant species tested	

Intensive Agricultural Practices

Fig. 29.18 Abandoned land formerly used for ranching. Note the hard, blocky appearance of the soil.

Cattle ranching was responsible for the **majority of deforestation** that occurred in the Amazon from the 1960s to the 1980s. **Seventy-five per cent of deforested areas** are now used for **cattle pasture.** An increased **demand for beef** in the 1980s led to more **intense deforestation** as trees were cleared by MNCs for ranching. **Slash and burn** was the technique used to remove trees.

This method was very unproductive, as many of the trees that were **burned** were **valuable hardwoods** that could have been sold. Instead, trees for industry and timber were cut down elsewhere, meaning the rate of deforestation was much higher than it needed to be. Brazil is one of the **largest producers of beef** in the world, with the government on target to **double beef production** between 2014 and **2018.**

This target seems to be in direct opposition to the government's **aim of reducing the rate of deforestation** in the Amazon.

Cash crops are widely grown in Brazil as a means of paying off its **international debt**. **Soya bean** is the most widely grown cash crop in Brazil, which is then exported to the US and UK as animal feed. This crop was originally grown in the south and south-east of the country, but **increase in global demand** has seen production move north to the **Amazon Basin**. Genetically modified soya bean seed was created in Brazil that made it suitable to grow in the Amazon's climate. This **intensive growth** has led to Brazil becoming the **second-largest producer** of soya bean in the world.

Environmental Consequences

Typically, **rainforest is first cleared** for **ranching** before being **sold on to soya bean producers**. Huge amounts of **artificial fertiliser** are required to make the soil **fertile enough for arable** agriculture. Cattle ranchers then move further into the Amazon, clearing vegetation for **new pastoral land**. This intensive agriculture has very serious **environmental consequences**.

🔺 **Fig. 29.19** Head to head: two soya bean plantations meet two remaining edges of rainforest

- Slash-and-burn techniques **destroy the ecosystems** as plants and animals are destroyed. By removing the natural vegetation, the **nutrient cycle is stopped**. As plant litter no longer falls on the ground, the **soil becomes infertile** within a few years.

- Clearing new land in the Amazon is **cheaper for farmers** than using **artificial fertilisers** to keep the land they already have fertile. As a result, **land is abandoned** and new areas of forest are cleared. The **abandoned soil** is left **exposed to the climate** and is baked into an **impermeable laterite soil**.

- The abandoned **soil** is quickly **eroded by the torrential rain** and **washed away** into the region's rivers. The **increased load** causes rivers to rise and **flood** surrounding areas of lowland forest, further **damaging the natural ecosystem**.

EDUCATE YOURSELF

Intensive Agricultural Practices	
Cattle ranching	Majority of deforestation, 75% of deforested areas cattle pasture, demand for beef, intense deforestation, slash and burn, burned valuable hardwoods, one of largest producers of beef, doubling beef production by 2018, at odds with aim of reducing rate of deforestation
Cash crops	International debt, soya bean, increase in global demand, Amazon Basin, intensive growth – second-largest producer, rainforest first cleared for ranching, sold on to soya bean producers, artificial fertiliser for arable, land now sold, new pastoral land
Environmental consequences	Destroy ecosystems, nutrient cycle stopped, soil becomes infertile, cheaper for farmers to clear new land than use artificial fertilisers, land abandoned, abandoned soil exposed to the climate, impermeable laterite soil, soil eroded by torrential rain, washed away, river increased load – flooding, damaging natural ecosystem

GEO DICTIONARY

Genetically modified: living things with genetic material that has been artificially altered so as to produce a desired characteristic, e.g. drought resistant crops

ACTIVE LEARNING

1. What is meant by the term 'slash and burn' and why is it considered unproductive?

2. Describe three consequences of intensive farming in the Amazon.

OPTION 7 CHAPTER 29

Industrial Activity

As Brazil becomes more industrialised, the **demand for raw materials has increased.** The Amazon Basin has a wealth of **valuable raw materials** for industry, leading to the increased exploitation of the region over the past 30 years. The main destructive industrial activities include:

- Mining
- Hydroelectric power
- Blast furnaces

Fig. 29.20 Deforestation at the site of a bauxite mine

Mining

The Amazon Basin has large deposits of valuable materials such as iron ore, gold, bauxite and diamonds, which has led to increased exploitation of the area. Mining is extremely **destructive to the rainforest** for a number of reasons:

- In order to mine an area in the rainforest, **large areas are cleared** through the forest to **gain access** to the proposed site of the mine.

- Areas of forest are cleared to provide **temporary housing for the mine workers.** Land is also cleared to make way for pipelines and other machinery.

- Fewer trees are felled by mining operations than activities such as cattle ranching. However, the **roads** which are constructed to transport material from the mine give **illegal loggers better access** to the rainforest. This leads to increased deforestation.

- **Environmental regulations** are not as strict in Brazil as they should be. **Toxic materials** such as lead and mercury have been washed into the region's rivers. This has led to **water pollution,** which has **damaged aquatic ecosystems** and contaminated the food chain in the region. Many native **tribes** have been **wiped out** as a result of pollution to their **water supply.**

- **Indigenous people** have been **forced to abandon their homes** in places where valuable raw materials have been found. Much of this displacement has been as a result of illegal mining operations threatening the native people until they move. In many cases, **native people have been murdered** to intimidate others into cooperating.

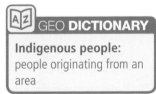

GEO DICTIONARY

Indigenous people:
people originating from an area

Hydroelectric Power (HEP)

Roughly **79 per cent of Brazil's electricity** is produced by HEP, although two-thirds of the country's hydroelectric potential remains untapped. The country has 158 HEP plants in operation, with a further 48 dams planned to be built by 2020. Thirty of these dams are located in the Amazon Rainforest. While HEP is seen as a clean energy, it has had negative effects on the Amazon's ecosystem.

An example of this is the **Balbina Dam** near Manaus, which **flooded 2400 km² of rainforest,** but failed to

Fig. 29.21 The effects of the Balbina Dam

produce any significant electricity. Instead, the reservoir became a **stagnant swamp** and a **methane 'factory'**.

Despite generating carbon-free electricity, HEP dams produce **huge amounts of carbon dioxide** and **methane gas**. This occurs as dam construction **floods** large areas of **uncleared rainforest**. The **vegetation** is **submerged in water and rots**, releasing previously absorbed carbon dioxide. As trees and plants rot, they **produce methane gas** which builds up before eventually being **released into the atmosphere**.

The flooding of large areas also leads to the **displacement of populations,** especially the indigenous tribes of the area. Their **culture** and **way of life are destroyed** and, in many cases, they are not properly compensated.

Blast Furnaces

The **Carajás region** in Brazil has close to **50 blast furnaces,** which have destroyed **75 per cent of its forests**. With forest running out, **illegal logging** has occurred in **conservation areas** and **indigenous lands**. The law now states that **80 per cent of the forest** must be **left untouched,** but this law is **not enforced,** resulting in large-scale destruction of the Amazon.

Fig. 29.22 Blast furnaces release greenhouse gases into the atmosphere and cause widespread deforestation.

EDUCATE YOURSELF

Industrial Activity		
Demand for raw materials increased, valuable raw materials		
Mining	Destructive to the rainforest, large areas cleared to gain access, temporary housing for miners, roads – easier access illegal loggers, environmental regulations, toxic materials, water pollution, damaged aquatic ecosystems, tribes destroyed, drink contaminated water, indigenous people forced to abandon homes, have been murdered	
Hydroelectric power (HEP)	79% Brazil's electricity, Balbina Dam flooded 2400 km² of rainforest, stagnant swamp, methane factory, huge amounts of carbon dioxide and methane gas, floods uncleared rainforest, vegetation submerged in water and rots, produce methane gas, released into atmosphere, displacement of populations, culture and way of life destroyed	
Blast furnaces	Carajás region, 50 blast furnaces, 75% of forests, illegal logging of conservation areas, indigenous lands, law 80% of forest left untouched, not enforced	

ACTIVE **LEARNING**

1. Explain how mining damages the ecosystem of the rainforest.

2. What causes a build-up of methane gas in HEP reservoirs?

3. How do blast furnaces damage the tropical rainforest?

Settlement

Destruction of the Amazon Rainforest has had a **devastating effect** on the **native tribes** who have lived there for thousands of years. Today, there are an estimated **900 000 native people remaining** from the 11 million who were living in Brazil when the Portuguese arrived in the 1500s. It is believed that over **100 tribes** have been completely **wiped out.**

Fig. 29.23 The Yanomami tribe build communal shelters, with individual sleeping areas for each family.

The most common cause of death is contact with people from the east coast. These **isolated** peoples have **not built up immunity** to diseases that are common elsewhere. This makes them **vulnerable** as increasing areas of the rainforest are exploited by the Brazilian government. Statistics show that it is likely that **50 per cent of tribespeople will die within the first year** of **making contact with people** from outside the Amazon due to diseases such as measles, **influenza** and the common cold.

The largest native tribe is the **Yanomami,** which has a population of roughly **19 000**. They are a relatively **isolated tribe** who occupy **9.4 million hectares** of land in the northern Amazon. They survive by using **sustainable slash-and-burn farming** to grow bananas, **fishing** and **hunting**.

With **increased exploitation** of the rainforest, more and **more of the tribe are being forced off** their land to allow for further **industrial development**. The Brazilian government has refused to accept an international agreement recognising land ownership for native tribes.

Twenty-five per cent of the tribe's population has died of illnesses such as colds, influenza and measles introduced by loggers and miners.

Manaus

As the cities of the east become more densely populated, settlements have developed further inland to **accommodate rising populations**. Manaus is one such settlement which has experienced rapid growth. The Brazilian government has designated Manaus a 'growth pole'. Originally a river port, Manaus was founded as a **trading centre for rubber**. However, further growth has led to the area becoming **highly industrialised**, with **modern industry** such as chemical production, **car manufacturing,** ship building and electronics locating there. This industrialisation has seen the **population grow** to **2 million** as people **migrated** from the east in search of employment.

This growth has had a negative impact on the Amazon Rainforest. The city's increasing population has led to its **boundaries expanding** into the **surrounding ecosystem**. Vast areas of forest are **cleared for agriculture,** as the growing population led to an increased demand for food. Waste from the city, especially **sewage, is untreated** and released into the **River Negro,** leading to severe **pollution**.

ACTIVE LEARNING

1. What is the main cause of tribal decline in the Amazon?
2. Why did the population of Manaus experience such rapid population growth?
3. What impact has the growth of Manaus had on the Amazon Rainforest?

EDUCATE YOURSELF

Settlement
Destruction – devastating effect native tribes, 350 000 natives remaining, 100 tribes wiped out, isolated, not built up immunity, vulnerable, 50% will die within the first year of making contact with outside people, influenza; Yanomami – 19 000, isolated tribe, 9.4 million hectares, sustainable slash-and-burn farming, fishing and hunting, increased exploitation – more of tribe are being forced off, industrial development, 25% died of illness

Manaus	Accommodate rising populations, growth pole, trading centre for rubber, highly industrialised, modern industry, car manufacturing, population 2 million, migration, boundaries expanding into surrounding ecosystem, cleared for agriculture, is untreated, River Negro, pollution

HIGHER LEVEL

1. Examine, with reference to one biome that you have studied, how plants and animals have adapted to specific climatic and soil conditions. *2015 Q18 80M*

2. Biomes are altered by human activity. Discuss. *2014 Q18 80M*

3. With reference to one biome that you have studied, account for the type of climate experienced in this biome and explain how this climate impacts on soils and vegetation within the biome. *2014 Q17 80M*

Common Marking Scheme for Geoecology Questions

Marks awarded	Discussing 3 aspects	Discussing 4 aspects
Total marks for each aspect	27m + 27m + 26m	20m + 20m + 20m + 20m
Identifying an aspect	4m each	4m each
Examination of each aspect	8 SRPs @ 2m each	6 SRPs @ 2m each
Overall coherence	7/6m per aspect	4m per aspect

The following 'structure sheet' will help you to plan your Geoecology answers. Many students try to learn off sample answers. This can take a long time and forgetting one sentence can lead to a person forgetting all of the sentences that follow it. It is always better to focus on understanding key words.

Try using the structure sheet to write your own answer to the question.

HIGHER LEVEL

EXAM QUESTION

'The development of economic activities can alter biomes.' Discuss this statement with reference to appropriate examples that you have studied. *2011 Q18 80M*

Structure Sheet

Aspect 1: Logging in the Amazon Rainforest	Aspect 2: Intensive agriculture in the Amazon Rainforest	Aspect 3: Industrial activity in the Amazon Rainforest
Commercial logging greatly altered biome	Ecosystem destroyed – plants and animals extinct	Areas cleared for access for machinery/transport
Loss of biodiversity – destruction of habitat	Nutrient cycle stopped	Roads allow easy access for illegal logging
Interdependency breaks down	Slash-and-burn technique	Toxic materials, e.g. mercury released
Loss of soil fertility – removal of canopy	Soils become infertile	Hydroelectric power – flooding
Laterite formed from exposure to climate	Cheap land – infertile land abandoned	Methane and CO_2 released into atmosphere
Soil erosion – wind and rain	Soil erosion – torrential rain – washed into rivers – flooding	Blast furnaces – burn trees for charcoal
Evapotranspiration stopped – drought	Soil turns to desert – laterisation	Carajás region – 75% of forest destroyed
Destroys carbon sink – CO_2 released	Impossible to cultivate – indigenous people displaced	Air pollution – greenhouse gases

Note that these are not SRPs, but act as SRP 'cues'. This method should improve your understanding of the topic. When you have chosen your key points, practise writing your answer with the aid of your notes and this book. You will gradually become more comfortable with the topic and eventually find that you need only these cues to write the answer.

TOPIC MAP

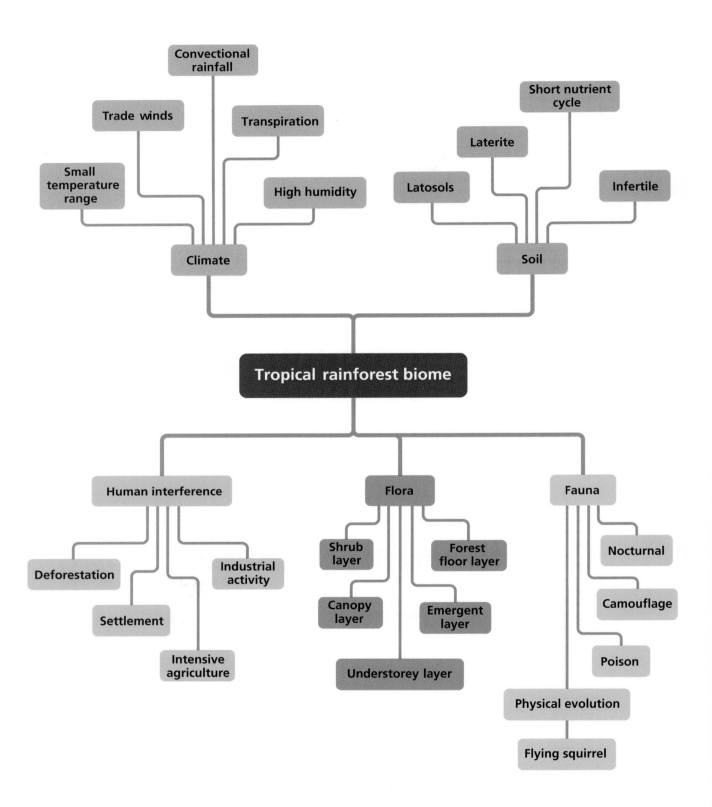

Tropical rainforest biome

Climate
- Convectional rainfall
- Trade winds
- Transpiration
- Small temperature range
- High humidity

Soil
- Short nutrient cycle
- Laterite
- Latosols
- Infertile

Human interference
- Deforestation
- Settlement
- Intensive agriculture
- Industrial activity

Flora
- Shrub layer
- Canopy layer
- Forest floor layer
- Emergent layer
- Understorey layer

Fauna
- Nocturnal
- Camouflage
- Poison
- Physical evolution
- Flying squirrel

Index